Lecture Notes in Artificial Intelligence 4626

Edited by J. G. Carbonell and J. Siekmann

Subseries of Lecture Notes in Computer Science

Rosina O. Weber   Michael M. Richter (Eds.)

Case-Based Reasoning
Research
and Development

7th International Conference
on Case-Based Reasoning, ICCBR 2007
Belfast, Northern Ireland, UK, August 13-16, 2007
Proceedings

 Springer

Series Editors

Jaime G. Carbonell, Carnegie Mellon University, Pittsburgh, PA, USA
Jörg Siekmann, University of Saarland, Saarbrücken, Germany

Volume Editors

Rosina O. Weber
The iSchool at Drexel
College of Information Science & Technology
3141 Chestnut Street, Philadelphia, PA 19104, USA
E-mail: rweber@ischool.drexel.edu

Michael M. Richter
TU Kaiserslautern
Department of Computer Science
P.O. Box 3049, 67618 Kaiserslautern, Germany
E-mail: richter@informatik.uni-kl.de

Library of Congress Control Number: 2007932197

CR Subject Classification (1998): I.2, J.4, J.1, F.4.1

LNCS Sublibrary: SL 7 – Artificial Intelligence

ISSN   0302-9743
ISBN-10   3-540-74138-0 Springer Berlin Heidelberg New York
ISBN-13   978-3-540-74138-1 Springer Berlin Heidelberg New York

Springer is a part of Springer Science+Business Media

springer.com

© Springer-Verlag Berlin Heidelberg 2007
Printed in Germany

Typesetting: Camera-ready by author, data conversion by Scientific Publishing Services, Chennai, India
Printed on acid-free paper   SPIN: 12105106   06/3180   5 4 3 2 1 0

Preface

The International Conference on Case-Based Reasoning (ICCBR) is the pre-eminent international meeting on case-based reasoning (CBR). ICCBR 2007 (http://www.iccbr.org./iccbr07/) was the seventh in this series, presenting the most significant contributions in the field of CBR. The conference took place in Belfast, Northern Ireland, UK, during August 13-16, 2007. ICCBR and its sister conferences ECCBR (European Conference on Case-Based Reasoning) alternate every year. ICCBR 2007 followed a series of six successful international conferences previously held in Sesimbra, Portugal (1995); Providence, Rhode Island, USA (1997); Seeon, Germany (1999); Vancouver, Canada (2001); Trondheim, Norway (2003); and Chicago, Illinois, USA (2005). The European Conferences on Case-Based Reasoning (ECCBR) were held as European workshops in Kaiserslautern, Germany (1993); Chantilly, France (1994); Lausanne, Switzerland (1996); Dublin, Ireland (1998); and Trento, Italy (2000); and as European conferences in Aberdeen, UK (2002); Madrid, Spain (2004); and Lykia World, Turkey (2006).

Days one, two, and four comprised presentations and posters on theoretical and applied CBR research. In order to emphasize the importance of applications, the traditional industry day was converted into an Industry Program held on the second day, in the middle of the conference. Day three was devoted to five workshops: Case-Based Reasoning and Context-Awareness; Case-Based Reasoning in the Health Sciences; Textual Case-Based Reasoning: Beyond Retrieval; Uncertainty and Fuzziness in Case-Based Reasoning; and Knowledge Discovery and Similarity.

There were four distinguished invited speakers. Two speakers from the CBR community, David W. Aha (Naval Research Laboratory, USA) spoke about perceptions of CBR, while Eva Armengol (IIIA-CSIC, Spain) talked about usages of generalization in CBR. Hans-Dieter Burkhard (Humboldt University, Germany) described the use of cases in robotic soccer, and Larry Kershberg (George Mason University, USA) presented the role of XML databases in CBR. Thanks to their commitment and ideas.

The presentations and posters covered a wide range of topics, including adaptation, planning, learning, similarity, maintenance, textual CBR, and recommender systems. This volume includes 15 papers from oral presentations and 18 from posters. These were chosen from a total of 64 submissions originating from 25 different countries. In addition, the volume contains three papers from invited speakers. The accepted papers were chosen based on a thorough and highly selective review process. Each paper was reviewed and discussed by four reviewers and revised according to their comments.

There were many people who participated in making ICCBR possible. First of all, David W. Patterson (University of Ulster, Northern Ireland, UK) –the Conference Chair who had the initiative to propose ICCBR 2007. The organization team was very diverse, having David C. Wilson (University of North Carolina, USA) and Deepak Khemani (IIT Madras, India) as coordinators of the Workshop Program. Thomas Roth-Berghofer (DFKI, Germany) chaired a Steering Committee for the Industry Program that included Kareem S. Aggour (General Electric CRD, USA), Bill

Cheetham (General Electric CRD, USA), Mehmet H. Göker (PricewaterhouseCoopers, USA), and Kalyan Moy Gupta (Knexus Research Corp., USA).

Mirjam Minor (University of Trier, Germany) coordinated the contacts with CBR researchers who have published work outside ICCBR and ECCBR conferences. We invited those researchers because we wanted to bring to the ICCBR audience a complete view of recent advances in CBR.

This diverse team together with the authors, the Program Committee, and additional reviewers are the stars of the CBR community in 2007. They made the conference happen and we want to thank them for their brilliant performances that are recorded in this volume.

We would also like to acknowledge the thoughtfulness of David W. Aha, whose constant leadership and concern for the community are crucial to the success of ICCBR and ECCBR conferences.

We gratefully acknowledge the generous support of the sponsors of ICCBR 2007 and their, partly long-time, sponsorship of ICCBR and ECCBR.

Additional help was given by doctoral students from the iSchool at Drexel University. Thanks to Caleb Fowler for serving as webmaster and to Sidath Gunawardena and Jay Johnson for their help with this volume. In support of local arrangements, thanks to the Local Arrangements Committee from the University of Ulster: Patricia Kearney, Niall Rooney, Mykola Galushka, and Juan Carlos Augusto.

The submission and reviewing process was supported with the use of Conf Master.net - The Conference Management System. We would like to express our gratitude to Thomas Preuss. Finally, we thank Springer for its continuing support in publishing this series of conference proceedings.

June 2007   Rosina O. Weber
                                                          Michael M. Richter

Organization

Program Chairs

Rosina O. Weber, Drexel University, USA
Michael M. Richter, Technical University of Kaiserslautern, Germany

Conference Chair

David W. Patterson, University of Ulster, Northern Ireland, UK

Workshop Chairs

David C. Wilson, University of North Carolina, USA
Deepak Khemani, IIT Madras, India

Industry Program Committee

Thomas Roth-Berghofer, DFKI, Germany (Chair)
Kareem S. Aggour, General Electric CRD, USA
Bill Cheetham, General Electric CRD, USA
Mehmet H. Göker, PricewaterhouseCoopers, USA
Kalyan Moy Gupta, Knexus Research Corp., USA

Program Committee

Agnar Aamodt, Norwegian University of Science and Technology, Norway
Kareem S. Aggour, General Electric CRD, USA
David W. Aha, Naval Research Laboratory, USA
Klaus-Dieter Althoff, University of Hildesheim, Germany
Josep Lluís Arcos, IIIA-CSIC, Spain
Eva Armengol, IIIA-CSIC, Spain
Kevin Ashley, University of Pittsburgh, USA
Paolo Avesani, The Centre for Scientific and Technological Research, Italy
Ralph Bergmann, University of Trier, Germany
Enrico Blanzieri, University of Trento, Italy
L. Karl Branting, MITRE, USA
Derek Bridge, University College Cork, Ireland
Stefanie Brüninghaus, University of Pittsburgh, USA
Robin Burke, DePaul University, USA

David C. Wilson, University of North Carolina, USA
Nirmalie Wiratunga, The Robert Gordon University, Scotland, UK
Ronald R. Yager, Iona College, USA
Qiang Yang, University of Hong Kong, China

Additional Reviewers

Jörg Denzinger
Susan Fox
Andrew Golding
Stewart Massie
Lisa Cummins
Miltos Petridis
Stefania Montani
Conor Hayes
Alexandre Hanft
Régis Newo
Qhang Nhat Nguyen
Steve Bogaerts
Frode Sormo

Sponsoring Institutions

ICCBR 2007 was supported by these organizations: DFKI (http://www.dfki.de/web), Drexel iSchool (http://www.ischool.drexel.edu/), empolis (http://www.empolis.com/), University of Ulster (http://www.ulster.ac.uk/), and Zerosolution Inc. (http://www. zerosolution.com/).

Table of Contents

Application Papers

Cases in Robotic Soccer

Hans-Dieter Burkhard and Ralf Berger

Humboldt University Berlin
Institute of Informatics
D-10099 Berlin
{hdb,berger}@informatik.hu-berlin.de

Abstract. Soccer playing robots are a well established test bed for the development of artificial intelligence for use in real environments. The challenges include perception, decision making and acting in a dynamic environment with only unreliable and partial information. Behaviors and skills for such environments must be optimized by experiences. Case Based Reasoning provides an excellent framework for learning as discussed in this paper.

1 Introduction

Early AI was based on symbolic descriptions of problems using logics, theorem provers and search techniques for solutions. There was a common understanding that chess programs could be a milestone to understand and implement intelligent behavior. Now we have machines that can play chess, but these machines are not considered to be really intelligent. We have learned that acting in the real world is much more difficult for machines. Machines are still far away from performing daily tasks. Therefore, the development of soccer playing robots has become a new challenge. The competitions in RoboCup are used to evaluate scientific and technological progress, similarly to the role of chess in the past.

The key problem of AI is the knowledge about daily life, how it is like to ride bicycle or to climb a tree, or simply to walk. Such skills are necessary to understand language, to interpret a scene given by visual sensors, or to decide what to do next. Human beings do acquire this knowledge by learning, by experiencing the environment, by collecting cases about good and bad behavior. Therefore, Case Based Reasoning (CBR) can be used as a basic technology together with other methods from Machine Learning. At the same time, CBR meets again its roots in cognitive science. It is still a challenge to understand how the experience can be stored and organized for later use. The scenario of soccer playing robots provides a lot of different tasks in dynamic real environments. The tasks include perception, skills and deliberation.

Because lack of space, we cannot give a detailed introduction to RoboCup. There are recently five different leagues, introduced to tackle different problems on the base of the available hard- and software. Real robots are investigated in the

– **Middle Size League (MSL)** with robots not exceeding a 50 cm diameter.

R.O. Weber and M.M. Richter (Eds.): ICCBR 2007, LNAI 4626, pp. 1–15, 2007.

- **Small Size League (SSL)** with robots not exceeding 15 cm in diameter.
- **4-Legged League (4LL)** with Sony's AIBO robots.
- **Humanoid League (HL)** with robots of human shape.

The **Simulation League (SL)** was established in order to explore more complex strategic and tactical behaviors which cannot be realized with real robots up to now. Besides individual programs for the 11 players, each team has a coach program for directing the playing style (while analyzing an ongoing match).

More information about RoboCup can be found on the website [1]. Recent developments are discussed in the article [2].

The paper is organized as follows: In Section 2 we start with a very short overview on the programming of soccer robots. It is the basis for the discussion of the Machine Learning tasks in Robotic Soccer in section 3. A discussion of the CBR related general problems is given in section 4, and section 5 gives short overviews about existing work using CBR in RoboCup.

2 Programming Soccer Robots

The robots in RoboCup have to act autonomously, no human interaction is allowed. In the so-called sense-think-act cycle they have to recognize the environment, to decide about their next goals and related actions, and to perform the actions using their skills.

The robots have to gather all needed information using their sensors. They have to process the sensory input to obtain a picture about the situation, the localization of the robot itself, of the other robots, and of the ball. Today, visual sensors are widely used to perceive the environment. Sophisticated algorithms for picture processing and scene interpretation are needed. Statistical methods like Kalman filters or particle filters are used for localization tasks. Not only the place but also the the direction and the speed of the ball are very important. Latency modeling (a good team in SSL has a latency of approx. 110ms) and prediction methods are important as well.

Especially the biped (humanoid) and quadruped robots (AIBO) need various proprioceptive sensors for observing and controlling their movements. Sensors for joint angles, forces, and torques measure the positions, directions and movements of different parts of the body.

Having a belief (not necessarily a true knowledge) about the environment, the robot has to decide for its next goals and actions. This means to check and to evaluate the own chances in comparison to the opportunities of other robots (team mates and opponents) on the playing ground. Therefore the robot needs knowledge about his own skills and about the results it can hopefully achieve.

There are different levels of control. On the lowest level, the robot has to control its body movements. In the case of humanoid robots it has to keep balance while walking or kicking. This needs a continuous interaction between sensor inputs and appropriate actions at the related joints. The compensation of an unexpected force by an adjustment of the heap is an example. It is still an open problem in the worldwide research on humanoid robots how this can be

achieved best: how to couple sensors and actors, which sensors to use and where
to place them, how to program the control etc. Recent efforts try to implement
some kind of a spinal cord inspired by solutions from nature. Because of the
lack of complete models, methods from Machine Learning are tested for the
development of efficient (distributed) sensor-actor loops.

Having such basic skills like dribbling, intercepting or kicking the ball, the
next level of control concerns the choice of an appropriate skill for a given goal.
While the skill is performed, the robot has continuously to check the performance
of the skill, e.g. maintaining control over the ball while dribbling. Again, a close
interaction is necessary between sensors, control, and actuators.

On the highest level(s), tactical and strategic decisions can actually take place.
Related reasoning procedures are especially studied in the simulation league
because it is the only league which already uses 11 players per team.

3   Machine Learning Tasks in Robotic Soccer

As discussed in the previous section, a soccer program consists of modules according to a "horizontal" structure regarding the sense-think-act cycle, and a
"vertical" structure of the levels (layers). The related modules can cooperate
in different ways depending on the architecture in use. Visual perception, for
example, is performed vertically starting with primitive image operations on the
lowest level up to the scene interpretation using background knowledge (physical properties, design of the playground etc.) at the higher levels. Horizontal
cooperation is necessary for the sense-think-act cycle.

Many of the processes inside the modules as well as the interconnections of
the modules are subject to Machine Learning. Available data are incomplete and
unreliable such that programming by hand leads to sub-optimal solutions. Moreover, optimal solutions are often too costly because of real-time requirements.
Hand crafted systems in RoboCup were sufficient only during the first years.
Now, all the good teams in simulation as well as in the real robot leagues use
various Machine Learning techniques to a great extend. RoboCup has become
an important scenario for development and evaluation of Machine Learning. The
scenario of keep away soccer [3] has become a standard evaluation test bed for
Machine Learning.

It is not possible to train all aspects of successful soccer playing in a single
learning process. The overall learning task (how to win) has to be decomposed
into smaller tasks. Up to now, the most scenarios investigated for Machine Learning in RoboCup are rather granular, but because of the interdependencies of the
processes, the scenarios for learning are depending on each other. Actually, the
pioneering work for multi layered learning came from the RoboCup community
[4]. We will give some examples in section 5.

3.1   Perception

The players need to have beliefs about the movement of the ball, about their own
position and the position of other players. In the early days of RoboCup teams

used distance data provided by range finders. But driven by the recent cheap camera prices, visual data are most important today. Useful constraints between relative and absolute data (distances, angles, positions, speed) can be exploited. Absolute data are measured with respect to global coordinates, relative data are measured with respect to the player itself (egocentric world model). The data are collected and analyzed over time, usually with an underlying Markov assumption. Statistical methods try to overcome the unreliability of the measurements. Particle filters and Kalman filters are used for positioning tasks today. The tuning of their parameters is a special learning task.

Up to now, the environment of the robots is carefully designed with color coded objects. In the near future, the robots are to play in arbitrary environments, e.g. in a gym. The only spatial background knowledge the robots can rely on is the fact that there should be two goals and maybe some field lines on the ground. Therefore the robots will have to learn orientation also from other landmarks available in a concrete room.

An intensively studied field is opponent modeling, especially in the simulation league. The coach agent can observe the match and try to find out useful information about the other team. There are different player types, and the coach can try to find out which opponent players are on which positions. Moreover he can try to identify special patterns (cases!) about the style of playing. The findings can be used to improve the own strategy. The coach can analyze the behavior recorded from log files as well as online during a match.

3.2   Act

Reliable basic skills are essential for the success in robotic soccer as well as in human soccer. The simulation league provides an ideal test bed for the investigation of different skill learning techniques. The league can provide as many data as wanted with low cost. In the real robot leagues, experiments are expensive regarding the costs for the equipment, and they are time consuming. This leads to more sophisticated experimental designs. Accompanying simulations are used to get a better understanding, and special methods help for off line pre-selection of promising trials [5].

With the arrival of legged robots, especially the humanoid ones, internal sensors for measurement of forces and joint angles are used for the stabilization and for fast movements including omni-directional walking, running, kicking and dribbling. With about 20 degrees of freedom and frame rates of more than 100 fps, learning methods are mandatory to tune appropriate sensor-actor-loops.

Learning basic skills, like approximation of the best interception point for a moving ball was already an early learning task in RoboCup simulation league [6]. It is one of the characteristic properties of RoboCup, that skill learning does not concern only a single action. In most cases, the success depends on the learning of a suitable sequence of actions. This is obvious for the chain of motor commands for legged robots, but it was even necessary in the simulation league from the very beginning. A prominent example was the success of AT Humboldt over the favorite team CMUnited in 1997. A successful shoot consists of a sequence of well tuned kick actions, and CMUnited was not prepared for such kicks. But it is only a nice tale, that AT-Humboldt team could kick "the ball around themselves, continually increasing its velocity so that it ended up moving towards the goal faster than was imagined possible. Since the soccer server did not enforce a maximum ball speed, a property that was changed immediately after the competition, the ball could move arbitrarily fast, making it impossible to stop"[4]. Since faster velocities would make the ball to leave the kickable range immediately, it was not possible to get a higher speed than the later defined maximum speed.

3.3   Decision Making

The control tasks can range from basic reactive behaviors up to high level deliberative behaviors. The overall performance depends on appropriate interconnections. Using weak skills, learning of decision criteria will result in optimization of doing what is possible. Replacing the skill by a better one will need a new learning of the higher level decisions.

There are obvious tasks for Machine Learning approaches like classifiers for the selection of appropriate skills for a situation. Likewise, simple tasks concern the choice of skills for the player in possession of the ball. The player may choose between scoring, passing, dribbling etc. Next he may choose between different ways to perform the chosen action, e.g. by a kick selection procedure and the determination of parameters like direction and speed of the kick.

More complex deliberation concerns the behavior of the players not controlling the ball. Typical tasks are supporting or marking, more complex behavior concerns standard situations. Deliberation of this kind needs more understanding of tactical options. Certain patterns can be identified. The fine tuning or even the detection of useful patterns is very challenging. Besides well developed basic skills, the performance in high level cooperative play is already mandatory for teams in the simulation league, and it becomes more and more important in the real robot leagues. An exquisite example are the Tribots MSL team from University of Osnabrueck (world champion 2006) with successful transformations of methods from their simulation team Brainstormers (vice champion in 2006).

There are different implementations for cooperative team play. Explicit planning and data structures for resulting plans do not seem to be mandatory. Neural networks have been trained using reinforcement learning to determine just the next action useful in the recent situation. Of course, Reinforcement Learning did consider the later progress of playing, but the neural net computes only the immediate action [7]. A related concept with symbolic representations was used by AT Humboldt in 1997 [8]. The idea behind such concepts is the following presumption: If there exists a good potential plan, then the subsequent choices will lead to actions consistent with the potential plan. Problems may arise from oscillations between different potential plans. Therefore the teams with such approaches take some additional care for stability.

Other approaches use explicit symbolic plans. Symbolic approaches permit the description of behavior patterns and standard situations of soccer, like change of wings, wall passes, offside trap, free kicks, corner kicks, etc. The suitable behavior in such situations can be described in a script-like manner, where concrete parameters are filled in as appropriate. Such a behavior is started with only a rough partial plan (the "idea" how to perform the behavior). In the beginning of a wall pass, the both players involved know about the sequence of dribbling (player 1)/positioning(player 2), pass from 1 to 2, intercept (2)/run over opponent (1), pass back from 2 to 1, intercept by player 1. This is only a rough script not a complete plan. The concrete parameters are determined during the progress of the behavior depending on the opponents behavior, the movement of the ball etc. (least commitment). The higher levels of layered architectures are commonly used for the long term commitments. The choice of appropriate plans may be considered again as a classification task. Tuning for optimization is useful to find good parameters.

The coordination of different players can rely on different approaches. Communication is useful to some extend, but limited in bandwidth and subject to losses (especially for wireless communication). Cooperation without communication is also possible since all players act in the same environment. Therefore RoboCup provides a lot of interesting challenges for multi-agent learning.

3.4   Machine Learning Methods in RoboCup

As we have seen, RoboCup needs learning for classification and for optimization. Neural networks and Case Based Reasoning are often used for classification purposes. Evolutionary approaches provide good results for scenarios with large parameter spaces, e.g. complex situations or locomotion of legged robots. Learning of skills with delayed rewards are treated with methods from Reinforcement Learning, where various function approximations for the large parameter spaces are in use.

There is no space to discuss all methods in detail. Instead it can be stated that rather all Machine Learning methods can be applied – and have been applied in different soccer scenarios and for different modules. There are several hundred teams in RoboCup competitions year by year, and there are a lot of people working in Machine Learning.

4   CBR in RoboCup – Some General Remarks

4.1   What Are Cases, and Where Do They Come from?

As in many other CBR systems, the classical distinction between problem part and solution part (rule type cases) is useful for soccer applications, too. For simple classification tasks, the problem part contains examples from the classes, while the solution gives the correct class. The selection of actions or skills can be considered as classification. The solution may also contain a quality measure which evaluates the suitability of the proposed solution. Negative numbers indicate that the solution was not successful or not correct. The contents (vocabulary) of the cases are often given by attribute-value pairs of positions, speeds, teams, score, time, intentions etc. Similarity is then calculated by the local-global principle [9]: Local similarities of the attributes (e.g. inverse distances of positions) are combined by a certain function. Weighted sums are very popular, whereby the weights can be adjusted by learning.

The data of the matches provide a large pool for case bases. For skill learning, the cases can be recorded from special experimental settings (e.g. for intercepts or dribbling). The simulation league can produce data as much as one needs. For the real robots, the collection of data is more limited by time and by the efforts needed for recording.

The case data are then extracted from the recorded files. This means to identify related situations and related sequences of actions from a stream of recorded events. A pass e.g. consists of a kick by the first player, then the ball moves freely for some time, and then the second player intercepts the ball. Thereby, the second player must belong to the same team. It is difficult to judge if a pass was actually performed by intentions of both players. But often it is only important that a pass occurred, regardless for what reasons.

There are useful methods for the analysis originally developed for commentator programs and for coaches, respectively. Such programs can find the co-occurrences of pre-situations, action sequences, and post-situations. They can find the successful passes in the recorded games. But there are also situations in the matches where a pass could have been successfully performed, but the player did not try. Such situations would need a more careful analysis. This addresses an old problem of experience based learning: If there was no trial, then there is no experience (exploration problem). A human expert could consider such situations and design related cases. More sophisticated analysis tools can be used for such tasks at least to some extend.

Moreover, typical cases can be designed completely by humans. There are a lot of standard situations in soccer. They are often explained by related cases in human soccer. This provides a good alternative approach for programming soccer robots. Instead of defining the conditions for the application of a maneuver in terms of spatial relations between the players and the ball, one can provide a set of typical cases and use CBR methods.

The use of cases is often appropriate since the decision are ordered by time: A recent situation (problem) is mapped to subsequent actions (solution).

One drawback of the rule type case format is the need for different cases while dealing with the same standard situation, e.g. during a wall pass. There we have a unique script with ongoing decisions (when to pass to whom, where to run to, where to intercept). Using rule type cases, we would need different cases for each of these decisions.

This problem can be solved using the ideas of case completion as proposed in [10]. A case describes a whole episode (e.g. of a wall pass) with concrete decisions and actions. While performing a new episode, those cases are retrieved step by step from the case base which correspond to the recent belief (initial part of the recent course of events and situations, e.g. after performing the pass from player 1 to player 2 in the wall pass). These cases can then provide more data from their stored experience: How the problem was solved with further decisions (e.g. where the player 2 should intercept the ball, where the player 1 should run to etc.).

Such cases are of constraint type: Unknown values are determined from given data using cases as constraints. Systems using constraint type cases can be implemented with Case Retrieval Nets (CRN, [10]). Such a case is a set of information entities which have occurred together in the stored episode. Their usage consists of retrieving remaining (unspecified) information entities (IEs) to a partially described situation.

Another example of constraint type cases comes from perception. There, a case may contain the positions of objects (e.g. players and ball) in world coordinates, and the distances between the objects. The description is redundant (e.g. distances could be calculated from positions and vice versa if some fixed positioned objects are involved). Therefore a case with all these data can be retrieved by some of its IEs and serve for specifying the unknown IEs (they could also be calculated by trigonometry – but humans do not).

4.2   Maintenance

Maintenance of cases is substantial for the success of CBR in soccer programs. Large case bases are not useful because of the needs for real-time processing. It is necessary to keep a bounded number of cases using related techniques.

Moreover, cases may become invalid over time. This may happen due to changes in other modules, for example after collecting new cases there. It may also occur for cases collected online, e.g. for opponent models. If a team uses such models and changes its style of play, then the opponent usually responds with other patterns of behavior (besides the fact that opponents may also change their behavior using their related modeling methods for our team).

Another problem concerns the consistency of the case bases of different players of a team. If the players use the same CBR system, they have a chance to obtain the same proposals. It then depends on comparable world models. But if the players have different case bases (due to online collected experiences), then their decisions may not lead to a joint intention.

4.3   Generalization (Adaptation)

In the soccer domain, adaptation is usually closely related to the similarity measure. This concerns spatial transformations (positions, symmetries etc.) and seems to be continuous for a first look. Actually, there can be substantial discontinuities according to quantization effects. They are explicitly implemented even in the soccer server of the simulation league.

5   CBR in RoboCup – An Applicational View

In the last 10 years CBR has been applied to a broad variety of aspects of robot control. We know of more than 20 international publications from the RoboCup community in this field. In the following sections we will have a more detailed look on how Case Based Reasoning is incorporated.

5.1   CBR Methods for Self-localization

Sensing a camera image with some striking features similar to an image corresponding to a known position (case) usually implies that the current position is similar to the known one.

The paper [11] utilizes local visual information of landmarks for self localization (position and orientation) of an AIBO robot in the 4-Legged League. The problem part of a case represents an omni-directional view from a certain position. The solution is the according position on the field.

The playground was divided into cells of $20cm \times 20cm$. For each of these partitions a case was generated, that consists of information about all landmarks. In detail these are the following features: the width, height and color of the appearances of all landmarks as well as the angles between pairs of landmarks. Thus every case consists of 68 (out of 859 possibly different) information entities.

In the application, only some landmark features are available (since the robot camera has a view angle of 50 degrees). Hence cases must be retrieved according to partial problem descriptions. This was implemented with the help of Case Retrieval Nets [10]. To find the robot's position a weighted sum is computed over all solutions of cases that are sufficiently similar to the given camera image. The main advantage of this approach is its flexibility and its robustness even against some strongly incorrect visual information.

5.2   CBR Methods for Opponent Modeling

The overall problem of opponent modeling is defined as "building up a model of the opponent's behavior based on observations within a game". The particular practicability of Case Based Reasoning is given since human players seem to solve this problem in a similar way and there are usually only few learning samples to exploit. At least three different research groups applied CBR methods to opponent modeling in RoboCup.

Wendler et al. [12,13] use a combined system for recognizing and predicting of behaviors. The prediction is based on the recognition of associated triggers, which are assumed to cause the agents to start the corresponding behavior. For each particular behavior they define a set of relevant attributes such as positions or relative angles. Cases are generated automatically during the behavior recognition learning phase. Potential triggers have to be identified for the retrieval, and then the case base is searched for cases with similar triggers. Finally, the case is adapted according to the current situation by comparing the observed trigger and the trigger stored in the case.

The work of Steffens [14,15] investigates improvements of prediction accuracy for case-based opponent modeling. The approach also enhances efficiency since it exploits the same observations during learning for different purposes. While the observations remain the same, the similarity measure is adapted to the type or role of the agents. This adaptation is done by integrating problem solving knowledge represented in goal dependency networks (GDN). The GDNs are defined manually and contain very general but domain dependent information. It could be shown that using an adaptive similarity measure regarding the role of the agents leads to a better prediction of a player's actions.

The approach of Ahmadi et al. [16] is similar to the last one. It also tries to optimize the actual CBR process by adapting its meta-parameters. It uses a second case-based subsystem for this task, building a two-layered CBR architecture. The complexity of the problem is split into two subproblems, each of which works with a relatively small number of cases. The features of the ordinary ('lower') cases are defined relative to the ball. These cases provide local solutions which can be applied everywhere in the field. Adapting these cases for different game situations requires information about the current focus of the play. This information is provided by the 'upper' cases and incorporates the position and velocity vector of the ball and a rough estimation of the position of all the players. The second layer provides optimal case parameters (representation, retrieval and adaptation). It monitors the performance of the lower layer. Ahmadi et al. could show that the the system is able to learn a competent opponent model by the iterative application of this approach to only very few games.

5.3   CBR Methods for Situation Analysis and Decision Making

In this paragraph we will address the problems of situation analysis and (individual) decision making. These are probably the tasks where the application of case-based methods is most apparently.

Probably the first application of Case Based Reasoning in RoboCup is shown by the 'AT Humboldt' team [17]. CBR was used for dynamic situation assessment in the Simulation League. The task is to find a 'preference position' where the player should move to. Cases are represented by a feature vector of a game snapshot including the following properties: occupancy of the segmented playground by other players, time until a teammate will control the ball, preference directions, available power resources, distance to the ball and to the other players. The work again uses Case Retrieval Nets.

In [18] the prior work was continued towards decision making of the goalkeeper. He has to decide whether to stay in front of the goal and defend the goal-line or to run towards an attacker to decrease the possible shooting angles to the goal. The logfiles of previous games were analyzed for situations in which a goal attack was running and the goalie had to decide what to do. From each of such situations a case was generated which basically contained the positions of the players and the ball, the ball's velocity, the decision of the goalie regarding the discussed scenario, and the success of this behavior. The problem of finding a suitable similarity measure was tackled by using a combination of an inverse distance and a relevance function that provides a rating of the estimated impact of a players position on the goalie's decision. An interesting aspect of this work is that the whole procedure from processing and analyzing hundreds of logfiles to building up the index and the runtime structure works fully automatically and takes just a few hours.

The work of 'AT Humboldt' was recently extended to a comprehensive CBR-framework [19,20] for decision making for cooperative tasks. Perhaps the most interesting feature is its twofold case-base optimization process.

Firstly only the significant pieces of information from each case are extracted. This is done by defining areas of interest based on the spatial relations between the ball and the relevant players. The deletion of the non-essential information speeds up the retrieval and leads to more general cases. The second optimization task is to delete the redundant cases. To determine whether a case is redundant (it can be deleted without decreasing the competence of the case-base), the individual competence contribution model based on the concepts of coverage and reachability is used. It turned out that the deletion of the redundant cases shrinks the case-base significantly. Furthermore the information density of the case-base decreases and the dispersion of the information becomes more homogeneous which again speeds up the retrieval. First applications of the system used the game play 'wall pass' to successfully show it's performance.

A very comprehensive work comes from the group of Raquel Ros [21,22]. They propose an almost complete methodology for case-based decision making applied to the 4-legged League. Their work covers:

Case-acquisition: The idea of this work is to start with an initial case base of prototypical cases that was manually designed with the help of expert knowledge. A supervised training is installed afterwards where an expert reviews the retrieved solution of the system. The robot can then adopt the scope of the case accordingly.

Case format: As usual a case represents a snapshot of the environment at a given time. The case definition is composed of three parts: $case = (P, K, A)$. P is the problem description containing a set of spatial attributes as well as some game-based attributes (timing of the match and current goal difference). K indicates the scope of the case defined as the regions of the field within which the ball and the opponents should be located in order to retrieve that case. A is the solution description – a sequence of actions the robots should perform. This is often denoted as 'game play'.

Retrieval: The retrieval is implemented as a twofold process: It considers the similarity between the problem and the case, and the cost of adapting the problem to the case. The similarity function indicates how similar non-controllable features (cannot directly be influenced) are between the problem and the case using local similarities and a global aggregation function. The cost function defines the cost of modifying the controllable features (own and teammates' positions) of the problem to match the case.

Reuse: The reuse phase refers to the adaptation of case features before executing the associated actions. Its basic idea is to transform the controllable features of the current problem in a way that the relation between these features w.r.t. the ball is the same as in the retrieved case.

5.4   CBR Methods for Planning

There are a lot of different possibilities for the integration of Case Based Reasoning into the robot's planning process (from multi-agent decision making to complete architectural models). Since the spectrum is too broad we will only pick some exemplary work and outline its ideas briefly.

A complete single-player hybrid architecture (CBRFuze) is introduced in [23]. It combines a deliberative problem solver using Case Based Reasoning and a reactive part using fuzzy behavioral control. The problem description part of the cases uses a set of fuzzy linguistic variables which is also helpful for case indexing and provides an easy similarity measure.

Marling et al. [24] show how Case Based Reasoning can be integrated into various tasks of their Small Size team. They present three CBR prototypes, for the tasks of positioning the goalie, selecting team formations, and recognizing game states. So far the prototypes are only realized in simulation yet.

In [25] a system for strategic behavior selection in the Small-Size League is proposed. It utilizes Case Based Reasoning for dynamic situation assessment in offensive and defense game situations. In addition Bayesian classifiers are used to choose between optimal behaviors. The approach was tested using the formerly mentioned 'keepaway' task.

Karol et al. [26] propose a theoretical model for high level planning in the Four-Legged League. Their model supports game play selection in common and key game situations. It is argued that developing a case base for robot soccer game plays can capture creative genius and enduring principles of how to play the game. The proposed approach uses the conceptual spaces framework for categorization of cases by well-defined similarity measures.

5.5   CBR Methods for Coaching

Until now coaching is available exclusively in the Simulation League. A coach may give advises to adapt the team's game strategy. Furthermore, the coach can initially choose between varying player types that differ from each other in their physical attributes. He can assign them their roles in the game, and he can substitute players up to three times during a match.

The problem of finding a good line-up is investigated using a case-base approach in [27]. The problem part of a case consists of the individual properties of all available heterogenous players. The solution part presents some alternative solutions. Each solution features descriptive elements like formation type, main strategy or opponent team as well as the assignment of the player types. It also provides some measure of the quality of the solution. This was done by analyzing the performance of games played with the related formation. The second important issue was the definition of appropriate similarity measures between heterogeneous player types, i.e. the question which of the properties have a significant impact on the similarity between two player types.

5.6   CBR Methods for Acting

There is some published work of using Case Based Reasoning for acting in general robotics (e.g. for navigation and parameter optimization) but we know only one paper in RoboCup. In [28] an interesting combination of Reinforcement Learning and CBR is presented. Case-based methods are used for approximating a high-dimensional, continuous state value function of the Reinforcement Learning task. A case is regarded as pair of state representation and state value estimation learned from exploration examples. To determine a specific state value, k-nearest neighbor regression is used based on Euclidean distances. Special maintenance procedures are implemented. They handle the growth of the case base and serve for deleting older cases. Since early cases may be due to early insufficient approximations, such cases should be removed from the case base when approximation becomes better. The approach was evaluated using the ball interception task and could produce good behavior policies within a very short time and with comparatively little case data.

6   Conclusion

Intelligent behavior in restricted domains – as today already implemented in numerous assistance systems or in chess – can be achieved using special methods and techniques (e.g. search, statistics, artificial neural networks). But complex intelligent behavior needs the solution of lots of different combined problems using a large variety of methods and technical staff. Many skills which humans seem to perform easily are of that kind. Perception and action, language understanding and communication are examples.

Soccer playing robots provide a very challenging test bed with a lot of different requirements similar to the requirements of intelligent behavior in real world scenarios. It is impossible to program such robots in all its details. Instead, methods from Machine Learning are needed for the development and the tuning of suitable features, skills and behaviors. Since acting in the real world is based on experiences, Case Based Reasoning is best suited for the tasks on hand.

We have shown, that CBR can be used for all aspects of the sense-think-act-cycle, and we have discussed the existing work in this field. There are in fact a lot of interesting results and useful applications. Nevertheless, there are more open than solved problems to date. Especially the integration of different solutions is a challenging task for CBR-methods.

The development of autonomous intelligent robots is a challenge which can only be achieved by the integration of different fields. The soccer playing robots are an attempt to study these problems and to use the framework of friendly competitions for scientific research. Thus it does not really matter if robots can win against human players in 2050. Nevertheless it is important to have this vision in mind as a long term goal to consider new questions and to foster new results.

Acknowledgments

The authors wish to thank all the thousands of researchers within the RoboCup Federation. All of the exciting work in RoboCup is possible only with the help of this world wide community.

References

1. The RoboCup Federation: Official Website URL: http://www.robocup.org
2. Visser, U., Burkhard, H.D.: RoboCup – 10 years of achievements and future challenges. AI Magazine (to appear)
3. Stone, P., Kuhlmann, G., Taylor, M.E., Liu, Y.: Keepaway Soccer: From Machine Learning Testbed to Benchmark. In: Bredenfeld, A., Jacoff, A., Noda, I., Takahashi, Y. (eds.) RoboCup 2005. LNCS (LNAI), vol. 4020, pp. 93–105. Springer, Heidelberg (2006)
4. Stone, P.: Layered Learning in Multiagent Systems. PhD thesis, Carnegie Mellon University, Computer Science Department (1998)
5. Quinlan, M.: Machine Learning on AIBO Robots. PhD thesis, The University of Newcastle, Faculty of Engineering and the Built Environment (2006)
6. Stone, P., Veloso, M.: A Layered Approach to Learning Client Behaviors in the RoboCup Soccer Server. Applied Artificial Intelligence 12, 165–188 (1998)
7. Riedmiller, M., Gabel, T.: On Experiences in a Complex and Competitive Gaming Domain: Reinforcement Learning Meets RoboCup. In: Proceedings of the 3rd IEEE Symposium on Computational Intelligence and Games (CIG 2007)
8. Burkhard, H.-D., Hannebauer, M., Wendler, J.: AT Humboldt – Development, Practice and Theory. In: Kitano, H. (ed.) RoboCup-97: Robot Soccer World Cup I. LNCS, vol. 1395, pp. 357–372. Springer, Heidelberg (1998)
9. Burkhard, H.-D., Richter, M.M.: On the Notion of Similarity in Case Based Reasoning and Fuzzy Theory. In: Pal, S.K., Dillon, T.S., Yeung, D.S. (eds.) Soft Computing in Case Based Reasoning, pp. 29–46. Springer, Heidelberg (2000) CISM Courses and Lectures No. 408, pp. 141–152. Springer, Wien, New York (2000)
10. Burkhard, H.D.: Extending some Concepts of CBR – Foundations of Case Retrieval Nets. In: Lenz, M., Bartsch-Spörl, B., Burkhard, H.-D., Wess, S. (eds.) Case-Based Reasoning Technology. LNCS (LNAI), vol. 1400, pp. 17–50. Springer, Heidelberg (1998)
11. Wendler, J., Brüggert, S., Burkhard, H.-D., Myritz, H.: Fault-tolerant self localization by Case-Based Reasoning. In: Stone, P., Balch, T., Kraetzschmar, G.K. (eds.) RoboCup 2000. LNCS (LNAI), vol. 2019, pp. 259–268. Springer, Heidelberg (2001)
12. Wendler, J.: Automatisches Modellieren von Agenten-Verhalten - Erkennen, Verstehen und Vorhersagen von Verhalten in komplexen Multi-Agenten-Systemen. Dissertation, Humboldt Universität zu Berlin (2003)
13. Wendler, J., Bach, J.: Recognizing and Predicting Agent Behavior with Case Based Reasoning. In: Polani, D., Browning, B., Bonarini, A., Yoshida, K. (eds.) RoboCup 2003. LNCS (LNAI), vol. 3020, pp. 729–738. Springer, Heidelberg (2004)
14. Steffens, T.: Enhancing Similarity Measures with Imperfect Rule-Based Background Knowledge. Dissertation, University of Osnabrueck (2006)
15. Steffens, T.: Adapting Similarity Measures to Agent Types in Opponent Modelling. In: Kudenko, D., Kazakov, D., Alonso, E. (eds.) Adaptive Agents and Multi-Agent Systems II. LNCS (LNAI), vol. 3394, Springer, Heidelberg (2005)

16. Ahmadi, M., Lamjiri, A., Nevisi, M., Habibi, J., Badie, K.: Using two-layered case-based reasoning for prediction in soccer coach. In: Proc. of the Intern. Conf. of Machine Learning; Models, Technologies and Applications (MLMTA'04) (2004)

17. Wendler, J., Gugenberger, P., Lenz, M.: CBR for Dynamic Situation Assessment in an Agent-Oriented Setting. In: Proc. AAAI-98 Workshop on CaseBased Reasoning Integrations (1998)

18. Berger, R., Gollin, M., Burkhard, H.-D.: AT Humboldt 2003 – Team Description. In: Polani, D., Browning, B., Bonarini, A., Yoshida, K. (eds.) RoboCup 2003. LNCS (LNAI), vol. 3020, Springer, Heidelberg (2004)

19. Lämmel, G.: Fallbasierte Verhaltenssteuerung im RoboCup – Ein Verfahren zum Fallbasierten Erkennen von Doppelpass-Situationen und der Steuerung eines entsprechenden Verhaltens in der RoboCup Simulationsliga. Diploma Thesis, Institut für Informatik, Humboldt Universität zu Berlin (2006)

20. Berger, R., Lämmel, G.: Exploiting Past Experience – Using Case-Based Techniques for Decision Support in Soccer Agents. Technical report (2007)

21. Ros, R., Veloso, M., de Antaras, R.L., Sierra, C., Arcos, J.L.: Retrieving and Reusing Game Plays for Robot Soccer. In: Roth-Berghofer, T.R., Göker, M.H., Güvenir, H.A. (eds.) ECCBR 2006. LNCS (LNAI), vol. 4106, pp. 47–61. Springer, Heidelberg (2006)

22. Ros, R., Arcos, J.L.: Acquiring a Robust Case Base for the Robot Soccer Domain. In: Proceedings of the 20th International Joint Conference on Artificial Intelligence (IJCAI 2007), pp. 1029–1034. AAAI Press, California (2007)

23. Lin, Y., Liu, A., Chen, K.: A Hybrid Architecture of Case-Based Reasoning and Fuzzy Behavioral Control Applied to Robot Soccer. In: International Computer Symposium ICS'02, Workshop on Artificial Intelligence (2002)

24. Marling, C., Tomko, M., Gillen, M., Alexander, D., Chelberg, D.: Case-Based Reasoning for Planning and World Modeling in the RoboCup Small Sized League. In: IJCAI Workshop on Issues in Designing Physical Agents for Dynamic Real-Time Environments (2003)

25. Srinivasan, T., Aarthi, K., Meenakshi, S.A., Kausalya, M.: CBRRoboSoc: An Efficient Planning Strategy for Robotic Soccer Using Case Based Reasoning. In: International Conference on Computational Intelligence for Modelling Control and Automation (CIMCA'06) (2006)

26. Karol, A., Nebel, B., Stanton, C., Williams, M.-A.: Case Based Game Play in the RoboCup Four-Legged League – Part I The Theoretical Model. In: Polani, D., Browning, B., Bonarini, A., Yoshida, K. (eds.) RoboCup 2003. LNCS (LNAI), vol. 3020, Springer, Heidelberg (2004)

27. Gabel, T.: A CBR Approach to the Heterogeneous Players Problem in Robotic Soccer Simulation. Student theses, University of Kaiserslautern (2002)

28. Gabel, T., Riedmiller, M.: CBR for State Value Function Approximation in Reinforcement Learning. In: Muñoz-Ávila, H., Ricci, F. (eds.) ICCBR 2005. LNCS (LNAI), vol. 3620, pp. 206–221. Springer, Heidelberg (2005)

A Case-Based Framework for Collaborative Semantic Search in Knowledge Sifter

Larry Kerschberg[1], Hanjo Jeong[1], Yong Uk Song[2], and Wooju Kim[3]

[1] E-Center for E-Business and Department of Computer Science
Volgenau School of Information Technology and Engineering
George Mason University, Fairfax, Virginia USA
{kersch,hjeong}@gmu.edu
http://eceb.gmu.edu/
[2] Department of MIS, Yonsei University Wonju Campus, Kangwon, Korea
yusong@yonsei.ac.kr
[3] Department of Information and Industrial Engineering
Yonsei University, Seoul, Korea
wkim@yonsei.ac.kr

Abstract. This paper addresses the role of case-based reasoning in semantic search, and in particular, as it applies to Knowledge Sifter, an agent-based ontology-driven search system based on Web services. The Knowledge Sifter architecture is extended to include a case-based methodology for collaborative semantic search, including case creation, indexing and retrieval services. A collaborative filtering methodology is presented that uses stored cases as a way to improve user query specification, refinement and processing.

Keywords: Agents, Semantic Search, Collaborative Filtering, Case-Based Frameworks, Knowledge Sifter.

1 Introduction

This paper addresses an important problem, that of assisting users in posing queries to multiple heterogeneous sources over the Internet and the World Wide Web. There is a *semantic mismatch* between how a person conceptualizes a query and how that query must be expressed using the limited keyword-based query interfaces of traditional search engines. This "semantic mismatch" has been addressed by WebSifter [1]; it performs a preprocessing step in which the user develops a semantic taxonomy tree of concepts – terms and their synonyms – which are then transformed into queries submitted to traditional search engines. The resulting best matches from the individual search engines are then rated by means of a multi-attribute decision model that associates weights to the syntactic, semantic, categorical and authoritative components of each page retrieved. The results are presented to the user who then has the opportunity to rate those URLs that best match his or her requirements. WebSifter served as the preferred embodiment for a recently-awarded patent [2].

R.O. Weber and M.M. Richter (Eds.): ICCBR 2007, LNAI 4626, pp. 16–30, 2007.

Knowledge Sifter [3] is the successor to WebSifter in that the lessons learned in designing and building WebSifter have been used to create an agent-based system that coordinates the search for knowledge in heterogeneous sources, such as the Web, semi-structured data, relational databases and the emerging Semantic Web.

This paper begins with an overview of the Knowledge Sifter (KS) agent-based architecture. The artifacts created by the agents during the formulation, refinement, processing and results ranking of a user query are captured and described in terms of a meta-schema. The artifacts can be indexed and stored in a repository as user-cases. A case-based framework is presented for specifying, storing, retrieving and recommending user-cases to assist in query formulation, recommendation and processing. The cases are represented in terms of an XML schema, are stored in a case repository and are managed by a case management agent. Finally, an algorithm is presented that uses a hybrid approach which combines both content-based and collaborative filtering techniques.

2   The Knowledge Sifter Agent-Based Architecture

The Knowledge Sifter project, underway at George Mason University, has as its primary goals: 1) to allow users to perform ontology-guided semantic searches for relevant information, both in-house and open-source; 2) to access heterogeneous data sources via agent-based knowledge services; and 3) to refine searches based on user feedback. Increasingly, users seek information from open sources such as the Web, XML-databases, relational databases and the emerging Semantic Web. The Knowledge Sifter project makes use of open standards for both ontology construction – the Web Ontology Language (OWL) – and for searching heterogeneous data sources – Web services. The Knowledge Sifter (KS) architecture, depicted in Fig. 1, may be considered a service-oriented architecture consisting of a community of cooperating agents. The rationale for using agents to implement intelligent search and retrieval systems is that agents can be viewed as autonomous and proactive.

The information domain we address is that of Image Analysis, but multiple ontologies and domains can be supported. The architecture has three layers: User Layer, Knowledge Management Layer and Data Sources Layer. Specialized agents reside at the various layers and perform well-defined functions. They support interactive query formulation and refinement, query decomposition, query processing, result ranking and presentation. The KS architecture is general and modular so that new ontologies[4] and new information resources can be incorporated easily, in almost a "plug-and-play" fashion. The various KS agents and services are presented below.

User and Preferences Agents. The User Agent interacts with the user to elicit user preferences that are managed by the Preferences Agent. These preferences include the relative importance attributed to terms used to pose queries, the user-perceived authoritativeness of Web search engine results, the biases a user has towards data sources, etc., used by the Ranking Agent. The Preferences

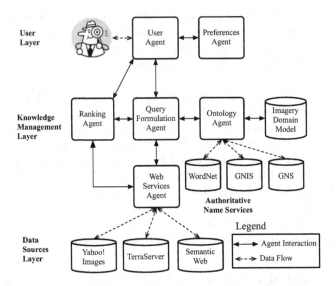

Fig. 1. The Knowledge Sifter Agent-Based Architecture

Agent can also learn the user's preference based on experience and feedback related to previous queries.

Ontology Agent. The Ontology Agent accesses an imagery domain model, specified in OWL, and depicted in Fig. 2. In addition, there are three authoritative name services: Princeton University's WordNet [5], the US Geological Survey's GNIS, and the National Geospatial-Intelligence Agency's GNS. They allow the Ontology Agent to use terms provided by the name services to suggest query refinements such as generalization, specialization and synonyms. For example, WordNet can provide a collection of synonyms for a term, while GNIS and GNS translate a physical place name – in the US and the World, respectively – into latitude and longitude coordinates that are required by a data source such as TerraServer. Other appropriate name and translation services can be added in a modular fashion, and the domain model can be updated to accommodate new concepts and relationships.

Authoritative Name Services. The three name services are WordNet, GNIS and GNS. When the initial query instance, specifying a person, place, or thing, is sent to the Ontology Agent, it then consults WordNet to retrieve synonyms. The synonyms are provided to the Query Formulation Agent to request that the user select one or more synonyms. The decision is communicated to the Ontology Agent which then updates the appropriate attribute in the instantiated version of the OWL schema. If the attribute value is the name of a class of type place then the Ontology Agent passes the instance to the both GNIS and GNS. These take the place name as input and provide the latitude-longitude coordinates as output. This information can then be communicated to the Query Formulation

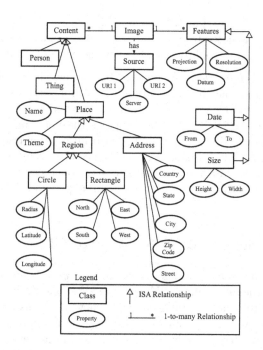

Fig. 2. Imagery Ontology Schema in Unified Modeling Language Notation

Agent which then forwards the information in the reformulated queries to the Web Services Agent for processing.

Query Formulation Agent. The User Agent poses an initial query to the Query Formulation Agent. This agent, in turn, consults the Ontology Agent to refine or generalize the query based on the semantic mediation provided by the available ontology services. Once a query has been specified by means of interactions among the User Agent and the Ontology Agent, the Query Formulation Agent decomposes the query into subqueries targeted for the appropriate data sources. This involves semantic mediation of terminology used in the domain model ontology and name services with those used by the local sources. Also, query translation is needed to retrieve data from the intended heterogeneous sources.

Web Services Agent. The main role of the Web Services Agent is to accept a user query that has been refined by consulting the Ontology Agent, and decomposed by the Query Formulation Agent. The Web Services Agent is responsible for the choreography and dispatch of subqueries to appropriate data sources, taking into consideration such facets as: user preference of sites; site authoritativeness and reputation; service-level agreements; size estimates of subquery responses; and quality-of-service measures of network traffic and dynamic site workload [6].

Ranking Agent. The Ranking Agent is responsible for compiling the sub-query results from the various sources, ranking them according to user preferences, as supplied by the Preferences Agent, for such attributes as: 1) the authoritativeness of a source which is indicated by a weight – a number between 0 and 10 – assigned to that source, or 2) the weight associated with a term comprising a query.

Data Sources and Web Services. At present, Knowledge Sifter consults two data sources: Yahoo Images and the TerraServer. Yahoo Images supports Representational State Transfer (REST)-based [7] web services which simply returns XML result data over HTTP. Yahoo Images supports the name and description for images; this allows the Ranking Agent to perform more precise evaluation for the semantic criteria. The Ranking Agent also uses the size of images contained in Yahoo Images metadata to filter images based on user preference, but the metadata does not contain the creation time of images which is a good measure of temporal aspect.

3   Emergent Semantics in Knowledge Sifter

This section presents some notions related to *emergent behavior and patterns* that arise from 1) the functioning of Knowledge Sifter, and 2) the use of composable Web services to create reusable search frameworks. This topic is discussed in detail in [3], so we present an overview here. Our approach to Emergent Semantics in Knowledge Sifter is to collect, index, organize and store significant artifacts created during the end-to-end workflow for KS. The KS workflow manages the entire search process, including, query specification, query reformulation, query decomposition, web service selection, data source selection, results ranking and recommendation presentation.

By stepping back and abstracting the agents, classes, their relationships and properties, one can construct the Knowledge Sifter Meta-Model (KSMM) [3]. Fig. 3 depicts the UML Static Model for the KSMM. What follows is a brief overview of the classes and relationships depicted in Fig. 3.

At the top is the Class Agent, which is specialized to those agents in the KS architecture, specifically the UserAgent, PreferencesAgent, OntologyAgent, QueryFormulationAgent, RankingAgent and WebServicesAgent. These agents manage their respective object classes, process specifications, and WebServices. For example, the UserAgent manages the User Class, the UserInterfaceScenario, the User PatternMiningAlgorithm, and the WebServices. The User specifies User Preferences that can be specialized to Search Preferences and Source Preferences. The User poses UserQuery that has several QueryConcept, which in turn relates to an OntologyConcept. The Ontology Agent manages both the UserQuery and the OntologyConcept that is provided by an OntologySource. Both OntologySource and DataSource are specializations of Source. Source is managed by the WebServicesAgent and has attributes such as provenance, coverage, access protocol and history. DataSource has attributes such as Quality-of-Service Service-Level-Agreements (QoS-SLAS) and Certificate.

A UserQuery consists of several RefinedQuery, each of which is posed to several DataSource. DataSource provides one-or-more DataItem in response to a RefinedQuery as the QueryResult. Based on the returned QueryResult, the User

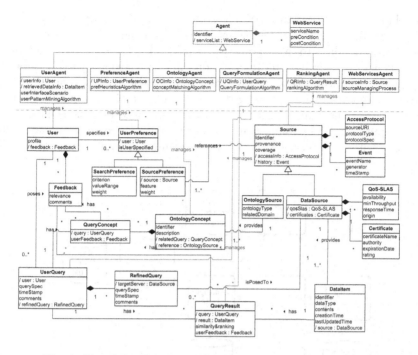

Fig. 3. Knowledge Sifter Meta-Model Schema in UML Notation

may provide Feedback as to the result relevance and other comments. These may impact the evolution of metadata associated with UserPreference, query formulation, data source usage and result ranking. The KSMM can be implemented as a relational database schema, which can be used to organize, store and interrelate the artifacts associated with a user query. The data can then be mined emergent properties related to the use of Knowledge Sifter resources.

4   Case-Based Knowledge Sifter Framework

The original Knowledge Sifter [3] creates a repository of user queries and artifacts produced during the search process. In this section, a case-based framework is proposed for KS in order to recommend query specifications and refinements based on the previously-stored user-query cases. A user query case is generated only when a user provides relevance feedback for results returned for a query. The user feedback is the user's evaluation of the degree of relevance of a result to the refined query; e.g., highly relevant; relevant; highly not relevant, or unclear. This relevance feedback can also be regarded as a user rating of the result's information quality.

The role of the Case Management Agent in Fig. 4 is to communicate with the User Agent, and to obtain cases from the User Query Case Base that have user feedback annotations. The Query Formulation Agent communicates with the

Case Management Agent to retrieve cases according to a user query and user preferences. To efficiently retrieve cases, the Case Management Agent maintains ontology-based indices to cases as described in Sect.4.2. From the retrieved cases, a refined query with data source information will be selected using a collaborative filtering approach which is described in Sect.4.3. KS also maintains pre-compiled component repository for accessing data sources for each information domain such as places, music, movies, scholarly papers, etc. Based on the collaborative filtering approach, KS semi-automatically selects data sources and is dynamically configured with Web Services-based wrapper components for each selected data source.

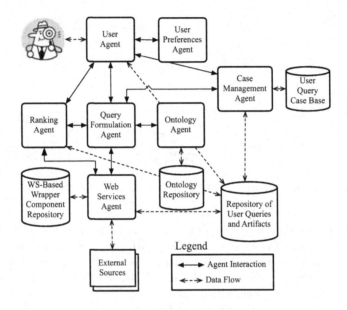

Fig. 4. Knowledge Sifter Case-Based Framework

4.1   Semantic Case Representation

Case-based Knowledge Sifter maintains cases representing a user query and its artifacts; these are required to recommend a refined query for each user-selected information domain. Fig. 5 shows an XML-based structure for the case representation. A case contains a username to identify its user, and this user identifier will be used to perform collaborative filtering and to retrieve the user's preferences. Also, each case has an associated user query and multiple refined queries, because KS generates a refined query for each information domain.

A user query can have multiple concepts which consist of a user term, multiple ontology references, and a weight. For example, suppose one wishes to visit the Washington Monument and then dine at a steakhouse in DC, then the keyword terms in a query might be "Washington monument" and "steakhouse". The ontology reference is a concept identifier in an ontology which contains the concept. WordNet is employed as a general upper ontology and several domain-specific ontologies such as places, restaurants, and wine can be linked and used to represent user concepts. This referenced ontology concept serves as an index of the user query as described in Sect.4.2. The concept weight is a degree of importance the user assigns to a concept. A refined query has exactly one information domain for which the query is specified. The refined query is a weighted multi-dimensional/multi-valued query as represented in Fig. 5. The feature name is also a variable since the schema of a refined query will be determined by its information domain and the user-selected data source. The data source information is also a feature of the refined query and it can be represented as $FeatureName : data - source, FeatureValue : imdb.com$, where IMDB denotes the Internet Movie Data Base.

Thus, a feature can be not only content-based metadata, but also metadata created during on the information object's life-cycle[9]. The feature name may be standardized in the scope of KS to remove the ambiguity which can occur during the search and recommendation processes described in Sect.4.3. Some standardized metadata such as Dublin Core Metadata can be used to describe feature attributes.

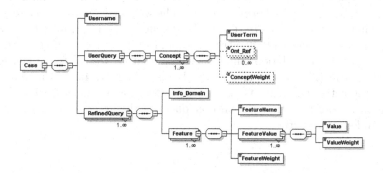

Fig. 5. XML-Based Semantic Representation of a User Case

4.2   Case Retrieval Via Ontology-Based Indices

The Case Management Agent maintains ontology-based indices for entire cases. As represented in Fig. 5, each user term of the query concept can have referenced ontology concepts. For each ontology concept, case identifiers referencing the ontology concept can be stored as the indices. Fig. 6 represents a simple index structure for an ontology which has an ontology identifier, several concept indices consisting of ontology concept identifiers of that ontology, and case identifiers for each of the ontology concepts. This approach allows for efficient retrieval of similar cases because it explores related ontology concepts first, rather than navigating a large number of the user query cases. Fig. 7 represents an algorithm for retrieving cases similar to the user query via ontology-based indices. First, the algorithm generates expanded queries of every possible combinations of

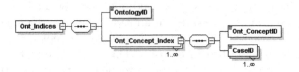

Fig. 6. XML-Schema for Ontology Index

concepts, including their equivalent and generalized concepts. For example, a user query {Washington Monument, steakhouse} can be expanded via ontology navigation as: {Washington Monument, chophouse}{Washington Monument, restaurant}{DC, steakhouse}, etc. The DC concept is obtained from WordNet through the "Part Holonym" relationship of the "Washington Monument" concept to the "DC" concept, and this can be regarded as a *spatial generalization*.

The algorithm then retrieves cases which are indexed by all the concepts of an expanded query, but limiting the number of the cases to a prespecified maximum. For efficiency purposes, whether the required number of cases are retrieved or not will be checked before expanding one element query of powerset of the user query because the expanded queries cannot be more similar to the user query than the original element query. The weighted sum of each query can be calculated from (1). The $sim(C_a, C_i)$ in the algorithm is a similarity between the expanded user query of the active case and the user query of the retrieved cases using cosine correlation which is widely used for the vector model in IR [8] as defined in (2). This similarity will be used in Sect. 4.3 as the similarity between the active case and its similar cases in terms of the similarity of their user queries. Note that the original user query of the active case is also one of the expanded user queries.

$$w(uq_i) = \sum_j tw(c_{ij}) * uw(c_{ij}) \qquad (1)$$

$$tw(c_{ij}) = \begin{cases} 1.0 & \text{if } c_{ij} \text{ is a user concept} \\ syw & \text{if } c_{ij} \text{ is an equivalent concept of the user concept} \\ hyw & \text{if } c_{ij} \text{ is a generalized concept of the user concept} \\ syw * hyw & \text{if } c_{ij} \text{ is a generalized concept of the equivalent concept} \end{cases}$$

where uq_i represents a user query for case i and $tw(c_{ij})$ represents a predefined weight for the type of jth concept in uq_i. The terms syw and hyw denote the predefined weight for an equivalent (synonym) concept and a generalized (hypernym) concept, respectively. The term $uw(c_{ij})$ is a user defined weight for a concept c_{ij}.

$$sim(C_a, C_i) = \frac{\sum_{j \in EQ_a} cw_{aj} \cdot cw_{ij}}{\sqrt{\sum_{j \in EQ_a} cw_{aj}^2} \cdot \sqrt{\sum_{j \in EQ_a} cw_{ij}^2}} \qquad (2)$$

where cw_{aj} and cw_{ij} represent the weights of jth concept in the expanded user query of the active case EQ_a and the user query of the retrieved case respectively.

```
Input: the active user query uqₐ
Output: a number (maxnc) of cases similar to the user query

maxnc ← 10
A set of retrieved cases RCS ← the Empty Set
A set of expanded queries EQS ← the Empty Set
CQS ← the powerset of uqₐ except the empty set
Sort elements of CQS in descending order of their weights
FOREACH cq in CQS
 IF #RCS < maxnc THEN
  FOREACH concept in cq
   EC ← a set containing the concept and its equivalent concepts
  END
  CPECS ← Cartesian product of EC sets
  FOREACH cpec in CPECS
   FOREACH concept in cpec
    HC ← a set containing the concept and its generalized concepts
   END
   CPHCS ← Cartesian product of HC sets
   FOREACH cphc in CPHCS
    WeightOfeq ← a weighted sum of concept weights in cphc
    Add cphc to EQS
   END
  END
  Sort elements of EQS in descending order of WeightOfeq
  FOREACH eq in EQS
   If WeightOfeq > WeightOfNextcq THEN
    Remove eq from EQS
    CASES ← a set of cases indexed by every concept in eq
    IF #RCS < maxnc THEN
     FOREACH case in CASES
      sim(Cₐ,Cᵢ) ← a cosine similarity of eq and case's user query
     END
     Sort elements of CASES in descending order of sim(Cₐ,Cᵢ)
     FOREACH case in CASES
      IF #RCS < maxnc THEN
       Add case to RCS
      END
     END
    END
   END
 END
END
```

Fig. 7. Case Retrieval Algorithm via Ontology Index

4.3 Collaborative Incremental Query Specification

Content-based filtering is a method for recommending unseen items to a user based on the contents of items they have already seen and are stored in their profile. It can assist users in refining a query based on the artifacts of their past queries which are similar to the active query. However, similar queries may not yet exist in the active user's profile, or the acceptable number of the user-preferred data items cannot be easily obtained because of insufficient feedback data provided thus-far.

This situation is ameliorated by using collaborative filtering, which attempts to predict usefulness of as yet unseen items for an active user, by proposing items based on those previously rated by other users. The basic idea is to recommend a set of unseen items that are preferred by other users who have tastes similar to the active user. Thus, the drawbacks of content-based filtering can be addressed with a higher level of confidence.

However, collaborative filtering cannot be applied directly to our case-based KS framework because more than one user-query case, stored in the case repository, may be similar to the active user query. A better approach is to recommend a single *aggregated* refined query from the cases having a certain level of user-query similarity. Therefore, a hybrid filtering approach which combines both collaborative filtering and content-based filtering can be used effectively in this architecture. However, if there is no previously-stored user query posed by the active user in the selected similar cases, the collaborative filtering cannot be directly used for the active refined query because the recommendation of the query specification should be made before retrieving results from data sources, i.e., no user feedback on results of the query which is required for the collaborative filtering exists on the recommendation time. To address this problem, an aggregated refined query from the refined queries of the selected cases can be recommended.

The case-based KS recommends the refined query and the user confirms that this is to now be the active refined query. During this confirmation step, the user can fine-tune the query parameters, e.g., for the data source feature, the user might add or remove data sources and adjust the weights for each data source. Then, KS retrieves results from the data sources in the user-confirmed refined query by dynamically translating it to one or more queries according to each data source's schema/ontology. The active user can provide feedback on some results and can request another recommendation of the specification. At this time, collaborative filtering can be used because the artifacts of active refined query will have been stored in the case base as a new case, it can then be selected as a similar case because the case's user query would be identical to the current specification of the active user query.

Data Item Recommendation via Query-to-Query Collaborative Filtering. With the user rating values for result data items of the active refined query, the active user's rating value of unseen data items can be predicted from the results and their rating values for the active refined query and neighbor refined queries which can be found from the KS repository. The prediction can be calculated from (3) and (4) which are derived from the well-known collaborative filtering approach used in GroupLens [10].

This refined query-based collaborative filtering allows KS to show the unseen data items immediately because the data items are found in a neighbor's search history in the repository. The mismatch problem between user queries and refined queries can be alleviated by using a threshold for the similarity between the active refined query and neighbor refined query, i.e., only the neighbor refined query having a certain high similarity value will be selected for this prediction process.

$$p_{rq_{ad},dt_u} = \overline{r_{rq_{ad}}} + \frac{\sum\limits_{i \in NC} (r_{rq_{id},dt_u} - \overline{r_{rq_{id}}}) \cdot sim(rq_{ad}, rq_{id}) \cdot sim(C_a, C_i)}{\sum\limits_{i \in NC} |sim(rq_{ad}, rq_{id})| \cdot sim(C_a, C_i)} \quad (3)$$

$$sim(rq_{ad}, rq_{id}) = \frac{\sum\limits_{s \in SD} (r_{rq_{ad},dt_s} - \overline{r_{rq_{ad}}}) \cdot (r_{rq_{id},dt_s} - \overline{r_{rq_{id}}})}{\sigma_{rq_{ad}} \cdot \sigma_{rq_{id}}} \quad (4)$$

where p_{rq_{ad},dt_u} represents a prediction for an unseen (unrated) data item dt_u for the active refined query rq_{ad}. rq_{ad} represents a refined query for the active user case a for the domain d. $sim(rq_{ad}, rq_{id})$ is the correlation weight for user rating patterns of the refined queries rq_{ad} and rq_{id} as defined by the Pearson Correlation Coefficient shown in (4). $sim(C_a, C_i)$ represents the similarity between the active case C_a and a neighbor case C_i as defined in (2). NC is a set of neighbor cases selected as similar to the active case. SD is a set of common seen (rated) items between rq_{ad} and rq_{id}. $\overline{r_{rq_{ad}}}$ and $\overline{r_{rq_{id}}}$ represent mathematical means for the ratings of the result data items of the queries rq_{ad} and rq_{id}, respectively.

Incremental Refined Query Specification. The active refined query can be incrementally specified based not only on the data items rated by the active user, but also on the data items whose rating value predicted from (3) and (4). That is, the refined query can be specified by content patterns of the rated data items and a new result set can be retrieved from a new data source set. More unseen data items can be found from above collaborative filtering with the new search artifacts. Thus, the refined query can be incrementally specified by aggregating the rated and predicted data items.

At first, the value weight for each feature of the active refined query can be found from (5) and (6). Then, the feature weight can be determined by (7) and (8) which also uses the Pearson Correlation Coefficient. This is based on an idea that if the similarity value patterns for a criterion (feature) and the user rating patterns are similar, the feature would be an important factor (feature) for the user to determine his likeness on the data. Therefore, this approach also takes into account the negative examples which have a negative feedback from users whereas content-based filtering systems [11][12] consider only the positive examples to refine queries in terms of weight adjustments. Furthermore, the negative correlation weight will become zero via the $n(x)$ function because the negative correlation would not necessarily mean that the user rated a data item as an relvant one since it is dissimilar to his query in the dimension of the feature or vice versa.

$$vw_{adfv} = \frac{\overline{rvv_{adfv}}}{\sum\limits_{l=1}^{m_{adf}} \overline{rvv_{adfl}}} \quad (5)$$

$$\overline{r_{vv_{adfl}}} = \frac{\displaystyle\sum_{m \in MD} r_{rq_{ad}, dt_m} \cdot O(vv_{adfl}, dt_m)}{\displaystyle\sum_{m \in MD} O(vv_{adfl}, dt_m)} \tag{6}$$

$$fw_{adf} = \frac{n(sim(f_{adf}, rq_{ad}))}{\displaystyle\sum_{k=1}^{m_{ad}} n(sim(f_{adk}, rq_{ad}))}; \quad n(x) = \begin{cases} x \text{ if } x > 0 \\ 0 \text{ otherwise} \end{cases} \tag{7}$$

$$sim(f_{adk}, rq_{ad}) = \frac{\displaystyle\sum_{m \in MD} (sim(f_{adk}, dt_m) - \overline{sim(f_{adk})}) \cdot (r_{rq_{ad}, dt_m} - \overline{r_{rq_{ad}}})}{\sigma_{f_{adk}} \cdot \sigma_{rq_{ad}}} \tag{8}$$

where vw_{adfv} represents the weight of the value vv_{adfv} for a feature f_{adf} of the query rq_{ad}. MD is a set of data items representing the union of the set of the seen data items and the set of predicted unseen data items.

$\overline{r_{vv_{adfv}}}$ represents an average rating value for data items in the set MD having a value vv_{adfv}. $O(vv_{adfl}, dt_m)$ is a binary variable which represents whether the data item dt_m has the value vv_{adfl}, and if yes, its value is 1, otherwise 0. $sim(f_{adk}, rq_{ad})$ represents the correlation weight between the criterion (feature) similarity and the original and predicted user ratings for the query rq_{ad}. $sim(f_{adk}, dt_m)$ represents the similarity value between the values of the query rq_{ad} and the data item dt_m in terms of the dimension of the feature f_{adk}.

Fig. 8 represents an example of the feature weight adjustment using the multiple weighted-valued query generated only from the positive examples via (3) and (4) and increased user feedback information via the query-to-query collaborative filtering. For the explanation purpose, the queries and data items in the example have only binary values for each features, but the equations surely work for the real values. The left table represents the feature vectors of the query and data items. The right table represents similarity values of the query and data items for each feature and rating values of the data items for the query. In this example, the similarity value of the query and a data item for a feature is 1 if they have same value, otherwise 0. Intuitively, the feature f_{ad1} would be regarded as an important criterion for which the user determines the relevance of the data items; therefore, it would be beneficial to have a higher weight on the feature for the efficiency of the system's automatic rating/search process. This approach would be advantageous for adjusting criterion weights for the systems of using the weighted/multi-valued query-based and heterogeneous types of values in each criterion thereby requiring different metrics for evaluating the values.

The incrementally specified query can seem to degrade the prediction ratio and efficiency of the search process because it aggregates contents of multiple data items. However, clearly it can have better recall ratio. The prediction ratio can be alleviated by using the weights so that the results can be automatically rated and sorted by a similarity measure based on the weights. The efficiency

	f_{ad1}	f_{ad2}	f_{ad3}	f_{ad4}
dt_1	1	0	1	0
dt_2	0	1	0	1
dt_3	1	1	1	0
dt_4	0	1	1	0
rq_{ad}	1	0	1	0

	dt_1	dt_2	dt_3	dt_4	$sim(f_{adk},rq_{ad})$	fw_{adk}
$sim(f_{ad1},dt_i)$	1	0	1	0	4	0.63
$sim(f_{ad2},dt_i)$	0	1	0	1	-4	0
$sim(f_{ad3},dt_i)$	1	1	1	0	2.31	0.37
$sim(f_{ad4},dt_i)$	0	1	1	0	0	0
$rating(rq_{ad},dt_i)$	1	0	1	0		

Fig. 8. An Example of Feature Weight Adjustment

problem can be caused if the refined query has more values because the number of data sources can be increased and some data sources do not provide multi-valued queries so that the refined query can be translated to a number of data source-specific queries. To address this problem, the translated queries having higher weight values can be priorly posed to a data source with a certain degree of parallel processing and the partial results can be shown to the users.

5   Conclusions

The Case-Based Knowledge Sifter framework expands on the original KS architecture by incorporating a novel XML-based index together with an indexing scheme for the efficient storage and retrieval of user-query cases. A methodology is presented for specifying, refining and processing user queries, based on a hybrid filtering approach that combines the best aspects of both content-based and collaborative filtering techniques.

The XML-based indexing scheme uses ontology-based concepts to index user-query cases. This leads to efficient algorithms for associative retrieval of relevant related cases, thereby avoiding a sequential search of the case base, as is the case in other case-based collaborative filtering systems [13][14][15].

Acknowledgments. This work was sponsored in part by a NURI from the National Geospatial-Intelligence Agency (NGA). This work was also sponsored in part by MIC & IITA through IT Leading R&D Support Project.

References

1. Kim, W., Kerschberg, L., Scime, A.: Learning for Automatic Personalization in a Semantic Taxonomy-Based Meta-Search Agent, Electronic Commerce Research and Applications (ECRA) 1, 2 (2002)
2. Kerschberg, L., Kim, W., Scime, A.: Personalizable semantic taxonomy-based search agent. USA: Patent Number 7,117,207, George Mason Intellectual Properties, Inc (Fairfax, VA) (October 3, 2006)
3. Kerschberg, L., Jeong, H., Kim, W.: Emergent Semantics in Knowledge Sifter: An Evolutionary Search Agent based on Semantic Web Services. In: Spaccapietra, S., Aberer, K., Cudré-Mauroux, P. (eds.) Journal on Data Semantics VI. LNCS, vol. 4090, pp. 187–209. Springer, Heidelberg (2006)

4. Morikawa, R., Kerschberg, L.: MAKO-PM: Just-in-Time Process Model. In: Althoff, K.-D., Dengel, A., Bergmann, R., Nick, M., Roth-Berghofer, T.R. (eds.) WM 2005. LNCS (LNAI), vol. 3782, pp. 688–698. Springer, Heidelberg (2005)

5. Miller, G.A.: WordNet a Lexical Database for English. Communications of the ACM 38(11), 39–41 (1995)

6. Menascé, D.A.: QoS Issues in Web Services. IEEE Internet Computing 72–75 (November/December 2002)

7. Fielding, R.: Architectural styles and the design of network-based software architectures. Ph. D. Dissertation, University of California at Irvine (2000)

8. Baeza-Yates, R., Ribeiro-Neto, B.: Modern Information Retrieval. ACM Press, New York (1999)

9. Smith, J.R., Schirling, P.: Metadata Standards Roundup. IEEE MultiMedia 13(2), 84–88 (2006)

10. Herlocker, J.L., Konstan, J.A., Borchers, A., Riedl, J.: An Algorithmic Framework for Performing Collaborative Filtering. SIGIR 230–237 (1999)

11. Porkaew, K., Chakrabarti, K.: Query refinement for multimedia similarity retrieval in MARS. ACM Multimedia (1), 235–238 (1999)

12. Wu, L., Faloutsos, C., Sycara, K., Payne, T.: Falcon: Feedback adaptive loop for content-based retrieval. In: Proceedings VLDB Conference, pp. 297–306 (2000)

13. Bradley, K., Smyth, B.: An Architecture for Case-Based Personalised Search. In: Funk, P., González Calero, P.A. (eds.) ECCBR 2004. LNCS (LNAI), vol. 3155, pp. 518–532. Springer, Heidelberg (2004)

14. Coyle, L., Doyle, D., Cunningham, P.: Representing Similarity for CBR in XML European Conference on Advances in Case-Based Reasoning, Spain (2004)

15. McCarthy, K., McGinty, L., Smyth, B., Salamo, M.: The Needs of the Many: A Case-Based Group Recommender System. In: Roth-Berghofer, T.R., Göker, M.H., Güvenir, H.A. (eds.) ECCBR 2006. LNCS (LNAI), vol. 4106, pp. 196–210. Springer, Heidelberg (2006)

Usages of Generalization in Case-Based Reasoning

Eva Armengol

IIIA, Artificial Intelligence Research Institute
CSIC, Spanish Council for Scientific Research
Campus UAB, 08193 Bellaterra, Catalonia (Spain)
eva@iiia.csic.es

Abstract. The aim of this paper is to analyze how the generalizations built by a CBR method can be used as local approximations of a concept. From this point of view, these local approximations can take a role similar to the global approximations built by eager learning methods. Thus, we propose that local approximations can be interpreted either as: 1) a symbolic similitude among a set of cases, 2) a partial domain model, or 3) an explanation of the system classification. We illustrate these usages by solving the Predictive Toxicology task.

1 Introduction

One of the main differences between eager and lazy methods used for concept learning is that the former generalizes a set of examples and builds a *global approximation* of a concept. Then, this global approximation is used for classifying unseen examples. Instead, lazy learning methods do not explicitly generalize the examples but they always use the complete set of examples. Thus, an unseen problem is classified according to its similitude to a subset of known examples. In this sense, lazy learning methods can be seen as building *local approximations* of concept [27] since the similar examples define an area around the new example which can be taken as a general description of that area. However sometimes the general knowledge, in the sense of global approximations of concepts, could also be useful inside lazy learning methods. PROTOS [24], one of the early Case-based Reasoning (CBR) systems, takes the idea of generalization commonly used on inductive learning methods to define categories of cases and also defines *exemplars* representing each category. Then, a new case is classified into a category if a match can be found between an exemplar and the new case. Notice that the exemplars play the same role as general descriptions of a class induced by some inductive learning method. Bergmann et al [10] proposed the idea of generalized cases, i.e. a case does not represent a single point of the problem-solution space but a subspace of it. The use of generalized cases can be seen as general descriptions of parts of the problem space.

In this paper we are interested in analyzing how generalizations can be used inside CBR. In particular, from both the literature and our experience we

R.O. Weber and M.M. Richter (Eds.): ICCBR 2007, LNAI 4626, pp. 31–45, 2007.
© Springer-Verlag Berlin Heidelberg 2007

identified some usages that generalization can have in the context of CBR. Thus, a generalization can be taken as a representative of a subset of cases as in PRO-TOS or in the work of Bergmann et al. [10], but also it could be interpreted as a symbolic similitude of a subset of cases as we proposed in [5]. In addition, we also propose the hypothesis that a set of local approximations can be seen as a partial model of a domain. The idea is that a lazy method can produce a generalization that explains the classification of a new problem, in a sense similar to the explanations produced by *explanation-based learning methods* [28]. A set of such explanations can be seen as a partial model of the domain since that model is able to classify only a subset of the available cases.

The structure of this paper is the following. Firstly we briefly introduce LID the method that we used in our experiments. LID produces a generalization that we call *similitude term* and that serves as the basis for the analysis of generalizations inside CBR. In particular, in section 3 we describe how generalizations can be interpreted as a symbolic similitude among a subset of cases. Then, in section 4 we explain how generalizations produced by a lazy method can be used to build a lazy model of the domain. In section 5 we describe how lazy generalizations can be interpreted as the explanation of the classification proposed by a CBR method. Finally, in section 6 we describe an application domain where we applied all the usages of generalizations we described in the previous sections.

2   Lazy Induction of Descriptions

In this section we briefly describe a lazy learning method called *Lazy Induction of Descriptions* (LID) we introduced in [5]. LID determines which are the more relevant features of a problem p and searches in the case base for cases sharing these relevant features. The problem p is classified when LID finds a set of relevant features shared by a subset of cases all belonging to the same solution class C_i. Then LID classifies the problem as belonging to C_i (Fig. 1). We call *similitude term* the description formed by these relevant features and *discriminatory set* the set of cases satisfying the similitude term. In fact, a similitude term is a generalization of both p and the cases in the discriminatory set.

The similitude term can be interpreted in several ways. Firstly, the similitude term can be seen as a partial discriminant description of C_i since all the cases satisfying the similitude term belong to C_i (according to one of the stopping conditions of LID). Therefore, the similitude term can be used as a generalization of knowledge in the sense of either PROTOS or inductive learning methods. On the other hand, because the similitude term contains the important features used to classify a problem, it can be interpreted as a justification or *explanation* of why the problem has been classified in C_i. Finally inside the context of multi-agent systems, where agents collaborate for solving problems, similitude terms could be taken as the basis for both exchanging knowledge and negotiation. In next sections the different usages of similitude terms is explained.

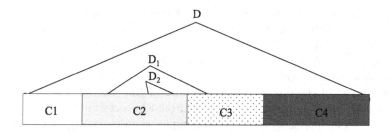

Fig. 1. From a description D that is satisfied by all the cases of the case base, LID builds successive specializations of D, until finding a similitude term (D_2 in this Fig.) that only is satisfied by cases of one class

3   Generalizations as Symbolic Similitude

Similarity among cases is one of the key issues of lazy methods in general and of CBR in particular. The usual approach to assess this similarity is by defining similarity measures. Since features defining domain objects can have different relevance concerning the classification task, some of these measures allow us to to weigh the features differently. Emde and Wettscherek [16] analyzed how the similarity measure influences the result of Instance-based Learning algorithm [1].

Eager learning methods induce discriminant descriptions of classes, i.e. they build descriptions with features that are only satisfied by examples belonging to one of the classes. For instance, an inductive learning method such as ID3 [30] produces a decision tree where each path from the root to a leaf gives the pairs attribute-value that are important to classify an example as belonging to a class C_i. Notice that, in fact, a path is a general and discriminant description d_i of C_i that can be interpreted as a *symbolic similitude* among the cases in C_i. In other words, d_i contains the features shared by a set of examples belonging to C_i.

What is the role of the similitude term produced by LID? On one hand, LID classifies a new problem p as belonging to a class C_i *because* it is similar to a subset of cases in C_i that share some features that have been considered as the most important for the classification. Therefore, in this sense the similitude term plays the role of symbolic similitude as the paths of a decision tree. On the other hand, because LID is a lazy method, that similitude term shows the similitude of the particular problem p to the subset of cases belonging to C_i that satisfy the similitude term.

4   Lazy Generalizations for Building Lazy Domain Models

Lazy learning methods classify a new problem based on the similarity among that problem and a subset of known cases. Commonly, once the system proposes the solution, all the generalizations used to achieve the solution are rejected. The justification of this is that any generalization is constructed based on the new problem. Our point is that, although these generalizations define a local approximation to the concept defined by the new problem, they can be useful for solving other problems inside such area. Therefore, as well as a CBR system is solving new problems, it can store all the local approximations supporting the classification of these problems. The set of such approximations can be seen as a *partial* model of the domain. The partiality of that domain comes from the fact that each local approximation is build from a subset of examples instead of being a model including all the known examples as in eager learning methods.

This lazy way to build a domain model can be useful in domains such as Predictive Toxicology [21] or some medical problems, where experts are interested in finding models about the domain. The usual tool in such domains is an eager learning method inducing general domain knowledge. The main problem of these approaches is that sometimes the models have to be induced from a set of cases with high variability and the result is a set of rules that are too general to be useful for classification. An example of a lazy construction of a domain model is the *Lazy Decision Trees (LDT)* proposed by [17]. Differently from pure eager techniques, LDT build a decision tree in a lazy way, i.e. each time that a new problem has to be classified, the system reuses, if possible, the existing tree. Otherwise, a new branch classifying the new problem is added to the tree. Notice that, in fact, the decision tree represents a general model of a domain and LDT builds it in a lazy way. The main difference between inductive learning methods and LDT is that the former generalize from all the examples of a class whereas the latter takes into account only the characteristics of the problem at hand.

A similar idea is behind the method C-LID [8]. C-LID is implemented on top of LID by storing the similitude terms provided by LID and using them as domain knowledge useful for solving new problems. C-LID uses two policies: the caching policy and the reuse policy. The *caching policy* determines which similitude terms (patterns) are to be retained. The *reuse policy* determines when and how the cached patterns are used to solve new problems. The caching policy of C-LID states that a similitude term D is stored when all cases covered by a pattern belong to one class only. The *reuse policy* of C-LID states that patterns will be used for solving a problem p only when LID is unable to univocally classify p.

The assumption of C-LID is that the similitude term is a partial description of the solution class in the same sense as in inductive learning methods. Thus the set of patterns stored by C-LID can be seen (an used) as a domain model, even if this model is partial because it does not cover all the available examples.

5   Generalizations and Explanations

Explaining the outcome of a CBR system has been an issue of growing interest in recent years. In 2004 was the first workshop on explanations in the framework of the EWCBR held in Madrid [18]. The focus of this workshop was to analyze how CBR applications from very different domain explain their result to the user. Then, in 2005 Roth-Berghofer and his colleagues organized an international workshop in the framework of the AAAI conference [9] with the same focus: to analyze different forms to explain the results. In the latter workshop the scope was not only CBR but authors participating in it coming from very different fields.

Focusing on CBR, in particular in recommender systems, the most common form of explanation is to show the user the set of cases that the system has assessed as the most similar to the new case at hand. Nevertheless some authors agree that in some situations this may not be a good explanation. For instance, McSherry [26] argues that the most similar case (in addition to the features that have been taken as relevant for selecting that case) also has features that could act as arguments against that case. For this reason, McSherry proposes that the explanation of a CBR system has to explicitly distinguish between the case features in favor of an outcome and the case features against it. In this way, the user could decide about the final solution of the problem. A related idea, proposed in [25], is to use the differences among cases to support the user in understanding why some cases do not satisfy some requirements.

Explanations had received attention from the early rule-based systems, that explained the result by showing the user the chain of rules that produce the solution. Inductive learning methods can also explain their results by showing the general descriptions satisfied by the new problem. The explanation of a decision tree outcome could be formed by showing the conditions satisfied in the path from the root to a leaf used to classify a new problem. *Explanation-based learning (EBL)* [28] is a family of methods that build explanations by generalizing examples. In short, EBL solves a problem and then analyzes the problem solving trace in order to generalize it. The generalized trace is an *explanation* that, in fact, is used as a new domain rule for solving new problems. This explanation is represented using the same formalism as the problems, therefore it is perfectly understandable and usable by the system. In other words, the generalization of the process followed for solving a problem has been taken as explanation of the result and can be also used for solving future problems. Conceptually similar is the use that [8] makes of the similitude terms given by LID. The similitude term can be seen as a justification of the classification given by LID since it contains all the aspects considered as relevant to classify an example.

An explanation scheme for CBR based on the concept of *least general generalization* was introduced in [9]. The relation *more general than* ($\geq_g$) forms a lattice over a generalization language $\mathcal{G}$. Using the relation $\geq_g$ we can define the *least general generalization* or *anti-unification* of a collection of descriptions (either generalizations or instances) as follows:

- $AU(d_1, ..., d_k) = g$ such that $(g \geq_g d_1) \wedge ... \wedge (g \geq_g d_k)$ and not exists $(g' \geq_g d_1) \wedge ... \wedge (g' \geq_g d_k)$ such that $g' >_g g$

In other words the anti-unification g of a set of descriptions is the most specific generalization of these descriptions in the sense that there is no other generalization g' of all these descriptions that is more specific than g. The anti-unification is a description composed of all the properties shared by the descriptions. Therefore, the anti-unification can be seen as a symbolic description of the similarity among these descriptions.

Thus, descriptions resulting from the anti-unification of a collection of cases can be used to provide explanation of the classification of a new problem in CBR systems. Let us explain in more detail the explanation scheme based on the anti-unification concept we introduced in [9].

Let C be the set of cases that have been considered as the most similar to a problem p. For the sake of simplicity we assume that there are only two solution classes: $C_1 \subseteq C$ and $C_2 \subseteq C$ ($C = C_1 \cup C_2$). The explanation scheme is composed of three descriptions:

- AU^*: the anti-unification of p with all the cases in C. This description shows what aspects of the problem are shared by all the compounds in C, i.e. cases in C are similar to p because they have in common what is described in AU^*.
- AU_1: the anti-unification of p with the cases in C_1. This description shows what has c in common with the cases in C_1.
- AU_2: the anti-unification of p with the cases in C_2. This description shows what has p in common with the cases in C_2.

Thus the explanation of why a case p is in a class C_i is given by what p shares with the retrieved cases in that class. In other words, the anti-unification $AU(c_1...c_k, p)$ is an explanation of why the cases in C are similar to p, since it is a description of all that is shared among the retrieved cases and the new problem. Section 6.4 shows an example of ow this explanation scheme is used on the Predictive Toxicology task.

In the next section we explain in detail an application on Predictive Toxicology, where all the usages of generalizations explained in the previous sections have been applied.

6   A Case Study: Predictive Toxicology

In this section we explain the approach we introduced to solve the predictive toxicology task, i.e. to assess the carcinogenic activity of chemical compounds. This is a complex problem that most approaches try to solve using machine learning methods. The goal of these approaches is to build a general model of carcinogenesis from both domain knowledge and examples of carcinogen and non-carcinogen chemical compounds. Because these general models give not enough predictivity, we take a completely different vision of the problem. Our idea is that the low predictivity of the induced models is due to the high variability of the chemical compounds that produces overgeneralizations. Thus, we decided to take a lazy approach and to consider that the goal is to classify a chemical compound as carcinogen or non-carcinogen. Therefore all the efforts have to focus on the features allowing the classification of the chemical compound at hand. In other words, we do not try to build a general model of carcinogenesis as ML techniques do but we only try to classify a particular chemical compound.

Nevertheless, we benefit from the classification of that compound to build some patterns of carcinogenesis.

In the next sections we explain how we solved the problem. First we describe the predictive toxicology problem and a new representation of chemical compounds using feature terms. Then we describe how C-LID can be used as a lazy problem solving method but also as a form to build some domain knowledge. Finally, we detail how the system can explain the results to a chemist by means of the explanation scheme introduced in section 5.

6.1   The Toxicology Domain

Every year thousands of new chemicals are introduced in the market for their use in products such as drugs, foods, pesticides, cosmetics, etc. Although these new chemicals are widely analyzed before commercialization, the effects of many of them on human health are not totally known. In 1973 the European Commission started a long term program consisting of the design and development of toxicology and ecotoxicology chemical databases. The main idea of this program was to establish lists of chemicals and methods for testing their risks on people and the environment. Similarly, in 1978 the American Department of Health and Human Services established the National Toxicology Program (NTP) with the aim of coordinating toxicological testing programs and developing standard methods to detect potentially carcinogenic compounds (see more information in www.ntp-server.niehs.nih.gov). When a chemical compound is suspected to be toxic, it is included in the NTP list in order to perform standardized experiments to determine its toxicity degree.

The use of computational methods applied to the toxicology field could contribute to reduce the cost of experimental procedures. In particular, artificial intelligence techniques such as knowledge discovery and machine learning (ML) can be used for building models of compound toxicity (see [20] for a survey).

6.2   Representation of Chemical Compounds

Predictive toxicology is a complex task for ML techniques. There is no ML technique providing excellent results [21], a likely explanation is that the current representation of chemical compounds is not adequate. The usual representation of chemical compounds is using *structure-activity relationship (SAR)* descriptors coming from commercial tools from drug design such as CODESSA [22], TSAR (Oxford molecular products, www.accelrys.com/chem/), DRAGON (www.disat.inimib.it/chm/Dragon.htm). By means of these descriptors a natural way to represent a chemical compound is as a set of attribute value pairs (propositional representation). A challenge on Predictive Toxicology held in 2001 [21] was focused on ML techniques and most contributions proposed a relational representation based on SAR descriptors and used inductive techniques for solving the classification task. Moreover the relational representation and the ILP techniques also allow the representation and use of chemical background knowledge.

Other approaches to represent chemical compounds have been proposed. For instance [14,19,12] represent the compounds as labeled graphs and this allows

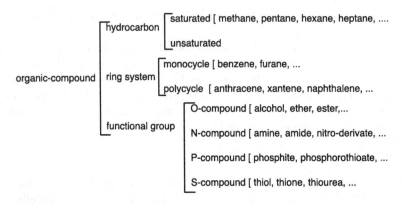

Fig. 2. Partial view of the chemical ontology

the use of graph search algorithms for detecting frequent substructures of the molecules in the same class. Particularly interesting are SUBDUE [12] and SMILES [35] that follow this approach. A completely different approach was introduced in [11] where the compounds are organized according to their active centers (chemically identified with weak bonds).

The representation of chemical compounds we propose is based on the chemical terminology, i.e the IUPAC (*International Union of Pure and Applied Chemistry*) nomenclature (www.chem.qmul.ac.uk/iupac/). Also we take into account the experience of previous research (specially the works in [19,15,11]) since we represent a chemical compound as a structure with substructures. Our point is that there is no need to describe in detail the properties of individual atom properties in a molecule (like some relational representations based on SAR do) when the domain ontology has a characterization for the type of that molecule. For instance, the *benzene* is an aromatic ring composed by six carbon atoms with some well-known properties. While SAR models would represent a given compound as having six carbon atoms related together (forming an aromatic ring), in our approach we simply state that the compound is a benzene (abstracting away the details and properties of individual atoms).

Figure 2 shows a partial view of the chemical ontology we used for representing the compounds in the Toxicology data set. This ontology is based on the chemical nomenclature which, in turn, is a systematic way of describing the molecular structure of chemical compounds. In fact, the name of a molecule using the standard nomenclature, provides chemists with all the information needed to graphically represent its structure. According to the chemical nomenclature rules, the name of a compound is usually formed in the following way: *radicals' names + main group*. Commonly, the *main group* is the part of the molecule that is either the largest or that is located in a central position; however, there is no general rule to establish them. *Radicals* are groups of atoms usually smaller than the main group. A main group can have several radicals and a radical can, in turn, have a new set of radicals. Any group of atoms could be a main group

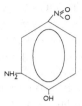

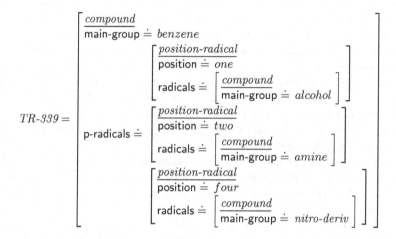

Fig. 3. Representation of the *2-amino-4-nitrophenol*, with feature terms

or a radical depending on their position or relevance on the molecule, i.e. the benzene may be the main group in one compound and a radical in some other compounds.

Figure 3 shows the representation of the chemical compound, *2-amino-4-nitrophenol*, using feature terms [4]. The *2-amino-4-nitrophenol* has a benzene as its main group and a set of three radicals: an *alcohol* in position one; an *amine* in position two; and a *nitro-deriv* in position four. Notice that this information directly comes from the chemical name of the compound following the nomenclature rules. This kind of description has the advantage of being very close to the representation that an expert has of a molecule from the chemical name.

6.3   Assessing Carcinogenic Activity to Chemical Compounds

Inductive learning techniques applied to the Predictive Toxicology try to extract general rules describing the cases in each class. These kinds of techniques have some difficulties in dealing with domains, like toxicology, where entities are subject to high variability. The goal of predictive toxicology is to develop models able to predict whether or not a chemical compound is carcinogen. The construction of these models using inductive learning methods takes into account the toxicity observed in some molecules to extract theories about the carcinogenecity on families of molecules. Early systems focused on predictive toxicology were DEREK [31] and CASE [23]. PROGOL [34] was the first ILP program used to induce SAR models. PROGOL's results were very encouraging since the final rules were more understandable than those obtained using the other methods.

Lazy learning techniques, on the other hand, are based on the retrieval of a set of solved problems similar to a specific problem. Several authors use the concept of similarity between chemical compounds: HazardExpert [13] is an expert system that evaluates the similarity of two molecules based on the number of common substructures; Sello [32] also uses the concept of similarity but the representation of the compounds is based on the energy of the molecules.

We conducted a series of experiments focused on the use of lazy learning techniques for classifying chemical compounds. In [7] we report the results of using the *k-nearest neighbor* (*k-NN*) algorithm with Shaud as similarity measure. Results of these experiments show that our approach is comparable to results produced by inductive methods in terms of both accuracy and ROC analysis. We want to remark that our approach only handles information about the molecular structure of the chemical compounds whereas the other approaches use more information (SAR descriptors).

Clearly, in Predictive Toxicology the classification of a particular chemical compound its important, nevertheless, experts are also interested in finding a general model of carcinogenesis. In this sense, we think the use of C-LID can satisfy these expert's interests. On one hand it can classify a chemical compound and also justify this classification; on the other hand, it can produce general knowledge about carcinogenesis thanks to the similitude term. Thus, we conducted some experiments with a main goal: to build a (partial) model of carcinogenesis using C-LID. These experiments are composed of two steps: 1) using LID with the leave-one-out in order to generate similitude terms for classifying the cases; and 2) select a subset of these similitude terms to build a partial carcinogenesis model. We consider that the model is partial because given a class, we can only assure that the similitude term generated by LID is satisfied by a subset of compounds of that class. The idea behind these experiments comes from the observation of the similitude terms given by LID to justify the classification of a chemical compound (step 1). By analyzing these similitude terms we note that some of them are given several times and that they are good descriptions of carcinogen (or non-carcinogen) compound. This means that there are some features (those included in the similitude terms) that are good descriptors of a class since they are often used to classify compounds as belonging to that class. consequently, they can be used by C-LID as general domain knowledge for assessing the carcinogenic activity of new chemical compounds (step 2).

In [6] we report some domain knowledge contained in the carcinogenesis model built thanks to the similitude terms of LID and that have been successfully used by C-LID for predecting the carcinogenesis of unseen chemical compounds. Some of the patterns detecting positive toxicity are also reported in the literature. For instance, LID founds that compounds with a radical chlorine are carcinogenic and Brautbar (www.expertnetwork.com/med2.htm) describes some experiments confirming the toxicity of chlorinated hydrocarbons. Nevertheless, there are other patterns whose positive carcinogenic activity is not clearly reported in the literature. An example of this are the chemical compounds with the polycycle *anthracene*. An analysis of the chemical compounds with *anthracene* included in the data set of the NTP shows that they are positive in rats, nevertheless there are no laboratory experiments confirming this result, even there are reports explaining that *anthracene* is a molecule with a high tendency to make associations with other molecules and these associations could easily be carcinogenic. Other patterns included in the partial domain knowledge built by C-LID concern the carcinogenecity of chemical compounds containing *epoxydes, bromine* and long *carbon* chains. Some of these patterns are confirmed by the experimental knowledge, therefore they could be directly included as rules of a model. Nevertheless, because C-LID is lazy it can include in the model some knowledge that is not general enough to be induced but that is true for a known subset of compounds (like the case of the long chains of *carbons*).

6.4 The Explanation Scheme

A common situation in toxicology is that chemical compounds with similar molecular structure have different carcinogenic activity. Therefore, the use of lazy learning methods, based on the similarity among structures of the compounds, can produce non univocal classifications. That is to say, a chemical compound can share some structural aspects with carcinogen compounds but it can also also share other aspects with no carcinogen compounds. Let C be the set of chemical compounds that have been considered by a lazy learning method (say k-NN) as the most similar to a compound c. Let $C^+ \subseteq C$ be the subset of positive (carcinogen) compounds and $C^- \subseteq C$ the subset of negative (non-carcinogenic) compounds ($C = C^+ \cup C^-$). In such situation the final prediction about the carcinogenic activity of c is taken using the *majority rule*, i.e. the compound is classified as belonging to the same class as the majority of the compounds in C. The application of the majority rule seems appropriate when there is a "clear" majority of compounds belonging to one of the classes. Nevertheless this is not always the case, consequently the result has to be explained to the user. In fact, more important than the classification should be to show the user the similitude that the compound has with compounds of both classes. In other words, if the user can analyze by themself the reasons that explain the classification of the compound in each one of the classes, then s/he could decide the final classification of the compound.

Let us illustrate the complete explanation scheme with an example. The right hand side of Fig. 4 shows a chemical compound, namely C-356, for which we want to assess its carcinogenicity for male rats. The set C of retrieved cases (*retrieval set*), formed by five chemical compounds considered the most similar to C-356 is also shown on the right hand side of Fig. 4. The set C is divided in $C^- = \{C$-$424, C$-$171\}$ and $C^+ = \{C$-$084, C$-$127, C$-$142\}$ according to the carcinogenic activity of the compounds.

Following our approach, the explanation scheme (left hand side of Fig. 4) for chemical compound C-356 is as follows:

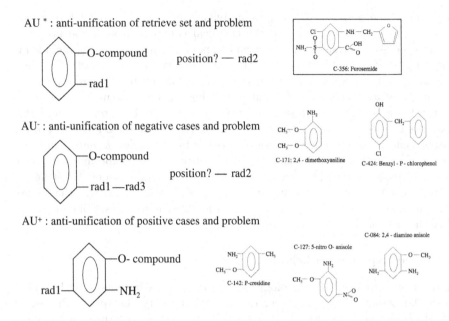

Fig. 4. AU^* is the chemical structure common to all the compounds in Fig. **??**. AU^- is the chemical structure common to C-356 and the negative compounds (i.e. C-424 and C-171). AU^+ is the chemical structure common to C-356 and the positive compounds (i.e. C-084, C-127 and C-142).

- The description AU^* shows that C-356 and the compounds in C have in common that they are all benzenes with at least three radicals: one of these radicals is a functional group derived from the oxygen (i.e. an alcohol, an ether or an acid) called O-compound in the figure; another radical (called rad1 in the figure) is in the position next to the functional group (chemically this means that both radicals are in disposition *ortho*). Finally, there is a third radical (called rad2 in the figure) that is in no specific position.
- The description AU^- shows that C-356 and the chemical compounds in C^- have in common that they are benzenes with three radicals: one radical derived from an oxygen (O-compound), a radical rad1 with another radical (rad3 in the figure) in position *ortho* with the O-compound, and finally a third radical (rad2) with no specific position.
- The description AU^+ shows that C-356 and the chemical compounds in C^+ have in common that they are benzenes with three radicals: one of the radicals is derived from an oxygen (O-compound), another radical is an *amine* (NH_2) in position *ortho* with the O-compound, and a third radical (rad1) is at distance 3 of the O-compound (chemically this means that both radicals are in disposition *para*).

Using the majority rule, the compound C-356 will be classified as positive. The explanation scheme explicitly shows the user the similarities among the compound and the retrieved compounds (with known activity). Nevertheless, the user can also easily compare all the descriptions and analyze the differences between them. Thus, from AU^- and AU^+ the user is able to observe that the presence of the *amine* (NH_2) may hypothetically be a key factor in the classification of a compound as positive for carcinogenesis. Once the symbolic similarity description gives a key factor (such as the *amine* in our example), the user can proceed to search the available literature for any empirical confirmation of this hypothesis. In this particular example, a cursory search in the Internet has shown that there is empirical evidence supporting the hypothesis of *amine* presence in aromatic groups (i.e. benzene) being correlated with carcinogenicity [33], [2].

Notice that a similar explanation scheme could be proposed when using LID instead of the k-NN algorithm for solving the classification task. In such case the similitude term takes the role of the description AU^*, i.e. the anti-unification of the k cases similar to a problem p. The difference among both AU^* and the similitude term is that the former contains *all* that is shared by the k cases whereas the later contains only the relevant features used for classifying p. A detailed description of the use of the similitude term as explanation can be found in [3].

7 Conclusions

Lazy learning methods can build local approximations of concepts. In this paper we analyzed how these approximations can be used in a CBR method. In particular, we analyzed the usages as 1) symbolic similitude among a set of cases; 2) partial model of the domain, when they are stored to be used for solving new problems; and 3) as explanations, since they can be interpreted as the justification of the classification given by the system.

We show an example of these usages of generalization for solving the Predictive Toxicology task. Moreover, the generalization can also be used in the same terms in the context of multi-agent systems as is proposed by Ontañón and Plaza in [29]. In fact, these authors propose to use the generalizations build by a CBR method as a means for the communication of knowledge among the agents.

Acknowledgments

Author thanks Enric Plaza, Ramon López de Mántaras and Josep Lluis Arcos for all the helpful discussions during the elaboration of this paper. This work has been supported by the MCYT-FEDER Project MID-CBR (TIN2006-15140-C03-01)

References

1. Aha, D.W., Kibler, D., Albert, M.K.: Instance-based learning algorithms. Machine Learning 6(1), 37–66 (1991)
2. Ambs, S., Neumann, H.G.: Acute and chronic toxicity of aromatic amines studied in the isolated perfused rat liver. Toxicol. Applied Pharmacol. 139, 186–194 (1996)

3. Armengol, E.: Discovering plausible explanations of carcinogenecity in chemical compounds. In: Perner, P. (ed.) MLDM 2007. LNCS (LNAI), vol. 4571, pp. 756–769. Springer, Heidelberg (2007)
4. Armengol, E., Plaza, E.: Bottom-up induction of feature terms. Machine Learning 41(1), 259–294 (2000)
5. Armengol, E., Plaza, E.: Lazy induction of descriptions for relational case-based learning. In: Flach, P.A., De Raedt, L. (eds.) ECML 2001. LNCS (LNAI), vol. 2167, pp. 13–24. Springer, Heidelberg (2001)
6. Armengol, E., Plaza, E.: Discovery of toxicological patterns with lazy learning. In: Palade, V., Howlett, R.J., Jain, L. (eds.) KES 2003. LNCS, vol. 2774, pp. 919–926. Springer, Heidelberg (2003)
7. Armengol, E., Plaza, E.: Relational case-based reasoning for carcinogenic activity prediction. Artif. Intell. Rev. 20(1-2), 121–141 (2003)
8. Armengol, E., Plaza, E.: Remembering similitude terms in case-based reasoning. In: Perner, P., Rosenfeld, A. (eds.) MLDM 2003. LNCS, vol. 2734, pp. 121–130. Springer, Heidelberg (2003)
9. Armengol, E., Plaza, E.: Symbolic explanation of similarities in case-based reasoning. Computing and informatics 25(2-3), 153–171 (2006)
10. Bergmann, R., Stahl, A.: Similarity measures for object-oriented case representations. In: Smyth, B., Cunningham, P. (eds.) EWCBR 1998. LNCS (LNAI), vol. 1488, pp. 8–13. Springer, Heidelberg (1998)
11. Blinova, V., Bobryinin, D.A., Kuznetsov, S.O., Pankratova, E.S.: Toxicology analysis by means of simple jsm method. In: Procs. of the Predictive Toxicology Challenge Workshop, Freiburg, Germany (2001)
12. Chittimoori, R., Holder, L., Cook, D.: Applying the subdue substructure discovery system to the chemical toxicity domain. In: Procs. of the Twelfth International Florida AI Research Society Conference, 1999, pp. 90–94 (1999)
13. Darvas, F., Papp, A., Allerdyce, A., Benfenati, E., Gini, G., et al.: Overview of different ai approaches combined with a deductive logic-based expert system for predicting chemical toxicity. In: Gini, G.C., Katrizky, A.R. (eds.) Predictive Toxicology of Chemicals: Experiences and Impacts of AI Tools, pp. 94–99. AAAI Press, Stanford (1999)
14. Dehaspe, L., Toivonen, H., King, R.D.: Finding frequent substructures in chemical compounds. In: Agrawal, R., Stolorz, P., Piatetsky-Shapiro, G. (eds.) 4th International Conference on Knowledge Discovery and Data Mining, pp. 30–36. AAAI Press, Stanford (1998)
15. Deshpande, M., Karypis, G.: Automated approaches for classifying structures. In: Proc. of the 2nd Workshop on Data Mining in Bioinformatics (2002)
16. Emde, W., Wettschereck, D.: Relational instance based learning. In: Saitta, L. (ed.) Machine Learning - Procs. 13th International Conference on Machine Learning, pp. 122–130. Morgan Kaufmann Publishers, San Francisco (1996)
17. Friedman, J.H., Kohavi, R., Yun, Y.: Lazy decision trees. AAAI/IAAI 1, 717–724 (1996)
18. Gervás, P., Gupta, K.M.: Explanations in CBR. In: Funk, P., González Calero, P.A. (eds.) ECCBR 2004. LNCS (LNAI), vol. 3155, pp. 142–144. Springer, Heidelberg (2004)
19. Gonzalez, J.A., Holder, L.B., Cook, D.J.: Graph based concept learning. In: AAAI/IAAI, p. 1072 (2000)
20. Helma, C., Gottmann, E., Kramer, S.: Knowledge discovery and data mining in toxicology. Statistical Methods in Medical Research 9, 329–358 (2000)

21. Helma, C., Kramer, S.: A survey of the predictive toxicology challenge 2000-2001. Bioinformatics (page in press, 2003)
22. Katritzky, A.R, Petrukhin, R., Yang, H., Karelson, M.: CODESSA PRO. User's manual. University of Florida (2002)
23. Klopman, G.: Artificial intelligence approach to structure-activity studies: Computer automated structure evaluation of biological activity of organic molecules. Journal of the America Chemical society 106, 7315–7321 (1984)
24. Kolodner, J.: Case-based reasoning. Morgan Kaufmann, San Francisco (1993)
25. McCarthy, K., Reilly, J., McGinty, L., Smyth, B.: Thinking positively - explanatory feedback for conversational recommender systems. In: Procs of the ECCBR 2004 Workshops. TR 142-04, pp. 115–124. Dep. de Sistemas Informáticos y Programación, Universidad Complutense de Madrid, Madrid, Spain (2004)
26. McSherry, D.: Explanation in recommendation systems. In: Procs. of the ECCBR 2004 Workshops. TR 142-04, pp. 125–134. Dep. de Sistemas Informáticos y Programación, Univ. Complutense de Madrid, Madrid, Spain (2004)
27. Mitchell, T.M.: Machine Learning (International Editions). Computer Science Series. McGraw-Hill, New York (1997)
28. Mitchell, T.M., Keller, R.M., Kedar-Cabelli, S.T.: Explanation-based learning: A unifying view. Machine Learning 1(1), 47–80 (1986)
29. Ontañón, S., Plaza, E.: Justification-based multiagent learning. In: Procs. 20th ICML, pp. 576–583. Morgan Kaufmann, San Francisco (2003)
30. Quinlan, J.R.: Induction of decision trees. Mach. Learn. 1(1), 81–106 (1986)
31. Sanderson, D.M., Earnshaw, C.G.: Computer prediction of possible toxic action from chemical structure: the derek system. Human and Experimental Toxicology 10, 261–273 (1991)
32. Sello, G.: Similarity, diversity and the comparison of molecular structures. In: Gini, G.C., Katrizky, A.R. (eds.) Predictive Toxicology of Chemicals: Experiences and Impacts of AI Tools, pp. 36–39. AAAI Press, Stanford (1999)
33. Sorensen, R.U.: Allergenicity and toxicity of amines in foods. In: Procs. of the IFT 2001 Annual Meeting, New Orleans, Louisiana (2001)
34. Srinivasan, A., Muggleton, S., King, R.D., Sternberg, M.J.: Mutagenesis: Ilp experiments in a non-determinate biological domain. In: Procs. of the Fourth Inductive Logic Programming Workshop (1994)
35. Weininger, D.J.: Smiles a chemical language and information system. J. Chem. Inf. Comput. Sci. 28(1), 31–36 (1988)

Team Playing Behavior in Robot Soccer: A Case-Based Reasoning Approach*

Raquel Ros[1], Ramon López de Màntaras[1], Josep Lluís Arcos[1],
and Manuela Veloso[2]

[1] IIIA - Artificial Intelligence Research Institute
CSIC - Spanish Council for Scientific Research
Campus UAB, 08193 Barcelona, Spain
{ros,mantaras,arcos}@iiia.csic.es
[2] Computer Science Department, Carnegie Mellon University
Pittsburgh, PA 15213 USA
veloso@cs.cmu.edu

Abstract. This paper presents extensions and improvements of previous work, where we defined a CBR system for action selection in the robot soccer domain. We show empirical results obtained with real robots, comparing our team playing approach with an individualist approach.

1 Introduction

Action selection in robotics is a challenging task: the robot has to reason about its world beliefs (the state of the environment), and rationally act in consequence in order to complete a task (typically divided in subtasks). Moreover, in the case of a robot team, robots must agree on the decisions made (who and what to do to complete the subtasks), jointly execute the actions, and coordinate among them to successfully perform the task. Working with real robots has additional difficulties that must be considered while developing their reasoning system. Thus, the reasoning engine must be capable of dealing with high uncertainty in the robot's perception (incoming information of the world), and be robust in case of failure, since the outcomes of the actions performed are unpredictable. Not to mention that decision must be made on real time and in our case, with limited computational resources.

This paper presents extensions and improvements of previous work [7], where we defined a CBR system for the robot soccer domain. Given a state of the environment the aim of the approach is to define the sequence of actions the robots should perform during a game. In this first attempt, we presented a preliminary model of our CBR system and we also showed initial experiments with one robot in a simulated environment.

* Partial funding by the Spanish Ministry of Education and Science project MID-CBR (TIN2006-15140-C03-01) and partly sponsored by BBNT Solutions, LLC under contract no. FA8760-04-C-0002. Raquel Ros holds a scholarship from the Generalitat de Catalunya Government. The views and conclusions contained herein are those of the authors and should not be interpreted as representing any sponsoring institutions.

R.O. Weber and M.M. Richter (Eds.): ICCBR 2007, LNAI 4626, pp. 46–60, 2007.

Because of the high uncertainty in our domain, in [5] we introduced the concept of "scope" of a case. With this concept we refer to regions in the field where a case should be retrieved. Dealing with regions is much more intuitive and feasible than dealing with points in the field, since we are interested in observing if the ball or a robot is in a given region, rather than if it is in an exact position. Once we verified the effectiveness of this new concept, we have now introduced it in the system as part of the description of a case.

In several different domains it has been proved that teamwork improves the performance of a task. Robot soccer is one of these domains. Having a single player running across the field with the ball may result in success if no problems arise during the performance. But, what if while attempting to reach the attacking goal it loses the ball? It could be a perfect opportunity for an opponent to take the ball. Having teammates that can help during the task is essential to increase robustness in case of failure. Therefore, in [6] we presented our first multi-robot case-based approach, where cases may include explicit passes between robots, which for the best of our knowledge, has not been presented before in this domain. In this preliminary work a fixed robot was in charge of the reasoning process (retrieving cases) and coordinating the execution of the case with the rest of the teammates. In order to increase the robustness of our multi-robot approach, we now present an additional mechanism, where the best candidate among the available robots is selected as the coordinator for each cycle of the CBR process.

Based on the successful results obtained in our previous work, we have extended our system including the opponents. Due to the incorporation of new cases with teammates and opponents, the complexity of the case base has also increased. Thus, in this paper we also present a new representation of the case base to facilitate the access during retrieval. Furthermore, since now we are working with teammates, we have emphasized cooperation between robots, i.e. we prefer to retrieve a case with teammates, than a case with a single robot. To this end, we define a retrieval process that prioritizes cases with multiple robots, rather than cases with a single robot.

In this paper we present the current version of our system and the empirical results obtained with real robots. We compare our approach with an individualist approach in two scenarios with a team of two robots. The aim of the experiments is to prove that the performance of the robots using the extended system is more cooperative, and hence, more robust in case of failure since more than one robot participates as much as possible during the execution of the task.

We focus our work on the the Four-Legged League (RoboCup). Teams consist of four Sony AIBO robots. The robots operate fully autonomously and they can communicate with each other by wireless. The field represents a Cartesian plane as shown in Figure 1. There are two goals (cyan and yellow) and four colored markers the robots use to localize themselves in the field. A game consists of two parts of 10 minutes each. At any point of the game, if the score difference is greater than 10 points the game ends. For more details on the official rules of the game refer the RoboCup Four-Legged League Rule Book.

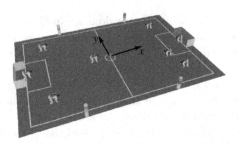

Fig. 1. Snapshot of the field (image extracted from the Official Rule Book)

The paper is organized as follows. Section 2 reviews the related work. In Section 3 we define the case structure and related details and the retrieval process is described in Section 4. We present the multi-robot approach and the case reuse in Section 5 and we show empirical results in Section 6. Finally, we conclude the paper in Section 7.

2   Related Work

Researchers have focused their work on different techniques to model the agents' behaviors in the action selection domain. In the CBR field, Wendler et al. [8] describe an approach in the Simulation League to select actions based on previously collected experiences encoded as cases. Thus, many parameters they take into account are not considered in our domain, and also they do not have to deal with the major problems involved when working with real robots. Marling et al. [3] introduce three CBR prototypes in their robot team (RoboCats, in the Small Size League): the first prototype focused on positioning the goalie; the second one, on selecting team formations; and the third one, on recognizing game states. All three systems are mainly based on taking snapshots of the game and extracting features from the positions of the robots during the game.

Lam et al. [1] focus their research on learning from observation. The aim of this technique is to model agents that learn from observing other agents and imitating their behavior. As in CBR, the learning agent selects the most similar past observed situation with respect to the current problem and then reproduces the solution performed at that time. The main difference between these approaches is that the learning agent is not able to improve the observed agent since there is no feedback in the model. Although our work does not include yet the revise step, the main differences with this work are: the number of agents implied in the scenes (we include teammates which interact among them); the solution of the problem (we deal with a sequence of actions for each teammate instead of a single action in [1]); and the objects locations (robots and ball are within fixed regions of field in [1], whereas we deal with variable regions).

In the Simulation League, Riedmiller et al. [4] focus their work on Reinforcement Learning applied to two different levels: moving level and tactical level. The former refers to learning a specific move (learning to kick). While the latter refers to which move should be applied at a certain point (*pass the ball*). Lattner et al. [2] present an approach that creates patterns based on the qualitative information of the environment. The result of learning is a set of prediction rules that give information about what (future) actions or situations might occur with some probability if certain preconditions satisfy. They all address their work to the Simulation League.

3   Case Definition

A case represents a snapshot of the environment at a given time from a single robot point of view. We call this robot the *reference* robot, since the information in the case is based on its perception and internal state (its beliefs). The case definition is composed of three parts: the problem description, which corresponds to the state of the game; the knowledge description, which contains additional information used to retrieve the case; and finally, the solution description, which indicates the sequence of actions the robots should perform to solve the problem. We formally define a case as a 3-tuple:

$$case = ((R, B, G, Tm, Opp, t, S), K, A)$$

where:

1. R: robot's relative position (x_R, y_R) with respect to the ball and heading θ.

   $$x_R \in [-2700..2700]\text{mm} \quad y_R \in [-1800..1800]\text{mm} \quad \theta \in [0..360)\text{degrees}$$

2. B: ball's global position (x_B, y_B)

   $$x_B \in [-2700..2700]\text{mm} \quad y_B \in [-1800..1800]\text{mm}$$

3. G: defending goal
   $$G \in \{\text{cyan}, \text{yellow}\}$$

4. Tm: teammates' relative positions with respect to the ball.

   $$Tm = \{tm_1, tm_2..., tm_n\}$$

   where tm_i is a point (x, y) and $n = 1..3$ for teams of 4 robots. This set could be empty for cases where no teammates are implied in the case solution.

5. Opp: opponents' relative positions with respect to the ball.

   $$Opp = \{opp_1, opp_2, ..., opp_m\}$$

   where opp_i is a point (x, y) and $m = 1..4$ for teams of 4 robots. This set could be empty for cases where no opponents are described in the case.

6. t: timing of the match. Two halves parts of 10 min.

   $$t \in [0..20]\text{min}, t \in \mathbb{N}$$

7. S: difference between the goals scored by our team and the opponent's team. The maximum difference allowed is 10. The sign indicates if the team is losing (negative) or winning (positive).

$$S \in [-10..10]$$

8. K: scope of the case. We define the scope as the regions of the field within which the ball and the opponents should be positioned in order to retrieve that case. We represent the scope as ellipses centered on the ball's and opponents' positions indicated in the problem description.

$$K = (\tau_x^B, \tau_y^B, \tau_x^1, \tau_y^1, \ldots, \tau_x^m, \tau_y^m)$$

where τ_x^B and τ_y^B correspond to the x and y radius of the ball's scope, τ_x^i and τ_y^i, to the radius of opponent i's scope ($i = 1..m$).

9. A: sequence of actions, called gameplays, each robot performs.

$$A = \{tm_0 : [a_{01}, a_{02}, \ldots, a_{0p_0}], \ldots, tm_n : [a_{n1}, a_{n2}, \ldots, a_{np_n}]\}$$

where $n = 0..3$ is the Id of the robot, and p_i the number of actions teammate tm_i performs (tm_0 corresponds to the *reference* robot). The actions are either individual actions, such as "get the ball and kick", or joint actions, such as "get the ball and pass it to robot tm_i".

Case Description Details

Problem description. Each robot constantly reports its position to the rest of the robots in the same team. Thus, the *reference* robot can update Tm at every time step. Regarding the opponents' positions, the robots may include a vision processing system to detect them. However, in this work we do not use this system because it is not robust enough. The purpose of this research is to study the performance of the CBR approach, and not to improve robustness to the perception system. Therefore, to test our system independently from vision issues, the robots from the opponent team also report their positions to all the robots in the field. Since we are only interested on the opponents near the ball (an opponent far from the ball does not take part in the immediate gameplay) the *reference* robot only considers the existence of an opponent (active opponent) if it is within a given radius from the ball's position.

Knowledge description. We are more interested in defining qualitative positions of the ball and opponents rather than using precise positions. Hence, describing the scope of cases based on ellipses is beneficial in two aspects: first, because of the high degree of uncertainty in our domain, dealing with exact positions is not feasible; and second, we can easily describe the opponents' positions with respect to the ball by means of qualitative positions. Figure 2a shows in a section of the field an example of the ball's and opponent's scope of a given case. Given a new problem, if the ball and the opponent are within the scopes, i.e. the

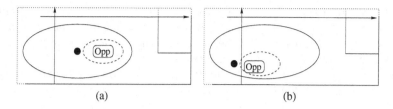

(a)   (b)

Fig. 2. (a) Example of the scope of a case. (b) Example of a problem. The scope of the opponent is translated with respect to the ball.

ball (black circle) is within the solid ellipse, and the opponent in front of it, the case would be considered as a potential solution. Note that the opponent's scope (dashed ellipse) is computed with respect to the actual ball's position. Figure 2b illustrates an example of a new problem to solve, where the ball is within the ball's scope, and the scope of the opponent is located with respect to this position. To solve this problem, the case shown in Figure 2a would be retrieved.

The initial scopes of the cases (values of τ_x and τ_y for the ball and opponents) are initially given by hand when creating the cases and then automatically adjusted by means of a learning mechanism presented in [5].

Solution description. Although actions have different durations, through the execution of joint actions there is no need of explicit action synchronization between robots, nor to specify timings to actions. This is so because each action corresponds to low level behaviors which are triggered when a set of preconditions are fulfilled. For instance, a pass between two robots corresponds to two sequences: "pass the ball" and "wait for ball". The first robot (the one that initiates the pass) gets the ball and then kicks it towards the second robot. Meanwhile, the robot receiving the ball remains in its position until the ball is close enough to it. Once the ball approaches the second robot, it will catch the ball and continue with whatever action is indicated in the gameplay (such as "kick to goal").

4   Case Retrieval

A case can be retrieved if we can modify part of the current problem description in order to adapt it to the description of the case. We separate the features of the problem description in two sets: *controllable* indices and *non-controllable* indices. The former ones refer to the *reference* robot and teammates (since they can move to more appropriate positions), while the latter refers to the ball, opponents, defending goal, time and score difference (which we cannot directly modify). The modification of the *controllable* features leads to a planning process where the system has to decide how to reach the positions of the robots indicated in the retrieved case in order to reuse its solution. We compute two measures for each set. We briefly describe them next (see [7] for details).

Similarity function. This measure indicates how similar the *non-controllable* features are between the problem and the case. We define different functions for each domain of features and we then compute the overall similarity using the harmonic mean of the individual similarities.

The similarity sim_B for the ball and the similarities sim_{Opp_i} for the opponents are computed using a 2D Gaussian function:

$$sim(x_1, y_1, x_2, y_2) = e^{-\left[\left(\frac{x_1-x_2}{\tau_x}\right)^2 + \left(\frac{y_1-y_2}{\tau_y}\right)^2\right]}$$

where the point (x_1, y_1) refers to either the robots' or the ball's position in the problem and (x_2, y_2) refers to the positions in the case. τ_x and τ_y correspond to the scopes (K) of either the ball or the opponents described in the case.

To compute the opponents' similarity we first must determine the correspondence between the opponents of the problem and the case, i.e. which opponent opp_i from the problem description corresponds to which opponent opp_j in the case description. In [7] we presented a Branch&Bound algorithm to efficiently obtain the best match between n robots. However, since in this work n is low (at most three robots per team) we perform an exhaustive search to obtain the correspondences, which has a lower computational complexity than implementing the B&B search. Once we obtain the correspondences, we compute the similarity for each pair using the Gaussian function defined above.

We model the strategy of the game based on the time and the score difference. As time passes and depending on the score of the game, we expect a more offensive or defensive behavior. We define the strategy function as:

$$strat(t, S) = \begin{cases} \frac{t}{20(S-1)} & \text{if } S < 0 \\ \frac{t}{20} & \text{if } S = 0 \\ \frac{t}{20(S+1)} & \text{if } S > 0 \end{cases}$$

where $strat(t, S) \in [-1..1]$, with -1 meaning a very offensive strategy and 1 meaning a very defensive strategy. The similarity function for the strategies is:

$$sim_{tS}(t_1, S_1, t_2, S_2) = 1 - |strat(t_1, S_1) - strat(t_2, S_2)|$$

where t_1 and S_1 corresponds to the time and scoring features in the problem and t_2 and S_2, the features in the case.

Finally, the overall similarity is defined as:

$$sim = f(sim_B, sim_{tS}, sim_{Opp_1}, \ldots, sim_{Opp_m})$$

where f is the harmonic mean, m is the number of opponents in the case, and each argument of f corresponds to the similarity value obtained for each feature. For more details regarding the similarity functions refer to [7].

Cost function. This measure computes the cost of modifying the *controllable* features, i.e. the cost of adapting the problem to the case. It is computed as the sum of the distances between the positions of the robots in the problem and the adapted positions specified in the case (after obtaining their correspondences).

The adapted positions correspond to the global locations where the robots should position in order to execute the solution of the case. To compute them, we transform the robots' relative coordinates to global coordinates, having the position of the ball in the problem as the reference point. Figure 3 illustrates a simple adaptation example with one robot.

Retrieving a Case

Since we are working in a real time domain and because of computational limitations in the robots, it is essential to minimize the time invested during the retrieval process. To speed up the search we use an indexed list to store the cases. Thus, when a new problem enters the system we can easily access the subset of cases (CB^s) we are interested in by indexing the case base using the value of the defending goal (yellow or cyan) and the number of opponents involved in each case. Searching in the rest of the case base is useless since those cases will not match the current problem at all. In Section 6 we show some examples of cases.

After computing the similarities between the problem and the cases in the subset CB^s, we obtain a list of potential cases. From this list, we compute the cost for each case and select those cases that have a cost lower than a given threshold. From this list of potential cases (PC) we must select one case for the reuse step.

We consider a compromise between the similarity degree between the problem and the case and the cost of adapting the problem to the case. Moreover, since we are working in a multi-robot domain (teams of robots), we are also interested in stimulating cooperation between them as much as possible. Thus, given two candidate cases, one described with a single robot, and the other, with two robots that cooperate during the execution of the solution, the system would select the second case as the retrieved case (although it might have a lower similarity).

Therefore, given the list of potential cases (PC), we first classify the cases based on the number of robots described in the case (number of teammates, n, plus one -the *reference* robot-). Each subset is further classified into four lists based on different similarity intervals: $H = [0.8, 1.0]$, $h = [0.6, 0.8)$, $l = [0.4, 0.6)$ and $L = (0.0, 0.4)$. Finally, each list is sorted based on the cost, where the first case of the list corresponds to the case with lower cost. Formally:

$$PC = [[sim_H^{n+1}, sim_h^{n+1}, sim_l^{n+1}, sim_L^{n+1}], \ldots, [sim_H^1, sim_h^1, sim_l^1, sim_L^1]]$$

where $sim_s^i = [c_{s1}^i, c_{s2}^i, \ldots]$ is an ordered list of cases based on their cost (i.e. $cost(c_{s1}^i) < cost(c_{s2}^i)$); $s \in \{H, h, l, L\}$ stands for the similarity interval; and $i = 1..n+1$ is the number of players in the case. The retrieved case corresponds to the first element of the flatten[1] list PC: $ret\_case = first(flat(PC))$.

In summary, when a new problem enters the system, the system retrieves a case maximizing both the number of players implied in the solution and the similarity, while minimizing the cost.

---

[1] We define a flatten list as a list with one single level, i.e. no nested lists.

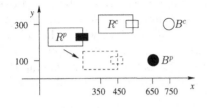

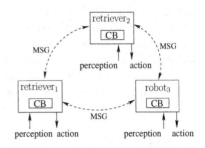

Fig. 3. Case description (R^c, B^c), and current problem description (R^p, B^p). The robot in dashed lines represents the adapted position of the robot with respect to the ball's position described in the problem.

Fig. 4. Case-based multi-robot architecture for $n = 3$ robots and $k = 2$ *retrievers*

5   Multi-robot Architecture and Case Execution

Next we describe the architecture for our multi-robot system integrating the retrieval and reuse steps of the CBR approach. The multi-robot system is composed of n robots. All robots interact with the environment and among them, i.e. they perceive the world, they perform actions and they send messages (MSG) to each other to coordinate and to exchange information about their internal states.

We distinguish a subset of k $(1 \le k \le n)$ robots, called *retrievers*. These robots are capable of retrieving cases as new problems arise. All robots have a copy of the same case base so they can gather the information needed during the case reuse. Figure 4 shows the architecture described. Given a new problem to solve, the first step of the process is to decide which of the *retrievers* is going to actually retrieve a case to solve it (since only one case can be executed at a time). We believe that the most appropriate robot to perform this task should be the one that has the most accurate information about the environment. From the set of features described in a case, the only feature that might have different values from one robot to another, is the ball's position. Moreover, this is the most important feature in order to retrieve the correct case and we must ensure as less uncertainty as possible. The remaining features are either shared among the robots, or given by an external system, i.e. defending goal, the score and time of the game. Therefore, we propose that the robot retrieving the case should be the one closer to the ball, since its information will be the most accurate (the further a robot is from an object, the higher the uncertainty about the object's information). From now on, we will refer to this robot as the *coordinator*.

Since we are working with a distributed system, the robots may have different information about each other at a given time. Their beliefs about the state of the world are constantly updated. They are also constantly sending messages about their current internal states (position, ball's position, etc.) to the rest of the robots. As a consequence, we cannot ensure that all robots agree on who is the one closer to the ball at a given time. To solve this issue, only one robot is responsible for selecting the *coordinator*. In order to have a robust system (robots may crash, or be removed due to a penalty), the robot performing this task is always the one with lower Id among those present in the game (since the robots always have the same Id). Once it selects the *coordinator*, it sends a message to all the robots indicating the Id of the new *coordinator*.

After the *coordinator* is selected, it retrieves a case according to the process described in Section 4 and informs the rest of the team which case to reuse. It also informs the correspondences between the robots in the current problem and the robots in the retrieved case (so they can know which actions to execute accessing their case bases).

At this point the case execution begins. Firstly, all robots that take part of the solution of the case move to their adapted positions (computed as showed in Section 4). Once they reach them, they send a message to the *coordinator* in order to synchronize the beginning of the gameplays execution with the rest of the robots. Next, they all execute their actions until ending their sequences. Finally, they report the *coordinator* that they finished the execution and wait for the rest of the robots to end. When the *coordinator* receives all messages, it informs the robots so they all go back to the initial state of the process, i.e. selecting a new *coordinator*, retrieving a case and executing its solution.

The execution of a case may be aborted at any moment if any of the robots either detects that the retrieved case is not applicable anymore or an expected message does not arrive. In either case, the robot sends an aborting message to the rest of the robots so they all stop executing their actions. They once again go back to the initial state in order to restart the process. For more details on the behaviors presented refer to [6].

6   Evaluation

To evaluate the approach presented in this paper, we have compared it with the behavior-based approach used by the CMDash team in the US Open'05. We briefly introduce the basic ideas of this approach.

The behavior-based approach consists in defining high level behaviors (state-based behaviors) the robot executes based on the state of the environment. For example, a robot defending its goal should get the ball and clear it from the defense region. They coordinate to prevent from going towards the ball at the same time and to collide between them as they move with the ball. When a robot decides to go after the ball it informs its teammates so they try to move away from its trajectory. Therefore, they do not have explicit passes between them, and passes occur by chance. The roles are used to maintain the robot's positions within certain regions of the field. Therefore, the robots can be organized in different layouts on the whole field as needed.

There are four main differences with our approach: (*i*) behaviors are applicable only if all preconditions are fully satisfied (true or false); (*ii*) there are few behaviors, and therefore, they are very general; (*iii*) the approach has an implicit

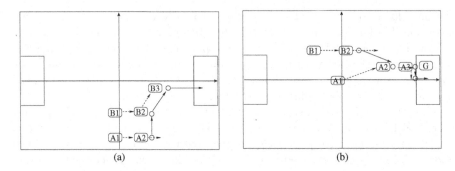

Fig. 5. The letters correspond to the robots (A, B and G), the numbers to the time step of the execution (1, 2 and 3) and the arrows represent the ball's and robots' movement, solid and dashed respectively. (a) Scenario 1 using the case-based approach: "multiple right side" case followed by "single right middle" case. (b) Scenario 2 using the case-based approach: "multiple left middle" case followed by "single goalie front" case.

coordination mechanism, where coordination results as an emerging property (robots actually play always individually and passes are unintentional); and, (iv) the approach does not have a representation model. Thus, modifying the behaviors results in a very tedious task if the user is not familiar with it.

The goal of our experimentation is to prove that the resulting behavior of the robot team using our approach is more cooperative than a robot team using the behavior-based approach. In other words, our approach results in a collective or "team playing" behavior (participation of more than one robot of the same team during the execution of a task through passes), as opposed to individual behavior (only one robot executing the task).

A trial consists in positioning the robots and the ball on the field and the robots' task is to move the ball until reaching the penalty area (rectangular box in front the attacking goal). Two sets of experiments where performed, each composed of 15 trials. Figure 5a illustrates the first scenario, where two robots (A and B) initiate the task in the right side of the field (negative y). While in the second scenario, Figure 5b, two robots are positioned in the left middle side of the field, and an opponent is also included (the goalie) in the left side of the attacking goal (cyan goal). Both approaches (case-based and behavior-based) were tested in the two scenarios. Next, we describe the results obtained for each approach.

6.1   Behavior-Based Approach

During the experiments with the behavior-based approach, we observed that due to its individualistic nature, in general only one robot was implied in the execution of the task. From the 30 trials (15 for each scenario), 4 times the ball went out of field, failing the experiment. Although the remaining trials were fulfilled, a single robot was always after the ball while the second robot remained behind it to avoid intercepting either the first robot or the ball. Hence, for

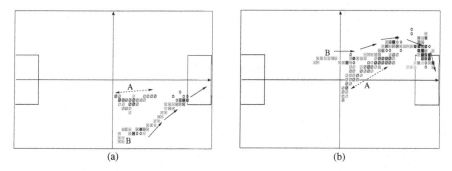

Fig. 6. Behavior-based approach. (a) Scenario 1. (b) Scenario 2.

an external observer, the performance was lacking of teamwork or cooperation (although the robot was actually avoiding to cross the path of the first robot as part of its teamwork mechanism).

Figure 6 shows examples of the robots' paths in both scenarios. We can observe how robot B is the robot that goes after the ball constantly, while robot A remains behind it, moving back and forth to avoid robot B. This behavior may be reasonable when there are no opponents, but is not effective when there are opponents around.

6.2   Case-Based Approach

Given the symmetric properties of the features of the field, for each manually created case in any of the four quadrants of the field, we can easily generate three more cases using symmetric transformations. Our case base is composed of 56 cases, even though only 14 cases were manually created.

Because of the non-deterministic nature of the real world we are working on, although the initial layout of robots and ball is always the same, different outcomes can occur after executing the same actions several times. For instance, the ball's trajectory is not exactly the same, a robot may lose the ball when attempting to grab it, the kick strength can be stronger or weaker, etc. Therefore even if the first case that the robots retrieve is the same at different times, the next retrieved case may not be the same because it will depend on the outcome of the actions performed during the execution of the first case (the final positions of the robots and the ball).

After studying the results obtained from the experiments, we can classify the trials in different groups based on the sequence of retrieved cases during the performance. For space reasons we only describe the second scenario which is more interesting since an opponent is included. However, the ideas discussed are based on both sets of experiments.

Figure 5b shows the execution scheme for the second scenario: robot B passes the ball to robot A, who then kicks it near the penalty area ("multiple left middle" case). The interesting situation occurs next, when the ball is near the penalty area but there is an opponent between the player and the goal. Hence,

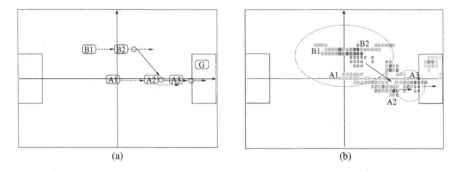

Fig. 7. Scenario 2 using the case-based approach: (a) "multiple left middle" case followed by "single goalie diagonal" case. (b) robots' real paths performed during the execution of both cases.

the retrieved cases must include an opponent. We classified the 15 trials in two groups based on the retrieved cases for this second part of the execution:

Opponent: The goalie is either in between the ball and the goal (Figure 5b) or diagonally located with respect to the ball, i.e. not obstructing the trajectory of the ball to the goal (Figure 7). In the first case, the attacking robot must grab it under its chin, move sideways to the right with the ball to avoid the goalie and kick forward. In the second case, since the goalie is diagonally located, there is no need to avoid it, and the robot can directly kick the ball.

No opponent: The task is achieved with a single case (Figure 8a and 8b)), or the opponent was not considered during the next retrieval because the opponent is not within the radius of the ball (not an active opponent as mentioned in Section 3). Therefore, a case with no opponents is retrieved next (Figure 8c and 8d).

In both scenarios the first retrieved cases are always the same since the initial positions are fixed. From that point on, depending on the events occurred during the execution, the next case may vary. In any case, the robots always made a good decision and performed the task successfully in a cooperative way.

After discussing the qualitative results of the experimentation, we now show the most significant data obtained from the experiments with the case-based approach. Figure 9 shows a table with the number of retrieved cases in both scenarios. As we can see, from a total of 65 cases, 57 were correctly retrieved and successfully executed. The 8 remaining where aborted during execution because the robots realized that the cases were not applicable anymore. From an observer point of view, these 8 cases were incorrectly retrieved since the states of the environment were not similar to the cases descriptions. However, from the robots' point of view, the cases indeed matched the states of the environment at the retrieving stage, but due to localization errors, the robots' beliefs were wrong. From the moment they correctly relocalized (and therefore, correctly localized the position of the ball), they realized that the cases did not match the state of the environment and aborted the execution. Figure 10 depicts the regions of the

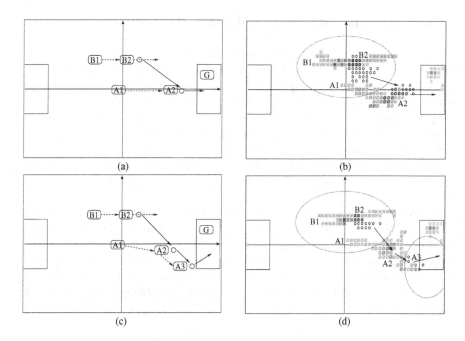

Fig. 8. Scenario 2 using the case-based approach: "multiple left middle" case followed by (a) no more cases; (c) "single right front" case; and (b) and (d) robots' real paths performed during the execution of both executions

field covered during the performance of both experiments. From the case base, a total of 11 different cases were retrieved in both scenarios.

We also noticed that during the experiments with the behavior-based approach, the robots collided between them 8 times and 4 times the ball went out of the field. While with our approach, the robots never collided, neither kicked the ball out of the field.

Finally, we must also point out that during a game our approach results in a more controlled strategy, rather than an aggressive one where the robots are constantly trying to individually get the ball and score. This is because we include a reasoning module which takes care of higher level decisions. Although the chances of scoring increases with an aggressive strategy, it also increases the number of lost balls, which may allow the opponent team to score more goals.

	retrieved cases	lost cases	completed execution
Scenario 1	36	6	30
Scenario 2	29	2	27
Total	65	8	57

Fig. 9. Case results in both scenarios

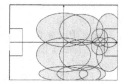

Fig. 10. Case execution coverage

7   Conclusions and Future Work

We have presented an extension of our CBR system for action selection in the robot soccer domain. Since we have increased the complexity of the system (including teammates and opponents), we have developed a new representation of the case base (an indexed list) as well as a retrieval process that prioritizes the participation of more than one robot. Hence, as shown in the evaluation, the robots behavior results in a "real" team playing performance (more cooperative with explicit passes) instead of an individualistic performance, which we believe is more adequate for robot soccer. To this end, we also presented a mechanism to select the robot in charge of the retrieval process and the coordination of the team.

As future work we propose to have the different robots retrieving cases, and therefore, the need of an agreement mechanism will arise. For instance, it would be interesting to integrate a negotiation mechanism based on appropriate information (e.g. how well localized a robot is) to allow the robots to decide the most appropriate case in a better informed manner. We also plan to further extend the system by a more complete coverage of the possible situations that arise during a game after introducing more teammates and opponents.

References

1. Lam, K., Esfandiari, B., Tudino, D.: A Scene-based Imitation Framework for RoboCup Clients. In: MOO - Modeling Other Agents from Observations (2006)
2. Lattner, A., Miene, A., Visser, U., Herzog, O.: Sequential Pattern Mining for Situation and Behavior Prediction in Simulated Robotic Soccer. In: Bredenfeld, A., Jacoff, A., Noda, I., Takahashi, Y. (eds.) RoboCup 2005. LNCS (LNAI), vol. 4020, pp. 118–129. Springer, Heidelberg (2006)
3. Marling, C., Tomko, M., Gillen, M., Alexander, D., Chelberg, D.: Case-based reasoning for planning and world modeling in the robocup small size league. In: IJCAI Workshop on Issues in Designing Physical Agents for Dynamic Real-Time Environments (2003)
4. Riedmiller, M., Merke, A., Meier, D., Hoffmann, A., Sinner, A., Thate, O., Ehrmann, R.: Karlsruhe brainstormers — A reinforcement learning approach to robotic soccer. In: Stone, P., Balch, T., Kraetzschmar, G.K. (eds.) RoboCup 2000. LNCS (LNAI), vol. 2019, Springer, Heidelberg (2001)
5. Ros, R., Arcos, J.L.: Acquiring a Robust Case Base for the Robot Soccer Domain. In: Proc. of 20th International Joint Conference on Artificial Intelligence, pp. 1029–1034 (2007)
6. Ros, R., Veloso, M.: Executing Multi-Robot Cases through a Single Coordinator. In: Proc. of Autonomous Agents and Multiagent Systems (to appear)
7. Ros, R., Veloso, M., Màntaras, R.L.d., Sierra, C., Arcos, J.L.: Retrieving and Reusing Game Plays for Robot Soccer. In: Roth-Berghofer, T.R., Göker, M.H., Güvenir, H.A. (eds.) ECCBR 2006. LNCS (LNAI), vol. 4106, pp. 47–61. Springer, Heidelberg (2006)
8. Wendler, J., Lenz, M.: CBR for Dynamic Situation Assessment in an Agent-Oriented Setting. In: Proc. AAAI-98 Workshop on CBR Integrations (1998)

Acquiring Word Similarities with Higher Order Association Mining

Sutanu Chakraborti, Nirmalie Wiratunga, Robert Lothian, and Stuart Watt

School of Computing,
The Robert Gordon University
Aberdeen AB25 1HG, Scotland, UK
{sc,rml,nw,sw}@comp.rgu.ac.uk

Abstract. We present a novel approach to mine word similarity in Textual Case Based Reasoning. We exploit indirect associations of words, in addition to direct ones for estimating their similarity. If word A co-occurs with word B, we say A and B share a first order association between them. If A co-occurs with B in some documents, and B with C in some others, then A and C are said to share a second order co-occurrence via B. Higher orders of co-occurrence may similarly be defined. In this paper we present algorithms for mining higher order co-occurrences. A weighted linear model is used to combine the contribution of these higher orders into a word similarity model. Our experimental results demonstrate significant improvements compared to similarity models based on first order co-occurrences alone. Our approach also outperforms state-of-the-art techniques like SVM and LSI in classification tasks of varying complexity.

1 Introduction

Textual Case Based Reasoning (TCBR) is based on the idea of modelling unstructured documents as cases. A knowledge light approach towards TCBR would use a bag of words directly to represent cases. The set of distinct terms and key-phrases in the document collection is treated as the feature set. One is tempted to believe that this line of thinking undermines the importance of domain-specific knowledge and thus blurs the distinction between CBR and Information Retrieval (IR) [2][3]. However, it may be argued that knowledge light approaches facilitate the application of statistical techniques to significantly lower knowledge acquisition overheads, in comparison to knowledge intensive techniques.

This paper presents a novel knowledge light technique for acquiring word similarities for TCBR. Our discussion is centred on a Case Retrieval Network (CRN) formalism, which has been demonstrated to be effective and efficient in retrieval over large and high dimensional case bases, typical with textual data [18]. CRNs have two main knowledge containers: knowledge about how words in a domain are related to each other (similarity knowledge); and knowledge about relatedness of words to cases (relevance knowledge). Typically statistical approaches model similarity between two words based on the number of documents in the corpus where these words co-occur.

R.O. Weber and M.M. Richter (Eds.): ICCBR 2007, LNAI 4626, pp. 61–76, 2007.
© Springer-Verlag Berlin Heidelberg 2007

Notwithstanding significant amount of both philosophical and pragmatic debate on whether co-occurrence is a robust basis for semantic similarity [3], this simple approach works fairly well in the presence of large and representative collections [17]. Also, unlike domain-independent linguistic resources like WordNet or Roget's Thesaurus, this approach can be used for estimating domain specific word similarities. In this paper, we show that we can do even better. We incorporate the notion of higher-order co-occurrence into our model of word similarity. The basic idea is to use indirect associations between words, in addition to direct ones. For example if words *car* and *chassis* co-occur in one document, and words *automobile* and *chassis* in another, we can infer that *car* and *automobile* are related to each other, even if they do not co-occur in any document. Such a relation is called a second-order association. We can extend this to orders higher than two. Several interesting examples showing the importance of second order associations have been reported in studies on large corpora. Lund and Burgess [4] observe that near-synonyms like *road* and *street* fail to co-occur in their huge corpus. In a French corpus containing 24-million words from the daily newspaper *Le Monde* in 1999, Lemaire and Denhiere [5] found 131 occurrences of *internet*, 94 occurrences of *web*, but no co-occurrences at all. However, both words are strongly associated. Experiments [5] show that higher order co-occurrences can be exploited to infer "semantic relatedness" [19] between *road* and *street*, and between *web* and *internet*. Throughout this paper, we use the word "similarity" as a measure of semantic relatedness, as opposed to a rigid semantic relation (like synonymy or hyponymy).

This paper presents algorithms for mining higher order associations between words. The strengths of these associations are combined to yield an estimate of word similarity. One primary goal of this work is to evaluate the goodness of the learnt similarity knowledge. In addition, we show how our approach can be extended to incorporate class knowledge in supervised classification tasks. We compare our approach with state of the art text classifiers like Support Vector Machines (SVM) and k Nearest Neighbours (kNN) based on Latent Semantic Indexing (LSI). The comparison with LSI is particularly significant in the light of empirical evidence [6] that LSI implicitly exploits higher order co-occurrence relations between words to arrive at a reduced dimensional representation of words and documents. We make a comparative study to illustrate the advantages of explicitly capturing higher order associations, as opposed to doing so implicitly as in LSI.

The rest of the paper is organized as follows. Section 2 introduces the CRN. Section 3 explains the concept of higher order associations, along with algorithms to mine the same. Section 4 describes our model of word similarities. Section 5 presents experimental findings comparing the performance of our model at the empirically determined best choice of parameters, with other approaches. All experiments reported in this paper were carried out on four text classification tasks of varied complexity. In Section 6, we present a novel approach of influencing the similarity values based on class knowledge, along with empirical results. Section 7 shows that the parameters of this model can be determined automatically. Possible extensions of the current work are discussed in Section 8. In Section 9, we situate our work in the context of other related work. Finally, section 10 summarizes our main contributions and concludes the paper.

2 Case Retrieval Networks

The CRN has been proposed as a representation formalism for CBR in [1]. To illustrate the basic idea we consider the example case-base in Fig. 1(a) which has nine cases comprising keywords, drawn from three domains: CBR, Chemistry and Linear Algebra. The keywords are along the columns of the matrix. Each case is represented as a row of binary values; a value 1 indicates that a keyword is present and 0 that it is absent. Cases 1, 2 and 3 relate to the CBR topic, cases 4, 5 and 6 to Chemistry and cases 7, 8 and 9 to Linear Algebra.

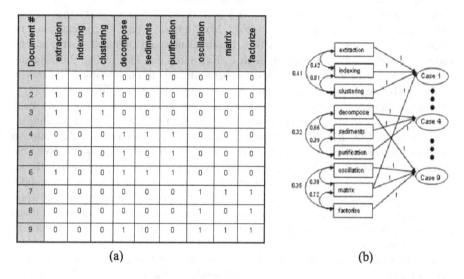

Document #	extraction	indexing	clustering	decompose	sediments	purification	oscillation	matrix	factorize
1	1	1	1	0	0	0	0	1	0
2	1	0	1	0	0	0	0	0	0
3	1	1	1	0	0	0	0	0	0
4	0	0	0	1	1	1	0	0	0
5	0	0	0	1	0	1	0	0	0
6	1	0	0	1	1	1	0	0	0
7	0	0	0	0	0	0	1	1	1
8	0	0	0	0	0	0	1	0	1
9	0	0	0	1	0	0	1	1	1

(a)   (b)

Fig. 1. CRN for Text Retrieval

Fig. 1(b) shows this case-base mapped onto a CRN. The keywords are treated as feature values, which are referred to as Information Entities (IEs). The rectangles denote IEs and the ovals represent cases. IE nodes are linked to case nodes by relevance arcs which are weighted according to the degree of association between terms and cases. In our example, relevance is 1 if the IE occurs in a case, 0 otherwise. The relevances are directly obtained from the matrix values in Fig. 1(a). IE nodes are related to each other by similarity arcs (circular arrows), which have numeric strengths denoting semantic similarity between two terms. For instance, the word "indexing" is more similar to "clustering" (similarity: 0.81) than to "extraction" (similarity: 0.42). Knowledge acquisition in the context of CRNs boils down to acquiring similarity and relevance values. This paper focuses on an approach to acquire similarity values automatically from a given collection of texts.

To perform retrieval, the query is parsed and IEs that appear in the query are activated. A similarity propagation is initiated through similarity arcs, to identify relevant IEs. The next step is relevance propagation, where the IEs in the query as well as those similar to the ones in the query spread activations to the case nodes via relevance arcs. These incoming activations are aggregated to form an activation score for each case node. Cases are ranked accordingly and the top k cases are retrieved.

A CRN facilitates efficient retrieval compared with a linear search through a case-base. While detailed time complexity estimates are available in [1], intuitively the speedup is because computation for establishing similarity between any distinct pair of IEs happens only once. Moreover, only cases with non-zero similarity to the query are taken into account in the retrieval process.

3 Higher Order Associations

The idea of higher order associations is illustrated through an example in Fig. 2. Terms A and B co-occur in Document 1 in Fig. 2(a), hence they are said to have a first order association between them. In Fig. 2(b), terms A and C co-occur in one document, and terms C and B in another. In our terminology, A and B share a second order association between them, through C. Extending this idea to Fig. 2(c), we say that A and B share a third order association between them through terms C and D. The similarity between two terms A and B is a function of the different orders of association between them. When modelled as a graph as shown in Fig. 2(d), each higher order association defines a path between the two vertices corresponding to terms A and B. (A,C,B) is a second order path and (A,C,D,B) is a third order path. An arc between any two nodes stands for a first-order co-occurrence relation between the corresponding words. A slightly more involved version is the weighted graph shown in Fig. 2(e). The weight of an arc connecting two nodes is proportional to the number of documents in the collection where they co-occur. It is important to note that while we have considered co-occurrence over entire documents, the context can be localized to arbitrary length word windows or sentences to restrict the number and scope of mined associations.

The basic idea is to estimate the strengths of different higher order co-occurrences and combine them into a word similarity model. Details of our similarity model appear in the next section. To estimate higher order strengths, we first tried a simple approach using goal driven unification supported by Prolog. The Prolog program has two parts to it: a fact base and a set of rules. The fact base was constructed automatically from the non-zero entries of the term document matrix, by taking all possible pairwise combinations of terms that appear in any document. From the matrix of Fig 1(a) we can construct facts such as

```
first_order(extraction, clustering).
first_order(extraction, matrix).
first_order(extraction, indexing).
```

Defining rules for higher order association is straightforward using Prolog. Second and third order associations are defined in the following statements:

```
second_order(X, Y ,Z) :- first_order(X, Z), first_order(Z, Y), X \== Y.
third_order(X,Y,Z,W) :- second_order(X,W,Z), first_order(W,Y), X \== Y,
Z\== Y.
```

Often, we are not interested in the actual words that act as links between words, as extracted by the Prolog unifications, but more in the *number* of distinct paths linking up words. This is easy in Prolog, as well:

```
lengthOfList([], 0).
lengthOfList ([_|Tail], N) :- lengthOfList (Tail, N1), N is 1 + N1.
no_of_2ord_paths(X,Y,N, List) :- setof(Z, second_order(X,Y,Z), List),
lengthOfList(List,N).
no_of_3ord_paths(X,Y,N, List1) :- setof((K,L), third_order(X,Y,K,L),
List1), lengthOfList(List1,N).
```

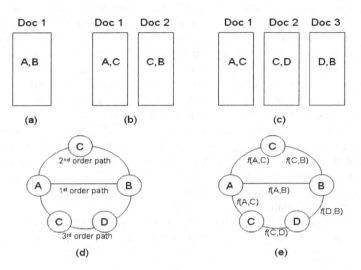

Fig. 2. Graphical Representation of Higher Order Co-occurrences

One main limitation of Prolog in this task is the combinatorial explosion in the number of first order associations that had to be recorded in the fact-base. In realistic tasks over several hundreds of documents, our version of Prolog (SWI-Prolog) often ran out of memory. To address this limitation, we explored the applicability of matrix operations to directly compute the strengths of higher order associations. We first implemented an approach reported by [7], where the authors start by computing a first order co-occurrence matrix. For |W| words in the feature set, this is a |W| × |W| matrix which has a value 1 in the i,jth element if word i co-occurs with word j in at least one document. For all pairs of words that do not co-occur in any document, the corresponding element in the matrix is 0. The diagonal values are set to zero since we are not interested in trivial co-occurrence of a word with itself. The first-order co-occurrence matrix is calculated using the following steps:

Step 1: The term document matrix A is multiplied with its transpose A^T to obtain the |W| × |W| matrix T_0.
Step 2: All non-zero values of T_0 are set to 1, and the diagonal values are set to zero to yield a binary first order co-occurrence matrix T.
Step 3: The second order co-occurrence matrix T_2 can be calculated by squaring T. The third order matrix T_3 is given as T^3. Other higher order co-occurrence matrices can be calculated similarly.

Before a matrix is reduced to binary, the value of its i,jth element is the number of co-occurrence paths between words i and j. The strength of a first order co-occurrence path is the number of documents in which two words co-occur. The strength of a second order co-occurrence path between words a and b is the number of distinct words c such that a co-occurs with c and b co-occurs with c.

Implementing the above algorithm revealed a critical shortcoming. Let us consider a third order association between terms a and b via terms c and d. Thus pairs a and c, c and d, and d and b co-occur with each other. In finding distinct pairs of terms c and d, we need to ensure that they are not the same as either a or b. By setting the diagonal elements to 0 in Step 2 above, the algorithm ensures that a and c are different, and so are d and b. But in addition we also need to ensure that d is not the same as a, and c is not the same as b, and this is not taken care of. Thus the strengths of third order associations were over-estimated by the algorithm. We need to make a correction to the algorithm to address this limitation. The brute force approach of explicitly counting terms that satisfy the above-mentioned constraint instead of blindly cubing the binary matrix T, turned out to be computationally expensive. We present below a technique that rewrites this procedure as an equivalent matrix manipulation, which can be implemented efficiently in matrix processing environments like Matlab.

Let T be the matrix of first order connections with diagonal elements set to zero. For third-order co-occurrences, we seek to enumerate paths of type i-j-k-l for all i and l. Now

$$\left(T^3\right)_{il} = \sum_{j,k} T_{ij}T_{jk}T_{kl}$$

is the total number of such paths, including paths of type i-j-i-l and i-l-k-l, which we wish to exclude. Let n_i be the number of paths of type i-j-i. This is equal to the total number of paths originating from i. We may evaluate n_i by summing the rows (or columns) of T:

$$n_i = \sum_j T_{ij}$$

Now, the number of paths of type i-j-i-l is n_iT_{il} and for type i-l-k-l the count is n_lT_{il}. If $T_{il} \neq 0$, then we have counted the path i-j-i-j twice, so the total number of invalid paths is $(n_i+n_l-1)T_{il}$. Equivalently, if we construct a discount matrix D whose elements $D_{il} = (n_i+n_l-1)$, then the number of invalid paths between words i and j is given by the i,j th element of the pointwise product $D*T$. We use the following procedure:

(1) Calculate T^3.

(2) Enumerate and discount the invalid paths as above. T^3- $D*T$ is the revised third order matrix.

3.1 An Example

We illustrate the above ideas on a toy case base comprising 4 terms and 4 documents as shown in Fig.3. The third order matrix T_3' says that there are two third-order paths between terms $t2$ and $t3$, one third order path between $t1$ and $t2$, another between terms $t1$ and $t3$, and none between $t1$ and $t4$. A closer inspection of matrix T reveals that that this is indeed true. Fig. 4 shows a graphical representation of matrix T, where an arc exists between any two nodes iff the corresponding entry in the matrix is 1, denoting that there is at least one document in the collection that has both of these terms. The two third order paths between $t2$ and $t3$ are $t2$-$t1$-$t4$-$t3$ and $t2$-$t4$-$t1$-$t3$. The only third order path between $t1$ and $t2$ is $t1$-$t3$-$t4$-$t2$, and between $t1$ and $t3$ is $t1$-$t2$-$t4$-$t3$. There are only two possible candidates for a third order path between $t1$ and $t4$: $t1$-$t2$-$t3$-$t4$ and $t1$-$t3$-$t2$-$t4$. Either would require a first order association between $t2$ and $t3$, which in our example does not exist, since there are no documents that contain both $t2$ and $t3$. Hence any third order association between $t1$ and $t4$ is ruled out.

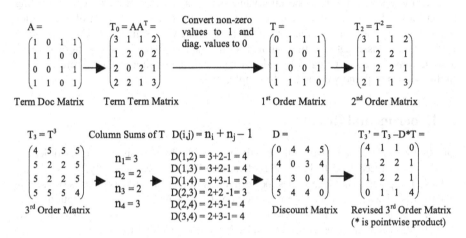

Fig. 3. An Example

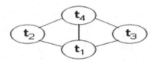

Fig. 4. The Term-Term Association Graph

4 Modeling Word Similarities

Once higher order co-occurrences are mined, we need to translate them into a measure of similarity between words. Intuition suggests that very high order co-occurrences do not really indicate similarity. In a study of higher order associations in the context of LSI [5], the authors report experimental evidence to confirm that associations beyond an order of 3 have a very weak influence on similarity modeled by LSI. In our word similarity model, we ignore the effects of orders higher than 3. In the last section, we have defined the strength of a higher order association between two terms as the number of co-occurrence paths between those terms. Let $first\_order(a,b)$, $second\_order(a,b)$ and $third\_order(a,b)$ denote the strengths of first, second and third order associations between terms a and b respectively. The similarity between terms a

and b can be expressed as a weighted linear combination of the strengths of the first three orders of co-occurrence as follows:

$$similarity(a,b) = \alpha \; first\_order(a,b) + \beta \; second\_order(a,b) + \gamma \; third\_order(a,b) \qquad (1)$$

Note that higher the order of association, the larger the number of co-occurrence paths (since $T^n_{i,j} > T^m_{i,j}$, if $n>m$ and if for all $T_{i,j} \neq 0$, $T_{i,j} \geq 1$, which is true in our case), and hence the greater the strength of association. Thus, to make α, β and γ comparable to each other, we need to normalize $first\_order(a,b)$, $second\_order(a,b)$ and $third\_order(a,b)$ to values in $[0,1]$. In our implementation, we achieve this by dividing each of these values by the maximum value between any pair of words corresponding to that order. Each distinct choice of α, β and γ leads to a different set of similarities between terms, which can then be used as similarity arcs in the CRN to perform retrieval or classification. In complex domains, we would expect higher order associations to play a critical role and hence such domains should show preference for higher values of β and γ compared to simpler ones.

5   Experimental Results

Our first experiment has two goals. Firstly, we test the hypothesis that higher order co-occurrences indeed lead to better classification effectiveness. Secondly, we study the values of α, β and γ that lead to best performances in four classification tasks of varying complexity. These experiments are carried out by varying α, β and γ, computing term similarities at each of these settings as given by (1) above, and observing the classification accuracies achieved by the CRN with these similarity values.

5.1   Experimental Methodology

Experiments were conducted on four datasets, of which two involve text classification in routing tasks and two involve Spam filtering. It may be noted that while the results reported are based on classification tasks for ease of evaluation, the techniques presented in this paper are fairly general and can easily be adapted for unsupervised retrieval tasks as well.

The two datasets used for text classification in routing were formed from the 20 Newsgroups [8] corpus which has about 20,000 Usenet news postings organized into 20 different newsgroups. One thousand messages (of discussions, queries, comments etc.) from each of the twenty newsgroups were chosen at random and partitioned by the newsgroup name. We form the following two subcorpuses:

- HARDWARE which has 2 hardware problem discussion groups, one on Apple Mac and the other on PC
- RELPOL which has two groups, one concerning religion, the other politics

The two datasets used for evaluating performance on Spam filtering include

- USREMAIL contains 1000 personal emails of which 50% are spam
- LINGSPAM dataset which contains 2893 email messages, of which 83% are non-spam messages related to linguistics, the rest are spam

We created equal sized disjoint training and test sets, where each set contains 20 % of the dataset of documents randomly selected from the original corpus, preserving the class distribution of the original corpus. For repeated trials, 15 such train test splits were formed.

Textual cases were formed by pre-processing documents by removing stopwords (common words) and special characters such as quote marks, commas and full stops. Some special characters like "!", "@", "%" and "$" were retained since they have been found to be discriminative for some domains. Remaining words are reduced to their stem using the Porter's algorithm [9]. The word stems that remain after preprocessing constitute the set of IEs.

In our experiments, we took into account first, second and third order associations, as given by (1). α is set to 1, and β and γ are incremented steps of 0.1 in the range [0,1.9] to examine the effect of second and third orders. $\beta = 0$, $\gamma = 0$ corresponds to the situation where only first order associations are used. At each unique choice of the three parameters, the term–term similarities obtained with those settings are used to define the similarity arcs in a CRN. The relevance arcs were set to 1 or 0 based on whether an IE(word) is present or absent in a case. The CRN produces the dot product of the incoming case with each of the existing cases. These values are normalized using the query and case norms to obtain the cosine similarity. A weighted 3-nearest neighbour algorithm is used to classify the test document.

We compare the classification accuracies with two other classifiers. The first is Support Vector Machines (SVM) which is reported to yield state-of-the-art performance in text categorization. The second is Latent Semantic Indexing (LSI), which maps terms and documents to a lower dimensional "concept" space, which is hypothesized to be more robust to variations due to word choice. Cases are represented using the reduced dimensions obtained with LSI, and a usual k-NN approach can then be used for retrieval. The comparison of our approach with LSI is motivated by the observations in [6], which attribute LSI performance to its ability to implicitly model higher order associations between words. However unlike our approach, LSI is constrained by the need to maximize variance across the concept dimensions, and by the need to produce the best k-rank approximation to the original term document matrix, in the least-squares sense. Our intuition was that these constraints are unnecessarily restrictive in a classification domain and could be relaxed to obtain better performance. Unlike LSI, our approach *explicitly* captures higher order associations and embeds this into term-term similarity knowledge. This also opens avenues for better visualization as discussed in Section 8.

LSI performance is critically dependent on the number of concept dimensions used for representing terms and documents. To make a fair comparison, we report LSI performance at the dimension at which its performance was found to be optimal. For SVM, we used a linear kernel as this was reported to yield best results in text categorization tasks [10].

5.2 Analysis of Results

Table 2 presents a summary of the results. The figures in bold are the best results after paired t-tests between each classifier over results from the 15 trials. In situations where the differences between the top ranking classifiers is not statistically significant (p > 0.05), all top figures have been marked in bold. We observe that using second and third order co-occurrences at parameter settings that yield best performance results in better classification accuracies compared to using first-order co-occurrences alone ($\beta,\gamma = 0$). While the differences are statistically significant on all four datasets, the magnitude of improvement is more conspicuous in HARDWARE and RELPOL, which are harder domains, compared to USREMAIL and LINGSPAM, which already recorded high accuracies with simpler approaches. In the RELPOL domain, 16 terms provided second order path between *Bible* and *sin*; interestingly these include *Christ, Jesus, faith, scripture, heaven, roman, kill, genocide* and *biblical.* It may be noted that the use of higher order co-occurrences leads to better accuracies compared to LSI and the differences are statistically significant on all four domains. This is all the more noteworthy in the light of our paired tests that reveal that LSI does better than first order co-occurrences on both HARDWARE and RELPOL, while results are statistically equivalent on the other two datasets. These two observations show LSI does better than using first order associations alone, but is outperformed comprehend-sively when higher orders are used.

We also note that our approach outperforms SVM on all datasets except HARDWARE where SVM performs significantly better. One possible reason for the relatively poor performance in HARDWARE could be a significant overlap in vocabularies used to describe problems in Mac and PC. The problem is compounded by the fact that we ignore class knowledge of training documents while constructing similarity relations between terms. In contrast this is a critical input to SVM. Motivated by this observation, we investigated a novel way of introducing class knowledge into the higher order mining algorithm, which is described in Section 6.

Table 1 reports α, β and γ values at which best performances are observed. Easier domains like USREMAIL and LINGSPAM appear to prefer lower values of β and γ compared to HARDWARE and RELPOL. We will re-examine this observation in the light of more experimental results in Section 7.

Table 1. Empirically determined best values of α,β and γ

	HARDWARE	RELPOL	USREMAIL	LINGSPAM
$(\alpha,\beta,\gamma)_{\text{optimal}}$	(1,0.37 ,1.15)	(1,0.61 ,1.04	(1,0.21,0.15)	(1,0.27, 0.31)

Table 2. Comparing classifier accuracies

	HARDWARE	RELPOL	USREMAIL	LINGSPAM
BASE(VSM) (Euclidean)	.5951	.7054	.5923	.8509
LSI-mined Similarities	.7240	.9339	.9583	.9832
SVM	**.7883**	.9228	**.9583**	.9636
First Order Similarities	.7171	.9309	.9577	.9826
Higher Order Similarities	.7451	**.9530**	**.9640**	**.9859**

6 Incorporating Class Knowledge into Word Similarities

In a supervised classification context, we have class knowledge of training documents in addition to the co-occurrence knowledge. Our intention is to incorporate this class knowledge as part of pre-processing. The idea is very similar to the approach described in [11], where LSI was extended to supervised classification tasks. Each document in the training set is padded with additional artificial terms that are representative of class knowledge. For example in the Hardware domain, all documents belonging to Apple Mac are augmented with artificial terms A, B , C and D, and all documents belonging to PC are padded with E, F, G and H. The padded terms, which we refer to as *sprinkled* terms, appear as new IEs in the CRN and are treated like any existing IE node. The revised architecture is shown in Fig. 5. When co-occurrences are mined on this new representation, terms representative of the same class are drawn closer to each other, and terms from disjoint classes are drawn farther apart. This happens because the sprinkled terms provide second-order co-occurrence paths between terms of the same class. For the test documents, the class is unknown; hence none of the artificial terms are activated. One important question is to decide the number of additional terms to be added for each class; an empirical solution is to use as many as yields best results over a cross validation dataset. While sprinkled terms help in emphasizing class knowledge, using too many of them may distort finer word association patterns in the original data [11]. In our experiments, we used 8 additional terms per class, as this was empirically found to yield good results.

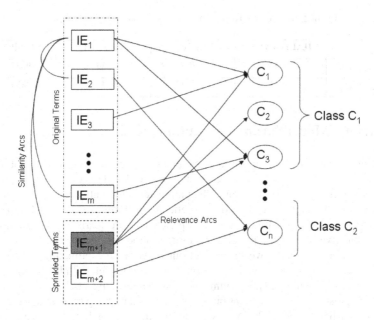

Fig. 5. A CRN Architecture after Sprinkling Terms that carry class knowledge

6.1 Empirical Results

The results are summarized in Tables 3 and 4. Sprinkling led to conspicuous improvement in performance over the HARDWARE dataset from 74.51% to 80.44%. This unambiguously points to the importance of class knowledge in this dataset. Table 3 suggests that sprinkled higher orders outperforms SVM on all datasets; in the USREMAIL dataset, the improvement is not statistically significant. This is possibly because the domain is simple and had already high recorded accuracies. For the RELPOL domain however, adding class knowledge led to a slight drop in the performance from 95.30% to 93.93% (Table 4), which was still significantly better than both LSI and SVM. The drop in RELPOL performance indicates that in this domain, class knowledge is not as important as in HARDWARE. In our current implementation, we have used uniform number of sprinkled terms over all domains. Performance could be improved by optimising the number of sprinkled terms for each individual domain. For example, HARDWARE would be more heavily sprinkled than RELPOL.

Table 3. Comparing Sprinkled Higher Orders against SVM

	HARDWARE	RELPOL	USREMAIL	LINGSPAM
Sprinkled HO	**.8044**	**.9393**	**.9630**	**.9838**
SVM	.7883	.9228	**.9583**	.9636

Table 4. Comparing Higher Orders with and without Sprinkling

	HARDWARE	RELPOL	USREMAIL	LINGSPAM
Sprinkled HO	**.8044**	.9393	**.9630**	**.9838**
Higher Order	.7451	**.9530**	**.9640**	**.9859**

7 Learning Model Parameters Automatically

Performing exhaustive search on the parameter space allows us to empirically ascertain the contributions of each co-occurrence order. However, in practice, we would need a mechanism to determine the parameters automatically based on a given text collection. We have investigated a Genetic Algorithm based approach to achieve this in supervised classification tasks. The parameters are learnt on the training set, with the objective of maximizing classification accuracy on the unseen test set. Since the test set is not available, we instead set our objective to optimizing classification accuracy over 5-fold cross validation on the training set. While details of our approach can be found in [21], we summarize our main findings below.

Table 5 presents the classification accuracies when the parameters were learnt using the GA-based approach. We used the architecture of Fig. 5 where sprinkled terms were used as carriers of class knowledge. The accuracy figures with the learnt

Table 5. Comparing effectiveness of empirically determined and GA-learnt parameters

	HARDWARE	RELPOL	USREMAIL	LINGSPAM
Sprinkled HO (parameter learning)	.7938	.9304	**.9593**	.9814
Sprinkled HO	**.8044**	**.9393**	**.9630**	**.9838**

Table 6. Parameter values learnt by GA

	HARDWARE	RELPOL	USREMAIL	LINGSPAM
$(\alpha,\beta,\gamma)_{optimal}$	(1,1.88 ,1.56)	(1,1.01 ,1.15)	(1,0.97,0.85)	(1,0.73, 0.96)

parameters are very similar to the figures obtained by the approach of Section 6 where the best values are chosen after exhaustively searching the parameter space in fixed increments. While there is still a statistically significant difference in three of four datasets, the very close average values suggest that the GA-based approach holds promise in significantly lowering manual overheads in parameter setting, while still continuing to deliver good performance. We need further research into better tuning of our approach for facilitating faster and more effective search in the parameter space. Table 6 shows the values of α,β and γ that were learnt by our algorithm for each of the four datasets. Comparing these values with the corresponding ones in Table 1, we observe a significant increase in the values of β. This can be attributed to the fact that sprinkled terms provide second order co-occurrence paths between terms of the same class. Increasing β thus helps in boosting similarity between terms of the same class, and decreasing similarity between terms of disjoint classes. This explains the greatly improved performance in the HARDWARE domain with sprinkling.

8 Discussion

While we have evaluated our ideas in the context of classification domains, it would be possible to apply the basic idea to unsupervised retrieval scenarios as well. One interesting metric to evaluate goodness of a TCBR configuration in unsupervised domains was recently proposed by Luc Lamontagne [12]. The measure, which the author calls case cohesion, measures the degree of correspondence between problem and solution components of textual cases. Using case cohesion instead of classification accuracy as a measure of the fitness function in our optimization algorithm would be a first cut towards applying our approach to retrieval tasks.

The importance of modeling similarity using higher order co-occurrences extends beyond textual CBR. In the context of recommender systems, several authors have reported problems due to sparseness of user-item matrices [16]; Semeraro et al [15] for example, report that 87% of the entries in their user-item matrix are zero. Knowledge representations used in collaborative recommenders (like concept lattices [24]) fail to exploit associations beyond the first order. Higher order associations can help reduce the sparseness and allow for better recommendation. In this context, analysis of higher-order associations in user item matrices will help discover novel product recommendation rules that would normally be implicit in the user ratings. Our approach can also be applied to link analysis in social networks [23], for clustering similar words, and resolving ambiguity of words spanning several clusters.

While our approach has outperformed SVM, the important thing to note is the explicit nature of our similarity relations as compared to SVM. It is not clear how SVM can be used to mine similarity between words, or incorporate expert feedback. The comparison with SVM illustrates that our techniques can outperform the best-in-line classifier while being able to explicitize its knowledge content, and supporting lazy incremental updates, both of which are strengths of CBR. The Prolog-based system described in Section 3 has its own advantages for visualization. For any given pair of words, all higher order associations can be depicted in graphs of the kind shown in Fig.2, which may be useful for explanation or for initiating expert feedback.

9 Related Works

Several works in the past have pointed to the importance of higher order co-occurrence in modeling word similarity. However we have not come across any work that explicitly attempts to obtain a parameterized model of similarity based on these co-occurrences, and learn optimal values of these parameters based on a fitness criterion. The work by Kontostathis and Pottenger [6] provides empirical evidence to show that LSI implicitly exploits higher order co-occurrence paths between words to arrive at its revised representations. This provides a fresh explanation for improvements obtained using LSI in text retrieval applications. Edmonds [13] examines the role of higher order co-occurrence in addressing the problem of lexical choice, which is important to both machine translation and natural language generation. Broadly speaking, the goal is to determine which of the possible synonyms is most appropriate for a given communication (or pragmatic) goal. The authors show that using second order co-occurrence has a favourable influence on the performance of their lexical choice program. Recent work by Lemaire and Denhiere [5] makes an in-depth study of the relationship between similarity and co-occurrence in a huge corpus of children's texts. They show that while semantic similarity is largely associated with first order co-occurrence, the latter overestimates the former. Higher order co-occurrences as well as lone occurrences (occurrence of word a but not b and vice versa) were used to account for LSI-inferred term similarities. Unlike our work, the authors do not propose an algorithm to arrive at word similarities; their approach is more analytic than synthetic. Two other recent approaches potentially useful for mining word similarities are distributional word clustering for textual case indexing [20][22], and Propositional Semantic Indexing [2] which mines word relationships using Association Rule Mining (ARM) with the goal of feature generalization. However, probability estimates used in the first approach and the ARM approach used in the second currently fail to accommodate associations beyond the first order. It appears that both approaches can potentially benefit from higher-order knowledge.

10 Conclusion

The main contribution of this paper is an approach for exploiting higher-order associations between words to acquire similarity knowledge for CRNs. We demonstrated the importance of higher order co-occurrences in determining word similarity, presented both supervised and unsupervised algorithms for mining such associations and proposed a word similarity model, whose parameters are learnt using an evolutionary approach. We have demonstrated the effectiveness of the learnt similarity knowledge and shown that using second and third order-co-occurrences yields better results than using first-order co-occurrence alone. Another contribution of the current work is to incorporate class knowledge into the process of mining higher order associations. We have demonstrated the effectiveness of this extension as our approach outperforms state of the art classifiers like SVM and LSI/kNN on classification tasks of varying complexity. Though the work has been presented in the context of CRNs, in essence we have presented a general approach to mine feature similarities, which can be easily integrated into other retrieval formalisms. Future work will aim at improving the parameter learning algorithm, and forming an easy-to-use workbench for similarity knowledge mining, for textual and non-textual CBR applications.

References

1. Lenz, M., Burkhard, H.: Case Retrieval Nets: Foundations, Properties, Implementation, and Results, Technical Report, Humboldt-Universität zu Berlin (1996)
2. Wiratunga, N., Lothian, R., Chakraborti, S., Koychev, I.: A Propositional Approach to Textual Case Indexing. In: Jorge, A.M., Torgo, L., Brazdil, P.B., Camacho, R., Gama, J. (eds.) PKDD 2005. LNCS (LNAI), vol. 3721, pp. 380–391. Springer, Heidelberg (2005)
3. Jarmasz, M., Szpakowicz, S.: Roget's thesaurus and semantic similarity. In: Proceedings of the International Conference on Recent Advances in NLP (RANLP-03), pp. 212–219 (2003)
4. Lund, K., Burgess, C.: Producing high-dimensional semantic spaces from lexical co-occurrence. Behavior Research, Methods, Instruments and Computers 28(2), 203–208 (1996)
5. Lemaire, B., Denhière, G.: Effects of High-Order Co-occurrences on Word Semantic Similarity. Current Psychology Letters 18(1) (2006)
6. Kontostathis, A., Pottenger, W.M.: A framework for understanding LSI performance. Information Processing and Management 42(1), 56–73 (2006)
7. Mill, W., Kontostathis, A.: Analysis of the values in the LSI term-term matrix, Technical report, Ursinus College (2004)
8. Mitchell, T.: Machine Learning. Mc Graw Hill International (1997)
9. Porter, M.F.: An algorithm for suffix stripping. Program 14(3), 130–137 (1980)
10. Joachims, T.: Text Categorization with Support Vector Machines: Learning with Many Relevant Features. In: Proc. of ECML, pp. 137–142. ACM Press, New York (1998)
11. Chakraborti, S., Mukras, R., Lothian, R., Wiratunga, N., Watt, S., Harper, D.: Supervised Latent Semantic Indexing using Adaptive Sprinkling. In: Proc. of IJCAI, pp. 1582–1587 (2007)

12. Lamontagne, L.: Textual CBR Authoring using Case Cohesion, in TCBR'06 - Reasoning with Text. In: Proceedings of the ECCBR'06 Workshops, pp. 33–43 (2006)
13. Edmonds, P.: Choosing the word most typical in context using a lexical co-occurrence network. Meeting of the Association for Computational Linguistics, 507–509 (1997)
14. Lenz, M.: Knowledge Sources for Textual CBR Applications. In: Lenz, M. (ed.) Textual CBR: Papers from the 1998 Workshop Technical Report WS-98-12, pp. 24–29. AAAI Press, Stanford (1998)
15. Semeraro, G., Lops, P., Degemmis, M.: WordNet-based User Profiles for Neighborhood Formation in Hybrid Recommender Systems. In: Procs. of Fifth HIS Conference, pp. 291–296 (2005)
16. Xue, G.-R., Lin, C., Yang, Q., Xi, W., Zeng, H.-J., Yu, Y., Chen, Z.: Scalable Collaborative Filtering Using Cluster-based Smoothing. In: Procs. of the 28th ACM SIGIR Conference, pp. 114–121 (2005)
17. Terra, E., Clarke, C.L.A.: Frequency Estimates for Word Similarity Measures. In: Proceedings of HLT-NAACL 2003, Main Papers, pp. 165–172 (2003)
18. Lenz, M., Burkhard, H.-D.: CBR for Document Retrieval - The FAllQ Project. In: Leake, D.B., Plaza, E. (eds.) Case-Based Reasoning Research and Development. LNCS, vol. 1266, pp. 84–93. Springer, Heidelberg (1997)
19. Budanitsky, A.: Lexical semantic relatedness and its application in natural language processing, Technical Report CSRG390, University of Toronto (1999)
20. Patterson, D., Rooney, N., Dobrynin, V., Galushka, M.: Sophia: A novel approach for textual case-based reasoning. In: Proc. of IJCAI, pp. 1146–1153 (2005)
21. Chakraborti, S., Lothian, R., Wiratunga, N., Watt, S.: Exploiting Higher Order Word Associations in Textual CBR, Technical Report, The Robert Gordon University (2007)
22. Wiratunga, N., Massie, S., Lothian, R.: Unsupervised Textual Feature Selection. In: Roth-Berghofer, T.R., Göker, M.H., Güvenir, H.A. (eds.) ECCBR 2006. LNCS (LNAI), vol. 4106, pp. 340–354. Springer, Heidelberg (2006)
23. Mori, J., Ishizuka, M., Matsuo, Y.: Extracting Keyphrases To Represent Relations in Social Networks from Web. In: Proc. of the Twentieth IJCAI Conference, pp. 2820–2825 (2007)
24. Boucher-Ryan, P., Bridge, D.: Collaborative Recommending using Formal Concept Analysis. Knowledge-Based Systems 19(5), 309–315 (2006)

Label Ranking in Case-Based Reasoning

Klaus Brinker and Eyke Hüllermeier

Department of Mathematics and Computer Science
Marburg University, Germany
{brinker,eyke}@informatik.uni-marburg.de

Abstract. The problem of label ranking has recently been introduced as an extension of conventional classification in the field of machine learning. In this paper, we argue that label ranking is an amenable task from a CBR point of view and, in particular, is more amenable to supporting case-based problem solving than standard classification. Moreover, by developing a case-based approach to label ranking, we will show that, the other way round, concepts and techniques from CBR are also useful for label ranking. In addition to an experimental study in which case-based label ranking is compared to conventional nearest neighbor classification, we present an application in which label ranking is used for node ordering in heuristic search.

1 Introduction

As a generic problem solving methodology, case-based reasoning (CBR) has already been applied successfully for various types of problems [21]. An especially simple yet relevant problem class for CBR is *prediction*, including classification (predicting one among a finite set of class labels) and regression (predicting a numerical output) as special cases. In this context, CBR overlaps with the field of machine learning and is typically referred to as case-based, instance-based, or memory-based learning [20,2,1]. The core of case-based learning algorithms is built upon the nearest neighbor estimation principle [7].

From a CBR point of view, prediction is arguably one of the least complex problem types, mainly because the crucial subtask of *adaptation* is not an intricate issue. In fact, the adaptation of previous solutions, retrieved from a case library, to the current problem at hand is still one of the most challenging steps of a CBR process and quite difficult to automate [9]. For prediction problems, however, adaptation can be done in a rather straightforward way: In the case of regression, one can hardly do better than deriving an average of the k nearest neighbors' outputs (in which the neighbors are weighted according to their similarity to the query [17,4]). In the case of classification, the "solution space" is given by the finite set of class labels, and the classes of the nearest neighbors are typically combined through majority voting.

Despite the fact that (nearest neighbor) classification methods have been used extensively in the CBR field, e.g., for problems such as diagnosis, one may argue that the classification framework in its standard form is not fully satisfactory

R.O. Weber and M.M. Richter (Eds.): ICCBR 2007, LNAI 4626, pp. 77–91, 2007.
© Springer-Verlag Berlin Heidelberg 2007

from a *problem solving* point of view, simply because problem solving usually goes beyond predicting a single solution:

- A first crucial problem is that a simple classification does not imply a possible course of action in the case where it fails: If the classification is wrong, the problem is not yet solved, so the question is how to continue.
- Besides, in the case of failure, conventional classification does not offer a means to properly *learn* from the unsuccessful trial, because a problem in conjunction with a suboptimal solution is not an "example" in the sense of supervised learning; and even if an optimal solution is eventually found, the corresponding problem/solution pair will usually not comprise the complete experience (e.g., differences in the quality of suboptimal solutions) that has been gathered in the course of the problem solving episode.

To avoid these problems, we propose a (case-based) approach to *label ranking* and elaborate on its application in case-based reasoning. Label ranking is an extended classification task that has recently been studied in machine learning. The goal in label ranking is to predict a complete ranking of all class labels instead of only a single class (top-label). Obviously, a prediction of that kind can be very useful in CBR. For example, it suggests a simple problem solving strategy, namely a trial and error search process which successively tests the candidate solutions until the problem has been solved. Needless to say, to be effective, this strategy presupposes a solution space in the form of a finite set of small to moderate size (just like classification learning itself).

To illustrate, consider a fault detection problem which consists of identifying the cause for the malfunctioning of a technical system. Moreover, suppose that a (case-based) learning system is used to predict the true cause, e.g., on the basis of certain sensor measurements serving as input attributes (see, e.g., [3] for an application of that type). A prediction in the form of a label ranking then dictates the complete order in which the potential causes (which play the role of labels) should be searched.

The remainder of the paper is organized as follows: The problem of label ranking and its relation to CBR are discussed in Section 2. In Section 3, we present a case-based approach to label ranking which is an extension of nearest neighbor classification.[1] Section 4 is devoted to experimental studies in which our case-based label ranking method is compared to conventional nearest neighbor classification. Moreover, this section elaborates on the idea of using case-based label ranking for node ordering in heuristic search. Finally, Section 5 gives a summary and concludes the paper.

2   Label Ranking and CBR

In label ranking, the problem is to learn a mapping from instances x of an instance space $\mathcal{X}$ to rankings $\succ_x$ (total strict orders) over a finite set of labels

$$\mathcal{L} = \{\lambda_1, \lambda_2 \ldots \lambda_c\},$$

---

[1] Parts of this section can also be found in the companion paper [6].

where $\lambda_i \succ_x \lambda_j$ means that, for the instance x, label λ_i is placed ahead of λ_j; in this case, we shall also say that λ_i is preferred to λ_j (by x). As mentioned earlier, in the context of CBR, instances correspond to problems and labels correspond to candidate solutions. This should be kept in mind, since we shall subsequently use both the CBR and the machine learning terminology.

A ranking over $\mathcal{L}$ can be represented by a permutation τ of $\{1 \ldots c\}$, where $\tau(i)$ denotes the position of the label λ_i; thus, $\lambda_i \succ_x \lambda_j$ iff $\tau(i) < \tau(j)$. The target space of all permutations over c labels will subsequently be referred to as $\mathcal{S}_c$.

As training data, a label ranking algorithm can refer to a number of example instances together with different types of information regarding their preference for labels. Since this point is important for CBR, we will discuss it in this specific context.

2.1 Training Data in Label Ranking

Suppose that, in the course of a problem solving process in CBR, a subset of all candidate solutions has been tried to solve a query problem x_0. What can be learned from these trials, and what experiences can be memorized? One type of experience concerns the suitability of individual candidate solutions λ_i: Such candidates may be feasible or acceptable as a solution or not. Subsequently, we shall refer to this kind of distinction as an *absolute preference*.

Another type of experience concerns *relative preferences*: As soon as two alternatives λ_i and λ_j have been tried as solutions for x_0, these two alternatives can be compared and, correspondingly, either a preference in favor of one of them or an indifference can be expressed:

$$\lambda_i \succ_{x_0} \lambda_j \quad \text{or} \quad \lambda_i \prec_{x_0} \lambda_i \quad \text{or} \quad \lambda_i \sim_{x_0} \lambda_j.$$

Again, these preferences can be memorized and utilized for future problem solving. For example, a preference $\lambda_i \succ_{x_0} \lambda_j$ clearly holds if λ_j turned out to be unacceptable, while λ_i was found to be acceptable as a solution. However, even if both alternatives were acceptable, or both unacceptable, one may state that one of them is still better than the other one (e.g., because it is less expensive). Indeed, more often than not, there will be more than one acceptable solution, even though not all of them will be equally preferred.

To exploit experience of the above type, a CBR system may store a problem along with absolute and relative preferences in a case library. Thus, a *case* may look a follows:

$$\left\langle x, ([\lambda_2, \lambda_4]^+, [\lambda_1, \lambda_6]^-, \lambda_4 \succ \lambda_2, \lambda_1 \sim \lambda_6) \right\rangle. \tag{1}$$

The meaning of this example is that λ_2 and λ_4 are acceptable solutions for the problem x, λ_1 and λ_6 are unacceptable, λ_4 is preferred to λ_2, and indifference holds between λ_1 and λ_6. Note that a case such as (1) represents only partial preference information about labels; for example, nothing is known about λ_3, perhaps because it has not been tried as a solution for x.

As will be explained in more detail later on, cases of the form (1) correspond to the (most general) type of examples that label ranking algorithms can learn from. With regard to gathering experiences from a problem solving episode, label ranking is hence more flexible and expressive than conventional classification. In fact, the standard type of example in classification learning is a tuple consisting of an instance and an associated class or, using CBR terminology, a problem with its "correct" solution. Comparing these two approaches, label ranking clearly exhibits the following advantages:

- Label ranking can also learn from unsuccessful trials; in contrast, the information that a certain label is not the correct class is not directly utilizable by standard classification methods (unless, of course, in the case of binary problems with only two classes).
- Even if the problem was eventually solved, label ranking can learn more than the optimal solution, because it additionally makes use of the preferences between the alternatives that have been tried before.

Even though conventional classification has already been extended in one way or the other, the aforementioned limitations essentially persist. For example, in *multi-label classification*, an instance may belong to more than one class or, stated differently, a problem may have more than one solution. So, an example is a tuple consisting of an instance x together with an associated subset $L_x \subseteq L$ of class labels. In principle, it is hence possible to distinguish between acceptable and unacceptable solutions, as we have done above. Note, however, that L_x must indeed be known exactly, i.e., the representation of partial knowledge is still a problem. Besides, of course, a more refined discrimination between solutions in terms of relative preferences is not possible.

2.2 Prediction and Loss Functions on Label Rankings

Apart from increased flexibility with respect to the representation of experiences, label ranking has also advantages regarding the prediction of solutions for new problems. Conventional classification learning essentially allows a classifier to make a one shot decision in order to identify the correct label. A prediction is either correct or not and, correspondingly, is rewarded in the former and punished in the latter case. The arguably best-known loss function reflecting this problem conception is the misclassification or error rate of a classifier. However, in many practical applications, the problem is not to give a single estimation, but to make repeated suggestions until the correct target label has been identified. Obviously, this task is ideally supported by a label ranking.

To measure the quality of a predicted label ranking, a suitable loss function $\ell(\cdot)$ is needed. To this end, several meaningful metrics can be used, such as the sum of squared rank distances

$$\ell_2(\tau, \tau') \stackrel{\mathrm{df}}{=} \sum_{i=1}^{c} (\tau(i) - \tau'(i))^2. \tag{2}$$

The linear transformation of the latter loss function into a $[-1, 1]$-valued similarity measure is well-known as the *Spearman rank correlation coefficient* [19].

Remark 1. Regarding the relation between classification and label ranking, ordering the class labels according to their probability of being the top-label (i.e., the "true" label in classification) as suggested, e.g., by a probabilistic classifier, does not usually yield a good prediction in the sense of a ranking error such as (2). To illustrate, suppose that $\mathbb{P}(1 \succ 2 \succ 3) = 0.5$, $\mathbb{P}(3 \succ 2 \succ 1) = 0.3$, $\mathbb{P}(2 \succ 1 \succ 3) = 0.2$, while the probability of all other rankings is 0. The probability of being the top-label is, respectively, 0.5, 0.2, 0.3 for the three labels 1, 2, and 3, so sorting them according to these probabilities gives $1 \succ 3 \succ 2$. However, in terms of the sum of squared rank distances (2), this ranking is suboptimal as it has a higher expected loss than the ranking $2 \succ 1 \succ 3$. This result is not astonishing in light of the fact that, by only looking at the top-labels, one completely ignores the information about the rest of the rankings. In the above example, for instance, one ignores that label 2 is never on the lowest position.

In some applications, the quality of a ranking may not depend on the positions assigned to *all* the labels. For example, consider again a fault detection problem which consists of identifying the cause for the malfunctioning of a technical system. As mentioned earlier, a ranking suggests a simple (trial and error) search process which successively tests the candidates, one by one, until the correct cause is found. In this scenario, where labels correspond to causes, the existence of a single target label λ^* (the true cause) instead of a target ranking can be assumed. Hence, an obvious measure of the quality of a predicted ranking is the number of futile trials made before that label is found. To distinguish it from real *ranking errors* such as (2), a deviation of the predicted target label's position from the top-rank has been called a *position error* [3,16]. Needless to say, various generalizations of a position error thus defined are conceivable, depending on the type of search or problem solving process used to find the target label λ^*. For instance, imagine a process which tries exactly k solutions and then takes the best among these candidates, $\lambda^{(k)}$. In this case, a reasonable loss function is given by the quality of λ^* minus the quality of $\lambda^{(k)}$.

3   Case-Based Label Ranking

For the time being, let us make the idealized assumption that the training data submitted to the learning algorithm consists of a set of examples

$$\mathcal{D} = \{(\boldsymbol{x}_1, \tau_1), (\boldsymbol{x}_2, \tau_2) \dots (\boldsymbol{x}_m, \tau_m)\},$$

where each example contains a *complete* label ranking. As discussed in Section 2.1, the preference information being available in practice will usually be much weaker. However, by reducing the technical complexity, this assumption will allow us to focus on the main conceptual elements of case-based label ranking. In Section 3.2, we will discuss how to handle more general scenarios that relax the above assumption and allow for dealing with examples such as (1).

In the following, we will introduce a general case-based framework for learning label rankings. The k-nearest neighbor algorithm (k-NN) is arguably the most basic case-based learning method [7]. In its simplest version, it assumes all instances to be represented by feature vectors $x = (x_1 \ldots x_N)^\top$ in the N-dimensional space $\mathcal{X} = \mathbb{R}^N$ endowed with a distance measure $d(\cdot)$ such as the Euclidean metric. Given a query input x_0, the k-NN algorithm retrieves the k training instances closest to this point in terms of $d(\cdot)$. In the case of classification learning, k-NN estimates the query's class label by the most frequent label among these k neighbors. As mentioned in the introduction, it can be adapted to the regression learning scenario by replacing the majority voting step with computing the (weighted) mean of the target values.

A unified view of both classification and label ranking as *discrete-valued* learning problems suggests a straightforward generalization of the k-NN algorithm which predicts the most common label ranking as a target object. However, on second thought, several obvious problems make this approach seem inappropriate in general:

- The cardinality of the target space in label ranking is $|\mathcal{S}_c| = c!$, a number exceeding the typical cardinality in classification learning abundantly clear. Therefore, if the local distribution of label rankings does not have sharp peaks, equal votes statistics are much more likely (except for $k = 1$). Random tie-breaking, a standard technique in k-NN learning, will hence be used rather frequently, resulting in randomly selecting a label ranking among the k nearest neighbors.
- In contrast to classification learning, where only the discrete metric (0/1 loss) is given on the target space, meaningful *non-trivial* metrics can be defined on label rankings (cf. Section 2.2), a property shared with regression learning. The conventional k-NN algorithm does not exploit this property in the aggregation step, which is typically realized as a simple majority vote among the neighbors instead of any sort of averaging.

To avoid these problems, a more sophisticated algorithm should incorporate the structured nature of the space of label rankings. Our approach, recently put forward in [6], considers aggregation techniques for label ranking which are conceptually related to averaging in k-NN regression learning. To this end, we incorporate a common rank aggregation model to combine the k nearest neighbors into a single ranking. Even though this model has already been used in a variety of applications, such as in combining meta-search results [8], it is a novel component in a label ranking algorithm. The *consensus label ranking* is computed such that it minimizes the sum of pairwise disagreement measures with respect to all k rankings, as will be detailed below.

3.1   Aggregating Label Rankings

Let $\tau_1 \ldots \tau_k$ denote rankings of the c alternatives (labels) $\lambda_1 \ldots \lambda_c$. A common method to measure the quality of a ranking

$$\tau = \mathrm{AGGR}(\tau_1 \ldots \tau_k)$$

as an aggregation of the set of rankings $\tau_1 \ldots \tau_k$ is to compute the sum of pairwise loss values with respect to a loss (distance) function $\ell : \mathcal{S}_c \times \mathcal{S}_c \to \mathbb{R}_{\geq 0}$ defined on pairs of rankings:

$$L(\tau) \stackrel{\text{df}}{=} \sum_{i=1}^{k} \ell(\tau, \tau_i)$$

Having specified a loss function $\ell(\cdot)$, this leads to the optimization problem of computing a ranking $\hat{\tau} \in \mathcal{S}_c$ (not necessarily unique) such that

$$\hat{\tau} \in \arg \min_{\tau \in \mathcal{S}_c} \sum_{i=1}^{k} \ell(\tau, \tau_i). \tag{3}$$

For the sum of squared rank distances as a loss function, a provably optimal solution of (3) is obtained by ordering alternatives according to the so-called *Borda count* [15], a voting technique well-known in social choice theory. The Borda count of an alternative is the number of (weighted) votes for that alternative in pairwise comparisons with all remaining options. This voting rule requires computational time on the order of $\mathcal{O}(kc + c \log c)$ and thus can be evaluated very efficiently[2].

In the experimental section, we will use the Borda-count ordering technique as it is computationally efficient and has a sound theoretical basis. However, as the aggregation component is an isolated module within our case-based framework, alternative aggregation techniques which may be suitable for the particular application at hand may be integrated easily (such as aggregation techniques which minimize loss functions focusing on correct top ranks rather than distributing equal weights to all positions).

3.2 Extensions of Label Ranking

Practical applications of (case-based) label ranking suggest several generalizations of the framework that we introduced above. Essentially, these generalizations concern the target space, that is, the set $\mathcal{S}_c$ of all rankings over $\mathcal{L}$. As an appealing property of the case-based framework, replacing $\mathcal{S}_c$ by any more general space, say, $\mathcal{S}_c^{ex}$ can be done quite easily without changing the framework itself, provided that $\mathcal{S}_c^{ex}$ can be endowed with a suitable distance measure. In the following, we give a brief overview of some important extensions, though without going into much technical detail.

Rankings with Ties. So far, we assumed rankings in the form of *strict* total orders, which means that, for any pair of alternatives λ_i, λ_j, either $\lambda_i \succ \lambda_j$ or $\lambda_j \succ \lambda_i$. More generally, as mentioned in Section 2.1, it might be reasonable to allow for the case of indifference ($\lambda_i \sim \lambda_j$), that is, to consider *rankings with ties*. A ranking of that kind is also referred to as a *bucket order* [8]. More precisely, a

---

[2] More technical details can be found in [6], where the aggregation problem is also considered for other loss functions.

bucket order is a transitive binary relation $\succ$ for which there exist sets $B_1 \ldots B_m$ that form a partition of the set of alternatives $\mathcal{L}$ such that $\lambda_i \succ \lambda_j$ if and only if there exist $1 \leq k < l \leq m$ such that $(\lambda_i \in B_k) \wedge (\lambda_j \in B_l)$. A bucket order induces binary preferences among labels and, moreover, forms a natural representation for generalizing various metrics on strict rankings to rankings with ties. To this end, we define a generalized rank $\sigma(i)$ for each label $\lambda_i \in \mathcal{L}$ as the average overall position $\sigma(i) = \sum_{l<j} |B_l| + \frac{1}{2}(|B_j| + 1)$ within the bucket B_j which contains λ_i. Fagin et al. [8] proposed several generalizations of well-known metrics such as Kendall's tau and the Spearman footrule distance.

Calibrated Rankings. A particularly interesting generalization of label ranking is *calibrated label ranking* as introduced in [5]. Roughly speaking, a calibrated ranking is a ranking with an additional neutral label which splits a ranking into two parts, say, a positive and a negative one. This way, it becomes possible to combine absolute and relative preference information as introduced in Section 2.1. For example, in a CBR context, the positive part may consist of those alternatives (solutions) λ_i which are feasible, while the alternatives in the negative part are not acceptable as solutions for the current problem. The ranking further refines this crude distinction, e.g., one alternative can be better than another one, even though both are feasible.

An elegant extension of distance measures for rankings to measures for calibrated rankings was proposed in [6]. The basic idea is to define the distance between two calibrated rankings by the distance between the associated extended rankings which include the neutral label. Moreover, the neutral label can be duplicated to broaden the gap between the positive and the negative part. This way, a deviation of a label's estimated position from its true position is punished more strongly if it furthermore leads to putting the label on the wrong side.

Partial Preference Information. The assumption that a *complete* ranking is given for every training example will generally not be satisfied in practice. Instead, only partial preference information will be available, e.g., a ranking of only a subset of the labels $\mathcal{L}$. The problem of extending distance measures to partial preference relations was studied by Ha and Haddawy [11]. Here, the basic idea is to consider the set of all consistent extensions of such rankings (to complete rankings), and to measure a distance between these extensions. Again, this is a quite elegant approach, even though it may become computationally complex.

4   Experiments

As already mentioned earlier, label ranking essentially assumes a finite label set $\mathcal{L}$ of small to moderate size, a property it shares with conventional classification. If this property is fulfilled for a solution space in CBR, label ranking can be applied immediately. A related experimental study, which deals with predicting a rational, decision-theoretic agent's ranking of actions in an uncertain environment, is presented in Section 4.1.

Moreover, in Section 4.2, we consider an interesting alternative, showing how label ranking can be usefully applied as a sub-component in the context of a search-based problem solving strategy operating on a complex solution space. More specifically, by determining the order of successor states in heuristic search, label ranking will be used for guiding a heuristic search process.[3] Roughly speaking, the idea is to assume that, if a certain ordering of successor nodes in a search state A turned out to be useful, the same or a similar ordering will also be useful in a similar state B.

4.1 Case-Based Decision Making

In our first experiment, we replicate a setting that has been used in the context of label ranking in [10]. The problem is to learn the ranking function of an expected utility maximizing agent. More specifically, we proceed from a standard setting of expected utility theory: $A = \{a_1 \dots a_c\}$ is a set of actions the agent can choose from and $\Omega = \{\omega_1 \dots \omega_m\}$ is a set of world states. The agent faces a problem of *decision under risk* where decision consequences are lotteries: Choosing action a_i in state ω_j yields a utility of $u_{ij} \in \mathbb{R}$, where the probability of state ω_j is p_j. Thus, the *expected utility* of action a_i is given by

$$\mathbb{E}(a_i) = \sum_{j=1}^{m} p_j \cdot u_{ij}. \tag{4}$$

Expected utility theory justifies (4) as a criterion for ranking actions and, hence, gives rise to the following preference relation:

$$a_i \succ a_j \iff \mathbb{E}(a_i) > \mathbb{E}(a_j). \tag{5}$$

Now, suppose the probability vector $\boldsymbol{p} = (p_1 \dots p_m)$ to be a parameter of the decision problem (while A, Ω and the utility matrix matrix $\mathbf{U} = (u_{ij})$ are fixed). A vector $\boldsymbol{p}$ can be considered as a description of the "problem" that the agent has to solve, namely as a characterization of the uncertain environment in which the agent must take an action.

The above decision-theoretic setting can be used for generating synthetic data for label ranking. The set of instances (problems) corresponds to the set of probability vectors $\boldsymbol{p}$, which are generated at random according to a uniform distribution over $\{\boldsymbol{p} \in \mathbb{R}^m \,|\, \boldsymbol{p} \geq 0, \, p_1 + \dots + p_m = 1\}$. The ranking associated with an instance is defined by the pairwise preferences (5). Thus, an experiment is characterized by the following parameters: The number of actions/labels (c), the number of world states (m), the number of examples (n), and the utility matrix which is generated at random through independent and uniformly distributed entries $u_{ij} \in [0, 1]$.

In this study, we applied our case-based approach to label ranking (CBLR), using the aggregation technique described in Section 3.1. For comparison, we

---

[3] The idea of using CBR to support heuristic search has already been put forward by several authors; see e.g. [18] for a very recent and closely related approach.

used the standard k-NN classification method, which simply orders the class labels according to the number of votes they receive from the neighbors (ties are broken at random). The main goal of this study is to show the benefit of the additional information contained in the comparison of suboptimal solutions, which is exploited by CBLR but not by the simple k-NN classifier.

In the experiments, we chose the problem dimensions to be $m \in \{5, 10, 15, 20\}$, $c \in \{5, 15, 20\}$, and fixed the number of training and test examples to $1,000$ each. For each value of the input dimension, we generated 10 different label ranking problems originating from independently sampled utility matrices. As evaluation measures, we considered the position error (i.e., the position assigned to the true top-label) and the Spearman rank correlation. In order to simplify the comparison, the position error was re-scaled into a similarity measure on $[-1, +1]$ in a straightforward way. For each learning problem and algorithm, the neighborhood parameter $k \in \{1, 3 \ldots 19, 21\}$ was determined based upon the performance (with respect to the particular evaluation measure at hand) on a random 70/30 split of the training data. The performance results on the test sets were averaged over all 10 runs.

Table 1. Results of the first experimental study. In each horizontal block, the first line shows the accuracy values for CBLR, the second line for the simple k-NN classifier.

m	pos. err.	rank. err.	pos. err.	rank. err.	pos. err.	rank. err.
5	.967 ± .020	.969 ± .011	.932 ± .026	.929 ± .019	.878 ± .0628	.880 ± .046
	.967 ± .020	.625 ± .080	.923 ± .025	.697 ± .071	.866 ± .0670	.706 ± .084
10	.980 ± .008	.979 ± .005	.959 ± .017	.951 ± .007	.924 ± .0333	.909 ± .023
	.977 ± .008	.437 ± .067	.950 ± .016	.484 ± .102	.907 ± .0373	.536 ± .114
15	.987 ± .005	.985 ± .002	.966 ± .011	.964 ± .007	.954 ± .0196	.926 ± .006
	.982 ± .006	.302 ± .065	.957 ± .015	.414 ± .094	.940 ± .0213	.425 ± .109
20	.988 ± .003	.988 ± .002	.972 ± .007	.968 ± .006	.948 ± .0204	.936 ± .019
	.984 ± .002	.266 ± .043	.958 ± .008	.337 ± .055	.926 ± .0232	.419 ± .099
	$c = 5$		$c = 10$		$c = 20$	

The results in Table 1 show that CBLR clearly outperforms the simple k-NN classifier. As it was to be expected, the differences in performance are indeed dramatic for the rank correlation which takes the complete ranking into account. However, CBLR is also superior for the position error, which is essentially a type of classification error. This result shows that exploiting information about suboptimal solutions can also improve the standard classification performance.

4.2   Label Ranking for Controlling Heuristic Search

Resource-based configuration (RBC) is a special approach to knowledge-based configuration [13]. It proceeds from the idea that a (technical) system is assembled from a set of primitive *components*. A resource-based description of components is a special property-based description in which each component (e.g. a lamp) is characterized by some set of *resources* or *functionalities* it provides (e.g. light) and some other set of resources it demands (e.g. electric current). The relation between components is modeled in an abstract way as an exchange of resources. A configuration problem consists of minimizing the price of a configuration while satisfying an external demand of functionalities. In its simplest form it corresponds to an integer linear program $\mathbf{A} \times \mathbf{z} \geq \mathbf{x}$, $\mathbf{c}^\top \mathbf{z} \to min$, where the matrix $\mathbf{A} = (a_{ij})$ specifies the quantities of functionalities offered and demanded by the components (a_{ij} = quantity of the i-th functionality offered by the j-th component, demands are negative offers), the vector $\mathbf{x}$ quantifies the external demand, and the vector $\mathbf{c}$ contains the prices of the components. A configuration is identified by the vector $\mathbf{z}$, where the j-th entry is the number of occurrences of the j-th component. In practice, it is reasonable to assume that different problems share the same *knowledge base* $\langle \mathbf{A}, \mathbf{c} \rangle$ while the external demand $\mathbf{x}$ changes. Thus, the instance (problem) space $\mathcal{X}$ can be identified by all possible demand vectors.

Since an RBC problem, in its basic form, is equivalent to an integer linear program, one could think of using standard methods from operations research for solving it. However, this equivalence is already lost under slight but practically relevant generalizations of the basic model (such as non-additive dependencies between components). Realizing a heuristic search in the *configuration space*, i.e., the set $\mathcal{Z}$ of possible configurations (identified by integer-valued vectors $\mathbf{z}$), seems to be a reasonable alternative which is more amenable toward extensions of the model. Besides, this approach is better suited for incorporating (case-based) *experience* from previously solved problems [14].

In fact, there are different ways of realizing the idea of *learning* from a set of (optimally) solved problems in connection with heuristic search. Here, we consider the possibility of employing (case-based) label ranking to guide the search process, i.e., to control the choice of search operators: By starting with the empty configuration (root of the search tree) and adding basic components one by one, every node η of the search tree can be associated with an (intermediate) configuration $\mathbf{z}(\eta)$ and a corresponding demand $\mathbf{x}(\eta) = \mathbf{x} - \mathbf{A} \times \mathbf{z}(\eta)$ which still remains of the original demand $\mathbf{x}$; the search process stops as soon as $\mathbf{x}(\eta) \leq \mathbf{0}$. The key idea of our approach is to use label ranking to predict a promising order τ in which to explore the successors of a search state, that is, the order in which adding the basic components is tried (see Figure 1); the latter hence correspond to the class labels, while the demand $\mathbf{x}(\eta)$ serves as an instance. As mentioned above, label ranking thus implements the heuristic (CBR) assumption that, to find a good solution for a problem $\mathbf{x}(\eta)$, the next component to be added to the current configuration should be one that turned out to be a good choice for a similar problem $\mathbf{x}'$ as well.

In our experiments, we generated synthetic configuration problems as follows: The components of a 5×5-matrix $\mathbf{A}$ were generated at random by sampling from a uniform distribution over $\{-1, 0, 1, 2, 3\}$ (the sampling process was repeated until a feasible solution with a cost ≤ 25 existed). Likewise, the components of

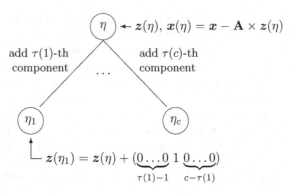

Fig. 1. Configuration as heuristic search: Every node η of the search tree is associated with an intermediate configuration $z(\eta)$. Each successor of η is obtained by adding one of the c available components, and the order in which components are tried is determined by the ranking (permutation) τ. The search stops if $x \leq 0$.

the cost vector c and the demand vector x were sampled, respectively, from a uniform distribution over $\{1, 2, 3\}$ and $\{1, 2, 3, 4, 5\}$.

We constructed a case library as follows: Given a matrix $\mathbf{A}$, a cost vector c and a demand vector x, we used iterative deepening search to determine a solution with minimum cost. Then, the search was repeated with a cost bound of twice the optimum value. In this "exploration phase", each node in the search graph corresponds to an intermediate configuration and a remaining demand vector. Moreover, each successor configuration can be associated with the minimum cost of all solutions within that subtree (which is set to infinity if no solution with bounded costs of twice the optimum value exists). Hence, from a label ranking point of view, we can see the remaining demand vector as an instance, the associated ranking of which is obtained by ordering the 5 possible successor configurations according to the subtree solution quality. We also used a calibration label (cf. Section 3.2) which corresponds to the maximum finite cost value, i.e., this label separates subtrees with finite-cost solutions from subtrees with no feasible solution.

An initial case library containing all remaining demand vectors and the associated rankings (with ties) we created for the search graph up to the maximum limit of twice the optimal cost. To reduce the number of ties and hence to increase the number of meaningful examples, we considered only those vectors for which the labels were associated with at least 2 different cost values. Fixing the matrix $\mathbf{A}$, the process was repeated 10 times for randomly sampled initial demand vectors x (see above). Finally, a subsample of constant size S was randomly selected from the the complete case library to equalize the knowledge base size for different matrices $\mathbf{A}$.

We gave this final case library to our CBLR approach (with $k = 3$) and used it as the main building block for a heuristic search strategy: Each search node corresponds to a remaining demand vector and the predicted ranking among the successor configuration can be interpreted as a qualitative ordering of the

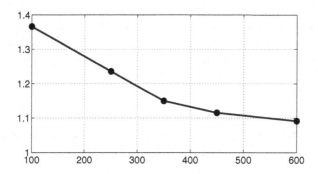

Fig. 2. Performance curve for case-based heuristic search: Average ratio between the cost of the solution found and the true optimum (minimal cost), as a function of the size of the case library (number S of stored cases)

utility for searching a particular subtree. Hence, we traverse the search graph in the order dictated by the predicted ranking, where the calibration label is associated with a back-tracking step. To evaluate this strategy, we sample a new initial demand vector, conduct 100 search steps, and store the solution with minimum cost found in the course of this process. Additionally, we determined an optimal solution using the iterative deepening strategy.

The overall process of sampling $\mathbf{A}$ and $\mathbf{c}$, building the case library, and testing on a new demand vector was repeated 100 times. Figure 2 shows the average ratio between the cost of the solution found by our CBLR search heuristic and the optimal cost obtained by iterative deepening, depending on the size S of the case library. As can be seen, for a large enough case library, the solution quality comes close to the optimum. For example, for $S = 600$, the quality of the heuristic approach (which is faster by at least one order of magnitude) deviates by not more than 10% on average, showing the effectiveness of the approach.

5   Summary and Conclusions

The aim of this paper is to establish a connection between CBR and the label ranking problem that was recently introduced in the field of machine learning. In fact, our claim is that this connection can be beneficial for both sides: Firstly, as we showed in [6], a case-based approach to the label ranking problem offers an interesting alternative to hitherto existing model-based methods [12,10]. Secondly, we have argued here that, for various reasons, label ranking can be useful in the context of case-based problem solving, especially when being compared to conventional classification learning. In particular, label ranking can better exploit the pieces of experience that accumulate in the course of a problem solving episode, and provides predictions that are potentially more helpful in finding a solution to a new problem.

To substantiate our claims, we presented experimental studies which, in absence of existing benchmark problems, are based on artificial scenarios and synthetic data. Despite the usefulness of these settings (e.g., for conducting controlled experiments), an obvious next step is to put the ideas outlined in this paper into practice, that is, to use label ranking in conjunction with CBR methods for solving real problems.

References

1. Aha, D.W.: Tolerating noisy, irrelevant and novel attributes in instance-based learning algorithms. International Journal of Man-Machine Studies 36, 267–287 (1992)
2. Aha, D.W., Kibler, D., Albert, M.K.: Instance-based learning algorithms. Machine Learning 6(1), 37–66 (1991)
3. Alonso, C., Rodríguez, J., Pulido, B.: Enhancing consistency based diagnosis with machine learning techniques. In: Conejo, R., Urretavizcaya, M., Pérez-de-la-Cruz, J.-L. (eds.) Current Topics in Artificial Intelligence. LNCS (LNAI), vol. 3040, pp. 312–321. Springer, Heidelberg (2004)
4. Atkeson, C.G., Moore, A.W., Schaal, S.: Locally weighted learning 11, 11–73 (1997)
5. Brinker, K., Fürnkranz, J., Hüllermeier, E.: A unified model for multilabel classi-fication and ranking. In: Proceedings ECAI–2006, 17th European Conference on Artificial Intelligence, Riva del Garda, Italy (2006)
6. Brinker, K., Hüllermeier, E.: Case-based multilabel ranking. In: Proc. IJCAI–07, 20th International Joint Conference on Artificial Intelligence, pp. 701–707, Hyder-abad, India (January 2007)
7. Dasarathy, B.V. (ed.): Nearest Neighbor (NN) Norms: NN Pattern Classification Techniques. IEEE Computer Society Press, Los Alamitos (1991)
8. Fagin, R., Kumar, R., Mahdian, M., Sivakumar, D., Vee, E.: Comparing and aggre-gating rankings with ties. In: Proc. PODS–04, 23rd ACM Symposium on Principles of Database Systems, pp. 47–58 (2004)
9. Fuchs, B., Lieber, J., Mille, A., Napoli, A.: Towards a unified theory of adaptation in case-based reasoning. In: Althoff, K.-D., Bergmann, R., Branting, L.K. (eds.) Case-Based Reasoning Research and Development. LNCS (LNAI), vol. 1650, pp. 104–117. Springer, Heidelberg (1999)
10. Fürnkranz, J., Hüllermeier, E.: Pairwise preference learning and ranking. In: Lavrač, N., Gamberger, D., Todorovski, L., Blockeel, H. (eds.) ECML 2003. LNCS (LNAI), vol. 2837, Springer, Heidelberg (2003)
11. Ha, V., Haddawy, P.: Similarity of personal preferences: theoretical foundations and empirical analysis. Artificial Intelligence 146, 149–173 (2003)
12. Har-Peled, S., Roth, D., Zimak, D.: Constraint classification: a new approach to multiclass classification. In: Cesa-Bianchi, N., Numao, M., Reischuk, R. (eds.) ALT 2002. LNCS (LNAI), vol. 2533, pp. 365–379. Springer, Heidelberg (2002)
13. Heinrich, M.: Ressourcenorientiertes Konfigurieren. Künstliche Intelligenz 1(93), 11–14 (1993)
14. Hüllermeier, E.: Focusing search by using problem solving experience. In: Pro-ceedings ECAI–2000, 14th European Conference on Artificial Intelligence, Berlin, Germany, pp. 55–59. IOS Press, Amsterdam (2000)
15. Hüllermeier, E., Fürnkranz, J.: Ranking by pairwise comparison: A note on risk minimization. In: FUZZ-IEEE–04, IEEE International Conference on Fuzzy Sys-tems, Budapest, Hungary (2004)

16. Hüllermeier, E., Fürnkranz, J.: Learning label preferences: Ranking error versus position error. In: Famili, A.F., Kok, J.N., Peña, J.M., Siebes, A., Feelders, A. (eds.) IDA 2005. LNCS, vol. 3646, pp. 180–191. Springer, Heidelberg (2005)
17. Kibler, D., Aha, D.W., Albert, M.: Instance-based prediction of real-valued attributes. Computational Intelligence 5, 51–57 (1989)
18. De la Rosa, T., Olaya, A.G., Borrajo, D.: Case-based recommendation of node ordering in planning. In: Proc. 20-th International FLAIRS Conference, Key West, Florida (2007)
19. Spearman, C.: The proof and measurement for association between two things. Amer. Journal of Psychology 15, 72–101 (1904)
20. Stanfill, C., Waltz, D.: Toward memory-based reasoning. Communications of the ACM, 1213–1228 (1986)
21. Watson, I.: Case-based reasoning is a methodology not a technology. In: Mile, R., Moulton, M., Bramer, M. (eds.) Research and Development in Expert Systems XV, pp. 213–223. London (1998)

When Similar Problems Don't Have Similar Solutions

Stewart Massie, Susan Craw, and Nirmalie Wiratunga

School of Computing,
The Robert Gordon University,
Aberdeen AB25 1HG, Scotland, UK
{sm,smc,nw}@comp.rgu.ac.uk

Abstract. The performance of a Case-Based Reasoning system relies on the integrity of its case base but in real life applications the available data used to construct the case base invariably contains erroneous, noisy cases. Automated removal of these noisy cases can improve system accuracy. In addition, error rates for nearest neighbour classifiers can often be reduced by removing cases to give smoother decision boundaries between classes. In this paper we argue that the *optimal* level of boundary smoothing is domain dependent and, therefore, our approach to error reduction reacts to the characteristics of the domain to set an appropriate level of smoothing. We present a novel, yet transparent algorithm, Threshold Error Reduction, which identifies and removes noisy and boundary cases with the aid of a local complexity measure. Evaluation results confirm it to be superior to benchmark algorithms.

1 Introduction

Case Based Reasoning (CBR) solves new problems by re-using the solution of previously solved problems. The case base is the main source of knowledge in a CBR system and, hence, the availability of cases is crucial to a system's performance. In fact, it is the availability of cases that often supports the choice of CBR for problem-solving tasks. However, in real environments the quality of the cases cannot be guaranteed and some may even be corrupt. Error rates in the order of 5% have been shown to be typical in real data [?,?].

Corrupt cases, also called noise, contain errors in the values used to represent the case. In classification tasks, noise can result from either the class labels being wrongly assigned or corruption of the attribute values [?]. The CBR paradigm typically employs a lazy learning approach, such as k-nearest neighbour [?], for the retrieval stage of the process. While the nearest neighbour algorithm can reduce the impact of noise to some extent by considering more than one neighbour, the existence of noise can still be harmful. This is particularly true where the retrieved cases are being used to support an explanation of the proposed solution [?]. Manually identifying noisy cases is at best time consuming and usually impractical, hence, automated pre-processing techniques that remove noisy cases are useful.

One of the assumptions underlying the CBR methodology is that similar problems have similar solutions. This assumption is challenged in classification tasks at class boundaries, where the solution changes abruptly as the location of a target case crosses

R.O. Weber and M.M. Richter (Eds.): ICCBR 2007, LNAI 4626, pp. 92–106, 2007.
© Springer-Verlag Berlin Heidelberg 2007

a decision boundary in the problem space. Previous work has identified the importance of boundary regions for case base maintenance [?,?]. We agree that boundary regions are critical for error reduction. While noisy cases are generally harmful, valid boundary cases can also reduce retrieval performance and may also be considered as harmful cases. Smoothing the decision boundary by removing selected, *harmful* cases located near boundaries can improve accuracy in some case bases, however, excessive smoothing of the boundary by removing too many cases will reduce accuracy. The *optimal* level of smoothing depends on the characteristics of the decision boundary and is not easily quantified.

In this paper we present a novel pre-processing technique for classification tasks to reduce the error rate in lazy learners by identifying and removing both noisy cases and harmful boundary cases. Our approach identifies potentially harmful cases with the aid of a case base complexity profile and uses a stopping criteria to vary the level of case removal at class boundaries to suit the domain. As an additional benefit, the technique provides an insight into the structure of the case base that can allow the knowledge engineer to make informed maintenance decisions.

The remainder of this paper describes our approach to error reduction for lazy learning classifiers and evaluates it on several public domain case bases. In Section 2 we review existing research on error reduction techniques. Section 3 discusses profiling of a case base and how it can aid the knowledge engineer make informed maintenance choices. Our new error reduction algorithms are introduced in Section 4 with experimental results, comparing them with two benchmark algorithms, being reported in Section 5. Finally, we draw our conclusions in Section 6.

2 Related Work in Noise Reduction

The retention stage of the CBR process is now considered to involve far more than simply incorporating the latest problem-solving experience into the case knowledge. Case base maintenance is now an integral part of a CBR process [?].

Considerable research effort has been aimed at case base maintenance and much of the research has focused on control of the case base size through case deletion or case selection policies. Two distinct areas have been investigated: the reduction of redundancy; and the control of noise. Redundancy removal generally aims to remove a large number of cases but retain, rather than improve accuracy. Most recent redundancy removal techniques apply a standard noise reduction algorithm as a pre-processing step [?,?,?].

Noise reduction algorithms aim to improve competence by removing cases that are thought to have a detrimental effect on accuracy. These may be corrupt cases with incorrect solutions or, alternately, cases whose inclusion in the case base results in other cases being incorrectly solved. These algorithms usually remove fewer cases. Wilson Editing [?], also called ENN, is one of the best known algorithms and attempts to remove harmful cases by removing cases that are incorrectly classified by their three nearest neighbours. Tomek extends ENN with the Repeated Wilson Editing method (RENN) and the All k-NN method [?]. RENN repeats the ENN deletion cycle with multiple passes over the case base until no more cases are removed. The All k-NN is similar, except that after each iteration the value of k is increased.

The Blame-Based Noise Reduction (BBNR) algorithm [?] takes a slightly different approach to error reduction: rather than removing cases that are themselves incorrectly classified, BBRN removes cases that causes other cases to be misclassified. BBNR achieves this by extending Smyth & Keane's competence model [?] with the introduction of a *liability* set which is used to identify cases that cause misclassification. Cases are then removed if they cause more *harm* than *good*. Exploiting the existing knowledge within the case base is common to all these approaches, likewise, we use this implicit knowledge source to calculate a complexity measure by comparing a case's spatial positioning in relation to neighbours belonging to the same and different classes. This complexity measure highlights areas of uncertainty within the problem space.

Identifying the level of a system's uncertainty, in its proposed solution, has been shown to be useful in identifying harmful cases. Brodley& Friedl employ an ensemble of different type classifiers and use the uncertainty within the results to inform an error reduction filtering algorithm [?]. A misclassified case is removed where there is a consensus among the ensemble.

These approaches have been shown to successfully remove noise by removing mislabelled cases plus a varying degree of boundary cases. However, all these approaches have the disadvantage that they provide no control over the level of reduction. Each case is simply identified as harmful or not giving no control over the number of cases removed. We introduce a novel pre-processing technique to reduce the error rate in lazy learners by identifying and removing both noisy cases and harmful boundary cases. Our approach identifies potentially harmful cases with the aid of a case base profile and uses a stopping criteria to vary the level of case removal at class boundaries to suit the domain.

In previous work, complexity-guided maintenance [?,?] explicitly identifies class boundaries with the aid of a local complexity metric that measures the alignment between problem and solution space. This metric is then used to aid the discovery of new cases and the identification of redundant cases. We also consider the local alignment between problem and solution space at a local level, but focus on identifying and removing harmful cases.

3   Profiling to Identify Harmful Cases

CBR systems can be built without passing through the knowledge elicitation bottleneck since elicitation becomes a simpler task of acquiring past cases. Hence, CBR is often applied to solve problems where no explicit domain model exists. However, in adopting CBR certain implicit assumptions are made about the domain.

The regularity assumption requires that *similar problems have similar solutions*. CBR systems solve new problems by retrieving similar, solved problems from the case base and re-applying their solutions to the new problem. If, on a general level, the solutions of similar problems do not apply to new target problems then CBR is not a suitable problem-solving approach for the domain. Fortunately, the world is generally a regular place and the fact that *similar problems have similar solutions* tends to apply in many domains. It is our contention that in local areas of the problem space, in particular at class boundaries, this assumption may not hold true and that these areas require special consideration. If we can measure the alignment between the problem and solution space in terms of the extent to which *"similar problems have similar solutions"* holds true at a local level we can then make informed maintenance decisions.

In previous work the alignment between problem and solution space has been measured by looking at the mix of solution classes present among a case's neighbours in the problem space [?]. However, for the identification of noisy cases we found the use of a measure that incorporates distance between cases to be more discriminating.

Our initial objective is to identify potentially harmful cases. By adopting the basic premise that cases whose neighbours belong to a different class are more likely to be harmful, we use a case distance ratio measure that provides a local measure of a case's position in relation to neighbours of its own class and neighbours with a different class. A ranked profile of this measure provides a view of the overall structure of the case base. The profile identifies the mix of local complexities. In the rest of this section we first define the local distance ratio used and then look at our profiling approach as a means of presenting a global picture of the composition of local ratios contained within the case base.

3.1   Assessing Confidence

The complexity measure we use to assess our confidence in a case compares distances to a case's nearest like neighbours (NLN's) with distances to its nearest unlike neighbours (NUN's), where the NLN is the nearest neighbour belonging to the same class and the NUN is the nearest neighbour belonging to a different class. We call the complexity measure the Friend:Enemy (F:E) ratio.

Figure 1 shows the calculation of the NLN distance (Dist(NLN)) for case c_1. A case is represented by a symbol with its class distinguished by the shapes circle and star. Two cases are identified (c_1 and c_2) and the distances to their three NLN's are represented by solid lines and the distances to their NUN's by dashed lines. D_k is the average distance to a case's k NLN's. In Figure 1(a), as the value of k increases, the sequence of D_k for c_1 starts $0.1, 0.15, 0.18$. A profile of D_k (Figure 1(b)) can now be plotted as k increases. Dist(NLN) is the average value of D_k for some chosen K. For c_1 with K=3, Dist(NLN) is 0.14; Dist(NUN) is 0.17 and the F:E ratio is 0.83 (0.14/0.17).

C_1 is a typical boundary case, positioned at a similar distance from its NLN's and NUN's, with a F:E ratio in the region of 1. Whereas, C_2 is a typical noisy case, positioned closer to cases belonging to a different class, with a F:E ratio greater than 1 (2.36). This complexity measure gives a higher weighting to nearer neighbours because they are included repeatedly in D_k and also allows the size of the neighbourhood to be easily varied to suit different sized case bases. A small neighbourhood is typically more suitable for identifying noise and K=3 has been used to calculate the F:E ratio for the experiments in this paper.

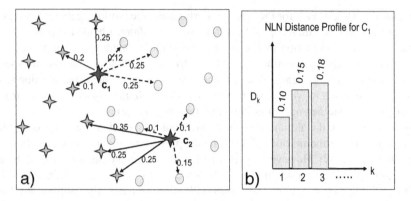

Fig. 1. Calculation of friend:enemy ratio

3.2   Profile Approach

The F:E ratio gives an indicator of the positioning of a case in relation to other cases of the same and different class within its own local neighbourhood. This ratio can provide an indication on the potential of a case to be harmful and we will show later that this indicator can be used to inform an error reducing case editing algorithm. However, it is difficult for the knowledge engineer to use this local information directly to gain an insight into the structure of a case base from a global perspective. Our approach to providing the knowledge engineer with meaningful access to this pool of local information is to present the data as a ranked profile of case complexities. In this approach the mix of complexities within the case base can be viewed as a profile allowing comparisons to be made between case bases.

The ranked complexity profile is created by first calculating the F:E ratio of each case to give a measure of case complexity. The cases are then ranked in ascending order of F:E. Then, starting with cases with the lowest complexity, case complexities

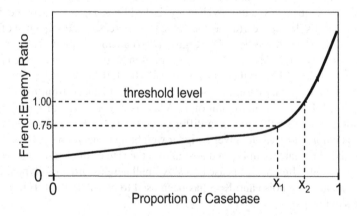

Fig. 2. Typical graph of Friend:Enemy ratio profile

are plotted against the relative position of the case in the ranking. Thus the x-axis shows the proportion of the case base and the y-axis gives the F:E value for the particular case at the relative position in the ranked list. If we accept the representativeness assumption, that the contents of the case base is a good approximation of the problems the system will encounter [?], then the profile of the case base also provides useful information about both the case base and the problem domain being faced. A typical case base profile is shown in Figure 2.

Two thresholds are marked on the plot corresponding to F:E ratio values of 0.75 and 1.00. The proportion of the case base corresponding to these thresholds is marked as x_1, and x_2 respectively. These indicators provide an insight into the structure of the case base. The proportion of cases above x_2 identifies cases closer to those belonging to a different class and gives an indication of the level of noise present in the case base. The proportion of cases between x_1, and x_2 identifies the number of cases close to class boundaries and gives an indication of the potential number of cases that could be removed while smoothing decision boundaries.

3.3 Interpreting Profiles

We have looked at a *typical* profile and claimed that these profiles provide a tool for making comparisons of the structure of the case base, including the level of noise, across different domains. To examine this claim we look at example profiles from three domains. Figure 3 shows the profiles for three public domain classification datasets from the UCI ML repository [?]: House Votes, Lymphography and Breast Cancer.

House votes (Figure 3(a)) is a binary classification problem with 435 cases represented by 16 boolean valued attributes containing some missing values. It can be seen from the profile that a high level of classification accuracy is expected. There is a low level of predicted noise (7%) based on the 1.0 threshold, and few cases (4%) lie between the 0.75 and 1.0 thresholds, indicating that few cases lie close to decision boundaries. Error reduction techniques would not be expected to give a large improvement in accuracy levels on this case base.

Lymphography (Figure 3(b)) is a smaller dataset with 4 classes and 148 cases represented by 19, mostly nominal, attributes with no missing values. There is a low level of predicted noise (10%), however, this appears to be quite a complex problem, with the shape the profile indicating many cases lie close to decision boundaries; 29% of the cases lie between the two thresholds. In this case base it is unclear if smoothing the decision boundary will improve accuracy.

Breast Cancer (Figure 3(c)) has 286 cases and is a binary classification domain with 9 multi-valued features containing missing data. There is a high estimated level of noise with 24% of cases with a ratio greater than 1 and a peak F:E value greater than 6. 12% of cases lie between the 0.75 and 1.0 thresholds. Pre-processing to remove harmful cases would be expected to greatly improve accuracy on this case base.

4 Complexity-Guided Error Reduction

Our aim in creating an error reduction algorithm is to identify and delete both noisy cases and harmful boundary cases from the case base. Noisy cases are expected to have

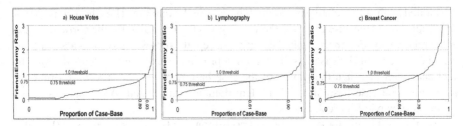

Fig. 3. Sample profiles for three classic dataset

a F:E ratio greater than 1 while boundary cases are expected to have a ratio in the region of 1. The basic approach we adopt is to set a threshold for the F:E ratio and delete all cases with values above the threshold.

4.1 Simple Threshold

An obvious threshold is 1 such that cases positioned nearer to those belonging to a different class will be removed from the case base. This approach provides our basic noise removal algorithm which we call Simple Threshold Error Reduction (TER-S). In this algorithm we

- Calculate the F:E ratio for each case in the case base.
- Rank cases in ascending order of the F:E ratio.
- Remove cases with an F:E ratio greater than 1 from the case base.

The proportion of cases being deleted can be read directly from the profile graph associating a level of explanation with the approach. However, there is no guarantee that setting a threshold of 1 is best for all domains. Conservative editing with only limited smoothing of the decision boundaries is possible by setting a threshold above 1 while, conversely, aggressive editing with strong smoothing of the decision boundaries is possible by setting a threshold below 1. In order to establish a suitable threshold across all domains we investigated the effect of setting different threshold values.

4.2 Setting the Threshold Level

Using a ten-times 10-fold cross-validation experimental set-up, giving 100 case base/test set combinations, cases with a F:E ratio above the specified threshold were deleted from the case base to form an edited case base. Test set accuracies were recorded on both the original and the edited case bases. The threshold was set at one of fourteen levels between 0.2 and 5. Figure 4 plots average test set accuracy on the original case base and on the edited case bases formed with the aid of the different thresholds for the three dataset discussed earlier: House Votes, Lymphography and Breast Cancer. Similar patterns of results were observed across other domains.

House Votes shows a small improvement in accuracy as the threshold falls toward 1 but the performance suffers as useful boundary cases are removed with lower thresholds. Lymphography shows no improvement in accuracy from case editing and any

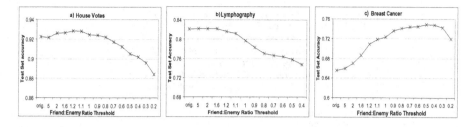

Fig. 4. Accuracy of edited case bases as cases with ratio above threshold are removed

boundary smoothing appears harmful. In contrast with Breast Cancer, the accuracy continues to rise until the threshold falls to 0.4, highlighting a domain in which aggressive smoothing of the decision boundaries helps performance.

The expected pattern of results was for the highest accuracy to be achieved with a threshold of about 1. However, this pattern was not observed consistently, as in some domains any boundary smoothing proved to be harmful and reduce accuracy while in others aggressive boundary smoothing with ratio thresholds as low as 0.4 gave the highest accuracy. It is clear that there is not one *optimal* threshold and a single threshold will not suit all domains.

4.3   Threshold Error Reduction Algorithm

The basic approach, of setting a single threshold, gives no control over the level of editing highlighting two problems.

– It is difficult to set a single threshold that works well across all domains. It would be better to set a threshold that suits the characteristics of the case base being considered. To overcome this problem and establish an appropriate threshold, we processes cases in batches by iteratively reducing the threshold in steps. After each editing step a leave-one-out accuracy check is performed to provide a possible stopping criteria. Leave-one-out accuracy is calculated initially on the original case base and then on the edited case base after each batch of cases are processed. If the accuracy falls the iterative process is stopped at the present threshold and the edited case base from the previous iteration is accepted as the final edited case base.
– The use of the F:E ratio to identify potential harmful cases can result in the neighbours of a noisy case being falsely considered to be noisy themselves, simply by the presence of the noisy case in their neighbourhood. This is particularly likely when looking at a very small neighbourhood and weighting the measure to the nearest neighbours as we do with the F:E ratio. To prevent useful cases being mistakenly removed we only delete cases if their complexity is higher than their neighbours. Of course, if a case, not deleted by this check, is truly noisy it will be identified on the next iteration and considered for deletion again.

Our Threshold Error Reduction (TER) algorithm, incorporating the stop criteria and neighbourhood check, is outlined in Figure 5.

```
T-set,          case-base of n cases (c₁ ....cₙ)
COM(S),         calculate F:E ratio, F:E(c), for
                each case in set S
ACC(S),         returns leave-one-out accuracy
                for set of cases, S
CHK(c),         returns true if F:E(c) is > F:E ratio of
                each of its k-nearest neighbours

E-set = T-set
R-set = T-set
accuracy  =  ACC(T-Set)
threshold = 1.25

while (ACC(E-Set) >= accuracy)
      COM(E-Set)
      for (each c in E-set)
         if (F:E(c) > threshold && CHK(c))
            E-Set = E-Set - c
         endif
      endfor
      If (ACC(E-set) >= accuracy)
            accuracy = ACC(E-set)
            threshold = threshold - 0.1
            R-set = E-set
      endif
endwhile
return  R-set
```

Fig. 5. Threshold error reduction algorithm

5   Evaluation of Threshold Error Reduction

In order to demonstrate that TER can improve accuracy we evaluate the algorithm's performance against several existing noise reduction algorithms. The algorithms are evaluated on two levels in this section. First we apply the algorithms to existing UCI datasets and compare accuracy and size reduction results achieved. Then in the second stage of the evaluation we artificially introduce higher levels of noise into the datasets to examine the algorithms performance in more challenging environments. TER is compared with two classic benchmark noise reduction algorithms: Wilson Editing (ENN) and Repeated Wilson Editing (RENN). The benchmark algorithms are described in Section 2.

5.1   Datasets

Eleven public domain classification datasets from the UCI ML repository [?] have been used in the evaluations reported in this paper. The selected datasets have been chosen to provide varying number of cases, features and classes and differing proportions of nominal to numeric attributes. Table 1 gives a summary of the datasets used including a measure of the difficulty of the classification problem in the form of test set accuracies

Table 1. Comparison of UCI datasets used for evaluation

CASE BASE	No. of CASES	No. of CLASS	NO. OF ATTRIBUTES			CLASSIFIER ACCUR. %		
			NOMINAL	NUMERIC	MISSING	3-NN	J48	N.BAYES
Anneal	898	6	32	6	29	96.9	98.4	86.3
Breast Cancer	286	2	9	0	2	72.4	75.5	71.7
Diabetes	768	2	8	0	8	72.7	73.8	76.3
Heart-C	303	5	7	6	2	81.2	77.6.8	83.5
Hepatitis	155	2	13	6	15	81.3	83.9	84.5
House Votes	435	2	16	0	16	92.6	96.3	90.11
Iris	150	3	0	4	0	95.3	96.0	96.0
Lymphography	148	4	15	3	0	80.4	77.03	83.11
Vowel	990	11	3	10	0	97.1	81.5	63.7
Wine	178	3	0	13	0	94.9	93.8	96.6
Zoo	101	7	16	1	0	92.1	92.1	95.1

achieved with three standard classifiers[1]. Some of the datasets are recognised to be noisy, e.g. Breast Cancer, and present more difficult problems while others, e.g. Wine, have no or low levels of erroneous data and present relatively easy problems with accuracies of over 95%. Some of the datasets contain missing data and column 6 shows the number of attributes which contain missing data.

5.2 Initial Experiments

A ten-times 10-fold cross-validation experimental set-up is used giving one hundred case base/test set combinations per experiment. The editing algorithms were applied to each case base and the resulting edited set size recorded. Test set accuracy, using 1-NN retrieval, was measured for the original case base and for each of the edited sets formed by the editing algorithms.

Comparisons have been made on eleven UCI datasets. Table 2 displays the experimental results with each row containing the results for the named dataset. The average test set accuracies for each dataset are shown in columns 2-6: column 2 has the accuracy for the original, unedited case base; column 3 and 4 show the accuracies for the benchmark algorithms; while column 5 and 6 displays the accuracies for our new threshold editing algorithms. Columns 7 gives the unedited case base size while column 8-11 contain the edited case base size as a proportion of the original for each of the editing algorithms. In both the accuracy and case base size results the editing algorithm that achieved the highest accuracy in each domain is highlighted in bold.

TER provides the highest accuracy in ten out of the eleven datasets. In the other dataset TER-S gives the highest accuracy with the accuracy of TER also above the benchmark algorithms accuracies. We checked the significance of these differences using a

---

[1] Classification accuracy is measured using standard 10-fold cross validation parameters with the WEKA machine learning workbench [?].

Table 2. Comparison of average test set accuracy and edited case base size

CASE BASE	TEST SET ACCURACY					CASE BASE SIZE				
	ORIG	ENN	RENN	TER	TER-S	ORIG	ENN	RENN	TER	TER-S
Anneal	0.990	0.973	0.969	*0.990*	0.975	809	0.99	0.99	**1.00**	0.99
Breast Cancer	0.671	0.746	0.753	**0.758**	0.751	258	0.69	0.67	**0.67**	0.80
Diabetes	0.695	0.745	0.739	0.748	**0.752**	692	0.70	0.66	0.61	**0.77**
Heart-C	0.761	0.808	0.816	**0.819**	0.809	273	0.76	0.74	**0.75**	0.86
Hepatitis	0.808	0.826	0.827	*0.837*	0.835	140	0.82	0.80	*0.70*	0.86
House Votes	0.921	0.919	0.911	**0.924**	0.923	392	0.93	0.91	**0.97**	0.95
Iris	0.940	0.951	0.951	**0.955**	0.951	135	0.95	0.95	**0.93**	0.95
Lymphography	0.812	0.777	0.765	*0.798*	0.795	134	0.84	0.81	*0.76*	0.90
Vowel	0.988	0.977	0.974	**0.988**	0.977	891	0.99	0.99	**1.00**	0.99
Wine	0.965	0.954	0.948	*0.965*	0.954	161	0.97	0.97	*1.00*	0.98
Zoo	0.957	0.919	0.895	*0.946*	0.941	91	0.94	0.93	*0.98*	0.97

2-tailed t-test with 95% confidence level. The superiority of TER was found to be significant over the two benchmark algorithms in 6 domains: Anneal, Hepatitis, Lymphography, Vowel, Wine and Zoo. TER achieves its performance gain by using the stopping criteria to vary the level of editing at the decision boundaries. In some datasets, where smoothing the decision boundary is found to improve accuracy, TER removes far more cases than the benchmark algorithms, for example in Hepatitis and Lymphography. In other datasets, where boundary smoothing is found to be harmful, TER removes less cases than the benchmarks, for example in Wine and Anneal, no cases are removed at all.

TER-S is a less complex algorithm that does not include an informed stopping criteria to control the level of editing. Overall it gives the best accuracy on only one dataset, however, it performs surprisingly well when compared with the benchmark algorithms. It outperforms the benchmarks in seven of the eleven datasets and in the remaining four datasets gives better or comparable performance than at least one of the benchmarks. Generally, TER-S takes a conservative approach to editing and removes less cases than either ENN or RENN.

In a comparison of the benchmark algorithms RENN removes more cases but is slightly outperformed by ENN which achieves higher accuracies in four domains compared to two for RENN. It would normally be expected that RENN would outperform ENN but the results are probably due to the low level of noise present in some of the original datasets.

It is worth noting that in two domains the original accuracy was higher than for any of the editing algorithms and in three other datasets accuracy is same as TER but higher than the other editing algorithms. In these datasets any editing appears harmful although TER appears least harmful. The poor performance of the noise reduction algorithms is largely due to the very low levels of noise present in some of the datasets, however, poor performance also appears more noticeable in multi-class problems. TER has the advantage that it will generally only remove cases if an improvement in accuracy is being achieved and obtains better results on these datasets.

5.3 Experiments on Datasets with Artificial Noise

The same experimental set-up, as used for the initial experiments, was adopted for these experiments with the exception that differing levels of noise were artificially introduced into the case base. Noise was introduced by randomly selecting a fixed proportion of the cases in the case base and changing the class of their solution. The algorithms were evaluated after the introduction of 5%, 10%, 20% and 30% noise levels. Table 3 gives sample results, with the average test set accuracy for different noise levels on Breast Cancer, Hepatitis and Lymphography shown in columns 2-6. Column 7 displays the unedited case base size and the remaining columns show the edited case base size as a proportion of the original, for the relevant dataset and noise level. Again, the algorithm that achieved the highest accuracy for each domain and noise level is highlighted in bold and also in italics if it significantly outperformed the other algorithms.

As expected the accuracy on the original case base falls dramatically with increasing noise levels. All the noise reduction algorithms help slow the degradation in accuracy and, unlike in our initial experiment, they dramatically improve on the accuracy achieved with the unedited case base. Overall TER gives the strongest performance, recording the highest accuracy in 9 of the 12 experiments. However, the improvement is only significant in 5 experiments (Breast Cancer 5%, Hepatitis 5%, and Lymphography 5%, 10% & 20%) and RENN gives the highest accuracy in the remaining three

Table 3. Comparison of average test set accuracy and edited case base size

	TEST SET ACCURACY					CASE BASE SIZE				
CASE BASE	ORIG	ENN	RENN	TER	TER-S	ORIG	ENN	RENN	TER	TER-S
Breast Cancer (5%)	0..653	0..719	0.733	*0.746*	0.719	258	0.66	0.63	**0.68**	0.78
Breast Cancer (10%)	0.631	0.708	0.729	**0.735**	0.683	258	0.63	0.61	**0.69**	0.76
Breast Cancer (20%)	0.605	0.677	**0.697**	0.696	0.663	258	0.59	**0.54**	0.65	0.73
Breast Cancer (30%)	0.583	0.646	*0.673*	0.655	0.639	258	0.56	*0.50*	0.63	0.72
Hepatitis (5%)	0.765	0.829	0.821	*0.846*	0.839	140	0.75	0.74	**0.66**	0.82
Hepatitis (10%)	0.744	0.823	0.819	**0.833**	0.827	140	0.73	0.71	**0.63**	0.79
Hepatitis (20%)	0.708	0.816	0.810	**0.817**	0.788	140	0.66	0.62	**0.56**	0.72
Hepatitis (30%)	0.663	0.783	*0.809*	0.792	0.749	140	0.60	*0.53*	0.47	0.70
Lymphography (5%)	0.776	0.768	0.761	*0.794*	0.781	134	0.76	0.73	*0.64*	0.86
Lymphography (10%)	0.753	0.762	0.758	*0.783*	0.768	134	0.74	0.69	*0.55*	0.80
Lymphography (20%)	0.713	0.734	0.731	*0.762*	0.743	134	0.65	0.60	*0.49*	0.72
Lymphography (30%)	0.641	0.688	0.718	**0.724**	0.708	134	0.58	0.50	**0.44**	0.71

experiments. RENN is particularly strong with data containing a high proportion of noise. It would appear that TER's competitive advantage gained by smoothing the boundary regions between classes is deminished slightly in some datasets containing high levels of noise, possibly because the noise creates false decision boundaries that the algorithm attempts to maintain.

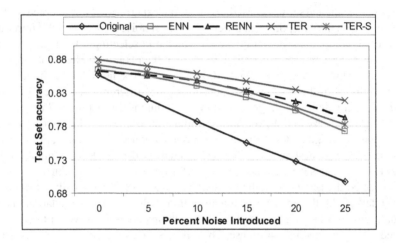

Fig. 6. Average accuracies over 11 datasets with varying levels of noise introduced

The detailed results from the three sample datasets give an indication of the ability of the algorithms when encountering different levels of noise in the original data. However, in order to evaluate a more general picture of the impact of noise on the individual algorithms the average accuracies obtained across all our experimental domains, with different levels of noise artificially introduced, are plotted in Figure 6. The y-axis shows the average test set accuracies achieved in the eleven datasets described earlier and the x-axis displays the level of noise (between 0 and 25%) artificially introduced by flipping the solution class on a percentage of the cases. While the comparisim between alternative algorithms from averages over different datasets can be misleading, the results demonstrate quite clearly the impact of noise.

The accuracies achieved by the original data without the use of a noise reduction algorithm falls very quickly as the level of noise increases. The benefit from applying noise reduction algorithms is quite clear as all the noise reduction algorithms are effective at improving accuracy. TER-S appears to marginally out perform ENN, however, both algorithms degrade at a similar rate as the level of noise increases. These algorithm give reasonable performance at low noise levels but their performance relative to TER and RENN fall away at higher noise levels. The accuracies of TER and RENN both degrade at a slower rate than the other algorithms and are the better performers at higher noise levels. To some extent the improved performance of these two algorithms is expected because they both take an incremental approach to noise removal. Overall TER clearly gives the strongest performance.

6   Conclusions

This paper introduces a novel error reduction algorithm. A local case distance ratio considers the distance to neighbours belonging to the same and different classes to aid identifying harmful cases. This ratio together with a case base profile guides the editing process for lazy learners. The algorithm, (TER), focuses on deleting harmful cases from boundary regions to give smoother decision boundaries between classes. A stopping criteria is used to ensure that the level of smoothing is adjusted to suit the domain.

We have demonstrated the effectiveness of TER on public domain datasets. In general, TER provides superior performance characteristics when compared to benchmark techniques for case bases containing low and medium levels of noise. One limitation of the approach may be its ability to identify harmful cases when the case base contains high levels of noise and boundaries become difficult to identify.

The evaluation results confirm that noise reduction can also harm performance. Careful consideration should be given to the domain and the structure of the case base to ensure there is a need for noise reduction before removing case knowledge with an editing algorithm. The complexity profile provides a tool for the knowledge engineer to make an informed decisions on the need for case base maintenance.

In this paper we have calculated a case's position in relation to neighbours of its own class and neighbours with a different class to give a measure of confidence that similar problems will have similar solutions. In classification tasks, such as those considered in this paper, where we know the solution or class of a case's neighbours this relationship is is relatively easy to measure. It is hoped to extend the approach to unsupervised tasks, in which cases are not assigned class labels but where instead we can to measure the similarity between solutions, for example, in textual CBR where both the problem and the solution are often in textual form.

References

1. Aamodt, A., Plaza, E.: Case-based reasoning: Foundations issues, methodological variations, and system approaches. AI Communications 7, 39–59 (1994)
2. Basu, M., Ho, T.K.: Data Complexity in Pattern Recognition. In: Advanced Information and Knowledge Processing, Springer, Heidelberg (2006)
3. Bernadó, E., Ho, T.K.: Domain of competence of XCS classifier system in complexity measurement space. IEEE Transaction Evolutionary Computation 9(1), 82–104 (2005)
4. Blake, C.L., Merz, C.J.: UCI repository of machine learning databases (1998)
5. Brown, M.: A Memory Model for Case Retrieval by Activation Passing. PhD thesis, University of Manchester (1994)
6. Chang, P., Lai, C.: A hybrid system combining self-organizing maps with case-based reasoning in wholesaler's new-release book forecasting. Expert Syst. Appl. 29(1), 183–192 (2005)
7. Demsar, J.: Statistical comparisons of classifiers over multiple data sets. Journal of Machine Learning Research 7, 1–30 (2006)
8. Fornells, A., Golobardes, E., Martorell, J.M., Garrell, J.M., Bernadó, E., Macià, N.: Measuring the applicability of self-organization maps in a case-based reasoning system. In: 3rd Iberian Conference on Pattern Recognition and Image Analysis. LNCS, vol. 4478, pp. 532–539. Springer, Heidelberg (2007)

9. Fornells, A., Golobardes, E., Vernet, D., Corral, G.: Unsupervised case memory organization: Analysing computational time and soft computing capabilities. In: Roth-Berghofer, T.R., Göker, M.H., Güvenir, H.A. (eds.) ECCBR 2006. LNCS (LNAI), vol. 4106, pp. 241–255. Springer, Heidelberg (2006)

10. Fornells, A., Golobardes, E., Vilasís, X., Martí, J.: Integration of strategies based on relevance feedback into a tool for retrieval of mammographic images. In: Corchado, E., Yin, H., Botti, V., Fyfe, C. (eds.) IDEAL 2006. LNCS, vol. 4224, pp. 116–124. Springer, Heidelberg (2006) (Selected to be published in the International Journal of Neural Systems)

11. Ho, T.K., Basu, M.: Complexity measures of supervised classification problems. IEEE Transaction on Pattern Analysis and Machine Intelligence 24(3), 289–300 (2002)

12. Kohonen, T.: Self-Organization and Associative Memory, 3rd edn. Springer Series in Information Sciences, vol. 8. Springer, Heidelberg (1984)

13. Lenz, M., Burkhard, H.D., Brückner, S.: Applying case retrieval nets to diagnostic tasks in technical domains. In: Smith, I., Faltings, B.V. (eds.) Advances in Case-Based Reasoning. LNCS, vol. 1168, pp. 219–233. Springer, Heidelberg (1996)

14. Myllymaki, P., Tirri, H.: Massively parallel case-based reasoning with probabilistic similarity metrics (1993)

15. Nicholson, R., Bridge, D., Wilson, N.: Decision diagrams: Fast and flexible support for case retrieval and recommendation. In: Roth-Berghofer, T.R., Göker, M.H., Güvenir, H.A. (eds.) ECCBR 2006. LNCS (LNAI), vol. 4106, pp. 136–150. Springer, Heidelberg (2006)

16. Pelleg, D., Moore, A.: X-means: Extending K-means with efficient estimation of the number of clusters. In: Proceedings of the 17th International Conference of Machine Learning, pp. 727–734. Morgan Kaufmann, San Francisco (2000)

17. Plaza, E., McGinty, L.: Distributed case-based reasoning. The Knowledge engineering review 20(3), 261–265 (2006)

18. Rissland, E.L., Skalak, D.B., Friedman, M.: Case retrieval through multiple indexing and heuristic search. In: International Joint Conferences on Artificial Intelligence, pp. 902–908 (1993)

19. Schaaf, J.W.: Fish and Sink - an anytime-algorithm to retrieve adequate cases. In: Aamodt, A., Veloso, M.M. (eds.) Case-Based Reasoning Research and Development. LNCS, vol. 1010, pp. 538–547. Springer, Heidelberg (1995)

20. Vernet, D., Golobardes, E.: An unsupervised learning approach for case-based classifier systems. Expert Update. The Specialist Group on Artificial Intelligence 6(2), 37–42 (2003)

21. Wess, S., Althoff, K.D., Derwand, G.: Using k-d trees to improve the retrieval step in case-based reasoning. In: Wess, S., Richter, M., Althoff, K.-D. (eds.) Topics in Case-Based Reasoning. LNCS, vol. 837, pp. 167–181. Springer, Heidelberg (1994)

22. Yang, Q., Wu, J.: Enhancing the effectiveness of interactive cas-based reasoning with clustering and decision forests. Applied Intelligence 14(1) (2001)

Mixed-Initiative Relaxation of Constraints in Critiquing Dialogues

David McSherry[1] and David W. Aha[2]

[1] School of Computing and Information Engineering, University of Ulster
Coleraine BT52 1SA, Northern Ireland
dmg.mcsherry@ulster.ac.uk
[2] Navy Center for Applied Research in Artificial Intelligence
Naval Research Laboratory, Code 5514
Washington DC 20375, USA
david.aha@nrl.navy.mil

Abstract. Eliminating previously recommended items in a critiquing dialogue prevents the user from navigating back to acceptable items she critiqued earlier in the dialogue. An equally serious problem if previous recommendations are not eliminated is that acceptable items may be unreachable by any sequence of critiques. Progressive critiquing solves this dilemma while also making it easier for users to recognize when none of the available items are acceptable. In this paper, we present theoretical and empirical results that demonstrate the benefits of a critiquing strategy in which the user gives priority to constraints that must be satisfied in a progressive critiquing dialogue. We also present a new version of progressive critiquing in which mixed-initiative relaxation of constraints introduced by user critiquing choices that depart from this strategy greatly reduces their impact on dialogue outcomes.

Keywords: Critiquing, recommender systems, case-based reasoning, constraint relaxation, explanation, mixed-initiative interaction.

1 Introduction

Critiquing in recommender systems is based on the idea that it is often easier for users to critique recommended items (e.g., products) than to construct formal queries [1-3]. For example, a *Like this but cheaper* critique reveals important clues about the user's preferences (e.g., make, color, size) as well as the maximum price she is willing to pay. In case-based reasoning (CBR) approaches, the initially recommended case may be retrieved on the basis of its similarity to an initial query, or may be one that is already familiar to the user. An early example is *Entrée*, a restaurant recommender that supports both directional critiques (e.g., *cheaper*, *livelier*, *quieter*) and replacement critiques (e.g., *Like this with French cuisine*) [1]. The case recommended in response to a critique is usually one that satisfies the critique, and among such cases, is maximally similar to the critiqued case.

Concern that progress towards an acceptable case can often be slower than might be expected has prompted significant research interest in the efficiency of critiquing

R.O. Weber and M.M. Richter (Eds.): ICCBR 2007, LNAI 4626, pp. 107–121, 2007.

dialogues [4-7]. There is also growing awareness of the need to help users recognize when none of the available cases are acceptable, and thus avoid commitment to a long and fruitless critiquing dialogue [5]. Another important issue is the *diminishing choices* problem that occurs when previously recommended cases are eliminated in a critiquing dialogue, thus preventing the user from navigating back to an acceptable case she critiqued earlier (e.g., having ruled out cheaper alternatives). At worst, the user may find that the only acceptable case has been eliminated. An equally serious problem if previous recommendations are not eliminated is that acceptable cases may be *unreachable* by any sequence of critiques [6].

Providing a solution to this dilemma is one benefit of progressive critiquing, a CBR approach in which a recommended case must, if possible, satisfy all previous critiques as well as the user's current critique [5-6]. As we have shown in previous work, this ensures that cases (if any) that satisfy a given set of constraints for which "remedial" critiques are available (i.e., critiques that bring the user closer to cases that satisfy her constraints) can always be reached without eliminating previous recommendations. Explaining the "progression failures" that occur when none of the available cases satisfy all the user's critiques also makes it easier for users to recognize the non-existence of an acceptable case.

However, as in any critiquing algorithm, the outcome of a progressive critiquing dialogue may depend as much on the user's critiquing choices as on the system's responses to her critiques. In this paper, we examine the effects of critiquing "pitfalls" such as critiquing attributes whose values are acceptable while ignoring attributes whose values are not acceptable. We also present a new version of progressive critiquing in which mixed-initiative relaxation of constraints introduced by such critiquing choices greatly reduces their impact on dialogue outcomes.

We summarize progressive critiquing in Section 2 and formally analyze the approach in Section 3 to demonstrate the benefits of a critiquing strategy in which the user gives priority to her *hard* constraints (i.e., those that *must* be satisfied for a recommended case to be acceptable). As we show in Sections 4 and 5, critiquing choices that depart from this strategy are likely to delay progress in a critiquing dialogue, and may even prevent the user from reaching an acceptable case. We also describe the role of mixed-initiative constraint relaxation in enabling users to undo the effects of such critiquing choices. In Section 5, we present empirical results that confirm the benefits of giving priority to hard constraints and the effectiveness of mixed-initiative constraint relaxation as a solution to some of the problems caused by user critiquing choices that depart from this strategy. We present our conclusions in Section 6 together with a brief discussion of future work.

2   Overview of Progressive Critiquing

As in other CBR approaches, an initially recommended case can be retrieved in progressive critiquing on the basis of its similarity to an initial user query. If an initial query is not provided, as in the examples we use to illustrate the approach, an initially recommended case can instead be randomly selected from the available cases. Cognitive load is an important issue in any approach to critiquing, as the user must often consider and critique several recommended cases before reaching an acceptable case. For this reason, and in common with most other CBR approaches, only a single case is recommended on each cycle of a progressive critiquing dialogue.

A progressive critiquing system maintains a list of active constraints, introduced by the user's previous critiques, which a recommended case must, if possible, satisfy as well as the user's current critique [5-6]. If no such case exists, this is recognized as a *progression failure*, and a maximally similar case among those that satisfy the current critique is recommended. In this situation, the recommended case may be one that the user critiqued earlier in the dialogue. An explanation is provided to inform the user that no case satisfies all the constraints that are currently active. The explanation also highlights the active constraint (or constraints) that the recommended case fails to satisfy. Finally, this constraint is relaxed to ensure that only constraints satisfied by the recommended case remain active. However, if the constraint relaxed at the system's initiative is one that must be satisfied, the user can immediately respond by navigating back in the direction of previously recommended cases that satisfy the constraint.

By leaving open the option of repeating a previous recommendation, progressive critiquing avoids the *diminishing choices* problem that occurs when previously recommended cases are eliminated in a critiquing dialogue [6]. However, a previous recommendation can be repeated only when a progression failure has occurred. Progressive critiquing also solves the unreachability problem [6] by ensuring that a case that satisfies a given set of constraints for which remedial critiques are available can always be reached if one exists.

Fig. 1 shows a progressive critiquing dialogue in a recommender system called *Tweak* that we use to demonstrate our approach. In this example, the case base

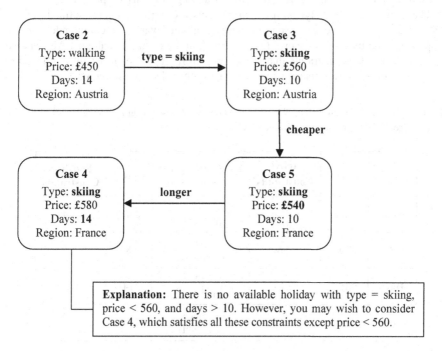

Fig. 1. A progressive critiquing dialogue in which a progression failure occurs

is a small set of holiday packages and the initially recommended case is a two-week walking holiday in Austria for £450. A progression failure has occurred in the example dialogue as Case 4, the case recommended in response to the user's *longer* critique, satisfies only two of her three critiques. As no case satisfies all the user's critiques, Case 4 is recommended because it is the most similar case that satisfies the user's current critique. Its failure to satisfy the user's *cheaper* critique on Case 3 is a possible compromise that the user may wish to consider.

If the user now critiques Case 4, her critiques on Case 2 and Case 5, but not her *cheaper* critique on Case 3, remain in force. For example, a holiday recommended in response to a *region* critique on Case 4 must also be a *skiing* holiday with *days* > 10 if such a case exists. If unwilling to compromise on price, the user may instead choose to navigate back in the direction of less expensive options by critiquing Case 4 on price. Such a critique may bring her directly back to Case 5, but only if there is no *skiing* holiday that is cheaper than Case 4 with *days* > 10. Fig. 1 also shows the explanation provided when a progression failure occurs in the example dialogue. If not prepared to compromise on the type, price, or length of her holiday, it should be clear to the user that none of the available holidays meet her requirements.

Progressive critiquing differs from other critiquing algorithms in that the retrieval of a recommended case in response to a critique is based on its similarity to an "ideal" case constructed from *assumed*, *explicit*, *predicted*, and *implicit* preferences that are continually revised in light of the user's critiques. Separately modeling the user's preferences and constraints, a feature that progressive critiquing shares with compromise-driven retrieval [8], plays an important role in enabling constraints to be relaxed without affecting the system's understanding of the user's preferences.

The four preference types used in progressive critiquing are defined below. Table 1 displays the "ideal" case used to guide the retrieval of a recommended case in response to the user's *longer* critique on Case 5 in the example dialogue. Also shown in the table are the constraints that are active before the price constraint is relaxed to ensure that only constraints satisfied by the recommended case remain active.

Table 1. Models of the user's preferences and constraints used to guide the retrieval of Case 4 in response to the user's *longer* critique on Case 5

	Case 5	Active Constraints	User Preferences (Ideal Case)	Case 4	Satisfied Constraints
Type	skiing	skiing	skiing (explicit)	skiing	skiing
Price	540	< 560	310 (assumed)	580	
Days	10	> 10	12 (predicted)	14	> 10
Region	France		France (implicit)	France	

Assumed Preferences. In the "ideal" case used to guide the retrieval of recommended cases, the values of *less-is-better* (LIB) attributes and *more-is-better* (MIB) attributes are based on assumed preferences. For example, the preferred value of a LIB attribute (e.g., *price*) is assumed to be the *lowest* value in the case base. One advantage is that no updating of the user's preferences is needed for critiques on LIB or MIB attributes. Instead, only the active constraints that recommended cases are required to satisfy are updated in response to such critiques.

Explicit Preferences. A replacement critique (e.g., type = *skiing*) provides an explicit preference that remains in force for the remainder of a critiquing dialogue unless changed by the user in a later critique. Such a critique also introduces an *equality* constraint that must, if possible, be satisfied as long as it remains active.

Predicted Preferences. Where a preferred value cannot reasonably be assumed for a numeric attribute (e.g., *days*), directional critiques (e.g., *longer*, *shorter*) may enable a preferred value to be predicted with reasonable accuracy. In progressive critiquing, the preferred value of such an attribute is predicted to be the *nearest* value in the case base that satisfies the most recent directional critique on the attribute.

Implicit Preferences. With respect to attributes for which no assumed, explicit, or predicted preferences are available to guide the retrieval process, progressive critiquing instead uses preferences that are implicit in the user's request to see another case that is *like* the critiqued case. In the "ideal" case, the preferred value of such an attribute is its value in the critiqued case. For example, region = *France* is used as an implicit preference, though not as an active constraint, in the retrieval of Case 4 in response to the user's *longer* critique on Case 5.

3 Analysis of Progressive Critiquing

Ultimately, the effectiveness of any critiquing system depends on the quality of feedback that the user provides to guide the search for an acceptable case. In this section, we present theoretical results that demonstrate the benefits of a critiquing strategy in which the user initially gives priority to her hard constraints in a progressive critiquing dialogue. An important role in our analysis is played by the concepts of "feasible" cases and "remedial" critiques that we now define.

Definition 1. *A* **feasible** *case is one that satisfies all constraints, whether known to the system or not, that must be satisfied for a recommended case to be acceptable to the user.*

Whether a feasible case is acceptable to the user may of course depend on how well it satisfies her overall requirements. Thus on reaching a feasible case, the user may wish to continue critiquing the system's recommendations. However, the non-existence of a feasible case implies the non-existence of an acceptable case.

Definition 2. *A critique is* **remedial** *if it is applied to an attribute that fails to satisfy one of the user's constraints, and is such that any case which satisfies the constraint must also satisfy the critique.*

As Fig. 2 illustrates, a remedial critique brings the user closer, if not directly, to cases (if any) which satisfy a constraint that a recommended case fails to satisfy. For example, *Like this but cheaper* is a remedial critique if the price of a recommended personal computer (PC) is more than the user is willing to pay. Similarly, *Like this with type = laptop* is a remedial critique if a recommended PC is a desktop and the user seeks a laptop.

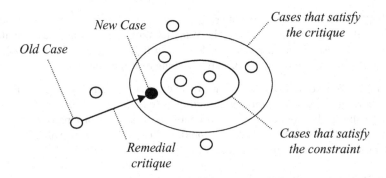

Fig. 2. A remedial critique brings the user closer, if not directly, to cases which satisfy a constraint that a recommended case fails to satisfy

As we show in Theorem 1, an important benefit of giving priority to hard constraints in progressive critiquing is that *any* sequence of remedial critiques must lead to a feasible case if one exists. It can also be seen from the theorem that giving priority to hard constraints, and initially choosing only remedial critiques, makes it easy for the user to recognize when no feasible case exists. If a progression failure occurs before a feasible case is reached in this strategy, then there can be no feasible case, and therefore no acceptable case. Our proof of this important result, and the discussion that follows, assumes that a remedial critique is available for any of the user's constraints that is not satisfied by a recommended case.

Theorem 1. *If at least one feasible case exists, then a progression failure cannot occur in progressive critiquing before a feasible case is reached provided the user chooses only remedial critiques and gives priority to her hard constraints.*

Proof. Let Q be the set of hard constraints, if any, among the user's requirements and let F be the non-empty set of feasible cases (i.e., cases that satisfy all the constraints in Q). If $C_1 \in F$, where C_1 is the initially recommended case, then a feasible case has been reached without any critiques. If $C_1 \notin F$, then there exists $q_1 \in Q$ such that $C_1 \notin matches(q_1)$, where $matches(q_1)$ is the set of cases that satisfy q_1. As we assume that a remedial critique is available for any constraint that a recommended case fails to satisfy, there must be a critique r_1 that the user can apply to C_1 such that $matches(q_1) \subseteq matches(r_1)$, where $matches(r_1)$ is the set of cases that satisfy r_1. If $C_2 \notin F$, where C_2 is the case recommended in response to r_1, then there exists $q_2 \in Q$ such that $C_2 \notin matches(q_2)$ and a critique r_2 that the user can apply to C_2 such that $matches(q_2) \subseteq matches(r_2)$. In progressive critiquing, the case recommended in response to r_2 must also satisfy r_1 if such a case exists. Moreover, as $F \subseteq matches(q_1) \cap matches(q_2) \subseteq$

$matches(r_1) \cap matches(r_2)$, the existence of at least one feasible case ensures the existence of at least one case that satisfies both critiques.

If $C_3 \notin F$, where C_3 is the case recommended in response to r_2, the user can continue as long as necessary to identify constraints $q_1, q_2, ..., q_k \in Q$ that cases C_1, $C_2, ..., C_k$ recommended by the system fail to satisfy and choose remedial critiques r_1, $r_2, ..., r_k$ such that, for $1 \leq i \leq k$, $matches(q_i) \subseteq matches(r_i)$. As $F \subseteq \bigcap_{1 \leq i \leq k} matches(q_i) \subseteq \bigcap_{1 \leq i \leq k} matches(r_i)$ the existence of at least one feasible case ensures that none of the critiques $r_1, r_2, ..., r_k$ can result in a progression failure. In particular, $C_{k+1} \in \bigcap_{1 \leq i \leq k} matches(r_i)$, where C_{k+1} is the case recommended in response to r_k. Moreover, $C_1, C_2, ..., C_{k+1}$ must be distinct cases, as a previous recommendation can be repeated in progressive critiquing only when a progression failure has occurred [6]. As the supply of distinct cases $C \notin F$ must eventually be exhausted, it must eventually be true that $C_{k+1} \in F$. $\square$

In progressive critiquing, therefore, the user can be certain of reaching a feasible case, or recognizing that no such case exists, by initially choosing only remedial critiques and giving priority to her hard constraints. This is an easy strategy for users to adopt when their requirements include constraints that obviously must be satisfied, such as the timing of a family holiday that can only be taken during a school vacation. However, in other situations, the user may not have a clear idea about what she is looking for initially and may begin to consider which constraints must be satisfied only when faced with the need to compromise. At this point in a critiquing dialogue, the user may be prepared to relax a constraint to which she initially gave priority, which means it is not a hard constraint as defined in Section 1.

There is also no guarantee that only remedial critiques will be chosen by the user before reaching a feasible case in a critiquing dialogue. For example, the user's reason for choosing a critique might be to improve the value of a LIB or MIB attribute whose value is already acceptable. We will refer to this type of "non-remedial" critique as an *optimizing* critique. In the following definition, we assume that the user's only constraints, if any, with respect to LIB and MIB attributes are maximum values for LIB attributes and minimum values for MIB attributes.

Definition 3. *A critique is an* **optimizing** *critique if it is applied to a LIB or MIB attribute whose value is acceptable and is such that any value of the attribute which satisfies the critique must be lower than the critiqued value for a LIB attribute or higher than the critiqued value for a MIB attribute.*

For example, *Like this but cheaper* is an optimizing critique if the price of the recommended case is already less than the maximum amount that the user is willing to pay. Optimizing critiques can be useful in the final stages of a critiquing dialogue (e.g., to check if an equally acceptable case is available at a lower price). However, as shown by our empirical results in Section 5, such critiques may delay progress towards an acceptable case if used before a feasible case has been reached.

Another type of non-remedial critique is one that carries the risk of taking the user *away* from cases that satisfy a constraint with respect to the critiqued attribute. We will refer to such a critique as an *exploratory* critique.

Definition 4. *A critique is* **exploratory** *if it is applied to an attribute whose value satisfies the user's constraints with respect to the attribute, and is such that a value of the attribute that satisfies the critique may fail to satisfy a constraint with respect to the critiqued attribute.*

The user's reason for choosing an exploratory critique might be to improve the values of attributes *other* than the attribute to which it is applied. For example, by asking to see something that is *more expensive* than a recommended PC, the user might be expecting to see improvements in attributes such as memory and processor speed. In this example, the risk for the user is that the price of a PC recommended in response to her critique may be more than she is willing to pay. A more serious problem with exploratory critiques is that they depart from the natural semantics of critiques on which the system's understanding of the user's preferences and constraints is based. While remedial and optimizing critiques are reliable indicators of desired improvements in the values of the critiqued attributes, the same cannot be said for exploratory critiques.

As we show in Section 4, another reason for choosing an exploratory critique might be to escape from a critiquing "loop" in which the user keeps returning to an unacceptable case. We also present a solution to the problem of critiquing loops that does not rely on exploratory critiques.

4 Mixed-Initiative Relaxation of Constraints

Our analysis of progressive critiquing in Section 3 focused on the benefits of a critiquing strategy in which the user initially chooses only remedial critiques and gives priority to her hard constraints. As we show in this section, user critiquing choices that depart from this strategy may result in a critiquing "loop" that prevents the user from reaching an acceptable case. We also describe how this problem is addressed in a new version of progressive critiquing by mixed-initiative relaxation of constraints introduced by the user's previous critiques.

Table 2 shows an example case base in the property domain that we use to illustrate the problem of critiquing loops. Attributes in the domain are bedrooms (3 or 4), property type (<u>det</u>ached or <u>semi</u>-detached), and price (in multiples of £1,000). The available critiques are *cheaper* critiques, *more* and *less* critiques on bedrooms, and replacement critiques on property type.

Fig. 3 shows an example critiquing dialogue in which the user is prepared to consider only 4 bedroom properties costing up to £200,000. She would also prefer a detached property but is prepared to consider another property type if necessary. Thus two of the user's three constraints (beds = 4, price ≤ 200, and type = det) must be satisfied, and Case 4 is the only feasible case. An initial query is not provided and the initially recommended case is Case 1, which satisfies none of the user's constraints.

Table 2. Example case base in the property domain

	Beds	Type	Price (£1,000)
Case 1	3	sem	209
Case 2	4	det	205
Case 3	3	det	180
Case 4	4	sem	195

The example dialogue shows how not giving priority to hard constraints may result in a critiquing loop. The user's first critique (type = det) is a remedial critique, but unlike the other two constraints that Case 1 fails to satisfy (beds = 4 and price ≤ 200), type = det is not a hard constraint. The case recommended in response to the user's second critique (more beds) also satisfies her first critique (type = det), but its price is more than the maximum (200) she is willing to pay. The user's *cheaper* critique on Case 2 results in a progression failure as there is no case that satisfies all three of her critiques. The case now recommended, Case 3, is one that the user critiqued earlier in the dialogue. It satisfies two of the user's critiques but involves a compromise (beds = 3) that the user is unwilling to accept.

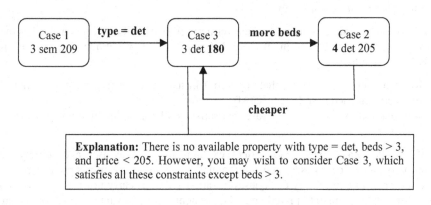

Fig. 3. A critiquing loop caused by not giving priority to hard constraints

Also as a consequence of not giving priority to her hard constraints, the user is unable to determine whether a feasible case exists from the system's explanation of the progression failure. A more serious problem for the user is that repeating the only available remedial critique on Case 3 (more beds) will take her again to Case 2, and the only remedial critique that applies to Case 2 (*cheaper*) will bring her back to Case 3. Thus by choosing only remedial critiques — a strategy we have shown to be very effective when priority is also given to hard constraints — the user is caught in a critiquing loop in which she keeps returning to an unacceptable case (Case 3).

In this example, the user can escape from the critiquing loop by resorting to an exploratory critique (Section 3). As the preference beds = 4 predicted from the user's second critique remains in force in spite of the constraint beds > 3 being relaxed by the system, the case recommended in response to an exploratory critique type = sem on Case 3 (3 det 180) will be Case 4 (4 sem 195). The user may think of this as relaxing the constraint (type = det) introduced by her first critique. However, instead of being relaxed, the previous constraint is replaced by another active constraint (type = sem) that is *inconsistent* with the user's requirements. Her exploratory critique also introduces an *incorrect* preference (type = sem) that remains in force even if the constraint is later relaxed at the initiative of the system.

As this example shows, exploratory critiques may provide the only means of escape from a critiquing loop, but at the expense of leaving the user's intentions open to misinterpretation by the system. In the new version of progressive critiquing that we now present, a solution to this problem is provided by "relaxation" critiques that enable users to relax constraints introduced by their previous critiques without the unwanted side effects of exploratory critiques. Relaxation critiques complement the existing mechanism for relaxation of constraints at the system's initiative (Section 2), thus providing the basis for *mixed-initiative* constraint relaxation. Recommender systems that do not support critiquing but in which constraint relaxation plays an important role include Adaptive Place Advisor, Intelligent Travel Recommender, and ShowMe [9-11].

Definition 5. *A* **relaxation** *critique is a request by the user to see a case that is like the currently recommended case, but with no restriction on the value of an attribute A that was previously critiqued by the user.*

A relaxation critique can be used whenever a progression failure occurs and takes the form "*relax A*", where A is an attribute that was previously critiqued by the user. It tells the system to:

1. Relax all active constraints that apply to A instead of the active constraints that the recommended case fails to satisfy
2. Retrieve a maximally similar case that satisfies all constraints that now remain active

If no such case exists, the system explains this to the user and retrieves a maximally similar case based on its current understanding of the user's preferences.

In contrast to exploratory critiques, relaxation critiques carry no risk of the user's intentions being misinterpreted by the system. No unwanted constraints are introduced, and separate modeling of the user's preferences and constraints in progressive critiquing (Section 2) ensures that the system's understanding of the user's preferences is unaffected by the relaxation process.

As Fig. 4 shows, the user can now escape from the critiquing loop in our example dialogue by applying the relaxation critique "*relax type*" to Case 3 after the progression failure that follows her *cheaper* critique on Case 2. This tells the system to relax type = det instead of beds > 3, the active constraint that Case 3 fails to satisfy. In response to the user's relaxation critique, the system recommends Case 4 (4 sem 195), the only case that satisfies the constraints (beds > 3 and price < 205) that remain active after type = det has been relaxed. A feasible case has thus been reached with no need for exploratory critiques.

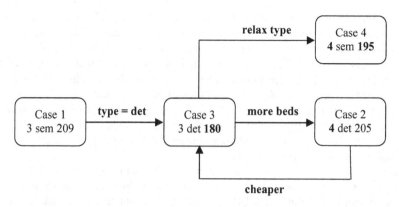

Fig. 4. Using a relaxation critique to delete a constraint introduced by a previous critique

Being caught in a critiquing loop may not be a problem that users are likely to experience often in practice, but it is not the only situation in which a user may feel she is making no progress in a critiquing dialogue. In progressive critiquing, a relaxation critique can now be used to guide the search for an acceptable case whenever a progression failure occurs (i.e., a critiquing loop need not have occurred). Thus if the case recommended after a progression failure fails to satisfy an active constraint that must be satisfied, but satisfies another active constraint that need not be satisfied, the user can now insist on the latter constraint being relaxed instead of the former. For example, a relaxation critique can be used to undo the effects of an optimizing critique (Section 3) that involves an unacceptable trade-off with respect to a previous critique.

As we show in Section 5, an important benefit of mixed-initiative constraint relaxation is to reduce the risk that the user will terminate a critiquing dialogue before reaching an acceptable case or recognizing the non-existence of an acceptable case.

5 Empirical Study

In this section, we evaluate the performance of progressive critiquing with and without mixed-initiative constraint relaxation (MICR), and in experimental conditions that are most challenging for a critiquing system:

- None of the available cases may be acceptable to the user
- An initial query is not provided by the user
- The user does not always make "good" critiquing choices

In this context, we investigate the following hypotheses:

Hypothesis 1. Dialogue outcomes and efficiency are adversely affected if users do not give priority to their hard constraints.

Hypothesis 2. Using optimizing critiques (Section 3) before a feasible case has been reached has a negative impact on critiquing performance.

Hypothesis 3. The risk that users will fail to reach an acceptable case (or recognize the non-existence of an acceptable case) due to their critiquing choices is reduced by enabling them to relax constraints introduced by their previous critiques.

Based on McGinty and Smyth's PC case base [12], our evaluation focuses on the initial stage of a critiquing dialogue that ends when a feasible case is reached, the non-existence of a feasible case is recognized, or the user abandons the search for an acceptable case without achieving either of these goals. Attributes in the PC case base and weights assigned to them in our experiments are make (1), chip (1), speed (1), screen size (1), type (1), memory (1), hard disk capacity (1), and price (7). In addition to relaxation critiques, the critiques available to simulated users in our experiments are *more* critiques on MIB attributes (speed, memory, and hard disk capacity), *more* and *less* critiques on screen size, replacement critiques on nominal attributes (make, chip, and type), and *cheaper* critiques.

We use a *leave-one-out* cross validation approach in which each of the 120 cases in the PC case base is temporarily removed and used to simulate ten different sets of user requirements. The value of a LIB attribute in a left-out case is treated as an upper limit (e.g., *price* $\leq$ 700), the value of a MIB attribute as a lower limit (e.g., *speed* $\geq$ 1.3), and the values of other attributes as equality constraints (e.g., *type* = *laptop*, *screen* = 14). We randomly select four of the eight constraints provided by a left-out case as the user's *hard* constraints. This step is repeated ten times for each left-out case, giving a total of 1,200 sets of simulated user requirements. A feasible case (other than the left-out case) is available in the PC case base in only 947 (or 79%) of these simulations, leaving 253 (or 21%) in which the most satisfactory outcome of a critiquing dialogue is that the user quickly recognizes the non-existence of an acceptable case.

For each left-out case and set of hard and soft constraints, one of the remaining cases is randomly selected as an initially recommended case, and presented to a simulated user interacting with *Tweak* 2, a progressive critiquing system that supports MICR. The critiquing dialogue that follows is allowed to continue until a feasible case is reached, the non-existence of a feasible case is recognized, or the critiquing dialogue is *inconclusively* terminated by the user.

We experiment initially with simulated users in three categories:

Class 1. Choose only remedial critiques and give priority to critiques on attributes, if any, that fail to satisfy their hard constraints

Class 2. Choose only remedial critiques but do not give priority to their hard constraints

Class 3. Do not give priority to their hard constraints and may also choose optimizing critiques on LIB and MIB attributes

The point at which a simulated user terminates a critiquing dialogue without reaching a feasible case or recognizing the non-existence of a feasible case depends on the user's critiquing strategy. For example, a Class 2 user abandons the search for an acceptable case if she has already tried all available remedial critiques on a currently recommended case. Similarly, a Class 3 user never repeats the same critique on a recommended case that she has already critiqued. As might be expected in practice, Class 2 and Class 3 users also adapt their critiquing behavior in light of the explanatory feedback provided in progressive critiquing when a progression failure occurs. Once an attribute has been involved in a progression failure, a Class 2 or Class 3 user never critiques it again before reaching a feasible case unless it fails to satisfy a hard constraint.

In two further experiments, we modify the critiquing behavior of Class 2 and Class 3 users so that they now choose a relaxation critique whenever the case recommended after a progression failure fails to satisfy an active constraint that must be satisfied, but satisfies another active constraint that need not be satisfied. For simulated users in Classes 1-3, Table 3 shows the percentages of dialogues with and without MICR in which a feasible case was reached, the non-existence of a feasible case was recognized, or the dialogue was terminated inconclusively by the user. Average dialogue length in each experimental category is also shown.

Table 3. Overall results of progressive critiquing dialogues on the PC case base for users in Classes 1-3 with and without MICR

	Class 1	Class 2	Class 2 + MICR	Class 3	Class 3 + MICR
Feasible case reached:	79%	73%	79%	72%	77%
Non-existence recognized:	21%	7%	20%	6%	17%
Inconclusive:	0%	20%	1%	22%	6%
Average dialogue length:	2.8	4.6	4.5	8.6	7.9

As predicted by our analysis of progressive critiquing in Section 3, the Class 1 strategy of choosing only remedial critiques and giving priority to hard constraints ensured that a feasible case was always reached if one existed (i.e., in 79% of dialogues). With an average dialogue length of less than 3 critiques, Class 1 users also never failed to recognize the non-existence of a feasible case. A detail not shown in Table 3 is that, on average, the feasible cases recommended in Class 1 dialogues satisfied 6.3 of the user's eight constraints. Only slight differences in this measure of critiquing performance were observed in the other experimental categories.

In Class 2, not giving priority to hard constraints had most impact on the user's ability to recognize the non-existence of a feasible case, while also increasing average dialogue length from 2.8 to 4.6. The results for Class 3 suggest that also using optimizing critiques before a feasible case is reached has little additional impact on dialogue outcomes, but a major impact on average dialogue length (8.6 compared to 4.6 for Class 2). These results support Hypotheses 1 and 2.

MICR greatly reduced the risk of inconclusive dialogues occurring in Class 2, with these users now reaching a feasible case or recognizing the non-existence of an acceptable case in 99% of dialogues. It also reduced the percentage of inconclusive dialogues in Class 3 from 22% to 6%. (Average dialogue lengths also decreased slightly.) These results support Hypothesis 3.

For simulated users in Classes 1-3, Fig. 5 shows the average lengths of critiquing dialogues, with and without MICR, in which a feasible case was reached or the non-existence of a feasible case was recognized. Average lengths of inconclusive dialogues (if any) are also shown. In Class 1, only 2.5 critiques were required on average to reach a feasible case, and 4.1 to recognize the non-existence of a feasible

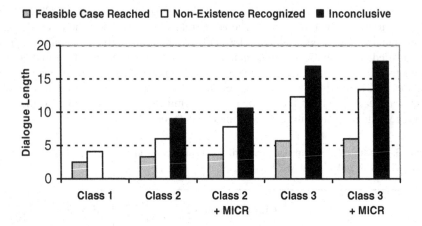

Fig. 5. Average lengths of critiquing dialogues in which a feasible case was reached, the non-existence of a feasible case was recognized, or the dialogue was terminated inconclusively

case. In conclusive Class 2 dialogues, not giving priority to hard constraints had most impact on the number of critiques required to recognize the non-existence of a feasible case. As shown by the results for Class 3, also using optimizing critiques before reaching a feasible case had an even greater impact on this aspect of critiquing performance, with 12.3 critiques required on average to recognize the non-existence of a feasible case. On average, more than twice as many critiques were needed to reach a feasible case in Class 3 (5.7) than in Class 1 (2.5). Another cause for concern in Class 3 is the average length of inconclusive dialogues (17.6).

MICR increased the average lengths of Class 2 and Class 3 dialogues (by 13% on average) in all three outcome categories. This is not surprising given the greater average lengths of dialogues that were previously inconclusive but in which the user now reaches a feasible case or recognizes the non-existence of a feasible case. It also seems a reasonable trade-off for the major reductions in the percentages of inconclusive dialogues (e.g., from 20% to 1% in Class 2). The observed increases in average dialogue lengths within outcome categories are also balanced by slight gains in *overall* dialogue efficiency (Table 3).

6   Conclusions

As shown by our analysis of progressive critiquing in Section 3, an important benefit of giving priority to hard constraints is that any sequence of remedial critiques must lead to a feasible case if one exists. In this strategy, the user can also be certain that none of the available cases are acceptable if a progression failure occurs before a feasible case is reached. Our empirical results confirm that user critiquing choices which depart from this strategy are likely to delay progress in a critiquing dialogue, and can even prevent users from reaching an acceptable case or recognizing the non-existence of an acceptable case.

Our paper also highlights the benefits of enabling users to relax constraints introduced by previous critiques that result in unacceptable trade-offs. In the recommendation task that we studied, mixed-initiative constraint relaxation reduced the percentage of dialogues that were inconclusively terminated by users as a result of not giving priority to their hard constraints from 20% to 1%. In our future work, we will extend the role of mixed-initiative interaction in progressive critiquing by adapting conversational CBR techniques [13-14] to guide users towards selecting critiques that lead more quickly to an acceptable case if one exists.

References

1. Burke, R., Hammond, K.J., Young, B.: The FindMe Approach to Assisted Browsing. IEEE Expert 12, 32–40 (1997)
2. Hammond, K.J., Burke, R., Schmitt, K.: A Case-Based Approach to Knowledge Navigation. In: Leake, D.B. (ed.) Case-Based Reasoning: Experiences, Lessons & Future Directions. AAAI Press/MIT Press, Menlo Park, CA, pp. 125–136 (1996)
3. Linden, G., Hanks, S., Lesh, N.: Interactive Assessment of User Preference Models: The Automated Travel Assistant. In: Proceedings of the 6th International Conference on User Modeling, pp. 67–78 (1997)
4. McCarthy, K., Reilly, J., McGinty, L., Smyth, B.: Experiments in Dynamic Critiquing. In: Proceedings of the International Conference on Intelligent User Interfaces, pp. 175–182 (2005)
5. McSherry, D., Aha, D.W.: Avoiding Long and Fruitless Dialogues in Critiquing. In: Bramer, M., Coenen, F., Tuson, A. (eds.) Research and Development in Intelligent Systems XXIII. BCS Conference Series, pp. 173–186. Springer, London (2006)
6. McSherry, D., Aha, D.W.: The Ins and Outs of Critiquing. In: Veloso, M. (ed.) Proceedings of the 20th International Joint Conference on Artificial Intelligence, pp. 962–967 (2007)
7. Reilly, J., McCarthy, K., McGinty, L., Smyth, B.: Incremental Critiquing. Knowledge-Based Systems 18, 143–151 (2005)
8. McSherry, D.: Similarity and Compromise. In: Ashley, K.D., Bridge, D.G. (eds.) ICCBR 2003. LNCS (LNAI), vol. 2689, pp. 291–305. Springer, Heidelberg (2003)
9. Thompson, C.A., Göker, M.H., Langley, P.: A Personalized System for Conversational Recommendations. Journal of Artificial Intelligence Research 21, 393–428 (2004)
10. Ricci, F., Arslan, B., Mirzadeh, N., Venturini, A.: ITR: A Case-Based Travel Advisory System. In: Craw, S., Preece, A.D. (eds.) ECCBR 2002. LNCS (LNAI), vol. 2416, pp. 613–627. Springer, Heidelberg (2002)
11. McSherry, D.: Incremental Relaxation of Unsuccessful Queries. In: Funk, P., González Calero, P.A. (eds.) ECCBR 2004. LNCS (LNAI), vol. 3155, pp. 331–345. Springer, Heidelberg (2004)
12. McGinty, L., Smyth, B.: Comparison-Based Recommendation. In: Craw, S., Preece, A.D. (eds.) ECCBR 2002. LNCS (LNAI), vol. 2416, pp. 575–589. Springer, Heidelberg (2002)
13. Aha, D.W., Breslow, L.A., Muñoz-Avila, H.: Conversational Case-Based Reasoning. Applied Intelligence 14, 9–32 (2001)
14. Aha, D.W., McSherry, D., Yang, Q.: Advances in Conversational Case-Based Reasoning. Knowledge Engineering Review 20, 247–254 (2005)

A Methodology for Analyzing Case Retrieval from a Clustered Case Memory

Albert Fornells, Elisabet Golobardes, Josep Maria Martorell,
Josep Maria Garrell, Núria Macià, and Ester Bernadó

Grup de Recerca en Sistemes Intel·ligents
Enginyeria i Arquitectura La Salle, Universitat Ramon Llull
Quatre Camins 2, 08022 Barcelona, Spain
{afornells,elisabet,jmmarto,josepmg,nmacia,esterb}@salle.url.edu
http://www.salle.url.edu/GRSI

Abstract. Case retrieval from a clustered case memory consists in finding out the clusters most similar to the new input case, and then retrieving the cases from them. Although the computational time is improved, the accuracy rate may be degraded if the clusters are not representative enough due to data geometry. This paper proposes a methodology for allowing the expert to analyze the case retrieval strategies from a clustered case memory according to the required computational time improvement and the maximum accuracy reduction accepted. The mechanisms used to assess the data geometry are the complexity measures. This methodology is successfully tested on a case memory organized by a Self-Organization Map.

Keywords: Case Retrieval, Case Memory Organization, Soft Case-Based Reasoning, Complexity Measures, Self-Organization Maps.

1 Motivation

The computational time of Case-Based Reasoning (CBR) [1] systems is mainly related to the case memory: the greater the size, the greater the time. This fact can be a problem for real time environments, where the user needs a fast response from the system. For this reason, a reduction of the number of cases is sometimes the only way for achieving this goal.

The case memory organization plays an important role because it helps CBR to concentrate on the potentially useful cases instead of the whole case memory. We focus on a case memory organization based on the definition of groups of similar cases by means of clustering techniques. The new retrieve phase selects the set of clusters most similar to the input case, and then it retrieves a set of cases from them. Although the reduction of cases improves the computational time, it may also imply a degradation of the accuracy rate if the clusters are not representative enough. This last issue depends on the data complexity[1].

---

[1] The data complexity refers to the class separability and the discriminant power of features, and not about its representation in the case memory.

R.O. Weber and M.M. Richter (Eds.): ICCBR 2007, LNAI 4626, pp. 122–136, 2007.
© Springer-Verlag Berlin Heidelberg 2007

We present a methodology for analyzing the behavior of the different ways in which the case retrieval can be performed from a clustered case memory according to the performance desired. The performance is defined as the relation between the required computational time improvement and the maximum accuracy reduction accepted with respect to using all the cases.

The first step is to know the performance of each one of the different case retrieval strategies. For this reason, we propose a taxonomy of them represented as a decomposition based on the number of clusters selected and the percentage of cases used from them in the retrieve phase. Thus, the strategies defined in the taxonomy are run over a wide set of datasets with the aim of evaluating its performance. The next step is to analyze the results. However, these executions generate a large volume of results which are very complex and difficult to study. That is why we have developed a scatter plot to understand in a more intuitive way these results instead of using huge results tables. This plot is a 2-D graphical representation in which the relations between the computational time improvement and the maximum reduction of the accuracy rate accepted are drawn for all the configurations from the last taxonomy. It allow us to compare the performance between the strategies and with respect to a CBR system based on a linear search of the case memory. Nevertheless, the behavior of the strategies depends on the definition of clusters, which are more closely related to data complexity. By taking into account the analysis of dataset complexity, we are able to identify separate behaviors that otherwise would remain hidden. The analysis of the scatter plot is done according to a priori classification of the dataset based on three levels of defined complexity.

The proposed methodology gives us a framework to understand the data mining capabilities of the clustering technique used to organize the case memory for a particular dataset characterized by its complexity, which heavily influences the case retrieval strategy. Therefore, there is not an absolute best strategy, the selection depends on the performance desired by the user.

The empirical test of the methodology is applied in a case memory organized by a Self-Organization Map (SOM) [12] over 56 datasets. We select SOM as clustering technique due to our experience using it [8,9,10]. However, this study could be easily extended to other clustering techniques.

The paper is organized as follows. Section 2 summarizes some related work about strategies for organizing the case memory and data complexity. Section 3 presents the methodology for setting up the case retrieval. Section 4 describes the experiments and discusses the results. Finally, Section 5 ends with the conclusions and further research.

2   Related Work

This section contains a brief review of the case memory organization and the importance of studying the data complexity.

The Case Memory Organization. This issue is tackled from several points of view in order to improve the computational time.

K-d trees [21] organize the features in nodes, which split the cases by their values. The main drawbacks are the treatment of missing values and the reduced flexibility of the method because of the tree structure. Both problems are successfully solved in Case Retrieval Nets [13], which organize the case memory as a graph of feature-value pairs. They employ a spreading activation process to select only the cases with similar values. Decision Diagrams [15] work in a similar way to the k-d trees but using a directed graph.

Other approaches link the cases by means of the similarity between them such as Fish-and-sink [19,22], or using relationships defined by the knowledge of the domain such as CRASH system [5]. In both cases, these links allow CBR to find out the similarity of cases in the case base.

The reduction of the number of operations can also be done by indexing the case memory using the knowledge from the domain like in the BankXX system [18], which is based on a conceptualization of legal argument as heuristic search. Another way of indexing the information is by the identification of clusters by means of clustering algorithms: X-means [16] in ULIC [20] or SOM [12] in [6,9].

On the other hand, there are approaches based on distributing the case memory through multi-agent architectures [17], or applying massive parallel solutions [14]. These solutions let CBR reduce the execution time, but they do not reduce the number of operations.

The Utility of the Complexity Measures. Complexity measures highlight the data geometry distribution offering an indicator that estimates to what extent the classes are interleaved, a factor that affects the accuracy. The dataset analysis allows us to understand the classifier behavior on a given dataset. Nowadays, the complexity measures are used to: (1) predict the classifier's error on a particular dataset, based on a study [3] where a linear relation was found between the estimated complexity of a dataset and the classifier's error; and (2) characterize the difficulty of a classification problem and provide a map that illustrates the domain of competence of classifiers in the complexity space. Basu and Ho [2] presented many metrics that measure the problem complexity from several aspects (power of discriminant attributes, class separability, degree of overlap, topology, etc.). However, it is difficult to set the complexity with only one measure. For this reason, their combination is a more reliable tool [8].

3   Description of the Methodology

This section explains the different parts of the methodology proposed for understanding the behavior of the case retrieval strategies from a clustered case memory. First, we present the strategy map as a taxonomy of the different ways in which the retrieval can be performed considering the clusters and cases used. Next, we detail the scatter plot for analyzing the results obtained from running over the strategies of the taxonomy. Finally, we introduce the characterization of the datasets according to its complexity.

3.1   The Strategy Map

The strategy map is a taxonomy of the case retrieval strategies from a clustered case memory based on two factors as Fig. 1 shows. The **factor of the selected clusters** identifies three possible situations on the basis of the number of clusters selected. Areas numbered 1 and 2 are situations where only the best cluster is retrieved. In contrast, areas numbered 5 and 6 represent the opposite situation where all the clusters are used. Finally, the intermediate situation is defined by the areas numbered 3 and 4, where a set of the clusters is selected. Note that area number 6 corresponds to a situation where all the cases are used in the same way as a CBR system that carries out a linear search over the whole case base: all the cases from all the clusters (*All_All*).

Although the number of selected clusters for retrieval can be set by the user, we could use a threshold (ϑ) for requiring the minimum similarity accepted between the input case C and a cluster M_X to select it. This similarity can be computed as the complement of the normalized Euclidean distance (see Eq. 1), and other metrics can be applied. N is the number of attributes.

$$similarity(C, M_X) = |1 - distance(C, M_X)| = \left| 1 - \sqrt{\frac{\sum_{n:1}^{N}(C(n) - M_X(n))^2}{N}} \right| \quad (1)$$

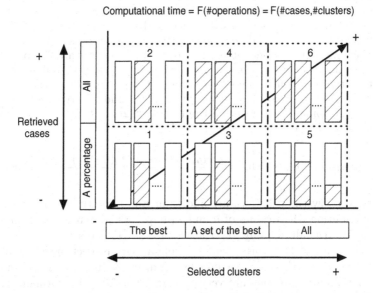

Fig. 1. The strategy map classifies the case retrieval strategies into six areas. Each one represents a combination of the number of clusters and cases selected for applying the case retrieval. The rectangles are the clusters and the lined area the retrieved cases from each cluster. The diagonal arrow from area number 1 to area number 6 shows the increase of the computational time as more cases are used.

Anyway, the selection of one of these situations depends on three issues: (1) the capability of the cluster for representing the data; (2) the desired computational time improvement; and (3) the maximum reduction of the accuracy rate accepted due to reduction of cases. For example, a high reduction of the computational time implies to select few clusters but the accuracy rate can be degraded if clusters are not representative. Therefore, the selection of the clusters is a compromise between issues 2 and 3, which are highly influenced by the capability of modeling the data complexity (issue 1).

On the other hand, the **factor of the retrieved cases** represents how many cases from the clusters are compared to C in the retrieve phase. The cases retrieved can be: (1) an arbitrary percentage or (2) all the cases. This issue is the difference between the areas 1-2, 3-4, 5-6 previously explained. Thus, the computational time can be reduced while the capability of exploring new clusters remains intact. To compute the percentage of retrieved cases, we propose two metrics based on the goodness of the clusters.

The first proposal defines a linear relation between the cluster contribution and its goodness. Eq. 2 computes the percentage as a normalized percentage between the similarity of the selected clusters K_M.

$$\% \ of \ cases \ from \ M_X = \frac{similarity(C, M_X)}{\sum_{m \in K_M} similarity(C, m)} \cdot 100 \qquad (2)$$

Furthermore, it could be interesting to promote the contribution of clusters with high goodness values and, at the same time, penalizing the contribution of clusters with lower goodness values. This is exactly the behavior of an *arctangent* function: linear in the central zone, restrictive in one extreme, and permissive in the other. Moreover, other interesting aspects to consider are the possibility of adjusting the gradient of the curve and defining for which similarity values the contribution of elements has to be more or less important (the inflection point). These behaviors are parametrized by the μ and x_0 arguments. Finally, the arctangent domain is transferred from $[-\pi/2, \pi/2]$ to $[0, 1]$ by dividing by π, and adding 0.5. These requirements define Eq. 3.

$$\% \ of \ cases \ from \ M_X = 0.5 + \frac{arctg(\mu * (similarity(C, M_X) - x_0))}{\pi} \cdot 100 \qquad (3)$$

Fig. 2 shows how the μ and x_0 arguments in Eq. 3 determine the percentage of the contribution. High values of μ and x_0 imply a highly restrictive selection. Alternatively, low values imply lower levels of restrictiveness.

However, if the selected clusters are not similar with respect to the input case, the global sum of the percentage will be less than 100%. In contrast, the sum will be greater than 100% if they are very similar. Therefore, the normalization of the last equation can help to adjust (increasing or decreasing) the total amount of cases to retrieve. Eq. 4 normalizes Eq. 3.

$$\% \ of \ cases \ from \ M_X \ (normalized) = \frac{\% \ of \ cases \ from \ M_X}{\sum_{m \in K_M} \% \ of \ cases \ from \ m} \cdot 100 \qquad (4)$$

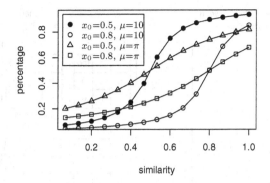

Fig. 2. Graphical representation of Eq. 3. The μ and x_0 arguments adjust the function according to the gradient and the inflection point desired. The pair $x_0 = 0.8$ and $\mu = 10$ is the most restrictive, and the pair $x_0 = 0.5$ and $\mu = 10$ is the most permissive. The other two configurations are intermediate situations.

Example. Fig. 3 illustrates the impact of the case retrieval strategies defined by Eq. 2, 3, and 4 through a case study. The left part represents a case memory clustered in nine clusters. Each cluster contains 100 cases and its goodness is computed by Eq. 1. The right part describes the behavior of twelve strategies, where each area is a combination of the two factors previously explained. Moreover, each area shows how many cases are retrieved from each one of the nine clusters. A value equal to zero means that the cluster is not selected. Therefore, the combination of both factors determines the degree of dispersion in which system explores the case memory. The definition of both issues depends on the performance desired by the user according to the capability of clusters for representing the domain, which is related to the data complexity. The greater the computational time improvement, the fewer clusters and cases have to be used.

Let's suppose a situation in which the user wants to improve the computational time but without reducing the accuracy rate. If the clusters are well defined, the best strategy is to select only the best cluster because it contains all the potentially useful cases.

Nevertheless, the clusters can present a lack of precision due to the data complexity. In this scenario, the best solution is to retrieve more than one cluster. Although this decision affects the computational time improvement, it can be compensated by applying strategies which focus on retrieving a percentage of cases from the selected clusters. The strategies based on Eq. 2 and 4 provide the same number of cases as the strategy that retrieves all the cases, the difference being that they explore other data clusters. The strategy built from Eq. 2 uses a linear contribution, and Eq. 4 uses a contribution weighted by the goodness of the cluster. On the other hand, Eq. 3 follows the same philosophy as the strategy based on Eq. 4 but increasing the total amount of cases as a consequence of the contribution not being normalized.

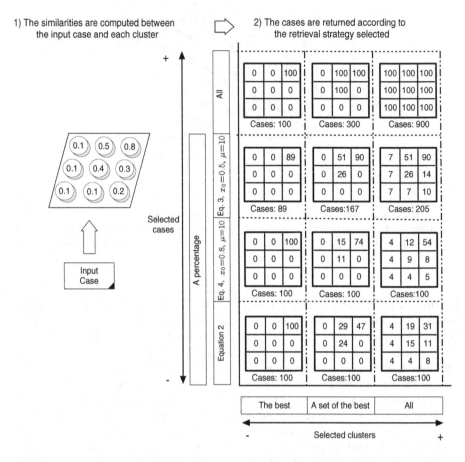

Fig. 3. The left part exemplifies a case memory clustered in nine clusters, and the right part shows the behavior of several case retrieval strategies. Each matrix corresponds to the cases retrieved from each cluster for a given configuration. A zero value means that the cluster is not selected. The total number of cases retrieved is below the matrix.

The extreme situation appears when the goodness of the clusters is small, and a full exploration of all the clusters is needed. In this case, the strategies of Eq. 2, 3, and 4 explore the case memory in different degrees of dispersion without utilizing all the case memory.

In summary, the performance is a balance between the computational time and the accuracy rate, where the goodness of clusters plays a crucial role.

3.2   Evaluation of the Case Retrieval Strategies

The evaluation of all strategies for a wide set of datasets implies the generation of huge tables which are complex to interpret. For this reason, we propose a 2-dimensional scatter plot to represent its performance as shown in Fig. 4.

The x axis depicts the ratio of the computational time of a case retrieval strategy (in this case $S2$ or $S3$) with respect to another strategy (in this case $S1$, which is the *All_All* situation featured by a linear search of the case memory) in logarithmic scale. A value closer to 0 indicates that there is no reduction in the number of operations, while growth in the negative direction implies a high reduction in this magnitude. A logarithm scale gives a better visual representation: for example, the value -1 of the logarithm in $S3$ means that $S3$ does 10% less operations than $S1$. As we can observe, the reduction in $S3$ is higher than in $S2$.

The y axis depicts the rank of each strategy averaged over all datasets. That is, if we consider m strategies tested over n datasets, $R_{i,j}$ is the rank-order assigned to the strategy i in comparison to the other ones, tested over the dataset j. From here, R_i is the medium rank for the strategy i, calculated as:

$$R_i = \frac{\sum_{j=1}^{n} R_{i,j}}{n} \tag{5}$$

Values next to 1 of this measure indicate that the strategy i is usually the best of the m tested, while values next to m indicate the opposite. Fig. 4 shows that S1 is better than S2, and S2 is better than S3 in terms of how many times each one has the best accuracy rate. The size of the drawn circumferences is proportional to the standard deviation of R_i. Thus, the bigger the circumference ($S2$, for example), the higher variability in the values obtained of $R_{i,j}$, and the smaller the circumference ($S1$ or $S3$), the lower the variability with respect to the medium rank.

Furthermore, the concept of critical distance (CD) is introduced to define the minimum distance from which the existence of a significant difference can be considered between the values of R_i, for a given confidence level [7]. The horizontal lines delimit the zone of equivalence between strategies. In this case, $S1$ and $S2$ are not significantly different but $S2$ reduces the cases used by almost by 50%. In contrast, $S3$ is significantly worse than $S1$ and $S2$.

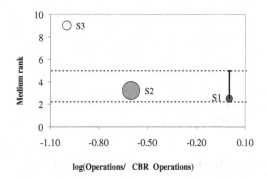

Fig. 4. Comparison of the performance between the strategies $S1$, $S2$, and $S3$. The x axis measures the computational time improvement, and the y axis represents how many times each strategy has the best accuracy rate. The vertical error bar is the CD value.

3.3   Data Complexity in the Case Retrieval Strategies

The data complexity influences the building of clusters and the strategy's behavior. We consider the boundary complexity [11] in order to evaluate how data geometry may affect the behavior of retrieval strategy.

The complexity space is defined by the complexity measures F3, N1, and N2 [8]. F3 is the feature efficiency, and it defines the efficiency of each feature individually describing to what degree the feature takes part in the class separability. The higher the value, the higher the power of class discrimination, implying a linear separation. N1 and N2 are the length of the class boundary and the intra/inter class nearest neighbor distances respectively. Both measures compute the distance between the opposite classes. Our metric is composed of the N1·N2 product because it emphasizes extreme behaviors. While a low value of these measures indicates a high class separability, a high value does not necessarily provide a conclusion about complexity. Thus, the dataset properties are evaluated by the discriminant power of features and the class separability.

Fig. 5 depicts the complexity space where the point (1,0) is considered the point of minimum complexity (mCP) whereas the point (0,1) corresponds to the maximum possible complexity (MCP). This is due to the meaning of each of the metrics and allows us to sort the complexity space into zones of low complexity (next to mCP) and zones of high complexity (next to MCP). As a matter of fact, the distance to the point mCP, in this space, distinguishes the studied datasets into three groups: (1) problems with a low complexity (type A, corresponding to distances to mCP less than 0.5), (2) problems with high complexity (type C, with value greater or equal than 1), and (3) problems in the middle of the two extremes (type B). Thus, we can evaluate the performance of each strategy in a more precise way.

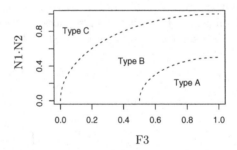

Fig. 5. The complexity space is divided into three types of complexity, where A is the less complex, and C the most complex

4   Experiments, Results, and Discussion

This section tests the methodology outlined in section 3. First, we briefly review how to integrate SOM in a Case-Based Reasoning system. Then, the datasets selected for the experimentation are described and classified by the complexity map. Finally, we present and discuss the results.

4.1 Self-Organization Map in a Case-Based Reasoning System

SOM projects the original N-dimensional input space into a new space with less dimensions by highlighting the most important data features to identify groups of similar cases. SOM is constituted of two layers: (1) the input layer composed of N neurons, where each neuron represents one of the N-dimensional features of the input case; and (2) the output layer composed of $M \times M$ neurons, where each one represents a set of similar cases by a director vector of N dimensions. Each input neuron is connected to all the output neurons. When a new input case C is introduced in the input layer, each neuron X from the output layer computes a degree of similarity between its director vector and the input case C applying a metric such as the normalized Euclidean distance (see Eq. 1). Thus, CBR can determine the clusters most similar to the input case. SOM is integrated into CBR in the SOMCBR framework (Self-Organization Map in a Case-Based Reasoning system) [9].

4.2 Testbed

The setting up of the case retrieval strategy according to the required performance is studied over several datasets of different domains and characteristics. There are 56 discrimination problems where miasbi, mias3c, ddsm, and μCa are related to breast cancer diagnosis [9] and the remaining datasets belong to the UCI Repository [4]. The datasets of D-classes are split in D datasets of two classes (each class versus all other classes) to increase the testbed. The dataset name, the number of features and instances, and the complexity type are described in table 1. The complexity map of datasets is drawn in Fig. 6.

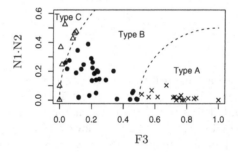

Fig. 6. Complexity map of the 56 analyzed datasets

4.3 Assessing the Performance of the Case Retrieval Strategies

The configurations from the strategy map studied for analyzing the behavior of the case retrieval strategy are summarized in Fig. 7. SOM is used for organizing the case memory. The strategies are executed applying a 10-fold stratified cross-validation with the following common configuration: (1) The retrieve phase uses

Table 1. Description of test datasets: name, number of attributes and instances, and complexity type. The suffix $2cX$ means that the dataset classifies the classes X versus the rest of classes. The datasets are sorted by their complexity.

Dataset	Attributes	Instances	Type	Dataset	Attributes	Instances	Type
segment2c2	19	2310	A	wav2c3	40	5000	B
iris2c2	4	150	A	wav2c1	40	5000	B
glass2c1	9	214	A	miasbi2c3	152	320	B
thy2c1	5	215	A	ddsm2c1	142	501	B
thy2c2	5	215	A	mias3c2c2	152	322	B
segment2c6	19	2310	A	thy2c3	5	215	B
segment2c7	19	2310	A	mias3c2c1	152	322	B
wine2c2	13	178	A	ddsm2c4	142	501	B
iris2c1	4	150	A	miasbi2c2	152	320	B
segment2c1	19	2310	A	wisconsin	9	699	B
wine2c1	13	178	A	wbcd	9	699	B
glass2c2	9	214	A	wav2c2	40	5000	B
miasbi2c4	152	320	A	sonar	60	208	B
glass2c4	9	214	A	wpbc	33	198	B
wine2c3	13	178	A	glass2c6	9	214	B
iris2c3	4	150	A	mias3c2c3	152	322	B
wdbc	30	569	A	biopsia	24	1027	B
segment2c3	19	2310	B	vehicle2c3	18	846	B
segment2c5	19	2310	B	vehicle2c2	18	846	B
glass2c3	9	214	B	bal2c3	4	625	C
vehicle2c1	18	846	B	bal2c2	4	625	C
segment2c4	19	2310	B	bal2c1	4	625	C
tao	2	1888	B	ddsm2c3	142	501	C
hepatitis	19	155	B	heartstatlog	13	270	C
glass2c5	9	214	B	μCa	21	216	C
ionosphere	34	351	B	ddsm2c2	142	501	C
vehicle2c4	18	846	B	pim	8	768	C
miasbi2c1	152	320	B	bpa	6	345	C

the Euclidean distance as similarity function. (2) The reuse phase proposes a solution using the most similar case. (3) The retain phase does not store new cases. Moreover, SOMCBR is tested with 10 random seeds and the size map is automatically computed as the map with the lowest error [9].

Next, the scatter plot for analyzing the strategies is built considering the complexity characterization in Fig. 8(a), 8(b), and 8(c). They show the accuracy (measured through the medium rank) versus the computational time (represented by the logarithm of the quotient of the number of operations). The strategy of reference is the *All_All* because it works like a CBR system with linear search of the case memory.

Fig. 8(a) represents the low complexity problems (type A). We observe a linear correlation between the values of the two axes, which indicates that the effect of the SOM is weak: the accuracy of the method is directly proportional to the number of retrieved cases (the correlation coefficient is 0.96 for the strategies

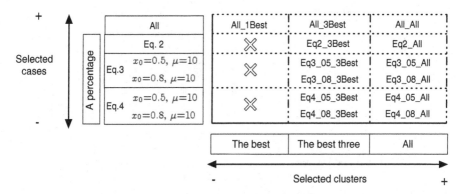

Fig. 7. Test experiments. The configurations marked with a cross has not been tested because they behave like *All_1Best*.

with a noticeable reduction in the number of operations). Even so, we note a set of strategies with values of medium rank inside the limit marked by CD, two of which have an important reduction in the number of operations while the accuracy rate is maintained: *Eq3_05_3Best* and *All_3Best*. Although the strategies *Eq3_05_All* and *Eq3_08_All* have a similar accuracy rate like *All_All*, they do not provide a significant computational time improvement.

Fig. 8(b) represents datasets with a complexity of type B, which has higher complexity than type A. The increase of the complexity entails two effects: (1) the number of operations is reduced in most strategies and (2) the linearity between the two variables is also decreased (the correlation coefficient is now 0.86). Similarly as before, *All_3Best* is the most suitable strategy because it maintains the accuracy rate while the computational is reduced. *Eq3_05_All* and *Eq3_08_All* works like *All_All* again.

Finally, Fig. 8(c) refers to datasets of the highest complexity (type C). In this case, the complexity accentuates the previous effects: (1) the mean number of operations continues to be reduced and (2) the linear correlation between both variables is even less than before (coefficient in 0.76). Although the strategies *Eq3_05_All* and *Eq3_08_All* continue without improving the computational time, they improve the accuracy rate of the *All_All* configuration. The strategy *All_3Best* improves the computational time and the accuracy rate, while the strategies *Eq3_05_3Best*, *Eq4_05_All* improve only the computational time and maintain the accuracy.

The analysis of SOMCBR using the proposed methodology can be summarized in the following aspects: (1) SOM is a suitable clustering technique for organizing the case memory because it is able to successfully index it. (2) SOM works best in complex domains. This idea corroborates a previous work of ours [8]. (3) The best configurations are those in which the retrieve phase uses all the cases from more than one cluster, or it uses a weighting percentage of cases from all the clusters. We understand such a good configuration those in which the computational time is improved and the accuracy rate is maintained. Notwithstanding, the rest of

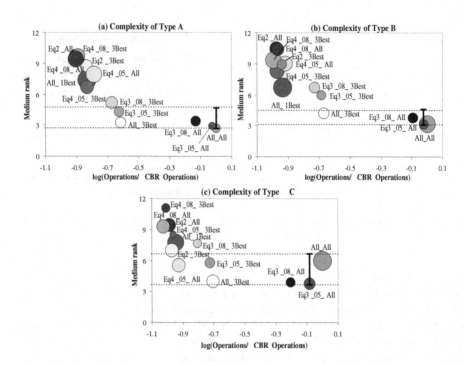

Fig. 8. Analysis of the case retrieval strategies according to the complexity types (A, B, and C)

configurations improve greatly the computational time because they use few cases, but this has a negative influence on the accuracy rate. The final selection of the strategy will depend on the user requirements.

5 Conclusions and Further Research

In this paper, we have presented a methodology for analyzing the behavior of the different ways in which the case retrieval from a clustered case memory can be performed while taking into account the performance expected by the user. The performance is a balance between the desired computational time improvement and the maximum acceptable reduction of the accuracy rate. Additionally, we have offered an innovative and intuitive way for analyzing the performance of the case retrieval strategies over a large set of datasets.

The proposed methodology is divided into three steps. The first step consists in running over all the possible case retrieval strategies from the clustered case memory. All the configurations are extracted from a previously taxonomy of several case retrieval ways. The taxonomy considers the number of clusters and cases used. Next, the datasets are split according to the three levels of complexity (A, B, or C) using the complexity measures N1, N2, and F3. Finally, the scatter plot is drawn for each one of the complexity types. The graphical representation compares the average rank with respect to the computational time improvement. These steps are applicable for any case memory organized by a clustering technique.

This methodology has been successfully tested using SOMCBR, which is a CBR system characterized by organizing the case memory by means of the SOM approach. The main conclusions of the analysis are that SOMCBR works better in complex domains, and that the best solution (improving the computational time while maintaining the accuracy rate) is often to use all the cases from more than one cluster or a part of cases from all the clusters. Anyway, the performed desired depends on the final user requirements: more speed, less accuracy.

The further work is focused on applying this methodology over other case memory organizations based on clusters, and trying to define a meta-relation level between the case memory organizations.

Acknowledgments

We would like to thank the Spanish Government for the support under grants TIN2006-15140-C03-03, TIN2005-08386-C05-04, and the *Generalitat de Catalunya* for the support under grants 2005SGR-302 and 2006FIC-0043. Also, we would like to thank *Enginyeria i Arquitectura La Salle* of Ramon Llull University for the support to our research group.

References

1. Aamodt, A., Plaza, E.: Case-based reasoning: Foundations issues, methodological variations, and system approaches. AI Communications 7, 39–59 (1994)
2. Basu, M., Ho, T.K.: Data Complexity in Pattern Recognition. In: Advanced Information and Knowledge Processing, Springer, Heidelberg (2006)
3. Bernadó, E., Ho, T.K.: Domain of competence of XCS classifier system in complexity measurement space. IEEE Transaction Evolutionary Computation 9(1), 82–104 (2005)
4. Blake, C.L., Merz, C.J.: UCI repository of machine learning databases (1998)
5. Brown, M.: A Memory Model for Case Retrieval by Activation Passing. PhD thesis, University of Manchester (1994)
6. Chang, P., Lai, C.: A hybrid system combining self-organizing maps with case-based reasoning in wholesaler's new-release book forecasting. Expert Syst. Appl. 29(1), 183–192 (2005)
7. Demsar, J.: Statistical comparisons of classifiers over multiple data sets. Journal of Machine Learning Research 7, 1–30 (2006)
8. Fornells, A., Golobardes, E., Martorell, J.M., Garrell, J.M., Bernadó, E., Macià, N.: Measuring the applicability of self-organization maps in a case-based reasoning system. In: 3rd Iberian Conference on Pattern Recognition and Image Analysis. LNCS, vol. 4478, pp. 532–539. Springer, Heidelberg (2007)
9. Fornells, A., Golobardes, E., Vernet, D., Corral, G.: Unsupervised case memory organization: Analysing computational time and soft computing capabilities. In: Roth-Berghofer, T.R., Göker, M.H., Güvenir, H.A. (eds.) ECCBR 2006. LNCS (LNAI), vol. 4106, pp. 241–255. Springer, Heidelberg (2006)

10. Fornells, A., Golobardes, E., Vilasís, X., Martí, J.: Integration of strategies based on relevance feedback into a tool for retrieval of mammographic images. In: Corchado, E., Yin, H., Botti, V., Fyfe, C. (eds.) IDEAL 2006. LNCS, vol. 4224, pp. 116–124. Springer, Heidelberg (2006) (Selected to be published in the International Journal of Neural Systems)

11. Ho, T.K., Basu, M.: Complexity measures of supervised classification problems. IEEE Transaction on Pattern Analysis and Machine Intelligence 24(3), 289–300 (2002)

12. Kohonen, T.: Self-Organization and Associative Memory, 3rd edn. Springer Series in Information Sciences, vol. 8. Springer, Heidelberg (1984)

13. Lenz, M., Burkhard, H.D., Brückner, S.: Applying case retrieval nets to diagnostic tasks in technical domains. In: Smith, I., Faltings, B.V. (eds.) Advances in Case-Based Reasoning. LNCS, vol. 1168, pp. 219–233. Springer, Heidelberg (1996)

14. Myllymaki, P., Tirri, H.: Massively parallel case-based reasoning with probabilistic similarity metrics (1993)

15. Nicholson, R., Bridge, D., Wilson, N.: Decision diagrams: Fast and flexible support for case retrieval and recommendation. In: Roth-Berghofer, T.R., Göker, M.H., Güvenir, H.A. (eds.) ECCBR 2006. LNCS (LNAI), vol. 4106, pp. 136–150. Springer, Heidelberg (2006)

16. Pelleg, D., Moore, A.: X-means: Extending K-means with efficient estimation of the number of clusters. In: Proceedings of the 17th International Conference of Machine Learning, pp. 727–734. Morgan Kaufmann, San Francisco (2000)

17. Plaza, E., McGinty, L.: Distributed case-based reasoning. The Knowledge engineering review 20(3), 261–265 (2006)

18. Rissland, E.L., Skalak, D.B., Friedman, M.: Case retrieval through multiple indexing and heuristic search. In: International Joint Conferences on Artificial Intelligence, pp. 902–908 (1993)

19. Schaaf, J.W.: Fish and Sink - an anytime-algorithm to retrieve adequate cases. In: Aamodt, A., Veloso, M.M. (eds.) Case-Based Reasoning Research and Development. LNCS, vol. 1010, pp. 538–547. Springer, Heidelberg (1995)

20. Vernet, D., Golobardes, E.: An unsupervised learning approach for case-based classifier systems. Expert Update. The Specialist Group on Artificial Intelligence 6(2), 37–42 (2003)

21. Wess, S., Althoff, K.D., Derwand, G.: Using k-d trees to improve the retrieval step in case-based reasoning. In: Wess, S., Richter, M., Althoff, K.-D. (eds.) Topics in Case-Based Reasoning. LNCS, vol. 837, pp. 167–181. Springer, Heidelberg (1994)

22. Yang, Q., Wu, J.: Enhancing the effectiveness of interactive cas-based reasoning with clustering and decision forests. Applied Intelligence 14(1) (2001)

Using Cases Utility for Heuristic Planning Improvement

Tomás de la Rosa, Angel García Olaya, and Daniel Borrajo

Departamento de Informática, Universidad Carlos III de Madrid
Avda. de la Universidad, 30. Leganés (Madrid). Spain
trosa@inf.uc3m.es, agolaya@inf.uc3m.es, dborrajo@ia.uc3m.es

Abstract. Current efficient planners employ an informed search guided by a heuristic function that is quite expensive to compute. Thus, ordering nodes in the search tree becomes a key issue, in order to select efficiently nodes to evaluate from the successors of the current search node. In a previous work, we successfully applied a CBR approach to order nodes for evaluation, thus reducing the number of calls to the heuristic function. However, once cases were learned, they were not modified according to their utility on solving planning problems. We present in this work a scheme for learning case quality based on its utility during a validation phase. The qualities obtained determine the way in which these cases are preferred in the retrieval and replay processes. Then, the paper shows some experimental results for several benchmarks taken from the International Planning Competition (IPC). These results show the planning performance improvement when case utilities are used.

1 Introduction

AI planning consists of the computational task of given a domain theory (problem space represented in a form of first order logic as a set of predicates, actions and types), and a problem to be solved (instances of types, initial state and goals), obtain a plan. The plan usually consists of an ordered set of instantiated actions that transform the initial state into a state where the goals are met. Some of the most useful current approaches to planning are based on heuristic planning. Heuristic planners (e.g., FF [1], YAHSP [2] or SGPLAN [3]) are mainly composed of an efficient search algorithm guided by a heuristic function. The standard heuristic used consists of computing a solution to a relaxed planning problem, and then returning the cost of that solution. It was first introduced by FF and has proven to be accurate enough to guide efficiently the planners towards reasonable solutions in most of the benchmark domains[1]. One of the drawbacks of this heuristic is its computational cost, since it consumes most of the total planning time. To address this issue, among other solutions, researchers have incorporated additional heuristics to make the heuristic values more accurate, thus reducing, for instance, the number of ties of heuristic values through

---

[1] Since the reader does not need to know how it actually works, we refer the reader to the FF papers for its details [1].

R.O. Weber and M.M. Richter (Eds.): ICCBR 2007, LNAI 4626, pp. 137–148, 2007.
© Springer-Verlag Berlin Heidelberg 2007

the search tree. Another option for improving planning time consists of ordering the way in which nodes are evaluated when a greedy algorithm is used. FF uses as the standard search algorithm a variation of hill-climbing called enforced hill-climbing (EHC). In order to select the next successor of the current node, EHC evaluates one successor after another, until it finds one that returns a heuristic value better than the current node. Therefore, if node evaluations are correctly ordered, it might imply a reduction on the number of evaluations: the sooner a good successor is evaluated, the more probable will be to continue the search further.

In our previous work [4,5], we showed that a CBR approach could improve the planning time deciding the node evaluation order in EHC. This domain-dependent knowledge is stored in a case base. The training phase consists of solving a set of planning problems, and then extracting cases from the solution path. Cases were structures called typed sequences which are abstracted state transitions incorporated with the set of actions performed to solve the problem for each object type in the domain, as we will describe in more detail in the next section. This CBR cycle worked very well in the tested domains. However, we did not assess how good the learned knowledge was, since the cases were extracted from non-optimal solutions. Furthermore, there was no maintenance of the case base, apart from merging new solutions to problems with previous ones. Also, cases were used regardless of their efficiency of replaying them previously. In this paper, we present an improved approach that dynamically learns the case qualities, in terms of how useful they were for supporting planning search.

In the following sections we present a summary of how typed sequences are used to support EHC. Then, we introduce the scheme for assessing case quality based on two utility measures, one related to the sequence steps and the other one related to the global use of the sequences during the replay process. Afterwards, we show the experimental results comparing EHC, the previous approach, and the use of cases based on their quality. We also include a study of training the case base to recognize how much it may be populated depending on a particular domain. We also use this study to select a good case base for assessing case qualities. Finally we discuss some conclusions and future work.

2   Typed Sequences Overview

Current planners use a common standard language for describing their inputs, the Planning Domain Definition Language (PDDL). This language is used in the planning competitions (IPC) held every two years for describing the domains and problems to be solved. Once of the features of the domain definitions is the possibility of assigning types to predicate arguments and action variables. This permits to recognize typical state transitions that each object type has [6]. In our work, we define a case as a sequence of these transitions, called typed sequence, which describes a particular episode of the object type. As an example, if we have a domain in which crates have to be moved among some depots, using trucks and hoists to load them into the trucks, we will have cases that refer to crates, cases that refer to trucks, and so on for each type in the domain.

A typed sequence of a given type is formed by an ordered list of pairs (typed sub-state, action to reach the state). A typed sub-state is a collection of all properties that an object has in a particular state. The notion of object properties was first introduced by TIM [6] with its domain analysis techniques. A property is defined as a predicate subscripted with the object position of a literal (e.g., at_1 is a property of object *truck1* in the literal *(at truck1 depot0)*. In addition, an object sub-state is the set of the state literals in which the object is present. Then, the set of object properties that forms the typed sub-state is extracted from the object sub-state. For instance, suppose we have an initial state like [*(at truck1 depot1) (on crate0 crate1) (at crate0 depot0) (available hoist1) (clear crate0)*...]. Then, the object sub-state of *crate0* would be [*(on crate0 crate1) (at crate0 depot0) (clear crate0)*]. This is generalized to $(on_1\ at_1\ clear_1)$ which is a typed sub-state of type *crate*. If action *lift(hoist1,crate0,crate1,depot0)* were applied in the initial state, we would generate first a pair with the initial state and no action, and a second pair with the state resulting from applying that action, and the action: [$(lifting_1\ at_1)$, *lift*].

The typed sequences grouped by domain types form the case base. In a training phase, the case base is populated, solving the training problems and extracting a sequence for each object of the problem instance. Figure 1 shows an example of a typed sequence for *crate0* and the plan from which it was generated. The two *no-op* in the sequence are steps in which the typed sub-state does not change (no action related to *crate0* was executed), so there is no relevant action to store in the sequence.

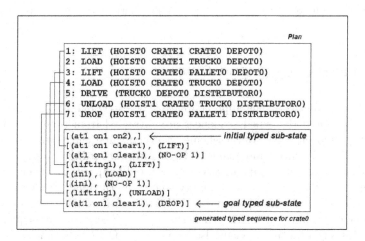

Fig. 1. An example of a typed sequence relevant to a crate

Typed sequences are used as follows. In a new problem, the planner retrieves from the case base the most similar sequence for each instance (object) in the problem. First, for each object in the problem instance, we generate two typed sub-state, one from the initial state and the other from the problem goals (goals are also described as state literals). Then, we match the typed sub-state from the goals against the last step of all sequences in the case base. Then, we do the same with the initial typed sub-state and the first step of the sequences that resulting from the first match. The retrieved sequences are generalizations of sub-states, so in order to use them properly, they are partially instantiated in the adaptation phase by using objects found in applicable actions from the initial state.[2]

Then, a modified version of EHC generates at any state S its successors, and checks if any successor is recommended by the retrieved cases. If there are, the successors are evaluated in order for obtaining their heuristic value $h(S')$. If $h(S')$ is strictly less than $h(S)$, the successor is selected, and the search continues from it, until a state achieving the problem goals is reached. If $h(S')$ is equal or greater than $h(S)$, a second attempt with the next successor is done, and so on, until a node with a better heuristic is found. If the CBR module could not recommend any node, all skipped successors are evaluated in order, and the standard EHC is used. A successor is recommended when its object sub-state (typed sub-state if it is not fully instantiated) matches the current sequence step in one of the retrieved sequences.

This approach has been implemented in SAYPHI, a learning architecture in which several techniques for control knowledge acquisition can be integrated with a heuristic planner. The SAYPHI planner is an FF-like heuristic planner. The planner includes several search algorithms and the same heuristic function as FF. Figure 2 shows its architecture. We are currently using EHC as the search algorithm, but we could use any other included in the planner, like the standard hill-climbing technique used in [4]. Also, there is one case base for each domain.

3   Computing Quality of Cases

One of the drawbacks of this approach is that heuristic planners generate non-optimal plans, and the typed sequences are extracted from those non-optimal solutions. Moreover, our retrieval scheme returns the first choice when it finds an exact match of the initial and goal typed sub-states, regardless of any other case with an exact match too. This suggests that we could improve the behavior of the CBR approach, by assessing cases quality, and using the quality to prefer useful cases in the retrieval. An additional issue is that CBR could recommend more than one node to evaluate in EHC, since the replay process uses one sequence per object. This suggests that we can also improve the CBR behavior by assessing how useful the steps in a sequence are, so we can break ties among cases when they provide different recommendations of nodes to be evaluated first. In this section we introduce two utility measures to address these issues.

---

[2] We refer for details to [5].

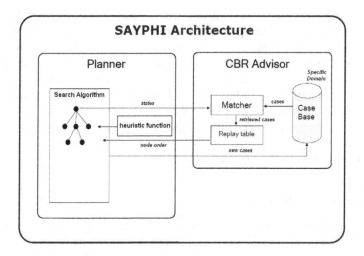

Fig. 2. The SAYPHI architecture

3.1   Step Utility Measure

During the search, the CBR approach continues following (advances to its next step) a retrieved case (typed sequence) in three different situations. The standard one is when a node (state) matches the current step of the case, and the evaluation of the recommended node improves the heuristic value of its parent. The second one is when the evaluation of the recommended node does not improve the heuristic value, but none of its siblings improve the heuristic value either. Even if it was not a good option, there was nothing better in the case base. The third one is when a node is recommended by two or more cases. All cases are then advanced to the next step if the node evaluation improves the heuristic value. Thus, we say that a "right choice" is a step sequence that recommended a node that belongs to the solution path (independently, of whether it improves the heuristic value of its parent). Likewise, we say that a "wrong choice" is a sequence step that recommended a node that does not belong to the solution path. If there is a wrong choice, there must be a sibling node that improves the heuristic value. The sum of right and wrong choices of a case is the number of recommendation attempts of the case. Thus, being g the number of right choices and A the number of recommendations, we define the step utility measure as:

$$\gamma = \frac{g}{A} \tag{1}$$

γ is the step frequency of recommending a good choice. This frequency can be easily computed after a problem is solved by just having a recommendation trace of evaluated nodes. We wanted to deal with the exploration vs. exploitation trade-off: when there is no good case for recommending a node, we can prefer the less used cases (exploration), or the most used ones (exploitation). Thus, we define a threshold μ_{step}, and a sorting function that orders the recommendations (steps of cases) by γ when $\gamma >= \mu_{step}$ (exploitation) and by increasing number of recommendation attempts when $\gamma < \mu_{step}$ (exploration: the less frequently used cases will be selected first).[3] Therefore, when none of the step options reaches the threshold we assume that no choice was good enough, and the less explored step is preferred. We can use high values of μ in a training phase if we want to explore the different options in order to learn the cases steps quality. In a test phase we can use lower values of μ to use the steps by their utility discarding only the known bad ones.

3.2   Sequence Utility Measure

Once a sequence is retrieved for an object, it stays selected regardless of whether it is used or not during the search. Though we could abandon it and select a different relevant sequence, this would lead to a higher computational load. Therefore, our replay process must deal with the problem of wrongly retrieved sequences, since either they produce wrong step choices or they are not followed at all. The problem of not using a retrieved sequence is different of the problem of having a sequence that produces wrong choices. For the sequence utility measure we have decided that is more important to recognize the "bad advisors" sequences, so the global utility measure for a sequence is a cumulative function of the step utilities. Thus, we define:

$$\lambda = \frac{\sum_{i=1}^{N} g_i}{\sum_{i=1}^{N} A_i} \qquad (2)$$

where λ is the global frequency for a sequence of giving a good choice, N is the number of steps in the sequence, and i represents each step. As the step utility measure, we have defined a threshold μ_{case} to decide when it is bad to select a given sequence. We keep our retrieval scheme of selecting the most similar sequence, but the first one with an exact match. Then, we sort the cases of each type by λ when they have $\gamma >= \mu_{case}$ and the rest of cases are ordered in ascending order by the number of total attempts of recommendation when $\gamma <= \mu_{case}$. This utility measure adds all attempts independently from where the attempts came. Frequently, the same sequence is retrieved more than once, but assigned to different objects (two or more instantiations). Then, the λ value of a case is computed adding the right choices and the attempts of all such instantiations of the sequence. High values of μ_{case} ensure that unused cases are selected if there is more than one with an exact match. Lower values μ_{case} will guarantee that reasonably good cases are selected to avoid bad selections of unknown ones.

---

[3] We could have used any other way of implementing this trade-off as ϵ-greedy approaches in reinforcement learning.

4   Experimental Results

Before doing the tests with the utility measures we decided to perform a study of the learning curve for each domain. Since one training planning problem produces many cases (one per object) we intuitively know that the case base may perform reasonably well after training the system with few planning problems. Then, we selected the best training problem-set for each domain and used it for learning their qualities using the two defined utility measures. We have used four domains of the IPC in their version of classical planning (known as STRIPS). These benchmark domains are among the difficult ones: Satellite, Rovers, Depots and Zenotravel. The Satellite domain involves planning a set of observation tasks among multiple satellites. The Rovers domain requires that a collection of rovers navigate a planet surface, finding samples, taking pictures and communicating them back to a lander. In the Depots domain trucks transport crates around depots and distributors, and crates must be stacked onto pallets or on top of other crates at their destination. The Zenotravel domain involves transporting people around in planes, using different modes of movement.

4.1   Study on Training Problems

To set up the training cases tests we have generated for each domain a training set and a test set with the random problem generators supplied by the IPC. A training set consists of 20 problems subdivided in 10 groups by their difficulty. The test set consists of 100 problems subdivided in 20 sub-sets of incremental difficulty. The last training sub-set has the same difficulty than the 10th of the test sub-sets, so the test set has more complex problems. The aim of the experiment is to solve the test set after training the case base with the first sub-set, then after training with the first two sub-sets and so on. We expect that at some point an extra training will not produce any advantage of time or plan quality, and in some cases it could produce a disadvantage due to the overhead that produces a larger case base.

Table 1 shows the results of the study in the cited domains. These are the average length and evaluated nodes of problems solved with all training sub-sets. In none of the domains a considerable difference of solved problems was encountered, and the trace of these differences does not reflect any kind of convergence. In the Satellite domain, between 85 to 92 problems were solved depending on the training sub-set. In the Rovers domain between 92 and 93 problems were solved, while in the Depots domain between 61 and 64 were solved. The average of the number of evaluated nodes reflects more interesting results because we can observe the improvement as the case base grows. Though the average plan length could be a good measure for selecting a training sub-set, we have chosen the best training set in terms of the average of number of evaluated nodes. For those sub-sets the average plan length is either the best or quite good. In the Satellite domain the sixth sub-set was selected. It has 12 problems and generated 66 cases. In the Rovers domain the fifth sub-set was selected, that has 10 problems and generated 75 cases. In the Depots domain the fifth sub-set was selected that has 10 problems and generated 55 cases. In the Zenotravel domain the second sub-set was selected that has 4 problems and 24 cases.

Table 1. Results of the study on the training problems

Cycle	Probs	Satellite			Rovers			Depots			Zenotravel		
		Cases	Len.	Eval.	Cases	Len.	Eval.	Cases	Len.	Eval.	Cases	Len.	Eval.
1	2	14	32.0	279.5	15	25.6	88.5	16	30.2	768.6	14	14.5	122.5
2	4	22	31.7	231.6	33	25.6	83.0	21	30.1	733.5	24	13.7	66.5
3	6	30	31.8	221.5	51	25.9	94.7	36	29.6	657.4	37	13.7	71.1
4	8	43	32.2	278.4	62	25.8	86.6	55	29.4	728.3	49	13.6	77.8
5	10	57	31.9	208.9	75	25.5	80.0	55	29.4	559.8	58	13.7	81.3
6	12	66	31.9	208.8	98	25.8	86.0	71	29.3	618.5	68	13.8	74.3
7	14	79	32.1	271.9	120	25.7	87.0	85	29.6	663.6	78	13.9	78.1
8	16	92	31.9	281.5	147	25.9	92.2	92	29.8	632.5	90	13.9	81.8
9	18	106	32.2	240.3	174	25.9	90.8	92	29.5	647.5	108	13.8	72.2
10	20	118	32.2	230.6	201	25.7	84.8	100	29.9	710.5	128	13.8	83.8

4.2 Test Using the Utility Measure

In the following experiments, we chose for each domain the best training problems-set in terms of the number of node evaluations. After the training phase, we performed a validation phase with a validation problems-set to determine the utility measures for each case. A validation set consists of 30 new problems with the same difficulty scheme as the training set. This validation is made with an on-line strategy, so the retrieval and the replay of sequences in one problem uses the utility measures of the previous problem in the validation set. The values of μ_{step} and μ_{case} for validation were set to 0.75 to prefer exploration.[4] Afterwards, with the test set of 100 problems, we compare the EHC performance by itself (no CBR advice), with the cases support (EHC-CBR), and with the cases support using both utility measures (EHC-CBR-Utility). The values of μ_{step} and μ_{case} for the test phase were set to 0.5 to use more exploitation, but not preferring cases that perform poorly more than half the time.

Table 2 shows the number of solved problems in each domain. In the Satellite and Rovers domains one problem more than EHC was solved. In the Depots domain the EHC-CBR does not perform quite well, but it was improved with the utilities. Table 3 shows the accumulated time, the average of plan length (solution quality) and the average of evaluated nodes for problems that were solved by all techniques.

Figure 3 shows the detail for the accumulated time using each technique. The results show that EHC-CBR-Utility greatly reduced the number of evaluations done by EHC-CBR in four domains. Compared with EHC, EHC-CBR-Utility

---

[4] We started with an "a priori" reasonable value for those thresholds. Since there are heuristic values, we will perform an analysis to understand the influence of those values in the results.

Table 2. Number of solved problems

Domains	EHC	EHC-CBR	EHC-CBR-Utility
Satellite	93	93	94
Rovers	94	95	95
Depots	74	69	74
Zenotravel	73	72	73

reduced the number of evaluations in three of four domains, specially in the Satellite domain, that had an improvement of 46%. In the Depots domain, both CBR approaches perform worse than EHC, even though EHC-CBR-Utility has improved EHC-CBR. The Depots domain is known as a hard benchmark in the IPC, but in spite of that, we can blame the poor performance to our current case representation. Typed sequences only store information about one object and do not take into account the relation that this object has in other problem goals. The Depots domain has strongly goal dependencies and the other domains are serializable (at least there is a sub-optimal plan that can solve each goal individually). However, the CBR approaches can partially deal with goal dependencies since the replay process holds more than one sequence at a time and selecting actions from different sequences interleaves actions within a plan to achieve the goals in the right order.

Table 3. Accumulated time of solved problems using EHC, EHC-CBR and EHC-CBR-Utility

Domains	EHC			EHC-CBR			EHC-CBR-Utility		
	Time	Len	Eval	Time	Len	Eval	Time	Len	Eval
Satellite	1291.9	35.1	316.2	1040.2	34.6	254.6	695.9	34.1	146.8
Rovers	669.4	26.8	116.5	590.0	26.4	93.0	553.9	26.4	81.7
Depots	529.5	33.8	744.6	943.8	33.8	1432.8	667.5	33.4	816.0
Zenotravel	505.3	18.1	133.6	499.4	17.9	126.1	395.3	17.9	101.6

We can also analyze the plan quality measured in terms of the plan length. In all domains, the plan length was either equal or slightly improved by both CBR approaches. In EHC, the heuristic function can suggest irrelevant actions even if the heuristic value is improved with that action, producing non-optimal plans. EHC uses an inconsistent heuristic. Therefore, search can generate nodes with successors that improve the heuristic value, but with different estimations among them (the search will go through the first node evaluated of them). This fact is specially observed in bigger problems (in terms of size of initial state), and since typed sequences are learned from easy problems, the sequences do not store many of these irrelevant actions. Thus, the CBR recommendation is giving an additional heuristic to suggest the best successor even if there is another successor that also improves the heuristic value.

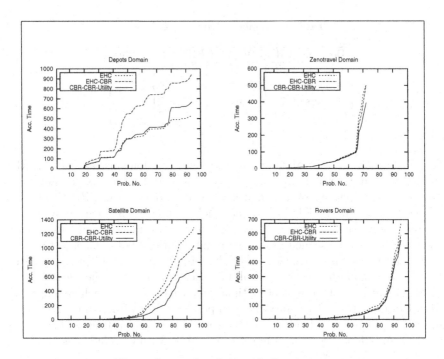

Fig. 3. Accumulated time of all techniques

5   Related Work

The relevance of object type transitions were shown by [6]. With a pre-processing
tool, they obtain Finite State Machines that represent states in which a type of
object can be and can move to (state invariants). A basic difference is that
state invariants help planners to build efficient action schemas, needed to compute applicable actions, and in our approach typed sequences are used to guide
the search ordering nodes during the search. Previous CBR approaches have
supported different kinds of planning tasks. PARIS [7] stores cases in different
abstraction levels of a solved problem, CAPLAN-CBC [8] performs plan-space
search and replay and ANALOGY [9] integrates CBR with generative planning
based on a derivational analogy process, in which lines of reasoning are trans-
fered and adapted to a new problem. More recently, in [10] CBR is applied to
Hierarchical Task Networks Planning, another AI paradigm for planning. Our
approach differs from these contributions, since ours is the first CBR approach
applied to heuristic planning. Nevertheless, heuristic planning has been applied
to support CBR retrieval. Tonidandel and Rillo [11] proposed a similarity metric
based on the FF heuristic function. They use the heuristic estimation to measure
the distance between the initial state of a problem and the initial state of a case,
and between the problem goals and the goal state stored in the case. This idea
was suitable for case-based planners that use whole plans as cases and needs

significant effort to transform the solution to fit in the new problem, but this idea was not implemented to support heuristic planning.

6   Conclusions and Future Work

We have presented an approach that is based on previous work. The starting point is a CBR approach that advises a heuristic planner which is the best successor of each node to evaluate first during the search. In this paper, we describe a way of assessing the quality of the learned cases and results show that it can reduce the total planning time in some benchmark domains. This improvement is basically due to the reduction of the number of calls to the heuristic function, which is computationally expensive for planners.

In our future work we want to extend our system to numeric domains (incorporate cost functions different than plan length and handle numeric fluents). The IPC benchmark domains are very challenging in their numeric versions, and most planners can not find good solutions even for easy problems. We believe typed sequences, together with the quality of the solutions, could improve not only planning time, but also quality of solutions.

Acknowledgments

This work has been partially supported by the Spanish MEC project TIN2005-08945-C06-05 and regional CAM-UC3M project CCG06-UC3M/TIC-0831.

References

1. Hoffmann, J., Nebel, B.: The FF planning system: Fast plan generation through heuristic search. Journal of Artificial Intelligence Research 14, 253–302 (2001)
2. Vidal, V.: A lookahead strategy for heuristic search planning. In: Proceedings of the Fourteenth International Conference on Automated Planning and Scheduling, pp. 150–160 (2004)
3. Chen, Y., Hsu, C.W., Wah, B.: SGPlan: Subgoal partitioning and resolution in planning. In: ICAPS'04. Proceedings of the 4th International Planning Competition (IPC4) in Conference, pp. 30–33 (2004)
4. DelaRosa, T., Borrajo, D., Garcfa-Olaya, A.: Replaying type sequences in forward heuristic planning. In: Ruml, W., Hutter, F. (eds.) Technical Report of the AAAI'06 Workshop on Learning for Search, Boston, MA, AAAI Press, Stanford (2006)
5. de la Rosa, T., García-Olaya, A., Borrajo, D.: Case-based recommendation for node ordering in planning. In: Dankel II, D. (ed.) Proceedings of the 20th International FLAIRS Conference, Key West, FL, AAAI Press, Stanford (2007)
6. Fox, M., Long, D.: The automatic inference of state invariants in TIM. Journal of Artificial Intelligence Research 9, 317–371 (1998)
7. Bergmann, R., Wilke, W.: Paris: Flexible plan adaptation by abstraction and refinement. In: Voss, A. (ed.) ECAI (1996). Workshop on Adaptation in Case-Based Reasoning, John Wiley & Sons, Chichester (1996)

8. Muñoz-Avila, H., Paulokat, J., Wess, S.: Controlling nonlinear hierarchical planning by case replay. In: in working papers of the Second European Workshop on Case-based Reasoning, Chantilly, France, pp. 195–203 (1994)

9. Veloso, M.M., Carbonell, J.G.: Derivational analogy in PRODIGY: Automating case acquisition, storage, and utilization. Machine Learning 10(3), 249–278 (1993)

10. Macedo, L., Cardoso, A.: Cased-based, decision-theoretic, HTN-Planning. In: Funk, P., González Calero, P.A. (eds.) ECCBR 2004. LNCS (LNAI), vol. 3155, Springer, Heidelberg (2004)

11. Tonidandel, F., Rillo, M.: An accurate adaptation-guided similarity metric for case-based planning. In: Aha, D.W., Watson, I. (eds.) ICCBR 2001. LNCS (LNAI), vol. 2080, pp. 531–545. Springer, Heidelberg (2001)

Case-Based Reasoning Adaptation
for High Dimensional Solution Space

Ying Zhang[1], Panos Louvieris[1], and Maria Petrou[2]

[1] Surrey DTC, University of Surrey, Guildford, UK
[2] Electrical and Electronic Engineering, Imperial College, London, UK
{Y.Zhang, Panos.Louvieris}@surrey.ac.uk, Maria.Petrou@imperial.ac.uk

Abstract. Case-Based Reasoning (CBR) is a methodology that reuses the solutions of previous similar problem to solve new problems. Adaptation is one of the most difficult parts of CBR cycle, especially, when the solution space with multi-dimension. This paper discusses the adaptation of high dimensional solution space and proposes a possible approach for it. Visualisation induced Self Organising Map (ViSOM) is used to map the problem space and solution space first, then a BackPropagation (BP) network is applied to analyse the relations between these two maps. A simple military scenario is used as case study for evaluation.

1 Introduction

Case-Based Reasoning is a methodology that reuses the solutions of previous similar problems to solve the new problems. Adaptation is considered to be one of the most difficult parts of CBR cycle. Wilke and Bergmann classify adaptation into three main types [1]: Null adaptation, transformation adaptation and generative adaptation.

Null adaptation simply applies the solution from the retrieved cases to the target case. It is the approach adopted by a simple Nearest Neighbour (NN) technique and maybe combined with taking the inverse distance weighted mean for K Nearest Neigbours (KNN) when K>1. *Transformation adaptation* modifies the old solution derived from the retrieved cases. There are structural transformations which are based on some function of the target and retrieved case feature vectors, and rule-based transformations. The rules are either elicited from the domain experts or learnt using an induction algorithm. *Generative adaptation* entails deriving the solution to the problem from scratch. The derivation is handled by the case based system, largely independent of the case base. In practical application, all the above adaptation could be combined. A general framework of case adaptation is proposed [13], which can be easily expanded if necessary.

Creating an automatic adaptation mechanism that is able to determine how the solution needs to be modified to fit the new circumstances is a complex affair. Case adaptation generally requires detailed knowledge of both the task and domain at hand. However, adaptation knowledge is not always accessible and available.

The simplest adaptation strategy consists of using adaptation rules to resolve differences and possible conflicts between the old case and the new problem. In order

R.O. Weber and M.M. Richter (Eds.): ICCBR 2007, LNAI 4626, pp. 149–163, 2007.

to overcome the difficulties and limitation of rule-based adaptation, Leake[2] proposed a hybrid case-adaptation process combining memory of previously applied adaptations with rules that are able to find in the system's memory the appropriate information for guiding and implementing the necessary transformation. The system's memory retains not only the transformation operation during any adaptation process, but also a trace of the steps taken during the memory's search. Although considered powerful [3], Leake's approach is limited by the need to consider only one adaptation target at any time. In addition, this approach is not appropriate for CBR systems that have a modest knowledge acquisition capability. This is because the method relies on the availability of substantial adaptation knowledge and its explicit representation. Finally this method also relies on the intensive involvement of the user whenever the system's adaptation knowledge is insufficient. Hanney and Keane[4] proposed building adaptation rules directly from the case-base by analysing the differences between cases and their corresponding solutions, and identifying, if possible, a plausible pattern. Jarmulak et al.[3] also developed an adaptation method based on the use of the CBR knowledge content. Each case in the system's memory is used as a test case and compared with the others in the case-base that are most similar to it. For each comparison made, an adaptation case is constructed. This contains information about the differences between the problems and solutions of the test case and the retrieved cases, as well as the description of the test case and the proposed solution. As a new problem arise, the adaptation case are utilised to estimate the correctness of the proposed solution and suggest the necessary adjustments.

The above mentioned methods are referred as "knowledge-light methods" [5], learn adaptation knowledge from the CBR system's own cases and treat them as sources of knowledge. They initially pre-process the information extracted and, afterwards, pass it to a learning algorithm. The learning algorithm must be designed with respect to the problem domain under investigation and the adaptation goal considered. It transforms the pre-processed knowledge to obtain the required adaptation solution. Knowledge-light adaptation methods must be supported by a significant amount and variety of knowledge contained in the CBR system. Insufficient knowledge can badly affect its performance. Furthermore, the adaptation knowledge obtained from a learning algorithm must be correctly and properly combined with knowledge already stored in the adaptation module, resolving, if necessary, possible contradictory and incompatible situations.

Many CBR systems' solution spaces are only one dimensional, such as the price of a property, the classification of a case etc. But in our project, CBR is applied to find the suitable course of action (COA) for the military scenario. A COA is represented by the entities' waypoints at the corresponding times. Therefore, our case solution space is multi-dimensional. We could simply treat it as several single dimensions, apply the same methodology on each individual dimension and then combine the results. This, however, would treat a COA as a collection of independent decisions. This clearly is not correct. That is why we propose another approach to solve case adaptation in this situation.

The rest of the paper is organised as follows. Section 2 discusses possible normal adaptation approaches. Section 3 introduces Self Organizing Map (SOM) and ViSOM. In section 4, we discuss how to find the target case solution using the techniques outlined in Section 3. In Section 5, we present the experimental design.

Evaluation and results are in section 6. Finally, our discussion and conclusions in section 7.

2 Normal Adaptation Approach

For our system, the easy and direct adaptation approach is based on domain knowledge. We could ask human commanders to revise the suggested solution directly, or adapt retrieved cases using the adaptation rules, which are also based on the domain knowledge acquired from human commanders. Gradually the performance of the system could be improved by adding new cases.

When domain knowledge is not available, a neural network can be used to adapt the retrieved cases automatically. This is the case in our project. In particular, we set up a three layers BP network. The network is trained by using as input the problem space differences between all pairs of cases, while the solution space differences between the corresponding cases are the target output for each pair. For example, suppose there are five cases (C1, C2, C3, C4, and C5). Then the input of the BP network consists of the problem space differences C1-C2, C1-C3, C1-C4, C1-C5, C2-C3, C2-C4, C2-C5, C3-C4, C3-C5 and C4-C5. The target outputs are the solution space differences between the same pairs of cases. Because CBR is based on the idea that similar problems have similar solutions, in this way we could analyse how similar these cases are, and how similar their solutions are. Once the BP network is trained, the problem space difference between the target case and its most similar case is input into the network, and then the solution space difference between these two cases is obtained. Thus the solution of the target case can be achieved.

However, when the case problem space and solution space both are of high dimensionality, the construction of the neural network must be complicated and a large size of cases are required to train the neural network. This is particularly difficult for our project, given only small size training samples we have. To solve this problem, we propose to employ SOM to the case problem space and the solution space first to reduce the size of the BP network. SOM can dramatically reduce the data dimensionality, and help us to visualise the case base as well.

3 SOM and ViSOM

The SOM is an unsupervised neural network algorithm that has been successfully used in a wide variety of applications, such as pattern recognition, image analysis and fault diagnosis etc. The basic algorithm was inspired by the way in which various human sensory impressions are neurologically mapped into the brain such that spatial or other relations among stimuli correspond to spatial relations among the neurons. This is called competitive learning. A SOM consists of two layers of neurons, an input layer with n input nodes, which are according to the n –fold dimensionality of the input vectors, and N output nodes, which are according to the N decision regions, with every input node connected to every output node. All the connections are weighted. A SOM forms a nonlinear projection from a high-dimensionality data manifold onto a low-dimensionality grid. The basic process is as follows.

1.   Initialization: choose the random value of weight vectors of all neurons
2.   Similarity matching: using the dot product or the Euclidean criterion as:

$$d_{ij} = \|x_i - x_j\| = \sqrt{\sum_{n=1}^{N}(x_{in} - x_{jn})^2} \qquad (1)$$

The smaller the Euclidean distance is, the closer the vectors are. Another measure of similarity is base on the inner product of the vectors.

$$\cos\theta = \frac{x^T y}{\|x\|\|y\|} \qquad (2)$$

Where $\|x\| = \sqrt{x^T x}$ is the Euclidean norm of the vector.

The bigger the cosine is, the similar the vectors are. So we can find the best-matching winner $i(x)$ at time t:

$$i(x) = \arg\min_j \|x(t) - w_j\|, \qquad j = 1,2,...,N \qquad (3)$$

3.   Updating: adjust the synaptic weight vectors of all neurons, using the update formula

$$w_j(t+1) = \begin{cases} w_j(t) + \eta(t)[x(t) - w_j(t)] & j \in \Lambda_{i(x)}(t) \\ w_j(t) & otherwise \end{cases} \qquad (4)$$

Where $\eta(t)$ is the learning rate and is the neighborhood function around the winner, the winning unit and its neighbors adapt to represent the input by modifying their reference vectors towards the current input. The amount the units learn will be governed by a neighborhood kernel, which is a decreasing function of the distance of the units from the winning unit on the map lattice. the largest weight adjustment which is positive occurs for the winner, and smaller positive changes are made to adjacent neuron, and so on until at some distance d the weight adjustment go to zero, all these can be implemented by Gaussian function,

$$\Lambda_{i(x)}(t) = \exp(\frac{-d(j)^2}{2\sigma(t)^2}) \qquad (5)$$

Where σ^2 is the variance parameter specifying the spread of the Gaussian function, and it is decreasing as the training progresses.

In order to speed up the computation, Chef Hat function can be used, in which only identical positive weight changes are made to those neurons within the r radius. Continue with these above steps until no noticeable changes.

4. Continuation. Continue with step 2, both $\eta(t)$ and $\Lambda_{i(x)}(t)$ are dynamically during the training, until no noticeable changes are observed. At the beginning of the learning process the radius of the neighborhood is fairly large, but it is made to shrink during learning. This ensures that the global order is obtained already at the beginning, whereas towards the end, as the radius gets smaller, the local corrections of the model vectors in the map will be more specific.

SOM is a very good tool for mapping high-dimensionality data into a low dimensionality feature map, typically of one or two dimensions. However, it does not faithfully portray the distribution of the data and its structure. Several measures can be used to quantify the quality of map for obtaining the best project result. The average quantization error is the average distances between the vector data to their prototypes. Generally, when the size of the map increase, there are more unit to represent the data, therefore each data vector will be closer to its best matching unit, thus the average quantization error will be smaller.

One of the most important beneficial features of SOM is the ability to preserve the topology in the projection. The accuracy of the maps in preserving the topology or neighbourhood relations of the input space has been measured in various ways. Topographic product introduced by Bauer and Pawelzik [6], try to find folds on the maps. Since the SOM approximates the higher dimension of input space by folding itself, topographic product can be an indicator about topographic error. However, it does not differentiate the correct folds following a folded input space and the actually erroneous folds. Kohonen himself proposed another approach to measure the proportion of all data vectors whose first and second best matching unit are not adjacent [7]. This is called topographic error. The smaller the topographic error is, the better the SOM preserves the topology. Generally, the higher dimensionality of input space has, the larger the topographic error is. This is because the increasing difficulty to project units in right order and the dimensionality of the prototype grows too.

There have been some research efforts to enhance topology preservation of SOM. In [8], SOM was trained to minimize the quantization error first, and then minimise the topological error in the second stage. A Double SOM (DSOM) uses dynamic grid structure instead of a static structure, together with the classic SOM learning rules to learn the grid structure of input data [9]. The Expanding SOM (ESOM) preserves not only the neighbourhood information, but also the ordering relationships, by learning the linear ordering through expanding [10].

ViSOM uses a similar grid structures as normal SOM [11]. The difference is, instead of updating the weights of neurons in the neighbourhood of the winner by

$$w_k(t+1) = w_k(t) + \alpha(t)\eta(v,k,t)[x(t) - w_k(t)] \tag{6}$$

where $\eta(v,k,t)$ is the neighbourhood function.

ViSOM updates the neighbourhood according to

$$w_k(t+1) = w_k(t) + \alpha(t)\eta(v,k,t)\left(\ [x(t) - w_v(t)] + [w_v(t) - w_k(t)]\frac{(d_{vk} - \Delta_{vk}\lambda)}{\Delta_{vk}\lambda}\ \right) \tag{7}$$

where $w_v(t)$ is the weight of winning neuron at time t.

d_{vk} is the distance between neurons v and k in the input space

Δ_{vk} is the distance between neurons v and k on the map.

λ is a positive pre-specified resolution parameter, the smaller it is, the higher resolution the map provide.

The key feature of ViSOM is that the distances between the neurons on the map can reflect the corresponding distances in the original data space. The map preserves the inter-neuron distances as well as topology as faithfully as possible.

We employ ViSOM on both the case problem space and the case solution space. Once two ViSOM are set up, the location of cases on the case problem space ViSOM can be used as input while the location of corresponding case on the case solution space ViSOM as output. Because these locations are only two dimensional, the BP network structure is much simpler than one created from directly inputting the original dataset. This approach tries to mimic the case problem space and the case solution space as input and output patterns respectively and map the problem to the solution by weight as the connections.

Instead of using the actual location, an alternative approach is to employ, as input, the location's difference between each case pair of case problem space ViSOM. Likewise, the location's difference between the same case pair of case solution ViSOM is the output.The difference between target case and its nearest case is input to the trained network after the network is trained, in this way the target case location on case solution space map is acquired.

Because the ViSOM can preserve the inter-point distances of the input data on the map, the located nearest case to the target case can be adapted to the target case solution. In our experiment, a 3-layer BP network was used. The input vector has 2 elements. There are 5 neurons in the hidden layer while 2 neurons in the output layer. The transfer function for both layers is tan-sigmoid. The training function is trainlm, the Levenberg-Marquardt algorithm, a very fast training method which is suitable for small network.

4   How to Find the Target Case Solution

After the target case location on the case solution space ViSOM is acquired, if there is a previous case projected on the same location, the solution of this case will be chosen as the target solution. If there are more than one previous cases projected on the location, then the mean of these case solutions will be used as the solution for the target case. However, if there is no previous case projected on this location, how can we find the corresponding high dimensional solution for this exact location? There are several possible solutions as follows.

First, the prototype vector of corresponding node of the case solution space ViSOM can be used. Once the solution space ViSOM is trained, each node has its corresponding prototype vector. As the location of target case on the solution space ViSOM is known, the corresponding node can be regarded as the winning node for the target case solution, therefore its weight can be regarded as the output suggestion.

Second, KNN with distance inverse weight can be used as well. However, instead of distances in the problem space, the distances between target case location and its neighbours in the solution space map are applied.

Third, an approach called kriging [12] which usually get better interpolation result can be used. Kriging is the best linear unbiased estimator. The estimation of an unsampled location is given as the weighted sum of the circumjacent observed pointes. It is unbiased since it tries to have the mean residual or error equal to 0, it is best because it aims at minimizing the variance of the errors. It is a powerful spatial interpolation technique and widely used throughout the earth and environment sciences. Kriging is normally suitable for 2 or 3 dimensional data, so it can not be applied directly on the original dataset. However, our case solution space map is only two dimensional now.

In general, in order to solve the problem we must model the covariance matrix of the random variable which was done by choosing covariance function and calculating all the required co variances form the function by modelling the "variogram" of the function. The variogram $\gamma(h)$ is defined as

$$\gamma(h) = 0.5E[Z(x+h) - Z(x)]^2 \tag{8}$$

Where x and $x+h$ are points in the n (n<4) dimension. For a fixed angel, the variogram indicates how different the values becomes as the distance increases. When the angle is changed, the variograms disclose direction features such as anisotropy [12].

In order to calculate experimental variogram of a solution space with m dimensions, for each dimension, $S_1, S_2, ..., S_m$, a variogram will be created as a function of the distance in the case solution space. Such as:

$$\gamma_1(h) = \frac{1}{2N(h)} \sum_{i=1}^{N(h)} (S_{1\alpha}^i - S_{1\beta}^i)^2 \tag{9}$$

Where $\gamma_1(h)$ is the variogram of first dimension of the solution.

$N(h)$ is the total number of pairs of cases in the solution space map which are separated by a distance h.

$S_{1\alpha}^i$ is the first parameter of solution of case α

$S_{1\beta}^i$ is the first parameter of solution of case β.

case α is h away case β in the case solution space.

Similarly, for the second dimension of case solution, we have

$$\gamma_2(h) = \frac{1}{2N(h)} \sum_{i=1}^{N(h)} (S_{2\alpha}^i - S_{2\beta}^i)^2 \tag{10}$$

And so on.

Actually, Kriging can be used directly on the case problem space map as well, instead of the solution space map. The same varigram formula can be used. The only difference is, this time h is the distance in the problem space map, and $N(h)$ is the total number of pairs of cases in the problem space map which are separated by a distance h.

5 Experiment Design

In our research, we apply CBR to military decision making. When the military commanders face a tactical mission, they will develop a set of COAs to achieve their objective. Generally, it is composed of commands for each entity in the troops. It is difficult to transform these human natural language commands into a form which the computer can understand. We choose MAK VR-Forces [14] as our simulation environment. It provides both a set of Application Program Interfaces (API) for creating computer generated forces and an implementation of those APIs. By using VR-Forces, we can interactively add individual entities to a simulation. The entities may include land vehicles, such as T-80 tank, BTR-80 combat vehicle, BMP-2 infantry fighting vehicle, air entities such as F-16 Falcon fighting aircraft, F/A-18 Hornet aircraft, and surface and subsurface entities such as Landing Craft Air Cushion (LCAC).

Because VR-Forces is our scenario simulation environment, our system directly outputs to it. No matter how complicated a COA is, (e.g. attack hasty, attack deliberately, drawback, remain stationary or occupy), it boils down to a series of movements of the entities in the VR-Forces. So a COA is represented by a series of positions of entities. Once the entities reach the suitable waypoints, they fire automatically. Therefore, we decide to represent a COA by the entities' waypoints and the corresponding times for each entity to reach its waypoint. In other words, a COA is represented by a matrix, quite similar to the synchronization matrix [15] which human commanders apply to decide COAs. The matrix is composed of each entity's waypoint location at different time steps during the scenario. Each row corresponds to one entity and each column at one time step.

In this paper, an example scenario in VR-Forces is presented as a test. In this exercise, four hostile vehicles (BMP2 1, BMP2 3, T80, and BMP2 2) are arrayed behind a minefield. Three platoons (Blue, Red and White) of four tanks each suppress the hostile vehicles, allowing two engineering vehicles to clear the minefield.

The scenario, which is shown by Fig.1, plays out as:

Blue platoon stays in position and fires on hostile forces.

Red platoon advances to waypoint red and provides cover for the engineers.

White platoon advances to waypoint white and provides cover for the engineers.

The engineering entities follow behind Red platoon. When Red platoon is at waypoint red and then hostile forces are destroyed, the engineering entities advance on the minefields to clear them.

5.1 Scenario Representation

In related military CBR systems, cases can be made up of war stories, prior experience, tactics and doctrine [17]. According to domain knowledge, METT-T (Mission, Enemy, Terrain, Troops, and Time) are factors human commanders usually consider in the real battle field. It is very convenient to use these parameters to represent a scenario.

In this simple scenario, the mission, namely to breach the minefield, is fixed. In order to simplify the scenario representation, we currently omit mission, but will include it in the future when it is necessary.

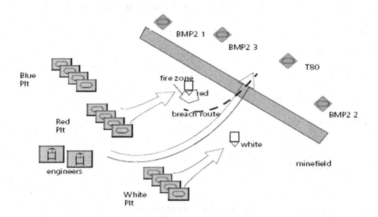

Fig. 1. Breaching Scenario

Each entity may be represented as a symbolic object, but comparing the effectiveness of the opposing sides then is a problem. So instead of representing each troop individually, we combine them together, and use their Scaled Strength Ratio to represent their capabilities. According to domain knowledge, T80 is assigned power 5 while M1A2 is assigned power 6, and BMP2 is assigned power 3 [16].Actually, it is not so easy to estimate an entity's power because its power may be affected by other factors, such as the location of the entity (e.g. even the entity is very powerful, it is useless when it is far away from the target) and the current terrain (e.g. even the most powerful tanks are not a major threat to an enemy on the other side of an impassable river). However, in order to simplify the problem, we currently omit this consideration. Meanwhile, we may treat Combat Effectiveness as ordinal data instead of symbolic. Therefore, "full capability" is represented by 1 while "Inoperable" is represented by 0 and "Degraded" is represented by ½. Then the scaled strength ratio is defined as:

$$\text{Scaled Strength Ratio} = \frac{\sum_{i=1}^{n} T_i C_{ti}}{\sum_{j=1}^{m} E_j C_{ej}} \tag{11}$$

Where T_i is the power assigned to friendly troop i and C_{ti} is its combat effectiveness. E_j is the power assigned to enemy j and C_{ej} is its combat effectiveness.

In VR-FORCES, the whole battle field is covered by a grid. Instead of using long complicated geocentric locations, we can use the grid information to represent an entity's location. The entities which are not exactly at the centre of a grid cell will be assigned to the closest grid cell. The following table shows an example.

We can store the grid information for all the entities as a matrix. If there is no entity in a grid cell, assign 0 to it. Otherwise, put the entity type in that grid cell. In Table 1, we have entities *a* and *b* in the battle field, so the corresponding matrix is:

(0, 0, 0, 0, 0... 0;

0, 0, *a*, 0, 0... 0;

0, 0, 0, 0, 0... 0;

0, 0, 0, 0, *b*... 0;

0, 0, 0, 0, 0... 0;

......

0, 0, 0, 0, 0... 0)

Table 1. Grid representation

0	1	2	3	4	5	..	N
1							
2			a				
3							
4					b		
5							
..							
N							

There are two kinds of enemy entities: BMP2 and T80. The numbers of each type of entity may vary. Suppose we represent BMP2 as 1 and T80 as 2. The enemy force then may be represented by a matrix the elements of which may take values 0, 1 or 2. We consider this type of representation as categorical data.

There is another way to represent the data in Table 1. The entity location can be stored according to the coordinate system used. For example, the entities in Table 1 can be represented by:

a= (3, 2)
b= (5, 4)

This approach is suitable for representing the friendly forces in our experimental scenario. There are four main parts of friendly troops, namely the Blue platoon, the Red platoon, the White platoon and the Engineers. So we can store their locations using the coordinate system. Because the terrain is fixed, only the X and Y axes values are needed. These are continuous data.

Finally, in order to simplify things even more, we omit time in the case representation. Table 2 shows the representation of this scenario.

Table 2. Scenario representation

Scaled Strength Ratio	Enemy Force Matrix (3 X 9)	Blue Platoon (Xb, Yb)	Red Platoon (Xr, Yr)	White Platoon (Xw, Yw)	Engineers (Xe, Ye)

5.2 Case Solution Part

As discussed earlier, COA can be represented by the matrix composed of the entities' waypoint locations at different time steps during the scenario. Each row corresponds to one entity and each column at one time step. For this simple scenario, we use the following four routes to represent the solution part: Blue platoon route, Red platoon route, White platoon route and Engineers route. Each route is composed of five waypoints at corresponding time steps, including the start point and the end point, which can be de derived from the case description part. For each waypoint, because the terrain is fixed, only X and Y are required. Therefore in the solution part we only need to describe another three waypoints, as shown in Table 3. In a more sophisticated version of this scenario, one should also include time to each waypoint to indicate the time in which the troops should reach that waypoint.

5.3 Data Collection

In order to collect data to populate our case base, we randomly choose values for the Scaled Strength Ratio, enemy entities locations and friendly troops entities' locations

Table 3. Troops section route representation

Blue Platoon Route
$(Xb^1, Yb^1), (Xb^2, Yb^2), (Xb^3, Yb^3)$
Red Platoon Route
$(Xr^1, Yr^1), (Xr^2, Yr^2), (Xr^3, Yr^3)$
White Platoon Route
$(Xw^1, Yw^1), (Xw^2, Yw^2), (Xw^3, Yw^3)$
Engineers' Route
$(Xe^1, Ye^1), (Xe^2, Ye^2), (Xe^3, Ye^3)$

to generate the case description part for 300 cases. Then according to each of the case description, we choose a suitable COA based on common sense and simulate it in VR-Forces. We record the result, including factors such as whether the goal was achieved or not, the enemy leftover power, the friendly troops leftover power, etc. The COA with the highest winning value W, which is a weighted function of these factors, will be chosen as the suitable solution.

Because it is impossible to exhaust all possible enemy plans, with different disposition, their waypoints may also be changed. We need to choose cases which are varied and cover most of the variations in the scenario. Fig.2 and Fig.3 show two examples of them.

6 Evaluation

There are not many military decision support systems, and even similar projects are based on different scenario data, so it is difficult to apply benchmarking. The direct approach is based on domain experts, such as military Subject Matter Experts (SME). We can utilize the Turing test on the evaluation cases, and compare the resultant outputs with the suggestions of SMEs. A more practical approach is to simulate the generated COAs in VR-Forces, and find whether the corresponding COA can help the friendly troops to achieve their goal or not. The feedback can be input back to the system to increase its learning ability.

There are 300 cases in our case base. We can divide the case base into two groups: one for training, and the other one for evaluation. Cases in the training group are input to the system for training the ViSOM and the BP networks while cases in the evaluation group will be used to judge how good the outputs are.

In Table 4, normalised average errors for cases in evaluation group are calculated, by comparing the output with the real solution in the case base. Loc-KNN represents using the location of map to train BP, with KNN to acquire the solution. Loc-Proto

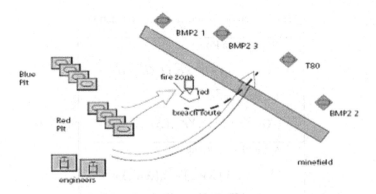

Fig. 2. Breaching exercise variation 1 (White platoon is missing)

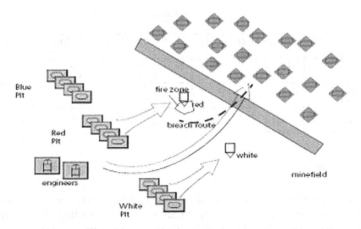

Fig. 3. Breaching exercise variation 2 (Enemy firepower is stronger than that of the friendly troops)

represents using the location of map to train BP, with map prototype vector for the solution. Loc-Krig represents using the location of map to train BP, with Kriging to acquire the solution.

Dif-KNN represents using the location's difference to train BP, with KNN to acquire the solution. Dif-Proto represents using the location's difference to train BP, with map prototype vector for the solution. Dif-Krig represents using the location's difference to train BP, with Kriging to acquire the solution. Kriging represents using kriging directly on the case problem space.

When Kriging is applied, we found this dataset is locally stationary, once we limit the neighbour size to 5, instead of using the whole case problem space to create the variogram, the result become better. The best result is obtained by using case pair location difference to train the BP and chose the prototype vector as the suggested solution.

We can also apply the k-fold cross-validation method [18] to reduce the possible bias which might be caused by the small sample. Table 5 shows the result of k-fold cross-validation, where k is 10 for Dif-Proto. The output COAs of cases in the evaluation group are often not exactly the same as the corresponding COAs stored in the case base. This is because for a given scenario, there is not only one successful COA. If all the waypoints in the suggested COA are reasonable, we think this COA is good, if only one or two waypoints deviate, we think the COA is satisfactory. Otherwise the COA is considered as an error.

Table 4. Experiment Results for all the methods discussed

Method	Loc-KNN	Loc-Proto	Loc-Krig	Dif-KNN	Dif-Proto	Dif-Krig	Kriging
Avg Err	0.435	0.458	0.447	0.421	0.393	0.407	0.396

Table 5. k-fold cross-validation ($k = 10$) for Dif-Proto

	Test1	Test2	Test3	Test4	Test5	Test6	Test7	Test8	Test9	Test10
Good	23	21	22	23	25	24	23	19	26	24
Satisfactory	5	8	3	5	1	4	4	7	2	3
Error	2	1	5	2	4	2	3	4	2	3

7 Conclusion

In this paper, we discuss how to achieve case adaptation for case base with high dimensional solution space. It is a very difficult task, esp. for high dimensional data and limited size of case base. We propose to map problem space and solution space in two different ViSOM. Then analyse the mapping between these two maps. A simple military scenario is used as a test. Although all the case attributes have numeric values in our example dataset. In fact, non-numeric attributes can be converted to numeric first. Thus our approach has the potential to be applied to other datasets as well.

Military application is very demanding area, but CBR is very suitable to mimic decision making process of human commander, thus using CBR to suggest possible COA for military scenario is reasonable. For this simple scenario, the result is promising. However it is still an initial endeavours, further effort need to be paid.

In order to evaluate the generality of this approach, we are looking for other simple direct datasets with high dimensional solution space. Once suitable dataset is available, additional experiments will be processed and further discussed.

References

1. Wilke, W., Bergmann, R.: Techniques and knowledge used for adaptation during case-based problem solving. In: Mira, J.M., Moonis, A., de Pobil, A.P. (eds.) Tasks and Methods in Applied Artificial Intelligence. LNCS, vol. 1416, pp. 497–505. Springer, Heidelberg (1998)
2. Leake, B., Kinley, A., Wilson, D.: Acquiring case adaptation knowledge: a hybrid approach. In: Proceedings of the Thirteenth National Conference on Artificial Intelligence, AAAI Press, Menlo Park, CA (1996)
3. Jarmulark, J., Craw, S., Rowe, R.: Using case-base data to learn adaptation knowledge for design. In: Proceedings of the Seventeenth IJCAI Conference, pp. 1011–1016. Morgan Kaufmann, San Mateo, CA (2001)
4. Hanney, K., Keane, M.T.: The adaptation knowledge: how to easy it by learning from cases. In: Leake, D.B., Plaza, E. (eds.) Case-Based Reasoning Research and Development. LNCS, vol. 1266, pp. 359–370. Springer, Heidelberg (1997)
5. Wilke, W., Vollrath, I., Althoff, K.D., Bergmann, R.: A framework for learning adaptation knowledge based on knowledge light approaches. In: Proceedings of the Fifth German Workshop on Case-Based Reasoning (1997)
6. Bauer, H.U., Pawelzik, K.R.: Quantifying the Neighbourhood Preservation of Self-Organizing Feature Maps. IEEE Transactions on Neural Networks 3(4), 570–579 (1992)

7. Kohonen, T.: Self-Organizing Maps, 3rd edn. Springer Series in Information Sciences, vol. 30. Springer, Heidelberg (2001)
8. Kirk, J.S., Zurada, J.M.: A two-stage algorithm for improved topography preservation n self-organizing maps. In: 2000 IEEE International Conference on Systems, Man, and Cybernetics, IEEE Service Center, 2000, vol.4, pp. 2527–2532 (2000)
9. Su, M.C., Chang, H.T.: A new model of self-organizing neual networks and its application in data projection. IEEE Transactions on Neural Networks 12(1), 153–158 (2001)
10. Jin, H.D., Shum, W.H., Leung, K.S., Wong, M.L.: Expanding Self-Orgainizing Map for data visulaization and cluster analysis. Information Sciences 163, 157–173 (2004)
11. Yin, H.: ViSOM-A Novel Method for Multivariate Data Projection and Structure Visualization. IEEE Transactions on Neural Networks 13(1), 237–243 (2001)
12. Armstrong, M.: Basic Linear geostatistics, pp. 25–57. Springer, Heidelberg (1998)
13. Chang, C.G., Cui, J.J., Wang, D.W., Hu, K.Y.: Research on case adaptation techniques in case-based reasoning. In: Proceeding of the third international conference on Machine Learning and Cybernetics, Shanghai, pp. 26–29 (August 2004)
14. MAK Technologies, MAK VR-Forces 3.7.1 User's Guide
15. Rasch, R., Kott, A., Forbus, K.D.: Incorporating AI into military decision making: an experiment. Intelligent Systems, IEEE 18(4), 18–26 (2003)
16. White, G.: Private communication (2005)
17. Pratt, D.R.: Case Based Reasoning for the Next generation Synthetic Force. Technical Report SAIC-01/7836&00, Science Applications International Corporation, Orlando, FL (2001)
18. Breiman, L., Friedman, J.H., Olshen, R.A., Stone, C.J.: Classification and Regression Trees. Wadsworth, Belmont, CA (1984)

Case-Based Planning and Execution for Real-Time Strategy Games

Santiago Ontañón, Kinshuk Mishra, Neha Sugandh, and Ashwin Ram

CCL, Cognitive Computing Lab
Georgia Institute of Technology
Atlanta, GA 303322/0280
{santi,kinshuk,nsugandh,ashwin}@cc.gatech.edu

Abstract. Artificial Intelligence techniques have been successfully applied to several computer games. However in some kinds of computer games, like real-time strategy (RTS) games, traditional artificial intelligence techniques fail to play at a human level because of the vast search spaces that they entail. In this paper we present a real-time case based planning and execution approach designed to deal with RTS games. We propose to extract behavioral knowledge from expert demonstrations in form of individual cases. This knowledge can be reused via a case based behavior generator that proposes behaviors to achieve the specific open goals in the current plan. Specifically, we applied our technique to the WARGUS domain with promising results.

1   Introduction

Artificial Intelligence (AI) techniques have been successfully applied to several computer games. However, in the vast majority of computer games traditional AI techniques fail to play at a human level because of the characteristics of the game. Most current commercial computer games have vast search spaces in which the AI has to make decisions in real-time, thus rendering traditional search based techniques inapplicable. For that reason, game developers need to spend a big effort in hand coding specific strategies that play at a reasonable level for each new game. One of the long term goals of our research is to develop artificial intelligence techniques that can be directly applied to such domains, alleviating the effort required by game developers to include advanced AI in their games.

Specifically, we are interested in real-time strategy (RTS) games, that have been shown to have huge decision spaces that cannot be dealt with search based AI techniques [2,3]. In this paper we will present a case-based planning architecture that integrates planning and execution and is capable of dealing with both the vast decision spaces and the real-time component of RTS games. Moreover, applying case-based planning to RTS games requires a set of cases with which to construct plans. To deal with this issue, we propose to extract behavioral knowledge from expert demonstrations (i.e. an expert plays the game and our system observes), and store it in the form of cases. Then, at performance time,

R.O. Weber and M.M. Richter (Eds.): ICCBR 2007, LNAI 4626, pp. 164–178, 2007.
© Springer-Verlag Berlin Heidelberg 2007

the system will retrieve the most adequate behaviors observed from the expert and will adapt them to the situation at hand.

As we said before, one of the main goals of our research is to create AI techniques that can be used by game manufacturers to reduce the effort required to develop the AI component of their games. Developing the AI behavior for an automated agent that plays a RTS is not an easy task, and requires a large coding and debugging effort. Using the architecture presented in this paper the game developers will be able to specify the AI behavior just by demonstration; i.e. instead of having to code the behavior using a programming language, the behavior can be specified simply by *demonstrating* it to the system. If the system shows an incorrect behavior in any particular situation, instead of having to find the bug in the program and fix it, the game developers can simply demonstrate the correct action in the particular situation. The system will then incorporate that information in its case base and will behave better in the future.

Another contribution of the work presented in this paper is on presenting an integrated architecture for case-based planning and execution. In our architecture, plan retrieval, composition, adaptation, and execution are interleaved. The planner keeps track of all the open goals in the current plan (initially, the system starts with the goal of winning the game), and for each open goal, the system retrieves the most adequate behavior in the case base depending on the current game state. This behavior is then added into the current plan. When a particular behavior has to be executed, it is adapted to match the current game state and then it is executed. Moreover, each individual action or sub-plan inside the plan is constantly monitored for success or failure. When a failure occurs, the system attempts to retrieve a better behavior from the case base. This interleaved process of case based planning and execution allows the system to reuse the behaviors extracted from the expert and apply them to play the game.

The rest of the paper is organized as follows. Section 2 presents a summary of related work. Then, Section 3 introduces the proposed architecture and its main modules. After that, Section 4 briefly explains the behavior representation language used in our architecture. Section 5 explains the case extraction process. Then sections 6 and 7 present the planning module and the case based reasoning module respectively. Section 8 summarizes our experiments. Finally, the paper finishes with the conclusions section.

2   Related Work

Concerning the application of case-based reasoning techniques to computer games, Aha et al. [2] developed a case-based plan selection technique that learns how to select an appropriate strategy for each particular situation in the game of WARGUS. In their work, they have a library of previously encoded strategies, and the system learns which one of them is better for each game phase. In addition, they perform an interesting analysis on the complexity of real-time strategy games (focusing on WARGUS in particular). Another application of case based reasoning to real-time strategy games is that of Sharma et al. [15], where they present a hybrid case based reinforcement learning approach able to learn which are the best actions to apply in each situation (from a set of high level actions). The main difference between their work and ours is that they learn a case selection policy, while our system constructs plans from the individual cases it has in the case base. Moreover, our architecture automatically extracts the plans from observing a human rather than having them coded in advance.

Ponsen et al [14] developed a hybrid evolutionary and reinforcement learning strategy for automatically generating strategies for the game of WARGUS. In their framework, they construct a set of rules using an evolutionary approach (each rule determines what to do in a set of particular situations). Then they use a reinforcement learning technique called *dynamic scripting* to select a subset of these evolved rules that achieve a good performance when playing the game. There are several differences between their approach and ours. First, they focus on automatically generating strategies while we focus on acquiring them from an expert. Moreover, each of their individual rules could be compared to one of our behaviors, but the difference is that their strategies are combined in a pure reactive way, while our strategies are combined using a planning approach. For our planner to achieve that, we require each individual behavior to be annotated with the goal it pursues.

Hoang et al. [9] propose to use a hierarchical plan representation to encode strategic game AI. In their work, they use HTN planning (inside the framework of Goal-Oriented Action Planning [13]). Further, in [11] Muñoz and Aha propose a way to use case based planning to the same HTN framework to deal with strategy games. Moreover, they point out that case based reasoning provides a way to generate explanations on the decisions (i.e. plans) generated by the system. The HTN framework is very related to the work presented in this paper, where we use the task-method decomposition to represent plans. Moreover, in their work they focus on the planing aspects of the problem while in this paper we focus on the learning aspects of the problem, i.e. how to learn from expert demonstrations.

The work presented in this paper is strongly related to existing work in case-based planning [8]. Case Based Planning work is based on the idea of planning by remembering instead of planning from scratch. Thus, a case based planner retains the plans it generates to reuse them in the future, uses planning failures as opportunities for learning, and tries to retrieve plans in the past that satisfy as many of the current goals as possible. Specifically, our work focuses on an integrated planning and execution architecture, in which there has been little work in the case based planning community. A sample of such work is that of Freßmann et al. [6], where they combine CBR with multi-agent systems to automate the configuration and execution of workflows that have to be executed by multiple agents.

Integrating planning and execution has been studied in the search based planning community. For example, CPEF [12] is a framework for continuous planning and execution. CPEF shares a common assumption with our work, namely that plans are dynamic artifacts that must evolve with the changing environment in

Fig. 1. A screenshot of the WARGUS game

which they are executing changes. However, the main difference is that in our approach we are interested in case based planning processes that are able to deal with the huge complexity of our application domain.

3 Case-Based Planning in WARGUS

WARGUS (Figure 1) is a real-time strategy game where each player's goal is to remain alive after destroying the rest of the players. Each player has a series of troops and buildings and gathers resources (gold, wood and oil) in order to produce more troops and buildings. Buildings are required to produce more advanced troops, and troops are required to attack the enemy. In addition, players can also build defensive buildings such as walls and towers. Therefore, WARGUS involves complex reasoning to determine where, when and which buildings and troops to build. For example, the map shown in Figure 1 is a 2-player version of the classical map "Nowhere to run nowhere to hide", with a wall of trees that separates the players. This maps leads to complex strategic reasoning, such as building long range units (such as catapults or ballistas) to attack the other player before the wall of trees has been destroyed, or tunneling early in the game through the wall of trees trying to catch the enemy by surprise.

Traditionally, games such as WARGUS use handcrafted behaviors for the built-in AI. Creating such behaviors requires a lot of effort, and even after that, the result is that the built-in AI is static and easy to beat (since humans can easily find holes in the computer strategy). The goal of the work presented in this paper is to ease the task of the game developers to create behaviors for these games, and to make them more adaptive. Our approach involves learning behaviors from expert demonstrations to reduce the effort of coding the behaviors, and use the learned behaviors inside a case-based planning system to reuse them for new situations. Figure 2 shows an overview of our case-based planning approach. Basically, we divide the process in two main stages:

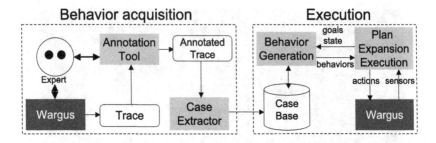

Fig. 2. Overview of the proposed case-based planning approach

- *Behavior acquisition*: During this first stage, an expert plays a game of WARGUS and the trace of that game is stored. Then, the expert annotates the trace explaining the goals he was pursuing with the actions he took while playing. Using those annotations, a set of behaviors are extracted from the trace and stored as a set of cases. Each case is a triple: situation/goal/behavior, representing that the expert used a particular behavior to achieve a certain goal in a particular situation.
- *Execution*: The execution engine consists of two main modules, a real-time plan expansion and execution (RTEE) module and a behavior generation (BG) module. The RTEE module maintains an execution tree of the current active goals and subgoals and which behaviors are being executed to achieve each of the goals. Each time there is an open goal, the RTEE queries the BG module to generate a behavior to solve it. The BG then retrieves the most appropriate behavior from its case base, and sends it to the RTEE. Finally, when the RTEE is about to start executing a behavior, it is sent back to the BG module for adaptation. Notice that this *delayed adaptation* is a key feature different from traditional CBR required for real-time domains where the environment continuously changes.

In the following sections we will present each of the individual components of our architecture.

4   A Behavior Reasoning Language

In this section we will present the Behavior Reasoning Language used in our approach, designed to allow a system to learn behaviors, represent them, and to reason about the behaviors and their intended and actual effects. Our language takes ideas from the STRIPS [5] planning language, and from the ABL [10] behavior language, and further develops them to allow advanced reasoning and learning capabilities over the behavior language.

The basic constituent piece is the *behavior*. A behavior has two main parts: a *declarative* part and a *procedural* part. The declarative part has the purpose of providing information to the system about the intended use of the behavior, and the procedural part contains the executable behavior itself. The declarative part of a behavior consists of three parts:

- A *goal*, that is a representation of the intended goal of the behavior. For every domain, an ontology of possible goals has to be defined. For instance, a behavior might have the goal of "having a tower".
- A set of *preconditions* that must be satisfied before the behavior can be executed. For instance, a behavior can have as preconditions that a particular peasant exists and that a desired location is empty.
- A set of *alive conditions* that represent the conditions that must be satisfied during the execution of the behavior for it to have chances of success. If at some moment during the execution, the alive conditions are not met, the behavior can be stopped, since it will not achieve its intended goal. For instance, the peasant in charge of building a building must remain alive; if he is killed, the building will not be built.

Notice that unlike classical planning approaches, postconditions cannot be specified for behaviors, since a behavior is not guaranteed to succeed. Thus, we can only specify what goal a behavior pursues.

The procedural part of a behavior consists of executable code that can contain the following constructs: *sequence, parallel, action,* and *subgoal*, where an *action* represents the execution of a basic action in the domain of application (a set of basic actions must be defined for each domain), and a *subgoal* means that the execution engine must find another behavior that has to be executed to satisfy that particular subgoal. Specifically, three things need to be defined for using our language in a particular domain:

- A set of *basic actions* that can be used in the domain. For instance, in WARGUS we define actions such as *move, attack,* or *build*.
- A set of *sensors*, that are used in the behaviors to obtain information about the current state of the world. For instance, in WARGUS we might define sensors such as *numberOfTroops*, or *unitExists*. A sensor might return any of the standard basic data types, such as boolean or integer.
- A set of *goals*. Goals can be structured in a specialization hierarchy in order to specify the relations among them.

A goal might have parameters, and for each goal a function *generateSuccessTest* must be defined, that is able to generate a condition that is satisfied only when the goal is achieved. For instance, *HaveUnits(TOWER)* is a valid goal in our gaming domain and it should generate the condition *UnitExists(TOWER)*. Such condition is called the *success test* of the goal. Therefore, the goal definition can be used by the system to reason about the intended result of a behavior, while the success test is used by the execution engine to verify whether a particular behavior succeeds at run time.

Summarizing, our behavior language is strongly inspired by ABL, but expands it with declarative annotations (expanding the representation of goals and defining alive and success conditions) to allow reasoning.

Table 1. Snippet of a real trace generated after playing WARGUS

Cycle	Player	Action	Annotation
8	1	Build(2,"pig-farm",26,20)	-
137	0	Build(5,"farm",4,22)	SetupResourceInfrastructure(0,5,2) WinWargus(0)
638	1	Train(4,"peon")	-
638	1	Build(2,"troll-lumber-mill",22,20)	-
798	0	Train(3,"peasant")	SetupResourceInfrastructure(0,5,2) WinWargus(0)
878	1	Train(4,"peon")	-
878	1	Resource(10,5)	-
897	0	Resource(5,0)	SetupResourceInfrastructure(0,5,2) WinWargus(0)
...	...	...	...

5   Behavior Acquisition in WARGUS

As Figure 2 shows, the first stage of our case-based planning architecture consists of acquiring a set of behaviors from an expert demonstration. Let us present this stage in more detail.

One of the main goals of this work is to allow a system to learn a behavior by simply observing a human, in opposition to having a human encoding the behavior in some form of programming language. To achieve that goal, the first step in the process must be for the expert to provide the demonstration to the system. In our particular application domain, WARGUS, an expert simply plays a game of WARGUS (against the built-in AI, or against any other opponent). As a result of that game, we obtain a game trace, consisting of the set of actions executed during the game. Table 1 shows a snippet of a real trace from playing a game of WARGUS. As the table shows, each trace entry contains the particular cycle in which an action was executed, which player executed the action, and the action itself. For instance, the first action in the game was executed at cycle 8, where player 1 made his unit number 2 build a "pig-farm" at the (26,20) coordinates.

As Figure 2 shows, the next step is to annotate the trace. For this process, the expert uses a simple annotation tool that allows him to specify which goals was he pursuing for each particular action. To use such an annotation tool, a set of available goals has to be defined for the WARGUS domain.

In our approach, a *goal* $g = name(p_1, ..., p_n)$ consists of a goal name and a set of parameters. For instance, in WARGUS, these are some of the goal types we have defined:

- $WinWargus(player)$: representing that the action had the intention of making the player *player* win the game.
- $KillUnit(unit)$: representing that the action had the intention of killing the unit *unit*.

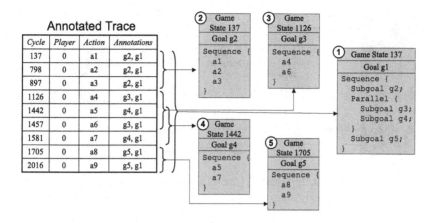

Fig. 3. Extraction of cases from the annotated trace

- *SetupResourceInfrastructure(player, peasants, farms)*: indicates that the expert wanted to create a good resource infrastructure for player *player*, that at least included *peasants* number of peasants and *farms* number of farms.

The fourth column of Table 1 shows the annotations that the expert specified for his actions. Since the snippet shown corresponds to the beginning of the game, the expert specified that he was trying to create a resource infrastructure and, of course, he was trying to win the game.

Finally, as Figure 2 shows, the annotated trace is processed by the *case extractor* module, that encodes the strategy of the expert in this particular trace in a series of cases. Traditionally, in the CBR literature cases consist of a problem/solution pair; in our system we extended that representation due to the complexity of the domain of application. Specifically, a case in our system is defined as a triple consisting of a game state, a goal and a behavior. See Section 7 for a more detailed explanation of our case formalism.

In order to extract cases, the annotated trace is analyzed to determine the temporal relations among the individual goals appearing in the trace. For instance, if we look at the sample annotated trace in Figure 3, we can see that the goal *g2* was attempted *before* the goal *g3*, and that the goal *g3* was attempted *in parallel* with the goal *g4*. The kind of analysis required is a simplified version of the temporal reasoning framework presented by Allen [7], where the 13 basic different temporal relations among events were identified. In our framework, we are only interested in knowing if two goals are pursued in sequence, in parallel, or if one is a subgoal of the other. We assume that if the temporal relation between a particular goal *g* and another goal *g'* is that *g* happens *during g'*, then *g* is a subgoal of *g'*. For instance, in Figure 3, *g2*, *g3*, *g4*, and *g5* happen *during g1*; thus they are considered subgoals of *g1*.

From temporal analysis, procedural descriptions of the behavior of the expert can be extracted. For instance, from the relations among all the goals in Figure 3,

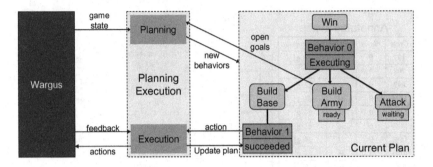

Fig. 4. Interleaved plan expansion and execution

case number 1 (shown in the figure) can be extracted, specifying that to achieve goal $g1$ in the particular game state in which the game was at cycle 137, the expert first tried to achieve goal $g2$, then attempted $g3$ and $g4$ in parallel, and after that $g5$ was pursued. Then, for each one of the subgoals a similar analysis is performed, leading to four more cases. For example, case 3 states that to achieve goal $g2$ in that particular game state, basic actions $a4$ and $a6$ should be executed sequentially.

6   Real-Time Plan Expansion and Execution

During execution time, our system will use the set of cases collected from expert traces to play a game of WARGUS. In particular two modules are involved in execution: a real-time plan expansion and execution module (RTEE) and a behavior generation module (BG). Both modules collaborate to maintain a current *partial plan tree* that the system is executing.

A *partial plan tree* (that we will refer to as simply the "plan") in our framework is represented as a tree consisting of two types of nodes: *goals* and *behaviors* (following the same idea of the task/method decomposition [4]). Initially, the plan consists of a single goal: "win the game". Then, the RTEE asks the BG module to generate a behavior for that goal. That behavior might have several subgoals, for which the RTEE will again ask the BG module to generate behaviors, and so on. For instance, on the right hand side of Figure 4 we can see a sample plan, where the top goal is to "win". The behavior assigned to the "win" goal has three subgoals, namely "build base", "build army" and "attack". The "build base" goal has already a behavior assigned that has no subgoals, and the rest of subgoals still don't have an assigned behavior. When a goal still doesn't have an assigned behavior, we say that the goal is *open*.

Additionally, each behavior in the plan has an associated state. The state of a behavior can be: *pending, executing, succeeded* or *failed*. A behavior is pending when it still has not started execution, and its status is set to failed or succeeded after its execution ends, depending on whether it has satisfied its goal or not.

A goal that has a behavior assigned and where the behavior has failed is also considered to be open (since a new behavior has to be found for this goal).

Open goals can be either *ready* or *waiting*. An open goal is ready when all the behaviors that had to be executed before this goal have succeeded, otherwise, it is waiting. For instance, in Figure 4, "behavior 0" is a sequential behavior and therefore the goal "build army" is ready since the "build base" goal has already succeeded and thus "build army" can be started. However, the goal "attack" is waiting, since "attack" has to be executed after "build army" succeeds.

The RTEE is divided into two separate modules, that operate in parallel to update the current plan: the *plan expansion* module and the *plan execution* module. The plan expansion module is constantly querying the current plan to see if there is any ready open goal. When this happens, the open goal is sent to the BG module to generate a behavior for it. Then, that behavior is inserted in the current plan, and it is marked as pending.

The plan execution module has two main functionalities: a) check for basic actions that can be sent directly to the game engine, b) check the status of plans that are in execution:

- For each pending behavior, the execution module evaluates the preconditions, and as soon as they are met, the behavior starts its execution.
- If any of the execution behaviors have any basic actions, the execution module sends those actions to WARGUS to be executed.
- Whenever a basic action succeeds or fails, the execution module updates the status of the behavior that contained it. When a basic action succeeds, the executing behavior can continue to the next step. When a basic action fails, the behavior is marked as failed, and thus its corresponding goal is open again (thus, the system will have to find another plan for that goal).
- The execution module periodically evaluates the alive conditions and success conditions of each behavior. If the alive conditions of an executing behavior are not satisfied, the behavior is marked as failed, and its goal is open again. If the success conditions of a behavior are satisfied, the behavior is marked as succeeded.
- Finally, if a behavior is about to be executed and the current game state has changed since the time the BG module generated it, the behavior is handed back to the BG and it will pass again through the *adaptation* phase (see Section 7) to make sure that the plan is adequate for the current game state.

7   Behavior Generation

The goal of the BG module is to generate behaviors for specific goals in specific scenarios. Therefore, the input to the BG module is a particular scenario (i.e. the current game state in WARGUS) and a particular goal that has to be achieved (e.g. "Destroy The Enemy's Cannon Tower"). To achieve that task, the BG system uses two separate processes: *case retrieval* and *case adaptation* (that correspond to the first two processes of the 4R CBR model [1]).

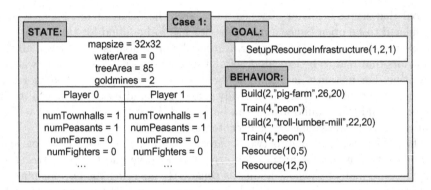

Fig. 5. Example of a case extracted from an expert trace for the WARGUS game

Notice that to solve a complex planning task, several subproblems have to be solved. For instance, in our domain, the system has to solve problems such as how to build a proper base, how to gather the necessary resources, or how to destroy each of the units of the enemy. All those individual problems are different in nature, and in our case base we might have several cases that contain different behaviors to solve each one of these problems under different circumstances. Therefore, in our system we will have an *heterogeneous* case base. To deal with this issue, we propose to include in each case the particular *goal* that it tries to solve. Therefore we represent cases as triples: $c = \langle S, G, B \rangle$, where S is a particular game state, G is a goal, and B is a behavior; representing that $c.B$ is a good behavior to apply when we want to pursue goal $c.G$ in a game state similar to $c.S$.

Figure 5 shows an example of a case, where we can see the three elements: a game description, that contains some general features about the map and some information about each of the players in the game; a particular goal (in this case, building the resource infrastructure of player "1"); and finally a behavior to achieve the specified goal in the given map. In particular, we have used a game state definition composed of 35 features that try to represent each aspect of the WARGUS game. Twelve of them represent the number of troops (number of fighters, number of peasants, and so on), four of them represent the resources that the player disposes of (gold, oil, wood and food), fourteen represent the description of the buildings (number of town halls, number of barracks, and so on) and finally, five features represent the map (size in both dimensions, percentage of water, percentage of trees and number of gold mines).

The case retrieval process uses a standard nearest neighbor algorithm but with a similarity metric that takes into account both the goal and the game state. Specifically, we use the following similarity metric:

$$d(c_1, c_2) = \alpha d_{GS}(c_1.S, c_2.S) + (1 - \alpha)d_G(c_1.G, c_2.G)$$

where d_{GS} is a simple Euclidean distance between the game states of the two cases (where all the attributes are normalized between 0 and 1), d_G is the distance metric between goals, and α is a factor that controls the importance of the game state in the retrieval process (in our experiments we used $\alpha = 0.5$). To measure distance between two goals $g_1 = name_1(p_1, ..., p_n)$ and $g_2 = name_2(q_1, ..., q_m)$ we use the following distance:

$$d_G(g_1, g_2) = \begin{cases} \sqrt{\sum_{i=1...n} \left(\frac{p_i - q_i}{P_i}\right)^2} & \text{if } name_1 = name_2 \\ 1 & \text{otherwise} \end{cases}$$

where P_i is the maximum value that the parameter i of a goal might take (we assume that all the parameters have positive values). Thus, when $name_1 = name_2$, the two goals will always have the same number of parameters and the distance can be computed using an Euclidean distance among the parameters. The distance is maximum (1) otherwise.

The result of the retrieval process is a case that contains a behavior that achieves a goal similar to the requested one by the RTEE, and that can be applied to a similar map than the current one (assuming that the case base contains cases applicable to the current map). The behavior contained in the retrieved case then needs to go through the adaptation process. However, our system requires *delayed adaptation* because adaptation is done according to the current game state, and the game state changes with time. Thus it is interesting that adaptation is done with the most up to date game state (ideally with the game state just before the behavior starts execution). For that reason, the behavior in the retrieved case is initially directly sent to the RTEE. Then, when the RTEE is just about to start the execution of a particular behavior, it is sent back to the BG module for adaptation.

The adaptation process consists of a series of rules that are applied to each one of the basic operators of a behavior so that it can be applied in the current game state. Specifically, we have used two adaptation rules in our system:

- *Unit adaptation*: each basic action sends a particular command to a given unit. For instance the first action in the behavior shown in Figure 5 commands the unit "2" to build a "pig-farm". However, when that case is retrieved and applied to a different map, that particular unit "2" might not correspond to a peon (the unit that can build farms) or might not even exist (the "2" is just an identifier). Thus, the unit adaptation rule finds the most similar unit to the one used in the case for this particular basic action. To perform that search, each unit is characterized by a set of 5 features: owner, type, position (x,y), hit-points, and status (that can be *idle*, *moving*, *attacking*, etc.) and then the most similar unit (according to an Euclidean distance using those 5 features) in the current map to the one specified in the basic action is used.
- *Coordinate adaptation*: some basic actions make reference to some particular coordinates in the map (such as the *move* or *build* commands). To adapt the coordinates, the BG module gets (from the case) how the map in the particular coordinates looks like by retrieving the content of the map in a 5x5 window surrounding the specified coordinates. Then, it looks in the current map for a spot in the map that is the most similar to that 5x5 window, and uses those coordinates.

Table 2. Summary of the results of playing against the built-in AI of WARGUS in several 2-player versions of "Nowhere to run nowhere to hide"

	map1	map2	map3
trace1	3 wins	3 wins	1 win, 1 loss, 1 tie
trace2	1 loss, 2 ties	2 wins, 1 ties	2 losses, 1 tie
trace1 & trace2	3 wins	3 wins	2 wins 1 tie

8   Experimental Results

To evaluate our approach, we used several variations of a 2-player version of the well known map "Nowhere to run nowhere to hide", all of them of size 32x32. As explained in Section 3, this map has the characteristic of having a wall of trees that separates the players and that leads to complex strategic reasonings. Specifically, we used 3 different variations of the map (that we will refer as *map1*, *map2* and *map3*), where the initial placement of the buildings (a gold mine, a townhall and a peasant in each side) varies strongly, and also the wall of trees that separates both players is very different in shape (e.g. in one of the maps it has a very thin point that can be tunneled easily).

We recorded expert traces for the first two variants of the map (that we will refer as *trace1* and *trace2*). Specifically, *trace1* was recorded in *map1* and used a strategy consisting on building a series of ballistas to fire over the wall of trees; and *trace2* was recorded in *map2* and tries to build defense towers near the wall of trees so that the enemy cannot chop wood from it. Each trace contains 50 to 60 actions, and about 6 to 8 cases can be extracted from each of them. Moreover, in our current experiments, we have assumed that the expert wins the game, it remains as future work to analyze how much the quality of the expert trace affects the performance of the system.

We tried the effect of playing with different combinations of them in the three variations of the map. For each combination, we allowed our system to play against the built-in AI three times (since WARGUS has some stochastic elements), making a total of 27 games.

Table 2 shows the obtained results when our system plays only extracting cases from *trace1*, then only extracting cases from *trace2*, and finally extracting cases from both. The table shows that the system plays the game at a decent level, managing to win 17 out of the 27 games it played. Moreover, notice that when the system uses several expert traces to draw cases from, its play level increases greatly. This can be seen in the table since from the 9 games the system played using both expert traces, it won 8 of them and never lost a game, tying only once. Moreover, notice also that the system shows adaptive behavior since it was able to win in some maps using a trace recorded in a different map (thanks to the combination of planning, execution, and adaptation).

Finally, we would like to remark the low time required to train our system to play in a particular map (versus the time required to write a handcrafted behavior to play the same map). Specifically, to record a trace an expert has to play a complete game (that takes between 10 and 15 minutes in the maps we used) and then annotate it (to annotate our traces, the expert required about 25 minutes per trace). Therefore, in 35 to 40 minutes of time it is possible to train our architecture to play a set of WARGUS maps similar to the one where the trace was recorded (of the size of the maps we used). In contrast, one of our students required several weeks to hand code a strategy to play WARGUS at the level of play of our system. Moreover, this are preliminary results and we plan to systematically evaluate this issue in future work. Moreover, as we have seen our system is able to combine several traces and select cases from one or the other according to the current situation. Thus, an expert trace for each single map is not needed.

9 Conclusions

In this paper we have presented a case based planning framework for real-time strategy games. The main features of our approach are a) the capability to deal with the vast decision spaces required by RTS games, b) being able to deal with real-time problems by interleaving planning and execution in real-time, and, c) solving the knowledge acquisition problem by automatically extracting behavioral knowledge from annotated expert demonstrations in form of cases. We have evaluated our approach by applying it to the real-time strategy WARGUS with promising results.

The main contributions of this framework are: 1) a case based integrated real-time execution and planning framework; 2) the introduction of a behavior representation language that includes declarative knowledge as well as procedural knowledge to allow both reasoning and execution; 3) the idea of automatic extraction of behaviors from expert traces as a way to automatically extract domain knowledge from an expert; 4) the idea of heterogeneous case bases where cases that contain solutions for several different problems (characterized as *goals* in our framework) coexist and 5) the introduction of *delayed adaptation* to deal with dynamic environments (where adaptation has to be delayed as much as possible to adapt the behaviors with the most up to date information).

As future lines of research we plan to experiment with adding a case retention module in our system that retains automatically all the adapted behaviors that had successful results while playing, and also annotating all the cases in the case base with their rate of success and failure allowing the system to learn from experience. Additionally, we would like to systematically explore the transfer learning [15] capabilities of our approach by evaluating how the knowledge learnt (both from expert traces or by experience) in a set of maps can be applied to a different set of maps. We also plan to further explore the effect of adding more expert traces to the system and evaluate if the system is able to properly extract knowledge from each of them to deal with new scenarios.

Further, we would like to improve our current planning engine so that, in addition to sequential and parallel plans, it can also handle conditional plans. Specifically, one of the main challenges of this approach will be to detect and properly extract conditional behaviors from expert demonstrations.

Acknowledgements. The authors would like to thank Kane Bonnette, for the java-WARGUS interface; and DARPA for their funding under the Integrated Learning program TT0687481.

References

1. Aamodt, A., Plaza, E.: Case-based reasoning: Foundational issues, methodological variations, and system approaches. Artificial Intelligence Communications 7(1), 39–59 (1994)
2. Aha, D., Molineaux, M., Ponsen, M.: Learning to win: Case-based plan selection in a real-time strategy game. In: Muñoz-Ávila, H., Ricci, F. (eds.) ICCBR 2005. LNCS (LNAI), vol. 3620, pp. 5–20. Springer, Heidelberg (2005)
3. Buro, M.: Real-time strategy games: A new AI research challenge. In: IJCAI'2003, pp. 1534–1535. Morgan Kaufmann, San Francisco (2003)
4. Chandrasekaran, B.: Design problem solving: a task analysis. AI Mag. 11(4), 59–71 (1990)
5. Fikes, R., Nilsson, N.J.: Strips: A new approach to the application of theorem proving to problem solving. Artificial Intellicence 2(3/4), 189–208 (1971)
6. Freßmann, A., Maximini, K., Maximini, R., Sauer, T.: CBR-based execution and planning support for collaborative workflows. In: Muñoz-Ávila, H., Ricci, F. (eds.) ICCBR 2005. LNCS (LNAI), vol. 3620, pp. 271–280. Springer, Heidelberg (2005)
7. Allen, F.G.: Maintaining knowledge about temporal intervals. Communications of the ACM 26(11), 832–843 (1983)
8. Hammond, K.F.: Case based planning: A framework for planning from experience. Cognitive Science 14(3), 385–443 (1990)
9. Hoang, M., Lee-Urban, S., Muñoz-Avila, H.: Hierarchical plan representations for encoding strategic game ai. In: Proceedings of Artificial Intelligence and Interactive Digital Entertainment Conference (AIIDE-05), AAAI Press, Stanford (2005)
10. Mateas, M., Stern, A.: A behavior language for story-based believable agents. IEEE intelligent systems and their applications 17(4), 39–47 (2002)
11. Muñoz-Avila, H., Aha, D.: On the role of explanation for hierarchical case-based planning in real-time strategy games. In: Funk, P., González Calero, P.A. (eds.) ECCBR 2004. LNCS (LNAI), vol. 3155, Springer, Heidelberg (2004)
12. Myers, K.L.: CPEF: A continuous planning and execution framework. AI Magazine, 20(4) (1999)
13. Orkin, J.: Applying goal-oriented action planning to games. In: AI Game Programming Wisdom II. Charles River Media (2003)
14. Ponsen, M., Muñoz-Avila, H., Spronck, P., Aha, D.: Automatically acquiring adaptive real-time strategy game opponents using evolutionary learning. In Proceedings of the 20th National Conference on Artificial Intelligence and the Seventeenth Innovative Applications of Artificial Intelligence, pp. 1535–1540 (2005)
15. Sharma, M., Homes, M., Santamaria, J., Irani, A., Isbell, C., Ram, A.: Transfer learning in real time strategy games using hybrid CBR/RL. In: IJCAI'2007, page to appear, Morgan Kaufmann, San Francisco (2007)

Case Authoring: From Textual Reports to Knowledge-Rich Cases

Stella Asiimwe[1], Susan Craw[1], Bruce Taylor[2], and Nirmalie Wiratunga[1]

[1] School of Computing
[2] Scott Sutherland School
The Robert Gordon University, Aberdeen, Scotland, UK
{sa, S.Craw, nw}@comp.rgu.ac.uk, B.Taylor@rgu.ac.uk

Abstract. SmartCAT is a Case Authoring Tool that creates knowledge-rich cases from textual reports. Knowledge is extracted from the reports and used to learn a concept hierarchy. The reports are mapped onto domain-specific concepts and the resulting cases are used to create a hierarchically organised case-based system. Indexing knowledge is acquired automatically unlike most textual case-based reasoning systems. Components of a solution are attached to nodes and relevant parts of a solution are retrieved and reused at different levels of abstraction. We evaluate SmartCAT on the SmartHouse domain looking at the usefulness of the cases, the structure of the case-base and the retrieval strategy in problem-solving. The system generated solutions compare well with those of a domain expert.

1 Introduction

Creating a case-based reasoning system can be quite challenging if the problem-solving experiences are captured as unstructured or semi-structured text [13]. This is because the system should be able to compare new problems with the textual case knowledge. Although IR-based techniques can be used to retrieve whole documents or snippets of documents, case comparison in this situation would only take place at word/phrase level. The features pertaining to the documents would still have to be compared using some domain/background knowledge or lexical source, in order to arrive at a useful ranking. Alternatively, a structured case representation can be created and the textual sources mapped onto it before they are used in reasoning [15]. This is quite difficult and the costs can be prohibitive if it is manually done by an expert.

It has been observed that humans do not interpret text at word-level but do so at a much higher level of abstraction where concepts are manipulated [4]. For example, an occupational therapist that reads about a *wheelchair user* immediately thinks about the person's *mobility*. Hierarchical organisation of cases enables effective retrieval at different levels of problem abstraction [2]. The humans' ability to organise information into concepts, in order to extract meaning that is beyond the words they read, is what we attempt to mimic in our work.

Our Case Authoring Tool SmartCAT creates knowledge-rich cases from textual SmartHouse reports. Figure 1 shows the expert interacting with SmartCAT to sanction authored cases. SmartCAT uses the information embedded in text to learn a concept

R.O. Weber and M.M. Richter (Eds.): ICCBR 2007, LNAI 4626, pp. 179–193, 2007.

hierarchy. During case authoring, it maps the textual reports onto appropriate domain-specific concepts. SmartH-CBR is the resulting SmartHouse case-based reasoning system where the cases are organised in a hierarchy. In this paper, we examine the usefulness of the SmartCAT cases and the goodness of the SmartH-CBR retrieval strategy.

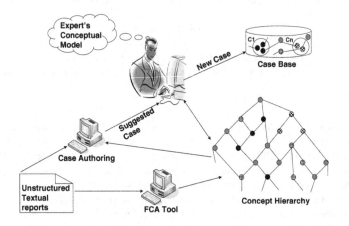

Fig. 1. Using the SmartCAT Tool

The rest of the paper is organised as follows. Related work is presented in Section 2 after which we describe the domain in Section 3. Section 4 details how relevant terms are extracted from the textual reports and used to represent the sub-problems. Section 5 presents the creation of the concept hierarchy which is used to organise the cases in Section 6. The usefulness of the cases and the adopted retrieval strategy are evaluated in Section 7 before our concluding remarks in Section 8.

2 Related Work

Early TCBR systems like FAQ Finder [5] retrieved whole unstructured documents or document snippets as cases. IR-based retrieval was typically employed and understanding case content was not a system requirement. More recent research has focused on creating more knowledge-rich case representations. One approach maps the textual case documents to a structured case representation, but in much of this work the case representations are acquired manually. This renders the systems more difficult to maintain. Examples include Wiratunga et. al.'s work [14] and systems created using frameworks like jCOLIBRI [10]. Further efforts have tried to acquire case representations automatically. Sophia [7] employs term distribution to create word-groups that co-occur in similar documents and the word clusters can represent the textual documents.

In domains like SmartHouse where adaptation knowledge is difficult to acquire, the effectiveness of the retrieval stage of CBR is also crucial. Both Bergmann & Wilke and Watson & Perera demonstrate that cases represented as a hierarchy of smaller cases lead to more efficient retrieval than using a simple flat case representation [2,12].

Déjà Vu [11] is a hierarchically organised system that designs plant-control software. Leaf nodes are tagged with sub-solutions. However, identifying abstract cases and discovering the relationships between them is done manually. We address this shortcoming by creating a concept hierarchy which enables us to automatically author cases and organise them in a hierarchy. Our earlier work was a first step towards building a concept hierarchy [1]. The availability of more reports allows us to incorporate Latent Semantic Indexing to identify relevant attributes for Formal Concept Analysis.

3   The SmartHouse Domain

SmartHouse problem-solving experiences are recorded as textual reports. Each report captures the problems/impairments of the person with disabilities and the SmartHouse devices that were installed in their home to assist them in carrying out different tasks. Figure 2 is an excerpt from a typical report. First, it briefly summarises the person's disabilities which are referred to as a type of *problem, difficulty, impairment,* or a disabling medical condition like *dementia.* Thus, a person with *impaired hearing* is referred to as having a *hearing difficulty, problem* or *impairment.* To distinguish disabilities from other terms in the text we refer to them as *disability terms.*

Ms M was a powered wheelchair user with very limited mobility. She had severe curvature of the spine, and this disability created difficulty when she attempted to carry out everyday tasks around her home. A number of problems were identified:

Door Opening

*Ms M did have a door-key fitted to a special fob that allowed her to unlock or lock her door, but once it was locked, she found it physically impossible to open the door due to her **mobility problem**...... and the final choice of equipment consisted of:*

Lighting Controls

The use of lighting controls was limited to two table lamps in the livingroom and one lamp in the bedroom... The lights were simply switched off or on by the operation of the GEWA control unit.

Door Opening Motor and Lock Release

These devices were intended to allow Ms M to unlock and open her door unaided...

Fig. 2. Report Excerpt

Next, sub-problem sections describe ways in which the person's disabilities manifest themselves. Each is dedicated to a given area of difficulty. The excerpt shows a sub-problem where the person found *door opening* to be cumbersome. Every sub-problem is given a summary heading, but they do not always accurately describe the area of difficulty. *Intercom operation* may refer to a person's difficulty in using their intercom but this could be due to a *hearing impairment* or a *mobility problem.* Typically, the person's disabilities are mentioned in the summary but these need not be repeated in the sub-problem text where symptoms and problem-areas are elaborated. The summary and all sub-problems make up the problem-part of each SmartHouse case. Each section that describes an area of difficulty is called a *sub-problem* since they describe only a part of the SmartHouse case problem.

Lastly, the report mentions the solution package which lists the SmartHouse devices, each with a description of how they help. Although it is not always obvious from the text, every sub-problem has a corresponding list of solutions. This is not always a 1-1 mapping because a particular sub-problem can generate the need for more than one SmartHouse device. However, it is possible to map each sub-problem to its correspond-ing solution components. In Figure 2 *Door Opening Motor and Lock Release* is the so-lution for the *Door Opening* sub-problem. A report records one or more sub-problems with accompanying solutions.

4   Identifying Relevant Terms

It is important for SmartHouse cases to capture useful problem features if they are to be re-used in problem-solving. However, the effectiveness of a case-based reasoning system also depends on its ability to compare cases. This requirement influences the choice of case representation. It has been observed that humans interpret text at a con-cept level and not merely at the level of words they read [4]. In fact, an occupational therapist will list problem features under predefined domain-specific concepts. For ex-ample the problem-features *uses walking sticks* and *abnormal gait* will be recorded under a *mobility* concept. Therefore, not only do our cases need to capture relevant do-main knowledge, we also need to be able to map the knowledge onto domain-specific concepts where concepts are useful groupings of disabilities, disabling conditions, or areas of difficulty.

In order to author cases that capture the relevant domain knowledge and allow for effective comparison and retrieval, we need to do the following steps:

1. extract knowledge embedded in the text and represent the textual reports with knowledge-rich terms;
2. use the knowledge to create a concept hierarchy;
3. map the problem representations onto the domain-specific concepts; and
4. attach solutions to the appropriate parts of the hierarchy.

In the real world, queries are lists of problem descriptors for which a list of Smart-House devices is sought. Therefore, we focus on creating problem concepts for the SmartHouse domain. Thus cases will be represented as groups of domain-specific prob-lem concepts and a corresponding list of SmartHouse devices that solve the problems. We start by trying to identify and extract terms that are meaningful with respect to SmartHouse problems. We will then use these terms to represent the problem parts of the textual reports.

4.1   Term Extraction from Textual Reports

We extract information in the form of trigrams, bigrams and a few necessary unigrams, since single words do not generally carry useful knowledge about the SmartHouse do-main. This is to ensure that only potentially knowledge-rich text is mined for domain-specific concepts. First, we carry out some pre-processing where, each problem part of a report is separated into sentences. A sentence is taken to be a group of words that is separated by a period, comma, bracket or other delimiting punctuation. Non-alphanumeric and numeric characters are removed next and the final pre-processing step applies the UEA-Lite [6] conservative stemmer that ensures words are reduced to forms that are complete words. The main aim is to make the case representations and the nodes in the concept hierarchy easy to comprehend and to allow manual refinement. Next, terms are obtained from each sentence as follows:

1. All word subsequences of length 3 (trigrams) are extracted, discarding all that begin or end with a stopword.
2. All word subsequences of length 2 (bigrams) are extracted, discarding all that begin or end with a stopword or are substrings of trigrams.
3. All non-stopword unigrams are extracted, discarding all that are sub-strings of trigrams or bigrams.

It should be noted that we discard only those terms that are substrings of other terms in the **same** sentence. This is to avoid unnecessary duplication, but at the same time ensuring that short terms are not discarded just because they happen to be sub-strings of terms that appear in other parts of the document. While limiting the incorporation of single-word terms, the process ensures that every word in the document can be represented as itself or as a part of a longer phrase. The assumption here is that in any given sentence, a single word is unlikely to occur independently of short phrases in which it occurs. For example in the sentence "*Case knowledge is a key knowledge source in case based reasoning*", phrases like "*case knowledge*" and "*case based reasoning*" will be extracted and the single word "*case*" will be ignored since it is a substring of the two phrases and can therefore be assumed not to occur independently of the two phrases. However, "*case*" will be extracted if it appears in a sentence like "*A case is made up of a problem and solution part*". The problem part of each SmartHouse report is transformed into a set of terms containing stemmed words. The terms may contain stopwords but will not start or end with one. Extracted terms are meaningful because they have not been distorted by the removal of stopwords. We obtain 731 terms from 38 problems. These terms will be filtered to obtain those that actually contain useful knowledge.

4.2 Latent Semantic Indexing

We make use of Latent Semantic Indexing (LSI) [3] to identify useful terms out of the trigrams, bigrams and unigrams we have extracted. The problem part of a SmartHouse report is regarded as a *document* because we identify useful terms by learning their associations at case level. We represent the terms and the documents as an incidence term $\times$ document matrix A. Entry a_{ij} is the product of a local log frequency weighting and a global log entropy weighting of a term i in document j.

$$a_{ij} = \log_2(f_{ij} + 1)(1 - \sum_{k=1}^{N} \frac{P_{ik} \log_2(P_{ik})}{\log_2(N)})$$

where f_{ij} is the frequency of term i in document j, and P_{ik} is the relative frequency of term i in document k, compared to the collection of N documents.

LSI employs Singular Value Decomposition to decompose the term × document $m \times n$ matrix A as:

$$A_{(m \times n)} = U_{O_{(m \times m)}} \times S_{O_{(m \times n)}} \times V_{O_{(n \times n)}}^{T}$$

U_O represents the term matrix, V_O^T the document matrix, and S_O is a diagonal matrix containing singular values arranged in descending order. Each column in U_O represents a *topic* or *concept* and it captures terms that appear in that concept. The r highest singular values identify the r most important concepts in U_O. These r concepts are referred to as *LSI-concepts* in order to disambiguate them from later concepts in the paper. Keeping only the r highest singular values removes noisy dimensions and gives the lower rank approximation $\tilde{A}$, of the original matrix A.

$$\tilde{A}_{(m \times n)} = U_{(m \times r)} \times S_{(r \times r)} \times V_{(r \times n)}^{T} \qquad \text{(shaded in Figure 3.)}$$

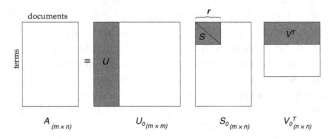

Fig. 3. Singular Value Decomposition and Latent Semantic Indexing

We accentuate the entries of $U_{(m \times r)}$ by multiplying it by $S_{(r \times r)}$ to obtain a *term × concept* matrix. The weights of terms in the matrix are a measure of the importance of the individual terms to the key LSI-concepts in the document collection. We use the top ten singular values ($r = 10$). Figure 4 illustrates a portion of the *term × concept* matrix obtained for the SmartHouse domain. The term *mobility problem* is most important in concept *C4* (weight *8.02*) and least important in concept *C2* (weight *-1.74*). It is the '*importance*' score and the groupings of terms as *LSI-concepts* that we exploit in order to identify knowledge-rich terms.

4.3   Term Filtering

We reduce the search space for finding relevant terms by making use of term weights in key LSI-concepts. In this domain, the areas of difficulty described in each sub-problem are a result of the person's disabilities and this helps us to target our search for relevant terms to only those terms that are related to disability terms. Pattern-matching with the words *difficulty*, *problem* and *impairment* and a list of disabling conditions are used to identify the disability terms. The list is compiled using brochures from the website of Tunstall, a leading provider of telecare solutions. The assumption we make here is that

	C1	C2	C3	C4	...	Cn
risk from fire	7.29	1.79	0.85	-1.93	...	0.76
weak grip	-0.36	1.28	1.48	6.55	...	0.87
unable to hear	0.31	6.11	0.71	-1.47	...	-1.98
mobility problem	**0.92**	**-1.74**	**1.12**	**8.02**	...	**2.51**
wheelchair	0.87	0.36	1.08	7.53	...	2.46
dementia	7.48	1.69	0.96	0.86	...	0.69
door open	1.39	1.30	1.87	6.95	...	2.30

Fig. 4. Term-Concept Matrix Showing Term Importance

"in a linear combination of terms in which the disability term is important, all other terms that are nearly as important, will be relevant to the disability." Thus disability terms are used as anchor terms to identify relevant terms.

We shall use the example in Figure 2 to illustrate the term filtering process. Consider the section describing the *door opening* sub-problem. The underlying disability is mentioned here as a *mobility problem*. Therefore terms that are relevant to the *door opening* problem are closely related to the disability term *mobility problem*. In Figure 4 we take the row in the *term × concept* matrix that represents the term *mobility problem* and look for the LSI-concept in which it has the highest weight. In the example, this is concept *C4*. We then set a threshold and extract terms whose weights are nearly as high in this concept. So the terms *wheelchair*, *weak grip* and *door open* are identified as being important. We look for those terms that *actually* appear in the sub-problem text. These will be the representative terms for this sub-problem. The effect is that we extract terms that are 'important' in LSI-concepts in which the disability term is *most important*. Thus we extract terms that are as informative as the disability term. This leaves only 238 terms rather than the 731 we had originally.

A sample of the discovered relevant terms is compared to text where an expert was asked to highlight key phrases. Figure 5 shows (stemmed) text highlighted in bold by the expert and LSI respectively for one sub-problem. The different n-grams are underlined in the latter case. Generally, the text highlighted using LSI compares very well with that highlighted by the expert. Although the expert does not highlight the heading *door open*, it clearly is an important term since both the expert and LSI agree that *difficult to open the door* is important in that context. It is not possible for LSI to highlight the whole term *poor flexibility in the joint* as important since the terms it is presented with are not more than 3 words long (trigrams). However, it highlights the important parts of the term.

We use the relevant terms obtained to represent the sub-problems. We also include the disability terms among the sub-problem representative terms since they may not be explicitly repeated in the description.

Expert's Highlighting

---

door open

when mr. M wish to open the front door, he had to project himself forward to **reach the door handle and lock.** *because of* **poor flexibility in the joint,** *he found this task to be extremely difficult and physically tiring.* *also, the* **position of the lock** *made it both* **difficult to open the door** *from the inside upon leave, or from the outside when return home.*

LSI Highlighting

---

door open

when mr. M wish to open the front door, he had to project himself forward to <u>**reach the door**</u> <u>**handle and lock.**</u> *because of* <u>**poor flexibility**</u> *in the* <u>**joint,**</u> *he found this task to be extremely* <u>**difficult and physically tiring.**</u> *also, the* <u>**position of the lock**</u> *made it both* <u>**difficult to open the door**</u> *from the inside upon leave, or from the outside when return home.*

Fig. 5. Text Highlighted by Expert and LSI

5   Creation of a Concept Hierarchy

Concept-superconcept relationships do not exist in the semantic structure captured by LSI. However, Formal Concept Analysis (FCA) yields a concept hierarchy where the concepts are ordered according to their concept-superconcept relationships. We employ FCA to create a concept hierarchy using the knowledge we have extracted using LSI. A brief description of FCA and how its use to create the concept hierarchy now follows.

5.1   Formal Concept Analysis

FCA is used to represent and analyse data in information science [8,9]. A formal context is a triple (O, A, I) where O is a set of objects, A a set of attributes and $I \subseteq O \times A$ is a binary incidence relation between O and A. I indicates which objects have which attributes. A formal context is often represented as in Figure 6. The different SmartHouse sub-problems form the set of objects, and some possible features of the sub-problems form the set of attributes. For example *telephone operation* has an attribute *hearing impairment* arising from a person with a *hearing impairment* who has difficulties operating their telephone. FCA uses a formal context to produce formal concepts.

A concept is a pair $(o \subseteq O, a \subseteq A)$ such that every object in o is described by every attribute in a and conversely, every attribute in a covers every object in o. In Figure 6, the set of objects {*intercom operation, window operation, door operation*} have the set of attributes {*mobility problem*} in common. Conversely, the set of attributes {*mobility problem*} shares a common set {*intercom operation, window operation, door operation*} of objects to which they belong. No other object has this set of attributes.

The concept lattice resulting from the context in Figure 6 is shown in Figure 7. Every node represents a concept and the nodes are ordered by a concept-subconcept relationship. The highest node represents the most general concept while the lowest one represents the most specific concept. So as you descend the hierarchy and therefore

ATTRIBUTES

OBJECTS	hearing impairment	wheelchair	mobility problem	poor flexibility in the joints	unable to stretch	cerebral palsy	lack of strength in hands	multiple sclerosis
intercom operation		X	X		X	X		
telephone operation	X							
window operation			X				X	X
door opening			X	X				

Fig. 6. Context for some SmartHouse Problems

become more specific (and less general), the number of objects at a node reduces while the number of attributes increases. Conversely, the number of objects increases and the number of attributes reduces as one ascends the hierarchy.

The objects associated with a concept are called its extent, and the attributes describing the concept are called its intent. Node 1 is the concept created as a result of the object set {*intercom operation, window operation, door operation*} having a common set of attributes {*mobility problem*} and the set of attributes {*mobility problem*} covering a common set of objects {*intercom operation, window operation, door operation*}. This concept has intent {*mobility problem*} and extent {*intercom operation, window operation, door operation*}. Similarly, the concept shown as node 2 has intent {*hearing impairment*} and extent {*telephone operation*}.

To prevent cluttering, reduced labeling is used. An attribute is attached to the topmost concept that has the attribute in its intent. The attribute occurs in all intents of concepts that are reachable by descending the subtree from which it is attached. Node 3 represents a concept whose intent is {*mobility problem, lack of strength in hands, multiple sclerosis*}. Conversely, an object is attached to the bottom-most concept where it is part of the extent. Every concept that is reachable by ascending from this point to the top-most concept has the object in its extent. Node 1 represents a concept whose extent is {*intercom operation, window operation, door operation*}. A description of how we obtain the objects and attributes for use in FCA now follows.

5.2 FCA Objects and Attributes

Each FCA object and associated attributes result in a concept and super-concepts if the object has common attributes with other objects. Each sub-problem of a SmartHouse report represents a specific need for a set of SmartHouse devices. We want to create a hierarchy of concepts pertaining to people's areas of difficulty which are described in the sub-problems. It is for this reason that we use each sub-problem as an FCA object. For easy identification, we name the FCA objects using the problem summary heading

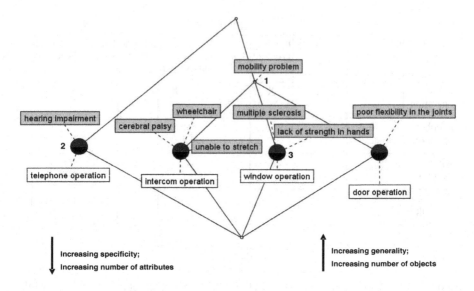

Fig. 7. Example Lattice

and the underlying disability. Thus the objects can be easily identified in the lattice which in turn, makes it easier for an expert to refine the hierarchy as necessary.

FCA attributes are features of the FCA objects. Each sub-problem is an FCA object and it follows that the terms describing the objects are used as FCA attributes. Thus the sub-problem representative terms identified using LSI, and the corresponding disability term, become the attributes for the sub-problem FCA objects. FCA is applied to a context of attributes and their corresponding objects to create a concept hierarchy.

6   Case Representation and Organisation

The concept hierarchy is used to define and organise cases in the SmartHouse domain. Figure 8 shows a portion of the SmartHouse problem concept hierarchy we have built. Normally, an occupational therapist would record a person's disabilities, problem areas and symptoms, under pre-defined groupings: *wheelchair* would be recorded under *mobility*; *learning difficulties* under *cognitive problems*. Similarly, the case representation task involves mapping the problem-representative terms onto the discovered concepts in the hierarchy and attaching a set of solutions that assists with the problem.

We map each sub-problem on to a concept by finding one whose *whole* intent is *all* of the sub-problem's representative terms. Node 5 in Figure 8 represents a concept whose intent is {*mobility problem, door open, reach the door handle and lock, poor flexibility, joint, difficult and physically tiring, position of the lock, difficult to open the door*}. This intent is also *all* the terms identified using LSI in the *door opening* sub-problem illustrated in Figure 5 plus the corresponding disability term. Thus the *door opening* sub-problem is mapped on to the concept represented by node 5. We shall use the term *concrete* to refer to those concepts onto which a sub-problem is

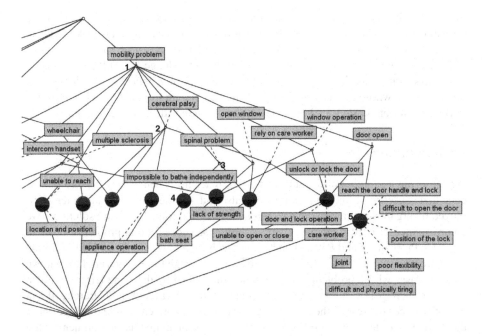

Fig. 8. Concept Activation During Retrieval

mapped. Concrete concepts include all of the most specific concepts in the hierarchy, and some abstract concepts whose intent *completely* represents a sub-problem in the document collection. We also refer to abstract concepts on to which no sub-problem is mapped, as *completely-abstract*. Mapping each sub-problem on to a concept transforms the problem-part of the original textual case to a list of concrete concepts. A case that contains n sub-problems is mapped onto n concrete concepts in the concept hierarchy.

We map each sub-problem on to a corresponding list of SmartHouse devices by making use of overlaps between the words in the sub-problem and solution description text. We also take advantage of device names because sometimes they reflect the sub-problems they assist with. For example, *Door Opening Motor and Lock Release* in Figure 2 is the solution to the *door opening* sub-problem mentioned in the report excerpt. Thus we map each sub-problem and invariably each concrete concept on to a list of SmartHouse devices. Consequently, a case becomes a list of concrete concepts each of which is tagged with a list of SmartHouse devices that solve the different sub-problems. All this is implemented in a case-based reasoning system called SmartH-CBR.

During problem-solving, the concept hierarchy is searched for the most specific concepts matching the query terms. Ideally, a concept is activated by a query term that forms part of its intent. However, since a query term cannot always be the same as that in the intent, substring matching of the query and intent strings is used to ensure that the two need not be exactly the same for a concept to be activated. A path ending at a concrete concept node leads to retrieval of the attached solution. However, when a path ends at a completely-abstract node, it is not possible to predict the next point in the path without further knowledge about the problem. In this situation, SmartH-CBR returns the **disjunction** of all solutions of concrete concepts that are reachable by descending the subtree from which the completely-abstract concept is attached. If all we knew about a problem was that the person has *cerebral palsy* and a *mobility problem*, nodes 1 and 2 in Figure 8 would be activated. Without any further knowledge, it is difficult to predict if the person also has a *door opening* problem, an *appliance operation* problem or any other problem whose concepts are reachable by descending from node 2. Generally, the retrieved solution depends on how much of the problem is described in the query.

7 Evaluation

We judge the usefulness of the authored cases by testing whether they capture knowledge that is useful for finding solutions. We also test whether the retrieval strategy employed by organising the cases in a hierarchy results in retrieval of useful solutions. We compare SmartH-CBR's and the expert's solution packages for four problems shown in Figure 9. Problems A and B were handcrafted by the expert who ensured the description terms were the same as the ones in the case base. Although these terms are familiar, we have no cases whose problems are completely described by the same terms. Problem C is a problem part of a report that is excluded in the creation of the hierarchy. It is a test of whether the rest of the cases in the case base capture enough knowledge about the domain in order to give useful solutions to this problem that has not influenced the case representation. It is also a test of SmartH-CBR's ability to find appropriate parts of useful cases in order to reuse them for problem-solving. Problem D is another test of the same sort as Problem C. Hence, problems C and D are more challenging.

Problem A	window opening, door opening, spinal problem, wheelchair user, unable to bathe independently
Problem B	cognitive problems, aphasia, confusion, disorientation, fully ambulant, perseveration, no insight into condition
Problem C	intercom operation, unable to hear buzzer, telephone operation, problem hearing the caller, unable to listen to television, can only watch pictures on television
Problem D	paralysis, ataxia, chair bound, body constricted, poor hand to eye coordination, left sided weakness, copious aspiration

Fig. 9. Test Problems

Sometimes the occupational therapist has a list of terms describing the person's complications and she is required to *anticipate* the needs of the person. Therefore, we test the system's ability to recognise terms as belonging to given sub-problems and subsequently retrieving their solutions. In problems B and D, the person's complications are given but the specific needs like *door* or *window opening* are not enumerated. This makes the problems harder to solve than those where the specific needs can be targeted in the search for a solution. Thus problem B is harder to solve than A and problem D is harder than C.

SmartH-CBR attempts to index each problem in order to retrieve the appropriate so-lutions. The possession of features that are familiar to SmartH-CBR makes problems *A* and *B* easier to index than problems *C* and *D*. Figure 10 illustrates the solution packages offered by SmartH-CBR and the expert for problems *A*, *B*, *C* and *D*. The similarity of solutions for SmartH-CBR and the expert are compared using precision and recall. In the SmartHouse domain, precision is the proportion of SmartHouse devices proposed by SmartH-CBR that occur in the expert solution package; recall is the proportion of devices proposed by the expert that are also proposed by SmartH-CBR. Recall is more important than precision because SmartHouse solution recommendation is typically a supervised task. An occupational therapist prefers to be presented with a list of devices to choose from than to have a list of devices that perfectly solve only a part of the prob-lem and be required to formulate the rest of the solution from scratch. Altogether, there are 38 composite cases (reports) and 90 sub-problems, each of which can be solved by one or more SmartHouse devices.

Solution A	CBR	Expert
powered windows	Yes	Yes
powered external doors	Yes	Yes
community alarm	Yes	No
electrically operated locks	Yes	Yes
environmental controls	Yes	No
shower with sitting facility	Yes	Yes
Precision = 0.7	**Recall = 1.0**	

Solution C	CBR	Expert
video intercom	No	Yes
visual doorbell	Yes	Yes
telephone amplifying unit	Yes	Yes
video interface to telephone	No	Yes
television/audio amplifying headset	Yes	Yes
Precision = 1.0	**Recall = 0.6**	

Solution B	CBR	Expert
smoke/heat/gas alarms	Yes	Yes
stove shutoff isolator	Yes	Yes
intelligent microwave	Yes	No
community alarm	Yes	Yes
environmental controls	Yes	Yes
out-of-house alert	Yes	No
flashing lights as prompts to check PC for next activity	No	Yes
Precision = 0.7	**Recall = 0.8**	

Solution D	CBR	Expert
smoke/heat/gas alarms	Yes	Yes
video entry phone	No	Yes
door entry system	Yes	No
community alarm	Yes	Yes
environmental controls	Yes	Yes
very sheltered accommodation	Yes	No
needs assistance with toileting and feeding	No	Yes
Precision = 0.6	**Recall = 0.6**	

Fig. 10. SmartHouse Devices for Test Problems

Problem *A* was the easiest to solve and this is confirmed by the high values of recall obtained by SmartH-CBR. It activates nodes 3, and 4 in Figure 8. Node 4 is a concrete node which results in the return of the attached solution *shower with sitting facility*. However, two of the paths end at completely-abstract concept nodes which results in the generation of two additional devices. Nevertheless, SmartH-CBR recommends all the solutions that are proposed by the expert hence obtaining high recall for this problem.

Problem *B* was harder to solve as SmartH-CBR was required to find devices that would help the person, without knowledge of the person's specific needs. It has a wider space to search and was therefore more prone to returning solutions for completely-abstract concept nodes. Hence the poorer values of precision and recall.

In its search for a solution to the *intercom operation* sub-problem in problem *C*, SmartH-CBR activates a concrete node that results in the return of the solution *visual doorbell*. One interesting thing to note though is that, for the *television* sub-problem, SmartH-CBR returns the solution *television amplifier* OR *audio amplifying headset* because this particular path ends at a completely-abstract node. However, in real-life, either solution would assist with the sub-problem that is why the expert gives the solution as being either the *television amplifier* or the *audio amplifying headset*. Thus SmartH-CBR recommends the right solution by returning solutions of sub-cases attached to a completely-abstract node at which the search path ends.

Problem D was the most challenging. The fact that SmartH-CBR obtains reasonable values of precision and recall shows that there is good coverage of cases in the case base and that the vocabulary used is fairly standard since previously unseen terms can activate concepts in the hierarchy. However, the hierarchy has to expand its vocabulary and incorporate new terms. For example neither the query term *poor hand to eye coordination* nor its sub-strings activate any concept node. This could be done by the expert refining the concept hierarchy when she saw a need during problem-solving.

8   Conclusions and Future Work

We have presented SmartCAT, a case authoring tool that creates knowledge-rich cases from semi-structured textual reports. SmartCAT uses SmartHouse problem-solving experiences to learn a concept hierarchy. It then organises the knowledge-rich cases into a structure based on concept-superconcept relationships in the concept hierarchy. The result is SmartH-CBR, a hierarchically structured case-base where abstract cases and sub-cases exist at several levels of abstraction and all nodes whose intents completely represent a sub-problem are tagged with sub-solutions.

We obtain good results for precision and recall on the test cases. This is partly because tagging sub-problems with their solutions helps SmartH-CBR to retrieve only the relevant part of an otherwise composite solution. SmartH-CBR's ability to recommend sensible solutions can also be attributed to the retrieval mechanism. The use of the hierarchy as the basis for retrieval ensures the return of some form of solution. This is particularly important in domains where high recall is preferred to high precision.

Unlike most textual case-based reasoning systems, SmartH-CBR's case knowledge and the structure of the case-base are generated automatically. This feature makes the case knowledge for SmartH-CBR easy to acquire and maintain from textual records. This is the main novelty in our work. The use of FCA and LSI in CBR is not novel but using LSI to enrich FCA in order to exploit the resulting FCA hierarchy in CBR has not been explored by others.

The concept hierarchy could benefit from interaction with a human expert who would refine the relations and thus supplement existing knowledge with more background knowledge. For this the knowledge determining the structure of the case base has to be comprehensible. The extents in the concept hierarchy have been named using both a sub-problem header and the discovered disability term. These should be informative descriptions of the underlying problem for the expert. The intents consist of terms that an expert is likely to have chosen as key phrases. Therefore it is easy for an expert to see the attributes in context and amend the hierarchy as necessary.

References

1. Asiimwe, S., Craw, S., Taylor, B.: Discovering a concept hierarchy from SmartHouse reports. In: Proc 3rd Textual Case-Based Reasoning Workshop, 8th European Conference on Case-Based Reasoning (2006)
2. Bergmann, R., Wilke, W.: On the role of abstraction in case-based reasoning. In: Proc 3rd European Workshop on Advances in Case-Based Reasoning, pp. 28–43. Springer, Heidelberg (1996)
3. Deerwester, S., Dumais, S.T., Furnas, G.W., Landauer, T.K., Harshman, R.: Indexing by latent semantic analysis. Journal of the American Society for Information Science 41(6), 391–407 (1990)
4. Gabrilovich, E., Markovitch, S.: Computing semantic relatedness using Wikipedia-based explicit semantic analysis. In: Proc 20th International Joint Conference for Artificial Intelligence (2007)
5. Hammond, K., Burke, R., Martin, C., Lytinen, S.: FAQ Finder: a case-based approach to knowledge navigation. In: Proc 11th Conference on Artificial Intelligence for Applications, p. 80. IEEE Computer Society, Los Alamitos (1995)
6. Jenkins, M.-C., Smith, D.: Conservative stemming for search and indexing. Special Interest Group on Information Retrieval (2005)
7. Patterson, D., Rooney, N., Dobrynin, V., Galushka, M.: Sophia: A novel approach for textual case-based reasoning. In: Proc 19th International Joint Conference on Artificial Intelligence, pp. 15–20 (2005)
8. Petersen, W.: A set-theoretical approach for the induction of inheritance hierarchies. Electronic Notes in Theoretical Computer Science 53, 296–308 (2004)
9. Priss, U.: Formal concept analysis in information science. Annual Review of Information Science and Technology, 40 (2006)
10. Recio, J.A., Díaz-Agudo, B., Gomez-Martin, M., Wiratunga, N.: Extending jCOLIBRI for textual CBR. In: Muñoz-Ávila, H., Ricci, F. (eds.) ICCBR 2005. LNCS (LNAI), vol. 3620, pp. 421–435. Springer, Heidelberg (2005)
11. Smyth, B., Keane, M.T., Cunningham, P.: Hierarchical case-based reasoning integrating case-based and decompositional problem-solving techniques for plant-control software design. IEEE Transactions on Knowledge and Data Engineering 13(5), 793–812 (2001)
12. Watson, I.D., Perera, S.: A hierarchical case representation using context guided retrieval. Knowledge Based Systems 11(5-6), 285–292 (1998)
13. Weber, R.O., Ashley, K.D., Brüninghaus, S.: Textual Case-Based Reasoning. Knowledge Engineering Review 20(3), 255–260 (2005)
14. Wiratunga, N., Craw, S., Taylor, B., Davis, G.: Case-based reasoning for matching Smart-House technology to people's needs. Knowledge Based Systems 17(2-4), 139–146 (2004)
15. Wiratunga, N., Koychev, I., Massie, S.: Feature selection and generalisation for textual case retrieval. In: Funk, P., González Calero, P.A. (eds.) ECCBR 2004. LNCS (LNAI), vol. 3155, pp. 806–820. Springer, Heidelberg (2004)

Case Provenance:
The Value of Remembering Case Sources

David Leake and Matthew Whitehead

Computer Science Department, Indiana University, Lindley Hall 215
150 S. Woodlawn Avenue, Bloomington, IN 47405, U.S.A.
{leake, mewhiteh}@cs.indiana.edu

Abstract. Case-based reasoning systems routinely record the results of prior problem-solving, but not the *provenance* of new cases: the way in which the new cases were derived. This paper proposes the value of tracking provenance information in CBR, especially when timely feedback may not be available. It illustrates the use of provenance information with studies of the application of provenance information to guide case-base maintenance. Experiments with two data sets illustrate the benefit of using provenance to propagate maintenance and to target maintenance effort.

1 Introduction

In case-based reasoning (CBR), memory of prior problems and solutions plays a central role: new solutions are generated by retrieving and adapting prior solutions, and are added to the case library for future use. However, standard CBR systems do not remember the *provenance* of the cases in their case libraries: how those cases came to be. This paper proposes that the storage of simple provenance information can play a valuable role in CBR for estimating solution confidence and guiding case base maintenance.

When a case is provided to a CBR system externally, provenance information records the external source. When a CBR system generates a case internally, a minimal provenance trace records the case(s) from which it was generated; a richer approach could also record information such as the adaptation strategies used. Such information provides many potential opportunities for refining system performance. For example, provenance information on externally-provided cases may be a useful source of clues to the case's applicability [1] or its reliability [2]. As an illustration, an ethnographic study on remote naval troubleshooting support for sailors showed that not all cases captured were treated equally: the reliability of the sailor who captured problem information was a crucial concern to experts who consulted the cases later [3].

When a CBR system generates cases internally by case adaptation, both the cases taken as starting point and the adaptations used may affect the quality of solutions; unreliable adaptations may cause quality loss, decreasing expected quality in cases generated by long sequences of unreliable adaptations. Thus considering case derivations may provide useful clues to solution quality. Simple provenance-based reasoning may enable increasing system robustness to other problems as well. For example, the effects of learning in a CBR system may depend on the order of case presentation; a CBR

R.O. Weber and M.M. Richter (Eds.): ICCBR 2007, LNAI 4626, pp. 194–208, 2007.

system may learn different things from a single set of cases, based on case presentation order. Tracking the history of case generation provides data which may be used to detect and discount presentation-order effects.

This paper presents an argument for the importance of case provenance. It begins by considering an implicit assumption of much CBR research, that feedback will be available. It shows that this assumption may not always hold in practice, and that provenance can be a useful tool to help alleviate some of the problems caused by absent or delayed feedback. The paper then considers a wider set of motivations for studying case provenance, including guiding maintenance, which may be needed even if the system receives timely feedback at case generation time. The discussion of motivations is followed with a series of five experiments. The experiments first focus on feedback issues, studying the effects of delayed feedback on solution quality and the use of provenance to propagate feedback information that becomes available to related cases. They then examine issues related to quality loss through repeated adaptations, examining solution quality trends and the use of the number of adaptations as a predictor for cases likely to require maintenance. The results illustrate how provenance information can guide the case-base maintenance process.

2 The Fallacy of Feedback

Given the potential uses of case provenance information, it is interesting to consider why provenance has not been a routine consideration within CBR systems. One possible explanation for considering only cases, rather than cases' origins, is that early CBR research commonly assumed that the cases in the case-base were correct, due to the CBR system receiving feedback on the success of its solutions as they are generated. Feedback was seen as essential for successful CBR, to assure that the system would not be led astray by reapplying failed solutions. However, the feedback assumption merits re-visiting for two reasons. First, in practice, feedback may be delayed or even unavailable, making it desirable to increase the robustness of CBR in the face of missing feedback. Second, even in domains for which feedback appears to be available, it may be incomplete. The goodness of solutions may depend on multiple dimensions, with feedback available only for some of them. In such situations, robustness to incomplete feedback is desirable as well.

Missing Feedback: In contexts such as CBR systems which provide advice to end users, feedback may be hard to obtain. User feedback rates are notoriously low; for example, the annual report of one help desk reports an average response rate under 8% [4]. Even when feedback eventually will be available, the reasoner may need to act before feedback is provided. In asynchronous troubleshooting, there may be a lag of hours or days before a help desk receives the response to its advice on a new problem, during which time similar problems may need to be solved. In product design, there may be a time lag of months or even years before product use and maintenance reveal problems, during which time new designs must still be generated.

Lack of feedback can cause problems for a CBR system. For example, without feedback, a CBR system's conclusions from a given set of problems may be radically different depending on problem presentation order. As a simple example, consider the task

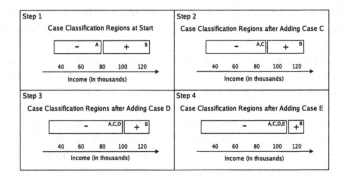

Fig. 1. Cases C, D, and E in sequence extend the negative classification region

of predicting loan eligibility based on the loan amount and the borrower's income. Assume that a CBR system predicts using 1-NN, with similarity determined by Euclidean distance, and that the system starts with seed cases A and B. Case A records a request for a $20,000 loan, an income of $40,000, and a negative decision; B records a request for a $20,000 loan, an income of $125,000, and a positive decision. Given the sequence of problems (C = ($20,000, $60,000), D = ($20,000, $80,000), E = ($20,000, $100,000)), cases C, D, and E will each extend the negative region, as illustrated in the 1-dimensional view of Figure 1. The same problems in the reverse order will successively extend the positive region, for the reverse effect. In either scenario, considering how the solutions were generated makes clear the need to treat the results with caution.

Incomplete Feedback: Even when feedback is available, it may be partial. In case-based planning, feedback may be available concerning a plan's success or failure, but not its comparative efficiency: The planner will know the number of plan steps but not whether alternative plans might have involved fewer steps. In an example from CHEF [5], the planner repairs an interaction problem by cooking two ingredients separately instead of together. If the resulting recipe is later modified, replacing the two ingredients with others which do not interact, they will be cooked separately, even if that is unnecessary. If a planner starts out with a set of high-quality expert plans, new plans generated with minor variations might be expected to have reasonable efficiency, but each successive adaptation may risk carrying forward aspects unneeded for the current situation and missing possible optimizations, regardless of whether feedback confirms successful accomplishment of goals. Here provenance information—how the new plan was generated from an expert plan—may be useful as a proxy for estimating aspects of quality not available from feedback to the system.

3   Motivations for Studying Case Provenance

While case provenance has not yet been studied as a CBR area in its own right, provenance considerations could contribute both to assessing case quality and to guiding case-base maintenance.

Provenance and Confidence: Recent research has observed the importance of methods for assessing confidence in the solutions of a CBR system. For example, Cheetham and Price [6] argue persuasively for the importance of internal methods for assessing confidence, and present an extensive set of confidence indicators, based on analyzing individual cases and their relationships (e.g., the sum of similarities of retrieved cases with the best solution). These provide rich criteria, provided that the cases in the case base are themselves assumed to be trustworthy. However, their trustworthiness depends on their own provenance.

In real-world case-based reasoning, cases may be collected from many distributed sources (e.g., [7]). Confidence in externally-provided cases may vary by source, making knowledge of sources important to balance tradeoffs between case similarity and source-based factors if one source is less reliable than another [1].

For internally-generated cases, confidence may depend both on the original cases and on their connections—the adaptation procedures generating one case from another. It is commonplace in rule-based systems to assign confidence values to rules, and to estimate the confidence of conclusions based on their derivations (e.g., [8]). For CBR systems, the quality of solutions may be estimated based on the quality of the original case and the chain of adaptation steps performed. In this paper, we explore the use of a very simple provenance-based metric for estimating quality, the length of the adaptation chain: the number of intermediate cases generated from an initial case before generating the current solution. This may enable estimating adaptation-based case quality decay for use in assessing confidence in a solution.

Provenance and Explanation: Beyond the direct use of provenance to assess confidence, provenance information may be useful to explanation of a CBR system's conclusions to the user. Understanding how a solution was derived from confirmed cases—perhaps through a chain of intermediate problem-solving—can provide users with a deeper understanding of how a solution was generated.

Provenance and maintenance: Case-base maintenance research has extensively examined case-base growth issues, focusing primarily on retention decisions for individual cases and factors such as consistency and coverage (for a sampling of this work, see [9]). This focus examines the contents of the cases in the case base at maintenance time, rather than their sources (one exception is the HOMER project [2], which distinguishes between cases captured directly from help desk operators and confirmed cases verified by a case author).

Tracking provenance information gives a new source of maintenance information, with many potential uses:

– *Responding to delayed feedback:* When feedback is delayed, an unconfirmed case may already have been used to solve other problems before its confirmation is received. If the original case is erroneous, the cases derived from it may require repair as well. Likewise, the error in the current case may suggest that the cases from which it was derived need repair as well. Provenance information enables identifying related cases for repair.

– *Focusing case-base maintenance effort:* In addition, internal case provenance information enables an analysis of the case-base's growth over time, and of the influences cases have on each other over time. If labor-intensive methods are needed to maintain cases, cases which led to more adaptations are a natural candidate for confirmation; in instances of conflict, derivations may be useful as well, to check other regions of the case-base which are potentially affected.

– *Focusing similarity and adaptation knowledge maintenance effort:* Provenance information can suggest cases which may require attention, even in the absence of feedback. Conversely, when feedback is available and shows problems in a derived solution, provenance information about how the erroneous solution was generated can provide data to analyze for flaws in the system's similarity metric (if the case used as a starting point was a poor choice) or adaptation knowledge (if case quality decays quickly along paths involving particular adaptations).
– *Guiding maintenance based on trends as cases are applied:* There is a long history of CBR systems using feedback about problem solutions to repair the cases generated to solve them (e.g., [5]). The commonplace approach it that a new solution is generated, compared to feedback, and fixed if needed. Thus the repairs address the current solution, but assume that the previous case is correct and is a good precedent to use for similar cases.

However, even correct cases may not be good precedents. For example, in a property value estimation domain, if the case for a particular house results in an erroneous estimate for a new problem, a new case, with the correct price for that problem, is stored; the initial case is retained unchanged. Nevertheless, if the original case repeatedly yields faulty predictions, the original case may require adjustment as well. If the previous house sold at an unusually high price, because the specific buyers were willing to pay a premium for personal reasons (e.g., proximity to their babysitter), using the case to predict the prices of other houses might often produce estimates which are too high. If a system retains information about both the cases to which a given case is adapted, and the success of those cases, analysis of this information could prompt repair of the case—e.g., in this example, an annotation to adjust how it is applied (e.g., "this case tends to suggest values 10% too high)—or an adjustment of the similarity metric in that region of the case base.

4   Experimental Design and Results

The previous section hypothesizes that maintenance guided by case provenance information can improve the overall performance of the CBR system. One way provenance information might be exploited is for automatic feedback propagation. Human experts can improve the quality of CBR systems by giving accurate reference solutions to cases already in the case base, but it may be infeasible for a human expert to correct a large number of cases. Therefore, we would like to maximize the benefit of each instance of feedback a human expert is able to give, by applying that feedback to improve the quality of related cases. Our experiments simulate a scenario in which human expert feedback completely corrects a solution for a single case in the case base and then that solution is used to repair the solutions for cases that were derived from the corrected case. This approach was implemented using IUCBRF [10], a freely-available Java case-based reasoning framework developed at Indiana University, extended with the needed maintenance functionality. The experiments explored the following questions:

- How do feedback delays affect overall solution quality?
- Is the length of the adaptation chain generating a case predictive of its solution quality?
- Is provenance-based maintenance propagation a beneficial strategy, and what are its computation costs?
- Is provenance information useful for selecting cases for which to solicit external feedback (e.g., from a human expert)?

Case Base Datasets and Setup. Our tests used two separate case bases, the Boston Housing Database and Abalone Database from the UCI [11] machine learning repository. The Boston Housing Dataset contains 506 cases, capturing attributes of house types in the Boston metro area. The dataset has one class attribute, the median price of houses of the given house type. In the experiments, the CBR system's goal was to predict median housing prices. Seed case bases for these experiments included 100 house types chosen at random, with the test sets composed of the remaining house types. The Abalone Dataset includes 4177 cases with one class attribute, the age of the abalone, which is continuously valued. This dataset was used to populate case bases with 100 cases along with their reference solutions, with the other data points used for testing. A new case base was generated for each trial run.

The problems presented to the CBR systems were solved by adapting prior cases using simple heuristics. For the Boston Housing Database, new solutions were formed by taking the case with the most similar problem features and offsetting its median house price by the relative difference in the sizes of the houses. A similar technique was used for the Abalone Age Dataset using the age of the nearest neighbor case and the relative lengths of the abalones.

Provenance Information Used. As our testbed system generates new cases by adaptation, it records the cases from which new cases are derived. This information is used to define the following relationships, considered by provenance-based maintenance processes: Case C is a *child* of *parent* case P if C was generated by adapting P; case D is a *descendant* of *ancestor* case A if case D was generated through some chain of adaptations from A (either a single adaptation or adaptations through a chain of intermediate cases). Any *descendant* or *ancestor* of C is considered *related* to C.

4.1   Test 1: Solution Quality with Delayed Feedback

The first experiment measured the solution quality decay of a CBR system given feedback delayed by various time intervals. At each time step a new problem was presented to the system to solve. The new adapted case, C, was then added to the case base, with a case removed at random if the case base size limit was exceeded. After n steps, feedback in the form of a reference solution was given for C and adapted solutions were propagated to all related cases.

We used the values $1, 5, 10, 50$ as the number of steps of delay before giving feedback to the system. The mean absolute error (MAE) average of all the cases in case base was graphed at each time step.

Test 1: Results. Figure 2 illustrates the dramatic benefit of feedback in the sample domains. Each plot line starts with increasing error up until the problem number when expert feedback is first received. At this point the error for each stops increasing and gradually decreases over the remainder of the problems. We note that the initial slope, while error increases, depends on the effectiveness of the adaptation method; better adaptation methods will yield gentler slopes, meaning less error added per adaptation.

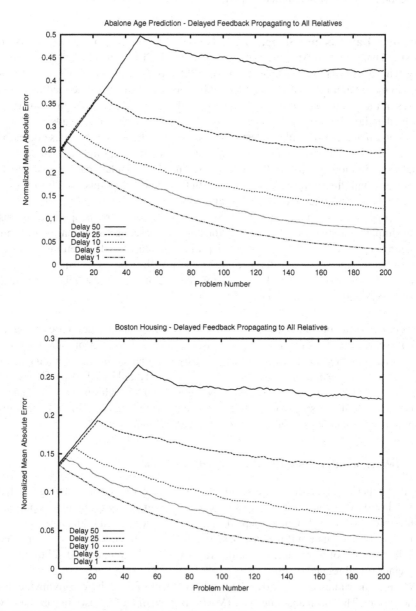

Fig. 2. MAE with varying feedback delays for the Abalone Age and Boston Housing datasets

4.2   Test 2: MAE Per Adaptation

This test measured the amount of error introduced into the case base for each adapted solution that was added. For this test we initialized case bases with 100 reference cases and then presented them 1000 randomly chosen new problems. The CBR system solved each problem, added the newly created case for the problem, and then performed maintenance by randomly deleting a case. No feedback was used for this test.

After each problem was solved, the MAE was computed for the entire case base along with the average number of adaptation generations for all the cases. These two values were stored after each problem presentation and later graphed to show the relationship between error and the number of adaptation generations.

Test 2: Results. Results were similar for both case bases, so only the results from the Boston Housing dataset are shown. Figure 3 shows the relationship between a case base's average number of adaptation generations per case and the normalized MAE for the entire case base. As expected, the greater the number of adaptation generations, the higher the overall error for the case base. As with Test 1, the slope of the linear fit line reflects the effectiveness of the system's adaptation method.

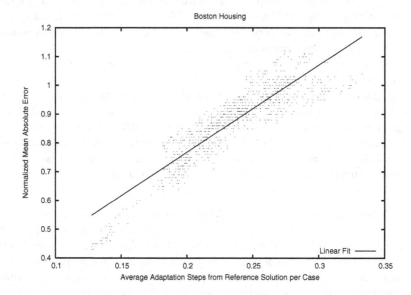

Fig. 3. The average number of adaptation generations per case in a case base is directly related to the case base's overall quality in the Boston Housing Database

4.3   Test 3: Using Feedback Propagation to Improve Case Base Quality

The third test examined different feedback propagation strategies using case provenance information, using MAE of all the cases in the case base to measure solution quality.

For each trial, the case base was initialized with 100 randomly-selected cases with known correct reference solutions, and a series of 200 test problems was presented to the system to solve. For each test problem, the system retrieved the most similar stored case and adapted its solution to the current problem. The adapted solution and current problem then formed a new case that was inserted back into the case base. Case base size was limited to 100 cases throughout the tests, with a randomly-chosen case removed from the case base for each addition, to keep the case base size constant. The entire test was repeated 100 times and the resulting MAE values were averaged over all the runs.

After each test problem, feedback was given for a single random case R in the case base. This was meant to simulate a human expert giving the system feedback. Once the feedback was given, one of the following solution propagation strategies was applied.

- *No Propagation:* Only the single case, R, that was given the reference solution was changed. This is the baseline method that has been common in past CBR systems.
- *Propagation to Similar Cases:* The entire case base is searched for cases that are similar to R within a given similarity threshold T. Sufficiently similar cases are then given new solutions adapted directly from R's reference solution. In our tests T was 0.2 for the Boston Housing dataset and 0.1 for the Abalone Age dataset.
- *Propagation to Children:* Any child cases of R are given new solutions adapted directly from R's reference solution.
- *Propagation to Parent:* Any parent case of R is given a new solution adapted directly from R's reference solution.
- *Propagation to Descendants:* Any descendant cases of R are given new solutions adapted from their immediate parent cases. This corresponds to recursively adapting solutions through generations of descendants from R's reference solution.
- *Propagation to Ancestors:* Any ancestor cases of R are given new solutions adapted from their immediate children cases. This corresponds to recursively adapting solutions up through generations from R's reference solution.

Test 3: Results. Figure 4 shows the results of different types of feedback propagation for the two data sets. No propagation results in the highest error across the problems (approximately 0.46 normalized MAE), i.e., every form of feedback propagation helped decrease overall error to some degree. *Propagation to children* and *propagation to descendants* outperformed *propagation to parents* and *propagation to ancestors*, which can be attributed to the greater number of cases reached by propagation to children and descendants: multiple cases may be adapted from a single parent case but each case has only a single parent. Overall, automatically propagating feedback to relative cases appears promising. The best performing feedback propagation methods reduced the error between 12% and 17% for the two test case bases.

On the Abalone dataset, performance of *propagation to similar cases* was nearly equivalent to *propagation to children*, but was only roughly comparable to *propagation to parent* and *propagation to ancestor* for the Boston Housing dataset. This difference is

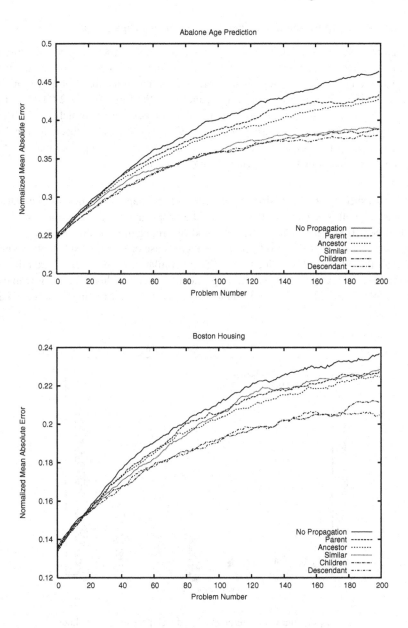

Fig. 4. MAE for varying propagation methods for the Abalone Age and Boston Housing datasets

a subject for further study. It may be attributable to inherent differences in the datasets or to the similarity thresholds used to determine which cases in the case base were considered similar enough to be given new solutions. However, additional tests adjusting the similarity thresholds were not conclusive.

4.4   Test 4: Computational Efficiency of Feedback Propagation

Propagating feedback by adapting case relatives increases processing cost, raising the question of tradeoffs between propagation time and improvement in solution quality for candidate methods. To examine this tradeoff, we compared feedback propagation time for each method. Propagation time was defined as CPU time (on a 1.2 GHz Pentium 4 with 768 MB of RAM) from presentation of feedback until completion of all case base updating. This test used case bases with 100 cases for each dataset and ran 1000 randomly chosen problems selected from the case bases with replacement. We then graphed the propagation times for each different technique.

Test 4: Results.   Figure 5 shows the feedback propagation times of the various propagation methods for both datasets. All the propagation methods took less than 2 seconds per 1000 test problems. The method of propagating feedback to any similar cases (whether directly adapted from the corrected case or not) took substantially more time than the other methods, due to identifying similar cases by linear search through the case base. Indexing strategies could significantly decrease this cost, but provenance-based methods might still be preferable to similarity-based methods for very large case bases.

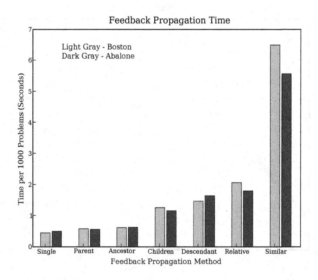

Fig. 5. Computational overhead of feedback propagation methods

4.5   Test 5: Targeted Feedback

Section 3 hypothesized that provenance information may be useful for predicting case quality in systems for which quality is expected to decay with repeated adaptations. Similarly, provenance information may be useful for directing limited maintenance resources, e.g., by directing a human expert towards those cases that when updated will maximize the benefit to the CBR system. This is especially important when the feedback process is time-consuming and costly. If the system can identify which cases are likely to have ineffective solutions, then the expert can focus on correcting those cases first, with the aim of maximizing the benefit of human effort. Likewise, if verifying a case requires additional costs (e.g., for running tests, etc.), the ability to target the right cases may be valuable.

For this test, recorded provenance information included a count of the length of the provenance path, i.e., the number of adaptations that a particular case is from a known accurate solution. We expected that given the imperfect case adaptation strategy used, cases closer in lineage to accurate solutions would be more accurate themselves, due to compounding of errors as repeated adaptations are performed.

The test compared resulting quality with four different maintenance techniques. The first, the baseline, used no feedback at all. The second, in each trial, used feedback to correct a random case in the case base. The third requested feedback on the case in the case base which was the highest number of generations from a reference solution, and corrected that case. The fourth corrected the case with the maximum error. We used 100 randomly chosen problems for each technique on case bases of size 100. We ran 25 trials and averaged the MAE for each problem.

Test 5: Results. Figure 6 shows that targeting feedback towards cases with the longest adaptation chain substantially improves overall solution quality, compared to randomly picking cases for feedback. This can be explained by the feedback improving the cases expected to account for the greatest error.

For the two datasets, targeting based on adaptation history reduced the error obtained using random feedback by 75% on the Abalone dataset, and 82% on the Boston dataset. This suggests the value of targeted feedback, and that the number of adaptations performed provides a useful proxy for identifying cases with the most error, when the actual amount of error is not known. For comparison, the bottom line on each graph shows the effect which would be achieved with the optimal strategy of always correcting the case with greatest error.

Other methods for targeting feedback are an interesting topic for future research. For example, targeting feedback to the case with the most descendants and then using the corresponding propagation method from Test 3 might provide additional benefits.

4.6   General Observations

Overall, the tests are encouraging for the use of case adaptation history information to guide maintenance for systems with weak adaptation. If a CBR system already has a very accurate adaptation method, then there is little error introduced per adaptation and the feedback propagation and targeting methods do not have as dramatic an impact. If a CBR system has a poor method of adaptation that on average adds substantial error per adaptation, then the methods tested above are even more beneficial.

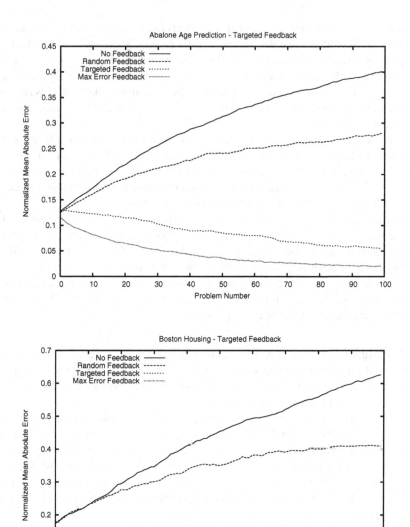

Fig. 6. Effect of selection of cases to correct on MAE for the Abalone Age and Boston Housing datasets

5   Related Work

The general notion of provenance is now attracting much attention in the e-Science community [12], for tasks such as enabling replication of results and estimating quality of scientific data. It is also attracting interest in Semantic Web research, for example, to support explanation (e.g., [13]). Tracking the derivations of beliefs and using those derivations to guide belief updating has a long history in AI, dating back to work on truth maintenance systems [14].

In the CBR literature, Goel and Murdock [15] proposed meta-cases to capture the reasoning underlying the CBR process, to support explanation of the reasoning underlying the processing of an individual case; such a reasoning trace is stored by the ROBBIE system as well [16]. However, in both these systems, the focus is on applying the trace to understand current reasoning, rather than understanding the extended derivation history of a case through the chain of cases from which it was derived.

6 Conclusion

This paper has argued for the value of studying of case provenance, and has illustrated the potential value of provenance-based strategies for estimating case confidence and guiding maintenance. The provenance-based approach is innovative in that—unlike maintenance work which only detects and fills gaps, or responds to problems revealed by feedback or inconsistencies—provenance-based methods can make *a priori* suggestions of candidates for case replacements or confirmations.

The paper explores simple strategies with much room for refinement. Interesting questions include how to use richer provenance information, such as information on the specific adaptations performed, and how to exploit such information for finer-grained prediction of case quality and for case base maintenance propagation strategies.

Provenance considerations may also prove useful for explanation, to enable grounding explanations of new solutions in authoritative cases connected to the current situation by short adaptation chains. The CBR community has long noted the value of supporting a conclusion by the known prior case from which it is derived (e.g., [17]). However, when solutions are based on cases generated by the system, simply showing the prior system case may not be as compelling. An interesting question is whether user trust may be increased by showing the full derivation of a solution, back to an externally-provided or externally-confirmed case.

Acknowledgment

We thank Steven Bogaerts and the anonymous reviewers for helpful comments.

References

1. Leake, D., Sooriamurthi, R.: Case dispatching versus case-base merging: When MCBR matters. International Journal of Artificial Intelligence Tools 13(1), 237–254 (2004)
2. Göker, M., Roth-Berghofer, T.: Development and utilization of a case-based help-desk support system in a corporate environment. In: Althoff, K.-D., Bergmann, R., Branting, L.K. (eds.) Case-Based Reasoning Research and Development. LNCS (LNAI), vol. 1650, pp. 132–146. Springer, Heidelberg (1999)

3. Evans, M.: Knowledge and Work in Context: A Case of Distributed Troubleshooting Across Ship and Shore. PhD thesis, Indiana University (2004)
4. Partington, N.: CIS helpdesk feedback statistics (2006) last modified (October 2, 2006), Accessed at http://www.ljmu.ac.uk/cis/aboutCIS/79910.htm
5. Hammond, K.: Case-Based Planning: Viewing Planning as a Memory Task. Academic Press, San Diego (1989)
6. Cheetham, W., Price, J.: Measures of solution accuracy in case-based reasoning systems. In: Funk, P., González Calero, P.A. (eds.) ECCBR 2004. LNCS (LNAI), vol. 3155, pp. 106–118. Springer, Heidelberg (2004)
7. Borron, J., Morales, D., Klahr, P.: Developing and deploying knowledge on a global scale. In: Proceedings of the Thirteenth National Conference on Artifical Intelligence, vol. 2, pp. 1443–1454. AAAI Press, Menlo Park, CA (1996)
8. Shortliffe, E.: Computer-based medical consultations: MYCIN. American Elsevier, New York (1976)
9. Leake, D., Smyth, B., Wilson, D., Yang, Q. (eds.): Maintaining Case-Based Reasoning Systems. Blackwell (2001) Special issue of Computational Intelligence, 17(2) (2001)
10. Bogaerts, S., Leake, D.: IUCBRF: A framework for rapid and modular CBR system development. Technical Report TR 617, Computer Science Department, Indiana University, Bloomington, IN (2005)
11. Blake, C., Merz, C.: UCI repository of machine learning databases (2000), http://www.ics.uci.edu/~mlearn/MLRepository.html
12. Simmhan, Y., Plale, B., Gannon, D.: A survey of data provenance in e-science. SIGMOD Record 34(3), 31–36 (2005)
13. Murdock, J., McGuiness, D., da Silva, P.P., Welty, C., Ferrucci, D.: Explaining conclusions from diverse knowledge sources. In: Cruz, I., Decker, S., Allemang, D., Preist, C., Schwabe, D., Mika, P., Uschold, M., Aroyo, L. (eds.) ISWC 2006. LNCS, vol. 4273, pp. 861–872. Springer, Heidelberg (2006)
14. Doyle, J.: A truth maintenance system. Artificial Intelligence 12, 231–272 (1979)
15. Goel, A., Murdock, J.: Meta-cases: Explaining case-based reasoning. In: Smith, I., Faltings, B.V. (eds.) Advances in Case-Based Reasoning. LNCS, vol. 1168, pp. 150–163. Springer, Heidelberg (1996)
16. Fox, S., Leake, D.: Modeling case-based planning for repairing reasoning failures. In: Proceedings of the 1995 AAAI Spring Symposium on Representing Mental States and Mechanisms, pp. 31–38. AAAI Press, Menlo Park, CA (1995)
17. Cunningham, P., Doyle, D., Loughrey, J.: An evaluation of the usefulness of case-based explanation. In: Ashley, K.D., Bridge, D.G. (eds.) ICCBR 2003. LNCS, vol. 2689, pp. 122–130. Springer, Heidelberg (2003)

Mining Large-Scale Knowledge Sources
for Case Adaptation Knowledge

David Leake and Jay Powell

Computer Science Department, Indiana University, Lindley Hall 215
150 S. Woodlawn Avenue, Bloomington, IN 47405, U.S.A.
{leake, jhpowell}@cs.indiana.edu

Abstract. Making case adaptation practical is a longstanding challenge for case-based reasoning. One of the impediments to widespread use of automated case adaptation is the adaptation knowledge bottleneck: the adaptation process may require extensive domain knowledge, which may be difficult or expensive for system developers to provide. This paper advances a new approach to addressing this problem, proposing that systems mine their adaptation knowledge as needed from pre-existing large-scale knowledge sources available on the World Wide Web. The paper begins by discussing the case adaptation problem, opportunities for adaptation knowledge mining, and issues for applying the approach. It then presents an initial illustration of the method in a case study of the testbed system WebAdapt. WebAdapt applies the approach in the travel planning domain, using OpenCyc, Wikipedia, and the Geonames GIS database as knowledge sources for generating substitutions. Experimental results suggest the promise of the approach, especially when information from multiple sources is combined.

1 Introduction

Case adaptation is a classic challenge for case-based reasoning (CBR). One of the impediments to endowing CBR systems with automated case adaptation is that adaptation often requires substantial domain knowledge, which may be difficult to capture. Knowledge-based adaptation methods have been widely explored in research systems (see [1] for a survey), but their application is limited by practical concerns: the difficulty and expense of hand-coding knowledge, as well as difficulties in anticipating how cases may be used, may make it infeasible to encode adequate adaptation knowledge in advance. Machine learning methods have been explored to extract adaptation rules from the case base for future use (e.g., [2]), and to capture adaptation experiences (e.g., [3]). Nevertheless, it is still common in CBR applications to follow the advice which Barletta [4], Kolodner [5], and others advanced in the 1990's: leave adaptation to the user.

This paper proposes addressing the knowledge capture problem for case adaptation by exploiting the large-scale, publicly-available knowledge sources now available on the Web. The goal is to develop largely domain-independent methods for "just in time" mining of domain-specific information as needed for specific adaptations, to give CBR systems robust adaptation capabilities without requiring the specific details of the adaptation domain to be precoded by CBR system-builders. To our knowledge, this is the first application of Web mining to the adaptation task.

R.O. Weber and M.M. Richter (Eds.): ICCBR 2007, LNAI 4626, pp. 209–223, 2007.

The success of Web mining to support case adaptation will depend both on the form and the coverage of the Web knowledge sources and on the ability of the CBR system to extract relevant knowledge. Not all Web sources are currently suitable for simple knowledge extraction, but we hypothesize that enough useful sources exist to make Web mining a valuable approach for enabling CBR systems to adapt a greatly increased set of problems. As initial support for this hypothesis, the paper presents a feasibility study exploring the use of three sources to support case adaptation in the travel planning domain: OpenCyc, a formalized knowledge-base of general-purpose knowledge [6], Wikipedia, a natural language encyclopedia including some structured information [7], and the Geonames GIS database, a database of site types and locations [8].

The paper begins by identifying key issues for harnessing general-purpose knowledge sources for case adaptation. It then explores some of these issues through a study introducing the WebAdapt system, a program which mines Web information to propose adaptations to tourists' sight-seeing itineraries. WebAdapt applies largely domain-independent strategies to extract domain-specific information as it is needed for substitution adaptation; this makes the methods applicable to adapt tourism itineraries without manual knowledge capture of details of local attractions or pre-processing of knowledge sources. The paper presents encouraging results from initial system tests, and closes by discussing prospects, limitations, and open questions for developing general frameworks for mining the Web to support case adaptation.

2   Framing the Problem

Any general approach to the adaptation problem must be based on a characterization of the task and required knowledge. For many tasks, case adaptation can be characterized in terms of two parts: (1) a small set of abstract structural transformations (e.g., [9]), and (2) memory search strategies for finding the information needed to apply those transformations, by substituting appropriate components into the case structure. For example, this view can be applied to tasks such as case-base planning (e.g., when a new ingredient must be substituted into a recipe [10]) and case-based explanation (e.g., when a plausible alternative cause must be substituted to replace a previous cause which does not apply to the current situation [11]).

The adaptation system's assessment of suitability for a substitution must be based on a characterization of the role to be filled. This can be described by a set of constraints to be satisfied, which can guide a search or "knowledge planning" through the internal knowledge of the CBR system, following the basic model of Kass's Tweaker [12] and Leake, Kinley and Wilson's DIAL [3]. Such a process assumes that the system will be endowed with sufficient background knowledge to address any adaptation problem it may encounter, forcing the system developer to confront the knowledge acquisition bottleneck. However, if the system could effectively mine pre-existing external knowledge sources, the burden on the system builder might be significantly reduced. This paper explores the use of knowledge mined from large-scale sources both (1) to hypothesize constraints which a replacement element must satisfy, and (2) to find replacement elements satisfying such constraints.

The proposed approach is consistent with recent general observations, by Hendler [13] and others, that the World Wide Web may provide the infrastructure to break the knowledge acquisition bottleneck. As ontologies become increasingly prevalent, carefully-crafted knowledge covering task domains of interest will become more widely available, perhaps significantly alleviating the burden of capturing formalized case adaptation knowledge. However, because the availability of formalized knowledge is currently outstripped by that of more informal, human-centered knowledge sources built collaboratively by individuals for human use, the aim of the WebAdapt project is to explore how case adaptation can benefit from both types of sources, with special focus on informal sources with fairly constrained forms, such as Wikipedia. Recent work explores mining Wikipedia for natural language processing tasks such as computing semantic relatedness [14] and augmenting text categorization algorithms [15]. To our knowledge, the proposed approach is the first effort to harness such sources to support CBR.

Central Issues: Given the differences in knowledge coverage by different Web sources and the different adaptation needs for different domains, the practicality of a Web mining approach will vary with the domain, task, and candidate knowledge sources. For any domain, tasks, and knowledge sources, applying the approach will depend on answering the following questions:

1. Which knowledge sources (or combinations of sources) should be exploited?
2. Which strategies should be used to determine constraints for knowledge search?
3. Which strategies should be used to mine each source for information satisfying the constraints?
4. For the task, knowledge sources, and generated constraints,
   – Are the knowledge source coverage and search strategies sufficient to find suitable information?
   – Is the mining process sufficiently efficient to make its application practical?

3 The WebAdapt System

Our testbed system, WebAdapt, explores the use of large-scale knowledge sources for identifying substitution adaptations using three knowledge sources which exemplify some major dimensions in the space of Web knowledge sources:

– OpenCyc, the open source version of the Cyc general-purpose knowledge base of formalized knowledge. OpenCyc contains hundreds of thousands of terms, and millions of assertions intended to represent consensus commonsense knowledge.
– The English version of Wikipedia, a collaboratively-written encyclopedia in natural language, including over 1.6 million articles.
– The Geonames GIS database, a database of over 8 million geographical names with associated features, including location information.

WebAdapt's task domain is tourism, an area which has been explored in a number of previous CBR projects (e.g., to support a community through sharing tour cases [16]). This is a domain for which generalized coverage of possible destinations and

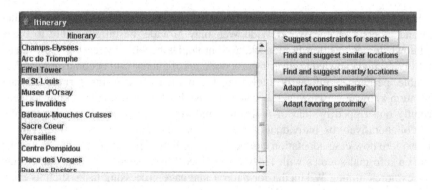

Fig. 1. Top level screen for WebAdapt

adaptations would require staggering amounts of precoded knowledge (e.g., Wikitravel includes guides to over 14,000 destinations, for each of which a traveler might consider multiple itineraries and substitutions).

WebAdapt's task is to aid user adaptation of plan itineraries, or to automatically adapt them. Its focus on the generation of substitutions for existing itinerary steps (e.g., if a user has already seen one of the proposed sights or prefers to see a different sight). The system's case-base contains itineraries drawn from the Frommer's travel guide to Paris [17], but because it processes itineraries in textual form and mines the Web for all additional knowledge needed, it could be applied to any domain for which sufficient Web coverage exists.

WebAdapt's user begins by selecting an itinerary case (e.g., "Best of Paris in 3 Days"). The system then presents the case's steps to the user. For steps which the user wishes to change, WebAdapt supports two adaptation modes, one in which the user interacts with the system to select constraints and alternatives from candidates proposed by the system, and another in which WebAdapt itself performs all adaptations.

Figure 1 shows the interface allowing a user to choose between interactively adapting an itinerary or having WebAdapt adapt it automatically. The steps in the itinerary are displayed on the left side of the screen, with user options on the right. For interactive adaptation, users can select the "Select constraints for search" button for WebAdapt to display a list of attributes hypothesized to be relevant for the selected item (e.g., reflecting that Notre Dame is a church and an example of Gothic architecture). The user can then select a constraint of interest, for WebAdapt to expand the constraint and display a hierarchy of retrieved sub-constraints and items. To have WebAdapt generate the suggestions autonomously, the user selects either "Find and Suggest Similar Locations" or "Find and Suggest Nearby Locations" for WebAdapt to generate constraints, use them to guide search, and display a ranked set of top suggestions to the user. The user may also select to have one of the top suggestions substituted into the itinerary.

3.1   Extracting Role-Filler Constraints

To generate constraints to guide the search for substitutions, WebAdapt applies a set of domain-independent search strategies. Each strategy calls on source-specific procedures to handle the format of information in each knowledge source (e.g., seeking Wikipedia category information at the bottom of the page, or examining all collections for an item in OpenCyc). However, it relies almost entirely on general-purpose approaches for its information search process in order to test the power of general approaches. We note that for any specific domain, it would be possible for a knowledge engineer to select a set of constraints *a priori*, or to hand-code task- and domain-specific constraint generation strategies, e.g., based on user profiles reflecting individual user interests, or to define domain-specific search procedures. This effort would be expected to increase the accuracy of results, and could be applied in conjunction with the more general methods investigated here.

Constraints are generated in a two-step process, first retrieving an initial set of "seed constraints," then performing refinement/filtering on the initial retrieval results. Given an item in an itinerary, the initial search strategies query the knowledge sources for information about the item. Currently, items in WebAdapt's cases undergo no re-coding from the text in Frommer's; each step is described by a set of keywords, which are used to query each knowledge source for an associated entry (e.g., to find substitutions for the Louvre, the system queries the sources for entries concerning the keyword "Louvre"). Entries for proper names or general categories may be found simply by matching keywords with the node labels in a formal representation (e.g., for OpenCyc), or by matching terms in the titles of associated Web pages (e.g., for Wikipedia). Keeping itineraries in textual form was chosen to test the ability of the system to function with minimal knowledge engineering.

Depending on the domain and representation scheme, additional pre-processing could be needed before constraints can be hypothesized. For textual role-fillers, NLP methods could be applied, using the context of the rest of the case to facilitate disambiguation; if items are encoded in a formal knowledge representation, role-based strategies could be used to select terms to generate Web queries [18].

Generating seed constraints: Each of the three Web knowledge sources includes an explicitly-defined abstraction hierarchy. If the knowledge source contains an entry (or entries) corresponding to the item to replace, WebAdapt considers each node in the source's abstraction hierarchy as a potential constraint. For the knowledge sources used in our tests, the seed constraints are:

1. Wikipedia - Categories under which an item falls
2. OpenCyc - General collections under which an item falls, regardless of any microtheories
3. Geonames GIS database - The feature class of an item

WebAdapt's core search process involves ascending and descending each source's abstraction hierarchy. The abstraction hierarchy is descended whenever a node is reached that can be expanded. In OpenCyc this will occur when a node corresponding to a collection is found, and in Wikipedia when a category node is found. The Geonames GIS abstraction hierarchy does not contain any child nodes which can be expanded (that is, the only node associated with each Geonames object is the item's feature class).

Expanding seed constraints to search for potential fillers: Once WebAdapt has generated a candidate set of role-filler constraints, it performs a breadth-first search for related information, expanding each constraint by searching its parents and recursively searching its children to find associated items. Individual items are listed in the order in which they are encountered. Search depth is limited, with no branch being searched to a depth greater than five nodes from a seed constraint; a limit is needed because the Wikipedia category structure occasionally contains cycles. Experience with these knowledge sources suggests that most relevant information is typically discovered at a depth of one or two nodes away from a seed constraint.

In our tests, WebAdapt finds one to eleven seed constraints when searching for role-filler information. Wikipedia routinely returns the largest number of role-filler constraints, averaging six per query. OpenCyc returns an average of three hypotheses, with a maximum of six, while the GIS Geonames database only returns one hypothesis per query. The retrieval of objects associated with a typical constraint for any of these knowledge sources usually returns approximately twenty objects. A retrieved object from OpenCyc is the name of an OpenCyc constant, an object from Wikipedia is a string of text describing a page, while an object from the Geonames database is the name of an item, it's feature class, and geographical coordinates.

Filtering result sets: For both Wikipedia and Geonames, WebAdapt relies on source-specific methods for filtering the retrieved items. For Wikipedia, WebAdapt's simple task-specific heuristic is to search for the name of the tour location in the first paragraph of the Wikipedia entry for each object in the initial retrieval set. If the name of the tour location is not found within the first paragraph, the item is rejected.

Geonames objects are filtered by location, requiring that objects must be within a three mile radius of the tour location (in this case, Paris, assuming that the user is primarily interested in items near the heart of a city). Tests of other radii between three and seven miles produced a fairly uniform set of results. No source-specific filtering is used for OpenCyc, as its knowledge is carefully encoded and any extra information that is associated with each object tends to be concise and unambiguous (e.g., the comment or 'pretty string' for the OpenCyc object Louvre-Museum is "the Louvre").

WebAdapt's other refinement processes include taking the intersection of the result sets returned by each knowledge source, or giving objects that simultaneously satisfy multiple constraints more weight. The intersection of two or more knowledge sources is taken by comparing each individual result set one element at a time, and retaining items that have the same name, or are judged equivalent based on another Web mining strategy, described in the following subsection. When searching for objects that simultaneously satisfy multiple constraints within one knowledge source, the number of constraints an object satisfies is stored. Objects satisfying the most constraints are displayed first.

3.2   Finding Replacement Elements That Satisfy Multiple Constraints

The initial search process often generates numerous candidate objects, many of which are irrelevant. To help refine this set, WebAdapt first attempts to resolve references described in different ways by different sources, then applies its role-filler constraint extraction process to each item, and then uses the constraints to estimate relevance, either automatically or based on user feedback about constraint importance.

Resolving naming inconsistencies: A system mining natural language must contend with the inconsistencies that presents. A particular sight may be referred to in different ways, but, ideally, the system should resolve these references to determine a unique set. In the spirit of exploiting large scale knowledge sources, WebAdapt uses Google to resolve naming conflicts. For each name mined from the text, WebAdapt queries Google and records the first URL returned. If the names from two knowledge sources are mapped to the same hyperlink address, they are considered to be equivalent items. For the examples in the experiments, this method had approximately 90% accuracy.

Determining object relevance: WebAdapt's automated strategy weights retrieved objects by the number of constraints that they share with the seed constraints for the initial role to be filled. Objects that share the greatest number of constraints are ranked highest; objects that share only one constraint with the seed constraint are ranked lowest.

In WebAdapt's interactive method, users define their preferred constraint types as they modify an itinerary. As a user modifies an itinerary, WebAdapt stores the final result of each modification and the system asks the user to select the constraint which was most important in his or her choice. For example, a user searching for a replacement for Notre Dame de Paris may prefer to look for other churches. If WebAdapt is using Wikipedia to suggest alternatives, the Wikipedia category "Churches in Paris" is most salient. WebAdapt keeps statistics on each constraint choice, building up an implicit model of user interests. The weighting of items mined in the future is adjusted, based on the number of high-ranked constraints they share with stored user preferences.

Filtering redundant candidates: Depending on the specificity of the constraints generated for a substitution, some of the retrieved items may duplicate objects already in the itinerary. To guard against suggestions for redundant items, WebAdapt compares each candidate result with every itinerary item already in the case, using the previously-described method for resolving naming ambiguities. Items from the result set that are determined to refer to the same sight as an element in the current case are discarded from the candidate set.

3.3   Generality of the Strategies

The WebAdapt system's constraint generation process is domain-independent; the system finds abstractions of the current role-filler. To find those abstractions, the system uses general strategies such as ascending and descending the abstraction hierarchy defined by a knowledge source. Likewise, the processes for generating and expanding seed constraints are independent of both the domain and knowledge source.

Because different sources organize knowledge differently, the procedures for tasks such as extracting abstractions are specific to the particular knowledge source, although not to any particular domain (e.g., the procedures for searching through the category hierarchy of Wikipedia are applicable to any domain, not only the tourism domain).

The filtering process involves some procedures specific to the type of knowledge involved and characteristics of the knowledge sources. For example, Geonames results are filtered by location, which applies only to spatial information; Wikipedia articles are filtered based on the assumption that the first paragraph of a Wikipedia article contains an overview of the most salient information on the article's topic. The process for resolving naming ambiguities applies to domains where items can be described by proper names which are easily queried.

4 Evaluation

Our evaluation studies the characteristics of alternative knowledge sources, explores the ability of the constraint generation and search processes to retrieve and rank relevant candidate substitutions, and tests the potential for the mining of multiple sources to improve performance. Specifically, the experiments were designed to provide information on the following questions:

1. How do the selected general purpose knowledge sources compare for suggesting useful adaptations?
2. Are the mining and ranking strategies successful at extracting information in the sources?
3. Can performance be improved by selecting items that simultaneously satisfy constraints from multiple sources?

For question 3, we considered both the combination of Web sources and a simple approach to refining use of Web sources by learning from interactive adaptations.

Experimental Design: The experiments tested adaptation suggestions for two itineraries taken from Frommer's Paris Travel Guide [17]:

1. The Best of Paris in 3 Days, a tour of 25 sights
2. Walking Tours: The Marias, Montmartre, The Literary and Artistic Left Bank, and The Latin Quarter, a tour of 60 sights

The 'Best of Paris' tour itineraries contain well-known Parisian tourist attractions; the 'Walking Tours' are small themed tours of less renowned attractions such as the living quarters of famous artists or small shops and cafes. One itinerary of each type was used in order to compare the system's ability to acquire adaptation information for (1) widely-recognized items likely to be contained in several knowledge sources, and (2) obscure items less likely to appear. Adaptation was performed on each of the steps in the itineraries, for a total of 85 adaptation problems.

Experiments were conducted using OpenCyc 1.0, the Geonames database updated as of January 7, 2007, and using Wikipedia pages last updated on February 10, 2007.

Performance Measures: Our experiments address two types of questions. First, they explore the domain coverage when WebAdapt's methods are applied to each particular source, i.e., the pool of items WebAdapt retrieves, given the constraints it generates from the problem and the source.

Second, they explore WebAdapt's ability to suggest the right items from that pool to present to the user, measured by standard precision and recall measures, applied to the sets of suggestions appearing in WebAdapt's top k suggestions, for $k \in \{1, 3, 5, 10\}$. As a coarse-grained impartial measure for which items in the pool are relevant, we consider an item relevant if it is mentioned in Frommer's Paris Travel Guide.

Table 1. Number of items returned from each knowledge source for various items to replace

Object		Wikipedia	OpenCyc	Geonames GIS
Notre Dame de Paris	Items returned	61	163	41
	Items within Paris	58	19	41
	In Frommer's Guide	40	16	20
Arc de Triomphe	Items returned	60	94	41
	Items within Paris	58	10	41
	In Frommer's Guide	32	10	20
St Germain Des Pres	Items returned	137	179	0
	Items within Paris	136	19	0
	In Frommer's Guide	17	16	0
Place Des Vosges	Items returned	63	0	5
	Items within Paris	62	0	5
	In Frommer's Guide	14	0	4
No. 20 Rue Jacob	Items returned	26	0	0
	Items within Paris	0	0	0
	In Frommer's Guide	0	0	0

Comparing knowledge sources: In our studies, Wikipedia provided substantially more coverage than OpenCyc or Geonames, as illustrated in Table 1 for five sample sights in an itinerary. The table lists the total number of items returned for each sight, how many of those were actually within Paris, and how many were listed in Frommer's. Notre Dame de Paris had a high percentage of relevant items returned from each knowledge source, while the more obscure No. 20 Rue Jacob had no relevant items returned from any knowledge source.

Case study of substitutions for the Eiffel Tower: To illustrate observed performance in more depth, we report results for the adaptation task of finding a substitution for the Eiffel Tower, which was chosen as a representative example illustrating variations in knowledge coverage and the quality of generated constraints. Table 2 shows the constraints generated using each knowledge source. Mining Wikipedia resulted in a rich set of constraints, ranging from describing the Eiffel Tower as a tourist attraction in Paris, to identifying the architectural time period under which the Eiffel Tower was constructed. Several of these constraints relate specifically to Paris or France itself, such as identifying the Eiffel Tower as a skyscraper in Paris, or as a tower or landmark in France. The results from Wikipedia also include some constraints, such as "Articles with unsourced statements" and "Eponymous places," which are irrelevant to identifying alternative sights.

OpenCyc provided fewer constraints than Wikipedia, but those returned tended to be more focused than the Wikipedia constraints. The OpenCyc and Wikipedia constraints agreed on several key features of the Eiffel Tower, such as being a tourist attraction, a landmark, and a tower. The Geonames GIS database allows for only one constraint per item, tending to describe a fairly broad range of items, as illustrated in Table 2. This makes it less useful as a constraint source, except for providing the ability to restrict items geographically.

218   D. Leake and J. Powell

Table 2. Hypothesized constraints for substitutions for the Eiffel Tower

Wikipedia	OpenCyc	Geonames GIS
Articles with unsourced statements	Landmark	Spot, building, farm, etc.
Visitor attractions in Paris	Tourist Attraction	Paris coordinates: 48.87° N, 2.33° E
1889 architecture	Tower	
Former world's tallest buildings		
Historic civil engineering landmarks		
Landmarks in France		
Michelin Guide		
Skyscrapers in Paris		
Towers in France		
Eponymous places		

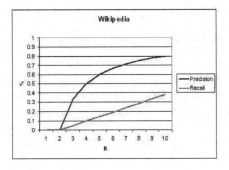

(a) Baseline Wikipedia precision

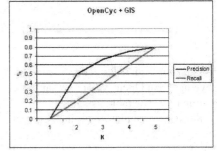

(b) OpenCyc ∩ GIS precision/recall

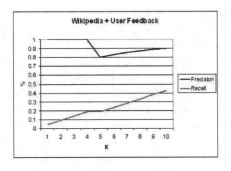

(c) Wikipedia + user feedback + compiled adaptation knowledge precision/recall

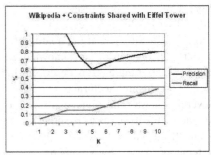

(d) Wikipedia + shared constraint information precision/recall

Fig. 2.

When WebAdapt used the generated constraints on substitutions for the Eiffel Tower, Wikipedia returned 32 items, 29 of which were within Paris, and 21 in Frommer's guide, compared to 170, 18, and 14 for OpenCyc and 41, 41, and 20 for Geonames (Geonames' high percentage within Paris is expected, due to WebAdapt's filtering for items within three miles of the center of Paris).

Of the items returned that were actually located in Paris, Wikipedia and OpenCyc contained a significant percentage of items identified by Frommer's as tourist attractions (approximately 75% in both instances). However, only 50% of the Geonames results were tourist related. Geonames contains a wealth of information about items within Paris, ranging from information on office buildings and communes, to the locations of several farms.

Figure 2(a) illustrates the precision and recall measures for the Wikipedia baseline example for the first ten items returned. The first two items displayed to the user when using Wikipedia alone are "2005 civil unrest in France" and "Visitor attractions in Paris." The object "2005 civil unrest in France" corresponds to the constraint "Articles with unsourced statements," while "Visitor attractions in Paris" is a general article elaborating on the phrase naming the constraint. Items two through ten each were displayed because they corresponded to the constraint "Visitor attractions in Paris," where each of the last eight items in this set appears in Frommer's Paris travel guide. The precision/recall measurements for OpenCyc were zero for the first ten items returned, while the precision measure for the Geonames GIS database was 60%, as six of the top ten items returned from the GIS database were found within the Frommer's tour guide. Recall at $k = 10$ for the GIS database was 49%.

Combining results from multiple sources: To test the effects of combining knowledge sources, after evaluating results using each knowledge source separately we compared the results of using intersections of the results from each of the individual sources, as well as of combining constraint information from the three sources and of using preferences learned from simulated user interactions. Conditions were:

1. Wikipedia ∩ OpenCyc ∩ Geonames GIS database (GIS)
2. Wikipedia ∩ OpenCyc
3. Wikipedia ∩ GIS
4. OpenCyc ∩ GIS
5. Wikipedia + Shared Constraint Information
6. Wikipedia + User feedback + Learned preference information

Conditions 5 and 6 favor items that simultaneously satisfy multiple constraints. In 5, a purely automated approach weights suggested items by the number of hypothesized constraints that intersect with the original item to be adapted. In 6, the system observes those constraints that the user of a system seems to prefer, and places greater weight on those items whose hypothesized constraints intersect with the user's preferences.

System results for intersections may sometimes have gaps, due to failures of WebAdapt's simple approach to resolving inconsistent naming. For the test example, the system-generated intersection of Wikipedia and OpenCyc produced five items, all of which were in the Frommer's Paris guide: the Arc de Triomphe, the Opera Garnier

Ceiling Painting, the Louvre, the Musée D'Orsay, and the Sacré Coeur. However, the true intersection also includes three more items, Notre Dame de Paris, the Pantheon, and Montmartre.

The intersection of Wikipedia and the Geonames database produced five results, each of which were found in the Frommer's travel guide. Each of these items simultaneously satisfied the constraints "Visitor attractions in Paris" and "Spot, building, farm." Figure 2(b) displays the results of the intersection of OpenCyc and the GIS database. The first item returned was the only irrelevant item, "Pantheon Rome." This item was incorrectly suggested due to the simple name merging strategy, which incorrectly mapped items corresponding to the Pantheon in Paris to the Pantheon in Rome.

Figure 2(c) and 2(d) illustrate precision and recall for a strategy that preferred items from one knowledge source that simultaneously satisfied multiple constraints. For the strategy that relied upon user feedback and user compiled adaptation knowledge, the only invalid suggestion was the object "Visitor attractions in Paris." Overall, filtering by constrains from several knowledge sources noticeably improved the precision and recall values compared to baseline strategies.

5 Related Work

Previous CBR research on acquiring adaption knowledge has explored a number of methods. Wilke et al. [19] propose approaches for refining adaptation knowledge using knowledge already contained in the CBR system; methods for mining adaptation knowledge from pre-existing cases include work by Hanney and Keane [2], Craw, Jarmulak and Rowe [20], and Patterson, Rooney, and Galushka [21]. Such approaches have proven valuable, but what they can glean is limited by the knowledge already contained within the case-base itself. Research on areas such as mining cases from databases has begun to address the question of leveraging external knowledge (e.g., the case mining of Yang and Cheng [22]), as has the use of case mining to extract cases from problem data, followed by mining adaptation rules from those cases, as by Patterson and Annad [23]. The WebAdapt approach contrasts in not acquiring its knowledge from an existing case-base or set of problems; instead, it mines large-scale, freely available knowledge sources developed for other purposes; the project's goal is to develop a flexible framework for enabling CBR systems to draw on multiple pre-existing knowledge sources. In addition, the goal of WebAdapt is not to generate new general adaptation rules, but to find the specific information needed to apply general adaptations.

The WebAdapt model of searching for adaptation knowledge is similar to that of the Leake, Kinley and Wilson's DIAL system, which also framed adaptations in terms of transformations and memory search. However, DIAL searched only internal structured knowledge, and relied on explicitly pre-specified role-filler constraints to provide goals for its search process. The WebAdapt system generates its own constraints and does a "just in time" search of external sources, taking a lazy approach to gathering adaptation knowledge and guided top-down by current needs, rather than bottom-up by the available data. McSherry's on-demand adaptation using adaptation triples [24] is in a similar spirit.

WebAdapt 's capture of user-selected adaptations to favor in the future is in the spirit of DIAL's manual adapter and of other case-based approaches to adaptation [25]; it also relates to Aquin et. al's CABAMAKA system, which combines case base mining with expert guidance [26].

Because WebAdapt searches sources which may vary greatly in its capabilities and internal structure, one of the challenges for WebAdapt is developing and managing the right search strategies. We anticipate that methods from information extraction and textual CBR research [27] to prove relevant.

6 Future Issues and Outlook

Current WebAdapt research has suggested many open issues for future study. The suitability of the Web mining approach for a particular domain will depend on its needs and sufficiently rich knowledge sources, but too much knowledge could impair the efficiency of the system, as the number of alternatives grows (currently, WebAdapt's constraints for the Louvre yield roughly 100 OpenCyc items, while its constraints for Place de la Concorde return 8,800). If the number of returned items becomes unmanageable, methods will be needed to increase search efficiency or generate more selective constraints (e.g., in the travel domain, to use Geonames information to only return alternatives within a small distance from the original tour location). Currently, WebAdapt mines a prespecified set of sources; another relevant question is how to automatically select a few on-point sources to which to dispatch queries for a particular problem (e.g., [28,29]).

Also, more sophisticated methods are needed for generating constraints in the context of the case as a whole, and for filtering and ranking search results. As mentioned previously, we are already exploring capturing user preferences from prior problems, for case-based reuse of successful adaptations across different users in similar contexts. Finally, human subjects studies will be needed to assess the overall success of the methods.

Despite the continuing challenges, we consider the initial results highly encouraging. WebAdapt can often propose good adaptations relying only on its cases, knowledge sources external to the system, and a few simple rules for mining them. Thus for domains with a good fit to available Web sources, the Web mining approach may be a promising avenue for helping to alleviate the knowledge bottleneck for case adaptation. The approach has great promise for adapting itineraries: With no additional knowledge capture effort, such a method could provide suggestions for an enormous number of destinations, limited only by the knowledge encoded in sources such as Wikipedia.

Procedures to learn constraints from prior adaptations to focus future choices, and to learn specific adaptations favored by users, could help to focus system results. We expect such procedures to be an important focus for the next phase of the project. In addition, based on the lessons from WebAdapt, we aim to develop a framework of general domain-independent methods for extracting constraints, defining knowledge source characteristics, and managing search, to facilitate application of the methods to new tasks and knowledge sources.

Acknowledgment

We thank Thomas Reichherzer, Matthew Whitehead and the anonymous reviewers for helpful comments on a draft of this paper.

References

1. Mantaras, R., McSherry, D., Bridge, D., Leake, D., Smyth, B., Craw, S., Faltings, B., Maher, M., Cox, M., Forbus, K., Keane, M., Aamodt, A., Watson, I.: Retrieval, reuse, revision, and retention in CBR. Knowledge Engineering Review 20(3) (2005)
2. Hanney, K., Keane, M.: The adaptation knowledge bottleneck: How to ease it by learning from cases. In: Leake, D.B., Plaza, E. (eds.) Case-Based Reasoning Research and Development. LNCS, vol. 1266, Springer, Heidelberg (1997)
3. Leake, D., Kinley, A., Wilson, D.: Learning to improve case adaptation by introspective reasoning and CBR. In: Aamodt, A., Veloso, M.M. (eds.) Case-Based Reasoning Research and Development. LNCS, vol. 1010, pp. 229–240. Springer, Heidelberg (1995)
4. Barletta, R.: Building real-world cbr applications: A tutorial. In: Haton, J.-P., Manago, M., Keane, M.A. (eds.) Advances in Case-Based Reasoning. LNCS, vol. 984, Springer, Heidelberg (1995)
5. Kolodner, J.: Improving human decision making through case-based decision aiding. AI Magazine 12(2), 52–68 (Summer 1991)
6. Cycorp: OpenCyc. Accessed (February 17, 2007) (2007), at http://www.opencyc.org/
7. Wikimedia Foundation: Wikipedia. Accessed (February 17, 2007) (2007), at http://www.wikipedia.org
8. Geonames: Geonames. Accessed (February 17, 2007) (2007), at http://www.geonames.org
9. Carbonell, J.: Learning by analogy: Formulating and generalizing plans from past experience. In: Michalski, R., Carbonell, J., Mitchell, T. (eds.) Machine Learning: An Artificial Intelligence Approach. Tioga, Cambridge, MA, pp. 137–162 (1983)
10. Hammond, K.: Case-Based Planning: Viewing Planning as a Memory Task. Academic Press, San Diego (1989)
11. Kass, A., Leake, D.: Case-based reasoning applied to constructing explanations. In: Kolodner, J. (ed.) Proceedings of the DARPA Case-Based Reasoning Workshop, pp. 190–208. Morgan Kaufmann, San Mateo, CA (1988)
12. Kass, A.: Tweaker: Adapting old explanations to new situations. In: Schank, R., Riesbeck, C., Kass, A. (eds.) Inside Case-Based Explanation, pp. 263–295. Lawrence Erlbaum, Mahwah (1994)
13. Hendler, J.: Knowledge is power: A view from the semantic web. AI Magazine 26(4), 76–84 (2005)
14. Strube, M., Ponzetto, S.: Wikirelate! computing semantic relatedness using wikipedia. In: Proceedings of the Twenty-first National Conference on Artificial Intelligence, AAAI Press, Stanford (2006)
15. Gabrilovich, E., Markovitch, S.: Overcoming the brittleness bottleneck using wikipedia: Enhancing text categorization with encyclopedic knowledge. In: Proceedings of the Twenty-first National Conference on Artificial Intelligence, AAAI Press, Stanford (2006)
16. Blanzieri, E., Ebranati, A.: Supporting touristic culture via cbr. In: Blanzieri, E., Portinale, L. (eds.) EWCBR 2000. LNCS (LNAI), vol. 1898, pp. 358–369. Springer, Heidelberg (2000)
17. Frommer's: Frommer's Paris 2006. Frommer's (2006)

18. Leake, D., Birnbaum, L., Hammond, K., Marlow, C., Yang, H.: Integrating diverse information resources in a case-based design environment. Engineering Applications of Artificial Intelligence 12(6), 705–716 (1999)
19. Wilke, W., Vollrath, I., Althoff, K.D., Bergmann, R.: A framework for learning adaptation knowedge based on knowledge light approaches. In: Proceedings of the Fifth German Workshop on Case-Based Reasoning, pp. 235–242 (1997)
20. Craw, S., Jarmulak, J., Rowe, R.: Learning and applying case-based adaptation knowledge. In: Aha, D.W., Watson, I. (eds.) ICCBR 2001. LNCS (LNAI), vol. 2080, pp. 131–145. Springer, Heidelberg (2001)
21. Patterson, D., Rooney, N., Galushka, M.: A regression based adaptation strategy for case-based reasoning. In: Proceedings of the Eighteenth Annual National Conference on Artificial Intelligence, pp. 87–92. AAAI Press, Stanford (2002)
22. Yang, Q., Cheng, S.: Case mining from large databases. In: Ashley, K.D., Bridge, D.G. (eds.) ICCBR 2003. LNCS, vol. 2689, pp. 691–702. Springer, Heidelberg (2003)
23. Patterson, D., Anand, S., Dubitzky, W., Hughes, J.: Towards automated case knowledge discovery in the M^2 case-based reasoning system. In: Knowledge and Information Systems: An International Journal, pp. 61–82. Springer, Heidelberg (1999)
24. McSherry, D.: Demand-driven discovery of adaptation knowledge. In: Proceedings of the sixteenth International Joint Conference on Artificial Intelligence (IJCAI-01), pp. 222–227. Morgan Kaufmann, San Mateo (1999)
25. Sycara, K.: Using case-based reasoning for plan adaptation and repair. In: Kolodner, J. (ed.) Proceedings of the DARPA Case-Based Reasoning Workshop, pp. 425–434. Morgan Kaufmann, San Mateo, CA (1988)
26. d'Aquin, M., Badra, F., Lafrogne, S., Lieber, J., Napoli, A., Szathmary, L.: Case base mining for adaptation knowledge acquisition. In: Proceedings of the Twentieth International Joint Conference on Artificial Intelligence (IJCAI-07), pp. 750–755. Morgan Kaufmann, San Mateo (2007)
27. Weber, R., Ashley, K., Brüninghaus, S.: Textual case-based reasoning. The Knowledge Engineering Review 20, 255–260 (2005)
28. Leake, D., Scherle, R.: Towards context-based search engine selection. In: Proceedings of the International Conference on Intelligent User Interfaces, pp. 109–112 (2001)
29. Leake, D., Sooriamurthi, R.: Case dispatching versus case-base merging: When MCBR matters. International Journal of Artificial Intelligence Tools 13(1), 237–254 (2004)

Representation and Structure-Based Similarity Assessment for Agile Workflows

Mirjam Minor, Alexander Tartakovski, and Ralph Bergmann

University of Trier
Department of Business Information Systems II
D-54286 Trier, Germany
minor@uni-trier.de
www.wi2.uni-trier.de

Abstract. The dynamics of the market requires workflow management systems that support agile workflows - workflows which are flexible concerning the adaptation to innovations. This paper presents a case-based approach to representation and index-based retrieval of past workflows in order to give authoring support for adaptation of recent workflow instances. The utility of the presented methods is demonstrated by an experimental evaluation.

1 Introduction

Thomas Herrmann reports the observation that many collaborative tasks in companies can be partly seen as recurrent routines but partly to contain innovation. ... This phenomenon will increase with the dynamics of the market and its requirements to the flexibility of the company and to the individual customer care." [1, p. 145, own translation]. Traditional workflow systems are able to support the recurrent tasks quite well. In order to deal with the flexible, innovative part, the workflows have to be adaptable to the innovation. Moreover, in highly flexible domains like medicine or chip design, situations occur where the ongoing workflows need to be changed. For instance, an alternative course of action has to be taken when a certain therapy is not successful for a patient or when a certain algorithm does not work for a new chip technology. This is not possible with traditional workflow systems.

Case-Based Reasoning (CBR) is a quite natural approach to support the flexibility of workflows. Experience from the adaptation of workflows in the past can be reused for the adaptation of an ongoing workflow. A case base contains past workflows in a certain state of execution together with the subsequent workflow modifications. When a current workflow has to be adapted it can be used as a query to the case base. Modifications of similar workflows from the case base can be reused in order to change the current workflow. In this paper, we present a new representation formalism for agile workflows [2] as well as a retrieval approach based on graph edit distances [3] that operates directly on the workflow structure. We show in some experiments that our approach is suitable for this kind of workflow.

R.O. Weber and M.M. Richter (Eds.): ICCBR 2007, LNAI 4626, pp. 224–238, 2007.

In the literature, a number of approaches for agile workflows exist that require further information in addition to the workflow structure such as context information [4,5] or conversational knowledge [6]. However, this information is not always available and can be processed automatically only with considerable effort. Furthermore, there is an approach that is related to our approach as it operates directly on the workflow structure: Luo et al. [7] have developed a building block similarity for traditional workflows. Unfortunately, this method is not suitable for changes of the order of workflow elements which are typical for agile workflows. Minor changes, for instance, moving a task to a different block leads to major restructuring activities within the building block tree and consequently seems to impact the similarity values to an excessive degree.

The remainder of this paper is organized as follows: Section 2 provides an introduction to agile workflows. In Sect. 3 we present a novel approach to representation and index-based retrieval of agile workflows. Section 4 provides an evaluation of our methods, while Sect. 5 concludes this paper with a discussion and an outlook.

2 Agile Workflows

In the following, we give an introduction to agile workflows [2] for which we have developed a retrieval approach based on graph edit distances. Agile workflows allow the incremental and flexible modeling of processes. Initial workflow instances are derived from a set of templates called workflow definitions. The instances can be adapted during the ongoing process. The term 'agile workflows' neither covers work on process mining [8] nor Herrmann's [1] approach to learning workflows from sets of loosely coupled tasks. We call these kinds of workflows 'emergent' rather than 'agile'. There is a small research community on agile workflow technology whose work we classify according to three types of process changes at run time:

- Ad-hoc changes that apply to individual workflow instances only [9,6],
- Modifications to a worflow definition that is already in use by instances [9], and
- Late-planning and hierarchical decomposition [4,5].

Our work fits in the first and third classifications.

Figures 1 and 2 show two UML activitiy diagrams of sample workflow definitions that we modeled for the chip design domain in order to support ad-hoc changes and late-planning. Each workflow consists of a control flow structure of tasks and of a context model. The context is described by a set of context factors with default values [10].

The control flow structure follows the design flow 'SciWay 2.0', i.e. a standardized description of the step by step design process for all digital design projects of our industrial partner Silicon Images GmbH (formerly sci-worx). The language to describe the control flow is based on the notation of workflow patterns introduced by van Aalst et al [11]. Workflow patterns "address business requirements in an imperative workflow style expression" [11, p. 4]; broadly speaking,

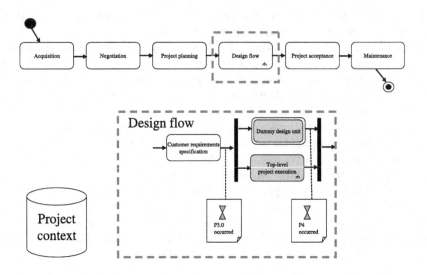

Fig. 1. The workflow definition of a design project following SciWay 2.0

they are useful routing constructs within workflows. In terms of van Aalst et al, our workflow modelling language consists of the five basic control flow elements (workflow patterns) *sequence*, *AND-split*, *AND-join*, *XOR-split*, and *XOR-join*, as well as loops. We regard loops as structured cycles with one entry point to the loop (LOOP-join) and one exit point from the loop (LOOP-split). A diamond with an ']L', one incoming and several outgoing arrows with conditions in squared brackets stands for the LOOP-split; a diamond with an 'L]', several incoming and one outgoing arrows stands for the LOOP-join (see Fig. 2). Loops cannot be interleaved but they can be nested, i.e. an inner loop may be set into one or several outer loops. For reasons of adaptability, we have extended this modelling language by three own workflow elements: (1) placeholder tasks for sub-workflows are depicted as rounded boxes with double borders (see 'Dummy design unit' in Fig. 1); (2) placeholder tasks for sub-diagrams are marked by a fork symbol (see the placeholder task for 'Design flow' in Fig. 1); (3) breakpoints are symbolized by stop signs (see Fig. 5). Sub-diagrams have only been introduced for reasons of clarity. In contrast to sub-workflows, sub-diagrams do not have an own workflow enactment service nor an own context model. Breakpoints are necessary for the implementation of long-term workflows. Decisions about how to modify a workflow region may take considerable time; setting a breakpoint prevents the workflow engine from overrunning tasks that are about to be modified.

Figure 3 shows a sample workflow instance that has been modified by late-planning. In comparison with the workflow definition in Fig. 1, the sub-workflow placeholder 'Dummy design unit' has been replaced by three sub-workflow place-holders for real design units. This has been done by the task 'Project planning'. Figure 4 expands the sub-workflow instance of the design unit '10a' which has

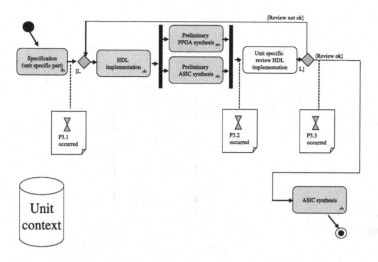

Fig. 2. The workflow definition of a design unit following SciWay 2.0

been derived from the template in Fig. 2. In addition to the workflow definition, it has the task 'Check whether feature set confirmed'. Figure 5 shows a further revision of this case that includes the implementation of additional features in hardware description language (HDL). This has been driven by a change request from the customer in a late project phase.

3   Representation and Retrieval of Workflow Instances

According to the above sample workflow instances, the representation has two parts: one for the control flow structure of tasks and another one for the context model.

The context is represented by a structural CBR approach with attribute-value pairs in a straightforward way. The representation of workflow structure makes use of the fact that the instances are derived from a particular workflow definition. As the instances usually differ only slightly from their templates, they can be described by means of the difference to their workflow definition.

A workflow definition is represented as a set of elements, such as tasks and control flow elements, as well as a successor-predecessor relation on this set. The difference between an ongoing instance and its workflow definition covers the following issues:

1. the structural modifications of tasks and control flow elements
2. the state of processing

Both can be encoded by sets of added and deleted workflow elements with respect to the original template. Hereby, completed tasks as well as passed control flow elements are regarded as deleted.

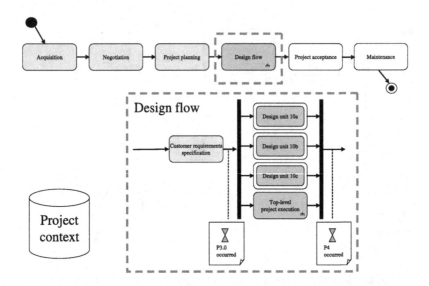

Fig. 3. Sample workflow instance of a design project

The experience that is contained in an ongoing workflow instance and the changes applied to it can be captured within cases according to the CBR approach. A case consists of a pair of subsequent revisions of a workflow instance $[X, X']$ (compare the two revisions in Figures 4 and 5). The previous revision X is the problem part of the case; X' is the solution part of the case.

3.1 Similarity Assessment and Index-Based Retrieval

The main challenge for the development of a similarity measure for agile workflows is comparing the structure of workflows. The comparison of context models can be realized according to the local-global-principle of the structural CBR approach. The similarity value for the context part is aggregated with the value for the structure part to an overall similarity value.

On the one hand the comparison of workflow structure should be kept computationally efficient and on the other hand the measure has to approximate the usability sufficiently well.

In the literature, several approaches have been developed for similarity assessment between graphs [12], among them graph matching measures and graph edit distance measures. To the first group belong measures which are based on such characteristics as "graph isomorphis" [13,14], "sub-graph isomorphism" [15], and "largest common sub-graph" [16,17]. To the second group belong algorithms dealing with graph edit distance, e.g. "weighted graph edit distance" [3].

For similarity assessment in our system we have chosen the idea of the weighted graph edit distance. The workflow definition (template) can be used to

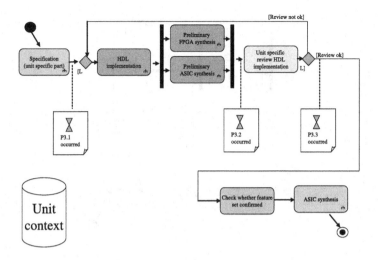

Fig. 4. Sub-workflow instance 'design unit 10a' from Fig. 3

accelerate the similarity assessment. However, this leads to completely different algorithms than those described in the literature.

Bunke and Messmer's [3] measure generalizes the string edit distance [18]. It is defined for attributed directed graphs but can be easily applied in a simplified form to standard graphs as well. Similarity is modeled through a set of edit operations on graphs. Each edit operation e transforms a graph into a successor graph performing a modification of the following kind: insert a new node or a new edge, delete a node or an edge, change a node or an edge label. Each edit operation has assigned a certain cost $c(e) \in [0,1]$. A difference can be defined based on the total cost of a sequence of edit operations which transform one graph into the other graph. The cheaper and the fewer the operations are that are required to transform a graph into another the smaller is the difference and hence the higher is the similarity between the two of them. These considerations lead to the following difference function:

$$\delta(x,y) = \min\{\sum_{i=1}^{k} c(e_i) \mid (e_1, \ldots, e_k) \text{ transforms } x \text{ to } y\} \qquad (1)$$

The computation of the graph edit distance measure is an NP-complete [3] problem and can be performed by a state-space search, e.g. by an A* algorithm. Hence, this similarity measure should be used quite carefully.

Our similarity measure for the structure of workflows will be explained in the two following sections. While the first section presents the similarity assessment only for restricted workflows, the second section presents an extension to this measure which can be applied to workflows with arbitrary tasks and control flow elements as well.

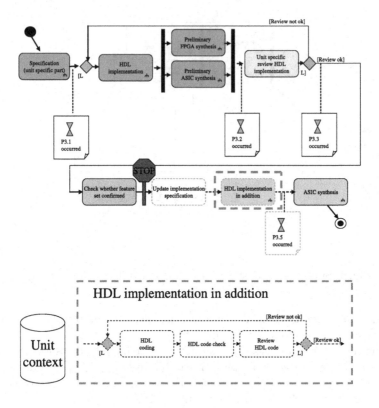

Fig. 5. Late revision of sub-workflow instance 'design unit 10a' from Fig. 3

3.2   Similarity Measure for Restricted Workflows

This section regards similarity assessment for restricted workflows that contain arbitrary tasks as well as control flow elements only of the type "sequence".

For the purpose of similarity assessment an abstract view on workflows will be defined. It includes only tasks, names of tasks, and ordering on tasks, given through control flow elements of the type "sequence". The view can be represented as a directed and attributed graph:

$$View =< N, E, name > \tag{2}$$

The nodes N in this graph represent workflows' tasks and the edges E represent the control flow elements of type "sequence". Furthermore, every node is labelled by the name of a respective task:

$$name : N \rightarrow TaskNames \tag{3}$$

There are two important characteristics of workflow instances that allow an efficient computation of the graph edit distance $\delta(V_1, V_2)$ between two arbitrary views $V_1 = < N_1, E_1, name_1 >$ and $V_2 = < N_2, E_2, name_2 >$. The first characteristic is that the name of every task is unique within a single workflow instance. The second characteristic is that two tasks, T_1 from one workflow and T_2 from another workflow, can be seen as identical if and only if their names are equal. This leads to following definitions:

$$\text{Nodes within } V_1 \text{ but not within } V_2 : \hat{N}_1 := N_1 \setminus N_2$$
$$\text{Nodes within } V_2 \text{ but not within } V_1 : \hat{N}_2 := N_2 \setminus N_1$$
$$\text{Edges within } E_1 \text{ but not within } E_2 : \hat{E}_1 := E_1 \setminus E_2$$
$$\text{Edges within } E_2 \text{ but not within } E_1 : \hat{E}_2 := E_2 \setminus E_1$$

(4)

Two nodes $n_1 \in N_1$ and $n_2 \in N_2$ are defined to be equal if and only if their labels are equal: $name(n_1) = name(n_2)$. Two edges $e_1 \in E_1$ and $e_2 \in E_2$ are defined to be equal if and only if $name(predecessor(e_1)) = name(predecessor(e_2))$ and $name(successor(e_1)) = name(successor(e_2))$.

We can now define the distance $\delta(V_1, V_2)$ between the views V_1 and V_2. Suppose, we are going to edit the view V_1 until it is equal to V_2. For this purpose the nodes $\hat{N}_1$ have to be deleted from V_1, since they are not in V_2. The number of edit operations is $|\hat{N}_1|$. Then the edges $\hat{E}_1$ have to be deleted for the same reason. The number of edit operations is $|\hat{E}_1|$. The sets $\hat{N}_2$ and $\hat{E}_2$ have to be added to the view V_1, since the nodes and edges are within V_2, but not within V_1. The number of operations is $|\hat{N}_2| + |\hat{E}_2|$. The overall sum of edit operations is $|\hat{N}_1| + |\hat{E}_1| + |\hat{N}_2| + |\hat{E}_2|$. It can be simply proven that this number of edit operations is minimal. Therefore the distance is set to:

$$\delta(V_1, V_2) = |\hat{N}_1| + |\hat{E}_1| + |\hat{N}_2| + |\hat{E}_2| \tag{5}$$

It should be mentioned that for this special case the complexity of the distance assessment is not exponential but quadratic. However, the average complexity could be further improved. The improvement is based on the fact that instances to be compared are created starting from the same workflow definition and differ only slightly from their template (with a view $V_T = < N_T, E_T >$). Therefore the respective views V_1 and V_2 can be redefined as follows:

$$V_1 = < N_T \cup add.nodes_{V_1} \setminus delete.nodes_{V_1}, E_T \cup add.edges_{V_1} \setminus delete.edges_{V_1} >$$
$$V_2 = < N_T \cup add.nodes_{V_2} \setminus delete.nodes_{V_2}, E_T \cup add.edges_{V_2} \setminus delete.edges_{V_2} >$$

(6)

Hereby the set $add.nodes_{V_1}$ defines nodes that should be added to the workflow definition in order to get the view V_1. The set of nodes $delete.nodes_{V_1}$ should be deleted from V_T. The sets $add.edges_{V_1}$ and $delete.edges_{V_1}$ have the same semantics but the objects to be altered are edges. The same consideration can be carried out for the view V_2. Now the sets $\hat{N}_1, \hat{E}_1, \hat{N}_2, \hat{E}_2$ can be redefined.

$$\hat{N}_1 := \{N_T \cup add.nodes_{V_1} \setminus delete.nodes_{V_1}\} \setminus$$
$$\{N_T \cup add.nodes_{V_2} \setminus delete.nodes_{V_2}\}$$
$$\hat{N}_2 := \{N_T \cup add.nodes_{V_2} \setminus delete.nodes_{V_2}\} \setminus$$
$$\{N_T \cup add.nodes_{V_1} \setminus delete.nodes_{V_1}\}$$
$$\hat{E}_1 := \{E_T \cup add.edges_{E_1} \setminus delete.edges_{E_1}\} \setminus \qquad (7)$$
$$\{E_T \cup add.edges_{E_2} \setminus delete.edges_{E_2}\}$$
$$\hat{E}_2 := \{E_T \cup add.edges_{E_2} \setminus delete.edges_{E_2}\} \setminus$$
$$\{E_T \cup add.edges_{E_1} \setminus delete.edges_{E_1}\}$$

Using results of the set theory the edit distance can be transformed to the following formula:

$$\delta(V_1, V_2) = |\hat{N}_1| + |\hat{E}_1| + |\hat{N}_2| + |\hat{E}_2| =$$
$$|\{delete.nodes_{V_1} \cup delete.nodes_{V_2}\} \setminus \{delete.nodes_{V_1} \cap delete.nodes_{V_2}\}|+$$
$$|\{add.nodes_{V_1} \cup add.nodes_{V_2}\} \setminus \{add.nodes_{V_1} \cap add.nodes_{V_2}\}|+$$
$$|\{delete.edges_{V_1} \cup delete.edges_{V_2}\} \setminus \{delete.edges_{V_1} \cap delete.edges_{V_2}\}|+$$
$$|\{add.edges_{V_1} \cup add.edges_{V_2}\} \setminus \{add.edges_{V_1} \cap add.edges_{V_2}\}| \quad (8)$$

Since the sets *add.nodes* and *del.nodes* become available with the construction of instances that starts from templates and since it normally has a low cardinality the computation time of the edit distance decreases significantly. The sets *add.nodes* and *del.nodes* can be understood as indexes.

Finally, the distance can be normalized and transformed to the compatible similarity measure with a range $[0, 1]$, e.g.:

$$sim(V_1, V_2) := 1 - \frac{\delta(V_1, V_2)}{|N_1| + |N_2| + |E_1| + |E_2|} \qquad (9)$$

This similarity measure can be enriched by the weights in order to emphasize some types of edit operations.

3.3   Similarity Measure for Workflows with Control Flow Elements

The distance measure introduced in the previous section does not support flow elements, such as AND-split, AND-join, XOR-split, XOR-join, and so on. However, taking them into consideration improves the approximation of usability (see Sect. 4).

The consideration of the flow elements in the similarity function entails several challenges. Contrary to tasks, which are unique within workflow instances and which could be identified by unique names, control flow elements do not have unique names and often occur several times within an instance. Because of this circumstance the computation of an exact edit distance becomes computationally more expensive. Therefore we regarded several approximation methods and evaluated the usability of the result sets empirically.

Approximation Method 1. The first approach supports workflows containing arbitrary control flow elements. However, it doesn't take the semantics of the control flow elements into account while computing the similarity value. The main idea of this straightforward approach is to represent every control flow element through one or several edges within a view. For this purpose every two tasks which are directly connected through control flow elements will be transformed to two nodes and one edge between them in the view. The "direct connection" means that there is a path in the workflows' structure connecting these tasks and this path does not contain any further tasks (but one or more control flow elements between them are allowed). E.g. regard two paths $(T_1, AND-split, T_2)$ and $(T_1, AND - split, T_3)$ within workflow instance $T_1 \rightarrow \begin{array}{l} \mapsto T_2 \\ \mapsto T_3 \end{array}$. The tasks T_1, T_2, and T_3 will be converted to nodes N_{T_1}, N_{T_2}, and N_{T_3} in each respective view. The control flow element will be substituted through two edges $e_1 = (N_{T_1}, N_{T_2})$ and $e_2 = (N_{T_1}, N_{T_3})$. The similarity assessment can then be carried out in the same way as presented in Sect. 3.2).

Approximation Method 2. The second approach is an extension of the first one. Also here every control flow element will be represented through one or several edges within a view. The difference is that every edge here is labelled by names of substituted elements. In order to realize this, a view on workflow instances will be extended to the following one:

$$View = < N, E, name_N, name_E > \qquad (10)$$

While $name_N$ is a function providing names (or labels) for nodes, $name_E$ does the same for edges. For two tasks T_1 and T_2 which are directly connected through some path $p = (Task_1, CFElement_1, \ldots, CFElement_n, Task_2)$ the function $name_E(e) = name_E((n_{T_1}, n_{T_2}))$ provides an ordered set of the elements' names: $name(CFElement_1), \ldots, name(CFElement_n)$. For example, consider the workflow instance introduced by the description of approximation method 1. The tasks T_1 and T_2 are directly connected by the path $p = (T_1, AND-split, T_2)$. For the edge $e = (n_{T_1}, n_{T_2})$ the function $name_E$ provides the value "$AND-split$". Now consider two tasks T_1 and T_2 which are directly connected by the path $p = (T_1, AND - split, XOR - split, AND - split, T_2)$. For that setup the function $name_E(e)$ provides the value "$AND-split, XOR-split, AND-split$".

The last thing to do is to redefine the equality of edges. Two edges $e_1 \in E_1$ and $e_2 \in E_2$ are defined to be equal if and only if $name(predecessor(e_1)) = name(predecessor(e_2))$ and $name(successor(e_1)) = name(successor(e_2))$ and $name_E(e_1) = name_E(e_2)$.

Using this extended model the similarity computation can be executed according to the approach presented in Sect. 3.2.

Approximation Method 3. The idea of this approximation method is to model the control flow elements of the type "sequence" as edges and other control flow elements (abbreviated with $\neg sequence$) as nodes. The only restriction is that for every $\neg sequence$-control flow element type (e.g. "$AND - split$") only one node will be introduced in the view, and this is independent from the real number of the same elements that occurred in a workflow instance. Thus, for all pairs of workflow elements e_1 and e_2, with e_2 being a direct successor of e_1, the following components will be introduced in the view:

- nodes n_{e_1}, $n_{successor(e_2)}$ and edge $e = (n_{e_1}, n_{successor(e_2)})$ if element e_1 is a task and e_2 is a control flow element of a type "sequence".
- nodes n_{e_1}, $n_{type(e_2)}$ and edge $e = (n_{e_1}, n_{type(e_2)})$ if element e_1 is a task and e_2 is a ¬sequence-flow element.
- nodes $n_{type(e_1)}$, n_{e_2} and edge $e = (n_{type(e_1)}, n_{e_2})$ if element e_2 is a task and e_1 is a ¬sequence-flow element.
- nodes $n_{type(e_1)}$, $n_{type(e_2)}$ and edge $e = (n_{type(e_1)}, n_{type(e_2)})$ if the both elements are ¬sequence-flow elements.

Here, the name of every node $n \in N$ representing a ¬sequence-flow element is set to the element type: $name_N(n) = type(n)$.

For example, the following two parts of one workflow instance $T_1 \rightarrow \begin{vmatrix} \rightarrow T_2 \\ \rightarrow T_3 \end{vmatrix}$ and $T_4 \rightarrow \begin{vmatrix} \rightarrow T_5 \\ \rightarrow T_6 \end{vmatrix}$ will be transformed to the following nodes and edges within a view:

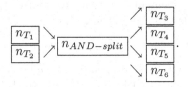

Also in this case the similarity computation can be carried out according to the approach presented in Sect. 3.2).

This approximation method could be further improved by counting the recurrent edges within a view. This can be achieved by using bags of edges instead of sets of edges. All operations on sets should be then replaced through operations on bags.

We have selected the approximation methods 1 and 3 for our empirical evaluation in order to get first insights whether and to what extent the results differ. In future, further experiments are required as well as a further extension of the described methods. For instance the control flow elements could be identified unambiguously by means of a naming function using their succeeding workflow elements.

4   Formative Evaluation

We did an experimental evaluation of the approximation methods 1 and 3. The test case base consists of 37 workflow instances from the chip design domain. They are derived from real change request documents of our industrial partner Silicon Image GmbH (formerly sci-worx). We presented each of the cases as a query to the remainder of the case base according to the leave-one-out approach. 35 of them have an empirically best matching case (EBMC) from the remainder of the case base. The EBMC has been selected by a human expert. As a quality criterion for the evaluation, we investigated whether the empirically best matching case was in the 10 most similar cases according to approximation methods 1 and 3. Method 3 is implemented with the bag approach that we sketched above.

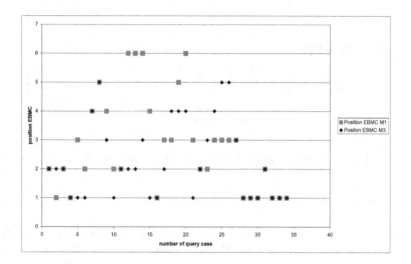

Fig. 6. Position of the empirically best matching case (EBMC) in the retrieval results

Both methods gave excellent results (compare Figures 6 – 7). For 34 of the queries, the EBMC was under the 10 most similar cases for both methods. For 21 of those, the EBMC was among the three most similar cases for both methods. Fig. 6 shows the positions of the particular EBMC's in the retrieval result lists. The squared dots stand for the results of method 1 and the diamonds for those of method 3. For example, for the case number five (x-axis) used as query the EBMC achieved position 3 (y-axis) for method 1 and the best position (position 1) for method 3. The expected position of the EBMC in a result set is with 2.91 for method 1 worse than for method 3 with 2.38. In 17 cases, the two methods gave the identical retrieval results. In 6 cases, method 1 achieved a better result and in 12 cases, method 3 was empirically more successful. In two of these cases of those, method 3 was significantly better; the empirically best matching case had a difference of 4 positions in the lists of most similar cases.

Figure 7 shows the frequency distribution of the positions of the EBMC's. Method 3 achieved better results than method 1, as the density of the distribution is higher for the better positions (the lower part of the distribution).

The representation according to method 1 required less nodes and edges for the same workflow instances. On average, this saved about a third of the size of the graph that was required by method 3.

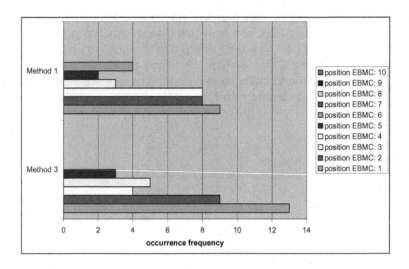

Fig. 7. Frequency distribution of the positions of the EBMC's

5 Conclusion

Handling the increasing dynamics of the market by means of agile workflow technology can be supported by CBR successfully. Our results have shown that the experience with the adaptation of ongoing workflows can be represented appropriately by the graph-based structure. Our new retrieval approach gave excellent experimental results showing that it provides a good approximation of the utility for the user. In addition, the experiments have clarified that it is worth-while to consider the control flow elements of the workflows explicitly within the similarity measure. The implementation seems to be computationally efficient due to our first experiments. The approximation graphs representing the agile workflows for retrieval purposes can be derived automatically from the process data and are available for further machine processing in future. We believe that our approach is suitable for developing a semi-automatic adaptation of workflows as well as for learning optimal weights for the distance measure, for instance by means of neural networks.

As next steps, we will conduct further experiments with approximation method 2 as well as with a more general distance model for agile workflows. Furthermore, we are going to do research on the employment of AI planning methods, for instance hierarchical planning [19], for semi-automatic, interactive adaptation of agile workflows.

Acknowledgements

The authors acknowledge the Federal Ministry for Education and Science (BMBF) for funding parts of our work under grant number 01M3075. We acknowledge the assistance we have received from our industrial partners in the chip design company Silicon Image GmbH (formerly sci-worx).

References

1. Herrmann, T.: Lernendes Workflow. In: Herrmann, T., Scheer, A.-W., Weber, H. (eds.) Verbesserung von Geschäftsprozessen mit flexiblen Workflow-Management-Systemen, pp. 143–154. Physica-Verlag, Heidelberg (2001)
2. Weber, B., Wild, W.: Towards the Agile Management of Business Processes. In: Althoff, K.-D., Dengel, A., Bergmann, R., Nick, M., Roth-Berghofer, T.R. (eds.) WM 2005. LNCS (LNAI), vol. 3782, pp. 409–419. Springer, Heidelberg (2005)
3. Bunke, H., Messmer, B.T.: Similarity Measures for Structured Representations. In: Wess, S., Richter, M., Althoff, K.-D. (eds.) Topics in Case-Based Reasoning. LNCS, vol. 837, pp. 106–118. Springer, Heidelberg (1994)
4. van Elst, L., Aschoff, F.R., Bernardi, A., Maus, H., Schwarz, S.: Weakly-structured Workflows for Knowledge-intensive Tasks: An Experimental Evaluation. In: 12th IEEE International Workshops on Enabling Technologies (WETICE 2003), Infrastructure for Collaborative Enterprises, pp. 340–345. IEEE Computer Society, Los Alamitos (2003)
5. Freßmann, A., Maximini, R., Sauer, T.: Towards Collaborative Agent-Based Knowledge Support for Time-Critical and Business-Critical Processes. In: Althoff, K.-D., Dengel, A., Bergmann, R., Nick, M., Roth-Berghofer, T.R. (eds.) WM 2005. LNCS (LNAI), vol. 3782, pp. 420–430. Springer, Heidelberg (2005)
6. Weber, B., Wild, W., Breu, R.: CBRFlow: Enabling Adaptive Workflow Management Through Conversational Case-Based Reasoning. In: Funk, P., González Calero, P.A. (eds.) ECCBR 2004. LNCS (LNAI), vol. 3155, pp. 434–448. Springer, Heidelberg (2004)
7. Luo, Z., Sheth, A., Kochut, K., Arpinar, B.: Exception Handling for Conflict Resolution in Cross-Organizational Workflows. Distributed and Parallel Databases 13(3), 271–306 (2003)
8. Schimm, G., van der Aalst, W.M.P., van Dongen, B., Herbst, J.: Workflow Mining: a Survey of Issues and Approaches. Data and Knowledge Engineering. 47(2), 237–267 (2003)
9. Reichert, M., Rinderle, S., Dadam, P.: ADEPT Workflow Management System: Flexible Support For Enterprise-wide Business Processes (Tool Presentation). In: van der Aalst, W.M.P., ter Hofstede, A.H.M., Weske, M. (eds.) BPM 2003. LNCS, vol. 2678, pp. 370–379. Springer, Heidelberg (2003)
10. Minor, M., Koldehoff, A., Schmalen, D., Bergmann, R.: Configurable Contexts for Experience Management. In: Gronau, N. (ed.) 4th Conference on Professional Knowledge Management - Experiences and Visions. Potsdam, University of Potsdam, GITO-Verlag, Berlin vol. 2. pp. 119–126 (2007)
11. van der Aalst, W.M.P., ter Hofstede, A.H.M., Kiepuszewski, B., Barros, A.P.: Workflow Patterns. Distributed and Parallel Databases 14, 5–51 (2003)
12. Bergmann, R. (ed.): Experience Management. LNCS (LNAI), vol. 2432. Springer, Heidelberg (2002)
13. Babai, L., Erdös, P., Selkow, S.M.: Random Graph Isomorphism. SIAM Journal of Computation 9, 628–635 (1980)
14. Babai, L., Kucera, L.: Canonical Labelling of Graphs in Linear Average Time. In: Proceedings of the 20th Annual IEEE Symposium on Foundations of Computer Science, pp. 39–46 (1979)

15. Ullman, J.R.: An Algorithm for Subgraph Isomorphism. Journal of the Association for Computing Machinery. 23(1), 31–42 (1976)
16. Brandstädt, A.: Graphen und Algorithmen. Teubner, Stuttgart (1994)
17. Mehlhorn, K.: Data Structures and Algorithms 2: Graph Algorithms and NP-Completeness. Springer, Heidelberg (1984)
18. Wagner, K., Bodendiek, R.: Graphentheorie I. BI-Wissenschaftsverlag, Mannheim (1989)
19. Nau, D.S., Cao, Y., Lotem, A., Muñoz-Avila, H.: SHOP: Simple Hierarchical Ordered Planner. In: Dean, T. (ed.) IJCAI 99. Proceedings of the Sixteenth International Joint Conference on Artificial Intelligence, Stockholm, Sweden, July 31 - August 6, 1999, vol. 2, pp. 968–975. 1450 pages, Morgan Kaufmann, San Francisco (1999)

Application of the Revision Theory to Adaptation in Case-Based Reasoning: The Conservative Adaptation

Jean Lieber

LORIA (UMR 7503 CNRS–INRIA–Nancy Universities),
BP 239, 54506 Vandœuvre-lès-Nancy, France
lieber@loria.fr

Abstract. Case-based reasoning aims at solving a problem by the adaptation of the solution of an already solved problem that has been retrieved in a case base. This paper defines an approach to adaptation called conservative adaptation; it consists in keeping as much as possible from the solution to be adapted, while being consistent with the domain knowledge. This idea can be related to the theory of revision: the revision of an old knowledge base by a new one consists in making a minimal change on the former, while being consistent with the latter. This leads to a formalization of conservative adaptation based on a revision operator in propositional logic. Then, this theory of conservative adaptation is confronted to an application of case-based decision support to oncology: a problem of this application is the description of a patient ill with breast cancer, and a solution, the therapeutic recommendation for this patient. Examples of adaptations that have actually been performed by experts and that can be captured by conservative adaptation are presented. These examples show a way of adapting contraindicated treatment recommendations and treatment recommendations that cannot be applied.

Keywords: case-based reasoning, knowledge-intensive case-based reasoning, adaptation, conservative adaptation, theory of revision, logical representation of cases, application to oncology.

1 Introduction

Case-based reasoning (CBR [1]) aims at solving a new problem thanks to a set of already solved problems. The new problem is called the *target problem*, denoted by tgt in this paper, and the already solved problems are the *source problems*, denoted by srce. A case is the representation of a problem-solving episode, that is, at least a problem pb and a solution Sol(pb) of pb. Hence a case is denoted by a pair (pb, Sol(pb)). A source problem srce is a problem that has already been solved in a solution Sol(srce). The pair (srce, Sol(srce)) is a *source case* and the set of source cases is the *case base*. A classical decomposition of the CBR inference points out three steps: retrieval, adaptation and memorization. *Retrieval* selects a source case (srce, Sol(srce)) that is judged similar to tgt, according to some similarity criterion. *Adaptation* aims at solving tgt thanks to the retrieved case (srce, Sol(srce)). Thus, a successful adaptation provides a solution Sol(tgt) to tgt, in general by modification of Sol(srce). Finally,

R.O. Weber and M.M. Richter (Eds.): ICCBR 2007, LNAI 4626, pp. 239–253, 2007.

memorization evaluates the utility of storing the new case $(\text{tgt}, \text{Sol}(\text{tgt}))$ in the case base and stores it when it is useful. Knowledge-intensive approaches of CBR are such that the domain knowledge plays a key role (and not only the case base) [2]. This holds for the conservative adaptation as it is shown hereafter.

1.1 CBR and Adaptation

In general, it is considered that the CBR inference is based on the following principle:

Similar problems have similar solutions.   (CBR principle)

This principle has been formalized in [3] by

$$\mathcal{T}(\text{Sol}(\text{srce}), \text{Sol}(\text{tgt})) \geq \mathcal{S}(\text{srce}, \text{tgt})$$

(translated with our notations) where $\mathcal{S}$ and $\mathcal{T}$ are similarity measures respectively between problems and solutions: the solution $\text{Sol}(\text{tgt})$ is constrained to be similar to $\text{Sol}(\text{srce})$. There are multiple ways of specifying the adaptation step in accordance to the CBR principle, starting from the so-called *null adaptation*:

$$\text{Sol}(\text{tgt}) := \text{Sol}(\text{srce})$$ (null adaptation)

Null adaptation is justified in [1] by the fact that "people often do very little adaptation". One limit of null adaptation is that the fact "$\text{Sol}(\text{srce})$ solves tgt" may contradict some domain knowledge. In this case, a strategy for adaptation is the following:

$\text{Sol}(\text{tgt})$ is obtained by keeping from $\text{Sol}(\text{srce})$ as much as possible features

while keeping the available knowledge consistent.   (conservative adaptation)

Conservative adaptation aims at following the CBR principle in the sense that it tends to make the similarity $\mathcal{T}(\text{Sol}(\text{srce}), \text{Sol}(\text{tgt}))$ maximal.

1.2 Overview of the Paper

In section 2, the principle of conservative adaptation is presented with more details. It relates this kind of adaptation with the theory of revision: both are based on minimal change. Section 3 presents the basic principles of the theory of revision. This theory consists of a set of axioms that a revision operator has to satisfy. Section 4 provides a formalization of conservative adaptation based on a given revision operator. This work is motivated by an application in oncology: the KASIMIR system, in which a problem represents a class of patients and a solution represents a treatment proposal for these patients. From our study of adaptations actually performed by experts in oncology, several adaptation patterns have emerged [4]. Several of these patterns can be implemented thanks to conservative adaptation; this is what is illustrated in section 5. Section 6 discusses this work. Finally, section 7 draws some conclusions and points out new directions of work following this study.

2   Principle of Conservative Adaptation

Let us consider the following example of conservative adaptation:

Example 1. *Léon is about to invite Thècle and wants to prepare her an appropriate meal. His target problem can be specified by the characteristics of Thècle about food. Let us assume that Thècle is vegetarian (denoted by the propositional variable v) and that she has other characteristics (denoted by o) not detailed in this example: $tgt = v \wedge o$. From his experience as a host, Léon remembers that he had invited Simone some times ago and he thinks that Simone is very similar to Thècle according to food behavior, except that she is not a vegetarian: $srce = \neg v \wedge o$. He had proposed to Simone a meal with salad (s), beef (b) and a dessert (d), and she was satisfied by the two formers but has not eaten the dessert, thus Léon has retained the case $(srce, Sol(srce))$ with $Sol(srce) = s \wedge b \wedge \neg d$. Besides that, Léon has some general knowledge about food: he knows that beef is meat, that meat and tofu are protein foods, and that vegetarians do not eat meat. Thus, his domain knowledge is*

$$DK_{Léon} \quad = \quad b \Rightarrow m \quad \wedge \quad m \Rightarrow p \quad \wedge \quad t \Rightarrow p \quad \wedge \quad v \Rightarrow \neg m \qquad (1)$$

where b, m, t and p are the propositional variables for "some beef/meat/tofu/protein food is appreciated by the current guest". According to conservative adaptation, what meal should be proposed to Thècle? $Sol(srce)$ itself is not a satisfactory solution of tgt: $Sol(srce) \wedge tgt \wedge DK_{Léon}$ is unsatisfiable. However, the features s and $\neg d$ can be kept in $Sol(srce)$ to solve tgt. Moreover, what conducts to a contradiction is the fact that there is a meat, not in the fact that it is a protein food. Therefore, a solution of tgt according to conservative adaptation could be $s \wedge p \wedge \neg d$. Another one could be to replace beef by tofu: $s \wedge t \wedge \neg d$.

As this example illustrates, the adaptation process consists of a shifting from the source context to the target context. If this process is conservative, then this shifting has to operate a minimal change and, in the same time, must be consistent with the definition of the target problem. Both contexts are interpreted in the framework of the "permanent knowledge", i.e., the knowledge of the CBR system, i.e., the domain knowledge. Therefore, conservative adaptation is based on three kinds of knowledge:

(KB$_1$) The old knowledge that can be altered (but must be altered *minimally*): the knowledge related to the context of the source problem and its solution;

(KB$_2$) The new knowledge, that must not be altered during the process: the knowledge related to the context of the target problem;

 (DK) The knowledge that is permanent (true in any context): the domain knowledge (i.e., the general knowledge of the domain of the CBR system under consideration, e.g., the ontology giving the vocabulary with which the cases are expressed).

The question that is raised is "What is the minimal change on the knowledge base KB$_1$ that must be done to be consistent with knowledge base KB$_2$?" When KB$_1$ and KB$_2$ do not contradict, there is no reason to change KB$_1$ and thus, a conservative adaptation process entails KB$_1$, which amounts to a null adaptation.

This principle of minimal change of knowledge can be found in the theory of *revision*: given two knowledge bases ψ and μ, the revision of ψ by μ is a knowledge base $\psi \circ \mu$ that entails μ and makes the *minimal change* on ψ to make this revision consistent [5].

Both KB_1 and KB_2 must be interpreted in consistency with the domain knowledge DK. Thus, conservative adaptation consists, given a *revision operator* $\circ$, in computing $(DK \wedge KB_1) \circ (DK \wedge KB_2)$ and to infer from this new knowledge base the pieces of information that are relevant to $Sol(tgt)$.

So, before formalizing conservative adaptation, it is necessary to introduce the notion of revision operator.

3   Revision of a Knowledge Base

Revision of a knowledge base has been formalized independently from a particular logic in the so-called AGM theory (called after the initials of the [5]'s authors). This theory has been applied, in particular, to propositional logic by [6] and it is this work that is presented here, since the current paper concentrates on this formalism.

3.1   Preliminaries

The propositional formulas are assumed to be built on $\mathcal{V}$, a finite set of propositional variables. An interpretation $\mathcal{I}$ is a function from $\mathcal{V}$ to the pair $\{\texttt{true}, \texttt{false}\}$. If $a \in \mathcal{V}$, $\mathcal{I}(a)$ is also denoted by $a^{\mathcal{I}}$. $\mathcal{I}$ is extended on the set of formulas in the usual way $((f \wedge g)^{\mathcal{I}} = \texttt{true}$ iff $f^{\mathcal{I}} = \texttt{true}$ *and* $g^{\mathcal{I}} = \texttt{true}$, etc.). A model of a formula f is an interpretation $\mathcal{I}$ such that $f^{\mathcal{I}} = \texttt{true}$. $Mod(f)$ denotes the set of models of f. f is satisfiable means that $Mod(f) \neq \emptyset$. f entails g (resp., f is equivalent to g), denoted by $f \vDash g$ (resp., $f \equiv g$), if $Mod(f) \subseteq Mod(g)$ (resp., $Mod(f) = Mod(g)$), for two formulas f and g. Finally, $g \vDash_f h$ (resp., $g \equiv_f h$) means that g entails h (resp., g is equivalent to h) under f: $f \wedge g \vDash h$ (resp., $f \wedge g \equiv f \wedge h$).

3.2   Katsuno and Mendelzon's Axioms

Let $\circ$ be a revision operator. $\psi \circ \mu$ is a formula expressing the revision of ψ by μ, according to the operator $\circ$: ψ is the "old" knowledge base (that has to be revised), μ is the "new" knowledge base (that contains knowledge revising the old one). The axioms that a revision operator on propositional logic has to satisfy are:

(R1) $\psi \circ \mu \vDash \mu$ (the revision operator has to retain all the knowledge of the new knowledge base μ);

(R2) If $\psi \wedge \mu$ is satisfiable, then $\psi \circ \mu \equiv \psi \wedge \mu$ (if the new knowledge base does not contradict the old one, then every piece of knowledge of the two bases has to be kept);

(R3) If μ is satisfiable then $\psi \circ \mu$ is also satisfiable ($\circ$ does not lead to an unsatisfiable knowledge base, unless the new knowledge is itself unsatisfiable);

(R4) If $\psi \equiv \psi'$ and $\mu \equiv \mu'$ then $\psi \circ \mu \equiv \psi' \circ \mu'$ (the revision operator follows the principle of irrelevance of syntax);

(R5) $(\psi \circ \mu) \wedge \phi \models \psi \circ (\mu \wedge \phi)$;
(R6) If $(\psi \circ \mu) \wedge \phi$ is satisfiable then $\psi \circ (\mu \wedge \phi) \models (\psi \circ \mu) \wedge \phi$.

for ψ, ψ', μ, μ', and ϕ, five propositional formulas. (R5) and (R6) are less obvious to understand than (R1) to (R4) and are explained in [6]. They are linked with the idea that a revision operator is supposed to perform a minimal change: $\psi \circ \mu$ keeps "as much as possible" from ψ while being consistent with μ.

3.3   Distance-Based Revision Operators and Dalal's Revision Operator

In [6], a characterization and a survey of revision operators in propositional logic is proposed. This paper highlights a class of revision operators based on distances between interpretations. Let $\mathtt{dist}$ be such a distance. For M_1 and M_2 two sets of interpretations and $\mathcal{J}$ an interpretation,

$$\text{let } \mathtt{dist}(M_1, \mathcal{J}) = \min\{\mathtt{dist}(\mathcal{I}, \mathcal{J}) \mid \mathcal{I} \in M_1\}$$
$$\text{and } \mathtt{dist}(M_1, M_2) = \min\{\mathtt{dist}(M_1, \mathcal{J}) \mid \mathcal{J} \in M_2\}$$
$$= \min\{\mathtt{dist}(\mathcal{I}, \mathcal{J}) \mid \mathcal{I} \in M_1 \text{ and } \mathcal{J} \in M_2\}$$

Now let ψ and μ be two formulas and $\Delta = \mathtt{dist}(\mathrm{Mod}(\psi), \mathrm{Mod}(\mu))$. Then, the revision operator $\circ_{\mathtt{dist}}$ based on $\mathtt{dist}$ is defined by

$$\mathrm{Mod}(\psi \circ_{\mathtt{dist}} \mu) = \{\mathcal{J} \mid \mathcal{J} \in \mathrm{Mod}(\mu) \text{ and } \mathtt{dist}(\mathrm{Mod}(\psi), \mathcal{J}) = \Delta\} \qquad (2)$$

This equation defines $\psi \circ_{\mathtt{dist}} \mu$ up to the equivalence between formulas (since we adhere to the principle of irrelevance of syntax, this is sufficient). The proof that axioms (R1) to (R6) hold for $\circ_{\mathtt{dist}}$ is a rather straightforward application of the definitions above. Note, in particular, that (R2) can be proven thanks to the equivalence $\mathtt{dist}(\mathcal{I}, \mathcal{J}) = 0$ iff $\mathcal{I} = \mathcal{J}$, for two interpretations $\mathcal{I}$ and $\mathcal{J}$.

The intuition of minimal change from ψ to $\psi \circ_{\mathtt{dist}} \mu$ is related to the distance $\mathtt{dist}$ between interpretations: $\psi \circ_{\mathtt{dist}} \mu$ is the knowledge base whose interpretations are the interpretations of μ that are the closest ones to those of ψ, according to $\mathtt{dist}$.

The Dalal's revision operator $\circ_D$ [7] is such a revision operator: it corresponds to the Hamming distance between interpretations defined by: $\mathtt{dist}(\mathcal{I}, \mathcal{J})$ is the number of propositional variables $a \in \mathcal{V}$ such that $a^{\mathcal{I}} \neq a^{\mathcal{J}}$. It is this operator that has been chosen for the examples of this paper.

4   Formalization of Conservative Adaptation

This section presents a formalization of conservative adaptation based on a revision operator in propositional logic, an example using Dalal's revision operator, and a discussion on the meaning of Katsuno and Mendelzon's axioms for conservative adaptation.

4.1   Conservative Adaptation Process Based on a Revision Operator

It is assumed that all the knowledge entities of the CBR system under consideration (problem, solution, domain knowledge) are represented in the formalism of propositional logic. The natural language assertion "pb is the current problem" is translated simply in pb. From this and the informal definition of conservative adaptation presented in section 1.1, it comes that, in order to solve tgt by conservative adaptation of (srce, Sol(srce)), the following knowledge bases are defined:

$$KB_1 = srce \wedge Sol(srce) \qquad KB_2 = tgt$$

Let ∘ be a revision operator. The ∘-conservative adaptation consists in computing $TSKCA = (DK \wedge KB_1) \circ (DK \wedge KB_2)$, where DK denotes the domain knowledge, and, second, entails from TSKCA pieces of information relevant to solve tgt (TSKCA is the target solution knowledge inferred by conservative adaptation).

4.2 Example

From this principle, the example 1 (section 2) can be treated as follows. The knowledge bases DK, KB_1, and KB_2 are:

$$DK = DK_{Léon} \qquad KB_1 = \neg v \wedge o \wedge s \wedge b \wedge \neg d \qquad KB_2 = v \wedge o$$

With $\circ_D$, the Dalal's revision operator on propositional logic (see section 3), it can be proven that

$$TSKCA = (DK \wedge KB_1) \circ_D (DK \wedge KB_2) \equiv_{DK_{Léon}} \underbrace{v \wedge o}_{(a)} \wedge \underbrace{s \wedge \neg b \wedge \neg m \wedge p \wedge \neg d}_{(b)}$$

The target problem $tgt = v \wedge o = (a)$ is entailed by TSKCA: this is true for any revision operator. Indeed, from axiom (R1), $TSKCA \vDash DK \wedge KB_2$, and $DK \wedge KB_2 \vDash tgt$ (since $KB_2 = tgt$).

In the example 1, two plausible solutions were proposed: $Sol_1(tgt) = s \wedge p \wedge \neg d$ and $Sol_2(tgt) = s \wedge t \wedge \neg d$. The former can be entailed from TSKCA: (b) $\vdash Sol_1(tgt)$. But (b) indicates more precisely that some protein food that is not meat ($\neg m \wedge p$) is appreciated by the guest. This does not involve that the guest appreciates tofu. Now, let $DK'_{Léon}$ be the knowledge of Léon with the additional knowledge that the only available protein food of Léon that is not meat is tofu: $DK'_{Léon} = DK_{Léon} \wedge (p \Rightarrow m \vee t)$. By substituting $DK_{Léon}$ by $DK'_{Léon}$ it comes:

$$TSKCA' = (DK'_{Léon} \wedge KB_1) \circ_D (DK'_{Léon} \wedge KB_2) \equiv_{DK'_{Léon}} \underbrace{v \wedge o}_{(a)} \wedge \underbrace{s \wedge \neg b \wedge \neg m \wedge t \wedge p \wedge \neg d}_{(b')}$$

and (b') $\vDash Sol_2(tgt)$.

4.3 Revision Axioms and Conservative Adaptation

Now, the Katsuno and Mendelzon's axioms (R1) to (R6) can be reconsidered at the light of conservative adaptation.

(R1) applied to conservative adaptation gives $TSKCA \vDash DK \wedge tgt$. If this assertion were violated, this would mean that there exists a model $\mathcal{I}$ of TSKCA such that $\mathcal{I} \notin Mod(DK \wedge tgt) = Mod(DK) \cap Mod(tgt)$. Therefore $\mathcal{I}$ would contradict

- Either the definition of the target problem (meaning that the conservative adaptation solves *another* target problem!);
- Or the domain knowledge (that has to be preserved by conservative adaptation).

Thus, using a revision operator that satisfies (R1) prevents from these two kinds of contradiction.

Let us assume that $DK \land KB_1 \land KB_2$ is satisfiable: in other words $srce \land Sol(srce) \land tgt$ is consistent under the domain knowledge DK. Then, (R2) entails that $TSKCA \equiv DK \land KB_1 \land KB_2$. Thus, $TSKCA \vDash srce \land Sol(srce) \land tgt$: if tgt is consistent with $srce \land Sol(srce)$ in DK, then it can be inferred by conservative adaptation that $Sol(srce)$ solves tgt. This is consistent with the principle of this kind of adaptation: $Sol(tgt)$ is obtained by keeping from $Sol(srce)$ as much as possible, and if the fact "$Sol(srce)$ solves tgt" does not contradict DK, then conservative adaptation amounts to null adaptation.

(R3) gives: if $DK \land KB_2$ is satisfiable then $TSKCA$ is satisfiable. The satisfiability of $DK \land KB_2 = DK \land tgt$ means that the specification of the target problem does not contradict the domain knowledge. Thus, (R3) involves that whenever the target problem is specified in accordance with the CBR domain knowledge, conservative adaptation provides a satisfiable result.

(R4) simply means that conservative adaptation follows the principle of irrelevance of syntax.

The conjunction of (R5) and (R6) can be reformulated as follows:

- Either $(\psi \circ \mu) \land \phi$ is unsatisfiable,
- Or $(\psi \circ \mu) \land \phi \equiv \psi \circ (\mu \land \phi)$.

Applied to conservative adaptation, it gives:

- Either $TSKCA \land \phi$ is unsatisfiable,
- Or $TSKCA \land \phi \equiv (DK \land KB_1) \circ (DK \land KB_2 \land \phi)$.

Let ϕ be a formula representing some additional knowledge about the target problem. If ϕ is consistent with the result of conservative adaptation ($TSKCA$ is satisfiable) then the conjunction of (R5) and (R6) entails that adding ϕ to tgt before the conservative adaptation process or after it gives the same result.

5   Application: Conservative Adaptation of Breast Cancer Treatments

The KASIMIR project aims at the management of decision protocols in oncology. Such decision protocols have to be adapted for some medical cases. This section shows some examples of adaptations performed by experts (oncologists) and how these examples can be modeled by conservative adaptation.

5.1   The KASIMIR Project

A huge research effort has been put on oncology during the last decades. As a consequence, the complexity of decision support in oncology has greatly increased. The KASIMIR project aims at the management of decision knowledge in oncology. A big part of this knowledge is constituted by decision protocols. For example, the protocol for breast cancer treatment is a document indicating how a patient suffering from this disease has to be treated. Therefore, this protocol can be seen as a set of rules Pat ⟶ Ttt, where Pat denotes a class of patients and Ttt, a treatment for the patients in Pat.

Unfortunately, for about one third of the patients, this protocol cannot be applied, for example because of contraindications (other examples are presented in section 5.3). Indeed, it is practically impossible to list all the specific situations that prevent the application of the protocol: this is an instance of what [8] calls the qualification problem. It has been shown that, in these situations, the oncologists often *adapt* the protocol for recommending a treatment to these patients (meaning that they reuse the protocol, but not in a straightforward manner). More precisely, given the description of a target patient, tgt, a rule Pat ⟶ Ttt is selected in the protocol, such that Pat is similar to tgt, and Ttt is adapted to fit the particularities of tgt. If the rules Pat ⟶ Ttt are assimilated to source cases (srce, Sol(srce)) –srce = Pat and Sol(srce) = Ttt– then this process is an instance of CBR, with the particularity that the source cases are *generalized cases* (as called in [9]), also known as *ossified cases* (in [1]).

5.2   The KASIMIR System

The KASIMIR system aims at assisting physicians in their decision making process. The last version of this system has been implemented as a semantic portal (i.e., a portal of the semantic Web [10]), using as representation language the W3C recommendation OWL DL that is equivalent to the expressive description logic $\mathcal{SHOIN}(D)$ [11].

This system performs protocol application: given a protocol written in OWL DL and the description of a patient, it highlights the treatments that the protocol recommends to the patient. It also implements adaptation processes, based on some adaptation knowledge [12]. Current studies aim at acquiring this adaptation knowledge: from experts [4] and semi-automatically [13].

Conservative adaptation appears as a promising research direction for adaptation within the KASIMIR system, as next section shows.

5.3   Examples

Two examples corresponding to real situations of decision problems of breast cancer treatment are presented below, followed by an explanation in term of conservative adaptation expressed in propositional logic. The first one deals with the adaptation of a contraindicated treatment. The second one deals with the adaptation of an inapplicable treatment. Other examples of conservative adaptation related to KASIMIR are presented in the research report [14].

Example 2. *Some hormones of the human body facilitate the development of cells. In particular, oestrogens facilitate the growing of some breast cells, including some cancerous breast cells. A hormonotherapy is a long term treatment that aims at inhibiting the development of hormons (or their actions) to lower the chance of having a new tumor developed after the other types of treatment (surgery, chemotherapy and radiotherapy) have been applied. Tamoxifen is a hormonotherapy drug that prevents from* *the action of oestrogen on breast cells. Unfortunately, tamoxifen is contraindicated for people having a liver disease. The protocol of breast cancer treatment does not take into account this contraindication and the physicians have to substitute tamoxifen by another treatment having the same therapeutic benefit (or a similar therapeutic benefit). For example, they can use anti-aromatases (a drug not contraindicated for people suffering from the liver) instead of tamoxifen or a treatment consisting of the ablation of ovaries (that are organs producing oestrogen).*

This example can be formalized as follows. The protocol rules leading to a recommendation of tamoxifen are formalized by $c_1 \Rightarrow tam$, $c_2 \Rightarrow tam$, ... $c_n \Rightarrow tam$. This can be expressed by a single rule $c \Rightarrow tam$, where $c = c_1 \vee c_2 \vee \ldots \vee c_n$. This rule corresponds to a source case $(\text{srce}, \text{Sol}(\text{srce}))$ with $\text{srce} = c$ and $\text{Sol}(\text{srce}) = tam$. Now, let us consider a woman suffering from breast cancer such that (1) the application of the protocol gives tamoxifen and (2) she suffers from a liver disease. This medical case can be formalized by $\text{tgt} = \gamma \wedge liver\text{-}disease$, where γ is such that $\gamma \vDash_{\text{DK}} c$ (see below). The domain knowledge is:

$$\text{DK} \quad = \quad \gamma \Rightarrow c \quad \wedge \quad liver\text{-}disease \Rightarrow \neg tam \quad \wedge \quad tam \Rightarrow anti\text{-}oestrogen \quad \wedge$$
$$anti\text{-}aromatases \Rightarrow anti\text{-}oestrogen \quad \wedge \quad ovary\text{-}ablation \Rightarrow anti\text{-}oestrogen$$

$liver\text{-}disease \Rightarrow \neg tam$ represents the contraindication of tamoxifen for people suffering from a liver disease. $tam \Rightarrow anti\text{-}oestrogen$ (resp., $anti\text{-}aromatases \Rightarrow anti\text{-}oestrogen$, $ovary\text{-}ablation \Rightarrow anti\text{-}oestrogen$) indicates that if tamoxifen (resp. anti-aromatases, ablation of ovaries) is recommended then an anti-oestrogen treatment is recommended.

The $\circ_D$-conservative adaptation leads to:

$$\text{TSKCA} = (\text{DK} \wedge c \wedge tam) \circ_D (\text{DK} \wedge \gamma \wedge liver\text{-}disease)$$
$$\equiv_{\text{DK}} \gamma \wedge c \wedge \neg tam \wedge anti\text{-}oestrogen$$

If the only anti-oestrogen treatments besides tamoxifen are constituted by anti-aromatases and ablation of ovaries then an additional piece of knowledge can be added to DK: $anti\text{-}oestrogen \Rightarrow (tam \vee anti\text{-}aromatases \vee ovary\text{-}ablation)$. With this additional knowledge, $anti\text{-}aromatases \vee ovary\text{-}ablation$ is involved by TSKCA. It can be noticed that this example is very similar to example 1: meat is (in a sense) contraindicated by vegetarians.

Example 3. *The large majority of persons suffering from breast cancer are woman (about 99%). This explains why the protocol of breast cancer treatment has been written for them. When the physicians are confronted to the medical case of a man suffering from this disease, they adapt the protocol. For example, let us consider a man with some characteristics c, such that, for a woman with these characteristics, the protocol recommends a radical mastectomy (surgery consisting of a breast ablation), a "FEC 100" chemotherapy and an ovary ablation. Both the surgery and the chemotherapy can be applied efficiently to the man, but no ovary ablation (for obvious reasons). The adaptation usually consists in keeping the surgery and the chemotherapy and in substituting the ovary ablation by an anti-oestrogen treatment, such as tamoxifen or anti-aromatases.*

The protocol rule used in this example is the source case $(\texttt{srce}, \texttt{Sol}(\texttt{srce}))$ with $\texttt{srce} = c \wedge woman$ and $\texttt{Sol}(\texttt{srce}) = radical\text{-}mastectomy \wedge FEC\text{-}100 \wedge ovary\text{-}ablation$: $radical\text{-}mastectomy$ (resp., $FEC\text{-}100$, $ovary\text{-}ablation$) denotes the persons for which a radical mastectomy (resp., a FEC 100 chemotherapy, an ovary ablation) is recommended. The target problem is $\texttt{tgt} = c \wedge man$. The domain knowledge is constituted by the domain knowledge of example 2 (denoted hereafter by $\texttt{DK}_{\texttt{ex.2}}$), the fact that ovary ablation is impossible for men, and the fact that men are not women:

$$\texttt{DK} \quad = \quad \texttt{DK}_{\texttt{ex.2}} \quad \wedge \quad man \Rightarrow \neg ovary\text{-}ablation \quad \wedge \quad \neg woman \vee \neg man$$

The result of conservative adaptation, TSKCA, is such that:

$$\texttt{TSKCA} \equiv_{\texttt{DK}} c \wedge man \wedge radical\text{-}mastectomy \wedge FEC\text{-}100 \wedge \neg ovary\text{-}ablation \wedge anti\text{-}oestrogen$$

If the only available anti-oestrogen therapies are tamoxifen, anti-aromatases, and ovary ablation, then DK can be substituted by

$$\texttt{DK}' = \texttt{DK} \wedge (anti\text{-}oestrogen \Rightarrow tam \vee anti\text{-}aromatases \vee ovary\text{-}ablation)$$

Then, the $\circ_{\texttt{D}}$-conservative adaptation gives TSKCA′ such that $\texttt{TSKCA}' \equiv \texttt{TSKCA} \wedge (tam \vee anti\text{-}aromatases)$.

6   Discussion

There have been several proposals in the CBR literature of adaptation approach taxonomies. In [14], conservative adaptation is situated among several such taxonomies. Below, the main part of this work is presented.

Conservative Adaptation and Adaptation by Generalization and Specialization. In [1] is introduced the *abstraction and respecialization* approach to adaptation that consists in (1) abstracting the solution $\texttt{Sol}(\texttt{srce})$ of $\texttt{srce}$ into a solution $\texttt{Sol}(\texttt{A})$ of an abstract problem A, and (2) specializing $\texttt{Sol}(\texttt{A})$ in order to solve $\texttt{tgt}$. According to [15], this adaptation can be better qualified as a generalization/specialization approach (versus an abstraction/refinement approach), but this distinction is not made in [1].

The examples of conservative adaptations presented in this paper may be seen as the application of some generalization and specialization adaptations. For instance, in example 3, $\texttt{Sol}(\texttt{srce})$ is generalized by substituting *ovary-ablation* by *anti-oestrogen* and then, whenever it is known that the only available anti-oestrogen treatments besides ovary ablation are tamoxifen and anti-aromatases, *anti-oestrogen* is specialized into *tam $\vee$ anti-aromatases*.

This behavior of $\circ_{\texttt{D}}$-conservative adaptation can be understood thanks to a definition of distance-based revision operators $\circ_{\texttt{dist}}$ (such as $\circ_{\texttt{D}}$), equivalent to the one given in section 3.3 and inspired from [7]. This definition is as follows. First, for any real number $\delta \geq 0$, let G^{δ} be a function that maps a propositional formula ψ based on a set of variables $\mathcal{V}$ to another formula $G^{\delta}(\psi)$ on $\mathcal{V}$, such that

$$\texttt{Mod}(G^{\delta}(\psi)) = \{\mathcal{I} \mid \mathcal{I}\text{: interpretation on } \mathcal{V} \text{ and } \texttt{dist}(\texttt{Mod}(\psi), \mathcal{I}) \leq \delta\}$$

G^δ realizes a generalization: $\psi \models G^\delta(\psi)$ for any ψ and any δ. Moreover $G^0(\psi) \equiv \psi$. Finally, if $0 \leq \delta \leq \varepsilon$, then $G^\delta(\psi) \models G^\varepsilon(\psi)$. For ψ and μ, two satisfiable formulas on $\mathcal{V}$, let Δ be the least value δ such that $G^\delta(\psi) \wedge \mu$ is satisfiable.[1] Then, $\psi \circ_{\text{dist}} \mu$ can be defined by $\psi \circ_{\text{dist}} \mu = G^\Delta(\psi) \wedge \mu$. If either ψ or μ is unsatisfiable, then $\psi \circ_{\text{dist}} \mu \equiv \mu$. It can be proven easily that this definition of $\circ_{\text{dist}}$ is equivalent to the one of section 3.3 (as soon as syntax is considered to be irrelevant). Thus $\psi \circ_{\text{dist}} \mu$ can be interpreted as follows: it is obtained by generalizing ψ in a minimal way (according to the scale $(\{G^\delta(\psi)\}_\delta, \models)$) in order to be consistent with μ, and then, it is specialized by a conjunction with μ.

Conservative Adaptation and Problem Decomposition. In [16], adaptation is considered within three taxonomies. One of them is the taxonomy of the adaptation operators used in adaptation procedures. Let us consider two of these operators: (1) subgoaling operators and (2) goal interaction operators. (1) A subgoaling operator aims at decomposing the adaptation task into subtasks while (2) a goal interaction operator handles interactions between solution parts: it detects and repairs bad interactions. It may be considered that conservative adaptation performs a combination of operations of types (1) and (2). The specification of a target problem –the formula tgt– can be viewed as a goal specification (the goal is to find a solution consistent with tgt). If tgt $\equiv$ tgt$_1$ $\wedge$ tgt$_2$ then tgt$_1$ and tgt$_2$ are two subgoals of the target problem. Conservative adaptation provides a solution that is consistent with both subgoals. Therefore, this approach to adaptation considers possibly interacting subgoals as a combined use of operators of types (1) and (2) would do. However, if the revision operator is considered as a black box, then the distinction between (1) and (2) operators is not visible.

Conservative Adaptation and Copy-Modify-Test Approach to Adaptation. In [17], a general model of adaptation in CBR is presented in a task formalism: starting from the analysis of several CBR systems implementing an adaptation process, they propose a hierarchical decomposition of adaptation in tasks and subtasks. The idea is that many (if not all) transformational adaptation procedures implemented in CBR systems may be modelled according to this scheme, considering a subset of these tasks. Conservative adaptation may be seen as a way of instantiating the following subset of tasks:

- Copy solution (that is similar to *null adaptation*);
- Select and modify discrepancies (by removing, substituting, and/or adding some pieces of information using the domain knowledge);
- Test consistency.

---

[1] In fact, $\Delta = \text{dist}(\text{Mod}(\psi), \text{Mod}(\mu))$ realizes this: (a) $G^\Delta(\psi) \wedge \mu$ is satisfiable and (b) if $\delta < \Delta$ then $G^\delta(\psi) \wedge \mu$ is unsatisfiable. (a) can be proven as follows. Let $\mathcal{J} \in \text{Mod}(\mu)$ such that $\Delta = \text{dist}(\text{Mod}(\psi), \mathcal{J})$ (this makes sense since $\text{Mod}(\psi) \neq \emptyset$). Thus, $\mathcal{J}$ also belongs to $\text{Mod}(G^\Delta(\psi))$ and so $\mathcal{J} \in \text{Mod}(G^\Delta(\psi)) \cap \text{Mod}(\mu) = \text{Mod}(G^\Delta(\psi) \wedge \mu)$, which proves (a). (b) can be proven by contradiction, assuming that there is some $\delta < \Delta$ such that $G^\delta(\psi) \wedge \mu$ is satisfiable. If so, let $\mathcal{J} \in \text{Mod}(G^\delta(\psi) \wedge \mu)$, thus $\mathcal{J} \in \text{Mod}(G^\delta(\psi))$ and $\mathcal{J} \in \text{Mod}(\mu)$. Therefore $\Delta = \text{dist}(\text{Mod}(\psi), \text{Mod}(\mu)) \leq \delta$, which is in contradiction with the assumption $\delta < \Delta$. Thus, (b) is also proven.

In fact, in conservative adaptation, it is the revision operator that processes all these tasks: it performs a minimal change that can be seen as a sequence of copy, modification, and test tasks. Moreover, it uses the domain knowledge in order to choose the features to be modified in order to reach consistency.

Therefore, conservative adaptation may also be seen as an instanciation of the reuse and revise steps of the Aamodt and Plaza's cycle [18]: reuse is performed by a simple copy and revise by a revision operator. It can be noticed that, to our knowledge, the revise step of the CBR cycle has not been related to the AGM theory of revision: we have found only one paper on CBR using revision techniques [19], but not for the purpose of the reasoning process itself, but for the maintenance of the case base and of a rule base when there are some evolutions in time (according to [20], this is more an update of a knowledge base than a revision of it).

7   Conclusion and Future Work

In case-based reasoning, adaptation is often considered as a difficult task, in comparison to retrieval that is supposed to be simpler to design and to implement. This paper presents an approach to adaptation, called conservative adaptation, that is based on the theory of revision: it consists in keeping as much as possible from the source case while being consistent with the target problem and the domain knowledge. Conservative adaptation is defined, formalized in the framework of propositional logic, and this formalism can be extended to other knowledge representation formalisms. Moreover, it is shown through examples that conservative adaptation covers some of the adaptations performed by experts in oncology. This approach to adaptation can be used for knowledge-intensive approaches to CBR, since it requires some domain knowledge. A noticeable feature of conservative adaptation is that the adaptation knowledge is part of the domain knowledge: it is not constituted by, e.g., a set of adaptation rules. This paper has also shown that the AGM theory of revision and the huge amount of research based on this theory may be of interest for adaptation in CBR: a revision operator should be considered as a tool for designing a conservative adaptation procedure.

Section 6 shows that conservative adaptation shares some common features with general approaches to adaptation defined in the CBR literature, in particular handling the problems of consistency, extending null adaptation (also called *copy of the source solution*), and, at least for $\circ_{\tt dist}$-conservative adaptation, being equivalent to an adaptation by generalization and specialization.

Several theoretical issues about conservative adaptation have been addressed in the research report [14], that deserve further investigations. Some of them are listed hereafter. One of them is the design of a retrieval procedure suited to conservative adaptation. It is based on the assumption that a conservative adaptation process is better than another one if the former requires less change thant the latter. This leads to prefer the source case $(\tt srce^1, Sol(srce^1))$ to the source case $(\tt srce^2, Sol(srce^2))$ if the former requires less change than the latter, which amounts to $\Delta^1 < \Delta^2$, with

$$\Delta^i = \mathtt{dist}(\mathtt{Mod}(\mathtt{DK} \wedge \mathtt{srce}^i \wedge \mathtt{Sol}(\mathtt{srce}^i)), \mathtt{Mod}(\mathtt{DK} \wedge \mathtt{tgt})) \quad (i \in \{1,2\})$$

However, on the one hand, this preference criterion may be insufficient to distinguish two source cases and, on the other hand, its naive implementation is intractable.

The knowledge required for conservative adaptation is the domain knowledge DK of the CBR system under consideration: DK is useful to point out the features of the source case that need to be adapted to the context of the target problem. Thus, with insufficient domain knowledge, conservative adaptation may provide an unsatisfying solution to the target problem: this solution contradicts the expert knowledge but does not contradict DK. In other words, the failed result of conservative adaptation is due to the gap between DK and the expert knowledge (a gap that cannot be completely filled in practice, due to the qualification problem mentioned in section 5.1). Thus, from an analysis of the failure, some new domain knowledge can be acquired and added to the current DK. Therefore, a CBR system may learn new domain knowledge from the explanations that follow failed conservative adaptation, which involves an improvement of its competence. The paper [21] proposes an approach to address this issue together with the description of a prototype that implements this approach.

Conservative adaptation covers only a part of the adaptations actually performed by experts. Some other adaptations could be covered thanks to extensions of conservative adaptation, as shown in the research report [14]. In particular, an approach to adaptation consists in (1) finding a substitution σ such that $\sigma(\text{srce}) \equiv_{\text{DK}} \text{tgt}$, (2) applying σ on $\text{Sol}(\text{srce})$ to provide a first solution of $\text{Sol}_1(\text{tgt})$, and (3) repairing $\text{Sol}_1(\text{tgt})$ to make it consistent with the domain knowledge. The step (3) can be performed by a revision operator. For instance, in [14], the well-known example of "beef and broccoli adaptation" of the CHEF system [22] is re-described using the revision operator $\circ_{\text{D}}$. This also shows, more generally, that revision operators can be used in various ways as tools for designing and implementing adaptation processes. The study of such extensions is another research direction.

Another future work is the combination of several source cases (srce^1, $\text{Sol}(\text{srce}^1)$), ...($\text{srce}^n, \text{Sol}(\text{srce}^n)$) to solve a sole target problem tgt. It is planned to study this issue thanks to the notion of merging of propositional knowledge bases [23]: given a multiset $\{\psi_1, \ldots \psi_n\}$ of knowledge bases to be merged and a consistent knowledge base μ (the "integrity constraint"), a merging operator builds a knowledge base $\triangle_\mu(\{\psi_1, \ldots \psi_n\})$ that is consistent with μ and keeps "as much as possible" information from the ψ_i's. This extends the notion of revision: $\circ$ defined by $\psi \circ \mu = \triangle_\mu(\{\psi\})$ is a revision operator. In the same way, an approach to case combination that extends conservative adaptation is to compute $\triangle_\mu(\{\psi_1, \ldots \psi_n\})$ with $\psi_i = \text{DK} \wedge \text{srce}^i \wedge \text{Sol}(\text{srce}^i)$ ($i \in \{1, 2, \ldots n\}$) and $\mu = \text{DK} \wedge \text{tgt}$. The relevance of this approach for practical problems of case combination in CBR remains to be studied.

From a practical viewpoint, future work will be the development and the use of a conservative adaptation tool to be integrated within the KASIMIR system. A first tool implementing the Dalal's revision operator has been implemented, but it can be optimized. As an example, the most complex computation of a revision presented in [14] is based on 16 propositional variables and requires about 25 seconds on a current PC. Another practical issue is the integration of conservative adaptation in the KASIMIR system, which raises two problems. The first one is that both the cases and the domain knowledge of KASIMIR are represented in a formalism equivalent to the description logic $\mathcal{SHOIN}(\text{D})$. Therefore, either adaptation problems expressed in $\mathcal{SHOIN}(\text{D})$

are translated in propositional logic and solved in this formalism, or a revision operator has to be implemented for a description logic compatible with KASIMIR (this second solution requires a formalization of conservative adaptation in description logics; a first proposal of such a formalization is given in [14]). When this integration issue is addressed, a comprehensive evaluation of the scope of conservative adaptation can be carried out. The second problem of integration is linked with the already existing adaptation module of KASIMIR [12], that is based on adaptation rules (roughly speaking). How conservative adaptation and this rule-based adaptation module can be integrated together in order to provide a unique adaptation module enabling complex adaptation processes (each of them being composed of a conservative adaptation and some rule-based adaptations)? This question should be addressed thanks to earlier work on adaptation composition and decomposition [24].

Acknowledgements

The author would like to thank greatly Pierre Marquis who, some years ago, has taught him the basis of the revision theory, has, more recently, suggested some interesting references about this theory, has made some interesting remarks on an earlier version of this paper, and has suggested him to use merging operators for case combination. He also wants to thank his beloved daughter who is, for some strange reason, at the origin of this study. Finally, he thanks the reviewers for their interesting comments.

References

1. Riesbeck, C.K., Schank, R.C.: Inside Case-Based Reasoning. Lawrence Erlbaum Associates, Hillsdale, New Jersey (1989)
2. Aamodt, A.: Knowledge-Intensive Case-Based Reasoning and Sustained Learning. In: Aiello, L.C. (ed.) ECAI'90. Proceedings of the 9th European Conference on Artificial Intelligence, August 1990 (1990)
3. Dubois, D., Esteva, F., Garcia, P., Godo, L., López de Màntaras, R., Prade, H.: Fuzzy set modelling in case-based reasoning. Int. J. of Intelligent Systems 13, 345–373 (1998)
4. d'Aquin, M., Lieber, J., Napoli, A.: Adaptation Knowledge Acquisition: a Case Study for Case-Based Decision Support in Oncology. Computational Intelligence (an International Journal) 22(3/4), 161–176 (2006)
5. Alchourrón, C.E., Gärdenfors, P., Makinson, D.: On the Logic of Theory Change: partial meet functions for contraction and revision. Journal of Symbolic Logic 50, 510–530 (1985)
6. Katsuno, H., Mendelzon, A.: Propositional knowledge base revision and minimal change. Artificial Intelligence 52(3), 263–294 (1991)
7. Dalal, M.: Investigations into a theory of knowledge base revision: Preliminary report. In: AAAI, pp. 475–479 (1988)
8. McCarthy, J.: Epistemological Problems of Artificial Intelligence. In: IJCAI'77. Proceedings of the 5th International Joint Conference on Artificial Intelligence, Cambridge (Massachussetts), pp. 1038–1044 (1977)
9. Maximini, K., Maximini, R., Bergmann, R.: An investigation of generalized cases. In: Ashley, K.D., Bridge, D.G. (eds.) ICCBR 2003. LNCS, vol. 2689, pp. 261–275. Springer, Heidelberg (2003)

10. Fensel, D., Hendler, J., Lieberman, H., Wahlster, W. (eds.): Spinning the Semantic Web. The MIT Press, Cambridge, Massachusetts (2003)
11. Staab, S., Studer, R. (eds.): Handbook on Ontologies. Springer, Berlin (2004)
12. d'Aquin, M., Lieber, J., Napoli, A.: Case-Based Reasoning within Semantic Web Technologies. In: Euzenat, J., Domingue, J. (eds.) AIMSA 2006. LNCS (LNAI), vol. 4183, pp. 190–200. Springer, Heidelberg (2006)
13. d'Aquin, M., Badra, F., Lafrogne, S., Lieber, J., Napoli, A., Szathmary, L.: Case Base Mining for Adaptation Knowledge Acquisition. In: Veloso, M.M. (ed.) IJCAI'07. Proceedings of the 20th International Joint Conference on Artificial Intelligence, pp. 750–755. Morgan Kaufmann, San Francisco (2007)
14. Lieber, J.: A Definition and a Formalization of Conservative Adaptation for Knowledge-Intensive Case-Based Reasoning – Application to Decision Support in Oncology (A Preliminary Report). Research report, LORIA (2006)
15. Bergmann, R.: Learning Plan Abstractions. In: Ohlbach, H.J. (ed.) GWAI-92: Advances in Artificial Intelligence. LNCS (LNAI), vol. 671, pp. 187–198. Springer, Heidelberg (1993)
16. Hanney, K., Keane, M.T., Smyth, B., Cunningham, P.: Systems, Tasks and Adaptation Knowledge: Revealing Some Revealing Dependencies. In: Aamodt, A., Veloso, M.M. (eds.) ICCBR'95. LNCS, vol. 1010, pp. 461–470. Springer, Heidelberg (1995)
17. Fuchs, B., Mille, A.: A Knowledge-Level Task Model of Adaptation in Case-Based Reasoning. In: Althoff, K.-D., Bergmann, R., Branting, L.K. (eds.) ICCBR-99. LNCS (LNAI), vol. 1650, pp. 118–131. Springer, Heidelberg (1999)
18. Aamodt, A., Plaza, E.: Case-based Reasoning: Foundational Issues, Methodological Variations, and System Approaches. AI Communications 7(1), 39–59 (1994)
19. Pavón Rial, R., Laza Fidalgo, R., Gómez Rodriguez, A., Corchado Rodriguez, J.M.: Improving the Revision Stage of a CBR System with Belief Revision Techniques. Computing and information systems journal 8(2), 40–45 (2001)
20. Katsuno, H., Mendelzon, A.: On the Difference Between Updating a Knowledge Base and Revising. In: Allen, J.F., Fikes, R., Sandewall, E. (eds.) KR'91: Principles of Knowledge Representation and Reasoning, pp. 387–394. Morgan Kaufmann, San Mateo, California (1991)
21. Cordier, A., Fuchs, B., Lieber, J., Mille, A.: Failure Analysis for Domain Knowledge Acquisition in a Knowledge-Intensive CBR System. LNCS, vol. 4626, pp. 448–462. Springer, Heidelberg (to appear)
22. Hammond, K.J.: Case-Based Planning: A Framework for Planning from Experience. Cognitive Science 14(3), 385–443 (1990)
23. Konieczny, S., Lang, J., Marquis, P.: DA^2 merging operators. Artificial Intelligence 157(1-2), 49–79 (2004)
24. Lieber, J.: Reformulations and Adaptation Decomposition (S. Schmitt and I. Vollrath (volume editor)). In: Lieber, J., Melis, E., Mille, A., Napoli, A. (eds.) Formalisation of Adaptation in Case-Based Reasoning, Third International Conference on Case-Based Reasoning Workshop, ICCBR-99 Workshop, vol. (3), University of Kaiserslautern, LSA (1999)

Methodological Assistance for Integrating Data Quality Evaluations into Case-Based Reasoning Systems

Annett Bierer

Chemnitz University of Technology
Faculty for economics and business administration
Chair of business process management and knowledge management
Reichenhainer Straße 39/611
D-09126 Chemnitz
Germany
Tel.: +49(0)371/531-33975; Fax: +49 (0) 371/531-26529
annett.bierer@wirtschaft.tu-chemnitz.de

Abstract. Case-based reasoning systems are used in more and more problem-solving domains supporting the long-term reusing and storing of experience. The performance of these systems essentially depends on the quality of the experience items in their knowledge base, represented as data. Defects in the quality of these data may interfere with the system's performance. By means of inspection and review the data quality is measured, evaluated, assured and improved. To support these activities in a case-based reasoning system, data quality criteria and control processes are required. Previous work in the field of data quality in case-based reasoning remains at a comparatively coarse-grained level. Existing approaches mostly do not provide sufficient methodological assistance in defining fine-grained quality criteria or designing and implementing control processes for the measurement and evaluation of the data quality. Therefore this paper proposes two approaches for methodological assistance in developing data quality inspections and data quality management for case-based reasoning systems.

Keywords: data quality, data quality management, closed loop control, goal-question-metrics-approach.

1 Introduction

Technologies for reusing and storing experience based on case-based reasoning (CBR)-methodology are now mature and case-based reasoning systems (CBR systems) are increasingly applied for long-term use in practice. The performance of CBR systems is essentially affected by the quality of the experience items, contained as data in their knowledge base (hereinafter referred to as data quality). If the current data quality level drops beyond an expected level, quality defects are indicated. They, in turn, are signs of errors. The notion of error includes all differences between a current data quality level and a required one,

R.O. Weber and M.M. Richter (Eds.): ICCBR 2007, LNAI 4626, pp. 254–268, 2007.

such as differences to the experience in the real world as well as entry errors and processing failures. Causes of insufficient data quality can be found in both the development and the use of a CBR system [14]. Causes of defects in system development may result from insufficient surveys and analyses of the relevant experience, from an inappropriate representation of the experience in the data and data structures, from implementation faults, or from testing and training. Causes of defects during system use, on which the paper focuses, may result from entry errors (e.g., entry of queries, acquisition of cases) and from changes in the relevant environment (e.g., incremental advances in the experience, radical or sudden technological and organisational changes).

To keep the data quality in the knowledge base at a constant level during the whole system's lifetime, the CBR system must be able to evaluate its current data quality level at any time. Developers and administrators are faced with the difficulty of several data structures for heterogeneous experience items, which will have different requirements for their measurement and evaluation. This is because:

- the data, representing heterogeneous experience items, show a varying sensitivity with respect to errors and failures,
- not necessarily every defect must directly result in triggering and executing maintenance operations, and
- no general criteria are applicable to the evaluation of the data quality of the knowledge base.

Numerous contributions in case-based reasoner maintenance provide learning algorithms for assuring the quality for several experience items. But there are only few criteria (e.g., problem-solution regularity, problem-distribution regularity, efficiency, competence) available which provide a sufficient granularity for the purposive execution of these algorithms. More analytical work is needed to identify potential sources for causes of defects in the knowledge base.

This paper presents initial steps towards an understanding of the importance of fine-grained evaluations of data quality in the knowledge base. After introducing a case study and the framework for the examination, an approach to define, analyse and interpret measures for the evaluation of data quality in CBR systems will be introduced. For the evaluation of data quality assurance and improvement, control processes based upon the principle of closed-loop control will be examined.

2   A CBR System for Quotation Processing

For a better understanding of main issues of the paper, the descriptions are illustrated by a simple case study. Its central components in the knowledge base will be presented in the following [19,22].

The knowledge base of a CBR system for assistance in quotation processing contains experience about the interrelation between technological features and manufacturing costs for rolls for the napping of fabrics. It consists of the following components:

- The cases in the case base are composed of the problem part that describes technological features in the form of attribute-value pairs, which are central for estimating manufacturing costs, and the solution part that describes among others cost accountings which will be dynamically generated in reference to a costing database. It also includes an explanation part for further information.
- The vocabulary contains characteristics of the technological features such as whether the feature is numeric or symbolic and referencing specifications for the data interchange with the costing database.
- The features are partly numeric (e.g., length of the roll, diameter) and partly symbolic (e.g., impact of fabric draft). Because of this, knowledge-intensive local similarity measures are used (for the notion of knowledge-intensive similarity measures see [27]).
- For the adaptation of a proposed solution to the current problem situation the solution transformation includes methods for similarity-based cost estimation as known from costing in early engineering stages [8,9].
- Additionally, membership functions are needed for the mapping of numeric features to linguistic terms in order to guarantee a numeric computation for vague feature values in queries (e.g., the length of the roll is given as "medium" to indicate that the length would probably be somewhere between 300 and 700 mm).

3   Framework for Examination

The performance preservation of the CBR system is an issue of operational data quality management. Its main task is the continuous improvement of the data quality in the knowledge base.

3.1   Why Data Quality?

CBR systems as for quotation processing combine functionalities and properties of CBR and database and data warehouse techniques respectively. CBR provides a structuring for the problem-solving processes and the idea of storing concrete technical and costing episodes as cases. The content of the knowledge base is represented as data in heterogeneous databases (e.g., the solution description is contained in a costing database, the vocabulary is described in a technical database). Reasoning algorithms process the data and present it to the users. The human user interprets the data as information. Knowledge is what the user needs in order to perform the interpretation process, and what he gets learned from the new information [1]. The focus of the paper centers the underlying data which are the basis for executing the problem-solving processes and enabling the users to make more precise decisions.

3.2   Data Quality and Data Quality Management

Today's comprehension of quality comes from the Latin term "qualitas", which means characteristics, constitutions or conditions of objects and is not valued

[31]. Data quality can be described from several perspectives such as the view of objective characterisations of the data or the view of the users [12]. Analogous to the general notion of quality in the norms of the Deutsches Institut für Normung (DIN e.V.) and based upon the user-based approach data quality means: the totality of features of the data in the knowledge containers that fulfil stated or implied needs [7]. It is a multidimensional measure for the applicability of the data in order to fulfil the purpose of their acquisition/generation, whereas this applicability may change if the underlying needs are changing with time [21,31].

Data quality management refers to all activities within the framework of a quality management system that constitutes data relevant aspects of the quality policy, goals and responsibilities and their transformation into operational planning, controlling, assurance and improvement processes [7]. The management of data quality is in fact an executive function, whereby the quality-related tasks have to be integrated (e.g., specification of data quality strategies) at all management levels. The higher the management level the more data quality abstracts from the specific information system, here from the CBR system.

This paper only considers operational criteria and means for the design of quality inspection processes for evaluating data quality within a CBR system based on the user's needs [15,28].

3.3   Phases of Operational Data Quality Management

The activities of operational data quality management are implemented with reference to the contexts of the enterprise and the considered CBR system. Against the background of continuous quality improvement the process-related plan-do-check-act-cycle (PDCA-cycle) by [5] has been established for structuring the activities. The cycle represents the idea of a continuous quality improvement process through the cyclic sequence of the phases data quality planning (plan), control (do), assurance (check) and improvement (act) (Fig. 1).

Data quality planning. In data quality planning the expectations and needs of the users (e.g., in the domain of quotation processing) are acquired and gradually transferred into guidelines for the design of the data in the knowledge base. Goals and requirements for data quality are defined, metrics are derived, categorized, weighted and appropriate measuring points and methods within the CBR cycle are selected [13,28]. The outcome of the phase is a data quality plan, which includes the requirements, the needed processes, resources, means and methods for measuring, and required records for the verification of conformity of the provided data with the experience in the real world [14].

Data quality control. After the planning the current data quality status has to be checked and verified every now and then. The execution of checking and verifying is the function of data quality control. The aim is to hold the fixed quality specifications and to guarantee the mastery of the required processes [13]. For the achievement of the objectives, data quality control is responsible for the monitoring and controlling of data quality and the initiation of maintenance

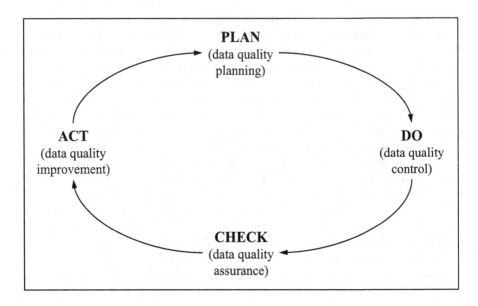

Fig. 1. Operational tasks in data quality management [24]

operations. Analysing to which extent the data quality and the requirements diverge is an issue of quality inspections [28].

Data quality assurance and improvement. Activities in data quality assurance and improvement are the initiation and execution of operations necessary to assure or to restore a required data quality level or even to increase it. Assurance, for instance, contains organisational arrangements like raising the user's awareness of data quality in the CBR system or automatically checking the inputs from users when entering queries or adding new cases. Restoring and improving are data administration tasks. These comprise maintenance operations, which in turn encompass case-based reasoner maintenance.

4   Metrics for Measuring and Evaluating Data Quality

The assessment of data quality presumes the setting of goals, metrics and measures respectively and their context-dependent interpretation derived from the goals. There are a variety of approaches and mechanisms to assist this top-down process. In this paper the Goal-Question-Metrics-Approach (GQM) will be used.

4.1   The Goal-Question-Metrics-Approach

For a CBR system to measure and to assess its data quality in a purposeful way, it requires (1) the specification of goals for the data quality in the knowledge base and the CBR system as whole, (2) their transfer to measuring data to operationalise the goals, and (3) the provision of a framework for domain-dependent interpretation of the measuring data to understand the goals [2]. First, the user requirements are acquired as accurately as possible in order to deliver quantifiable measures. These measures provide the basis of comparison for analysing the achievement of objectives with reference to the data quality level.

GQM is a systematic approach for defining and evaluating a set of operational measures, based on measurements. GQM can assist the adjustment and integration of goals, processes, components and component models into the CBR system. The approach assumes that measuring and evaluating the data quality requires [3]:

- the setting of goals for the quality of the data in the knowledge base (conceptual level),
- the refining of the goals into a set of quantifiable questions to characterize the assessment of specific goals (operational level), and
- the definition of measuring data associated with the questions in order to answer them in a quantitative way.

Every combination of these three levels builds up a hierarchical structure, which is called a GQM-model.

4.2   Deriving Data Quality Measures

Deriving data quality measures and evaluation models by means of the GQM-approach requires the existence of operationally defined data quality goals. In order to derive them the gap between the user's needs and their representation in goals has to be closed. In doing so, pyramids of needs may be built.

User requirements represent subjective expectations of the users regarding the performance of the CBR system. Usually, expectations are not directly transferable into data quality goals. They must be split up gradually until a suitable level for deriving questions is reached (Fig. 2) [16].

In a pyramid of needs each higher need (primary need) is decomposed step-by-step to partial needs (secondary, tertiary needs etc.) step-by-step until the transformation into product and process characteristics and the derivation of goals are feasible. For better understanding the figure below (Fig. 2) visualises the primary need "retrieval of experience-activating data for the efficient estimation of expected manufacturing cost", in short: *information*. Please note that this need has already been "translated". This means the voices of the users have already been transferred into a language understandable by the team of developers. The need information, for instance, can be split up into the three top-level-goals for CBR systems [25,26] *competence* (the range of cost estimation queries solved), *problem-solving efficiency* (e.g., the average retrieval time), and *solution quality* (e.g., the error level in the proposed solution). *Competence* may be split up further into *coverage* and *reachability* of the case base [25] or *problem-solution regularity* and *problem-distribution regularity* [18,30]. These tertiary needs have

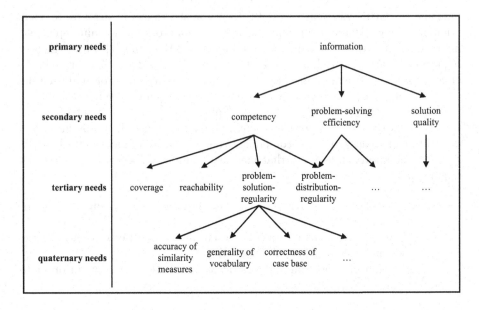

Fig. 2. Pyramid of needs for the example "information"

a relatively low granularity as a basis for assessing the data quality. Therefore an exclusive view on sinking *problem-solution regularity* in a CBR system is not sufficient for displaying directly whether there are defects in similarity measures, vocabulary or in the case base. Further analyses for identification of the knowledge base components causing the defects will be necessary. Therefore the tertiary need *problem-solution regularity* is here split up into quaternary needs like *accuracy of similarity measures, generality of vocabulary, correctness of the case base*.

The construction of pyramids of needs shows in a simple way the necessity for different goals and metrics for evaluating the data quality in a CBR system. Here, the quaternary needs are taken as a starting point for goal setting in GQM.

Data Quality Goals. Goals are defined for measuring objects (e.g., cases, retrieval, local similarity measures), for some purpose (e.g., evaluation, characterisation, improvement), with respect to various data quality criteria (e.g., minimality, consistency, speed), from various points of view (e.g., user, maintenance or experience engineer), and in relation to a relevant environment. Measuring objects are [3]:

- products: experience items, the data and data structures in the knowledge base, user queries or outcomes of the process steps retrieve, reuse and revise, which will be generated or processed during the system's lifetime;
- processes: activities associated with time like the processes of retrieve, reuse, revise itself;

– resources: employees as suppliers of experience, source systems etc., that are used in CBR for generating the outcomes.

The selection of an object must guarantee that it is possible to analyse and interpret its quality level directly with respect to a given data quality criterion, to expose the causes of its defects, and to repair the defect. As stated above a goal in GQM consists of the following components [2]:

purpose:
    Analyse   *(objects: products, processes, resources)*
    for purpose of   *(evaluation, decrease, improvement, ...)*
perspective:
    with respect to   *(quality criteria: timeliness, accuracy, validity, ...)*
    from the point of view *(user, maintenance engineer, developer, ...)*
environment:
    in the following context *(personal-, resource-, process-related factor, ...)*

Taking this scheme, an example for a concrete data quality goal is formulated as follows: "Analyse the *similarity assessment in the retrieval sets* for the purpose of *evaluation* of the *accuracy* from the point of view of an *experience engineer* depending on *advances in the experience of the human experts*".

Questions and Metrics. For assessing the achievement of goals they are refined into several questions. The questions must be qualified for characterizing the object of measuring with reference to the defined goal. The questions focused on the data quality goal break down the issues into major components for specific analyses. Please note that several GQM-models can have some questions in common.

After that each question is refined into a set of significant metrics. Several metrics may be used in order to answer different questions. For example the number of incorrect cases in a retrieval set for a given query may be a metric for both the generality of vocabulary and the accuracy of similarity measures.

Based on the metrics, skilled experience engineers and/or maintenance engineers as well as the CBR system, by itself, are able to evaluate the data quality of an object of measuring by analysing and interpreting its current values. In practice, several metrics may be aggregated to higher figures and key performance indicators respectively (e.g., the accuracy level of similarity measures and correctness level of the case base are aggregated for assessing the problem-solution regularity). When the domains of metrics differ, no aggregation by mathematical equations is feasible. But it is possible to combine and visualise their contribution to a higher-ranked figure by radar charts or other methods. The following table shows an example for questions and metrics using the GQM-goal defined above (Table 1).

The identification of questions and metrics is a nontrivial process, because both deriving questions and refining and relating appropriate metrics depend on various factors, among them (for the knowledge base of the case study):

Table 1. Example for questions and metrics for the data quality goal of evaluating the accuracy of similarity assessment

Goal:	Analyse the similarity assessment in the retrieval sets for the purpose of evaluation of the accuracy from the point of view of an experience engineer depending on advances in the experience of the human experts.
Question:	What is the current accuracy of similarity assessment?
	Metric: average maximum similarity of retrieved cases, average number of queries with no really "most similar" case in the retrieval set
Question:	Is the accuracy of similarity assessment improving with time?
	Metric: $$\frac{\text{current average of accuracy}}{\text{baseline average of accuracy}} \times 100$$ or a subjective rating by an experience engineer after consulting with the users

- The understanding of correlations between technological features and the manufacturing cost for the development of suitable similarity measures with the developers, experience engineers and users of the CBR system.
- The existence of assessable and generalisable cost effects that will be needed for the definition of universally valid local similarity measures.
- The approach used for case representation (for an overview of case representation approaches see [4]) which for example determines what kind of similarity measure is needed or what has to be included in the vocabulary.
- The maturity of the measuring object similarity measures depending on the status of the system's life cycle. If the CBR system has reached a steady state, the metrics must allow the comparison with the real-world experience. If the CBR system is at the training stage, the metrics and their interpretation must allow learning and tuning the similarity measures up to an acceptable level for practical application.
- The learning process for refining and adapting the GQM-models. The defined metrics, must help in evaluating not only the measuring objects but also the reliability of the evaluation models.

The GQM-approach enables experience and maintenance engineers to define and to interpret operational and measurable knowledge bases for CBR systems. Because of numerous and various factors affecting the construction of GQM-models, the GQM-processes are usually nontrivial and highly contextual.

5   Processes for Measuring and Evaluating Data Quality

The defined goals and metrics may not be sufficient without appropriate measurement, evaluation and maintenance processes. Specific control processes for data quality inspections must be designed in order to meet a high-quality knowledge base. In conventional quality management the control process design is often based upon the cybernetic principle of closed-loop control [13,20].

5.1   Role and Types of Data Quality Inspections

For the assessment of a current data quality level and its comparison with fixed requirements quality inspections are useful instruments. There are several types of inspections [28]:

- static inspections used for dated off-line reviews of the experience-related data in the knowledge base in order to check their conformance with the defined goals (e.g., checking the case base for inconsistencies or redundancies);
- dynamic inspections used for on-line and off-line reviews by counts and tests associated with time in order to check the performance of the knowledge base over time (e.g., changes in accuracy of the similarity measures since start of the system's use); and
- defects and error analyses used for checking and revising errors, faults or failures documented error lists by the users during an active problem-solving cycle (e.g., user documents erroneous cases).

5.2   Closed-Loop Control as a Process Framework

Closed loop control is a process cycle. It is based on serial measuring of controlled variables. The variables are compared with some external reference value and are modified when the resulting differences are outside the limits [6]. For visualising the process of control control loops are constructed.

In the following the process of closed loop control [11] will be described in terms of the data quality goal of "analysing the feature weights for the purpose of evaluation of their accuracy from the point of view of the experience engineer and in the following context: the company has bought a new machine reducing the manufacturing costs for lathing the diameter of the rolls" (Fig. 3).

Closed loop control in the example aims at evaluating the data quality level of the feature weights in the global similarity measure of the CBR system for quotation processing (*controlled system*). The reason for checking the accuracy of the feature weights is to account for changes in the distribution of the manufacturing costs because of the new lathe (*disturbance variable*). First, the current values of the feature weights and the cost distribution are measured (*controlled variables*: weights, cost distribution). The current values are compared with the changed cost distributions (*reference variables*: distributions of costs because of the new machine). Then potential modifications are investigated by test retrievals and when the differences in the similarity assessments with the old and the new cost distribution are too high, maintenance operations are initiated (*controller*: comparison, test retrievals, initiating operations). Maintenance operations that could solve the inaccuracy of the feature weights have to be selected and executed (*manipulating variable*: selection, timing and realisation of operations automatically or through interaction with the maintenance engineer).

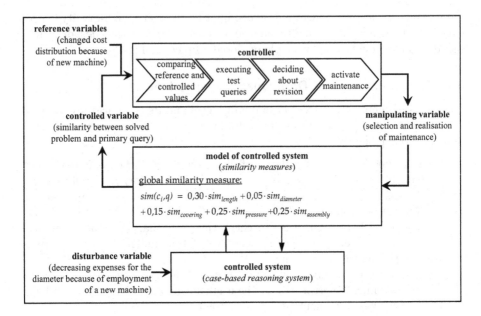

Fig. 3. Example of a control loop (following [11])

CBR systems bear some complexity in the knowledge base. Because of this, control processes do not operate directly on the controlled system but with models of the CBR system. The models contain only the components and relations of the knowledge base that are required for the respective process (*model of controlled system*: here the similarity measures and the case base is needed). The controlled system and its models interact by sensors (forwarding the disturbance and measuring data) and actors (reactivate the system after restoring the feature weights).

The example illustrated in Fig. 3 is only a simple instance of constructing and executing closed loop control. Usually, in real-world applications control loops are not as simple as that. In practice, hierarchically structured control loops are also needed. In this case, higher ranked loops will determine the reference variables and their values for subordinated stages and these in turn will be based upon the controlled variables of their subordinated control loops [13]. When assuming for the example above instead of changing the feature weights new features become necessary because of buying the new machine, changes are essential not only in the similarity measures but also in the vocabulary and the case base. The control loop for measuring, reviewing and restoring the vocabulary could provide disturbance variables and values for the controlled variables of the control loops for the evaluation of the similarity measures and the case base.

5.3 Integrating Control Loops in the Case-Based Reasoning Cycle

In addition to designing the basic sequences of closed loop control, the example above raises the question of when, where and how to specify and to integrate the three main tasks for controlling the data quality (measurements, evaluations and modifications) into the CBR system's processes efficiently. There are a variety of potential combinable strategies, which can be categorized as follows [17,29,30]:

- Strategies for the *scope* determine whether the main tasks affect only one component of the knowledge base (local), multiple components (multiple) or the whole knowledge base (global), or no inspections are made at all. Another differentiation would divide into operations affecting only a small data set (narrow) or a large data set or the whole knowledge base respectively (broad).
- Strategies for *triggering* determine the timing of the tasks. Triggering can be done at a set frequency (periodic), at every problem-solving cycle (continuous), in response to well-defined but nonperiodic conditions (conditional) or at externally given, nonperiodic and irregular conditions (ad hoc).
- Strategies for *integration* in the CBR cycle define whether one or all tasks are executed during an active problem-solving cycle (on-line) or during a pause of reasoning or in a separated maintenance cycle (off-line).
- Depending on the *integration of the users* into the control processes, especially the maintenance engineer, the tasks are executed by hand (manual), in interaction between the maintenance engineer and the system (interactive) or autonomously without human interaction (automatic).

By the combination of several strategies and their integration in the processes of control loops it will be possible to instantiate continuous data quality improvement processes. The postulation that the CBR system has to be able to evaluate the data quality of its knowledge base at any time requires at least the integration of measurement and evaluation into the CBR cycle.

For static quality inspections, measurement as well as the evaluation and modification are realised off-line in a separated maintenance cycle with the steps review and restore [23]. They are carried out off-line and may be periodic, interactive or automatic and local, multiple or global.

For dynamic quality inspections as well as defects and error analyses, collections of measuring data are carried out during an active problem-solving cycle (on-line, continuous, local, multiple, global). In order to enable the system to collect the measuring data the classical CBR steps retrieve, reuse, revise and retain will be enhanced by additional specific tasks (e.g., measuring data for number of queries) and methods (e.g., marking initially mismatches by an automatic counter). The continuous calculation of current averages of the metrics could be carried out during the active problem-solving cycle, too. The evaluation, in terms of comparisons of controlled variables and reference variables in the controller, is not integrated in the problem-solving cycle but in the maintenance cycle. The controller undertakes, autonomously or through interaction with the maintenance engineer, the task of reviewing the data quality level. When the measured and the required data quality level differ with reference to a particular quality goal, maintenance operations must be initialised. The selection and execution of these operations are issues of the restoring process and correspond with the tasks of the manipulating variables.

5.4   Combining Strategies for the Example in the Control Loop

For revising the feature weights to meet the changed distribution of manufacturing costs it is assumed that the revision can only be achieved by a manual adaptation executed by the maintenance engineer. At the time the revision has to be executed, no training data are available for the application of a learning algorithm for feature weighting. For this reason, a manual modification instead of an automatic learning is preferred here.

The control process is fully executed during a maintenance cycle (off-line). It is a static inspection because there are no dynamically collected measuring data that point out the technological change. The global similarity measure is the only component affected by the modifications (local). The process is triggered by the disturbing event of the new and more cost-effective machine (conditional). The activities in the controller, especially the comparison of weights before and after the reallocation and test retrievals for analysing the impacts of the changed weights, are triggered by the maintenance engineer in assistance with the experience engineer and the system (interactive). The maintenance operation consists of revising the feature weights in the global similarity measure and restoring the knowledge base for further application (manual).

After reactivation the case-based reasoning system data collection must be intensified for evaluating whether the accuracy of the modified weights meets the real world cost effects.

6   Conclusion

The growing and more long-term use of CBR systems requires fine-grained measurements and evaluations of the data quality in the whole knowledge base.

The presented methodologies are useful instruments for defining data quality goals and metrics as well as for designing and implementing control processes for continuous data quality improvement in the knowledge base. The integration of closed loop control processes into the CBR cycle as well as an enhanced maintenance cycle enable the measurement and evaluation of quality at a more fine-grained level. It is worthwhile to stress the fact out that both approaches are compatible with the strategies, frameworks, maintenance and learning algorithms developed for case-based reasoner maintenance.

The case study of the CBR system for quotation processing used to illustrate central aspects of the approaches is a relatively simple example. However, the idea of fine-grained quality evaluations and the approaches may be transferred to more complex CBR systems with different approaches for case representation and in several application domains.

References

1. Aamodt, A., Nygård, M.: Different roles and mutual dependencies of data, information, and knowledge - an AI perspective on their integration. In: Data and Knowledge Engineering, vol. 16(3), pp. 191–222 (1995)

2. Basili, V.R.: Software modelling and measurement: The Goal Question Metric Paradigm. Technical Report CS-TR-2956, Department of Computer Science, University of Maryland (September 1992)
3. Basili, V.R., Caldiera, G., Rombach, H.D.: The Goal Question Metric Approach. In: Marciniak, J.J. (ed.) Encyclopedia of Software Engineering, vol. 1, pp. 528–532. John Wiley & Sons, Chichester (1994)
4. Bergmann, R., Althoff, K.-D., Breen, S., Göker, M., Manago, M., Traphöner, R., Wess, S. (eds.): Developing Industrial Case-Based Reasoning Applications. LNCS (LNAI), vol. 1612. Springer, Heidelberg (2003)
5. Deming, W.E.: Out of the Crisis. MIT Press, Cambridge (1986)
6. Deutsches Institut für Normung e.V (Hrsg.): DIN 19226-1:1994-02. Leittechnik; Regelungstechnik und Steuerungstechnik; Allgemeine Grundbegriffe. Beuth Verlag, Berlin Wien Zürich (1994)
7. Deutsches Institut für Normung e.V (Hrsg.): Qualitätsmanagement, Statistik, Zertifizierung: Begriffe aus DIN-Normen. Beuth Verlag, Berlin Wien Zürich (1995)
8. Ehrlenspiel, K., et al.: Konstruktionsbegleitende Kalkulation in der Produktentwicklung. In: Kostenrechnungspraxis, vol. 1, pp. 69–76 (1996)
9. Ehrlenspiel, K.: Kostengünstig Konstruieren: Kostenmanagement bei der integrierten Produktentwicklung. Springer, Heidelberg (2005)
10. Eppler, M.J.: Managing Information Quality. Increasing the Value of Information in Knowledge-intensive Products and Processes. Springer, Heidelberg (2003)
11. Ferstl, O.K, Sinz, E.J.: Grundlagen der Wirtschaftsinformatik. Band I. Verlag Oldenbourg, München Wien (2001)
12. Garvin, D.A.: What Does Product Quality' Really Mean? In: Sloan Management Review, vol. 26(1), pp. 25–43 (1984)
13. Helfert, M.: Planung und Messung der Datenqualität in Data-Warehouse-Systemen. Dissertation Universität St. Gallen, Nr. 2648. Difo-Druck GmbH, Bamberg (2002)
14. Hinrichs, H.: Datenqualitätsmanagement in Data Warehouse Systemen. Dissertation Universität Oldenburg, Logos, Berlin (2002)
15. Institute of Electrical and Electronics Engineers (eds.): IEEE Standard 729-1983: Glossary of Software Engineering Technology (1983)
16. Juran, J.M.: Handbuch der Qualitätsplanung. Verlag Moderne Industrie, Landsberg/Lech (1991)
17. Leake, D.B., Wilson, D.C.: Categorizing Case-Base Maintenance: Dimensions and Directions. In: Smyth, B., Cunningham, P. (eds.) EWCBR 1998. LNCS (LNAI), vol. 1488, pp. 196–207. Springer, Heidelberg (1998)
18. Leake, D.B., Wilson, D.C.: When Experience is Wrong: Examining CBR for Changing Tasks and Environments. In: Althoff, K.-D., Bergmann, R., Branting, L.K. (eds.) Case-Based Reasoning Research and Development. LNCS (LNAI), vol. 1650, pp. 218–232. Springer, Heidelberg (1999)
19. Meyer, S.: Verarbeitung unscharfer Informationen für die fallbasierte Kostenschätzung im Angebotsengineering, Dissertation Technische Universität Chemnitz. Verlag der Gesellschaft für Unternehmensrechnung und Controlling, Chemnitz (2001)
20. Pfeifer, T.: Qualitätsregelkreis. In: Zollonds, H.-D. (ed.) Lexikon Qualitätsmanagement: Handbuch des modernen Managements auf Basis des Qualitätsmanagements, pp. 998–1002. Hanser Verlag, München Wien (2001)

21. Quix, Chr.J.: Metadatenverwaltung zur qualitätsorientierten Informationslogistik in Data-Warehouse-Systemen. Dissertation an der Rheinisch-Westfälischen Technischen Hochschule Aachen (2003) (request date: 26.07.2006) Online-Resource, http://sylvester.bth.rwth-aachen.de/dissertationen/2003/263/03_263.pdf

22. Rösler, M.: Kontextsensitives Kosteninformationssystem zur Unterstützung frühzeitiger Produktkostenexpertisen im Angebotsengineering. Dissertation Technische Universität Chemnitz. Verlag der Gesellschaft für Unternehmensrechnung und Controlling, Chemnitz (2005)

23. Roth-Berghofer, Th.: Knowledge Maintenance of Case-Based Reasoning Systems. The SIAM Methodology. Dissertation der Universität Kaiserslautern. Dissertationen zur Künstlichen Intelligenz Nr. 262. Akademische Verlagsgesellschaft Aka GmbH, Berlin (2003)

24. Seghezzi, H.D.: Integriertes Qualitätsmanagement – das St. Galler Konzept. Hanser Verlag, München Wien (1996)

25. Smyth, B., McKenna, E.: Modelling the Competence of Case-Bases. In: Smyth, B., Cunningham, P. (eds.) EWCBR 1998. LNCS (LNAI), vol. 1488, pp. 208–220. Springer, Heidelberg (1998)

26. Smyth, B., McKenna, E.: Footprint-Based Retrieval. In: Althoff, K.-D., Bergmann, R., Branting, L.K. (eds.) ICCBR'99: Case-Based Reasoning Research and Development. LNCS (LNAI), vol. 1650, pp. 343–357. Springer, Heidelberg (1999)

27. Stahl, A.: Learning of Knowledge-intensive Similarity Measures in Case-Base Reasoning. Dissertation Universität Kaiserslautern. Verlag dissertation.de, Berlin (2004)

28. Wallmüller, E.: Software-Qualitätssicherung in der Praxis. Hanser Verlag, München Wien (1990)

29. Wilson, D.C.: Case Based-Maintenance: The husbandry of experience. Dissertation of the Indiana University (2001)

30. Wilson, D.C., Leake, D.B.: Maintaining case-based reasoners: dimensions and directions. In: Computational Intelligence, May 2001, vol. 17, pp. 196–213 (2001)

31. Würthele, V.: Datenqualitätsmetrik für Informationsprozesse. Dissertation Eidgenössische Technische Hochschule Zürich. Books on Demand GmbH, Norderstedt (2003)

Case-Based Anomaly Detection

Alessandro Micarelli and Giuseppe Sansonetti

Department of Computer Science and Automation
Artificial Intelligence Laboratory
Roma Tre University
Via della Vasca Navale, 79, 00146 Rome, Italy
{micarel,gsansone}@dia.uniroma3.it

Abstract. Computer and network security is an extremely active and productive research area. Scientists from all over the world address the pertaining issues, using different types of models and methods. In this article we illustrate a case-based approach where the normal user-computer interaction is read like snapshots regarding a reduced number of instances of the same application, attack-free and sufficiently different from each other. The generic case representation is obtained by interpreting in numeric form the arguments and parameters of system calls deemed potentially dangerous. The similarity measure between a new input case and the ones stored in the case library is achieved through the calculation of the Earth Mover's Distance between the corresponding feature distributions, obtained by means of cluster analysis.

1 Introduction

Throughout the years, computer networks have evolved from a mere communication means to omnipresent computational infrastructure. They have become larger, faster and extremely dynamic. Indeed, the Internet has become a crucial tool serving governments, enterprises, cultural and financial institutions and millions of everyday users. The monitoring and surveillance of network infrastructure security are entrusted to the so-called *Intrusion Detection Systems* (IDS). These systems analyze information regarding the activities of computers and computer networks, searching for elements that may allow to detect possible malicious behaviors. Attacks against a system manifest themselves like events of different nature and level of granularity. The aim of an IDS is to analyze one or more event streams and detect attacks. This can be done through two different approaches, known as *misuse detection* and *anomaly detection*. Misuse detection systems feature a certain amount of attack descriptions (*signatures*) that are compared with the stream of audit data to look for elements that allow to identify the modeled attack. Anomaly detection systems, on the other hand, follow a complementary approach. They resort to historical data regarding system activities and to the specifications of the users' expected behavior, and applications needed to build a "normal" operation model (*profile*). Then they try to identify the activity patterns that deviate from the profile thus defined. Misuse

R.O. Weber and M.M. Richter (Eds.): ICCBR 2007, LNAI 4626, pp. 269–283, 2007.
© Springer-Verlag Berlin Heidelberg 2007

and anomaly detection systems both have benefits and setbacks. The former can run a detailed analysis of audit data and usually generate a restricted number of false positives. But they can only detect the previously modeled attacks, whose profile they already possess. The latter, on the other hand, allow to detect previously unknown attacks. This benefit, though, is offset by a large quantity of false positives and by the difficulty in training the system in very dynamic environments.

Another IDS classification criterion refers to the source of the data to be analyzed. When several header fields such as IP addresses or the source and destination port numbers are analyzed, a *network-based* IDS is used. On the contrary, should the attention focus on a generic network computer and on the behavior of the underlying operating system, a *host-based* IDS is deployed.

In this contribution we present a novel approach to realize a host-based, anomaly detection system. The basic idea is to interpret, in terms of images, the data achieved from monitoring computers and computer networks. Once this thesis is accepted, it becomes possible to include models and methods drawn from the realm of Computer Vision in the Intrusion Detection field, thus obtaining new and remarkable developments. In the system this work analyzes, the normal interaction between a user and network computer is read as a snapshot referring to a limited number of instances of the same application, attack-free and sufficiently different from each other, according to the chosen similarity metric. These images are collected in a library that is run according to a Case-Based Reasoning (CBR) approach. The single image is built by extracting the sequence of events pertaining to the relevant application from the audit logs collected from the Solaris Basic Security Module (BSM) and by interpreting, in terms of numbers, the arguments and output parameters of system calls deemed potential threats. The subsequent comparison between the input image and those stored in the system memory is performed by calculating the Earth's Mover Distance between the corresponding distributions of features obtained through cluster analysis.

The rest of this contribution breaks down as follows. Section 2 presents an overview of Anomaly Detection state-of-the-art. Section 3 illustrates our system, particularly stressing the case representation method and the dissimilarity metric. Section 4 presents the experiments led so far in order to evaluate the accuracy of our case-based classifier. In the last section we draw up our conclusions and outline the developments we expect to achieve in the near future.

2   Previous Work

In literature, several approaches have been proposed for anomaly detection. The foremost systems resort to statistical methods, data mining, expert systems and neural networks [25]. Statistical methods are the most widespread. They rely on variables sampled over time to capture the user-network computer interaction, and build the profiles according to the values of such variables during the system normal operation. The deviation of current values from those associated to profiles is considered anomalous and signaled with an alarm. For this purpose, parameters such as login and logout time and the amount of resources (processor, memory, disk) consumed during each session, are used. Sampling time periods range from a few minutes to several months. Two statistical IDSs, for instance, are EMERALD [26] and IDES [6,22,18]. The former, developed at Stanford Research Institute (SRI), aims at detecting intrusions into large networks, and focuses on the system scalability. As a matter of fact, it originates as a hybrid IDS, since it executes both anomaly and misuse detections, and consists of a rule-based, forward-chaining expert system and of a statistical anomaly detector. EMERALD allows a hierarchical composition of decentralized service monitors that apply statistical analysis to network data. IDES too is an hybrid IDS developed at SRI. In particular, it employs audit data to characterize user activity and detects deviations from the expected user behavior. The extracted information regards user login and logout, program execution, directory modifications, file access and network activity.

Data mining-based systems extract implicit and potentially useful information from data. Such systems include ADAM [3], developed at the George Mason University Center for Secure Information Systems, which is based on the combination between association rules mining and classification, to identify attacks in TCP dump data. Another system belonging to this category is IDDM [1], the result of the work led by the Defense Science and Technology Organization, in Australia. It characterizes the variations between the descriptions of network data collected in different times, and raises an alarm whenever it detects significant deviations among them. The main drawback of IDDM is its difficulty in operating in real-time. Basically, this system produces its output only once it has collected and analyzed a considerable amount of data.

The expert systems developed within the Anomaly Detection domain describe the users' normal behavior through sets of rules. Examples of these systems include Wisdom & Sense [35] and ComputerWatch [7]. The former is an IDS that detects statistical anomalies in users' behavior. In order to achieve this goal, it initially builds a set of rules that statistically describes users' behavior by recording their activities over a certain time period. It then compares these rules with the input behavior in hand, showing, with an alarm, any possible inconsistent behavior. The set of rules is updated on a constant basis, to track down new user models. ComputerWatch monitors user activities by means of a rule set describing the proper usage policy of the system, and triggers an alarm for any action that does not comply with it. Such an approach is not as efficient as the statistical one in processing large quantities of audit data.

AUTOGUARD [12,9] is an alternative solution to the previously mentioned systems. It is a case-based reasoner for intrusion detection. In this system, a translator model converts the low level audit trail into a high level class representing the events. This information is stored in memory as a case library. An approach based on fuzzy logic allows to assess the similarity between the input case and every case of the system memory.

Even neural networks have been adopted in setting up anomaly IDSs. Indeed, such algorithms are used to learn the behavior of system actors (e.g., users and demons). Actually, a form of equivalence between neural networks and statistical methods has been proved [29]. The benefit of using the former is in having a simple and straightforward method to express non-linear relations between variables. Neural networks, for example, have been employed in [5] to predict user behavior. Specifically, the behavior of UNIX root users, and the most users without root privileges, is - to a great extent - predictable. The problem of neural networks is the high computational burden they require, and this is why they are not widely used in the Intrusion Detection context.

Alternative solutions to the aforesaid approaches include completely different solutions, such as sonification techniques [36], which suggest using no-speech audio as a means to convey information, and haptic technologies [11], that can reproduce tactile sensations. More tangible proposals include visualization techniques, that convert textual datasets into digital images. These techniques are mostly used to represent, in graphical form, the performance and bandwidth usage, rather than as a support tool in Intrusion Detection. Other proposed approach include tools to assess the attack level the monitored system is undergoing [31,15], and sophisticated visual user interfaces that make it easier for the user to read IDS output data [19,4,17,16,24,8,32]. These systems, in spite of their relevance, can only make the human's activities easier, but cannot replace the human itself.

As far as we know, there currently are no works in literature on automatic approaches for Intrusion Detection that employ Computer Vision techniques. However, we do believe that these techniques are now ready to be successfully adopted in non-traditional application areas [10,30,14]. Indeed, the Content-Based Image Retrieval systems are nowadays widespread. They use describers such as texture, color, shape and spatial relationships to represent and retrieve the information requested by the user [37]. Their number, but above all the high quality of their performances, convinced us to explore the possibility of exploiting these techniques for Intrusion Detection purposes.

3   Case-Based IDS Architecture

The architecture of the system we propose is shown in Figure 1. The input data are collected from monitoring computers and computer networks, while the system evaluates the relative anomaly score. Such value depends on the highest similarity value, obtained by comparing the input image with those stored in the system. The relevance feedback phase is crucial to keep the case library updated. In order for an input representation to be really useful - and hence stored in the case library to optimize the system performance should similar situations occur again in future - two requirements must be met

1. the environment (term that includes the contribution of a human expert, for instance the system administrator) must confirm the classifier indications;
2. the input representation must really provide new information, namely the case library must not already include an image that represents the category the input snapshot belongs to.

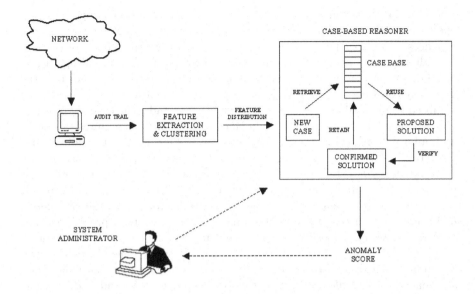

Fig. 1. System architecture

As for the second requirement, it can be met by introducing, for example, a double similarity threshold: an upper threshold (*reliability threshold*), beyond which the input case is not stored in memory, and a lower threshold (*identity threshold*), below which the anomaly score cannot be deemed reliable. Basically, the input case is added to the system knowledge base, thus assuming the profile role when its dissimilarity value, compared with all other cases in the library referring to the same application, is comprised between the two threshold values. This guarantees that the cases gradually added to the library reproduce a behavior that is not already present in memory. It is worthwhile noticing that the domain expert can intervene in the decision-making process, not only in the initial training phase of the system, but also during while the normal operation of the classifier. Indeed, the system is capable of gathering knowledge at run-time. The ease and straightforwardness of the learning phase are some of our case-based IDS real assets. Now we analyze in detail the key elements of an expert system of this kind, i.e., the case representation method and the selected similarity metric.

3.1 Case Representation

The basic assumption of the proposed approach is the following: in order for a program to cause real damages to the monitored system, it must interact with the underlying operating system through system calls. These are library functions (ranging from 70 to over 200, depending on the Unix version) that allow the programmer to use operating system services, and form the interface between user programs and the kernel.

Several host-based anomaly detection approaches have been proposed in recent years [13,38]. Such approaches build profiles starting from the system calls sequences. More specifically, these systems are based on the models of the system call sequences produced by the applications during the normal operation. In the detection phase, every monitored sequence that does not conform to the previously collected profiles is considered part of an attack.

Subsequent contributions proved, however, that intruder can easily bypass this type of monitoring [33,34,39]. A really efficient solution thus requires the use of extra information, still to be obtained from audit files. In [20] it is pointed out that return values and - above all - system call arguments can play a crucial role in the intrusion detection process. As far as return values are concerned, their conversion into graphic features is immediate, since they are already expressed in numerical terms. The process is somewhat complex for system call arguments. In this case, it is necessary to define some *models*, i.e., sets of procedures that allow to assess, in numerical terms, a certain argument feature, for instance the length of a string. The definition of a model clearly depends on the type of argument involved. In case of system calls, arguments can be subdivided into four categories: *file name, execution parameter, user ID* and *flag* [20]. The first two are `string` types, the other two `integer` types. In this first version of the system we only considered the `string` type, for which we can assess three features: length, distribution of characters and structural inference. The models relating to length and character distribution are immediate, since we are only interested in the general behavior of character frequency, regardless of the single character. As for structural inference, i.e., the deduction of the argument grammar, two processing stages are necessary. In the first stage, each character is replaced by the token that corresponds to its class; in the second stage, the possible repetitions of elements belonging to the same class are merged [20]. As regards the classes, we considered three main character categories: `lowercase` letters, `uppercase` letters and `digits`. Any character that does not belong to such categories will be included in new, separate categories. A different numerical identifier is associated with each class. For instance, considering the following class-identifier association

$$N_1: \text{lowercase letter}$$
$$N_2: \text{uppercase letter}$$
$$N_3: \text{digit}$$
$$N_4: \text{slash}$$
$$\ldots : \ldots$$

string `/etc/usr/bin` corresponds to the following ten features

$$N_4, N_1, N_4, N_1, N_4, N_1, 0, 0, 0, 0.$$

An $X = \{x_1, x_2, \cdots\}$ ordered sequence of system calls invocations is the input of the system; this stream represents an application instance. Following the previously mentioned considerations, each system call $x \in X$ is represented by the following features

$$< f_1^x, f_2^x, f_3^x, f_4^x, f_5^x, \cdots, f_{14}^x, f_{15}^x, \cdots, f_{24}^x >$$

where

f_1^x:	system call class
f_2^x:	return value
f_3^x:	error status
f_4^x:	argument length
$f_5^x, \cdots, f_{14}^x$:	argument character distribution
$f_{15}^x, \cdots, f_{24}^x$:	argument grammar inference

In the case at hand, we monitored the six system calls `execve()`, `chmod()`, `chown()`, `exit()`, `open()`, `setuid()`, since they were the only ones considered potentially dangerous. In [2] it is shown how such a choice, besides allowing to save resources, also enables to obtain more accurate results than other logging methods. In order to track down, within the audit trail, the system call sequence referring to a generic application instance, it is necessary to locate the audit record that represents system call `execve()`, which shows the path name of the relevant application, and record the *process ID* the operating system assigned to the process. The system calls to be considered are all those that follow each other, up to the relevant record at the `exit()` command, that terminates the process with that ID. Out of the entire system call sequence we have represented only the ones belonging to the aforesaid categories. For such audit events we then converted into numerical features the information on output parameters (second and third column) and arguments (remaining columns). For example, if we consider the instance of application `ps`, consisting of the system calls included in those shown in Figure 2, we can associate them with a feature matrix $(m \times n)$, where m is the number of system calls `execve()`, `chmod()`, `chown()`, `exit()`, `open()`, `setuid()` and n is 24, i.e., the number of features we decided to consider, with the matrix elements forming the corresponding values. By doing so, we obtain a snapshot of the temporal behavior of the `ps` application to be monitored. This can be successively compared with the different `ps` application profiles stored in the system. However, in order to compare the input application instance with those stored in the library, a preliminary clustering process is required.

Cluster Analysis. A cluster analysis is needed to compare system call sequences that may result rather different in terms of structure and number. In this version of the proposed architecture, we decided to run a *Hierarchical Clustering* with *Jaccard Distance*, defined as one minus the *Jaccard Coefficient*, which expresses the percentage of non zero coordinates differing from each other.

```
header,118,2,execve(2),,Fri Mar 05 06:59:01 1999, + 153037600 msec
path,/usr/bin/ps
attribute,104555,root,sys,8388614,22927,0
exec_args,1,
ps
subject,2117,root,100,2117,100,577,576,0 0 0.0.0.0
return,success,0
trailer,118

...


header,68,2,exit(2),,Fri Mar 05 06:59:01 1999, + 163035969 msec
subject,2117,root,100,2117,100,577,576,0 0 0.0.0.0
return,success,0
trailer,68
```

Fig. 2. Snippet of an application **ps** audit trail

Given a feature matrix X $(m\,x\,n)$ referring to an application generic instance, formed by m $(1\,x\,n)$ row vectors, which represent the relevant system calls, the Jaccard Distance between line vectors x_r and x_s has the following expression

$$d_{rs} = \frac{\#\left[(x_{rj} \neq x_{sj}) \wedge ((x_{rj} \neq 0) \vee (x_{sj} \neq 0))\right]}{\#\left[(x_{rj} \neq 0) \vee (x_{sj} \neq 0)\right]} \tag{1}$$

where $\#$ is the cardinality. Then, we set a threshold for the *inconsistency coefficient* so as to subdivide into clusters the objects belonging to the hierarchical tree. Such a coefficient expresses the ratio between the height of the generic link present in the cluster hierarchy and the average height of the contiguous links. This way, it is possible to determine the natural subdivisions in the database, which does, however, imply a variable number of clusters for each application instance. Every application instance is thus represented by a set consisting of different numbers of clusters, each one being represented by its centroid coordinates and by a weight equal to the total distribution fraction that belongs to it. The information thus obtained forms the generic *case*, which therefore assumes the structure of a three-field record

- a **string** type field, which contains the name of the application it refers to, obtained from the path of the relevant system call **execve()**;
- a field consisting of an array of N records (N being the number of clusters, function of the threshold value of the inconsistency coefficient) of 24 **double** type fields, which contain the values of represented features and that form the coordinates of the relative centroid;
- a field consisting of an array of N **double** values, each one expressing the weight of the corresponding cluster.

3.2 Dissimilarity Metric

Once the numerical representation is generated following the aforesaid modalities, it is necessary to select the most suitable similarity metric to compare the input case with those stored in memory. Recently, the *Earth Mover's Distance* (EMD) [27] has been suggested as a metric to assess the similarity between two distributions. EMD is based on the minimum cost to be paid to transform one distribution into another. In the case of Content-Based Image Retrieval it turned out to be more solid than histogram-based techniques, since it can also operate with representations that vary in length. If used to compare distributions with the same overall mass, it can be proved to be a real metric [28], that allows to adopt more efficient data structures and research algorithms. EMD enables us to assess the dissimilarity between two multidimensional distributions. Within our architecture context, the two distributions are located by two sets of weighted clusters. The number of clusters of each distribution can vary, and the sum of their weights can differ from the sum of the weights of the other distribution. This is why the EMD expression has a smaller sum at the denominator. In order to calculate the EMD in some feature space, it is necessary to define a distance measure - known as *ground distance* - between the single features.

The EMD value is obtained by solving the following linear programming problem: X indicates the distribution with cluster m, referring to an input instance of a certain application

$$X = \{(x_1, w_{x_1}), (x_2, w_{x_2}), \cdots, (x_m, w_{x_m})\} \tag{2}$$

where x_i represents the generic cluster and w_{x_i} the relative weight, and Y indicates the distribution with cluster n of the input instance of the same application, contained in the case library

$$Y = \{(y_1, w_{y_1}), (y_2, w_{y_2}), \cdots, (y_n, w_{y_n})\} \tag{3}$$

We then use $D = [d_{ij}]$ to indicate the matrix containing ground distances d_{ij} between clusters x_i and y_i. The goal is to calculate the value of flow $F = [f_{ij}]$, which minimizes the overall cost

$$WORK(X, Y, F) = \sum_{i=1}^{m} \sum_{j=1}^{n} f_{ij} d_{ij} \tag{4}$$

under the following constraints

$$f_{ij} \geq 0 \qquad 1 \leq i \leq m, 1 \leq j \leq n \tag{5}$$

$$\sum_{j=1}^{n} f_{ij} \leq w_{x_i} \qquad 1 \leq i \leq m \tag{6}$$

$$\sum_{i=1}^{m} f_{ij} \leq w_{y_j} \qquad 1 \leq j \leq n \tag{7}$$

$$\sum_{i=1}^{m} \sum_{j=1}^{n} f_{ij} = min \left(\sum_{i=1}^{m} w_{x_i}, \sum_{j=1}^{n} w_{y_j} \right) \tag{8}$$

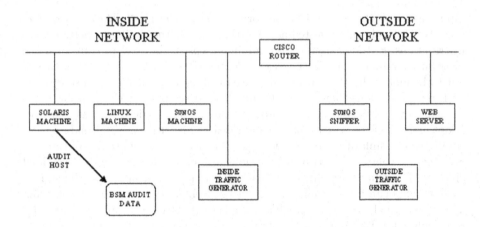

Fig. 3. Test bed network for the DARPA dataset

Once such value is calculated, the EMD assumes the following expression

$$EMD(X,Y) = \frac{\sum_{i=1}^{m} \sum_{j=1}^{n} f_{ij} d_{ij}}{\sum_{i=1}^{m} \sum_{j=1}^{n} f_{ij}} \tag{9}$$

4   Experimental Results

This section presents the experiments we led to evaluate the classification effectiveness and performance characteristics of our case-based IDS. We led these experiments using the DARPA Intrusion Detection Evaluation Data Set [21]. Despite some aspects of this *corpus* have been criticized [23], it is still the most commonly used one, both in the IDS development phase and in performance evaluation. In order to build this database, the Lincoln Laboratory researchers recreated, on a private network, the normal context in which a generic IDS runs, and to this end they employed real hosts, normal background traffic and both old and new types of attacks. The block diagram shown in Figure 3 illustrates the test bed network used at the Lincoln Laboratory. A more thorough description lies outside the purposes of this work, hence interested readers should turn to the indicated bibliographic references.

Experimental sessions were subdivided into a training phase and a testing phase. During the first phase, we set up - for each one of the relevant applications - a library of instances, representing the system normal behavior. Then, the second phase began. For these sessions we used the 1999 data of the MIT, specifically the two weeks with no attack (week 1 and week 3), to train the system. We then used the data of another two weeks (week 4 and week 5) to assess the proposed architecture ability to correctly distinguish an application with attacks from those featuring a normal user behavior. Some of the attacks included in the evaluation data did not result in the BSM logs of Solaris, hence

Table 1. Experimental results

	Total	With Attack	Identified	False Alarms
eject	9	3	3	0
fdformat	9	6	6	0
ffbconfig	2	2	2	0
ps	315	14	14	0
	335	25	25	0

we discarded them. Among the ones visible in the BSM audit trail, we focused on intrusion attempts based on *buffer overflow* vulnerability, which represent most of the current attacks on computers and computer networks. We did not try to detect the so-called *policy violations*, where the intruder tries to exploit possible misconfigurations of the system administrator, since they are linked to the normal system operation. During the experimentation, we assigned a value of 0.9 to the inconsistency coefficient threshold. We chose the Jaccard Distance as clustering distance, and the Euclidean Distance as ground distance to calculate the EMD. On the whole, we led two separate testing sessions. In the first one, we memorized all the 117 instances of the eject, fdformat, ffbconfig and ps applications we came across during the system training stage. We considered these four applications because they were the only ones subject to attack in the database provided by the Lincoln Laboratory. We then submitted the system to the test phase, setting value 5 for the reliability threshold. The input application was compared with all the instances of the same application contained in the library. With a minimum value lower than the threshold value, the application was deemed free from attacks; on the contrary, it was classified as under attack.

In the following session the database was initially empty. During the training phase, every input application was submitted to a hierarchical clustering and compared with all the instances of the same application stored in the case library. If a *rather* similar distribution, according to the EMD similarity metric, was found in the database (i.e., below the 0.5 identity threshold), this new case was then discarded, since it was already adequately represented in the database. On the contrary, the distribution (cluster and relative weights) corresponding to the new input case was included in the database. Once the training phase was over, the library contained 19 cases. We then ran the test phase, assigning the same values of the previous session to the parameters.

Table 1 shows the results obtained after the two experimental sessions. Having obtained the same values in both sessions proves that storing in memory only one case for every type of situation encountered in the training phase entails benefits in terms of calculation resources use, without hindering, in any way, the system performance, in terms of classification.

As for the results obtained, no false positives were achieved when the system underwent a testing phase comprising 335 input application instances, while the 25 applications being attacked were all correctly detected.

5   Conclusions

In this paper we have presented a host-based CBR anomaly detection system, which takes cue from the interpretation, in terms of snapshots, of system call sequences extracted from the log of the Solaris C2 Basic Security Module. This has allowed to leverage the Content-Based Image Retrieval techniques for implementing our system. These techniques - along with a CBR approach in the management of the knowledge base and in the representation of cases based on the information regarding arguments and output parameters of system calls - allowed us to obtain no false positives whatsoever, even with very few cases stored in the library. In particular, it was possible to discern the 25 application instances under attack from the 310 referring to the normal operation of the system, with a considerable accuracy margin, confirmed by the significant deviation recorded amidst EMD values referring to the corresponding feature distributions. Aside from that, the possibility of intervening on different parameters of the classification procedure (i.e., inconsistency coefficient threshold, reliability threshold, identity threshold,...) allows to duly tune the classifier sensitivity, so as to detect even the so-called *mimicry attacks* [33,34,39], through which the intruder imitates the system normal activities to bypass IDS identification.

As for the developments we plan to implement in the near future, we will focus firstly on the clustering procedure, particularly on the weight assignment mechanism. The goal is to take into account other factors too, such as the semantic differences between the several features, and the presence of outliers obtained through host monitoring activities. We will pursue the experimental appraisal of the system performance, employing new benchmarks, in order to verify its ability to detect new types of attacks, such as *policy violations*, through which the intruder tries to gain access to classified information through the normal operation of the system. In order to achieve this result it is necessary to develop case representation modalities further, considering new models, based on the information contained in audit trails, such as the *execution parameter*, the *user ID* and the *flag*, for example. We will also look into the possibility of integrating profiles with signatures referring to known attacks. Finally, we will work on a network-based version of the system, to lead a combined analysis of the data obtained from the monitoring of the entire network configuration.

Acknowledgments. We would like to thank Dick Kemmerer, Giovanni Vigna, and Luca Lucchese for the opportunity to work at the Reliable Software Laboratory, Computer Science Department, University of California, Santa Barbara (CA), USA, and at the Projects Laboratory, School of Electrical and Computer Science, Corvallis (OR), USA.

References

1. Abraham, T.: IDDM: Intrusion Detection using Data Mining Techniques. Technical Report DSTO-GD-0286, DSTO Electronics and Surveillance Research Laboratory (May 2001)

2. Axelsson, S., Lindqvist, U., Gustafson, U., Jonsson, E.: An Approach to UNIX Security Logging. In: Proceedings of the 21st NIST-NCSC National Information Systems Security Conference, Crystal City, VA, October 1998, pp. 62–75 (1998)

3. Barbara, D., Wu, N., Jajodia, S.: Detecting Novel Network Intrusions using Bayes Estimators. In: Proceedings of the First SIAM Conference on Data Mining, Chicago, IL (April 2001)

4. Couch, A.: Visualizing Huge Tracefiles with Xscal. In: LISA '96. 10th Systems Administration Conference, pp. 51–58. Chicago, IL, October 1996 (1996)

5. Debar, H., Becker, M., Siboni, D.: A Neural Network Component for an Intrusion Detection System. In: Proceedings of the IEEE Symposium on Security and Privacy, Oakland, CA, May 1992, pp. 240–250. IEEE Computer Society Press, Los Alamitos (1992)

6. Denning, D.: An Intrusion Detection Model. IEEE Transactions on Software Engineering 13(2), 222–232 (1987)

7. Dowell, C., Ramstedt, P.: The ComputerWatch Data Reduction Tool. In: Proceedings of the 13th National Computer Security Conference, Washington, DC, October 1990, pp. 99–108 (1990)

8. Erbacher, R.: Visual Traffic Monitoring and Evaluation. In: Proceedings of the Second Conference on Internet Performance and Control of Network Systems, Denver, CO, August 2001, pp. 153–160 (2001)

9. Esmaili, M., Safavi-Naini, R., Balachandran, B.M.: AUTOGUARD: A Continuous Case-Based Intrusion Detection System. In: Proceedings of the 20th Australasian Computer Science Conference (1997)

10. Smeulders, A.W., et al.: Content-Based Image Retrieval at the End of the Early Years. IEEE Transactions on Pattern Analysis and Machine Intelligence 22(12), 1349–1380 (2000)

11. Nyarko, K., et al.: Network Intrusion Visualization with NIVA, an Intrusion Detection Visual Analyzer with Haptic Integration. In: Proceedings of the 10th Symposium on Haptic Interfaces for Virtual Environment and Teleoperator Systems, Orlando, FL (2002)

12. Esmaili, M., et al.: Case-Based Reasoning for Intrusion Detection. In: Proceedings of the 12th Annual Computer Security Applications Conference, San Diego, CA (1996)

13. Forrest, S.: A Sense of Self for UNIX Processes. In: Proceedings of the IEEE Symposium on Security and Privacy, Oakland, CA, pp. 120–198. IEEE Computer Society Press, Los Alamitos (1996)

14. Forsyth, D., Ponce, J.: Computer Vision: A Modern Approach. Prentice-Hall, Upper Saddle River, NJ (2003)

15. Frincke, D., Tobin, D., McConnell, J., Marconi, J., Polla, D.: A Framework for Cooperative Intrusion Detection. In: Proceedings of the 21st National Information Systems Security Conference, Crystal City, VA, October 1998, pp. 361–373 (1998)

16. Girardin, L., Brodbeck, D.: A Visual Approach for Monitoring Logs. In: LISA XII. Proceedings of the Second Systems Administration Conference, Boston, MA, October 1998, pp. 299–308 (1998)

17. Hughes, D.: Using Visualization in System and Network Administration. In: LISA '96. Proceedings of the 10th Systems Administration Conference, Chicago, IL, October 1996, pp. 59–66 (1996)

18. Javitz, H.S., Valdes, A.: The SRI IDES Statistical Anomaly Detector. In: Proceedings of the IEEE Symposium on Security and Privacy, Oakland, CA, May 1991, IEEE Computer Society Press, Los Alamitos (1991)
19. Karam, G.: Visualization using Timelines. In: Proceedings of the International Symposium on Software Testing and Analysis, Seattle, WA (August 1994)
20. Kruegel, C., Mutz, D., Valeur, F., Vigna, G.: On the Detection of Anomalous System Call Arguments. In: Snekkenes, E., Gollmann, D. (eds.) ESORICS 2003. LNCS, vol. 2808, pp. 326–343. Springer, Heidelberg (2003)
21. MIT Lincoln Laboratory. DARPA Intrusion Detection Evaluation Data Set (1999) http://www.ll.mit.edu/IST/ideval
22. Lunt, T.: Real-time Intrusion Detection. In: Proceedings of the IEEE Symposium on Security and Privacy, Oakland, CA, April 1988, IEEE Computer Society Press, Los Alamitos (1988)
23. McHugh, J.: Testing Intrusion Detection Systems: A Critique of the 1998 and 1999 DARPA Intrusion Detection System Evaluations as Performed by Lincoln Laboratory. ACM Transaction on Information and System Security 3(4) (2000)
24. Mizoguchi, F.: Anomaly Detection Using Visualization and Machine Learning. In: Proceedings of the 9th International Workshop on Enabling Technologies: Infrastructure for Collaborative Enterprises (WET ICE'00), Gaithersburg, MD, pp. 165–170 (March 2000)
25. Noel, S., Wijesekera, D., Youman, C.: Applications of Data Mining in Computer Security. In: chapter Modern Intrusion Detection, Data Mining, and Degrees of Attack Guilt, pp. 2–25. Kluwer Academic Publisher, Boston, MA (2002)
26. Porras, P., Neumann, P.: EMERALD: Event Monitoring Enabling Responses to Anomalous Live Disturbances. In: Proceedings of the 20th National Information Systems Security Conference, Baltimore, MA (October 1997)
27. Rubner, Y., Tomasi, C., Guibas, L.J.: A Metric for Distributions with Applications to Image Databases. In: Proceedings of the IEEE International Conference on Computer Vision, Bombay, India, pp. 59–66 (January 1998)
28. Rubner, Y., Tomasi, C., Guibas, L.J.: The Earth Mover's Distance as a Metric for Image Retrieval. International Journal of Computer Vision 28(40), 99–121 (2000)
29. Sarle, W.S.: Neural Networks and Statistical Models. In: Proceedings of the Nineteenth Annual SAS Users Group International Conference, Cary, NC, pp. 1538–1550 (April 1994)
30. Shapiro, L.G., Stockman, G.C.: Computer Vision. Prentice-Hall, Inc. Upper Saddle River, NJ (2001)
31. Snapp, S.: DIDS (Distributed Intrusion Detection System): Motivation, Architecture and An Early Prototype. In: Proceedings of the National Information Systems Security Conference, Washington, D.C., pp. 167–176 (October 1991)
32. Takada, T., Koike, H.: Tudumi: Information Visualization System for Monitoring and Auditing Computer Logs. In: Proceedings of the 6th International Conference on Information Visualization (IV'02), London, England, pp. 570–576 (July 2002)
33. Tan, K., Killourhy, K., Maxion, R.: Undermining an Anomaly-Based Intrusion Detection System Using Common Exploits. In: Wespi, A., Vigna, G., Deri, L. (eds.) RAID 2002. LNCS, vol. 2516, Springer, Heidelberg (2002)
34. Tan, K., Maxion, R.: "Why 6?" Defining the Operational Limits of Stide, an Anomaly-Based Intrusion Detector. In: Proceedings of the IEEE Symposium on Security and Privacy, Berkeley, CA, pp. 188–202 (May 2002)
35. Vaccaro, H., Liepins, G.: Detection of Anomalous Computer Session Activity. In: Proceedings of the IEEE Symposium on Security and Privacy, Oakland, CA, pp. 208–209 (May 1989)

36. Varner, P.E., Knight, J.C.: Security Monitoring, Visualization, and System Surviv-
    ability. In: 4th Information Survivability Workshop (ISW-2001/2002), Vancouver,
    Canada (March 2002)
37. Veltkamp, R.C., Tanase, M.: Content-Based Image Retrieval Systems: A Survey.
    Technical Report 2000-34, UU-CS, Utrecht, Holland (October 2000)
38. Wagner, D., Dean, D.: Intrusion Detection via Static Analysis. In: Proceedings of
    the IEEE Symposium on Security and Privacy, Oakland, CA, pp. 40–47 (2001)
39. Wagner, D., Soto, P.: Mimicry Attacks on Host-Based Intrusion Detection Systems.
    In: Proceedings of the 9th ACM Conference on Computer and Communications
    Security, Washington, D.C., pp. 255–264 (2002)

Case-Based Reasoning in
Robot Indoor Navigation

Alessandro Micarelli, Stefano Panzieri, and Giuseppe Sansonetti

Department of Computer Science and Automation
Roma Tre University
Via della Vasca Navale, 79, 00146 Rome, Italy
{micarel,panzieri,gsansone}@dia.uniroma3.it

Abstract. In this paper, we advance a novel approach to the problem of autonomous robot navigation. The environment is a complex indoor scene with very little a priori knowledge, and the navigation task is expressed in terms of natural language directives referring to natural features of the environment itself. The system is able to analyze digital images obtained by applying a sensor fusion algorithm to ultrasonic sensor readings. Such images are classified in different categories using a case-based approach. The architecture we propose relies on fuzzy theory for the construction of digital images, and wavelet functions for their representation and analysis.

1 Introduction

Indoor robot navigation poses a unique challenge to Artificial Intelligence researchers. Mobile robots are inherently autonomous and they compel the researcher to tackle key issues such as uncertainty (in both sensing and action), reliability, and real time response. In particular, a still open problem is the devising of efficient strategies able to cope with the problem of *self-localization* in unstructured environments, i.e., the ability of estimating the position of the mobile platform when no artificial landmarks can be used to precisely indicate to the robot its position. To better explain this concept consider indoor navigation: the motion planning phase, that has to identify the best path through the environment must rely on the process of collection and interpretation of sensory data. This means that the robot, having no artificial landmarks, is asked to extract from natural features, like shape of corridors or lamps in the ceiling or even the number of encountered doors, the best estimate of its position. Moreover, the accuracy of such a process must be sufficient to plan its future actions. For this reason, to solve the self-localization problem for an autonomous mobile robot carrying out a navigation task consisting in moving between two points of a complex environment, the first step to take is characterizing an effective environment representation. This *map* must describe all the essential information being, at the same time, compact and easy to handle. Indeed, self-localization is always a multi-level process, usually consisting of more than one algorithm each

R.O. Weber and M.M. Richter (Eds.): ICCBR 2007, LNAI 4626, pp. 284–298, 2007.

one related to the accuracy requested for the subsequent motion steps. When covering large distances, motion accuracy along the path is not demanding and the environment representation itself can be more rough. On the contrary, when approaching the goal, this ability must be improved to allow fine motion. So, assuming that the motion planning step has to be performed within this representation, the map must allow the description of the calculated path. This means that the efficiency of the map, in terms of flexibility, extendibility, and adaptability, must be considered as first goal in its design.

Now, suppose to restrict the problem and choose the environment in a particular class, still very wide: an office-like environment with corridors, corners and other similar features. Then, the task to perform can be described in linguistic terms containing topological elements such as "go straight along the corridor, turn right at first corner, and follow the next corridor as far as the second door on the left". Suppose also that only low cost sonar sensors can be used: all localization information, that at this point has a topological character, should be easily extracted from sensory data and used to guide the platform along the path. Unfortunately, in a dynamic environment, those features (*natural landmarks*) can vary and some unknown configurations could be found leaving to the robot the choice on several strategies: one could consist in finding the nearest matching topological element in a static library; an other one could include a supervised learning stage in which the new pattern is used to increase the base library itself. This second approach is often referred as Case-Based Reasoning (CBR) [1,7] and tries to catch all the learning opportunities offered both by the environment and, in an initial phase, by an external supervisor, to improve robot skill in analyzing its exteroceptive sensorial view.

The rest of this paper is organized as follows. In Section 2, we review different approaches to constructing a model of the environment based on sensor measurements. Section 3 presents the case-based architecture, in particular the signal representation and the similarity metric. Section 4 describes the experiments performed to evaluate the accuracy of the proposed system. Our final remarks are given in Section 5.

2   Mapping the World

In literature, the way the world is represented is found to be grouped into two main classes: *metric maps*, giving absolute geometric information about objects, and *topological maps* containing only relations between objects with no metric at all [2]. In general, topological maps can be more flexible due to their abstract world representation and can be successfully employed when there is no metric information or its quality is extremely poor. Moreover, a planar graph can be used to describe a topological map, and metric information, when present, can be introduced as weights on arcs or nodes.

Nevertheless, the semantic associated to nodes and arcs can differ depending on the authors. For example, in maps defined by [8] nodes represent *places* and are associated to sensory data and arcs represent *paths* between places and are characterized by control strategies. On the contrary, maps defined by [14] are obtained by analyzing probabilistic gridmaps (metric maps divided into small cells) and partitioning them into *regions* (nodes) separated by *narrow passages* (arcs). Finally, a different approach can be found in [6], where concepts from digital topology, extended to fuzzy gridmaps, are used to build a *topology-based map* in which structure and shape of the free-space is analyzed and classified: nodes of the graph represent connected components (usually rooms and corridors) and arcs represent adjacency relationships between these components. In this paper, we make use of a similar representation, that has been presented in [11], where connected components (nodes) are classified using a semantic induced by the particular shape, like corridors or corners, and arcs are again an adjacency relationship. The high level planner can force a navigation strategy associating to the particular node a behavior that the mobile robot must bind to while moving in that portion of the environment. This kind of autonomous navigation implies, therefore, a recognition phase for each step taken by the robot to estimate its position, or better, to understand the particular shape of the environment (the topological feature) inside its actual range of view.

In our case, this can be done comparing the actual sonar output with a set of reference signals associated with particular topological features. In most cases, association is done by comparing the actual view with a static list of models obtained with *a priori* considerations on the environment itself [5]. However, following a CBR philosophy, a learning approach can be devised in which real-world cases obtained from a supervised navigation are used to build and update a dynamic library.

In this paper, we want to show how such a method can be successfully applied to help the robot during navigation in dynamic environments containing features that only partially correspond to previously known cases. In particular, the problem we intend to address concerns the recognition of a sonar-based digital image and its classification under one category belonging to a set of predetermined topological situations (Corridor, Corner, Crossing, End Corridor, Open Space).

Basically, the surrounding of the robot is represented in terms of *Fuzzy Local Maps (FLM)*, i.e., *Fuzzy Maps* [10,11], that turned out extremely useful in many sensor fusion problems, obtained from a preprocessing stage applied to the sonar signals. Each FLM consists of 40 x 40 cells and, for each cell of an FLM, two values specifying the degree of membership to the set of empty cells and to the set of occupied cells are computed. An FLM, usually derived at each step merging the last n sets of collected data, is thereafter represented by two fuzzy sets: the empty cells set $\mathcal{E}$, and the occupied cells set $\mathcal{O}$. As an example, in Figure 1 the $\mathcal{E}$ set of a FLM obtained in a corridor is reported. Different gray levels in the image represent different fuzzy values. Pixels with darker gray levels correspond to lower values of membership to the empty cell set $\mathcal{E}$, white pixels are unexplored regions, with a fuzzy value of membership to $\mathcal{E}$ equal to zero.

Now, with reference to the scheme depicted in Figure 3, let us assume that the robot has acquired a new FLM. As first step, a feature-based representation of the new FLM is evaluated by the feature extraction module. This representation

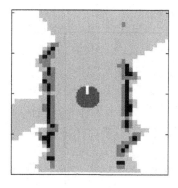

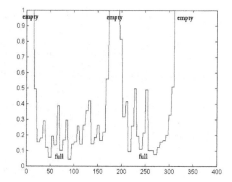

Fig. 1. Map of a corridor   **Fig. 2.** Worldmark

constitutes the "new case" of the proposed CBR system. The retrieval module shown in the figure will effect a search in the Case Library containing the old cases, based on a *<problem representation, solution>* structure, which in this specific case will be *<FLM based representation, topological category index>*. The solution given in the old case can therefore be seen as a pointer to the "Library of Objects", containing the categories (i.e., "topological features") that could appear in the maps to be analyzed. The "recognized object" is at this point taken into consideration by the robot navigation system to plan its motion. This object, which constitutes the old solution of the case retrieved from the Case Library, will also be considered as a candidate solution of a new problem (basically, there is no need for an adaptation of the old solution to suit the new case) and if the human supervisor accepts it, the pair *<new FLM based feature representation, recognized object index>* can be inserted as a new case in the Case Library.

3   Case-Based Architecture

For sake of clarity and for an immediate understanding of the problems addressed and the relative proposed solutions, the pseudo-code of a rather simplified version of the classification algorithm is reported in Table 1. The complete solution, employed for the experimental performance assessment, was implemented in C language under the Linux operative system, for reasons of porting and efficiency. To handle both the new case and any of those cases dwelling in the Case Library, the use of a record structure comprising the three fields below was adopted:

– a one-dimensional fuzzy *worldmark* summarizing the content of the FLM;
– *object*, designed to store the label associated to the recognized object;
– *time*, reserved to the storage of information regarding the utility of the case of reference.

As indicated above, the first field is dedicated to the representation of the FLM. In order to guarantee the applicability of the current approach to real-time

Table 1. Pseudo-code for CBR

```
Function REC(NewImage) returns RecObject
inputs : NewImage; the input image
variables : CaseLib; the case library
            C_j; the generic old case
            T_nouse; the inactivity time
            S_a; the reliability threshold
            S_b; the identity threshold
local variables : D.image; the image representation
                  D.object; the recognized object
                  s_j; the metric value
                  tempvalue; the temporary metric value
                  tempind; the temporary case index

D.image ← WAVELET(NewImage)
D.object ← 0
tempvalue ← 0
tempind ← 0
for each old case C_j in CaseLib do
    begin
        s_j ← COMPARE_CASE(D.image, C_j.image )
        if (tempvalue < s_j) then
            begin
                tempvalue ← s_j
                tempind ← j
            end
    end
if (tempvalue < S_a) then
    begin
        D.object ← HumanExpertSolution
        C_{n+1}.image ← D.image
        C_{n+1}.object ← D.object
        C_{n+1}.time ← 0
    end
else
begin
    if (C_{tempind}.object = HumanExpertSolution) then
        begin
            D.object ← C_{tempind}.object
            C_{tempind}.time ← 0
        end
    else
        D.object ← HumanExpertSolution
    if (tempvalue < S_b) then
        begin
            C_{n+1}.image ← D.image
            C_{n+1}.object ← D.object
            C_{n+1}.time ← 0
        end
end
CLEAN_LIB(CaseLib,T_nouse)
RecObject ← D.object
returns RecObject
```

control, a simplification has been introduced: the bi-dimensional fuzzy map of Figure 1 is replaced with a one-dimensional fuzzy signal, named *worldmark*. The worldmark is computed by determining, for each direction around the robot, the value of the cell with the highest matching score to the set of empty cells, or, in other words, the cell for which the risk of belonging to a possible obstacle is minimum (see fig. 2). Therefore the "new case" that appears in Figure 2 consists of

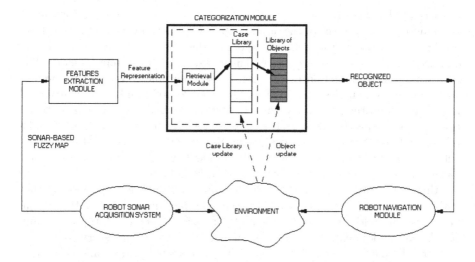

Fig. 3. Navigation architecture with Case-Based Reasoning

a vector of N elements (typically N=360) with values in the interval [0,1]. Before launching into the detailed description of the representation modalities of the aforementioned three fields, we believe it useful to provide a general overview of the entire algorithm. The domain expert's possibility to intervene in the decision task is certainly of primary interest. Such an intervention is possible both in the initial training phase of the system as well as during the verification phase for the retrieved solutions. The human element is, in fact, deemed indispensable not only when the robot begins to navigate without the support of any kind of information regarding the different topological configurations it may encounter, but also in the course of the regular operation of the system. In this way it is possible – *in fieri* – to remedy possible training shortcomings due to the limited information available. Another aspect worthy of attention is the one related to the adoption of a double similarity test. It is manifest that as the pertinence of the Case Library increases, so does the probability of retrieving a candidate with a good value of similarity to the case under examination and, therefore, that the associated solution to will prove to be valid even in a contingent situation. On the other hand, a rather voluminous library presents the two following inconveniences:

– more time necessary for the retrieval of the required information;
– a depletion in terms of available space.

It is evident that these problems relate across the board to any practical application of the CBR method. This becomes obvious when considering the considerable amount of work dedicated to the matter by the Artificial Intelligence community (see for instance [13]). In order to avoid, at least partially, this state of affairs, the proposed architecture uses two different tests, respectively, named *reliability test* and *identity test*. The former provides indications on the possibility of successfully apply the solution of the retrieved case to the new situation. It is a kind of measurement of the actual extent to which the case extracted from the library represents the class of the one under observation. Instead, the second test controls the insertion of the new case into the system memory. The reason for the introduction of the identity test parameter is owed to circumstances where it is useless to include a new case, "quite" similar to a case stored in the library in the system memory. In fact, such lesser information contribution would not justify the depletion of resources its storage would entail. The reliability test is performed by comparing the current similarity metric value s_j with the reliability threshold S_a, while the identity test is performed by comparing the same value s_j with an identity threshold S_b. In Tables 3, 4 and 5 the threshold values determined by a heuristic procedure are reported together with the percentage of coincidence between the responses given by the system and those provided by a domain expert. Specifically, for the setup of S_a and S_b, the available memory space, the amount of resources necessary to keep in memory the pair $<representation\ of\ signal,\ represented\ object>$ and the statistics of the similarity index were considered. The results obtained by adopting such a strategy are more than satisfactory, but this does not deny the fact that an adaptive mechanism would certainly be preferable, i.e., one capable of dynamically determining the optimal values for the two thresholds on the basis of certain parameters established by the user, and in conformity with the structure of the overall system. This option is not yet a reality, but we believe that the resources necessary for developing such a solution could be actually quite contained. Keeping in mind an "intelligent" management of the resources available to the system, a third test has been introduced. The idea that has, concretely, lead to its introduction, stems from the need to keep track, for all cases stored in memory, of the *frequency* of their appearance and the *effectiveness* of the solution associated to them. The record field *time* was specifically introduced in consideration of these aims. Once more, the *clean library* test compares this value with a threshold T_{nouse}. If *time* exceeds T_{nouse} the case is removed from the library. For the determination of the optimal value to assign to the indicator T_{nouse}, the same considerations expressed above for the parameters S_a and S_b still apply. However, for a full understanding of the architecture proposed in this article there are still two major aspects that, as always, in any case-based system, constitute the heart around which all the rest revolves, that is,

- the signal representation;
- the similarity metric.

These aspects are, furthermore, strongly interrelated.

3.1   Signal Representation

Choosing the most efficient representation for a current problem constitutes the crucial moment of any application of signal processing. In fact, it is certain that the availability of a representation that makes the extraction of characteristics simple and immediate is of vital importance for the positive outcome of subsequent applications. Here, we resorted to a wavelet representation of the worldmark. The wavelet representation expresses the signal of interest as super-imposed elementary waves and, therefore, in this respect does not introduce any innovation compared to traditional methods, such as Fourier series expansion. However, the innovative aspect offered by wavelet functions consists in the possibility of subdividing the available data in components with differing bandwidths and time durations. Each of these components is subsequently analyzed by a resolution associated to its scale. The advantages offered by this procedure are tangible, above all, in respect to the analysis of physical situations where typical signals show discontinuity and sudden peaks, exactly as happens with world-marks. The advantages of adopting representations in similar situations through wavelet functions, instead of traditional methods, are extensively expounded in the literature [4,9,3].

The analysis procedure through wavelets is based on the use of a prototype function, called *mother wavelet*, whose translated and scaled versions constitute the basis functions of a series expansion which it is possible to represent the original signal with, by way of coefficients. Operations involving signals can, therefore, be developed – in a decidedly more straightforward and efficient way – directly on corresponding wavelet coefficients. If the choice of the mother wavelet is performed in an appropriate manner, i.e., if the coefficients below a certain threshold value are shrinked, it is possible to represent the original data *sparsely*, meaning with few coefficients different from zero. As a consequence, the wavelet constitute a formidable tool in the context of data compression and noise filtering in temporal series. Computation of the wavelet transform can be performed in a fast way (at a computational cost $O(n)$, where n is the number of signal samples) by means of the *Fast Wavelet Transform* (FWT) [9], a computationally efficient implementation of the Discrete Wavelet Transform (DWT) that exploits a surprising relationship between the coefficients of the DWT at adjacent scales. DWT can, moreover, be easily extended to multi-dimensional data, such as images, which may turn out to be useful in view of a possible application of our architecture to direct treatment of FLM, instead of the respective worldmarks. All these considerations induced us to rely heavily on the transformed wavelet in the context of our experiments.

3.2   Similarity Metric

The last aspect to be examined concerns the choice of the metric necessary for the evaluation of the *similarity* existing between case f in input and the generic case g belonging to the Case Library. The importance of this choice is due to its fundamental role in determining the quality of the selection procedure for the most promising case, which is the very essence of a CBR system. A review of any kind of CBR application will easily confirm this priority since the crucial role of the similarity metric selection is obvious in every instance.

Regardless of the application context, a good metric must anyhow be able to guarantee an efficient compromise between the two main requisites, which are the *quality* of the recognition and the *computational complexity*. Clearly, an evaluation procedure that offers excellent success rates but, at the same time, also requires excessive processing lengths, is not suitable for an autonomous mobile robot for which real time response is a mandatory requirement. On the other hand, it would be just as inexpedient to have a robot colliding, at high speed, against the first possible obstacle.

Accordingly, during the experimental activity several different metrics were tested, each of which revealed assets and shortfalls. Among them, the relatively best results were obtained by using the *cross-correlation factor* as metric, whose expression is:

$$\underset{\theta \in [0, 2\pi]}{Max} \frac{\langle f(x), g(x - \theta)\rangle}{\sqrt{\langle f(x), f(x)\rangle \langle g(x), g(x)\rangle}}$$

In addition, when the worldmark is too noisy the similarity between the shrinked versions of the new and old worldmarks can be applied. This quantity was calculated both in the time and frequency domains, respectively, obtaining in both cases significant results with moderate processing time, through computation resources available on the market today.

4   Experimental Results

For our tests, we used the simulator of Nomad200 by Nomadic Technologies, a mobile robot equipped with a ring of 16 equally spaced ultrasonic sensors. The procedure consists of tracing a number of global maps of hypothetical office-like environments, simulating the robot dynamics and, finally, collecting the output data. For these operations we used the real time navigation software A.N.ARCH.I.C. [12] which, together with the aforementioned simulator, made the robot virtual navigation inside the mapped environment possible producing the sequence of FLMs and corresponding worldmark, each pair related to a different position taken during the followed path. Each sequence, therefore, includes hundreds of FLMs and worldmarks, which constitute the input for the tests that we performed on our classifier. The values reported below were obtained by using a machine equipped with a Pentium M processor, 1700 MHz, and 512 MB RAM. Before discussing the results obtained during the system test experiments, we deem it useful to set out here below some pertinent considerations. The recognition and classification of a digital image in one of the possible categories belonging to a predetermined set is a complicated task, not only for the machine itself, but also for humans. For example, imagine having to determine exactly the topological configuration that appears in the digital image shown in Figure 4.   In this case, as may be easily discerned, it is not possible to affirm with absolute certainty that the robot is advancing along a corridor or is at a crossing, or an angle. This problem becomes increasingly complex as the robot approaches a transition situation between a perfectly defined configuration and its subsequent position. Similar considerations are clearly valid also for the corresponding worldmark, represented in Figure 5. Thus, one must generally bear these factors in mind during the analysis and evaluation phase of the results given by the experimentation. Indeed, the performance, as for any

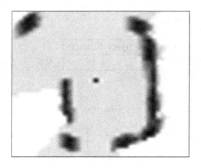   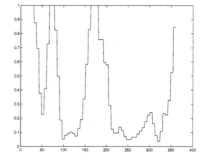

Fig. 4. Ambiguity map   **Fig. 5.** Ambiguity worldmark

knowledge-based system, depends above all on the quality and quantity of the training effected before operating directly on the input data. Accordingly, during the testing phase, we initialized the system through representations related to four different configurations:

- corridor
- crossing
- end of corridor
- angle

providing, for each of these, three different standard schemes, in practice as it appears in the initial phase, at its basic level, and in the final phase. Table 2 shows the configuration of the system memory, at the time when the robot begins its navigation. We believe it necessary to stress how, in an architecture based on cases such as the one described here, the initial training constitutes only the first stage for the system acquisition of a knowledge base. Subsequently, during the normal course of recognition operations, the domain expert may intervene at any time if s/he deems it opportune, in order to enrich the Object Library. In practice, if it appears that the FLM does not represent any of the categories already in memory, following the similarity metric values adopted, nothing prevents the expert from envisaging and consequently introducing a new category. For example, if the robot goes against a well defined obstacle, say a desk, the human expert would have the possibility to intervene and assign the corresponding worldmark to a new class. All other worldmarks deemed similar to the one mentioned above, would subsequently belong, according to the used metric, to the new class. The ease and immediacy of such an operation constitute the strong points of the system presented herein. Tables 3, 4, and 5 show the results recorded during different series of tests of the system. Table 3 illustrates the results obtained by performing the similarity evaluation between the input signal and the generic one inside the Case Library directly in the time domain. Instead, for Tables 4 and 5, the same operation was effected in the wavelet domain, i.e., the matching evaluation of the two signals was not made by estimating the cross-correlation between sequences of temporal samples, but between the corresponding residual low-frequency components,

Table 2. Initial system memory

Number of cases represented	Case library	Object library
12	12	4

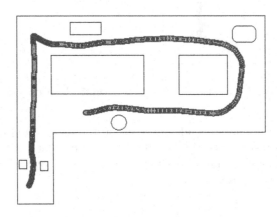

Fig. 6. Global map

obtained through DWT. Consequently, it is possible to appreciate in a more tangible way the extent of the possible advantages granted by the expansion of signals in series of waveform, perfectly located in time and in frequency. To perform this experimentation, we simulated the robot navigation in an environment that Figure 6 illustrates as a global map. In the same figure we have also traced the path followed by the robot, planned on the basis of specific methods for which further explanation is out of the scope of this paper. A sequence of 636 FLMs is thus generated, as well as a corresponding number of worldmarks. In order to streamline the experimental procedure, without, however, penalizing its efficiency, since the variation between one FLM and the subsequent one was practically insignificant, we decided to consider only one over three samples and to discard the others. As a result, the map effectively input to the system consists of only 212 FLMs. Initially, we shall examine the values reported in Table 3. As anticipated earlier, the tests were performed by running the system beforehand through the same training session, for each test series. This fact becomes apparent by looking at the data in the 6th column, since the same value recurs systematically in each line (12 cases). As a matter of fact, the coincidence does not only concern the number of cases used, but also the samples themselves. In this way, we attempted to guarantee the same initial condition in each test series. A reading of the data discloses the consistency of the recorded fluctuations, in respect to the varying values assigned to the two similarity thresholds. For example, it is noticeable that when the reliability threshold S_a decreases, there is a proportional decrease in the number of interventions required of the domain expert by the system. Similarly, there is a clear increase in the number of cases

Table 3. Experimental results obtained in the time domain

S_a	S_b	Input Cases	Expert Interventions	Coincidence Percentage	Cases Before	Cases After	Processing Time (s)
0.88	0.91	212	12	90.1% (191)	12	37	8.07
0.88	0.93	212	12	85.4% (181)	12	51	9.97
0.88	0.95	212	11	84.4% (179)	12	74	13.55
0.89	0.91	212	14	90.1% (191)	12	37	8.17
0.89	0.93	212	15	85.4% (181)	12	51	10.07
0.89	0.95	212	14	84.9% (180)	12	74	13.71
0.90	0.91	212	15	90.1% (191)	12	37	8.32
0.90	0.93	212	15	85.4% (181)	12	51	10.04
0.90	0.95	212	14	84.9% (180)	12	74	13.66
0.91	0.93	212	23	91.9% (195)	12	51	10.35
0.91	0.95	212	19	89.6% (190)	12	74	13.89
0.93	0.95	212	30	90.6% (192)	12	74	14.30

inserted in the relative library matching an increase in the identity threshold S_b. However, the phenomenon of major importance and interest relates to the trend recorded by the factor indicated in the table as *coincidence percentage*. In previous sections of this paper, we dealt with the problem of finding a parameter that could, albeit roughly, provide an idea of the quality of the recognition and classification operations performed by the system. In accordance to such evaluations and also taking into account that it is necessary to assess the performance of a system that requires training, we deemed it expedient to adopt as evaluation factor the coincidence percentage gathered by a comparison between the system responses and those that would have been given by the same expert who performed the training, when examining the corresponding FLM. Clearly, such a strategy is inevitably damaged by the loss of information that occurs during the passage from a bi-dimensional fuzzy map (FLM) to the corresponding polar map (worldmark). However, notwithstanding this additional source of uncertainty, the results obtained may be considered more than satisfactory. Proceeding with the analysis of the data reported in Tables 4 and 5, which refer to the same experimental tests, but performed on the wavelet coefficients and not on their corresponding original signals, the gain is noteworthy, both in terms of coincidence percentage as well as computational complexity. In particular, it can be observed how the first factor is affected to a significant lesser degree by the variation of the values assigned to the two thresholds S_a and S_b. Although we do not wish to dwell upon too many details of the experimentation, it should be noted, however, that to obtain the wavelet coefficients relating to sequences of 360 temporal samples we applied a four-level DWT with analysis filters of the type of the Haar wavelet (Table 4) and the Daubechies wavelet with four coefficients (Table 5). The choice of these wavelets was due to the support size, that is, the size of the domain in which the wavelet function is nonzero. Selecting a wavelet with a small size of support is fundamental in order to characterize

Table 4. Experimental results obtained through DWT with the Haar wavelet

S_a	S_b	Input Cases	Expert Interventions	Coincidence Percentage	Cases Before	Cases After	Processing Time (s)
0.88	0.91	212	12	91.9% (195)	12	38	0.41
0.88	0.93	212	11	91.5% (194)	12	48	0.58
0.88	0.95	212	10	90.1% (191)	12	74	0.75
0.89	0.91	212	16	91.9% (195)	12	38	0.46
0.89	0.93	212	14	91.5% (194)	12	48	0.53
0.89	0.95	212	13	90.1% (191)	12	74	0.74
0.90	0.91	212	22	94.8% (201)	12	38	0.68
0.90	0.93	212	18	91.5% (194)	12	48	0.62
0.90	0.95	212	15	90.6% (192)	12	74	0.68
0.91	0.93	212	21	91.5% (194)	12	48	0.67
0.91	0.95	212	15	90.6% (192)	12	74	0.78
0.93	0.95	212	28	93.8% (199)	12	74	0.93

Table 5. Experimental results obtained through DWT with the Daubechies-4 wavelet

S_a	S_b	Input Cases	Expert Interventions	Coincidence Percentage	Cases Before	Cases After	Processing Time (s)
0.88	0.91	212	7	95.8% (203)	12	31	0.42
0.88	0.93	212	7	95.3% (202)	12	43	0.57
0.88	0.95	212	7	95.3% (202)	12	64	0.62
0.89	0.91	212	12	96.2% (204)	12	31	0.51
0.89	0.93	212	11	95.8% (203)	12	43	0.56
0.89	0.95	212	10	95.8% (203)	12	64	0.77
0.90	0.91	212	13	96.2% (204)	12	31	0.52
0.90	0.93	212	12	95.8% (203)	12	43	0.58
0.90	0.95	212	10	95.8% (203)	12	64	0.75
0.91	0.93	212	15	95.8% (203)	12	43	0.61
0.91	0.95	212	13	95.8% (203)	12	64	0.79
0.93	0.95	212	25	97.2% (206)	12	64	0.91

a signal with only few nonzero components in the transformed data. The Haar wavelet and the Daubechies-4 wavelet are the wavelets with the smallest support size [4]. This can be seen by the number of filter coefficients needed to represent each of them (two for Haar and four for Daubechies-4). Of the 360 coefficients of the complete DWT (it should be noted that being an orthogonal transformation there is coincidence between the number of signal samples to be transformed and the number of coefficients of the transformed signal) it was sufficient to only consider the 22 comprising the residual low-frequency component. The results show how the Daubechies-4 wavelet enabled us to better understand the dynamics of the input signal and to discard the phenomena ascribed to noise superimposed on the signal, which, on the contrary, considerably pollutes the values obtained when the entire original signal is analyzed. Another observation should be made on the processing time. In order to finalize this experimentation, for sake of clarity, we decided to operate on the group of worldmarks generated during the course of the overall navigation inside the simulated environment. Consequently, the time necessary to operate in real-time is decidedly less than that reported in the tables and, above all, significantly lower than the time allowed during the robot actual navigation.

5   Conclusions

Traditional methodologies of pattern recognition usually require the availability of templates of the objects we want to classify. This template collection reflects the a priori knowledge we have about the problem to be solved by the image classifier. However, in practical cases, as for the robot autonomous navigation, the prior knowledge could be rather poor, thus leading to a risk of misclassifications. In our contribution, we included a feature extraction algorithm into a CBR shell, which allows a constant update of the environment knowledge. We point out that, in principle, there is no limit to the number and complexity of information that may be collected in the Object Library, as well as in the Case Library. Future work will be focused on introducing the possibility of fusing more information coming from different kind of sensors (e.g., laser scanners or cameras) into a more detailed worldmark to supply the classifier with a better and more robust input data.

References

1. Aamodt, A., Plaza, E.: Case-Based Reasoning: Foundational Issues, Methodological Variations, and System Approaches. AI Communications 7(1), 39–59 (1994)
2. Borenstein, J., Everett, H.R., Feng, L.: Navigating mobile robot: sensors and techniques. A.K. Peters, Ltd. Wellesley, MA (1996)
3. Chui, C.K.: An Introduction to Wavelets. Academic Press, London, England (1992)
4. Daubechies, I.: Orthonormal bases of compactly supported wavelets. Commun. Pure Appl. Math. 41(7), 909–996 (1988)
5. Fabrizi, E., Panzieri, S., Ulivi, G.: Extracting topological features of indoor environment from sonar-based fuzzy maps. In: Proc. of the 6th International Conference on Intelligent Autonomous Systems, Venice, Italy (2000)
6. Fabrizi, E., Saffiotti, A.: Extracting topology-based maps from gridmaps. In: Proc. of Int. Conf. on Robotics and Automation, San Francisco, CA (2000)
7. Kolodner, J.: Case-Based Reasoning. Morgan Kaufmann, San Mateo, CA (1993)
8. Kuipers, B., Byun, Y.T.: A robot exploration and mapping strategy based on a semantic hierarchy of spatial representation. Journal of Robotics and Autonomous Systems 8, 47–63 (1991)
9. Mallat, S.G.: A Theory for Multiresolution Signal Decomposition: the Wavelet Representation. IEEE Transactions on Pattern Analysis and Machine Intelligence 11(7), 674–693 (1989)

10. Oriolo, G., Vendittelli, M., Ulivi, G.: Real-Time Map Building and navigation for Autonomous Robots in Unknown Environments. IEEE Transactions on Systems, Men and Cybernetics - Part B: Cybernetics 28(3), 316–333 (1998)
11. Panzieri, S., Petroselli, D., Ulivi, G.: Topological localization on indoor sonar-based fuzzy maps. In: Intelligent Autonomous System, pp. 596–603. IOS Press, Amsterdam, NL (2000)
12. Panzieri, S., Pascucci, F., Petroselli, D.: Auton. Navigation ARCHitecture for Intelligent Control (2002), www.dia.uniroma3.it/autom/labrob/anarchic
13. Schank, R.: Dynamic Memory: A Theory of Learning in Computers and People. Cambridge University Press, New York (1982)
14. Thrun, S.: Learning Metric-Topological Maps for Indoor Mobile Robot Navigation. Artificial Intelligence 99(1), 21–71 (1998)

Case-Based Group Recommendation: Compromising for Success*

Kevin McCarthy, Lorraine McGinty, and Barry Smyth

Adaptive Information Cluster, School of Computer Science & Informatics,
University College Dublin, Belfield, Dublin 4, Ireland
{firstname,lastname}@ucd.ie

Abstract. There are increasingly many recommendation scenarios
where recommendations must be made to satisfy groups of people rather
than individuals. This represents a significant challenge for current recommender systems because they must now cope with the potentially
conflicting preferences of multiple users when selecting items for recommendation. In this paper we focus on how individual user models can be
aggregated to produce a group model for the purpose of biasing recommendations in a critiquing-based, case-based recommender. We describe
and evaluate 3 different aggregation policies and highlight the benefits
of group recommendation using live-user preference data.

1 Introduction

Recommender systems are playing an increasingly important role in many online
scenarios. E-commerce services in particular are benefiting from the ability of recommender systems to provide even the most tentative shoppers with compelling
and timely product suggestions. Over the past number of years the definition
of a recommender system has been evolving in a variety of ways. For example,
early recommender systems typically focused on making *single-shot* suggestions
to individual users on the basis of some initial assessment of user preferences
[16]. More recently, many recommender systems have adopted a more conversational approach, whereby multiple recommendation-feedback cycles help the
user navigate through more complex product spaces [17].

Another recent departure for recommender systems is the idea of *group recommendation*, where the objective is to generate a set of suggestions for a group
of users rather than a single individual. Of course there are no guarantees that
individuals in the group will share preferences and the task of generating recommendations that will meet the potentially competing preferences of individual
members becomes a very challenging one. The job of the group recommender is
to make suggestions that reflect the preferences of the group as a whole, while
offering reasonable and acceptable compromises to individual group members.
In this regard, a key aspect of group recommendation concerns the way in which

---

* This material is based on works supported by Science Foundation Ireland under
Grant No. 03/IN.3/I361.

R.O. Weber and M.M. Richter (Eds.): ICCBR 2007, LNAI 4626, pp. 299–313, 2007.
© Springer-Verlag Berlin Heidelberg 2007

individual user profiles are combined to generate a recommendation (or set of recommendations) for the group.

The work presented in this paper extends previous work [12] on group recommendation, which described a recommender system implementing an asynchronous model of conversational group recommendation via a collaborative Web-based interface. In particular, this previous work proposed a specific group recommendation approach and focused on interfacing functionality that assists individual group members in better understanding the evolving needs of the group. This helps group members to appreciate the compromises that may be required for a satisfactory conclusion to be reached (see also [7]). Here we focus on the core profiling and recommendation technique, describing and evaluating three different approaches for integrating the preferences of group members. In addition, we describe the results of an evaluation, based on live-user data, as a means to explore the relationship between group diversity and recommendation compromise. We demonstrate how group recommendation strategies can actually deliver higher quality recommendations to the individuals of the group when compared with single-user recommendation techniques. In effect, the individual complimentary preferences of similar group members combine in a constructive way to provide an improved preference picture. This leads to a higher quality of recommendation than would have be obtained from a single user profile on its own. However, we go on to show that such *constructive interference* is short-lived in many group recommendation scenarios. For example, for moderately and highly diverse groups of users, we find that competing individual preferences tend to *interfere destructively* to drive recommendation compromises. The resulting recommendations will inevitably be less optimal for an individual group member (compared to the case that would have been recommended based on their profile alone) but we demonstrate how our particular recommendation strategies manage to suggest cases that are a better fit to overall group preferences.

The remainder of this paper is organised as follows. In the next section we review related work on case-based recommendation and group recommender systems that provides a context for the work presented in this paper. Section 3 describes our overall group recommendation architecture, focusing on key areas such as individual and group profiling and recommendation generation. In particular, this section introduces a number of alternative recommendation strategies, which differ in the way that they combine individual profiles during recommendation generation. Next, in Section 4 we describe a comprehensive evaluation, based on live-user preference information, in which we compare the performance of different recommendation strategies on different types of user groups, ranging from groups with very similar preferences to more diverse groups with competing preferences. Finally, we discuss the main results and implications of this work.

2   Related Work

Recent changes in information technology have uncovered many new situations where recommendation technology can have a critical role to play, and in many of these situations there may be more than one individual designated as the recipient of the recommendation. For example, the way in which we watch TV with our families is rapidly changing as fixed-schedule, channel-based broadcasting gives way to TV-on-demand services. Accordingly a group of friends, or family members, now have access to hundreds of hours of programming content from which to choose. Recommendation technologies will help them to more effectively navigate through this content space, but in doing so must cater for a set of viewers rather than a single viewer. These types of scenario have motivated recent interest in group recommendation and to date a variety of early-stage systems have been developed in domains such as group web-page recommendation [9,14,18], recommending vacations or tours to groups of tourists [1,6,12], recommending music tracks and playlists to large groups of listeners [4,10], and, of course, recommending movies and TV programmes to friends and family [5,13]. Group recommenders can be distinguished according to their approach to 4 basic recommendation sub-tasks —(1) preference elicitation; (2) recommendation generation; (3) presentation and explanation; (4) consensus negotiation (see [8]).

2.1 Preference Elicitation

Preference elicitation refers to the manner in which information is acquired from users and in many cases methods similar to those used in single-user recommender systems are applied. For example, preferences may be acquired by asking users directly (*explicit preference elicitation*) or by inferring their preferences from their actions and feedback (*implicit preference elicitation*). In the case of the former, systems such as the Travel Decision Advisor [6] and Polylens [13] both acquire preferences by asking users to specify them explicitly; either in the form of preferred features or item ratings. In contrast, group systems such as FlyTrap [4] and Let's Browse [9] acquire the preferences by monitoring a user's interactions. FlyTrap, for example, learns about the preferences of individual users by mining each user's personal music usage habits. In this work we focus on a version of the latter, with preferences taking the form of product critiques [12]; for example, when presented with a $1000 holiday a user might indicate preference for holidays with *price < $1000*.

One advantage of preference elicitation, that is unique to group recommenders, is that the preference elicitation task can be shared, and group members can then view each others preferences. This can be beneficial on two fronts: it can save effort [3] because group members can save time by replicating the preferences of other members; and it can help members to learn from the stated preferences of others. For this reason, some group recommenders have explored different ways to promote and share group preferences during preference elicitation; for example [12], uses a common interface to share preferences among group members.

2.2 Recommendation Generation

In this paper we will focus mainly on the second subtask, the generation of group recommendations, and the related work in this regard identifies two basic approaches. One approach is called *ratings aggregation* and assumes that the recommender can predict the rating r_i that group member u_j would give to item/case/product c_k. Generating a set of recommendations then involves computing an aggregated ratings score, for each item, by combining the predicted ratings for each group member. The items with the highest aggregated ratings are then recommended; see [13]. Different aggregation policies can be used to introduce different group recommendation biases. For example, PolyLens applies a "least misery" strategy when recommending movies to groups; the aggregate ratings is the minimum of the individual ratings. Alternative policies include various ways to maximise average user satisfaction [11] or ways of ensuring fairness by making sure that no user is forced to compromise too much.

The alternative to ratings aggregation is to construct a group preference model prior to any item selection or recommendation taking place. In this approach the challenge is to combine the individual user models in to a meaningful model of group preferences that can be used to guide item selection and recommendation; in this way a single group model GM is used to predict a rating for each candidate item c_k. For example, the Let's Browse system [9] produces a group model from a linear combination of term-based individual models. In contrast the group model used by the Travel Decision Forum computes a group preference at the level of individual features of a holiday. In this way the group model is made up of a set of feature preferences with each preference computed as the average preference rating for that feature by the group [6].

2.3   Explanation and Consensus

The final two subtasks (presenting and explaining recommendations and helping group members to reach consensus) have received less attention from researchers. That said, there is an increasing interest in these areas. This is particularly evident in group recommendation scenarios because convincing group members that a particular recommendation is right for them is especially important. For instance, Let's Browse explains its Web page recommendations to group members by highlighting keywords from the page that are judged to be relevant to the group as a whole. As a collaborative filtering system, PolyLens does not have access to individual item content, and so instead attempts to explain its recommendations by presenting the predicted group ratings as well as an individual user rating for each recommendation.

Many group recommenders do not explicitly support consensus negotiation. Very often it is assumed that one particular group member is responsible for the final decision; Let's Browse, makes this assumption, because one group member typically controls the system interaction with other group members playing the role of viewers rather than actors. Alternatively the role of the recommender could be to produce a set of recommendations that will ultimately be debated by the group offline, before a consensus is reached. In the future it is likely that more active solutions will be proposed to help users to reach consensus, post-recommendation. It is easy to imagine how a simple voting system might be one way to achieve this. However, in general this remains an open issue for group recommenders.

3 A Group Recommender System

The Collaborative Advisory Travel System (CATS), previously described by [12], is a prototype recommender system that supports consensus decision-making for a group of users intending to book a ski-holiday together. Very briefly, in CATS, holiday candidates are represented as cases, each describing various features about the resort and ski-runs available. Sample case features include: *package price, number of ski runs/difficulty, location, accommodation type/rating* and *experience level of the skier*. CATS uses a common interface to share preferences among group members (see Figure 1). Importantly, a number of novel and interesting mechanisms have been put in place to maximise the amount of preference information captured from, as well as communicated to, group members (see [12]). This is so that the recommender can uncover useful information about their combined preferences and make more appropriate recommendations. In practice the recommendation interaction has three key steps: (1) individual group members each express their preferences over holiday options, (2) CATS generates recommendations by aggregating these evolving preference profiles, and (3) group consensus on a recommendation is arrived at through recommendation generation, group feedback, and preference compromise. The subsections that follow describe how our group recommender handles preference elicitation and profiling (Section 3.1), and recommendation generation (Section 3.2).

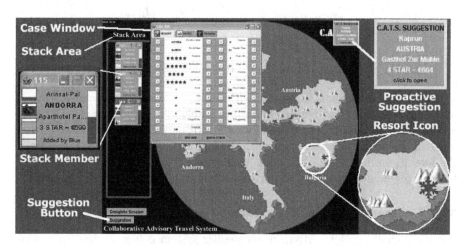

Fig. 1. The main CATS interface

3.1 Critique-Based Profiling and Recommendation

In our group recommender users provide feedback on holiday cases using critique-based feedback [2]. Once presented with a recommendation they can apply contextual critiques to case features in line with their preferences. For instance, they might seek a holiday that is less/more expensive, a higher/lower standard of accommodation, or one which provides access to more/less advanced ski runs. Next, we use the *incremental critiquing* technique [15] to maintain preference profiles for individual group members. A preference profile for a user U is made up of the set of critiques $\{I_1, .., I_n\}$ that they have applied so far. As new critiques are made by the user their preference profile is updated. This may involve removing past critiques if they conflict with, or are subsumed by, the most recent critique. For example, if a user had previously indicated a *Price < $900* critique and a new *Price < $750* critique is later applied, then the earlier critique will be removed to reflect the users refined *Price* preference. In this way the user's preference profile is a consistent reflection of their most recent preferences.

We will describe in Section 3.2 how this preference information is used to inform group recommendation generation by adapting the standard incremental critiquing approach. Importantly, recommenders that have implemented the standard incremental critiquing approach have concentrated on making recommendations to a single user [15]. As such, candidate recommendations are ranked for a user on the basis of their similarity to the preference case and their compatibility to that user's critiquing history. For each recommendation candidate, c_r, compatibility to the user's current preference profile, U, is measured as shown in Equation 1. Essentially, this compatibility score is equal to the percentage of critiques in the user's profile that are satisfied by the case; for example, if c_r is a $1000 ski holiday case then it will satisfy a *price* critique for less than $1200 ($I_i$) and so $satisfies(I_i, c_r)$ will return 1.

$$compatibility(c_r, U) = \frac{\sum_{\forall i} satisfies(I_i, c_r)}{|U|} \qquad (1)$$

$$quality(c_p, c_r, U) = \alpha * compatibility(c_r, U) + (1 - \alpha) * sim(c_p, c_r) \qquad (2)$$

The *quality* of a candidate case c_r with respect to a preference case c_p (previously recommended and critiqued case), is a weighted sum of feature similarity and critique compatibility. When a user U critiques c_p, the next case recommended will be the candidate case with the highest quality score; see Equation 2. By default, for incremental critiquing α is set to 0.5 in order to give equal weight to both preference similarity and critique compatibility.

3.2   Generating Group Recommendations

A critical challenge for a group recommender system is how to develop a comprehensive account of the evolving preferences of the group with a view to using their aggregate preferences to influence group recommendations. When generating recommendations it is important to prefer those cases that are likely to be acceptable to the group as a whole, as well as the individual participants. For this reason our group recommender maintains two types of preference model. Each group member (i.e., user U) is associated with an *individual preference* model, IM^U, that records the critiques that they have applied $(I_1, ..., I_n)$ (see Equation 3), with conflicting and redundant critiques removed as summarized in Section 3.1. In addition, a *group preference model*, GM, is also maintained by combining the individual models of each group member as shown in Equation 4.

$$IM^U = \{I_1, ..., I_n\} \tag{3}$$

$$GM = \{IM^{U_1} \cup IM^{U_2} \cup, ..., IM^{U_k}\} \tag{4}$$

A key difference when ranking candidate recommendations here, compared to the single-user approach taken in Section 3.1, is that the quality of a case c_r with respect to a critiqued case c_p, is now based on similarity to c_p and *group compatibility* (i.e., compatibility with those critiques stored in the group model, GM) according to Equation 5. Finally, the recommendation presented to a user is generated according to Equation 6.

$$Gquality(c_p, c_r, GM, IM^U) = \alpha * Gcompatibility(c_r, GM, IM^U) \tag{5}$$
$$+(1 - \alpha) * sim(c_p, c_r)$$

$$c_{rec} = argmax_{c_r}(Gquality(c_p, c_r, GM, IM^U)) \tag{6}$$

The aggregation policy employed when calculating group compatibility can take many forms. We have implemented and evaluated (see Section 4) three alternative strategies, which differ in the way that they combine individual profiles during recommendation generation; (1) The Weighted Average Group Model, (2)The Joint Group Model, and (3) The Average Individual Group Model.

The Weighted Average Group Model combines two weighted compatibility scores to measure group compatibility (i.e., *Gcompatibility*). First, a compatibility score is calculated for the case, c_r, in terms of critiques contained within the individual user model, IM^U, of the user applying the critique. Next, the compatibility of c_r to the preferences of the *other* group members is measured. Importantly, only a *partial group model* (i.e., $GM - IM^U$) is used for this part of the calculation. The final group compatibility metric leverages these scores as shown in Equation 7. The β parameter controls how much emphasis is placed on individual versus group compatibility. Thus, in this model, the case that is recommended to a particular user by Equation 7 will be chosen because it is both compatible with their own past critiques, and with the aggregated critiques of other group members.

$$WtdAveModel(c_r, IM^U, GM) = \beta * compatibility(c_r, IM^U) +$$
$$(1 - \beta) * compatibility(c_r, (GM - IM^U)) \tag{7}$$

The Joint Group Model differs from the weighted average model in that each group member model has *equal* influence over the group compatibility score generated for a candidate case. This means that no bias is introduced in favour of the user applying the critique. Group compatibility (i.e., *Gcompatibility*) for the Joint Model simply measures the compatibility of c_r (i.e., in terms of critique overlap) with the current aggregate group model, GM (see Equation 8).

$$JointModel(c_r, GM) = compatibility(c_r, GM) \qquad (8)$$

The Average Individual Group Model first calculates the compatibility of c_r for each group member using their own individual preference model, IM^U. The, *Gcompatibility* of c_r the preferences of the *all* group members is measured by calculating the average of these individual scores according to Equation 9. As above, in this aggregation approach each group member's model has equal influence over the group compatibility score generated for a candidate case.

$$AveIndividualModel(c_r, IM^{U_1, \ldots, U_k}) = \frac{\sum_{\forall i} compatibility(c_r, IM^{U_i})}{k} \qquad (9)$$

4   Evaluation

Previously we have described and evaluated a basic version of the CATS group recommendation system [12], implemented using one particular recommendation generation technique and evaluated as part of a limited live-user trial; for example, previous evaluations have been restricted to only 3 groups of 4 users. This previous work has helped to clarify the high-level response of users to the CATS system, focusing mainly on the interface components and a basic test of the group recommendation framework. In this paper our sights are set on a more thorough analysis of the core recommendation technique, one that will allow us to evaluate the quality of recommendations generated by a number of different group recommendation strategies across a large number of test groups with varying levels of inter-member similarity.

4.1   Data and Users

For our evaluation we use a casebase of 153 European ski packages as our product cases. Each case is made up of 42 different features related to the ski resort (25 features such as *country, transfer time, lift system, etc.*) and the type of accommodation (17 features such as *rating, price, ski room facilities, etc.*) As our trialists we enlisted the help of 34 postgraduate students with a range of skiing experience. Of the participants, 7 users had skied regularly before and so were very aware of their skiing preferences, while the other 27 users were novices or first-timers with a more limited idea of their preferences.

4.2   Methodology

The style of this evaluation is very different from our previous studies in that our test users do not participate in a live evaluation of different versions of the CATS system as members of a set number of well-defined groups. This time our goal was to evaluate group recommendation across a large number of different groups with very different characteristics. Ordinarily this would mean enlisting the help of very large numbers of users, which was judged to be prohibitively expensive. Therefore, instead we chose to spend significant effort eliciting the ski preferences of our test subjects and used these preferences as the basis for an off-line evaluation by combining the users into large numbers of different test groups. These test groups (and their member preferences) were then used to evaluate the recommendations made by different group recommendation strategies.

Preference Elicitation: To begin with, user preferences were recorded as each test subject browsed a collection of sample ski cases. No recommendation techniques were used during this phase as the objective was simply to allow the user to review the available holiday options and select a single preferred case (their *Final Case*) in their own time. Trial subjects were also asked to complete a Web form indicating which of the *Final Case* features they felt positively or negatively about in order to get a clearer picture of their preferences with respect to this case. Users were also asked to design their *"Perfect Case"* by completing a Web form to fill out their ideal set of ski holiday features. Users were instructed to make reasonable choices during this stage; it is unreasonable to expect a week in a 5-star hotel for $100, for example. Of course there are no guarantees that the resulting "case" will exist in the casebase — in fact it is highly unlikely — but it provides us with a clear picture of each user's true preferences, broadly unconstrained by the reality of what is available. At the end of this phase, the 34 trial subjects had chosen a total of 26 unique *Final Cases* after reviewing an average of 26 cases each (i.e., the typical user chose their preferred case after viewing approximately 17% of the available cases). On average each user annotated 11 features of their *Final Case* as positive and 3 features as negative and when they produced their *Perfect Case* they selected an average of 14 features.

Profiling Individual Users: Each of the preference profiles for the 34 trial subjects was then converted into a critique-based profile that could be used by our recommender system. To do this we inferred a set of critiques by comparing each user's *Final Case* features (positive and negative) to their corresponding *Perfect Case* features. For example, if a user indicated a positive preference for (*price* = *$1000*) and their corresponding *Perfect Case* feature for (*price* = *$800*) the inferred critique would be (*price* < *$1000*). Also for a negative preference, for example (*Ensuite* = *No*), a (*Ensuite* = *Yes*) critique would be generated. The result was a profile for each user made up of a set of feature-value critiques. On average, each profile contained just over 7 nominal critiques and 3-4 ordinal critiques; specifically, 6.029 *Equal to Nominal* critiques, 1.098 *Not Equal to Nominal* critiques, 1.059 *Less than Ordinal* critiques, 2.471 *Greater than Ordinal* critiques and 2.441 *Equal to Ordinal* critiques.

Constructing Group Profiles: From our set of 34 profiles we can generate combinatorially many groups made up of users with varying degrees of similarity. To compute inter-user similarity we compared users by their *Perfect Cases* in the usual way and randomly selected users to form 3 sets of 100 groups, with each group containing 4 users (as in CATS). Each set of groups was made up of members with certain similarity characteristics. For example, the *Similar* group-set contained groups of users with a high average pairwise similarity in the range of 0.64 to 0.87. The *Mixed* group-set contained groups of users with a mid-range pairwise similarities in the region of 0.4. Finally, the *Diverse* group-set contains groups of users with average pairwise similarities less than 0.25. Intuitively we would expect that more diverse groups will represent more challenging recommendation targets as their individual members tend to have conflicting preferences.

Generating Group Recommendation: For each test group we generate three sets of recommendations. Each set contains one recommended case for each group member. Thus, for each test group of 4 users we produce 4 recommendations. This is repeated for each of our 3 strategies (*WeightedAverage*, *Joint*, *IndividualAverage*) and the quality of the recommendations is evaluated.

Evaluating Group Recommendations: A number of different approaches are used to evaluate the recommended cases based on the *compatibility* between the user's known *Perfect Case* and each of the recommended cases; that is, the number of shared features. In fact, for each individual group member, in addition to the quality of the recommended cases (generated by the 3 recommendation strategies), we also consider the quality of their *Final Case* (the case they chose during their browsing session) and also the quality of their *Best Case*. The *Best Case* for a user is found by identifying that case in the casebase that is the closest match to their *Perfect Case*; remember that the *Perfect Case* does not correspond to an actual case in the casebase but rather is an ideal case for the user. In this way the quality of the *Final Case* and the *Perfect Case* allow us to benchmark the quality of the recommendations. The results of our evaluation are presented so that we may understand, on the one hand, how each individual group member has benefited from the group's recommendations, and on the other hand, how the group as a whole has benefited.

4.3   Results: The Individual's Perspective

During the preference elicitation phase of this experiment each individual trial subject selected a ski holiday case that they would be interested in purchasing (their *Final Case*). They also told us about their ideal ski holiday (their *Perfect Case*) and from this we selected the closest case available to this ideal in the case base (their *Best Case*). During the group recommendation phase of the experiment, when individual's were assigned to groups, recommendations were made for these groups using various strategies. Our first task is to analyse the relationship between the recommended cases and each user's *Perfect Case* to determine how well the group recommender has matched the preferences of each individual during the group recommendation process.

Thus, for each of the 4 members of a group we compute the compatibility between the member's *Perfect Case* (their true preferences) and their own recommended case; remember each group member is recommended an individual

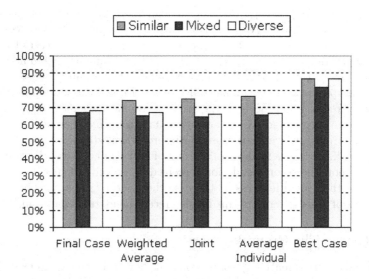

Fig. 2. Average Individual Perfect Case Compatibility

case (taking into account the group preferences as well as their own) so that overall the group receives 4 recommendations to chose from. Then for each group
we get the average of the resulting compatibility score to produce a single compatibility score for a particular set of group recommendations generated by one
recommendation strategy. This is repeated for all 3 recommendation strategies
and the same technique is also used to evaluate the average compatibility of the
final and best cases. The results are presented in Fig. 2 which charts the average
individual compatibility score for each of the 5 reference cases (final, best, and
the 3 types of recommended cases generated by the 3 different recommendation
strategies) across the 3 different set of groups (*similar*, *mixed*, and *diverse*).

The first point to highlight is that there is an improvement in the quality of the
recommended cases for the *similar* groups. For example, we see that on average,
the *Final Case* selected by a member of a *similar* group is approximately 65%
compatible with their ideal *Perfect Case* features. When we look at the quality
of the recommended cases produced for this type of group we see that they are
approximately 75% compatible with the user's ideal *Perfect Case*; significantly
closer to the average *Best Case* compatibility of about 85%. In other words the
cases recommended to users by the group recommender, which took account of
their own preferences and the preferences of others in their group, were actually
more compatible with their ideal than the cases they themselves chose. This
demonstrates the type of *constructive interference* effect mentioned earlier in
this paper: for groups of very similar users we find that their preferences combine
in a constructive way to produce better recommendations.

This improvement in case quality is short-lived however. Looking at the more
challenging *mixed* and *diverse* group results we see that there is a slight decrease
in the compatibility between recommended cases and each user's ideal. This is

to be expected. These groups are more challenging from a recommendation perspective because their individual members have competing preferences. Thus the group recommender must make compromises when selecting cases to recommend that will appeal to the group as a whole. The results presented here tell us something about the impact of such compromises. For example, we see that for *diverse* groups the average compatibility of the *Final Case* was approximately 68%, compared to about 65% for the group recommendations.

Thus, from the perspective of an individual group member we see that the recommendations received can represent improvements (compared to their own case choice) if they are a member of a group of very similar users. However, more often than not, the recommendations received by an individual will not satisfy as many of their ideal features as the case they select themselves, because the preferences of more diverse groups involve recommendation compromises.

4.4   Results: The Group Perspective

Our second main evaluation question concerns how well the recommended cases satisfy the combined preferences of the group members. To test this, for each group, we compute the compatibility of each member's *Perfect Case* with all 4 of the group's recommended cases to measure the overall satisfaction of each user with the full set of cases recommended to the group. Thus for each group member we compute an average compatibility score relative to all 4 recommended cases and for each group we calculate the average of these compatibility scores across all 4 members. Once again an analagous approach is used to measure the average group compatibility of the final and best cases and the results are presented in Figure 3, which charts the average overall compatibility score for each of the 5 reference cases (final, best, and the 3 types of recommended cases generated by the 3 different recommendation strategies) across the 3 different set of groups (*similar*, *mixed*, and *diverse*).

This time the results are more revealing. They show, for example, that the recommended cases enjoy significantly higher compatibility scores than the user's final and best cases. For example, for all group types we see that on average the recommended cases are compatible with upwards of 65% of the combined ideal features of the group's members; and in the case of the *similar* groups we see average compatibility scores in excess of 70%. By comparison, the average compatibility of the final and best cases is significantly lower, typically between 40% and 50%. In other words, when we evaluate the quality of a case (recommended, final, or best) with respect to the ideal preferences of *all* group members (as opposed to the single group member) we find that the recommended cases are significantly more compatible with the group's preferences as a whole than either the final or best cases.

4.5   Results Summary

In this evaluation, we have compared 3 different group recommendation strategies by their ability to generate recommendations for the individual's within a

Fig. 3. Average Overall Perfect Case Compatibility

group while taking the overall group preferences into account. The results high-light a number of important points. First, from the perspective of an individual group member, compromises sometimes have to be made when generating rec-ommendations that reflect the preferences of a group. That being said, we see in Figure 2 that these compromises are often not very significant and sometimes, if the group is made up of very similar members, then the recommended cases may even represent an improvement on the choices of any one individual. Second, the results clearly show that the recommendations being made are much more compatible with the preferences of a group as a whole than any case selected by an individual; see Figure 3. Interestingly we have found little difference between the 3 alternative recommendation strategies proposed. In particular, *Weighted Average* and *Joint* techniques have performed very similar with a slight benefit enjoyed by the *Average Individual* approach. An appropriate live-user evaluation with real user groups is needed to further examine the aggregation policies.

5   Conclusions

There are many recommendation scenarios in which recommendations must be made to groups of users with potentially competing preferences. This represents a significant challenge for recommender systems research and the inherent issues are only now being tackled head-on. In this paper we have described ongoing research in the area of group recommendation, focusing on how group preferences can be aggregated from the preferences of individual group members, and how these preferences can be used to generated recommendations that are likely to satisfy the individual as well as the group as a whole. The results of our recent evaluation show how group recommendation strategies can deliver higher quality recommendations to the individuals of the group when compared with single-user recommendation techniques. However, live-user evaluation may be the only way to investigate group strategies.

Also, in this paper we have explored the relationship between group diversity characteristics and their effect on recommendation compromise, and have confirmed that for moderately and highly diverse groups of users, that competing individual preferences tend to *interfere destructively* to drive recommendation compromises. However, while the resulting recommendations are inevitably less optimal for an individual group member, we have shown how our particular recommendation strategies manage to suggest cases that are a better fit to overall group preferences.

References

1. Ardissono, L., Goy, A., Petrone, G., Segnan, M., Torassol, P.: In-trigue: Personalized recommendation of tourist attractions for desktop and handset devices. Applied Artifcial Intelligence 17(8-9), 687–714 (2003)
2. Burke, R., Hammond, K., Young, B.C.: The FindMe Approach to Assisted Browsing. Journal of IEEE Expert 12(4), 32–40 (1997)
3. Chao, D., Balthrop, J., Forrest, S.: Adaptive radio: Achieving consensus using negative preferences. In: Proceedings of the 2005th International ACM SIGGROUP Conference on Support Group Work, pp. 120–123 (2005)
4. Crossen, A., Budzik, J., Hammond, K.J.: Flytrap: Intelligent group music recommendation. In: Gil, Y., Leake, D.B. (eds.) Proceedings of The International Conference on Intelligent User Interfaces (IUI-2002), pp. 184–185. ACM, New York (2002)
5. Goren-Bar, D., Glinansky, O.: Family stereotyping - a model to flter tv programs for multiple viewers. In: De Bra, P., Brusilovsky, P., Conejo, R. (eds.) AH 2002. LNCS, vol. 2347, Springer, Heidelberg (2002)
6. Jameson, A.: More than the sum of its members: Challenges for group recommender systems. In: Proceedings of the International Working Conference on Advanced Visual Interfaces, Gallipoli, Italy, pp. 48–54 (2004)
7. Jameson, A., Baldes, S., Kleinbauer, T.: Enhancing mutual awareness in group recommender systems. In: Mobasher, B., Anand, S.S. (eds.) Proceedings of the IJCAI 2003 Workshop on Intelligent Techniques for Web Personalization, AAAI, Menlo Park, CA (2003)
8. Jameson, A., Smyth, B.: Recommendations for multiple users: What a difference a group makes. In: Brusilovsky, P., Kobsa, A., Nejdl, W. (eds.) The Adaptive Web. LNCS, vol. 4321, Springer, Heidelberg (2007)
9. Lieberman, H., Van Dyke, N., Vivacqua, A.: Let's browse: A collaborative web browsing agent. In: Proceedings of the International Conference on Intelligent User Interfaces (IUI-1999), New York, page 65 (1999)
10. McCarthy, J.F., Anagnost, T.D.: Musicfx: An arbiter of group preferences for computer aupported collaborative workouts. In: Proc. of Conference on Computer Supported Cooperative Work, pp. 363–372 (1998)
11. McCarthy, J.F.: Pocket restaurantfinder: A situated recommender system for groups. In: Joseph, F. (ed.) Proceedings of the Workshop on Mobile Ad-Hoc Communication at the 2002 ACM Conference on Human Factors in Computer Systems, Minneapolis, ACM, New York (2002)

12. McCarthy, K., McGinty, L., Smyth, B., Salamó, M.: The Needs of the Many: A Case-Based Group Recommender System. In: Roth-Berghofer, T.R., Göker, M.H., Güvenir, H.A. (eds.) ECCBR 2006. LNCS (LNAI), vol. 4106, pp. 196–210. Springer, Heidelberg (2006)
13. O'Connor, M., Cosley, D., Konstan, J., Riedl, J.: PolyLens: A Recommender System for Groups of Users. In: Proc. of European Conference on Computer-Supported Cooperative Work, pp. 199–218 (2001)
14. Pizzutilo, S., De Carolis, B., Cozzolongo, G., Ambruoso, F.: Group modeling in a public space: Methods, techniques and experiences. In: Proceedings of WSEAS AIC 05, Malta, ACM, New York (2005)
15. Reilly, J., McCarthy, K., McGinty, L., Smyth, B.: Incremental Critiquing. In: Bramer, M., Coenen, F., Allen, T. (eds.) Research and Development in Intelligent Systems XXI. Proceedings of AI-2004, pp. 101–114. Springer, UK (2004)
16. Resnick, P., Iacovou, N., Suchak, M., Bergstrom, P., Riedl, J.: GroupLens: An open architecture for collaborative filtering of netnews. In: Proceedings of the 1994 Conference on Computer Supported Collaborative Work, pp. 175–186 (1994)
17. Smyth, B., McGinty, L.: An Analysis of Feedback Strategies in Conversational Recommender Systems. In: Cunningham, P. (ed.) Proceedings of the 14th National Conference on Artificial Intelligence and Cognitive Science, Dublin, Ireland (2003)
18. Smyth, B., Balfe, E., Freyne, J., Briggs, P., Coyle, M., Boydell, O.: Exploiting query repetition and regularity in an adaptive community-based web search engine. User Modeling User-Adapted Interaction 14(5), 383–423 (2004)

Catching the Drift:
Using Feature-Free Case-Based Reasoning for Spam Filtering

Sarah Jane Delany[1] and Derek Bridge[2]

[1] Dublin Institute of Technology, Dublin, Ireland
`sarahjane.delany@comp.dit.ie`
[2] University College Cork, Cork, Ireland
`d.bridge@cs.ucc.ie`

Abstract. In this paper, we compare case-based spam filters, focusing on their resilience to concept drift. In particular, we evaluate how to track concept drift using a case-based spam filter that uses a feature-free distance measure based on text compression. In our experiments, we compare two ways to normalise such a distance measure, finding that the one proposed in [1] performs better. We show that a policy as simple as retaining misclassified examples has a hugely beneficial effect on handling concept drift in spam but, on its own, it results in the case base growing by over 30%. We then compare two different retention policies and two different forgetting policies (one a form of instance selection, the other a form of instance weighting) and find that they perform roughly as well as each other while keeping the case base size constant. Finally, we compare a feature-based textual case-based spam filter with our feature-free approach. In the face of concept drift, the feature-based approach requires the case base to be rebuilt periodically so that we can select a new feature set that better predicts the target concept. We find feature-free approaches to have lower error rates than their feature-based equivalents.

1 Introduction

Spam filtering is a classification task. The filter must predict whether an incoming email is 'ham' (legitimate) or 'spam' (illegitimate).

Different filters work in different ways. In procedural approaches users deploy whitelists, blacklists and authentication protocols[1]; in collaborative approaches users share signatures computed from the spam they receive[2]; and in content-based approaches the filter inspects the header, body and attachments of each email, or features computed from these, for content that is indicative of spam. Of course, filters may also combine the different approaches.[3]

In content-based filters, the classifier may make its decisions using, for example, rules, decision trees or boosted trees [2], Support Vector Machines [3],

---

[1] E.g. www.email-policy.com/Spam-black-lists.htm, www.emailauthentication.org/
[2] E.g. http://razor.sourceforge.net/, http://www.rhyolite.com/anti-spam/dcc/
[3] E.g. http://spamassassin.apache.org/

R.O. Weber and M.M. Richter (Eds.): ICCBR 2007, LNAI 4626, pp. 314–328, 2007.

probabilities [4,5] or exemplars [5,6,7,8]. Except in the case of rules, which are most often human-authored, a learning algorithm usually induces the classifier from a set of labelled training examples. This is a form of concept learning. But spam has the following characteristics that make this form of concept learning especially challenging. First, there is a subjective and personal aspect to spam: what is spam to one person may not be spam to another [9]. Second, spam is a heterogeneous concept: spam that advertises replica watches shares little content with pornographic spam. Third, there is a high cost to false positives: it is unacceptable to most users if ham is incorrectly classified as spam. Finally, there is on-going concept drift: spam is constantly changing.

We have been taking a Case-Based Reasoning (CBR) approach to spam filtering [6,7,10], as have others [8], in the belief that this approach can overcome the challenges. First, individual users can maintain their own case bases to represent their personal, subjective interests. Second, instance-based approaches, such as CBR, often perform well when learning complex target concepts, including heterogeneous and disjunctive ones [11]. Third, as we explain in Section 2.1, by using a unanimous voting mechanism we can bias a k-nearest neighbours classifier away from false positives. Finally, lazy learners including CBR can easily be updated incrementally to cope with concept drift [12].

We recently introduced a 'feature-free' distance measure into our case-based spam filter, resulting in significant improvements in classification accuracy [10,13]. In this paper, we show that the feature-free distance measure is also more resilient to concept drift.

In Section 2, we describe our case-based approach to spam filtering. We describe both the feature-based distance measure that we used in earlier work and the feature-free distance measure, based on text compression, which we have been using in our more recent work. In Section 3, we describe concept drift in more detail and we review techniques for handling concept drift especially in instance-based learners. In Section 4, we present our new experimental results. These include a comparison of two different distance measures that are based on text compression; a comparison of instance selection and instance weighting approaches to tracking concept drift; and a comparison of feature-based and feature-free approaches to handling concept drift, based on periodically rebuilding the case base.

2   Case-Based Spam Filtering

2.1   Email Classification Using Examples (ECUE)

Our case-based spam filter is called ECUE [7,14]. Its case base is a set of labelled training examples, both ham and spam. ECUE retrieves an incoming email's k nearest-neighbours (k-NN) from the case base and uses unanimous voting in reaching the classification. In other words, ECUE classifies the incoming email as spam only if all k of the nearest-neighbours are spam. The case base is a Case Retrieval Net [15], which speeds up the retrieval process.

ECUE incorporates case base editing algorithms, which, prior to classification, can remove redundant or noisy cases from the case base. Such algorithms aim to reduce the size of the case base and hence reduce retrieval time, while endeavouring to maintain or even improve the generalisation accuracy [16,17,18].

The case base editing technique that we use is called Competence-Based Editing (CBE) [6]. CBE builds a competence model of the case base by identifying for each case its usefulness (represented by the cases that it contributes to classifying correctly) and also the damage that it causes (represented by the cases that it causes to be misclassified). A two step process uses these case properties to identify the cases to be removed. The first step, Blame-Based Noise Reduction, removes noisy cases that adversely affect classification accuracy. The second step, Conservative Redundancy Reduction, removes redundant cases that are not needed for correct classification. CBE has been shown to conservatively reduce the size of an email case base while maintaining and even improving its generalisation accuracy. We describe CBE in detail in [6].

We have recently been experimenting with two variants of the ECUE system, one which uses a feature-based case representation and distance measure (Section 2.2), and another which takes a feature-free approach, based on text compression (Section 2.3).

2.2   The Feature-Based Distance Measure

In the feature-based version of ECUE, we represent each email e_j as a vector of feature values, $e_j = (f_{1j}, f_{2j}, \ldots f_{nj})$. We use binary-valued features only: if the feature exists in the email the feature value $f_{ij} = 1$, otherwise $f_{ij} = 0$. We do not use numeric-valued features (e.g. occurrence frequencies) because we found that they resulted in only minor improvements in overall accuracy, no significant decrease in false positives, and much increased classification and case base editing times [7].

The distance between a target case (an incoming email) e_t and a case from the case base e_c is simply a count of features on which they disagree:

$$FDM(e_t, e_c) =_{\text{def}} \sum_{i=1}^{n} |f_{it} - f_{ic}| \tag{1}$$

We found it better, especially from the point of view of false positives, not to use *feature weighting* on the binary representation [7].

We compute features from some of the header fields and the body of the emails, with no stop-word removal or stemming. We have three types of features: word, character and structural. For word features, the feature is set to 1 if and only if the word appears in the email. For character features, whether the feature is set to 1 or 0 depends on the frequency of occurrence of the character in the email. The Information Gain (IG) is calculated for each character over the full dataset, where the character is represented as a continuous, and not binary, feature [19] (i.e. the value in each email is the frequency of the character normalised by the maximum character frequency). The normalised frequency that returns the highest IG value in this calculation is used as a threshold for that character across the dataset. The character feature value in each email is set to 1 if and only if the normalised frequency of the character in the email is greater than or equal to this threshold. For structural features (e.g. the proportion of uppercase characters, lowercase characters or white space in the email), we again use Information Gain as a threshold to give a binary representation.

Feature extraction on the training examples finds a large set of candidate features; *feature selection* on these candidates uses Information Gain to identify a subset that is predictive of ham and spam. Based on the results of preliminary cross-validation experiments, we chose to use 700 features for the evaluations in this paper. One observation, which we will return to in Section 3, is that to handle concept drift in spam filtering it is advantageous to periodically re-run the feature extraction and feature selection processes using the most recently received emails.

2.3   The Feature-Free Distance Measure

In the feature-free version of ECUE, we compute distance directly on the textual content of some of the header fields and the bodies of the emails using a distance measure that is based on text compression.

Distance measures based on data compression have a long history in bioinformatics, where they have been used, e.g., for DNA sequence classification [20]. Outside of bioinformatics, compression-based distance measures have been applied to *clustering* of time-series data [21] and languages [22,23]. They have also been applied to *classification* of time series data [21]. But, to the best of our knowledge, ours is the first application of these distance measures to text classification in general and spam filtering in particular[4] [10,13]. There have, however, been other classifiers based on text compression. In these classifiers, for each class an adaptive statistical compressor builds a compression model from training examples belonging to that class. The classifier assigns a target document to the class whose compression model best accounts for that document [24,25,26]. Bratko *et al.* have recently used classifiers of this kind for spam filtering [27,28]. Rennie and Jaakkola, on the other hand, propose using text compression to discover features indicative of spam [29].

Keogh *et al.* [21] and Li *et al.* [1] have both presented generic distance measures based on data compression and inspired by the theory of Kolmogorov complexity. The *Kolmogorov complexity* $K(x)$ of a string x can be defined as the size of the smallest Turing machine capable (without any input) of outputting x to its tape. The *conditional Kolmogorov complexity* $K(x|y)$ of x relative to y can be defined as the size of the smallest Turing machine capable of outputting x when y is already on its tape. This can be the basis of a distance measure. Informally, if $K(x|y) < K(x|z)$, then y contains more information content that is useful to outputting x than z does, and so y is more similar to x than z is.

---

[4] But see the discussion of the possibility of using compression in instance-based classification of email at www.kuro5hin.org/story/2003/1/25/224415/367.

Unfortunately, Kolmogorov complexity is not computable in general, and so we must approximate it. Since the Kolmogorov complexity of a string is in some sense the size of the smallest description of the string, one way of thinking of $K(x)$ is that it is the length of the best compression we can achieve for x. So, we can approximate $K(x)$ by $C(x)$, the size of x after compression by a data compressor.

We can define useful distance measures by comparing $C(x)$, $C(y)$ and $C(xy)$, where $C(xy)$ is the size after compression of y concatenated to the end of x. The intuition here is that compression of xy will exploit not only the redundancies within x and within y but also inter-document redundancies (similarities) between x and y too. If there are inter-document redundancies, then the amount of compression of xy should be greater than we obtain by compressing x and y separately. This still leaves the question of how to combine these into a normalized measure of distance.

Keogh et $al.$ [21] define the Compression-Based Dissimilarity between strings x and y as follows:

$$CDM(x, y) =_{\text{def}} \frac{C(xy)}{C(x) + C(y)} \tag{2}$$

CDM produces values in the range $(0.5, 1]$. Even with the best possible compression algorithm, the lowest value it can produce is slightly above 0.5 because, even if $x = y$, $C(xy)$ will be slightly greater than $C(x)$. In principle CDM's maximum value is 1. This would occur when x and y are so different that $C(xy) = C(x) + C(y)$. In other words, it occurs when there is no inter-document redundancy.

Li et $al.$ [1] offer an extensive theoretical analysis of their definition, which normalizes differently. They define the Normalized Compression Distance between strings x and y as follows:

$$NCD(x, y) =_{\text{def}} \frac{C(xy) - \min(C(x), C(y))}{\max(C(x), C(y))} \tag{3}$$

NCD produces values in the range $[0, 1 + \epsilon]$, where the upper bound allows for imperfections in the compression algorithm. Li et $al.$ say that values of ϵ above 0.1 are unlikely [1]. In fact, in a leave-one-out validation on a case base of 1000 emails, the range we obtained was $[0.02, 0.93]$.

In our previous work [10,13], we used CDM. In Section 4.2, we report the first empirical comparison of CDM and NCD, and we find in fact that NCD generally gives superior results. It is then NCD that we use in the remaining experiments in this paper.

Note that the properties expected of distance metrics do not in general hold for CDM and NCD. In general, it is not the case that $CDM(x, x) = 0$ iff $x = y$; $CDM(x, y) \neq CDM(y, x)$, i.e. CDM is not symmetric; and $CDM(x, y) + CDM(y, z) \not\geq CDM(x, z)$, i.e. the triangle-inequality does not hold. Similarly, these do not hold in general for NCD.

None of this prevents use of CDM or NCD in, for example, classification tasks, provided the classification algorithm does not rely on any of these properties. For example, an exhaustive implementation of k-NN (in which the algorithm finds the k nearest neighbours to the query by computing the distance between the query and *every* case in the case base) will work correctly. But retrieval algorithms that rely on these properties to avoid computing some distances (e.g. k-d trees [30] and Fish and Shrink [31]) are not guaranteed to work correctly.

CDM and *NCD* give us feature-free approaches to computing distances between textual cases. They can work directly on the raw text. Hence, this feature-free approach has negligible set-up costs. Cases are represented by raw text: there is no need to extract, select or weight features; there is no need to tokenise or parse queries or cases. This is a major advantage, especially if each user is to have a personalised case-based filter. By contrast, in the feature-based approach, we must extract and select features for each individual user case base.

We also believe that the feature-free approach should have an advantage in tracking concept drift. We explore and test this in the remainder of this paper.

3   Concept Drift

In some tasks, including spam filtering, the target concept is not static. It changes over time, and the characteristics that are predictive of the target concept change also. Spam changes according to the season (e.g. an increase after Christmas of spam that advertises weight loss products) and according to world events (e.g. the surge in spam related to religion following the death of Pope John Paul II). What people regard as spam also changes: their interests change (e.g. a person's interest in emails that advertise replica watches may cease after buying one) and their tolerances change (e.g. reminders of a conference or seminar can become increasingly unwelcome). But, above all, spam changes because there is an arms race between spammers and those who produce filters: each continually tries to outwit the other.

For many spam filters, this is a losing battle. But where classifiers are induced from examples, we can retrain the classifier using new examples of ham and spam, especially misclassified examples. Lazy learners, including the case-based approach, have the advantage that they can easily learn incrementally. The filter can insert into the case base new emails, along with their correct classifications, in the hope that this improves the competence of the system. However, incremental update is not enough. On its own, it results in an ever larger case base and ever longer classification times. Importantly also, because of the concept drift, some cases in the case base may no longer contribute to correct classification.

There are two main solutions: *instance selection* and *instance weighting*. The goal of instance selection is to identify, among all instances in the case base, those instances that define the current target concept. Other instances are deleted or, less commonly, are made ineligible for retrieval. Most instance selection algorithms are window-based. A window slides over the training examples, using, for example, only the most recent examples for prediction. Examples of window-based algorithms include the FLORA family of algorithms [32], FRANN [33] and Time-Weighted Forgetting [34]. Some algorithms use a fixed-size window, while others adjust the window size based on the rate and amount of drift [35,36,32].

In instance weighting, instances are weighted according to their age or performance. Instances with low weights are less likely to be used for classification and, if their weights become low enough, may even be deleted. Klinkenberg describes how to use Support Vector Machines in this way [36]. Instance-based approaches to instance weighting include Locally-Weighted Forgetting (LWF) and Prediction Error Context Switching (PECS) [34]. In LWF, each instance is weighted by a combination of its age and whether the learner has subsequently encountered new examples that are similar to it; new examples eventually oust older similar examples. In PECS, instances are weighted by their predictiveness. Specifically, if a stored example begins to disagree often with the correct classifications of its neighbours, then it is moved to an inactive set, from where it is no longer eligible for retrieval. This kind of performance weighting, and the use of confidence interval tests in deciding when to move instances between the active and inactive sets, gives PECS strong similarities with IB3 [37].

For completeness, we mention an altogether different way of handling concept drift: the use of ensembles of classifiers induced from different subsets of the training examples [38]. Further consideration of ensemble approaches is beyond the scope of this paper.

The research we have described above on instance selection, instance weighting and ensembles tracks concept drift by trying to use just the subset of examples that are predictive of the current target concept. But, it is important to realise that, additionally in feature-based approaches, the features that were once predictive may no longer be so. Hence the case-based filter must periodically extract and select a new feature set from the most recent examples and rebuild the case base so that it uses these new features. We investigated this in [14]. A related approach has subsequently been reported in [8], where a case-specific set of features is computed separately for each email when it arrives.

Of course, in this paper we are comparing a feature-based approach with a feature-free approach. We believe that the feature-free approach, which we have already found to be more accurate and to have lower set-up costs, will also be more resilient to concept drift precisely because its definition of the concept depends only on the current contents of the case base, and not on any features.

4   Spam Filtering Experiments

4.1   Evaluation Setup

The focus of the experiments reported in this paper is to investigate the effect of feature-free, compression-based distance measures on concept drift. To that end, we used two large datasets of date-ordered ham and spam.[5] Each dataset was collected by an individual from the email that they received over a period of approximately one year. For each dataset, we set up an initial case base using a training set of one thousand cases, five hundred consecutively received ham emails and five hundred consecutively received spam emails. This left the

---

[5] The datasets are available for download at www.comp.dit.ie/sjdelany/dataset.htm

Table 1. Profile of the test data in Datasets 1 and 2

	Feb '03	Mar	Apr	May	Jun	Jul	Aug	Sep	Oct	Nov	Dec	Jan '04	Total
Dataset 1													
spam		629	314	216	925	917	1065	1225	1205	1830	576		**8902**
ham		93	228	102	89	50	71	145	103	85	105		**1076**
Dataset 2													
spam	142	391	405	459	406	476	582	1849	1746	1300	954	746	**9456**
ham	151	56	144	234	128	19	30	182	123	113	99	130	**1409**

remainder of the data for testing and updating the case base. Table 1 shows the profile of the test data across each month for both datasets.

We presented each test email for classification to the case-based classifiers in date order. Results were accumulated over each month.

Since False Positive (FP) classifications (ham classified incorrectly as spam) are much more serious than False Negative (FN) classifications (spam classified incorrectly as ham), accuracy (or error) as a measure of performance does not present the full picture. Two filters with similar accuracies may have very different FP and FN rates. In addition, as the amount of ham is considerably lower than the amount of spam in the datasets, the actual error figure would follow the FN rate and not give adequate emphasis to FPs. The measure we use is the average within-class error rate, $Err = \frac{FPRate + FNRate}{2}$, rather than the actual error rate ($Err = \frac{number\ misclassified}{total\ emails}$). We also report the FP rate ($FPRate = \frac{number\ of\ false\ positives}{total\ negative\ examples}$) and FN rates (defined analogously) separately. Where differences exist, we use a two-tailed, paired t-test across the monthly results to test for significance.

The compression algorithm we use in all experiments reported here is GZip, a variant of Lempel-Ziv compression, in which a repetition of a string within a text may be replaced by a pointer to an earlier occurrence.

From the point of view of Kolmogorov complexity, one should use the best compression algorithm because the better the compression rate, the closer the compression algorithm will approximate the Kolmogorov complexity. But this does not necessarily mean that using the better compressor in a compression-based distance measure such as those defined in Equations (2) and (3) will result in a better approximation of the distance as it may effect different terms in the formulae differently [1]. We compared compression algorithms in [13], specifically GZip with PPM, an adaptive statistical compressor that is considered to achieve some of the best compression rates. We found GZip to compress the emails in our datasets slightly more than PPM with little difference in classification accuracy when used in a distance measure. PPM is considerably slower than GZip and by truncating each email to 8000 characters (exploiting the fact that substitutions in GZIP are confined to a 32 Kbytes sliding window) we were able to further speed up GZip with no appreciable loss of accuracy.

4.2   A Comparison of *CDM* and *NCD*

To compare the two distance measures, *NCD* and *CDM*, we presented each email in date order for classification against the full case base of 1000 training emails. The results are in Figure 1 which show that *NCD* performs better overall than *CDM*. The differences in overall error are significant in both datasets at the 99% level, but the differences in FP rate are not. Figure 1 also includes the results of adding each misclassified email as it is found into the case base: the error rates are considerably lower, with no significant difference between the two distance measures. These results show that even relatively simple attempts to track concept drift (in this case, retaining misclassified examples) can work well.

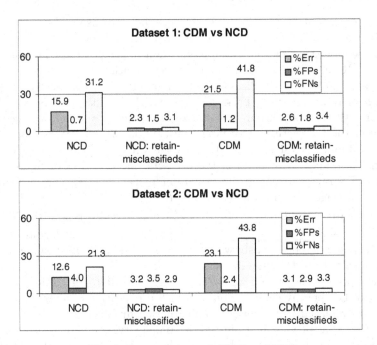

Fig. 1. A comparison of *CDM* and *NCD*

4.3   Handling Concept Drift with *NCD*

As we described in Section 3, one of the difficulties of handling concept drift by retaining examples is that the size of the case base increases. In the experiments performed in Section 4.2 above, when the case bases are updated with misclassified emails they increased in size by 32% and 30% respectively over the duration of the experiment.

It is necessary therefore to include a *forgetting* mechanism to remove instances that may no longer be useful in classification. We present results here of a variety of different approaches to retention and forgetting within an *add-1-delete-1* policy. The approaches to retention can be categorised as either *retain-all*, where all examples are added to the case base, or *retain-misclassifieds*, where just those examples that are misclassified are added. The forgetting mechanisms we considered were *forget-oldest* and *forget-least-accurate*. *Forget-oldest* is a simple form of *instance selection*, sliding a fixed-size window over the examples and deleting the oldest. *Forget-least-accurate* can be considered as a simple form of *instance weighting*, inspired by IB3 and PECS. In *forget-least-accurate*, the accuracy of a case is measured as the proportion of times the case is successfully retrieved. More formally, *accuracy = #successes/#retrievals*, where *#retrievals* is the number of times a case is retrieved as a nearest neighbour in k-NN classification and *#successes* is the number of times the case is both retrieved as a neighbour and has the same class as the target. In the case of ties, we delete the oldest of the least accurate cases. So that we compare like with like as much as possible, we use the accuracy records only for forgetting; they do not, as in IB3, influence which cases are retrieved as neighbours.

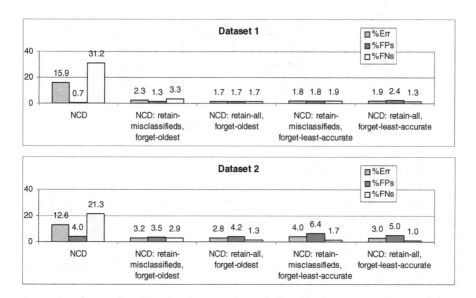

Fig. 2. *NCD* with various concept drift tracking mechanisms

It is evident from Figure 2 that all the approaches are successful at tracking the drift. It is difficult to identify any one approach that is the best, but *forget-least-accurate*, in spite of having a significant beneficial effect on FNs, appears to have a negative effect on FPs which is not desirable.

We also investigated using Competence-Based Editing on the initial case bases but found that it did not significantly improve on the results shown in Figure 2. The consequence of using an *add-1-delete-1* policy is that the case base size remains constant. If case base editing is also used then the sizes of the case bases will differ across systems.

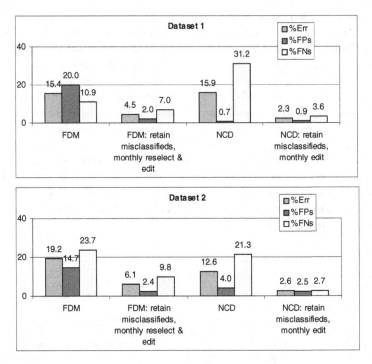

Fig. 3. *NCD* compared with *FDM*

4.4   Feature-Free Versus Feature-Based

Given that we have found that *NCD* can track concept drift, this section investigates how well it works compared with an approach that uses a feature-based
representation and distance measure, which we designate *FDM*. To track concept drift with our feature-based version of ECUE, we incorporate two levels
of learning [14]. Firstly, we retain misclassified emails as they are found. Secondly, the feature set needs to be periodically updated from the more recent
examples of email. Specifically, at regular intervals (monthly for the purposes of
our evaluation), we re-run feature extraction and selection on the most recent
emails; we rebuild the case base using only more recent examples of email, so
that each included case is now represented using the new set of features; and
we run Competence-Based Editing (CBE) on the rebuilt case base. Since CBE
deletes noisy and redundant cases, it gives us an implicit form of forgetting,
thereby limiting case base growth. Note that previously reported experiments
with *FDM* show this two-level form of learning to outperform a window-based
instance selection system [14].

Although *NCD* does not use features, in order to compare like with like we
implemented a version of ECUE that uses *NCD*, retains misclassified examples
and achieves a degree of forgetting by rebuilding the case base from the most
recent examples and running CBE on the rebuilt case base every month.

Figure 3 shows the results of comparing the *FDM* approach with the equivalent *NCD* approach. The Figure shows that when neither the feature-based nor the feature-free system incorporates any mechanism for handling concept drift, *NCD* has significantly lower FP rates; its FN rates are higher for one dataset and lower for the other.

However, the Figure also shows that when both systems retain misclassified examples and rebuild their case bases every month (in the way described above), the feature-free system tracks the concept drift better than the feature-based system with the differences in overall error significant at the 95% level for Dataset 2 and the 90% level for Dataset 1. There is, however, no significant difference in the FP rate.

The differences between the *NCD* tracking results presented in Figure 3 and those presented for the *add-1-delete-one* policies in Figure 2, although better in some cases and worse in others, are for the most part not significant. In any

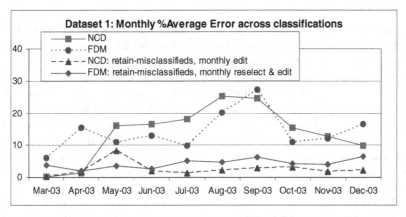

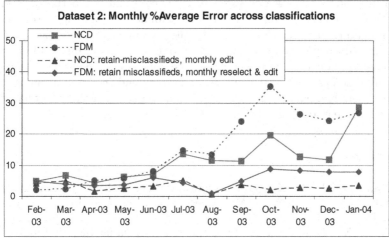

Fig. 4. Monthly average error across classifications

case, the case base rebuild and edit approach to forgetting offers advantages over the *add-1-delete-1* policies. Firstly it allows the spam filter to use smaller case bases, which speeds up classification. Secondly, it facilitates bootstrapping of a personalised spam filter. The system can be installed with small amounts of training data available from a user's email but over time will stabilise to appropriate amounts of training data as periodic rebuild and edit takes place.

A graphical representation of the average monthly error across classifications is shown in Figure 4. Although *NCD* is better overall than *FDM* (Figure 3), Figure 4 shows that, when the case base is never updated, *NCD* does not consistently outperform *FDM* in all months, in particular in Dataset 1. But when misclassified examples are retained and the case base is rebuilt and edited every month, the *NCD* results are as good as or better for all months in Dataset 2 and for all except one month in Dataset 1.

5   Conclusion

This paper continues our investigation of a feature-free distance measure based on text compression for case-based spam filtering. We have new results in which Li *et al.*'s *NCD* outperforms Keogh *et al.*'s *CDM*. But the real focus of the paper has been on concept drift.

We have shown that concept drift in spam is very real and, without a way of handling it, accuracy will be much the lower. We have shown too (Figures 1 and 2) that even quite simple retention and forgetting policies can be very effective. Finally, we have shown (Figures 3 and 4) that the feature-free approach can obtain accuracy that is better than or comparable to that of the feature-based approach but with lower set-up costs and simpler periodic maintenance demands.

In the future we would like to experiment with feature-free case-based spam filters using more sophisticated forms of instance weighting, perhaps closer to IB3 or PECS, and combining recency of use, amount of use and degree of success in the weighting formula. Encouraged by the success of the periodic case base rebuild and edit experiments, we would like to develop and evaluate a forgetting policy based on a competence model, that we hope would be cheaper than running a full case base edit. We would also like to extend the application of *NCD* to texts other than emails, to tasks other than classification, and to text other than raw text, e.g. text that has undergone POS-tagging.

References

1. Li, M., Chen, X., Li, X., Ma, B., Vitanyi, P.: The similarity metric. In: Procs. of the 14th Annual ACM-SIAM Symposium on Discrete Algorithms, Baltimore, Maryland, pp. 863–872 (2003)
2. Carreras, X., Marquez, L.: Boosting trees for anti-spam filtering. In: Procs. of the 4th International Conference on Recent Advances in Natural Language Processing, Tzigov Chark, Bulgaria, pp. 58–64 (2001)

3. Drucker, H., Wu, D., Vapnik, V.: Support vector machines for spam categorization. IEEE Trans. on Neural Networks 10, 1048–1054 (1999)
4. Sahami, M., Dumais, S., Heckerman, D., Horvitz, E.: A Bayesian approach to filtering junk email. In: Procs. of the AAAI-98 Workshop for Text Categorisation, Madison, Wisconsin, pp. 55–62 (1998)
5. Androutsopoulos, I., Paliouras, G., Karkaletsis, V., Sakkis, G., Spyropoulos, C., Stamatopoulos, P.: Learning to filter spam e-mail: A comparison of a naive Bayesian and a memory-based approach. In: Procs. of the PKDD-2000 Workshop on Machine Learning and Textual Information Access, pp. 1–13 (2000)
6. Delany, S.J., Cunningham, P.: An analysis of case-based editing in a spam filtering system. In: Funk, P., González Calero, P.A. (eds.) ECCBR 2004. LNCS (LNAI), vol. 3155, pp. 128–141. Springer, Heidelberg (2004)
7. Delany, S.J., Cunningham, P., Coyle, L.: An assessment of case-based reasoning for spam filtering. Artificial Intelligence Review 24, 359–378 (2005)
8. Méndez, J.R., Fdez-Roverola, F., Iglesias, E.L., Díaz, F., Corchado, J.M.: Tracking concept drift at feature selection stage in spamhunting: An anti-spam instance-based reasoning system. In: Roth-Berghofer, T.R., Göker, M.H., Güvenir, H.A. (eds.) ECCBR 2006. LNCS (LNAI), vol. 4106, pp. 504–518. Springer, Heidelberg (2006)
9. Gray, A., Haahr, M.: Personalised, collaborative spam filtering. In: Procs. of 1st Conference on Email and Anti-Spam, Mountain View, CA (2004)
10. Delany, S.J., Bridge, D.: Feature-based and feature-free textual CBR: A comparison in spam filtering. In: Procs. of the 17th Irish Conference on Artificial Intelligence and Cognitive Science, Belfast, Northern Ireland, pp. 244–253 (2006)
11. Aha, D.W.: Generalizing from case studies: A case study. In: Procs. of the 9th International Conference on Machine Learning, Aberdeen, Scotland, pp. 1–10 (1992)
12. Delany, S.J., Cunningham, P., Smyth, B.: ECUE: A spam filter that uses machine learning to track concept drift. In: Procs. of the 17th European Conference on Artificial Intelligence (PAIS stream), Riva del Garda, Italy, pp. 627–631 (2006)
13. Delany, S.J., Bridge, D.: Textual case-based reasoning for spam filtering: A comparison of feature-based and feature-free approaches. Artificial Intelligence Review (Forthcoming)
14. Delany, S.J., Cunningham, P., Tsymbal, A., Coyle, L.: A case-based technique for tracking concept drift in spam filtering. Knowledge-Based Systems 18, 187–195 (2005)
15. Lenz, M., Auriol, E., Manago, M.: Diagnosis and decision support. In: Lenz, M., Bartsch-Spörl, B., Burkhard, H.-D., Wess, S. (eds.) Case-Based Reasoning Technology. LNCS (LNAI), vol. 1400, pp. 51–90. Springer, Heidelberg (1998)
16. McKenna, E., Smyth, B.: Competence-guided case-base editing techniques. In: Blanzieri, E., Portinale, L. (eds.) EWCBR 2000. LNCS (LNAI), vol. 1898, pp. 186–197. Springer, Heidelberg (2000)
17. Wilson, D.R., Martinez, T.R.: Reduction techniques for instance-based learning algorithms. Machine Learning 38, 257–286 (2000)
18. Brighton, H., Mellish, C.: Advances in instance selection for instance-based learning algorithms. Data Mining and Knowledge Discovery 6, 153–172 (2002)
19. Quinlan, J.R.: C4.5 Programs for Machine Learning. Morgan Kaufmann, San Francisco (1997)
20. Loewenstern, D., Hirsh, H., Yianilos, P., Noordewier, M.: DNA sequence classification using compression-based induction. Technical Report 95-04, Rutgers University, Computer Science Department (1995)

21. Keogh, E., Lonardi, S., Ratanamahatana, C.: Towards parameter-free data mining. In: Procs. of the 10th ACM SIGKDD, International Conference on Knowledge Discovery and Data Mining, New York, USA, pp. 206–215 (2004)
22. Benedetto, D., Caglioti, E., Loreto, V.: Language trees and zipping. Physical Review Letters 88, 048702/1–048702/4 (2002)
23. Cilibrasi, R., Vitanyi, P.: Clustering by compression. IEEE Transactions on Information Theory 51, 1523–1545 (2005)
24. Frank, E., Chui, C., Witten, I.H.: Text categorization using compression models. In: Procs. of the IEEE Data Compression Conference, Utah, USA, pp. 200–209 (2000)
25. Teahan, W.J.: Text classification and segmentation using minimum cross-entropy. In: Procs. of the 6th International Conference on Recherche d'Information Assistee par Ordinateur, Paris, France, pp. 943–961 (2000)
26. Teahan, W.J., Harper, D.J.: Using compression-based language models for text categorization. In: Procs. of the Workshop on Language Modeling for Information Retrieval, Carnegie Mellon University, pp. 83–88 (2001)
27. Bratko, A., Filipič, B.: Spam filtering using character-level Markov models: Experiments for the TREC 2005 spam track. In: Procs. of the 14th Text REtrieval Conference, Gaithersburg, MD (2005)
28. Bratko, A., Cormack, G.V., Filipič, B., Lynam, T.R., Zupan, B.: Spam filtering using statistical data compression models. Journal of Machine Learning Research 7, 2673–2698 (2006)
29. Rennie, J.D.M., Jaakkola, T.: Automatic feature induction for text classification. In: MIT Artificial Intelligence Laboratory Abstract Book, Cambridge, MA (2002)
30. Wess, S., Althoff, K.D., Derwand, G.: Using k-d trees to improve the retrieval step in case-based reasoning. In: Haton, J.-P., Manago, M., Keane, M.A. (eds.) Advances in Case-Based Reasoning. LNCS, vol. 984, pp. 167–181. Springer, Heidelberg (1995)
31. Schaaf, J.W.: Fish and shrink. In: Smith, I., Faltings, B.V. (eds.) Advances in Case-Based Reasoning. LNCS, vol. 1168, pp. 362–376. Springer, Heidelberg (1996)
32. Widmer, G., Kubat, M.: Learning in the presence of concept drift and hidden contexts. Machine Learning 23, 69–101 (1996)
33. Kubat, M., Widmer, G.: Adapting to drift in continuous domains. In: Procs. of the 8th European Conference on Machine Learning, Heraclion, Crete, pp. 307–310 (1995)
34. Salganicoff, M.: Tolerating concept and sampling shift in lazy learning using prediction error context switching. Artificial Intelligence Review 11, 133–155 (1997)
35. Klinkenberg, R., Joachims, T.: Detecting concept drift with support vector machines. In: Procs. of the 17th International Conference on Machine Learning, San Francisco, CA, pp. 487–494 (2000)
36. Klinkenberg, R.: Learning drifting concepts: Example selection vs. example weighting. Intelligent Data Analysis 8, 281–300 (2004)
37. Aha, D.W., Kibler, D., Albert, M.K.: Instance-based learning algorithms. Machine Learning 6, 37–66 (1991)
38. Kuncheva, L.I.: Classifier ensembles for changing environments. In: Procs. of the 5th International Workshop on Multiple Classifier Systems, Italy, pp. 1–15 (2004)

Enhancing Case-Based, Collaborative Web Search*

Oisín Boydell and Barry Smyth

Adaptive Information Cluster
School of Computer Science and Informatics
University College Dublin, Dublin 4, Ireland
oisin.boydell@ucd.ie, barry.smyth@ucd.ie

Abstract. This paper describes and evaluates a case-based approach to personalizing Web search by post-processing the results returned by a Web search engine to reflect the interests of a community of like-minded searchers. The search experiences of a community of users are captured as a case base of textual cases, which serves as a way to bias future search results in line with community interests.

1 Introduction

Web searchers continue to struggle when it comes to efficiently locating precise information and recent evidence suggests that up to 50% of search sessions fail to deliver relevant results [20]. The types of queries used in Web search are a significant part of the problem due to *query ambiguity* and *vocabulary mismatches*. Web queries usually fail to clearly identify the searcher's true information needs and many studies have highlighted how a typical query contains only 2 or 3 terms [12]. For example, queries like *"jordan pictures"* offer no clues about whether the searcher is looking for images of the racing team, the middle eastern state, the basketball star, or the British celebrity. At the same time, recent evidence highlights the lack of correspondence between queries and target pages, suggesting that there is a vocabulary mismatch between search terms and index terms[5]; for example, [2] go so far as to dismiss the traditional view of there being a single conceptual space for information retrieval consisting of both query and document terms. As we shall see, encouraging users to submit more detailed queries is unlikely to provide a solution because such queries tend to exacerbate the *vocabulary gap*: users often add query terms that do not help to identify the document they are seeking.

The work of [1] described a case-based approach to Web search that involved maintaining a case base of *search cases* to reflect the combined search experiences of a community of like-minded searchers. Very briefly, each search case encoded the results that had been selected by community members in response to a particular query, q_i. When responding to some new target query, q_T, results

---

* This material is based on works supported by Science Foundation Ireland under Grant No. 03/IN.3/I361.

R.O. Weber and M.M. Richter (Eds.): ICCBR 2007, LNAI 4626, pp. 329–343, 2007.
© Springer-Verlag Berlin Heidelberg 2007

that are contained within search cases for similar queries are *promoted* within the result-list returned by some underlying search engine such as Google. In this way, results that are preferred by community members are promoted in response to recurring future queries. So if our searcher is a member of a community of motoring fans then their search for *"jordan pictures"* is more likely to refer to pictures of the racing team, and such results will be promoted assuming that they have been frequently selected for similar queries in the past.

One of the potential shortcomings of the work of [1] is the limited *retrievability* of search cases. Search cases are indexed using the query terms that led to a particular set of result selections, and these cases can only be retrieved (and their associated results promoted) if there is a term-overlap between the target query and case query. However, because search queries tend to be short (typically 2-3 terms in length [12]) such overlaps cannot always be guaranteed. For example, staying with our motoring community, a target query for *"F1 photos"* would not see the retrieval of a search case for *"jordan pictures"* and so relevant promotion opportunities will be missed. In this paper we describe an alternative approach, which seeks to provide a richer set of retrieval opportunities for search cases. Instead of indexing cases by their queries alone we describe how cases can also be indexed by the terms that occur in the snippet texts associated with the selected results. In this way case specifications contain a much richer vocabulary and offer far greater opportunities for retrieval and reuse during future searches.

The remainder of this paper is organised as follows. In the next section we motivate our work by highlighting the extent of the vocabulary gap in Web search. This is followed by a review of related work, focusing on recent attempts to bridge the vocabulary gap by harnessing context and experience within Web search. In particular, we review a number of case-based approaches to Web search that form the starting point for our own work. Sections 4 and 5 go on to describe and evaluate our approach to personalizing Web search across a number of different communities with a comparison to two separate benchmark search services.

2   How Wide Is the Vocabulary Gap in Web Search?

Further evidence in support of the vocabulary gap comes in the form of the recent emergence and popularity of tagging services such as *Del.icio.us*[1] and *Shadows*[2]. Such services allow users to explicitly *tag* Web pages with terms of their own choosing and they provide users with various ways to recall tagged pages. Thus, these services provide an alternative way for users to locate relevant and interesting pages. For example, *Del.icio.us* is a collaborative bookmarking service that allows users publish their tagged bookmarks online.

The availability of this tagging data can be considered as the basis for an experiment to estimate the extent of the vocabulary gap in Web search. It seems reasonable to view the set of terms used to tag a bookmarked page as a proxy for a search query that the user might submit to a search engine to locate this

---

[1] http://del.icio.us/

[2] http://www.shadows.com/

page. Indeed when we analysed 7692 *Del.icio.us* bookmarks and tags, we found that the tags share many of the same basic term distribution characteristics as search queries, such as average length, expected overlap, etc. This begs the question as to how Web search engines might respond to ambiguity and vocabulary problems among these 'queries': will they tend to return the bookmarked page, for example? To test this we submitted the 7692 queries to Google, Yahoo, and MSN search and noted whether their corresponding bookmarked pages occurred within the top ten pages returned. The results are presented in Figure 1 as a graph of the percentage of search sessions where the bookmarked result was located against different sizes of queries from the test set.

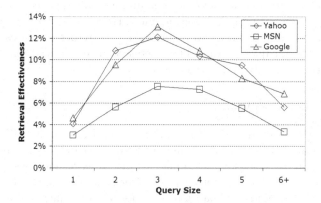

Fig. 1. Retreival Effectiviness vs. Query Size

There are a number of interesting observations to be made from these results.

1. The leading search engines only retrieve the target pages among their top ten results less than 15% of the time, with Yahoo and Google outperforming MSN Search.
2. All of the search engines achieve their maximum retrieval effectiveness for 3-term queries, which corresponds closely to the average size of the typical Web search query [12], suggesting that they are at least well-adapted to modern search queries.
3. Retrieval effectiveness degrades for longer, less ambiguous queries (the vocabulary gap at work) demonstrating a tendency for users to draw on increasingly less useful terms as part of more elaborate queries. Thus, retrieval performance is unlikely to be enhanced by encouraging Web searchers to extend their queries unaided.

3 Related Work

Primarily, this work is motivated by the need to bridge the vocabulary gap that obviously exists in Web search. Specifically we need to look for ways to improve how Web search engines cope with vague user queries and vocabulary mismatches.

3.1   Context Sensitive Search

Vague queries are often problematic because they lack context; to re-visit our previous example, the query *"jordan pictures"* does not help to distinguish between pages relating to motor racing, basketball, the country or the celebrity, any of which might be relevant to the searcher. One way, therefore, to improve a vague query is to expand it by including additional context terms. This can be done according to two basic approaches: either by explicitly establishing context up-front or by implicitly inferring it. For example, the Inquirus 2 meta-search engine [8] supplements keyword-based queries with a context category; users explicitly select from a set of categories such as "research paper", "homepage" etc. Alternatively, implicit context can be automatically inferred. Systems such as Watson [3] take advantage of user activity prior to the search to judge context; Watson monitors a user's word processing activities and uses document text as the basis for query terms. The interested reader is also referred to the Remembrance Agent [16] and Letizia [14].

3.2   Query-Log Analysis

Query-log analysis resonates well with a case-based approach to Web search, in the sense that it considers the value of historical search session information contained within query logs. For example, [6] mine a search engine's query log in order to discover correlations between query terms and document terms, which can then serve as candidate expansion terms as part of a query-expansion technique. The basic idea is that, if a set of documents is often selected for the same queries, then the terms in these documents must be strongly linked to the terms in the queries. Although this technique focuses on query-expansion rather than result re-ranking, it is similar in spirit to Collaborative Web Search which our work is based on.

3.3   Early Case-Based Approaches to Web Search

The use of case-based methods in information retrieval tasks has a long history. For example, the work of Rissland [18] looks at the application of CBR to legal information retrieval, and [4] describe a case-based approach to question-answering tasks. Similarly, in recent years there has been considerable research looking at how CBR techniques can deal with less structured textual cases. This has led to a range of so-called *textual CBR* techniques [13]. However these approaches have all tended to focus on particular application domains for textual CBR rather than the broader area of Web search. In the context of Web search, one particularly relevant piece of work concerns the *Broadway* recommender system [10], and specifically the Broadway-QR query refinement technique that uses case-based techniques to reuse past query refinements in order to recommend new refinements. Briefly, Broadway's cases reference a precise experience within a search session and include a problem description (made up of a sequence of behavioural elements including a sequence of recent queries), a solution (a new query refinement configuration), and an evaluation (based on historical explicit user satisfaction ratings when this case was previously recommended). The work of [9] apply CBR techniques to Web search in a different way. Their *PersonalSearcher* agent combines user profiling and textual case-based reasoning to dynamically filter Web documents according to a user's learned preferences.

3.4   A Review Collaborative Web Search

The work presented here is most directly influenced by the work of [1], on *Collaborative Web Search* (CWS), which adopted a case-based approach to personalizing search for communities of like-minded users. Very briefly, CWS is a form of personalized meta-search [7] with two novel features. First, personalization occurs at the level of a community of like-minded searchers. For a given target query q_T, the results returned by some underlying search engine(s) are modified so that those results which are most likely related to the learned preferences of the community are *promoted*. Second, personalization is based on the reuse of previous search sessions: the promotions for q_T are those results that have been previously selected by community members for queries that are *similar* to q_T.

$$c_i = (q_i, (r_1, h_1), ..., (r_k, h_k)) \tag{1}$$

Each community of searchers is a associated with a case base of *search cases* such that each case, c_i, is represented as a $k + 1$-tuple made up of the query component (a set of query terms, q_i used during some previous search session) plus k result-pairs; see Equation 1. Each result-pair is made up of a result page id (r_j) and a hit count (h_j) and reflects the number of times that a given community has selected r_j in response to q_i. In this way, each search case is a summary of the community's search experience relative to a given query. The *problem specification* part of the case (see Equation 2) corresponds to the query terms. The *solution* part of the case (see Equation 3) corresponds to the result-pairs; that is, the set of page selections that have been accumulated as a result of past uses of the corresponding query.

$$Spec(c_i) = q_i \tag{2}$$

$$Sol(c_i) = ((r_1, h_1), ..., (r_k, h_k)) \tag{3}$$

Each new target problem (corresponding to a new query q_T) is used to identify a set of similar cases in the case base by using a term-overlap similarity metric (such as that shown in Equation 4) to select the n most similar search cases $(c_1, ..., c_n)$ for q_T.

$$Sim(q_T, c_i) = \frac{|q_T \cap Spec(c_i)|}{|q_T \cup Spec(c_i)|} \tag{4}$$

These search cases contain a range of different result pages and their selection frequencies. Bearing in mind that some results may recur in multiple cases, the next step is to rank order these results according to their relevance for q_T. Each result p_j can be scored by its *relevance* with respect to its corresponding search case, c_i by computing the proportion of times that p_j was selected for this case's query q_i, as shown in Equation 5.

$$Rel(r_j, c_i) = \frac{h_j}{\sum_{\forall k} h_k \epsilon c_i} \tag{5}$$

Next the relevance of a result with respect to the current target query q_T is calculated by computing the weighted sum of the individual case relevance scores, weighting each by the similarity between q_T and each q_i. In this way, results which come from retrieved cases $(c_1, ..., c_n)$ whose query is very similar to the target query are given more weight than those who come from less similar queries; see Equation 6.

$$WRel(r_j, q_T, c_1, ..., c_n) = \frac{\sum_{i=1...n} Rel(r_j, c_i) \cdot Sim(q_T, c_i))}{\sum_{i=1...n} Exists(r_j, c_i) \cdot Sim(q_T, c_i)} \tag{6}$$

In this way, for given user u, a member of some community C, with query q_T we produce a ranked list of results R_C that come from the community's case base and that, as such, reflect the past selection patterns of this community. In parallel, q_T is used by a meta-search component to retrieve a set of *traditional* search results, R_M, from some underlying search engine(s). Finally, R_M and R_C are combined and returned to the user as R_T. This combination typically involves promoting prominent results in R_C ahead of those in R_M; for example, typically the top 3 results from R_C are promoted ahead of R_M results to the user while other results from R_C are marked as community-relevant within the final result-list, which follows the original R_M ranking. In this way, results that have been previously preferred by community members are either promoted or marked as relevant to provide community members with more immediate access to results that are likely to be relevant to their particular needs.

3.5   From Selections to Snippets

The work of [1,21,20] has shown that *CWS* can be effective in search scenarios where natural communities of searchers can be identified, but its case-based approach is ultimately limited to the promotion of previously selected results. Thus, *CWS* relies on *what* searchers have selected in the past rather than *why* they made their selections, an important limitation that motivates a new approach to collaborative Web search presented in this paper. While still fundamentally experience-based, we describe an alternative model of case representation, indexing, and retrieval that offers a much greater potential to influence future searches. In particular, we attempt to capture *why* a certain result has been selected by a community member by mining the terms that appear in selected result snippets (the short query-focused document summaries that are associated with documents in search engine result-lists). These terms then provide a much richer opportunity to index search cases than queries on their own.

As an aside, the use of snippets for document indexing in IR was first suggested in 1958 [15], and more recently by [19]. These works propose the use of generic document summaries as an alternative index to be queried in parallel to a full content index or for use as a source for pseudo relevance feedback. Our approach differs in its use of query sensitive snippets and the importance of user selection behaviour (real search experiences) when it comes to combining such snippets community-sensitive search cases. Alternatively, the work of [11] on *document transformation* modifies document indexes according to previous selection behaviour, but in a more limited way to our proposal: query terms are simply added to the default index for a selected document to boost the weight of these terms in the document. Over time, this allows the document to drift towards the query terms for which it was selected in the past. In our work a search case base corresponds to a community-level index, which can be updated separately by using the snippet terms of selected documents as well as the query terms that led to their selection.

4   A Snippet-Based Approach to Case-Based Web Search

The main contribution of this paper is an alternative approach to case-based Web search, which is inspired by the CWS model. We continue to encode the search experiences of a community as a case base of search cases, however, this time there are two important differences. First, each case now reflects the selection behaviour of the community with respect to a single result page, rather than a single query. Second, each case is indexed according to two separate sets of terms, the query terms (as in the traditional model of CWS) but also the snippet terms that were associated with the result when it was retrieved. By their nature, these snippet terms are likely to have played some role in attracting the attention of the searcher. In the following sections we will describe how community search behaviour is used to generate these so-called *snippet cases* and how these cases are retrieved and reused when responding to a new target query.

4.1   Snippet Surrogates as Cases

Let (C, u, q_T) denote a search for query q_T by user u in community C. Consider some result r_j selected in response to such a search. This result will have been accompanied by a snippet in the result-list that was presented to the searcher and we can reasonably assume that this snippet, $s(r_j, q_T)$, must have contained terms $t_1, ..., t_n$ that were relevant to the searcher's needs. Therefore these terms can be used to index future retrievals or r_j. In short, we create a search case whose solution is the result r_j and whose specification contains the queries that led to its selection (as in standard CWS) plus the terms that occurred in the snippets that led to these selections.

More generally then, a result r_j, which has been selected for a number of different queries, $q_1, ..., q_n$, will be associated by a number of different snippets, $s(r_j, q_1), ..., s(r_j, q_n)$. Then each search case will include these queries and the terms from these snippets, to capture the community's overall experiences as they relate to r_j. In this way each search case now includes the following components: (1) a solution, in the form of a selected search result r_j; (2) a set of queries, $q_1, ..., q_n$, that have led to r_j being selected; and (3) the union of the snippet terms. As in the traditional model of CWS, in each case, every query q_i is associated with h_i, the number of times that r_j has been selected for q_i. In addition, each snippet term t_i is associated with a frequency count f_i that counts the number of occurrences of this snippet term across the various snippets $(s(r_j, q_1), ..., s(r_j, q_n))$ that make up the selection history of r_j; see Equation 7. These hit counts and frequency counts will be used as part of the ranking procedure when it comes to retrieving cases and ranking result pages in response to a target query, as discussed in the following section.

$$c(r_j) = (r, (q_1, h_1), ..., (q_n, h_n), (t_1, f_1), ..., (t_m, f_m))$$ (7)

In this way, a given result page will be represented very differently in the search cases of different communities of users. For a start, each result will be indexed under different sets of queries, as in the standard model of CWS, to reflect the retrieval patterns of each community who has selected it. But in addition, according to our new snippet-based approach, each result will now also be indexed under the terms that occur frequently within the snippets shown for this result during retrieval. Because these snippets are query-sensitive they too will tend to reflect the preferences of particular communities. For example, a given community might use queries that probe a particular section within a given result page and so, for this community, this page will come to be indexed under the terms that occur within that particular section. In this case the document in question will be promoted in a limited set of circumstances. In contrast, if the same page is more broadly applicable to a different community, then it's snippets will tend to be extracted from a greater range of the page's contents and so its search case base will come to index this page under a broader set of snippet terms. In this case the page in question will be promoted for a much broader set of retrieval scenarios.

4.2   Ranking and Promotion

As in standard *CWS*, the final result-list R_T is made up of the set of meta results R_M and a complementary set of promotions R_C. As in CWS R_C is produced by retrieving relevant cases from the search case base, using the current target query q_T as a retrieval probe. This time, instead of comparing q_T to search cases only indexed by previous successful queries we can also compare q_T to the snippet terms of search cases as an alternative route to retrieval.

Thus, each search case c_j (representing the selection history of community for some result page r_j) is scored according to the *relevance* metric shown in Equation 8. As presented this metric is made up of two separate relevance components. First, similar to standard CWS, we compute the weighted relevance score for r_j with respect to a set of similar queries (queries which share terms with q_T), based on the proportion of times that r_j has been selected in response to each similar query (see equations 4 and 5); note that the notations used for

Sim and *Rel* in Equation 8 have been modified slightly because of the different case representation used in the current snippet-based approach.

$$SRel(c_j, q_T) = (1 + \sum_{i=1}^{n}(Rel(r_j, q_i) \cdot Sim(q_T, q_i))) * TFIDF(c_j, q_T) \qquad (8)$$

Secondly, r_j is scored, relative to q_T, based on the snippet terms encoded in c_j. Specifically, in the current implementation, we use a standard TFIDF (*term frequency, inverse document frequency*) term weighting metric commonly used by the information retrieval community. Very briefly, the TFIDF score of a term t_i with respect to the result page r_j, is calculated by dividing the frequency count of the term for c_j by the frequency count of the term across the case base as a whole. Thus, a higher score is given to those terms that occur frequently in a particular case but which are relatively rare among the snippet terms of other cases.

A more detailed account of TFIDF weighting is beyond the scope of this paper by the interetsed reader is directed to the work of [17]. For the purpose of the current work it is sufficient to understand that the TFIDF contributes an additional relevance component based on the relative frequency of snippet terms which overlap with the target query. Thus, result pages which are frequently selected for similar queries and whose snippets contain frequently recurring target query terms that are otherwise rare in the case base as a whole, will be ranked highly in R_C. Importantly, results that have never before been selected for q_T, or queries similar to q_T, may still come to be promoted if they have a high enough TF-IDF score, for example. As in the standard implementation of *CWS*, our promoted results R_C are returned ahead of the meta-search results R_M to produce the final results list R_T for the user.

5   Evaluation

So far we have described an approach to manipulate the results returned by a Web search engine so that they are better aligned to the learned preferences of the searcher's community. Our case-based approach is unique in the way it attempts to learn more about a community's implicit preferences by mining the terms that tend to occur within the snippets of selected results. In this section we seek to evaluate our research by comparing our snippet-based approach to the standard *CWS* and a leading search engine across four different communities of searchers.

5.1   Experimental Data

Ideally we would like to evaluate our techniques using real search data. Unfortunately the availability of comprehensive search logs, with query and selection information, is extremely limited, and so we have adopted an alternative strategy. As discussed previously, bookmarking services such as *Del.icio.us* can provide a reasonable source of search-like log-data if we interpret bookmark tags as queries for specific bookmarked documents.

In addition, it is possible to extract communities of 'searchers' from *Del.icio.us* by following sequences of related tags and extracting the bookmark data associated with these tag sequences. For example, consider the construction of an *iPod* community by starting with *'ipod'* as a seed tag. From this tag we can extract the top k ($k = 100$) bookmarked pages; for example, *'50 Fun Things To Do With Your iPod'* is the top page for the *ipod* tag at the time of writing. This page has been bookmarked by in excess of 1000 people and we can extract the tag-sets used to tag it, for a subset of u users; we extract the tag-sets for the first $p\%$ of all users who bookmarked the page. Thus, for example, one particular user has tagged the above page with *'ipod fun hacks'* and so this tag-set and page becomes a *query-result* pair in our *iPod* community. For each seed tag we can also get a list of related tags from *Del.icio.us* to expand the community and collect a new set of bookmarks. In this way we can, for example, expand the original seed to produce new tags such as *'ipod mp3'*, *'ipod apple'* or *'ipod hacks'*. We have used this community extraction technique to build four different communities of varying sizes from the *Del.icio.us* service as shown in Figure 4(a).

	Skiing	iPod	Travel	WebDev
Users	627	1287	1773	2206
Unique Queries	649	1485	1729	2545
Unique Pages	313	576	1025	1050
Selections	1042	2643	3218	3938
Queries/User	1.66	2.05	1.82	1.79
Queries/Page	2.07	2.58	1.69	2.42

Fig. 2. Community Statistics

5.2   Systems and Setup

Our evaluation uses Yahoo as the underlying search engine. Over this we implemented two case-bases systems: a standard version of *CWS* [20] and the new snippet-based approach. Thus we can compare three separate search services: (1) basic Yahoo; (2) *CWS* (with Yahoo); (3) *Snippet* (with Yahoo).

We randomly split the *query-result* pairs extracted from *Del.icio.us* in half to produce disjoint sets of training and test data and all results reported below are averaged over 10 such splits. The training data is used to build the necessary *CWS* and *Snippet* communities by 'replaying' the query-result pairs through *CWS* and *Snippet* as searches. Thus each community's case base was updated to reflect the selection of each result for its corresponding query and, in the case of *Snippet* each result was also represented by its corresponding snippet terms, generated using the Lucene snippet generator[3].

In this evaluation we are primarily concerned with overall *retrieval effectiveness*: the ability of a search engine to retrieve a target result for a given query.

---

[3] http://lucene.apache.org/

Using the 50% of search data that we held back as test data, for each query-result test pair we check to see if the target result (bookmarked page) was retrieved for the target query (bookmark tags) within the top 10 results. In this way retrieval effectiveness is expressed as the percentage of test searches for which the appropriate page was retrieved among the top 10 results. We will also look at the position of the test page within the result list.

5.3   Overall Retrieval Effectiveness

The overall retrieval effectiveness results are presented in Figure 3 (a). Each line refers to one of the evaluation systems and each data-point refers to the overall retrieval effectiveness for that system for a given configuration of promoted and baseline results. For example, the configuration $3 + 7$ refers to a maximum of 3 promoted results and 7 Yahoo results. Obviously the overall effectiveness of Yahoo remains unaffected (at 7.72%) by the promoted results, but we can see how *CWS* and *Snippet* systems benefit greatly from the availability of promotions. The *CWS* system can retrieve the target page within its top 3 results more than 3 times as often as Yahoo, and an even more significant benefit is seen for the *Snippet* system with retrieval effectiveness of over 4.5 times that of Yahoo. These benefits are largely due to the top 3 promotions and further promotions do not result in additional improvements in retrieval accuracy; this plateau effect is probably a result of our evaluation methodology as we are looking for the occurrence of a specific result in each search session and do not choose to assess the potential relevance of other promotions.

5.4   A Community-Based Analysis

In this section we take a more detailed look at retrieval performance on a community by community basis. Figure 3 (b) shows the average number of promotions per test query for *CWS* and *Snippet* for each of the test communities when a maximum of 10 promotions are allowed. As expected the *Snippet* system is capable of producing more promotions (8.5 on average) than the *CWS* system (7.7). But how relevant are these promotions to each community? We see from the results above that overall the *Snippet* promotions are contributing more positively

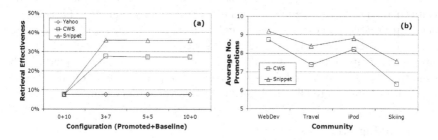

Fig. 3. The (a) overall retrieval effectiveness and the (b) number of promotions per community

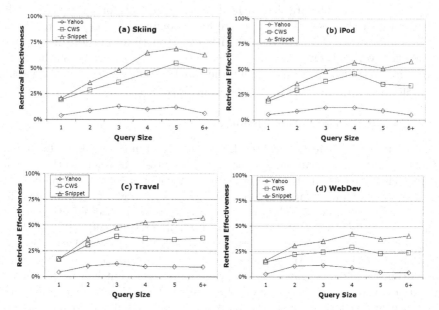

Fig. 4. Community Retrieval Effectiveness

to retrieval effectiveness than the *CWS* promotions but is this effect consistent across all communities? We know that the target result is likely to be one of the top 3 promotions, and for this reason, we will limit our next experiment to a 3+7 configurations (3 promotions plus 7 Yahoo results) and measure retrieval effectiveness on a community by community basis.

Figures 4 (a)-(d) compare retrieval effectiveness for *Snippet*, *CWS*, and Yahoo for test queries of different sizes, to investigate how retrieval effectiveness varies for the two community-based techniques with changes in query length; remember in Figure 1 we saw how traditional search engines were seen to suffer when faced with longer queries. This remains evident for the Yahoo system, as expected, but we see the retrieval effectiveness for *Snippet* improving with increasing query length. Both *Snippet* and *CWS* significantly out-perform Yahoo across all query categories, and *Snippet* in particular enjoys dramatic improvements in retrieval effectiveness, especially for the longer queries. These longer queries are the very ones that traditional Web search engines appear to struggle with — the vocabulary gap making its presence felt — and yet we find our new snippet-based approach is especially well able to cope with such queries. The terms that have been mined from the selected snippets as part of the community's snippet index are effectively bridging this vocabulary gap.

5.5 Ranking Analysis

Finally, it is worth considering the position of target results within successful sessions and in this experiment we look at the ranking of the target result within the top 10 promotions for *Snippet* and *CWS*, and Yahoo's top 10 results. Figures 5(a) and 5(b) present two different variations on average rank for each of the communities and all 3 search engines. Figure 5(a) shows the mean rank of the target result in those sessions where the target is actually retrieved and indicates that all 3 search engines perform similarly with no single approach winning outright. However, this version of average rank is clearly flawed since the 3 test systems locate the target pages in different search sessions and so this average rank is computed over different test sessions for each system; for example, the *Yahoo* rank is computed over only 8% of the sessions and the *Snippet* rank is computed over 43% of sessions. Hence, we report a *adjusted rank* in which every test session is considered, with those that do not contain the target page among their top-10 results penalized with a rank of 11; this is a conservative penalty since in all likelihood the real rank of the target will be much greater than 11. With this conservative penalty-based ranking function we see in Figure 5(b) that both community-based engines (*Snippet* and *CWS*) significantly outperform *Yahoo*. For example, in the *iPod* community *Snippet* locates the target result at an average adjusted rank of 7.6, compared to 8.41 for *CWS* and 10.36 for *Yahoo*. To put this another way, on average, over the 4 test communities, we find that the adjusted rank of *Yahoo* is 31% greater than *Snippet* and 20% greater than *CWS*.

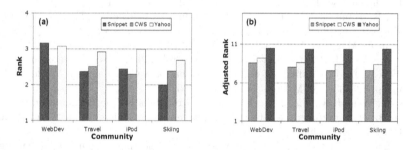

Fig. 5. (a) Average rank for successful sessions per community; (b) Adjusted rank per community

6   Conclusions

The main contribution of this work is a new experience-centric approach to the community-based personalization of Web search results that is based by the selection behaviour of a community of like-minded searchers. This work extends previous work in the use of case-based reasoning techniques for Web search [1] by minining the snippets of selected results to provide a much richer case representation that facilitates more flexible retrieval and result promotion. We have described a comprehensive multi-community evaluation of our unique snippet-based technique compared to a benchmark CWS case-based approach and a leading Web search engine. The results demonstrate the potential benefits of the two case-based approaches by highlighting how both are more successful than the standard Web search engine when it comes to locating target pages across a large set of realistic user data; these targets are located more frequently and positioned earlier in the result lists. In addition, we have shown that our novel snippet-based approach significantly outperforms the CWS benchmark across all 4 communities. Moreover, retrieval effectiveness tends to increase with query length, a desirable outcome that was not found for traditional term-based search engines, and an outcome which suggests our snippet-based cases provide a more effective representation with which to begin bridging the vocabulary gap that hampers Web search.

References

1. Balfe, E., Smyth, B.: Case-based collaborative web search. In: Funk, P., González Calero, P.A. (eds.) ECCBR 2004. LNCS (LNAI), vol. 3155, pp. 489–503. Springer, Heidelberg (2004)
2. Bollmann-Sdorra, P., Raghavan, V.V.: On the Delusiveness of Adopting a Common Space for Modeling IR Objects: Are Queries Documents? Journal of the American Society for Information Science and Technology 44(10), 579–587 (1993)
3. Budzik, J., Hammond, K.: User Interactions with Everyday Applications as Context for Just-In-Time Information Access. In: Proceedings International Conference on Intelligent User Interfaces, pp. 44–51. ACM Press, New York (2000)
4. Burke, R., Hammond, K., Kulyukin, V., Tomuro, S., Schoenberg, S.: Question Answering from Frequently-Asked Question Files: Experiences with the FAQ Finder System. AI Magazine 18(2), 57–66 (1997)
5. Cui, H., Wen, J.-R., Nie, J.-Y., Ma, W.-Y.: Probabilistic query expansion using query logs. In: Proceedings of the 11th International Conference on World Wide Web, pp. 325–332. ACM Press, New York (2002)
6. Cui, H., Wen, J.-R., Nie, J.-Y., Ma, W.-Y.: Probabilistic Query Expansion Using Query Logs. In: Proceedings of the 11th International Conference on World Wide Web, pp. 325–332 (2002)
7. Dreilinger, D., Howe, A.E.: Experiences with selecting search engines using metasearch. ACM Transactions on Information Systems 15(3), 195–222 (1997)
8. Glover, E., Lawrence, S., Gordon, M.D., Birmingham, W.P., Giles, C.L.: Web Search - Your Way. Communications of the ACM 44(12), 97–102 (2001)
9. Godoy, D., Amandi, A.: PersonalSearcher: An Intelligent Agent for Searching Web Pages. In: Monard, M.C., Sichman, J.S. (eds.) SBIA 2000 and IBERAMIA 2000. LNCS (LNAI), vol. 1952, pp. 62–72. Springer, Heidelberg (2000)
10. Kanawati, R., Jaczynski, M., Trousse, B., J-M, A.: Applying the Broadway Recommendation Computation Approach for Implementing a Query Refinement Service in the CBKB Meta-search Engine. In: Conférence Française sur le Raisonnement á Partir de Cas (RáPC'99) (1999)
11. Kemp, C., Ramamohanarao, K.: Long-term learning for web search engines. In: Elomaa, T., Mannila, H., Toivonen, H. (eds.) PKDD 2002. LNCS (LNAI), vol. 2431, Springer, Heidelberg (2002)
12. Lawrence, S., Giles, C.L.: Context and Page Analysis for Improved Web Search. IEEE Internet Computing, 38–46 (July-August 1998)
13. Lenz, M., Ashley, K.: AAAI Workshop on Textual Case-Based Reasoning, AAAI Technical Report WS-98-12 (1999)

14. Lieberman, H.: Letizia: An agent that assists web browsing. In: Mellish, C. (ed.) Proceedings of the International Joint Conference on Artificial Intelligence, IJ-CAI'95, pp. 924–929. Morgan Kaufman Publishers, Montreal, Canada (1995)
15. Luhn, H.P.: The automatic creation of literature abstracts. IBM Journal of Research and Development 2, 159–165 (1958)
16. Rhodes, B.J., Starner, T.: Remembrance Agent: A Continuously Running Automated Information Retrieval System. In: Proceedings of the 1st International Conference on the Practical Applications of Intelligent Agents and Multi-Agent Technologies, pp. 487–495 (1996)
17. Rijsbergen, C.J.V.: Information Retrieval, 2nd edn. Dept. of Computer Science, University of Glasgow (1979)
18. Rissland, E.L., Daniels, J.J.: A hybrid CBR-IR Approach to Legal Information Retrieval. In: Proceedings of the 5th international conference on Artificial intelligence and law, pp. 52–61. ACM Press, New York (1995)
19. Sakai, T., Sparck-Jones, K.: Generic summaries for indexing in information retrieval. In: SIGIR '01: Proceedings of the 24th annual international ACM SIGIR conference on Research and development in information retrieval, pp. 190–198. ACM Press, New York, USA (2001)
20. Smyth, B., Balfe, E., Boydell, O., Bradley, K., Briggs, P., Coyle, M., Freyne, J.: A Live-user Evaluation of Collaborative Web Search. In: Proceedings of the 19th International Joint Conference on Artificial Intelligence (IJCAI '05), pp. 1419–1424. Morgan Kaufmann, Ediburgh, Scotland (2005)
21. Smyth, B., Balfe, E., Freyne, J., Briggs, P., Coyle, M., Boydell, O.: Exploiting query repetition and regularity in an adaptive community-based web search engine. User Modeling and User-Adapted Interaction 14(5), 383–423 (2004)

An Analysis of Case-Based Value Function Approximation by Approximating State Transition Graphs

Thomas Gabel and Martin Riedmiller

Neuroinformatics Group
Department of Mathematics and Computer Science
Institute of Cognitive Science
University of Osnabrück, 49069 Osnabrück, Germany
{thomas.gabel,martin.riedmiller}@uni-osnabrueck.de

Abstract. We identify two fundamental points of utilizing CBR for an adaptive agent that tries to learn on the basis of trial and error without a model of its environment. The first link concerns the utmost efficient exploitation of experience the agent has collected by interacting within its environment, while the second relates to the acquisition and representation of a suitable behavior policy. Combining both connections, we develop a state-action value function approximation mechanism that relies on case-based, approximate transition graphs and forms the basis on which the agent improves its behavior. We evaluate our approach empirically in the context of dynamic control tasks.

1 Introduction

A key characteristic that has significantly contributed to the attractiveness of case-based reasoning (CBR) is that it allows for a *controlled* degree of inexactness during problem solving and, hence, can provide justifiable, though approximate solutions in situations where other approaches would fail. In this work, we consider learning agents that must solve some task in an unknown environment and that must adapt their behavior appropriately, solely on the basis of feedback concerning the suitability of actions taken that is obtained from the environment. Research in reinforcement learning (RL) has brought about a variety of learning algorithms for such problems. Most of them rely on learning a function that, given a situation, numerically expresses how appropriate each action is and that, logically, allows for choosing the right actions.

Aiming at the acquisition of such a value function, we will utilize the approximate nature of CBR methods in two stages. First, we will employ CBR in the obvious manner to represent the targeted value function by a finite number of instances distributed over a continuous state space. This utilization of case-based techniques represents a further development of our approach to state value function approximation using CBR [6] towards learning tasks where no model of the environment is available. Second, we utilize the CBR paradigm already

R.O. Weber and M.M. Richter (Eds.): ICCBR 2007, LNAI 4626, pp. 344–358, 2007.
© Springer-Verlag Berlin Heidelberg 2007

prior to the application of an RL algorithm that aims at the determination of a value function. To distinguish and properly evaluate the costs and benefits of a certain action in some situation, we must compare its effects to the effects other actions might yield. Here, CBR comes into play: If no information for trading off different actions is available, then it can be approximated in a case-based manner by retrieving the effects of identical or similar actions in similar situations. Based on that principle, we develop an approach that constructs an *approximate transition graph* (ATG) which serves as an ideal input to an RL algorithm.

In Section 2, we briefly review some basic concepts of RL and introduce necessary notation, focusing in particular on model-free batch-mode RL techniques that are relevant in the scope of this paper. Section 3 presents our learning framework, including the two mentioned stages of using CBR, and Section 4 continues with a discussion of important modelling variants and extensions. The results of a first empirical evaluation of our approach are presented in Section 5.

2   Model-Free Batch-Mode Reinforcement Learning

The basic idea of reinforcement learning [15] is to have an adaptive agent that interacts with its initially unknown environment, observes outcomes of its actions, and modifies its behavior in a suitable, purposive manner. In each time step, the learner observes the environmental state $s \in S$ and decides on an action a from the set of viable actions A. By executing a, some immediate costs $c(s, a)$ may arise and, moreover, the agent is transferred to a successor state $s' \in S$. The goal of the agent, however, is not to always decide in favor of the "cheapest" actions, but to minimize its long-term expected costs.

The behavior of the agent is determined by its decision policy $\pi : S \to A$ that maps each state $s \in S$ to an action $a \in A$ to be performed in that state. Accordingly, the overall goal of a reinforcement learning algorithm is to acquire a good policy π dynamically, only on the basis of the costs the agent perceives during interacting within the environment.

2.1   Model-Free Reinforcement Learning Methods

The majority of RL methods[1] is centered around learning value functions which bear information about the prospective value of states or state-action pairs, respectively, and which can be used to induce the best action in a given state. Usually, this is done by formalizing the learning problem as a Markov decision process $M = [S, A, c, p]$ [12], where S is the set of environmental states, A the set of actions, $c : S \times A \to \mathbb{R}$ is the function of immediate costs $c(s, a)$ arising when taking action a in state s, and $p : S \times A \times S \to [0, 1]$ is a state transition probability distribution where $p(s, a, s')$ tells how likely it is to arrive at state s' when executing a in s. Throughout this paper, we use S, A, $c(\cdot)$, and $p(\cdot)$

---

[1] There are exceptions such as direct policy learning methods that are not considered in the scope of this paper.

to refer to the components of the Markov decision process corresponding to the considered environment. In particular, we assume $S \subset \mathbb{R}^n$ and A to be finite.

A state value function $V^\pi : S \to \mathbb{R}$ estimates the future costs that are to be expected when starting in s and taking actions determined by policy π:

$$V^\pi(s) = E\left[\sum_{t=0}^{\infty} \gamma^t c(s_t, \pi(s_t)) | s_0 = s\right] \quad (1)$$

where $\gamma \in [0, 1]$ is a discount factor that models the reduced trust in future costs. Assuming an optimal value function $V^\star$ that correctly reflects the cost and state transition properties of the environment is available, the agent may infer an optimal behavior policy by exploiting $V^\star$ greedily according to

$$\pi^\star(s) := \arg\min_{a \in A}\left(c(s, a) + \gamma \sum_{s' \in S} p(s, a, s') V^\star(s')\right) \quad (2)$$

Unfortunately, Eqn. 2 can only be applied if we are in possession of a state transition model p of the environment. For most learning tasks with relevance to real-world problems, however, there is no such model available, which is why, in this paper, we are focusing on *model-free* scenarios. Under these circumstances, we consider *state-action* value functions and Eqn. 1 can be written as

$$Q^\pi(s, a) = E\left[\sum_{t=0}^{\infty} \gamma^t c(s_t, a_t) | s_0 = s, a_t = a \text{ if } t = 0 \text{ and } a_t = \pi(s_t) \text{ else}\right]. \quad (3)$$

The crucial question now is, how to obtain an optimal state-action value function $Q^\star$. Q learning [16] is one of the most prominent algorithms used to acquire the optimal state-action value function for model-free learning problems. Q learning directly updates estimates for the values of state-action pairs according to

$$Q(s, a) := (1 - \alpha)Q(s, a) + \alpha(c(s, a) + \gamma \min_{b \in A} Q(s', b)) \quad (4)$$

where the successor state s' and the immediate costs $c(s, a)$ are generated by simulation or by interaction with a real process. For the case of finite state and action spaces where the Q function can be represented using a look-up table, there are convergence guarantees that say Q learning converges to the optimal value function $Q^\star$ under mild assumptions. Then again, it is easy to infer the best action for each state and hence, the optimal policy $\pi^\star$ by greedy exploitation of $Q^\star$ according to

$$\pi^\star(s) := \arg\min_{a \in A} Q^\star(s, a). \quad (5)$$

2.2   Offline Q Learning with Value Function Approximation

Recent research in RL has seen a variety of methods that extend the basic ideas of Q learning. Aiming at the applicability to situations where large and/or infinite state spaces must be handled, two necessities should be considered. The approach to learning a (near-)optimal behavior policy we are pursuing in this paper adheres to both of these requirements, as we will show subsequently.

Value Function Approximation. To cover infinite state spaces, the value function must be represented using a function approximation mechanism. This means, we replace the optimal state-action value function $Q^\star(s, a)$ by an appropriate approximation $\tilde{Q}(s, a)$. For this, we will revert to case-based methods, building up an approximate state transition graph utilizing the CBR paradigm.

Exploitation of Experience. Standard Q learning is an online learning method where experience is used only once to update the value function. By contrast, there has recently been much interest in offline (batch-mode) variants of Q learning, and a number of algorithms were proposed that are subsumed under the term *fitted Q iteration* (e.g. NFQ [13] or FQI with decision trees [5]). Here, from a finite set of transition tuples $\mathbb{T} = \{(s_i, a_i, c_i, s'_i) | i = 1, \ldots, m\}$ that are made up of states, actions, immediate costs, and successor states, an approximation of the optimal policy is computed.

Aiming at fast and efficient learning, we will, on the one hand, store all transition tuples in an experience set as well, exploit it fully to construct an approximate state transition graph for the respective environment, and, on the other hand, employ k-nearest neighbor techniques to gain an approximated state-action value function for a continuous state space from which to infer a near-optimal policy.

3 Approximate Transition Graphs

Initially, the learning agent is clueless about state transitions that may occur when taking specific actions, as well as about the cost structure of the environment. During ongoing learning, however, it gains more experience and competence which it must utilize as smartly as possible in order to develop a good behavior policy. In this section, we present our learning approach by which the agent first creates an approximate transition graph (ATG) from its experience using case-based techniques and, second, performs RL on the ATG in order to finally induce a case-based policy that features near-optimal performance.

3.1 Basic Ideas of Approximate Transition Graphs

When the agent explores its environment by repeatedly acting within that environment, it steadily collects new pieces of experience that can be described as four-tuples (s, a, c, s') which the agent stores in its experience set $\mathbb{T} \subset S \times A \times \mathbb{R} \times S$. This set can also be interpreted as a partial transition graph.

Definition 1 (Partial Transition Graph)
Let $\mathbb{T} = \{(s_i, a_i, c_i, s'_i) | i = 1, \ldots, m\}$ be the transition set containing the experience the learning agent has gathered while interacting within its environment. Then, $\mathbb{T}$ determines a directed partial transition graph $\mathcal{P} = (V, E)$ whose set of nodes V is the union of all states s and s' that are components of elements from $\mathbb{T}$. Further, each transition $t \in \mathbb{T}$ is represented by an edge $(s, a, c, s') \in E$ pointing from s to s' that is annotated with the value of action a and costs c.

As we assume the state space to be continuous, the probability that, during its lifetime, the agent enters one particular state $s_x \in S$ more than once is zero. So, in general there is only one single transition tuple $t_x = (s_x, a_x, c_x, s'_x) \in \mathbb{T}$ that relates to state s_x, implying that $\mathbb{T}$ contains no information about what happens when taking an action $a \in A \setminus \{a_x\}$ in state s_x. This precludes the application of a Q learning style learning algorithm: In order to perform an update on the value function according to the Q update rule (Eqn. 4), it is necessary to calculate the minimum over all actions, i.e. $\arg\min_{b \in A} Q(s'_x, b)$ must be evaluated. This, of course, is impossible if no information about $Q(s'_x, b)$ for most $b \in A$ is available.

Thus, our goal is to create an extension of a partial transition graph – which we will call approximate transition graph – that contains sufficient information about actions and their effects to allow for the application of Q learning. The key to deriving such an ATG is CBR: In Figure 1, we outline the building blocks involved in the construction of a value function approximation mechanism based on transition graphs that are approximated using case-based reasoning.

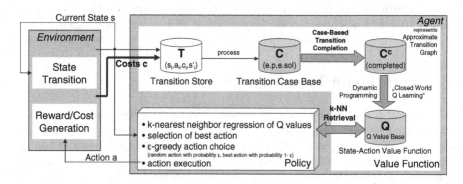

Fig. 1. Building Blocks of the Case-Based Approach to State-Action Value Function Approximation via Approximating State Transition Graphs: Descriptions for the individual components involved are given in Sections 3.2-3.4

3.2   Case-Based Transition Completion

In a first processing step, we employ the agent's stored transitions to build up a transition case base $\mathbb{C}$.

Definition 2 (Transition Case Base)
Given an experience set $\mathbb{T} = \{(s_i, a_i, c_i, s'_i)|i = 1, \ldots, m\}$, the transition case base is defined as a collection of cases[2] $\mathbb{C} = \{e = (e.p, e.sol)\}$ where each case consists of a problem part $e.p \in S$ and a solution $e.sol$ that is a set of up to $|A|$ elements. Each element of the solution $e.sol$ is itself a three-tuple (a_i, c_i, s'_i) for some $i \in \{1, \ldots, m\}$ with $e.p = s_i$. Further,

---

[2] Differing from common usage, we denote a single case by e instead of c throughout this work to avoid confusion with costs.

- *for all $(s_t, a_t, c_t, s'_t) \in \mathbb{T}$ with $s_t = s$ there is only one case $e \in \mathbb{C}$ with $e.p = s$*
- *for all $e \in \mathbb{C}$ with $e.p = s$ there is at least one $t \in \mathbb{T}$ with $s_t = s$.*

So, we refer to the starting state s of a transition as the case's problem part and to triples of second to fourth component (action, costs, and successor state) as a case's solution part. Note that transitions are clustered with respect to identical starting states and hence are assigned to the same case[3]. For ease of notation, we will also allow a specific element of a case's solution to be accessed with the index operator $[\cdot]$, such that $e.sol[a_x]$ refers to $(a, c, s') \in e.sol$ with $a_x = a$.

As emphasized, it is not possible to apply a Q learning style algorithm if no estimations about the values of *all* actions that may be taken in one state are available, so that the *argmin* operator (Eqn. 4) can be evaluated. One approach to solving that problem is represented by fitted Q iteration algorithms which employ estimates of $Q(s, a)$ for all states and actions provided by some function approximator already at any intermediate point of learning. Our approach to solving that problem, however, relies on the CBR paradigm. In particular, we assume that in similar situations similar actions yield a similar effect. More concretely, we assume that for a given pair of state and action (s, a), a nearby state – starting from which that action has actually been executed – may provide a good indicator regarding what immediate costs arise and regarding which successor state is entered upon executing a in s. Naturally, we formalize the vague phrase of a nearby state by defining a similarity measure $sim_S : S \times S \to [0, 1]$ over the state space and by employing the principle of nearest neighbors.

With that assumption, we define case completion rules that are used to approximate the effects of yet unexplored actions via the nearest neighbor principle.

Definition 3 (Case-Based Transition Completion)
Let $\mathbb{C}$ be a transition case base and $sim_S : S \times S \to [0, 1]$ be a similarity measure over the state space S. Further, denote by $\mathbb{C}_{a_x} = \{(e.p, e.sol) \in \mathbb{C} | \exists (a_i, c_i, s'_i) \in e.sol : a_i = a_x\}$ the subset of the case base $\mathbb{C}$ containing solution information about taking action a_x. Then, the case-based transition completion yields a new case base $\mathbb{C}^c$ where each $e \in \mathbb{C}^c$ results from applying the completion rule:

$$\text{For all } a \in A: \text{ If } \nexists(a_i, c_i, s'_i) \in e.sol \text{ with } a_i = a,$$
$$\text{then } e.sol := e.sol \cup NN^a(e).sol$$

where $NN^a(e)$ is defined as the nearest neighbor of case e from the sub case base $\mathbb{C}_a$, i.e. $NN^a(e) = \arg\max_{f \in \mathbb{C}_a} sim(e.p, f.p)$.

The key point regarding this completion method is that we have attached to each case a piece of information about the effects of taking any available action. Having started this section with the definition of a partial transition graph, we have now arrived at an approximate transition graph with completed actions that is represented by the completed transition case base $\mathbb{C}^c$ from Definition 3.

---

[3] As argued, the probability of entering the same state twice in a continuous environment approaches zero. However, some state may be re-entered if the system allows putting the agent into specific (starting) states.

Definition 4 (Approximate Transition Graph)
Let $\mathcal{P} = (V_\mathcal{P}, E_\mathcal{P})$ be a partial transition graph for an experience set $\mathbb{T}$ and $\mathbb{C}^c$ be the corresponding completed transition case base. An approximate transition graph $\mathcal{A} = (V_\mathcal{A}, E_\mathcal{A})$ corresponding to $\mathbb{C}^c$ is a proper extension of $\mathcal{P}$ where $V_\mathcal{P} \subseteq V_\mathcal{A}$. Further, each component $(a_j, c_j, s'_j) \in e.sol$ of the solution of each case $e \in \mathbb{C}^c$ is represented by an edge $(e.p, a_j, c_j, s'_j) \in E_\mathcal{A}$ that points from e.p to s'_j and that is annotated with the value of action a_j and costs c_j.

Figure 2 provides a simple example within a two-dimensional state space, two available actions (a_1 and a_2), the Euclidean distance as similarity measure, and an arbitrary set of transitions. By means of case-based transition completion, we have constructed an approximate transition graph (right part of the figure) from a partial transition graph (left), determined by the contents of the experience set $\mathbb{T}$. In the PTG, for example, there is no information about the effects of taking action a_2 in state s_5. Since the nearest neighbor of s_5 is s_3 and taking a_2 in s_3 yields a transition to s_4 with costs of zero, the approximate transition graph assumes that taking a_2 in s_5 leads the system to s_4 under zero costs, too.

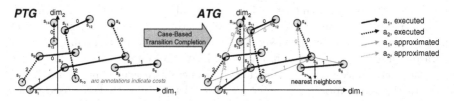

Fig. 2. From a Partial to a Completed, Approximate Transition Graph

3.3   Learning from a Completed Case Base

The output of the case-based transition completion is a case base $\mathbb{C}^c$ that is enriched by virtual state transitions and that represents an approximate state transition graph. Since $\mathbb{C}^c$ contains, in each of its cases $e \in \mathbb{C}^c$, solutions (i.e. tuples consisting of action, immediate costs, and successor state) referring to each available action $a \in A$, we are now in the position to calculate state-action values. The actual learning procedure we employ is termed closed world Q learning (CWQL), which is in tribute to the fact that this routine abstracts from the real system dynamics and considers the finite information in the completed case base only. CWQL operates like standard Q learning (Eqn. 4) on the finite set of points in state action space provided by $\mathbb{C}^c$ and is thus able to compute a value function that could be stored in a look-up table.

In our approach, the calculated state-action values are immediately attached to the case solution parts stored in $\mathbb{C}^c$, thus giving rise to a new, extended version of that case base which we subsequently call Q value base $\mathbb{Q}$ and whose individual state-action values for some state s and some action a can be accessed by: $\mathbb{Q}(s, a) = e.sol[a].Q$ where $e \in \mathbb{Q}$ with $e.p = s \in S$ and $e.sol[a] = (a, c, s', Q) \in e.sol$. So, starting with $e.sol[a].Q = 0$ for all $e \in \mathbb{Q}$ and all $a \in A$, all state-action pairs are repeatedly updated according to the Q update rule, giving rise to

repeat
   for all $e \in \mathbb{Q}$ **and all** $a \in A$
      $f \leftarrow g \in \mathbb{Q}$ with $f.p = e.sol[a].s'$

$$e.sol[a].Q \xleftarrow{\alpha} e.sol[a].c + \gamma \min_{b \in A} f.sol[b].Q \qquad (6)$$

   until *convergence*

We point to an important precondition that the realization of CWQL requires to work: For each state $e.p \in S$ and for each element (a_i, c_i, s_i') of the corresponding solution $e.sol$, there must either exist at least one case $f \in \mathbb{C}^c$ with $f.p = s_i'$ or s_i' must be a goal state of the system. This condition is fulfilled for all $e.sol[a_i] = (a_i, c_i, s_i')$ that were added to e in the scope of applying case completion rules (case-based transition completion, Section 3.2). For elements of case solutions that stem from real interaction with the environment (so, they are already included in $\mathbb{T}$ and $\mathbb{C}$, respectively), the requirement is fulfilled when the training data has been gathered along trajectories, which we assume for the remainder of this paper. Otherwise, prior to performing CWQL some sub case base of $\mathbb{C}^c$ fulfilling the requirement must be extracted.

3.4   Deriving a Decision-Making Policy

Being provided with the current state s of the system, the decision-making policy's task is to select one of the viable actions for execution. We determine the best (greedy) action with k-nearest neighbor regression, given the Q value base $\mathbb{Q}$, where the value of taking action a in state s is determined by

$$\tilde{Q}_k(s, a) = \frac{\sum_{e \in NN_k(s)} sim_S(e.p, s) \cdot \mathbb{Q}(s, a)}{\sum_{e \in NN_k(s)} sim_S(e.p, s)} \qquad (7)$$

where NN_k is the set of k nearest neighbors of s in case base $\mathbb{Q}$.

Given Eqn. 7 in combination with a suitable similarity measure sim_S defined over the state space S, the best action in state s can be derived according to $\pi(s) = \arg\min_{b \in A} \tilde{Q}_k(s, b)$. During learning, the agent pursues an ε-greedy policy to encourage exploration of the environment. With probability ε, a random action is chosen, whereas with probability $1 - \varepsilon$, the greedy action $\pi(s)$ is selected. During the evaluation of the learning results a purely greedy policy is applied.

The main computational burden of our algorithm lies in the case-based transition completion. Since for all cases and for all untried actions the nearest neighbors from $\mathbb{C}$ must be determined, the complexity is $O(|A||\mathbb{C}|^2)$ when linear retrieval is performed. Note that our actual implementation of the case-based ATG learning scheme realizes a policy iteration style learning algorithm, i.e. after having experienced one episode (terminated by reaching a goal state or by a time-out), the agent adds all transitions to $\mathbb{T}$ and initiates the processes of transition case base creation, case-based transition completion, and CWQL to obtain a new approximation $\tilde{Q}$ of the optimal value value function $Q^\star$. Then, the next episode is sampled by ε-greedily exploiting this new, improved Q function.

4   Modelling Variants

In Section 3, we have presented a method to approximate value functions for RL problems with CBR techniques based on the core idea of creating approximate, yet completed state transition graphs. The basic approach leaves much space for extensions and improvements, two of which shall be discussed in more detail below. Moreover, we clarify the connections to relevant related work.

4.1   Efficient Exploration

Choosing actions ε-greedily during learning means that the agent picks an arbitrary action a_{expl} with probability ε. Instead of doing that, the selection of a_{expl} may also be guided by the experience the agent has made so far. Here, we suggest the use of an efficient exploration strategy that is conducive for the construction of an approximate transition graph. This implies that we must foster a good performance of the case-based transition completion method from which an ATG (represented by case base $\mathbb{C}^c$) results.

We grant the policy access to the transition case base $\mathbb{C}$ to retrieve the nearest neighbor $NN(s)$ of the current state s. Then, the explorative action is determined as follows: Let $E = \{a \in A | \exists (a, c, s') \in NN(s).sol\}$ be the set of actions already explored in the nearest neighbor state of s. If $E = A$, then a purely random action is chosen, otherwise, however, the agent picks a_{expl} randomly from $A \setminus E$. This way, generally those actions are favored for which very little information about their effects is so far available. As a consequence, obtaining experience about taking differing actions in the neighborhood of s is fostered.

4.2   Transformational Analogy

The method of case-based transition completion (see Section 3.2) as the central step in creating an ATG performs null adaptation. As illustrated in Figure 3, the transition case base is searched for a similar case e where some action has in fact been executed, and the solution from that case is taken to solve, i.e. to complete the case considered, without any modifications (Definition 3).

Transformational analogy (TA) means that the solution of the similar case is transformed into a new solution for the current problem [4]. This basic idea can easily be integrated into case-based transition completion: Instead of adopting a solution $(a, c, s') \in NN(s).sol$ of a nearest neighbor case $NN(s)$, that solution – in particular, the solution's successor state s' – is adapted with respect to the shift[4] between s and $NN(s)$. Thus, we define:

---

[4] Recall that $S \subset \mathbb{R}^n$, which is why the vectorial shift $s_1 - s_2 \in \mathbb{R}^n$ between two states can easily be calculated.

Definition 5 (Case-Based Transition Completion Using Transformational Analogy). *Let all preconditions be as in Definition 3. Then, case-based transition completion using transformational analogy yields a new case base $\mathbb{C}^c$ where each $e \in \mathbb{C}^c$ results from applying the completion rule:*

$$\text{For all } a \in A: \text{ If } \nexists (a_i, c_i, s_i') \in e.sol \text{ with } a_i = a,$$
$$\text{then } e.sol := e.sol \cup \{\ T(e.p,\ NN^a(e).p,\ (a_j, c_j, s_j'))\ |$$
$$(a_j, c_j, s_j') \in NN^a(e).sol\}$$

where $NN^a(e)$ denotes the nearest neighbor of case e from sub-case base C_a.

The transformation operator $T : S \times S \times (A \times \mathbb{R} \times S) \to (A \times \mathbb{R} \times S)$ is defined as $T(s, s_{nn}, (a_{nn}, c_{nn}, s_{nn}')) = (a_{nn}, c_{nn}, s_t')$ with $s_t' = s_{nn}' + s_{nn} - s$.

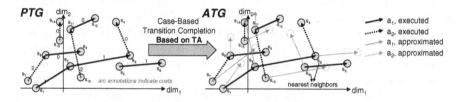

Fig. 3. Transformational Analogy During Case-Based Transition Completion

Using case-based transition completion with TA bears a disadvantage that can also be observed in Figure 3. The virtual successor states s' added to the cases' solution parts during completion do, in general, not correspond to goal states or to states for which there is an $e \in \mathbb{C}$ with $e.p = s'$. Accordingly, the precondition required for the execution of CWQL (see Section 3.3) is violated. To solve that problem, we now must apply a real fitted Q iteration algorithm where the "fitted" part, i.e. providing state-action values for states s' not covered by $\{e.p | e \in \mathbb{Q}\}$, is done by case-based estimation. We can achieve this, if we replace Equation 6 by

$$e.sol[a].Q \xleftarrow{\alpha} e.sol[a].c + \gamma \min_{b \in A} \tilde{Q}_k(e.p, b) \tag{8}$$

where $\tilde{Q}_k$ is defined according to Equation 7 and an intermediate version[5] of the Q value case base $\mathbb{Q}^t$ is forming the basis of the evaluation of $\tilde{Q}_k$. This change clearly increases the computational complexity of the algorithm since the evaluation of $\tilde{Q}_k$ requires the determination of the nearest neighbors of all $e.p$. We emphasize that this case-based Q iteration (CBQI) algorithm as determined by Equation 8 is also guaranteed to converge since the value function approximation it provides can be characterized as a contraction mapping [7].

---

[5] Intermediate refers to the fact that the learning process has not converged yet, i.e. that $\mathbb{Q}^t$ at iteration t of looping over all states and actions does not contain final state-action values.

4.3   Related Work

The idea of using instances of stored experience to represent value functions in the context of reinforcement learning is not new. For example, in [1] different versions of the k-NN algorithm are compared with the goal of teaching a robot to catch a ball. Several other control tasks and the use of different case-based methods with the focus on locally weighted regression are reviewed in [2]. In [6], we have analyzed the usability of case-based state value function approximation under the assumption that a transition model p is available and have evaluated our approach in the context of robotic soccer. By contrast, in this paper we exclusively focus on the model-free case and apply our algorithms to control and regulatory tasks. Highly related to ours is the work of Peng [10], where a memory-based dynamic programming (MBDP) approach is presented, that tries to learn a Q function [16] represented by finitely many experiences in memory, and uses k-nearest neighbor prediction to determine state-action values, as we do. Our work differs from MBDP insofar as we aim at the construction of a completed, approximate transition graph which is used as the starting point to acquire a state-action value function. Moreover, we also cover the issues of efficient exploration. A comprehensive article addressing the comparison of several instance- or memory-based methods to (value) function approximation is the one by Santamaria et al. [14].

The aspect of an agent learning from scratch has also been considered from a more CBR-centered perspective. For example, Macedo and Cardoso [9] focus in depth on the issue of efficient CBR-based exploration. While the agent uses a case base of entities encountered in the environment to generate expectations about missing information, our approach to efficient exploration is aimed at improving the accuracy of the value function approximation represented by an ATG. Powell et al. [11] introduce automatic case elicitation (ACE), an RL-related learning technique where the CBR system initially starts without domain knowledge and successively improves by interacting with the environment. While they focus on exact situation matching and develop a specialized action rating mechanism, our interest in this paper lies in domains with continuous states and on combining value function-based model-free RL with case-based methods.

5   Empirical Evaluation

For the purpose of evaluating our case-based approach to state-action value function with ATGs, we turn to two classical reinforcement learning benchmarks, the pole and the cart pole benchmark problems (see Figure 4).

The former represents a two-dimensional problem where the task is to swing up a pole, whose mass is concentrated in a mass point, from different starting situations. The learning agent controls a motor in the center that can apply left and right torques (-4N and +4N) to the pole. A swing-up episode is considered successful, if the agent has managed to bring the pole to a state $s = (\theta, \omega)$ with $|\theta| < 0.1$. The cart pole benchmark represents a more challenging, four-dimensional problem, where the state vector (θ, ω, x, v) consists of the pole's

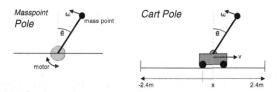

Fig. 4. Benchmark Problem Systems

angle θ and angular velocity ω as well as of the cart's position x and velocity v. Here, the task is to prevent the pole from falling down by accelerating the cart into the left/right direction ($\pm 10N$). A cart pole balancing episode is successful, if the agent manages to balance the pole for at least 1000 time steps and, to complicate the problem, the cart is positioned near the center of the track at the end ($|x| < 0.05m$). The agent fails if it hits the track boundaries ($|x| > 2.4$) or if the pole's angle exceeds the vertical position too much ($|\theta| > 1.0rad$), in which case the balancing episode is aborted. The starting states that system is initialized with during training, as well as during testing, are taken from $S = \{(\theta, 0, 0, 0)| - 0.2rad \leq \theta \leq 0.2rad\}$. The dynamics for the physical simulation of this system are taken from [3].

During all experiments, we measure similarity between states as an equally weighted amalgamation $sim_S(s_1, s_2) = \sum_{i=1}^{n} w_i sim_i(s_1(i), s_2(i))$ of local similarities where each sim_i refers to the similarity with respect to one single dimension: $sim_i(x, y) = (1 - \frac{|x-y|}{max_i - min_i})^2$ with max_i and min_i as the maximal/minimal value of the respective dimension (e.g. $max_x = 2.4$ and $min_\theta = -\pi$). Further, the exploration rate during all experiments was fixed to $\varepsilon = 0.1$.

5.1   Proof of Concept

We use the pole swing-up task to provide a proof of concept for the case-based ATG function approximator. For training, as well as for testing, we employ a set S of start situations equally distributed over the state space ($|S| = 100$), and we set $k = 1$ for k-nearest neighbor determination. Actions that do not lead to a goal state incur costs of $c = 1.0$, otherwise $c = 0.0$; no discounting is used. Figure 5 shows that the ATG-based agent is able to learn extremely quickly. The agent is able to swing up the pole for each start situation already after 5 training episodes; by then, the case base contains 485 cases. After about 60 training episodes (circa 1100 cases in memory), the performance has become very good and, during ongoing learning, continues to improve. Finally, the learning agent comes very near to the theoretical optimum (which can be calculated brute force for this problem) of 8.9 steps on average to swing up the pole for the considered set of test situations.

5.2   Results

For the cart pole benchmark it is not possible to provide some kind of optimal solution as in the case of the pole swing-up task. However, it is known that good policies which balance the pole for an arbitrary time can be learned within

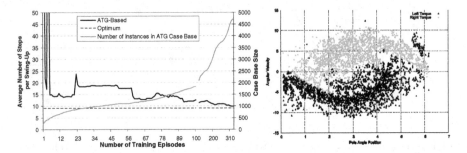

Fig. 5. Learning curve for the pole swing-up task and case base size (left). The right chart visualizes what happens during greedy exploitation of the resultant Q value base: It is shown which actions (left/right force) are considered best in which regions of the state space.

200 episodes. In the following, we show that achieving that goal is also possible using an ATG-based function approximation mechanism. For a comparison to the performance of other learning techniques, we refer to the RL benchmarking website [8].

The agent is punished with very high costs if it leaves its working area ($c = 1000$) by letting the pole fall down or leaving the track. Each action incurs immediate costs of 10, except for transitions in the target area (pole nearly upright with $|\theta| < 0.3rad$ and cart within $x \in [-0.05m, 0.05m]$) are free of costs. The discounting rate is set to $\gamma = 0.98$.

In Figure 6 (left), we compare the version of the ATG-based learning agent employed in Section 5.1 to 4 variants, where we incremented the value of k and utilized the efficient exploration mechanism suggested in Section 4.1, respectively. Performance curves are shown for the evaluation of the learned policies on the set of test situations. The empirical results suggest that choosing the number of nearest neighbors to be considered during retrieval must be larger than $k = 1$ in order to obtain satisfying results. Then, the resulting function approximator features better generalization capabilities and represents the value function in a smoother way. Moreover, the efficient exploration mechanism is capable of speeding up the learning process. We note that, during testing, we aborted an episode after $t = 1000$ steps (during learning after $t = 200$), as we observed that the agent is generally able to keep the cart pole in the target area for an arbitrarily longer time if it already manages to balance for 1000 steps. Thus, in our charts an episode time of 1000 steps represents an upper limit and corresponds to a zero failure rate.

Since the combination of using $k = 3$ in conjunction with efficient exploration yields best performance (100% from about the 135th episode onward; by then, there are nearly $20k$ instances in the Q value case base), we performed further experiments on top of that base configuration (see right part of Figure 6). The use of transformational analogy during the process of case-based transition completion (cf. Section 4.2) is computationally more expensive, but boosts the learning performance: Here, the agent attains a policy that yields no more failures already after about 50 training episodes.

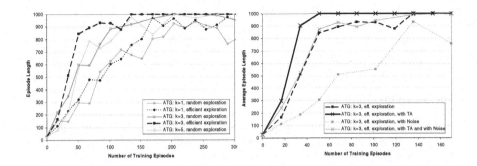

Fig. 6. Learning Curves for the Cart Pole Task

All experiments described so far were performed in a deterministic environment. To also examine non-deterministic environments, we added uniformly distributed noise to all state transitions. So, in *each* step the states $s = (\theta, \omega, x, v)$ resulting from taking an action were distorted subject to noise according to $(\theta \pm 1°, \omega \pm \frac{1°}{s}, x \pm 0.5cm, v \pm 0.5\frac{cm}{s})$. In the base configuration with added noise the learner now needs more than 200 training episodes to acquire a faultless policy for the first time (not included in the chart), whereas when using TA that goal is reached already after approximately 150 episodes.

6 Conclusion

We have presented an approach to state-action value function approximation for reinforcement learning agents that systematically relies on and employs case-based methods. Our approximate transition graph function approximation scheme utilizes case-based reasoning to replenish its transition experience and also represents the actual Q function in a case-based manner. Our empirical evaluations in the context of dynamic control tasks focused on established reinforcement learning benchmark problems and revealed that ATG-based function approximation employed by a Q learning agent brings about quick success and stable learning results.

A challenging issue for future work represents case base management. Currently, we make no attempts to discard redundant transitions gathered by the agent, which is why the case base's growth is not limited and retrieval times increase continuously. For an application scenario where, for example, the number of steps till reaching some terminal state is inherently large, using our approach in its current form may become infeasible. We also expect that the performance of an ATG-based value function approximator can significantly be improved when knowledge-intensive similarity measures are employed and when background knowledge about the respective application domain (e.g. the exploitation of symmetries) is utilized. Another topic for future work is the investigation of knowledge transfer from an ATG-based function approximator to another, preferentially more compact or computationally less demanding one.

Acknowledgment

This research has been supported by the German Research Foundation (DFG) under grant number Ri-923/2-3.

References

1. Aha, D., Salzberg, S.: Learning to Catch: Applying Nearest Neighbor Algorithms to Dynamic Control Tasks. In: Cheeseman, P., Oldford, R. (eds.) Selecting Models from Data: Artificial Intelligence and Statistics IV (1994)
2. Atkeson, C., Moore, A., Schaal, S.: Locally Weighted Learning for Control. Artificial Intelligence Review 11(1-5), 75–113 (1997)
3. Barto, A., Sutton, R., Anderson, C.: Neuronlike Adaptive Elements that Can Solve Difficult Learning Control Problems. IEEE Transactions on Systems, Man, and Cybernetics SMC-13(5), 835–846 (1983)
4. Carbonell, J.: Learning by Analogy: Formulating and Generalizing Plans from Past Experience. In: Michalski, R., Carbonell, J., Mitchell, T. (eds.) Machine Learning: An Artificial Intelligence Approach (1983)
5. Ernst, D., Geurts, P., Wehenkel, L.: Tree-Based Batch Mode Reinforcement Learning. Journal of Machine Learning Research (2005)
6. Gabel, T., Riedmiller, M.: CBR for State Value Function Approximation in Reinforcement Learning. In: Muñoz-Ávila, H., Ricci, F. (eds.) ICCBR 2005. LNCS (LNAI), vol. 3620, pp. 206–220. Springer, Heidelberg (2005)
7. Gordon, G.: Stable Function Approximation in Dynamic Programming. In: ICML, pp. 261–268. Morgan Kaufmann, San Francisco (1995)
8. Neuroinformatics Group. Reinforcement Learning Benchmarking Site (2007), www.ni.uos.de/index.php?id=930
9. Macedo, L., Cardoso, A.: Using CBR in the Exploration of Unknown Environments with an Autonomous Agent. In: Funk, P., González Calero, P.A. (eds.) ECCBR 2004. LNCS (LNAI), vol. 3155, pp. 272–286. Springer, Heidelberg (2004)
10. Peng, J.: Efficient Memory-Based Dynamic Programming. In: Proceedings of the Twelfth International Conference on Machine Learning (ICML 1995), Tahoe City, USA, pp. 438–446. Morgan Kaufmann, San Francisco (1995)
11. Powell, J., Hauff, B., Hastings, J.: Evaluating the Effectiveness of Exploration and Accumulated Experience in Automatic Case Elicitation. In: Muñoz-Ávila, H., Ricci, F. (eds.) ICCBR 2005. LNCS (LNAI), vol. 3620, pp. 397–407. Springer, Heidelberg (2005)
12. Puterman, M.: Markov Decision Processes: Discrete Stochastic Dynamic Programming. Wiley-Interscience, USA (2005)
13. Riedmiller, M.: Neural Fitted Q Iteration – First Experiences with a Data Efficient Neural Reinforcement Learning Method. In: Gama, J., Camacho, R., Brazdil, P.B., Jorge, A.M., Torgo, L. (eds.) ECML 2005. LNCS (LNAI), vol. 3720, Springer, Heidelberg (2005)
14. Santamaria, J., Sutton, R., Ram, A.: Experiments with Reinforcement Learning in Problems with Continuous State and Action Spaces. Adaptive Behavior 6(2), 163–217 (1998)
15. Sutton, R.S., Barto, A.G.: Reinforcement Learning. An Introduction. MIT Press/A Bradford Book, Cambridge, USA (1998)
16. Watkins, C., Dayan, P.: Q-Learning. Machine Learning 8 (1992)

From Anomaly Reports to Cases

Stewart Massie[1], Nirmalie Wiratunga[1], Susan Craw[1], Alessandro Donati[2],
and Emmanuel Vicari[2]

[1] School of Computing
The Robert Gordon University
Aberdeen AB25 1HG, Scotland, UK
{nw,sm,smc}@comp.rgu.ac.uk
[2] European Space Agency
European Space Operations Centre
64293 Darmstadt, Germany

Abstract. Creating case representations in unsupervised textual case-based reasoning applications is a challenging task because class knowledge is not available to aid selection of discriminatory features or to evaluate alternative system design configurations. Representation is considered as part of the development of a tool, called CAM, which supports an anomaly report processing task for the European Space Agency. Novel feature selection/extraction techniques are created which consider word co-occurrence patterns to calculate similarity between words. These are used together with existing techniques to create 5 different case representations. A new evaluation technique is introduced to compare these representations empirically, without the need for expensive, domain expert analysis. Alignment between the problem and solution space is measured at a local level and profiles of these local alignments used to evaluate the *competence* of the system design.

1 Introduction

In this paper we review the development of a case-based reasoning (CBR) application applied to the complex task of anomaly report matching for the European Space Agency (ESA). The cases are presented as semi-structured textual documents consisting, largely, of several sections of text describing the problem and one section of text describing the solution. In particular, we focus on the problem of deriving a structured case representation from unsupervised text data using feature selection and extraction techniques and on evaluating alternative design configurations.

Case representation is a key design issue for the successful development of any CBR system. This is particularly true for a Textual CBR (TCBR) system which generally requires the application of feature selection or extraction techniques to reduce the dimensionality of the problem by removing non-discriminatory and sometimes detrimental features. Dimensionality reduction has been shown to be successful in improving accuracy and efficiency for supervised tasks in unstructured domains [23]. However, in an unsupervised setting feature selection/extraction is a far more challenging task because class knowledge is not available to evaluate alternative representations.

We compare a TFIDF feature selection approach with a novel technique in which similarity between words is calculated by analysing word co-occurrence patterns

R.O. Weber and M.M. Richter (Eds.): ICCBR 2007, LNAI 4626, pp. 359–373, 2007.

followed by seed word selection using a footprint-based feature selection method. Applying feature selection only can result in sparse representations so we investigate feature extraction techniques using rules induced by either Apriori or from feature similarity neighbourhoods to generalise the seed words and reduce sparseness. The techniques are implemented in a prototype CBR Anomaly Matching demonstrator, called CAM, which retrieves similar reports when presented with a new anomaly and incorporates intuitive visualisation techniques to convey case similarity knowledge.

Evaluation in unsupervised TCBR systems also presents difficulties because the typical approach, which involves a domain expert rating a small number of retrievals, is very time consuming and depends on the availability of a willing domain expert. Evaluation is especially troublesome when following a typical incremental development approach in which a series of small changes are made to the design with evaluation required to measure the effect of the change after each stage. We introduce a novel approach to evaluation that measures the extent to which *similar problems have similar solutions* by investigating the alignment between local neighbourhoods in the problem and solution space. This approach reduces the requirement for human evaluations.

The problem domain is described in more detail in Section 2 along with CAM's key objectives. Section 3 discusses several feature selection and extraction techniques used to create alternative case representations. We describe how the prototype was implemented in Section 4. Evaluation results comparing five alternative system designs by measuring the alignment between problem and solution space are presented in Section 5. Related work is discussed in Section 6 before we provide conclusions and recommendations for future work in Section 7.

2   Anomaly Reporting

ESA is Europe's gateway to space. Its mission is to shape the development of Europe's space capability and ensure that investment in space continues to deliver benefits to the citizens of Europe. ESOC, the European Space Operations Centre, is responsible for controlling ESA satellites in orbit and is situated in Darmstadt, Germany. ESOC works in an environment in which safety and Quality Assurance is of critical importance and, as a result, a formal Problem Management process is required to identify and manage problems that occur both within the operations of the space segment and of the ground segment. Observed incidents and problems (the cause of the incidents), are recorded by completing anomaly reports.

Anomaly reports are semi-structured documents containing both structured and unstructured data. There are 27 predefined structured fields containing information such as: the originator's name; key dates relating to the report and the physical location of the anomaly. Structured fields are used to group and sort reports, for example by urgency or criticality. Importantly, for knowledge reuse purposes the anomaly reports also have four text sections: observation (the title of the report), description (facts observed), recommendation (first suggestion on recovery), and resolution (how the problem is analysed and disposed). These four unstructured sections contain free text that are not necessarily always spell-checked or grammatically perfect but contain valuable knowledge.

The work described in this paper involves the organisation and extraction of knowledge from anomaly reports maintained by the ARTS system. The overall goal is to extract knowledge and enable decision support by reusing past-experiences captured in these reports. An initial prototype CAM supports report linking and resolution retrieval.

- *Task 1:* Report linking aims to discover similar technical problems across multiple reports and to generate links between reports across projects. Reports can be related because they either describe symptoms of the same problem within the same project (indicating the re-occurrence of incidents associated with the same cause) or they report a similar anomaly shifted in time occurring in different projects / missions. Relating anomalies can highlight single problems that result in multiple incidents which are recorded in different (and sometimes un-related) reports. One goal is to find relationships in an automatic way.
- *Task 2:* Report reuse aims to retrieve similar reports so that their resolution can be re-applied to the current problem. This involves retrieval and reuse of anomaly reports with the requirement to compare new anomaly descriptions with past anomaly reports. In standard CBR terminology the resolution section provides the problem solution while the remaining sections decompose the problem description. Determining a suitable resolution for an anomaly is currently a manual decision making process (using Anomaly Review Boards) requiring considerable domain expertise. The prototype aids this decision-making process by providing the user with a list of anomaly reports that have similar problem descriptions to the current anomaly.

3   Report Representation

The first task for developing our prototype CBR system was to create a case representation for anomaly reports. The structured fields in the document were reduced to 13 relevant features following discussions with the domain experts.

Representation of the textual parts of the reports is a far harder task. The unstructured text has to be translated into a more structured representation of feature-value pairs. This involves identifying relevant features that belong to the problem space and solution space. The translation from text into a structured case representation can not be performed manually because the dimensionality of the problem is too great: there is a large vocabulary in the training sample of 960 reports which forms just 20% of the ESA's report database. An approach which can identify relevant features from the corpus is required. There are numerous approaches to feature selection and extraction on supervised problems where class knowledge can be used to guide the selection [10,23]. However since we are faced with an unsupervised problem the selection needs to be guided by knowledge other than class.

Our approach to unsupervised feature extraction (Figure 1) consists of three stages: an initial vocabulary reduction by pre-processing text using standard IR and NLP techniques; next seed word selection using word frequency counts or word distribution profiling; and finally feature extraction by considering word co-occurrence to avoid sparse representations using Apriori rules or seed word similarity neighbourhoods.

3.1   Text Pre-processing

The initial vocabulary is reduced to 2500 words by applying the following document pre-processing techniques:

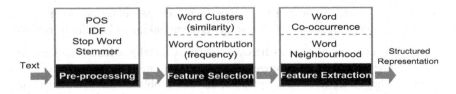

Fig. 1. Processing unstructured text to create structured representation

- Part of Speech Removal: text is first tokenised to identify word entities then tagged by its part of speech. Only nouns and verbs are retained.
- Stop Word Removal and Stemming: removes commonly occurring words and reduces remaining words to their stem by removing different endings, e.g., both anomaly and anomalous are stemmed to their root anomaly.
- Frequency Based Pruning: reduces the vocabulary, from approximately 8000 words to 2500 words, by considering the inverse document frequency (idf) of each word to determine how common the word is in all of the documents. We accept words that are common across several documents but not too frequent by accepting words with an idf value of between 3 and 6.

3.2 Feature Selection

Feature selection for structured data can be categorised into filter and wrapper methods. Filters are seen as data pre-processors and generally, unlike wrapper approaches, do not require feedback from the final learner. They tend to be faster, scaling better to large datasets with thousands of dimensions, as typically encountered in text applications.

Unlike with supervised methods, comparative studies into unsupervised feature selection are very rare. One of the few approaches explicitly dealing with unsupervised feature selection for text data [10] relies on heuristics that are informed by word frequency counts over the text collection. We compare this word contribution method with a novel similarity clustering approach that can consider contextual information.

Seed Word Selection by Word Contribution
Word frequency information can be used to gauge a word's contribution towards similarity computation for case comparison. Ideally we wish to ignore words that distribute over the entire case base whilst preferring those that are discriminatory of similar reports. TFIDF is commonly used in IR research to measure the discriminatory power of a word for a given document. The unsupervised feature selection approach introduced in [10] uses these TFIDF values to arrive at a feature ranking score. For a given word all its TFIDF values are combined using the vector product so that a word that is consistently discriminatory of small subsets of cases are preferred over those words that are discriminatory of only individual cases.

Seed Word Selection by Similarity Clustering
Seed words should be representative of areas of the problem space but also diverse so that together they provide good coverage of the problem space. Knowledge about word similarity enables the search process to address both these requirements. The question

then is how do we define similarity between words and thereafter how do we select representative but diverse words.

- **Word Similarity**
  One approach is to consider the number of times words co-occur in documents [14], however, a problem is that similar words do not necessarily co-occur in any document, due to sparsity and synonymy, and will not be identified as similar.

  Our approach is to analyse word co-occurrence patterns with the set of words contained in the solution, i.e., the remaining words from the resolution field. For example, to calculate the similarity between words in the observation field of the anomaly report, the conditional probability of co-occurrence is first calculated between each word in the observation field with each word in the resolution field. A distribution of these probabilities is then created for each observation word. A comparison between these distributions can then be made using the α-Skew metric derived from information theory [8]. This comparison provides an asymmetric similarity estimate between words in the observation field. We repeat the same process for all the text fields. Essentially similar words are those that have similar co-occurrence patterns with resolution words. A full description of this word similarity approach is given in [21].

- **Representative but Diverse Selection**
  We use the similarity knowledge derived from the conditional probability distributions to aid the search for a representative but diverse set of seed words. These words form the dimensions for the case representation. Smyth & McKenna developed a footprint-based retrieval technique in which a subset of the case base, called footprints, is identified to aid case retrieval [16]. We use a similar technique to cluster words and then select representative seed words from word clusters.

  Word clusters are created by first forming coverage and reachability sets for each word. In our scenario, the coverage set of a word contains all words within a predefined similarity threshold. Conversely, the reachability set of a word is the set of words that contains this word in its coverage set. Clusters of words are then formed using the reachability and coverage sets to group words that have overlapping sets. In Figure 2, six words (w_1 to w_6) are shown spaced in relation to their similarity to each other. The coverage of each word is shown by a circle with a radius corresponding to the similarity threshold. It can be seen that two clusters are formed: w_1 to w_5 in one cluster and w_6 in the other. A representative set of seed words is selected for each cluster by first ranking the words in descending order of relative coverage [16]. Each word is then considered in turn and only selected if it is not covered by another already selected word. The words are shown in Figure 2, in ranked order, with their coverage sets and related coverage scores. Hence w_1, w_5 and w_6 will be selected as the seed words. The composition of the coverage sets depends upon the similarity threshold chosen and so the number of seed words formed can be varied by adjusting this threshold.

3.3 Feature Extraction

Feature selection techniques are successful in reducing dimensionality, however, they tend to produce very sparse representations of text that can harm retrieval performance.

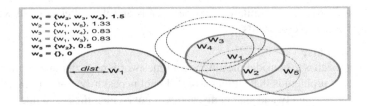

Fig. 2. Seed word selection using the footprint technique

We investigate two feature extraction techniques, that form a new set of features from the original features, to address the issue of sparseness.

Feature Extraction using Word Co-Occurrence

Each seed word forms a feature in the case representation. A feature value is derived based on the presence of a seed word in the report. Using seed words alone in this way to represent free text results in a sparse representation. This is because reports may still be similar even though they may not contain seed words. One way around this problem is to embed the context of the seed within the case. We achieve this by the induction of feature extraction rules [19,20].

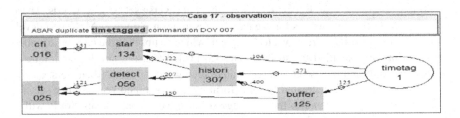

Fig. 3. Feature extraction rules

Each rule associates words with a selected seed word, such that the rule conclusion contains the seed word and the rule body (or conditions) consists of associated words. The presence of associated words in a report (in the absence of the seed word) activates the rule, inferring a degree of seed word presence in the report. Essentially with increasing rule activations the problem with sparse representation decreases.

Consider the text snippet in Figure 3 taken from the observation section of a particular anomaly report. Here the snippet happens not to contain any of the seed words discovered for observation parts of reports. This would typically lead to an *empty* representation, if only a feature selection approach is employed. However an associated word, "timetagged", identified by rule induction, and highlighted in the text, has led to a series of rule activations as shown in the lower part of Figure 3. The outcome of this is that six seed words, shown in the highlighted boxes, can now be instantiated because of their association with "timetagged". Importantly for case comparison this means that other cases containing these seed words that previously would have been considered distant can now be considered more similar.

Feedback for Seed Word	Context Relevance					Expert's Comments
	1	2	3	4	5	
TLM						
TLM <= lost				x		Also a type of problem about telemetry: we loose it!
TLM <= process & receive		x				We receive it and we process it. These are actions
TLM <= lock					x	Bingo: We sometimes have "Telemetry lock problems"
TLM <= telemetry						It is the abbreviation / synonym
TLM <= available & generated	x					a bit weird
TLM <= product & generated		x				A more elaborated processing of the telemetry

Fig. 4. Feature extraction rules concluding the seed word, TLM

Similarity computation requires that a mechanism is in place to facilitate the comparison of feature values. With CAM the process of translating rule activations into feature values involves combining evidence from multiple rule activations and propagating this evidence through rule chains. Key to this are rule accuracy values also referred to as confidence scores shown on the arcs between terms. Essentially when a rule with high confidence is activated it suggests higher belief in the presence of the seed word. We use a basic spreading-activation mechanism to propagate these confidence scores using an aggregation mechanism similar to the MYCIN approach to combining evidence for medical reasoning [4]. Here, if two rules x and y activate concluding the same seed word, then the confidences are aggregated to generate the feature value for the feature represented by the seed as follows: $conf(x) + conf(y) - conf(x)*conf(y)$. The aggregated confidence values derived from this approach, for our example, are shown below each seed word in Figure 3. The resulting representation now has 6 features instantiated with values between 0 and 1. It is interesting to note that when rules are triggered they implicitly capture latent higher order relationships (e.g. "timetag" associated with "tt" and "cfi" via "buffer"). These discovered relationships provide a more informed case comparison compared to one that is based solely on seed word presence alone.

We use the Apriori [1] association rule learner to extract feature extraction rules. Apriori typically generates many rules, and requires that confidence, support and discriminatory thresholds be set before useful rules are generated. Here expert feedback on the quality of generated rules is vital. The explicit nature of rules is an obvious advantage both to establish context and also to acquire expert feedback (see Figure 4).

Feature Extraction using Similarity Neighbourhoods
Our *seed word selection by similarity clustering* feature selection approach identifies seed words that are representative of a set of similar words and uses the seed words to represent the document. Similar words are those that have similar co-occurrence patterns with words contained in the solution. Rather than instantiating the feature only if the seed word itself is present it would appear sensible to instantiate the feature if either the seed word or any of the words it represents are present in the document. Feature extraction using similarity neighbourhoods does this. If the seed word is present the feature is given the value 1 as with the feature selection approach. However, sparseness is reduced by instantiating the feature if any related word contained in the seed word's coverage or reachability sets are present in the document. The feature value is set to equal the similarity between the seed word and the related word. Where multiple related words are present in the document the similarities are combined using the MYCIN approach discussed earlier.

4   The CAM Prototype

Our CAM demonstrator uses a structured representation of the anomaly reports, created by one or a combination of the feature selection/extraction processes described in Section 3. The representation process provides a 5 part case representation for each report. One of these contains the 13 features from the original structured report fields, while the remaining four parts are representations of the text data in the observation, description, recommendation and resolution fields of the report. These are represented by 70, 103, 94, and 156 features respectively, and correspond to the number of seed words extracted by the footprint-based feature selection. The similarity threshold controlling this extraction was set to encourage balanced word clusters. We are currently working with a sample of 960 reports, supplied by ESA.

The retrieval strategy implemented on CAM uses the k Nearest Neighbour algorithm (k-NN) to identify the k most similar cases to the current problem. The relative importance of each section or form (1 structured + 4 text) can be established by setting a form weight while at a more fine-grained level the importance of each feature within a form can be set with feature weighting. Three alternative distance measures can be selected in CAM to measure the relationship between anomaly reports: Manhattan, Euclidean, and Cosine. Because the representations are sparse the Manhattan and Euclidean measures have been adapted to consider only instantiated features and ignore zero valued features when calculating the distance between reports.

CAM provides an interface (Figure 5) that displays the current target report at the top with a ranked list of similar, retrieved reports below along with their similarity scores. Individual forms can be viewed by selecting the tab for the appropriate pane. Given the sparse representation, instantiated fields are colour highlighted to allow relationships between reports to be easily viewed. A gradient (darker for higher values) is applied to the highlighting to identify the confidence in a words presence in a report. The selected seed words are used in the structured representation to label the features.

The structured representation is the default report view, however, alternative views display the original text as displayed on the bottom left of Figure 5. A two colour word annotation is applied to the text. Seed words are annotated in yellow while any terms forming the body of induced rules are annotated in pink. Feature extraction rules induced from the text as part of the representation process, can be viewed as a list (displayed on the bottom left of Figure 5) or as a graph as shown in Figure 3.

Two additional visualisations are available to assist the user compare similarities and differences between retrieved reports [22]. A parallel co-ordinate plot shows the similarity of the retrieved nearest neighbours to the current report while a second visualisation uses the spring-embedder model to preserve the similarity relationship between cases as on-screen distances.

5   Experimental Evaluation

It is generally accepted that evaluation is a challenge for TCBR systems. Standard IR systems advocate precision and recall based evaluation on tagged corpuses. The manual tagging involves not only class assignment but often assignment of relevance

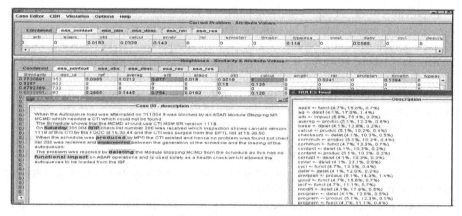

Fig. 5. Screen shot of CAM's interface

judgements on retrieved sets. In practical situations it is clearly prohibitive to expect a domain expert to tag substantial numbers of cases with relevance judgements.

Our initial evaluation approach was to acquire qualitative feedback on a few selected test cases. A structured representation was created for each case using our preprocessing techniques, seed word selection by word similarity clustering, and feature extraction rules. Five probe reports were randomly selected and for each probe the 3 most similar reports were retrieved by CAM. A further 3 randomly selected reports were then added to create a retrieval set size of 6. Each probe and corresponding retrieval set was presented to the domain expert to obtain our expert's feedback. The results of our initial study [22] show reasonable cases are being retrieved. However, qualitative evaluations are expensive, in terms of domain expert time, and only consider a small sample of available documents.

CAM requires choices to be made between major factors such as alternative feature selection and extraction techniques in addition to fine tuning numerous other factors that have an effect on retrieval performance e.g. between alternative distance measures or neighbourhood sizes to develop appropriate similarity knowledge. It soon became clear that manual evaluation of the iterative development cycle required to optimise our design would require an excessive level of involvement by the domain expert to the extent it was impractical. We require an empirical evaluation measure to allow us to choose between alternative system designs.

5.1 Alignment Measure

"Similar problems have similar solutions" is one of the fundamental assumptions that underpins CBR as a suitable problem-solving methodology for a particular problem domain. This assumption is often taken for granted, whereas, in fact it is a measure not only of the suitability of CBR for the domain but also of the competence of the system design in terms of case representation and similarity knowledge. If we can measure the alignment between the problem and solution space in terms of extent to which *"similar problems have similar solutions"* holds true for different system design configurations we have a measure of design competence.

In previous work, on supervised problems, the alignment between problem and solution space has been measured by looking at the mix of solution classes present among a case's neighbours in the problem space [11]. In unsupervised tasks cases are not assigned class labels, however, it is still possible to measure the local mix in solutions where the similarity between solutions can be measured e.g. where the solutions are in textual form. Weber et al. [18] use similarity in the solution space to cluster the case base and provide information on feature importance in the problem space. Case cohesion [9] measures level of overlap in retrieval sets retrieved independently from the problem and solution space, however, it is unclear on how to set suitable similarity thresholds that control the retrieval set sizes. We measure the alignment between the problem and solution space by considering the mix of similarities among solutions present in a set of neighbours retrieved in the problem space.

In a *good* design cases identified as having the most similar problems to a target case will also have the most similar solutions. This is exactly what our case alignment measures. If a CBR system processes problems in a problem space P and solutions for these problems belong to a solution space S. Let C be the set of cases in the case base containing cases $\{c_1, ..., c_n\}$. Cases consist problem/solution pairs such that $c_i = \{p_i, s_i\}$ where $p_i \in P$ and $s_i \in S$. Using the case base to represent future problems that will be faced, i.e. the representative assumption, each case becomes the target problem t in turn and we measure the alignment between P and S in the local neighbourhood of t. A distance function $D(t, p_i)$ or $D(t, s_i)$ measures the distance between t and c_i in either the problem or solution space giving a value between 0 and 1.

In Figure 6, t is identified in both P and S. Using $D(t, p_i)$, t's three nearest neighbours (NN) in P are found, shown as $p_1, p_2, \& p_3$. If we initially consider only c_1, consisting $\{p_1, s_1\}$, we can calculate the alignment of t in relation to c_1 ($Align(t, c_1)$) by comparing the distance in the solution space of t to s_1 with the distance to the nearest (Ds_{min}) and most distant solutions (Ds_{max}) in the case base, as shown below.

$$Align(t, c_1) = 1 - \frac{(D(t, s_1) - Ds_{min})}{(Ds_{max} - Ds_{min})}$$

The overall case alignment for t (CaseAlign(t)) is found by taking a weighted average of the alignment with its individual NN retrieved in the problem space. The size of the neighbourhood used would typically be the same as used for retrieval; a neighbourhood size of 3 is shown in Figure 6.

$$\text{CaseAlign(t)} = \frac{\sum_{i=1} (1 - D(t, p_i)) * Align(t, c_i)}{\sum_{i=1}(1 - D(t, p_i))}$$

In local areas where a case's NN in the problem space are also its NN in the solution space there is a strong alignment between problem and solution space and case alignment values will be close to 1; conversely, in areas in which a case's NN in the problem space are not close in the solution space the alignment is poor and case alignment values will be low. Case alignment allows us to evaluate alternative system design configuration and make informed maintenance decisions about individual cases.

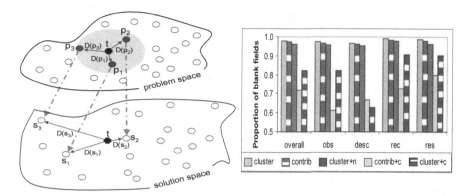

Fig. 6. Case alignment calculation

Fig. 7. Comparison of sparseness of different case representations

5.2 Representations

It is our contention that a *good* design will exhibit better alignment between the problem and solution space. Thus, looking at the mix of case alignments present in the case base provides an empirical evaluation technique and an alternative to the typical approach in which a domain expert manually tags a small set of retrieved documents. Using case alignments to evaluate alternative design configurations has several advantages: the burden on domain experts can be reduced; a more comprehensive evaluation is obtained rather being limited to a small sample; and fine-tuning of design variables becomes possible by adopting an iterative development process.

Our new alignment measure can now be used to evaluate 5 alternative case representations, constructed using a combination of the techniques described in section 3. The representations, all of which share the same pre-processing technique but differ in their combination of feature selection and extraction techniques, are described below.

- **CLUSTER:** Created using word similarity clustering to identify seed words only with no feature extraction rules.
- **CONTRIB:** Features are selected by the word contribution technique alone.
- **CLUSTER+N:** Case representation combines word similarity clustering with the word neighbourhood extraction technique.
- **CONTRIB+C:** Features selected by word contribution with feature extraction rules.
- **CLUSTER+C:** Uses word similarity clustering with feature extraction rules.

One of the key problems that needs to be addressed in creating structured representations of text is how to deal with the inherent data sparsity. Our five representations each take a different approach with the latter three representations, which include feature extraction techniques, being developed specifically to address the sparsity problem. Figure 7 gives a measure of sparsity, showing the proportion of blank fields present in the case base for each form and representation. The feature selection only representations are very sparse (0.981 for CLUSTER and 0.974 for CONTRIB). Surprisingly, the word similarity neighbourhood extraction technique used in CLUSTER+N does little to reduce sparsity with an overall value about 1% lower at 0.963. However, both

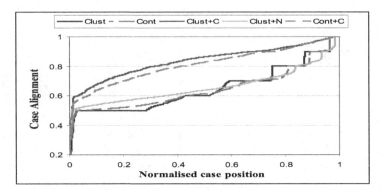

Fig. 8. Profiles of case alignment for alternative representations

representations using word co-occurrence extraction show a substantial reduction in sparsity with CONTRIB+C being least sparse at 0.720 compared to 0.825.

We create a profile of case alignments for each of the five representations. Case alignment is calculated for each case in the case base and the cases are ranked in ascending order of alignment. The profile shows the mix of individual case alignments present in the case base for a particular representation. Figure 8 plots the profile of the five representations being considered. Each profile is created by plotting case alignment against the normalised position of the case in the ranked list of case alignments. Thus each curve is a profile of the case alignments for one representation and a point on a curve gives the alignment value on the y-axis for a particular case whose relative position in the ranked list is shown on the x-axis. Representations that give profiles with higher case alignments are considered *better* designs. The alignment profiles fall into 2 groups coinciding with representation sparsity.

- representations incorporating the word co-occurrence feature extraction technique (CONTRIB+C and CLUSTER+C) give superior results showing a better alignment between problem and solution space providing support for the use of this approach. CLUSTER+C slightly outperforms CONTRIB+C with an average alignment of 0.836 compared to 0.810 even although its representation is more sparse. CLUSTER+C is our chosen representation for the domain.
- there is little to choose between the three representations showing poorer alignment. The 2 feature selection only approaches(CLUSTER and CONTRIB) both have an average alignment of 0.646 although CONTRIB gives a more even distribution across the case base. CLUSTER+N gave disappointing results with only marginal improvements in alignment as a result of the feature extraction stage with an average alignment of 0.662.

A similar evaluation approach was undertaken to evaluate and choose between alternative distance measure used in identifying the relationship between cases and for selecting a suitable neighbourhood size for the number of retrieved cases to return at the retrieval stage. Manhattan distance was seen to exhibit slightly better alignment than the Euclidean or Cosine measures while a neighbourhood size of 5 was found to give a good compromise between good alignment, found in smaller neighbourhoods, and minimising the impact of noise with larger neighbourhoods.

6   Related Work

A common problem for TCBR system development is the demand on knowledge acquisition. For instance in the EXPERIENCEBOOK project (aimed at supporting computer system administrators) all knowledge was acquired manually. This is not an exception, because current practice in TCBR system development show that the indexing vocabulary and similarity knowledge containers are typically acquired manually [17]. Consequently maintenance remains a problem since these systems are not able to evolve with newer experiences. These difficulties have created the need for fully or semi automated extraction tools for TCBR.

Tools such as stemming, stop word removal and domain specific dictionary acquisition are frequently used to pre-process text and are mostly automated. Acquiring knowledge about semantic relationships between words or phrases is important but is harder to automate. Although NLP tools can be applied they are often too brittle partly because they tend to analyse text from a purely linguistic point of view. Furthermore the reliance on deep syntactic parsing and knowledge in the form of generative lexicons still warrants significant manual intervention [6].

Research in text classification and information retrieval typically adopts statistical approaches to feature selection and extraction. The main pre-requisite is access to a significant number of cases. With the anomaly reporting problem domain case base size is not a constraint. Consequently, word co-occurrence based analysis becomes particularly attractive for automated indexed vocabulary acquisition. A common approach to determining representative features involve the use of distributional clustering approaches [13], and has since been adopted for feature extraction with supervised tasks [15,2]. Of particular importance for word clustering are distributional distance measures. These measures ascertain distance by comparison of word distributions conditioned over a disjoint target set. Typically, class labels are the set of targets and so cannot be applied to unsupervised tasks. However, in the SOPHIA retrieval system reliance on class labels was dropped by comparing word distributions conditioned on other co-occurring words (instead of class labels) [12]. Unlike with anomaly reports, SOPHIA operates on IR like documents, hence there is no requirement to learn from the differences between solution and problem space vocabulary. Our approach to calculating distributional distances is novel in that words from the problem space are compared conditioned on the solution space. This creates a distance measure that is guided by both the similarity and differences between problem and solution vocabularies.

Formation of newer and improved dimensions for case representation fall under feature extraction research. LSI is a popular dimensionality reduction technique particularly for text. Extracted features are linear combinations of the original features which unfortunately lack in expressive power [5]. Modelling keyword relationships as rules is a more successful strategy that is both effective and remains expressive. A good example is RIPPER [3], which adopts complex optimisation heuristics to learn propositional clauses for classification. Unlike RIPPER rules, association rules do not rely on class information and incorporates data structures that are able to generate rules efficiently making them ideal for large scale applications [24,7]. The seed generalisation approach discussed in this paper is similar to that employed by the PSI tool introduced in [20], but unlike PSI here generalisation does not rely on class knowledge.

7   Conclusions and Future Work

The paper presents an approach to case retrieval applied to anomaly reports and is implemented in the CAM prototype. It is a first step towards developing a CBR system to support the ESA's anomaly report processing task. Like most text applications, anomaly processing is unsupervised and requires automated knowledge acquisition tools that are not reliant on class knowledge.

The paper introduces a novel unsupervised index vocabulary acquisition mechanism to map unstructured parts of text data to a structured case representation. For this purpose word pair-wise distances are calculated according to similarity in co-occurrence patterns over the solution space. This facilitates problem space words to be considered similar with specific reference to the solution space vocabulary.

Seed words are identified using word clusters and forms the features vector for the case representation. The idea of using a footprint-based feature selection strategy is novel. It facilitates selection of representative and diverse words but importantly does not require that the number of seed words be pre-specified. It does however require a similarity threshold to be in place which directly controls the feature vector size.

A novel case alignment technique measures the extent to which *similar problems have similar solutions*. Alignment to some extent depends on the underlying characteristic of the problem domain, however, it is also a measure of the effectiveness of the particular system design configuration being evaluated. The problem and solution space was shown to be most aligned with CLUSTER+C, which combined word similarity clustering with feature extraction using co-occurrence rules. In addition to a global profile of the case base, individual case alignments also provide local information about the relationship between the problem and solution space. It is planned to utilise this local knowledge to develop maintenance approaches for unsupervised domains.

A common approach for setting retrieval weights in supervised problems is to learn feature importance from the available cases. Our alignment measure gives the opportunity to apply similar techniques to learn weights that improve alignment and will be investigated in future work. In a similar vein we have yet to establish a principled approach to setting Apriori's parameters and the similarity threshold for the feature vector size. Case alignment can assist in the optimisation of these design parameters. Future work will also extend CAM for the reuse and revision stages of the CBR cycle.

References

1. Agrawal, R., Mannila, H., Srikant, R., Toivonen, H., Verkamo, A.: Fast discovery of association rules. In: Advances in Knowledge Discovery and DM, pp. 307–327 (1995)
2. Baker, L., McCallum, A.: Distributional clustering of words for text classification. In: Proceedings of the 21st ACM Int Conf on IR, pp. 96–103. ACM Press, New York (1998)

3. Cohen, W., Singer, Y.: Context-sensitive learning methods for text categorisation. ACM Transactions in Information Systems 17(2), 141–173 (1999)
4. Davis, R., Buchanan, B., Shortliffe, E.: Production Rules as a Representation for a Knowledge-Based Consultation Program. Artificial Intelligence 8, 15–45 (1977)
5. Deerwester, S., Dumais, S., Landauer, T., Furnas, G., Harshman, R.: Indexing by latent semantic analysis. American Society of Information Science 41(6), 391–407 (1990)
6. Gupta, K., Aha, D.: Towards acquiring case indexing taxonomies from text. In: Proceedings of the 7th Int FLAIRS Conf, pp. 307–315 (2004)
7. Kang, N., Domeniconi, C., Barbara, D.: Categorization and keyword identification of unlabelled documents. In: Proceedings of the 5th IEEE Int Conf on Data Mining (2005)
8. Lee, L.: On the effectiveness of the skew divergence for statistical language analysis. In: Artificial Intelligence and Statistics, pp. 65–72 (2001)
9. Lamontagne, L.: Textual CBR Authoring using Case Cohesion. In: Roth-Berghofer, T.R., Göker, M.H., Güvenir, H.A. (eds.) ECCBR 2006. LNCS (LNAI), vol. 4106, Springer, Heidelberg (2006)
10. Liu, T., Liu, S., Chen, Z., Ma, W.: An evaluation on feature selection for text clustering. In: Proc. of the 12th Int. Conf. on ML, pp. 488–495 (2003)
11. Massie, S., Craw, S., Wiratunga, N.: Complexity profiling for informed Case-Base Editing. In: Roth-Berghofer, T.R., Göker, M.H., Güvenir, H.A. (eds.) ECCBR 2006. LNCS (LNAI), vol. 4106, pp. 325–329. Springer, Heidelberg (2006)
12. Patterson, D., Rooney, N., Dobrynin, V., Galushka, M.: Sophia: A novel approach for textual case-based reasoning. In: Proc of the 19th IJCAI Conference, pp. 1146–1153 (2005)
13. Pereira, F., Tishby, N., Lee, L.: Distributional clustering of English words. In: Proc of the 30th Annual Meeting of the Association for Computational Linguistics, pp. 183–190 (1993)
14. Salton, G., McGill, M.: An introduction to modern IR. McGraw-Hill, New York (1983)
15. Slonim, N., Tishby, N.: The power of word clusters for text classification. In: Proc of the 23rd European Colloquium on IR Research (2001)
16. Smyth, B., McKenna, E.: Footprint-based Retrieval. In: Althoff, K.-D., Bergmann, R., Branting, L.K. (eds.) Case-Based Reasoning Research and Development. LNCS (LNAI), vol. 1650, pp. 343–357. Springer, Heidelberg (1999)
17. Weber, R., Ashley, K., Bruninghaus, S.: Textual case-based reasoning. To appear in The Knowledge Engineering Review (2006)
18. Weber, R., Proctor, J.M., Waldstein, I., Kriete, A.: CBR for Modeling Complex Systems. In: Muñoz-Ávila, H., Ricci, F. (eds.) ICCBR 2005. LNCS (LNAI), vol. 3620, pp. 625–639. Springer, Heidelberg (2005)
19. Wiratunga, N., Koychev, I., Massie, S.: Feature Selection and Generalisation for Retrieval of Textual Cases. In: Funk, P., González Calero, P.A. (eds.) ECCBR 2004. LNCS (LNAI), vol. 3155, pp. 806–820. Springer, Heidelberg (2004)
20. Wiratunga, N., Lothian, R., Chakraborty, S., Koychev, I.: Propositional approach to textual case indexing. In: Jorge, A.M., Torgo, L., Brazdil, P.B., Camacho, R., Gama, J. (eds.) PKDD 2005. LNCS (LNAI), vol. 3721, pp. 380–391. Springer, Heidelberg (2005)
21. Wiratunga, N., Lothian, R., Massie, S.: Unsupervised Feature Selection for Text Data. In: Roth-Berghofer, T.R., Göker, M.H., Güvenir, H.A. (eds.) ECCBR 2006. LNCS (LNAI), vol. 4106, pp. 340–354. Springer, Heidelberg (2006)
22. Wiratunga, N., Massie, S., Craw, S., Donati, A., Vicari, E.: Case Based Reasoning for Anomaly Report Processing. In: Roth-Berghofer, T.R., Göker, M.H., Güvenir, H.A. (eds.) ECCBR 2006. LNCS (LNAI), vol. 4106, pp. 44–49. Springer, Heidelberg (2006)
23. Yang, Y., Pedersen, J.: A comparative study on feature selection in text categorisation. In: Proc. of the 14th Int. Conf. on ML, pp. 412–420 (1997)
24. Zelikovitz, S.: Mining for features to improve classification. In: Proc. of ML Models, Technologies and Applications (2003)

Assessing Classification Accuracy in the Revision Stage of a CBR Spam Filtering System

José Ramón Méndez[1], Carlos González[2], Daniel Glez-Peña[1],
Florentino Fdez-Riverola[1], Fernando Díaz[3], and Juan Manuel Corchado[4]

[1] Dept. Informática, University of Vigo, Escuela Superior de Ingeniería Informática,
Edificio Politécnico, Campus Universitario As Lagoas s/n, 32004, Ourense, Spain
{moncho.mendez,dgpena,riverola}@uvigo.es
[2] GFI Informatique,
C/ Salvatierra 5, 28034, Madrid, Spain
cgperez@gfi.es
[3] Dept. Informática, University of Valladolid, Escuela Universitaria de Informática,
Plaza Santa Eulalia, 9-11, 40005, Segovia, Spain
fdiaz@infor.uva.es
[4] Dept. Informática y Automática, University of Salamanca,
Plaza de la Merced s/n, 37008, Salamanca, Spain
corchado@usal.es

Abstract. In this paper we introduce a quality metric for characterizing the solutions generated by a successful CBR spam filtering system called SPAMHUNTING. The proposal is denoted as *relevant information amount rate* and it is based on combining estimations about relevance and amount of information recovered during the retrieve stage of a CBR system. The results obtained from experimentation show how this measure can successfully be used as a suitable complement for the classifications computed by our SPAMHUNTING system. In order to evaluate the performance of the quality estimation index, we have designed a formal benchmark procedure that can be used to evaluate any accuracy metric. Finally, following the designed test procedure, we show the behaviour of the proposed measure using two well-known publicly available corpus.

1 Introduction and Motivation

The greatest steps forward in the field of CIT (*Communications & Information Technologies*) were the Internet and mobile phone introduction. These have allowed the development of modern communication infrastructures which give the final user a wide range of ways to communicate, as well as the freedom of doing it everywhere. Moreover, some relationships have been established between these technologies and nowadays, users can have Internet access through their mobile phones [1] and talk or send SMS (*Short Message Service*) messages by using VoIP (*Voice over IP*) techniques [2].

Unfortunately, these technologies share the same problem: the massive dissemination of spam contents. Spam is not only present on the delivered e-mails. From a

R.O. Weber and M.M. Richter (Eds.): ICCBR 2007, LNAI 4626, pp. 374–388, 2007.

practical and broad perspective, spam can be viewed as a set of irritating techniques used for distributing information taking advantage of the newest communication technologies. Moreover, spam is generally unsolicited by those targeted. Spam communications can also be found in SMS messages, blogs (through commentaries of the posts), newsgroups, search engines, and of course, postal mail and e-mail messages. In this work, we are mainly concerned with the oldest form of spam: e-mails sent across the Internet.

Due to the exponentially increasing amount of spam messages transferred through Internet, several techniques have been introduced for fighting the delivery of spam messages. Although anti-spam filtering software is often classified as *collaborative* or *content-based* [3], most of the successful approaches are classical machine learning techniques with little adjustments for detecting and filtering spam e-mails [4].

In the context of content-based techniques, two innovative anti-spam filtering CBR models have been introduced during the last years. First of all, we highlight the relevance and accuracy of the results achieved by some well-known researchers from the Dublin Institute of Technology [5]. They have started a revolution on the spam filtering domain by introducing a successful CBR system called ECUE [6]. Recently, we have introduced a new way of filtering spam by using an innovative feature selection technique applied in the retrieval stage of our SPAMHUNTING CBR system [7]. All these previous successful results evidence how and why case-based reasoning is particularly suitable for classifying and filtering spam messages.

Among other deserving properties, one of the most relevant characteristics of CBR in the spam filtering domain is the possibility of generating a *null* solution. This situation is identified by CBR systems when not enough cases are recovered during their retrieval stage. Although in many domains a null solution is not suitable, in spam filtering domain it is equivalent to assert that the incoming e-mail is legitimate. These topics are supporting the quality of previous research works on CBR for spam filtering by Delany *et al* [5, 6] and Méndez *et al* [7, 8, 9, 10].

One of the most interesting issues for current techniques is the ability of evaluate the quality of each classification made by the system [11]. The most important question for computing this quality rate is related to measuring the quantity of relevant information available for the classification of a given e-mail. The definition of the above mentioned quality rate could be very useful for the final user and it can be used for reducing the amount of false positive errors (legitimate messages classified as spam e-mails).

Based on our previous work, we provide a study of different successful approaches for quality estimation in spam filtering domain. In this context, we introduce a novel method for computing the reliability of a given e-mail classification that outperforms the precision reached by other well-known techniques. Our proposal is integrated in the revision stage of our previous successful SPAMHUNTING CBR system.

The rest of the paper is structured as follows: section 2 summarizes the relevant findings of previous research works on spam filtering and classification accuracy. Section 3 presents our proposal for computing the quality of the final generated e-mail classification while section 4 introduces the design and configuration of the experiments carried out. Section 5 focuses on showing the experimentation results, discussing the preliminary findings. Finally, section 6 exposes the main conclusions reached as well as the future lines of our research work.

2 Previous Work

This section presents a short description of some previous findings that are relevant to the task addressed in this article. Our preceding and related work was mainly focused in corpus preprocessing, feature selection and message representation issues concerning spam filtering domain. From our previous experiments, we have concluded that all these issues are very relevant to guarantee the accuracy of filtering techniques. As a conclusion, a bad choice in selecting these parameters can severely degrade the precision of the model. Moreover, we have shown the benefits of keeping in mind the noise and concept drift problems while making decisions in the configuration of the experiments and models [7].

Subsection 2.1 contains a brief explanation of our previous successful SPAMHUNTING system, as well as other related questions about the problem domain. Complementing the work, Subsection 2.2 summarizes the main findings concerning the generation of confidence measures for existing spam filtering techniques.

2.1 SPAMHUNTING System

In [12] we introduced SPAMHUNTING, a new instance-based reasoning system for spam filtering. The main advantage of this model was the use of techniques for tracking concept drift [13] at the early stage of feature selection. In this publication we presented the system architecture, the instance representation model and the main basis of the system operation.

In our SPAMHUNTING system, an Enhanced Instance Retrieval Network (EIRN) is used for indexing the existing knowledge. In [14] we showed that the EIRN memory structure was able to outperform the classification capabilities achieved by using a simple Case Retrieval Network (CRN). For this purpose, we selected the messages of the SpamAssassin[1] corpus in order to execute a 5 stratified fold-cross validation test.

Later on, we worked on several improvements over the initial model. In this context, we studied the effect of relevant issues relative to tokenizing [9], stemming and stopword removal [15] and feature selection [8, 9]. All of these previous research contributions presented comparisons between SPAMHUNTING and other well-known techniques as Naïve Bayes [16], Support Vector Machines (SVM) [17], AdaBoost [18] and previous versions of the ECUE system [5] in different preprocessing and feature selection scenarios. All of these works evidenced the superiority of the SPAMHUNTING system in all the preprocessing and feature selection scenarios defined.

Finally, in [7] we have presented a feature selection improvement in order to boost SPAMHUNTING with the ability of handling concept drift. We have already suggested that concept drift should be kept in mind during both the preprocessing and feature selection stages.

Starting from the above mentioned ideas, we have introduced our novel feature selection technique based on computing the amount of achieved information (AI) by using a certain term. The main contribution of this technique is considering the effects of the passage of time that can be measured by using the difference between the

---

[1] Published and available at http://spamassassin.apache.org/publiccorpus/

number of spam and legitimate messages containing it. We have also considered the length and the frequency of a term w in a message e, as an important issue on spam filtering. Expression (1) shows the AI obtained when a term w is used for representing a message e at the instant t.

$$AI(w,e|t) = P(w \wedge e) \cdot \left[1 - \frac{1}{length(w)}\right] \cdot \left[\frac{|P(w \wedge Spam|t) - P(w \wedge Legitimate|t)|}{P(w \wedge Spam|t) + P(w \wedge Legitimate|t)}\right] \quad (1)$$

where $P(w \wedge e)$ represents the frequency of appearance of the term w in the considered message e, $P(w \wedge Spam \mid t)$ and $P(w \wedge Legitimate \mid t)$ are the frequencies of finding the term w in spam and legitimate instances at time t, respectively, and $length(w)$ measures the number of characters of the term w. If w does not appear in the vocabulary, last part of the equation combining the probabilities of finding it in spam and legitimate messages is assumed as 1.

The feature selection for a given message e, is computed as the smallest set of terms able to include those providing the greatest AI and having an information amount greater than a certain percentage (p) of the total AI retained by all features belonging to the given message e. Expression (2) enunciates this simple idea where $FS(e, t)$ represents the set of selected terms for the message e at the instant t, $AI(w_i, e, t)$ stands for the amount of information when a term w_i is selected (previously showed in Expression (1)) and p denotes the percentage of information selected from each message.

$$FS(e,t) = \left\{ w \in e \middle| \begin{array}{l} \{AI(w_a,e,t) > AI(w_b,e,t) \wedge w_b \in FS(e,t)\} \to w_a \in FS(e) \\[2ex] \nexists x \subset FS(e) \middle| \sum_{w_i \in x} AI(w_i,e,t) > \frac{p}{100} \cdot \sum_{w_i \in e} AI(w_i,e,t) \end{array} \right\} \quad (2)$$

As Expression (2) shows, the feature selection for a given e-mail, $FS(e, t)$, is a set of terms extracted from e that guarantees the following properties: (*i*) contains the most relevant features and (*ii*) the feature selection contains the minimum amount of terms having at least the percentage p of the total AI. We are currently using a value of 60 for the p parameter as this configuration has shown to be effective with different corpus and scenarios [7].

For accessing the stored instances in the knowledge base of the SPAMHUNTING system we use our successful EIRN indexation model [12]. The EIRN network is an efficient structure able to index all the existing messages. It was designed to provide the following features: (*i*) disjoint representation capabilities, (*ii*) weighted feature-instance relationships, (*iii*) easy and efficient algorithms for feature inserting and removal and (*iv*) efficient available message indexing and retrieval.

Assuming the above mentioned ideas, every time a new message arrives, a feature selection process is carried out in order to select its most informative terms. Then, we use the EIRN indexation structure to identify those instances sharing the maximum amount of relevant terms with the target e-mail. When this task has been finished, the retrieval stage is considered accomplished and the most relevant knowledge for the classification of the target e-mail is supposed to be recovered.

The obtained knowledge is used to generate an initial proposed classification for the target message using an Unanimous Voting Strategy (UVS) [19]. Therefore, SPAMHUNTING system labels a target message as spam when all the retrieved instances are also spam. This simple but effective reuse method has been successfully applied in several well-known and relevant research works [5, 7, 8, 9, 12, 14, 15, 19]. In the mean time we have been testing several meta-rules extracted from the e-mail headers to revise the proposed solution and assign a final class to it. Finally, every time an incoming e-mail is classified, it is stored on the knowledge base and indexed by using its most relevant features.

As we previously stated, one of our main research topics is the proposal and development of a complete solution for spam filtering. We believe that the calculation of a quality index for every generated solution is an essential feature for a spam filter. Therefore, we have analysed the main findings on this domain in order to evaluate the possibility of adapting an existing proposal for operating in conjunction with SPAMHUNTING or developing a new and more suitable solution. Subsection 2.2 presents a summary of the most relevant research work carried out in this area and the primary conclusions extracted from them.

2.2 Previous Work on Estimating Classification Accuracy

Some current techniques such as Naïve or Flexible Bayes [16] provide a natural mechanism for computing a confidence level estimation of the generated solution. Their outcome represents a probability estimation of the target message being spam taking into consideration its terms. Therefore, if the computed probability of a message being spam is near to 1, then the probability of an error in the filter is very small. On the other hand, if the probability of a message being spam is near to 0.5, then the classifier is not sure about its decision.

The SVM algorithm, which is based on creating a hyperplane able to lineally separate the spam and legitimate classes, can use the distance between the hyperplane and the target message as an estimation for the confidence of the solution. The most difficult task for a SVM model is the classification of a message being near the hyperplane, while e-mails clearly positioned in the spam and legitimate areas can be easily classified with a high security level.

From another point of view, AdaBoost technique works using a mixture of the results achieved from several weak learners. This combination is often carried out by applying voting strategies. Therefore, the amount of spam votes can be easily used as a confidence level for the target solution. Moreover, if a value in [0, 1] is needed as model outcome, the spam vote quantity can be normalized. A spam vote amount near to the number of classifiers means a reliable solution, but if the amount of spam votes is similar to the number of legitimate ones, the solution has a lower confidence level.

Unfortunately, the above mentioned strategies are not applicable on the CBR systems domain [11]. Moreover, other well-known spam filtering techniques such us Chung-Kwey [20], ECUE or SPAMHUNTING do not provide a natural way for computing this quality estimation rate. In fact, in [11] an explicit work on estimating the classification accuracy for ECUE was presented. In this work, a revision over the k Nearest

Neighbours (k-NN) confidence measures was carried out including: (*i*) Average NUN index, (*ii*) Similarity Ratio, (*iii*) Similarity Ratio within K, (*iv*) Sum of NN Similarities and (*v*) Average NN Similarity. These measures are computed by using the following distance criterions: (*i*) distance between a case and its nearest neighbours or $NN_i(t)$ (*ii*) distance between the target case t and its nearest like neighbours or $NLN_i(t)$ and (*iii*) distance between a case and its nearest unlike neighbours or $NUN_i(t)$.

As the main contribution of [11], the Aggregated Confidence Measure (ACM) is introduced. This measure is based on assigning confidence to the final classification if any of the above mentioned individual measures indicates confidence.

Despite the complexity of the metric, results showed in [11] are very promising and clearly evidence the benefits of using it over other well-known techniques such as Naïve Bayes. Nevertheless, we think that similarity is not enough for generating an accurate quality index. We believe that the classification quality index assigned to an incoming e-mail should be computed keeping in mind the amount of relevant information available for classifying this target message.

Summarizing these ideas, we have started our research work about how to improve the quality rate estimation, assuming that the following information is valuable: (*i*) the similarity among the retrieved cases (the recovered knowledge is relevant) and (*ii*) the existence of a significant amount of knowledge that clearly shows that a message has been successfully classified. With these background ideas in mind, we have defined an innovative confidence measure that is exposed in Section 3.

3   Defining a Relevant Information Amount Rate

In this section we introduce our successful quality rate estimation technique. As it has been previously stated, it is based on the use of relevance and amount of information estimations for computing a quality index for each generated classification.

We consider that the quality estimation for a given solution s related with a target message e is basically an evaluation of the suitability of the available information for correctly classifying e. As only retrieved instances are used to compute the classification for a target message, they should be exclusively considered for computing the quality index for the solution.

The most important issue in our SPAMHUNTING system is the role of the selected relevant terms for each instance. These terms are used both for indexing instances in our EIRN structure and for precisely representing the target message from two different points of view: (*i*) the relevance of the meaning of each term and the implication of this term in the global sense of the message and (*ii*) the usefulness of this term for accurately filtering in the present semantic context (due to the effects of concept drift) [7].

Those relevant terms selected when using our feature selection technique are considered as the basis for our proposal. A retrieved instance k_r^j is relevant for computing the solution of a target instance k_o if most of its relevant features are present in k_r^j. Otherwise, the quality of the generated solution will be very poor. We compute the quality of each generated solution by using the set of retrieved instances K_r for a given instance k_o by means of Expression (3). If no instances are fetched from the

SPAMHUNTING memory base during the retrieval stage, the legitimate class is assigned to the given instance k_o with a confidence ratio value of 0.

$$q(K_r, k_o) = \frac{\sum_{k_r^j \in K_r} card\left(\left\{terms\left(k_r^j\right) \cap relterms\left(k_o\right)\right\}\right)}{card\left(K_r\right) \cdot card\left(relterms\left(k_o\right)\right)} \tag{3}$$

where $card\left(\left\{terms\left(k_r^j\right) \cap relterms\left(k_o\right)\right\}\right)$ represents the number of features that are considered relevant in k_o and are also present in the instance k_r^j from K_r, $card(K_r)$ stands for the number of retrieved instances and $card\left(relterms\left(k_o\right)\right)$ symbolizes the number of features that have been selected as relevant for the target instance k_o.

As we can see from Expression (3), if the information used to construct a solution for a given message is relevant, then the computed solution will be excellent. In order to confirm whether the retrieved instances are relevant or not, we check for the presence of relevant terms belonging to the target message and the recovered instances.

The proposed technique and the ACM measures present an important advantage over other approaches because the classification of the target message and its quality can be concurrently computed. This feature can be successfully used in order to take advantage of the current multi-core processors.

Despite we are convinced about the performance of the introduced approach, we need to establish a procedure to check the suitability of the generated quality index. Next section introduces the benchmark set-up in order to estimate whether a final user will take advantage of applying the proposed quality ratio.

4 Experimental Setup Configuration

In this section we present a new technique for testing whether a quality ratio measure can be used for effectively improve the performance of our spam filter. Subsection 4.1 discusses the proposed benchmark procedure while Subsection 4.2 describes the training and testing corpus, the preprocessing techniques applied to them, the selected metrics and some configuration details for the SPAMHUNTING system.

4.1 Testing Procedure

This subsection introduces the procedure used for testing the suitability of the proposed quality index. Due to its simplicity and generic formulation it can be also used for testing the usefulness of other available quality index. The designed benchmark is based on using Receiver Operating Characteristic (ROC) curves [21]. They are a suitable tool for measuring the diagnostic performance of a test or its ability to discriminate between two kinds of classes [22], where the area under the ROC curve represents the performance of the classifier [23].

ROC curves are capable of showing the sensitivity of a filter as a function of the false positive error rate by means of using different cut values. Every time a message is received by a filter, it is able to analyze it and compute a numeric value, Z, useful for distinguishing between spam and legitimate classes. AdaBosst, Random Forests and SPAMHUNTING systems use a normalized amount of spam votes in order to assign a value to Z, whereas Bayesian approaches could use the probability of a message being legitimate. ROC curves can be used to check whether the computed Z value (filter classification) is predictive for distinguishing between spam and legitimate e-mails by using specific cut values.

If a model generates a value Z for a message m lower than a given cut value, we assume that the test is negative and assign the legitimate class for this message. Otherwise, the test result is positive and the spam class is assigned. A ROC curve is constructed by representing points (X_{cut}, Y_{cut}) in a two-dimensional coordinates graph for each cut value in the interval $[min(Z), max(Z)]$. The values X_{cut} and Y_{cut} are, in that order, the false positive rate (1-*specificity*) and the true negative rate (*sensitivity*) and can be computed by means of Expression (4).

$$X_{cut} = 1 - \frac{tn_{cut}}{fp_{cut} + tn_{cut}} \qquad Y_{cut} = \frac{tp_{cut}}{tp_{cut} + fn_{cut}} \qquad (4)$$

where for a given point (cut), tn_{cut}, tp_{cut}, fp_{cut} and fn_{cut} represent the amount of true negatives, true positives, false positives and false negatives, respectively.

In this work we use a version of our previous SPAMHUNTING system able to compute a value Z (useful for distinguish between legitimate and spam messages) and a quality estimation Q for the Z value (the proposed quality metric). A quality estimation Z will be useful for a final user if there is a function F, able to combine Z and Q in a form that its outcome is better in distinguishing spam and legitimate messages than Z.

As it has been previously mentioned, we will use the area under the ROC curve in order to compare the results computed using a function F and those achieved by SPAMHUNTING (Z). In order to compare behaviour of both methods we can compute the significance level for the hypothesis that the difference between the two areas under the ROC curves is zero [24], assuming that the z value showed in Expression (5) follows a Gaussian (0, 1) distribution shape.

$$z = \frac{(A_Z - A_F)}{\sqrt{EE(A_Z) + EE(A_F)}} \qquad (5)$$

where $EE(A_Z)$ and $EE(A_F)$ represent the standard error of the area computed for the Z and F ROC curves, while A_Z and A_F symbolize the are under the Z and F ROC curves.

Then, we can compare the effects of sensitivity and specificity measures for the best cut point of the ROC curves for F and Z. We can also compare the positive and negative likelihood ratios (+*LR* and –*LR*, respectively) achieved in this cut point in order to evaluate the amount of information provided by F and Z keeping in mind the information that is present before their calculation (the probability of spam and legitimate messages).

If Z presents a higher +*LR* value than F, then a positive result using Z is more effective than a positive result using F in order to confirm that a message is spam. Moreover, if Z achieves a value for –*LR* more close to 1 than F, then a negative result using F is more effective than a negative result using Z for confirming the hypothesis of a legitimate message. We should also compare the percentages of false positives, false negatives and correct classifications over the whole corpus, using the best criterion identified in the ROC analysis in order to manually check if the results achieved by using F are better than those obtained with Z.

Finally, we can use the test performance index δ introduced in [25] for comparing the behaviour of F and Z by means of Expression (6).

$$\delta = \sqrt{\frac{3}{\pi} \cdot \left(LN \frac{sen}{1-sen} + LN \frac{esp}{1-esp} \right)} \cong \sqrt{\frac{3}{\pi} \cdot LN \frac{+LR}{-LR}} \tag{6}$$

where sen and esp represent the sensitivity and specificity, respectively, and $+LR$ and $-LR$ stand for the positive and negative likelihood ratios.

The background idea behind the previous presented test performance is that a method obtaining a δ value near to 1 is not valid, while a method achieving a value near to 3 is considered to present good performance. Finally, if F presents a good value for δ and it is greater than the obtained by Z, then we confirm that the use of a quality index is adequate.

4.2 Corpus Selection, Preprocessing Tasks and Setup Model Configuration

In this section we discuss some configuration issues about the experimentation carried out including the corpus selection, tokenizing issues, preprocessing techniques used and miscellaneous setup details on our SPAMHUNTING system.

Despite the existence of many publicly available corpuses, some of them can not be used because they are distributed after a previous feature selection process (i.e., SpamBase[2]) or they contain only spam messages (i.e., DivMod[3], Junk-Email[4], Paul Judge message collection[5], Grant Taylor corpus[6] and Bruce Guenter[7] spam archive). This situation has motivated the choice of the public SpamAssassin and Ling-Spam[8] corpus.

Message tokenizing has been completed using only blanks (spaces, tabs and carriage return chars) as separators. This tokenizing method has been used in previous works in spam filtering obtaining successful results [9]. According to the findings of a previous work in preprocessing techniques [15], we have only applied a stopword removal process for the selected corpus. Finally, in order to increase the confidence level of the achieved results, all the experiments have been carried out using a 10-fold stratified cross-validation [26].

In order to configure our SPAMHUNTING system we have selected a value of 60 for the p parameter as it has shown to be a good election [7]. Once we have established the methodology and configuration issues relative to the experiments, we show in the next section the achieved results and some primarily conclusions.

---

[2] Available at http://www.ics.uci.edu/~mlearn/MLRepository.html
[3] Previously available at http://www.divmod.org/cvs/corpus/spam/
[4] Available at http://clg.wlv.ac.uk/projects/junk-email/corpus-no-duplications.tar.gz
[5] Previously available at http://www.spamarchive.org
[6] Previously available at http://www2.picante.com:81/~gtaylor/download/spam.tar.gz
[7] Available at http://untroubled.org/spam/
[8] Available at http://www.aueb.gr/users/ion/data/lingspam_public.tar.gz

5 Experimental Results and Evaluation

This section presents the results achieved by using the benchmark methodology and configuration details showed in Section 4. As we previously stated, the main objective is to find a function F combining the quality result Q and the model result Z able to go beyond the performance of Z. For this purpose, we have selected the function F showed in Expression (7) and executed the experiments following the benchmark procedure in order to test the suitability of the proposed Q quality index.

$$F = \begin{cases} \dfrac{Z-Q+2}{4} \textit{if } Z < 0.15 \\[3mm] \dfrac{Z+Q+2}{4} \textit{if } Z > 0.15 \end{cases} \qquad (7)$$

First of all, we have used the SpamAssassin corpus in order to complete a ROC analysis. Figure 1 shows a comparative ROC graph for the SpamAssassin corpus using Z as the normalized amount of spam votes and F as defined above.

Figure 1 clearly shows that F gets better performance than Z. The null hypothesis about the equality of areas under the F and Z ROC curves must be discarded since the p-value for the statistical test is lower than 0.01 ($p<0.001$). Therefore we can assert that from a statistical point of view, there is a very significant difference between F and Z measures. Consequently, the proposed quality measure can be used for improving the solution generated by using our SPAMHUNTING filter.

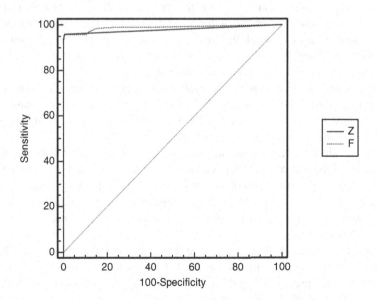

Fig. 1. ROC curve for the SpamAssassin corpus using Z and F

In order to provide a more detailed analysis, we have computed the area under the ROC curve, the standard error and the 95% confidence interval. Moreover, we have measured the sensitivity, specificity, the positive likelihood ratio, the negative likelihood ratio, percentages of false positives (FP%), false negatives (FN%) and correct classifications (OK%) over the whole corpus and the δ index for the best cut values of F and Z. These measures have been included in Table 1.

Table 1. ROC Analysis for the SpamAssassin corpus

	Z	F
Area under ROC	0.98	0.99
Standard error	0.002	0.002
95% Confidence Interval	0.98 – 0.98	0.99 – 0.99
Best cut value	0.0373	0.5
Sensitivity / Specificity	96.01 / 99.25	95.72 / 99.47
+LR / -LR	128.34 / 0.04	179.70 / 0.04
OK% / FP% / FN%	98.41 / 0.57 / 1.02	98.52 / 0.39 / 1.09
δ index	2.81	2.87

From the sensitivity values showed in Table 1 we can conclude that more spam messages can be detected if the quality ratio is not used. Nevertheless, we can also see from Table 1 that specificity measure for Z are lower than F. Therefore, the amount of false positives can be reduced by using the quality ratio index.

Analyzing the positive and negative likelihood ratios from Table 1 we can see that the use of F presents higher values for its ROC curve. Conceptually, this means that the F criterion has more reliability than the Z measure for detecting a spam message. Moreover, the Z and F measures show the same performance in order to detect legitimate messages since their $-LR$ measures are equal.

If we focus our attention to the evaluation of correct classifications and error percentages from Table 1, we can find that F generates a greater amount of good decisions and the smallest amount of false positive errors. This finding supports the suitability of the proposed quality measure metric.

Finally, values for test performance index δ are also showed in Table 1 confirming the results of the rest of measures. Therefore, as we have found a function F able to combine the results of the SPAMHUNTING classifier with the quality index improving the final solution, we can declare that the usage of the proposed quality index is suitable for complementing the solution generated by our previous successful SPAMHUNTING system.

In order to guarantee the validity of our proposed quality measure Q, we have also repeated the performance test using another well-known corpus, Ling-Spam. The function F is the previously used function for the SpamAssassin corpus (see Expression (7)). First of all, we have plotted the ROC curves for F and Z. The resultant graph is showed in Figure 2.

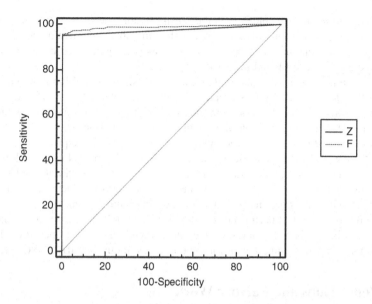

Fig. 2. ROC curve for the Ling-Spam corpus using Z and F

As we can realize from Figure 2, the area under the generated ROC curve using F is greater than the one computed with Z. We have executed a statistical test assuming that the area under Z is equal than the area under F as null hypothesis. As the computed p-value is lower than 0.05 ($p=0.01$), the null hypothesis must be discarded and we can state that there are statistically significant differences between Z and F measures.

In order to achieve more relevant conclusions, we have computed the area under the ROC curve, the standard error and the 95% confidence interval. Considering the best cut values for Z and F, we have also calculated the sensitivity, specificity, the positive likelihood ratio, the negative likelihood ratio, percentages of false positives, false negatives and correct classifications over the whole corpus and the δ index. All of these measures are showed in Table 2.

Table 2. ROC Analysis for the Ling-Spam corpus

	Z	F
Area under ROC	0.97	0.99
Standard error	0.01	0.00
95% Confidence Interval	0.97 – 0.98	0.98 – 0.99
Best cut value	0.01	0.48
Sensitivity / Specificity	95.01 / 99.71	95.43 / 99.79
+LR / -LR	327.38 / 0.05	459.95 / 0.05
OK% / FP% / FN%	98.93 / 0.24 / 0.83	99.03 / 0.21 / 0.76
δ index	2.93	2.99

As we can see from Table 2, both the sensitivity and the specificity achieved by the F function in the best cut value are greater than the obtained when using Z. From this finding we can conclude that the use of the proposed quality metric can contribute to reduce the amount of FP and FN errors.

From the positive and negative likelihood ratios showed in Table 2, we can see that the $+LR$ ratio achieved by F is greater than the one obtained by Z. This fact denotes that a positive value for the combination of the quality and the solution of SPAMHUNTING is more reliable than using only the solution generated by the filter. Moreover, the $-LR$ ratios achieved by the analyzed metrics are equal.

As we can realize from Table 2, the percentage of FP and FN errors is lower when the quality ratio is used. This fact confirms the findings of sensitivity and specificity measures. Moreover, as a direct consequence of the error reduction, the amount of correct classifications gets improved when the F measure is used.

Finally, from the test performance index δ showed in Table 2, we can realize that F measure is better than Z. Therefore, we can conclude that the proposed quality ratio represents a valuable complement for the outcomes of our SPAMHUNTING system.

6 Conclusions and Further Work

This paper presents a quality metric for complementing the classifications generated by our previous successful spam filtering system called SPAMHUNTING. In order to test our proposal, we have designed a benchmark protocol for assessing accuracy metrics based on ROC analysis. Using this test over two publicly available corpuses, we have shown the convenience of the proposed technique and its background behaviour.

The proposed technique is based on the study of the relevancy and amount of knowledge retrieved by a spam filter. Since we have shown the suitability of the quality estimation technique, we have also demonstrated that the relevancy and amount of retrieved knowledge are reliable data for computing the quality of the generated classification.

Although the amount of FP errors generated by SPAMHUNTING is low [7], the experimental results show that the proposed measure is able to reduce even more the number of FP errors. Therefore the *relevant information amount rate* is an excellent complementary metric for the computed classification of our SPAMHUNTING system.

The corpuses used to carry out the experiments have several semantic differences. While Ling-Spam contains only legitimate messages talking about linguistic issues, the SpamAssassin corpus comprises a wide variety of subject matter areas. The best cut values computed by the measures F and Z are similar when the underground testing corpus changes. This means that our SPAMHUNTING system is quite independent of the underlying corpus used. This hypothesis is confirmed because the percentage results achieved by using these different corpuses are similar.

One of the most relevant possibilities guaranteed for this work is the ability of concurrently computing the class for a message and the accuracy estimation for the solution. This fact makes possible to take advantage of the multi-core processors and multi-processor systems currently available at a low cost.

From the perspective of the future work, we think that the incorporation of semantic knowledge is a solution more and more promising. Moreover, previous work on text mining has introduced practical methods for achieving semantic information from publicly available resources such as the well-known free encyclopaedia *Wikipedia* [27, 28]. We believe in the relevance of these works and we think they will be useful for the integration of semantic information in our SPAMHUNTING filtering system.

References

1. Sharp Rock Technologies LTD: Dialer.net Mobile Internet Access (2000), http://mobile.dialer.net/
2. Zennstrm, N., Friis, J.: Skype (2003), http://www.skype.com
3. Oard, D.V.: The state of the art in text filtering. User Modeling and Use-Adapted Interaction 7, 141–178 (1997)
4. Androutsopoulos, I., Palioureas, G., Michelakis, E.: Learning to Filter Unsolicited Commercial E-Mail. Technical report TR-2004-2. NCSR: National Centre for Scientific Research "Demokritos" (2004)
5. Delany, S.J., Cunningham, P., Coyle, L.: An Assessment of Case-Base Reasoning for Spam Filtering. In: Proc. of the 15th Irish Conference on Artificial Intelligence and Cognitive Science, pp. 9–18 (2004)
6. Delany, S.J., Cunningham, P., Smyth, B.: ECUE: A Spam Filter that Uses Machine Learning to Track Concept Drift. In: Proc. of the 17th European Conference on Artificial Intelligence, pp. 627–631 (2006)
7. Méndez, J.R., Fdez-Riverola, F., Díaz, F., Iglesias, E.L., Corchado, J.M.: Tracking Concept Drift at Feature Selection Stage in SpamHunting: an Anti-Spam Instance-Based Reasoning System. In: Roth-Berghofer, T.R., Göker, M.H., Güvenir, H.A. (eds.) ECCBR 2006. LNCS (LNAI), vol. 4106, pp. 504–518. Springer, Heidelberg (2006)
8. Méndez, J.R., Fdez-Riverola, F., Iglesias, E.L., Díaz, F., Corchado, J.M.: A Comparative Performance Study of Feature Selection Methods for the Anti-Spam Filtering Domain. In: Proc. of the 6th Industrial Conference on Data Mining, pp. 106–120 (2006)
9. Méndez, J.R., Iglesias, E.L., Fdez-Riverola, F., Díaz, F., Corchado, J.M.: Tokenising, Stemming and Stopword Removal on the Spam Filtering Domain. In: Marín, R., Onaindía, E., Bugarín, A., Santos, J. (eds.) CAEPIA 2005. LNCS (LNAI), vol. 4177, pp. 449–458. Springer, Heidelberg (2006)
10. Fdez-Riverola, F., Iglesias, E.L., Díaz, F., Méndez, J.R., Corchado, J.M.: Applying Lazy Learning Algorithms to Tackle Concept Drift in Spam Filtering. Expert Systems With Applications 33(1), 36–48 (2007)
11. Delany, S.J., Cunningham, P., Doyle, D., Zamolotskikh, A.: Generating Estimates of Classification Confidence for A Case-Based Spam Filter. In: Muñoz-Ávila, H., Ricci, F. (eds.) ICCBR 2005. LNCS (LNAI), vol. 3620, pp. 177–190. Springer, Heidelberg (2005)
12. Fdez-Riverola, F., Iglesias, E. L., Díaz, F., Méndez, J. R., Corchado, J. M.: SpamHunting: An Instance-Based Reasoning System for Spam Labeling and Filtering. Decision Support Systems (in press) (2007)
13. Widmer, G., Kubat, M.: Learning in the Presence of Concept Drift and Hidden Contexts. Machine Learning 23(1), 69–101 (1996)
14. Fdez-Riverola, F., Méndez, J.R., Iglesias, E.L., Díaz, F.: Representación Flexible de E-mails para la Construcción de Filtros Anti-Spam: un caso práctico. In: Proc. of the first Spanish Conference on Computer Science, pp. 109–116 (2005)

15. Méndez, J.R., Iglesias, E.L., Fdez-Riverola, F., Díaz, F., Corchado, J.M.: A Comparative Impact Study of Corpus Preprocessing for the Construction of Anti-Spam Filtering Software. In: Proc. of the 10th Conference of the Spanish Association for the Artificial Intelligence, pp. 29–38 (2005)

16. John, G.H., Langley, P.: Estimating Continuous Distributions in Bayes Classifiers. In: Proc. of the 11th Conference on Uncertainty in Artificial Intelligence, pp. 338–345 (1995)

17. Vapnik, V.: The Nature of Statistical Learning Theory. 2nd Ed. Statistics for Engineering and Information Science (1999)

18. Carreras, X., Márquez, L.: Boosting Trees for Anti-Spam e-Mail Filtering. In: Proc. of the 4th International Conference on Recent Advances in Natural Language Processing, pp. 58–64 (2001)

19. Cunningham, P., Nowlan, N., Delany, S.J., Haahr, M.: A Case-Based Approach to Spam Filtering that Can Track Concept Drift. In: Ashley, K.D., Bridge, D.G. (eds.) ICCBR 2003. LNCS, vol. 2689, Springer, Heidelberg (2003)

20. Rigoutsos, I., Huynh, T.: Chung-Kwei: a Pattern-discovery-based System for the Automatic Identification of Unsolicited E-mail Messages. In: Proc. of the First Conference on Email and Anti-Spam (2004)

21. Egan, J.P.: Signal Detection Theory and ROC Analysis. Academic Press, New York (1975)

22. Metz, C.E.: Basic principles of ROC analysis. Seminars in Nuclear Medicine 8, 283–298 (1978)

23. Zweig, M.H., Campbell, G.: Receiver-operating characteristic (ROC) plots: a fundamental evaluation tool in clinical medicine. Clinical Chemistry 39, 561–577 (1993)

24. Griner, P.F., Mayewski, R.J., Mushlin, A.I., Greenland, P.: Selection and interpretation of diagnostic tests and procedures. Annals of Internal Medicine 94, 555–600 (1981)

25. Hasselband, V., Hedges, L.: Meta-analysis of diagnostics test. Psychological Bulletin 117, 167–178 (1995)

26. Kohavi, R.: A study of cross-validation and bootstrap for accuracy estimation and model selection. In: Proc. of the 14th International Joint Conference on Artificial Intelligence, pp. 1137–1143 (1995)

27. Gabrilovich, E., Markovitch, S.: Computing Semantic Relatedness using Wikipedia-based Explicit Semantic Analysis. In: Proc. of the 20th International Joint Conference on Artificial Intelligence, pp. 1606–1611 (2007)

28. Strube, M., Ponzetto, P.: WikiRelate! Computing Semantic Relatedness using Wikipedia. In: Proc. of the 22th American Association for Artificial Intelligence Conference (2006)

Intelligent Guidance and Suggestions Using Case-Based Planning

Javier Bajo[1], Juan Manuel Corchado[2], and Sara Rodríguez[2]

[1] Universidad Pontificia de Salamanca
Compañía 5, 37002, Salamanca, Spain
jbajope@upsa.es
[2] Departamento Informática y Automática
Universidad de Salamanca
Plaza de la Merced s/n, 37008, Salamanca, Spain
{corchado,srg}@usal.es

Abstract. This paper presents a multiagent system that provides guidance on leisure facilities and suggestions for shopping in malls. This paper presents a deliberative agent which incorporates a case based planner that provides suggestions in execution time. This agent is described together with its guidance and suggestion mechanism. The multiagent system has been tested, and the results obtained are presented in this paper.

Keywords: Planning; Learning; Shopping mall multiagent system; RFID.

1 Introduction

A shopping centre is a dynamic environment, in which shops change, promotions appear and disappear continuously, etc. This paper presents a multiagent system, developed for guiding and advising users in Shopping Centres (also known as shopping malls). The proposed system, SHOpping MulitAgent System (SHOMAS), helps users to identify a shopping or leisure plan as well as to identify other users within a given shopping mall. SHOMAS is an open wireless multiagent system and users require a wireless device (mobile or PDA) to download their own agent and to interact with the multiagent system. The user agents interact directly with a deliberative Case-Based Planning - Beliefes Desires Intentions (CBP-BDI) guiding agent which uses a case-based reasoning (CBR) [1], [21] architecture, that allows it to respond to events, to take the initiative according to its goals, to communicate with other agents, to interact with users, and to make use of past experiences to find the best plans to achieve goals. Moreover, SHOMAS incorporates Radio Frequency Identification (RFID) [28] technology to ascertain users' location in order to provide security and to optimize their time in the mall.

The core of SHOMAS is the CBP-BDI guiding agent. This particular agent uses a special type of CBR systems which we call Case-Base Planning (CBP) [12] system, specially designed for planning construction. CBP-BDI agent is a deliberative agent that works at a high level with the concepts of Believe, Desire, Intention (BDI) [7].

R.O. Weber and M.M. Richter (Eds.): ICCBR 2007, LNAI 4626, pp. 389–403, 2007.

The CBP-BDI agent has learning and adaptation capabilities, which facilitate its work in dynamic environments. A CBP-BDI agent is therefore a particular type of CBR-BDI agent [10], which uses case-based reasoning as a reasoning mechanism, which allows it to learn from initial knowledge, to interact autonomously with the environment as well as with users and other agents within the system, and to have a large capacity for adaptation to the needs of its surroundings.

This paper, then, presents a distributed architecture whose main characteristics are the use of a CBP-BDI guiding agent, wireless agents and RFID technology. The aim of this work is to obtain a model for recommending plans in dynamic environments. The proposal presented has been used to develop a guiding system for the users of a shopping mall that helps them to identify bargains, offers and leisure activities. An open wireless system has been developed, which is capable of incorporating agents that can provide useful guidance and advice services to the users not only in a shopping centre, but also in any other similar environment such as the labour market, educational system, medical care, etc. Users (clients in the mall) are able to gain access to information on shops and sales and on leisure time activities (entertainment, events, attractions, etc) by using their mobile phone or PDA. Mechanisms for route planning when a user wants to spend time in the mall are also available. Moreover, it provides a tool for advertising personalized offers (a shop owner will be able to publicise his offers to the shopping mall users), and a communication system between management, the commercial sector or shoppers.

SHOMAS has been tested in the Tormes mall in Salamanca (Spain) with interesting results. The system performance has been positive, after a period of technical adaptation, the user response has also been positive, and some aspects of the mall's management have improved substantially. The shops owners were the most reticent to using the system for several reasons as explained in the conclusions. Section two presents related work about planning, section three presents the SHOMAS wireless multiagent system, then section four introduces the CBP-BDI planning Agent and finally, the system is evaluated and the conclusions discussed.

2   Related Work

A shopping centre is a cluster of independent shops, planned and developed by one or several entities, with a common objective. As such, a shopping mall can be seen as a large dynamic problem, whose administration depends on the variability of the products, users, opinions, etc. [6]. The unstoppable advance of technology implies the need for alternatives to traditional commercial strategies. Between the new strategies it is worth mentioning the development of different E-Commerce systems [15], [22], [27]. E-Commerce allows users to shop through the Internet, receive personalized promotions or request guidance. The incorporation of artificial intelligence techniques has led to further studies and to the modelling of the mall problem in terms of agents and multi-agent systems [13], [14], [16], [23], [24]. These authors focus on the shopping problem and on the suggestions that can be made to users. The growing use of handheld devices in recent years has led to new necessities as well as to a great opportunity to extend traditional commerce techniques and apply new techniques.

These new devices facilitate the use of new interaction techniques, for instance, some systems focus on facilitating users with guidance or location systems [11], [13], [30] by means of their wireless devices. Bohnenberger *et al.* [6] present a decision-theoretic location-aware shopping guide in a shopping mall as a kind of virtual shop assistant. SHOMAS uses the CBP-BDI mechanism for replanning in execution time and incorporates RFID technology to automatically asses a user's location. Furthermore SHOMAS uses past experiences to take new decisions, which increases the personalization and adaptation capabilities of the system as well as the success of the guidance.

The generation of a new plan is made from plans or fragments of plans that have been previously generated [21], [25], [29]. The different planners based on cases differ from each other in the way that they represent and store the cases and the way in which they execute the CBP cycle (in algorithms executed in each of its stages). The case-based planner proposed within the framework of this article incorporates an adaptation algorithm that allows dynamic replanning in execution time. This fact means that our system is unique in terms of the response that it offers to changes in the environment during the execution of the plan.

The applications of the planning agents are increasingly prolific, especially in fields such as the web, games, tourism applications etc. Case-based Tactician (CAT) introduces a case-based planner with a plan retrieval algorithm that, by using three key sources of domain knowledge, removes the assumption of a static opponent [2]. In [25] it is ïdescribed an application of hierarchical case-based planning that involves reasoning in the context of real-time strategy games. Multiagent planning in the web (MAPWeb) presents a multiagent system for cooperative work among different intelligent software agents whose main goal is to solve user planning problems using the information stored in the Web [9]. The RETSINA agent architecture presents a planner module for every task agent, which interleaves HTN planning and process execution [19]. Furthermore [18] ïdescribe a prototype in which a conversational case-based reasoner, NaCoDAE, was agentified and inserted in the RETSINA multi-agent system. Some case-based planners have been used in tourism applications, such as the one presented by Corchado [11] in order to improve the traditional tourism techniques. Users of the case-based planner tourism application noticed the utility of the dynamic replanning, since it is quite usual for them change opinions/objectives in the middle of a plan. Another application field is intelligent guidance and suggestions in leisure or shopping. ïBohnenberger *et al.* [6] propose the use of decision-theoretic planning, but their system can't provide the option of replanning in execution time. SHOMAS uses the CBP-BDI mechanism for replanning in execution time and incorporates RFID technology to automatically asses a user's location. Furthermore SHOMAS uses past experiences to take new decisions, which increases the personalization and adaptation capabilities of the system as well as the success of the guidance. The CBP-BDI mechanisms enables the system to offer efficient plans in execution time that make it possible to choose optimum routes, and to react to changes that may be produced in the execution of the plan, responding with a dynamic replanning that avoids "retracing one's steps".

3 SHOMAS Architecture

The architecture of the SHOMAS multiagent systems incorporates "lightweight" agents that can reside in mobile devices, such as notebooks, phones or, PDAs [6], and therefore support wireless communication (Wi-Fi, Bluetooth) which facilitates the portability to a wide range of devices. These user agents make it possible for a user to interact with the MAS in a very simple way, downloading and installing a personal agent in his mobile phone or PDA. The system also incorporates one agent for each shop in the shopping mall. These agents can calculate the optimal promotions (those of greater sales success) and services at a given moment by considering the retails data and the user profiles. The core of the MAS is a guiding agent in charge of the generation of plans (routes) in response to a user's request, looking for the best shopping or leisure time alternatives. The agent has to take into account the user profile, the maximum amount of money that the user wants to spend and the time available. The generation of routes must be independent of the shopping mall management, in the sense that it is not appropriate to use the same knowledge base (or all the knowledge) controlled by the management. Only the knowledge corresponding to the offers and promotions at the moment of guidance should be used. Otherwise the user will be directed to the objectives of the shopping mall management. As can be seen in Figure 1 there are three types of agents in SHOMAS: the CBP-BDI guiding agent, Shop agents situated in each shop and User agents situated in the user mobile device. Each User agent communicates to the nearest shops and can communicate to the CBP-BDI agent. Shop agents communicate to CBP-BDI agent and User agents.

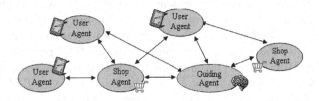

Fig. 1. SHOMAS: CBP-BDI agent, Shop agents and User agents

The User Agent plays three roles, the Communicator role manages all the communications of a user; the Finder role looks for devices nearby, trying to identify other users with similar preferences or locate a given user (in this case the use of RFID technology is fundamental); finally the Profile Manager role obtains a user profile.

The Shop agent plays two roles, the Store Operator is in charge of managing the store (operations on stored products database), and, moreover, monitors product shortages, in order to prevent under-supply; and the Promotions Manager role controls the retails in each shop, as well as the promotions that every shop is offering to its clients.

The CBP-BDI guiding agent plays four roles which are divided into seven capabilities: the Clients Manager role deals with the management of user profiles and controls the connected users at any given moment; the Analyst role carries out periodic evaluations on retails, promotions and surveys data trying to provide a good quality of service; the Incidents Manager role manages incidents in the mall, such as sending suggestions (user changes preferences, or a change affecting the time or economical restrictions happens), or solving a wide range of problems (security, alerts, lost children); the Planner role is the most important role in our system. The Planner creates a route printing the most suitable shops, promotions or events to the user profile and available resources at one particular moment. As can be seen in Figure 2, the Planner role is implemented through three capabilities (Update, KBase and VCBP – Variational CBP –), that make up the Case-based planning cycle explained in detail in section four of this paper. The use of RFID technology allows the CBP-BDI agent to locate persons in the mall for security or strategic reasons. Where there is a safety concern - as with young children or the elderly, for example - microchips or tags can be used (Sokymat ID Band Unique Q5 with a chip Hitag S 256) mounted on bracelets worn on the wrist or ankle [28]. These chips or transponders use a 125 kHz signal. The door readers (Hitag HT RM401 and mobile WorkAbout Pro RFID) sensors [28], are installed in strategic areas within the mall. Each reader sends a pulse of radio energy to the tags and listen for the tag's response. The signal received from a tag is sent to the CBP-BDI agent in order to be processed.

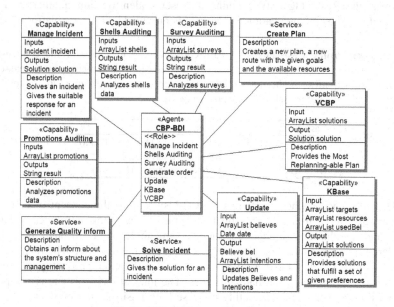

Fig. 2. CBP-BDI agent class diagram

3.1 SHOMAS in Operation

In the MAS presented in this paper the following protocols have been considered: RequestPromotionsData when the CBP-BDI or user (through his User agent) ask about promotions data and a Shop agent sends the response, RequestProductState when the CBP-BDI agent asks for the situation of any products. SolveConsult when a user in the mall interacts with the User agent and makes a query to a Shop agent and receives the response, AlertShortage for a Shop agent to inform the CBP-BDI agent about a product shortage, InformOrderSupplier for a Shop agent to inform the CBP-BDI agent about an order being carried out, InformProductsState when a Shop agent informs the CBP-BDI agent about the state of its products; InformPromotionsState for a shop to send periodic information about promotions to the CBP-BDI agent, SolveIncident for a Shop or User agent to indicate to the CBP-BDI agent that an incident has occurred and to receive the response, SolveGuidance when a user requests guidance from the User agent and the User agent asks the CBP-BDI agent about a plan and receives the response; finally, Notify is used for the CBP-BDI agent to send suggestions to User or Shop agents. For example, when an user asks for a new route, the User agent uses the SolveGuidance protocol. The CBP-BDI agent sends the guidance and keeps receiving the results of each of the subgoals proposed (each of the intermediate states proposed in the plan). If necessary a re-planning will be made.

The interactions have been implemented using a robust wireless LAN. In SHOMAS Wi-Fi and Bluetooth devices coexist together with RFID devices. A secure and authenticated access to the data is provided. The use of different authorisations for users, logins and passwords, and the encryption of messages using a public key infrastructure and SSL (Secure Socket Layer) have already been implemented. Moreover, the RFID tag only contains the user's identification number, and not personal data. The communication mechanism is provided by the Jade platform [4].

Table 1. User Profile Case Fields. A case corresponding to a user profile contains the description of the problem (personal data on the user and information about his purchases or attendance at activities within the commercial centre) and the solution to the problem description (interests of the user, tastes and tendencies)

Case Field	Measurement
PERSONALDATA	User Personal Data (UserData)
RETAILDATA	Retails (RetailsData)
INTEREST	User interests (UserInterest)

The main concept when working with CBR systems is the concept of case. The case structure for a user profile shown in Table 1. The items, attributes and their values and weights are labelled. In our problem, three main attributes have been considered: personal data, retail/leisure time data and interest data. The retail/leisure attribute is composed of business type, business identification, product type, product identification, price, units and date attributes. The interest data attribute is composed of retail time and frequency, monthly expense both business and product, extracted from retail data, and the explicit attributes obtained from questionnaires. Each attribute has a value, noun or adjective, and a weight assigned. Since the number and type of business is extensive, they were classified into leisure time (cinema and recreational), catering (restaurant, fast food and pizza) and public retail (clothes, shoes, computing, supermarket and optical). The products have been also classified, for example the films are divided in action, comedy, terror and drama.

The agent in charge of providing suggestions is a CBP-BDI agent and the case structure for guidance is shown in Table 2. The agent deals with multiple objectives, as shown in Figure 2, derived from the task of coordinating all the shops, user management and planning and optimising routes. The routes and promotions proposed to a user take into account the user profile and his resources (money and time) at the moment that the request for guidance is made. It contains a mall map and an estimation of the time employed walking by the user. The CBP-BDI agent is able to generate routes, analyze retails and promotion data, manage incidents and manage users at the same time. To solve the problem of routes guidance the CBP-BDI agent uses an innovative planning mechanism: the Case Based Planning. CBP provides the agent with capabilities for learning and adaptation to the dynamic environment. Moreover, the CBP-BDI is able to apply a dynamic replanning technique, which allows the agent to change a plan at execution time when an incident happens [21]. The CBP-BDI agent implements the reasoning cycle of the CBP system [12], [21] by means of three capabilities as can be seen in Figure 2: Update, KBase and VCBP (Variational CBP) capabilities. The Update capability implements the retrieve (the cases memory is organized as an efficiency pyramid, and only those plans with at least 4 similar businesses visited in the past, with the same user profile and restriction's limits are retrieved) and retain stages. The KBase capability implements the reuse stage (the optimum solution is sought among the base of solutions proposed in the retrieve stages) and the VCBP capability, the revise stage (system trusts user evaluation). The VCBP capability is also in charge of the dynamic replanning task. The use of the RFID technology enormously facilitates the planning and replanning processes incorporating a dynamic location within SHOMAS. Moreover, the RFID devices allow SHOMAS to provide a voluntary location service for its users.

Table 2. Guidance case fields

Case Field	Measurement
USER	User profile (UserProfile)
MONEY	Money to spend (Money)
TIME	Time (Time)
INIT	User initial location (Location)
PREF	User preferences (Preference)
SOLUTION	Solution and efficiency (Solution)

The platform chosen for the implementation was Jadex [26]. The Jadex agents deal with the concepts of beliefs, goals and plans. A belief can be any type of java object and is stored in the beliefs base. A goal is also a java object that has influence on the agent behaviour. A plan is a java procedure and is executed in order to achieve goals. Jadex has the advantage of allowing programmers to include their own deliberative mechanisms. Moreover it offers all the communication advantages that Jade [4] provides (including the LEAP add-on).

4   CBP-BDI Guiding Agent

The purpose of case-based reasoning (CBR) is to solve new problems by adapting solutions that have been used to solve similar problems in the past [1]. The CBP is a variation of the CBR which is based on the generation of plans from cases. The deliberative agents, proposed in the framework of this investigation, use this concept to gain autonomy and improve their guiding capabilities. The relationship between CBP systems and BDI agents can be established by implementing cases as beliefs, intentions and desires which lead to the resolution of the problem. In a CBP-BDI agent, each state is considered as a belief; the objective to be reached may also be a belief. The intentions are plans of actions that the agent has to carry out in order to achieve its objectives [7], so an intention is an ordered set of actions; each change from state to state is made after carrying out an action (the agent remembers the action carried out in the past, when it was in a specified state, and the subsequent result). A desire is any of the final states reached in the past (if the agent has to deal with a situation, which is similar to one in the past, it will try to achieve a similar result to the one previously obtained). Below, the CBP guiding mechanism, used by the CBP-BDI guiding agent, is presented: Let $E = \{e_0,...,e_n\}$ the set of the possible interesting places to visit and shop at.

$$a_j : \underset{e_i}{E} \quad \rightarrow \quad \underset{a_j(e_i)=e_j}{E} \tag{1}$$

An Agent plan is the name given to a sequence of actions (1) that, from a current state e_0, defines the path of states through which the agent passes in order to offer to the user the better path according to each user's characteristics. Below, in (2), the dynamic relationship between the behaviour of the agent and the changes in the environment is modelled. The behaviour of agent A can be represented by its action function $a_A(t)$ $\forall t$, defined as a correspondence between one moment in time t and the action selected by the agent,

$$Agent\ A = \{a_A(t)\}_{t \in T \subseteq N} \tag{2}$$

From the definition of the action function $a_A(t)$ a new relationship that collects the idea of an agent's action plan (3) can be defined,

$$p_A : \underset{(t,a_A(t))}{TxA} \quad \rightarrow \quad \underset{p_A(t)}{A} \tag{3}$$

in the following way,

$$p_A(t_n) = \sum_{i=1}^{n} a_{iA}(t_i - t_{i-1}) \tag{4}$$

Given the dynamic character that we want to print onto our agent, the continuous extension of the previous expression (4) is proposed as a definition of the agent plan, in other words (5) –

$$p_A(t_n) = \int_0^{t_n} a_A(t)dt \tag{5}$$

The variation of the agent plan $p_A(t)$ will be provoked essentially by: the changes that occur in the environment and that force the initial plan to be modified, and the knowledge from the success and failure of the plans that were used in the past, and which are favoured or punished via learning. O indicates the objectives of the agent and O' are the results achieved by the plan. R is the total resources and R' represents the resources consumed by the agent. The efficiency of the plan (6) is the relationship between the objectives attained and the resources consumed.

$$E_{ff} = \frac{\#(O' \cap O)}{\#R'} \tag{6}$$

Where # means cardinal of a set. The objective is to introduce an architecture for a planning agent that behaves – and selects its actions – by considering the possibility that the changes in the environment block the plans in progress. This agent is called CBP-BDI because it continually searches for the plan that can most easily be re-planned in the event of interruption. Given an initial point e_0, the term planning problem is used to describe the search for a way to reach a final point $e_i \equiv e^* \in E$ that meets a series of requirements. Given a problem E and a plan $p(t)$ the functions Ob and Rc accumulated are constructed from the objectives and costs of the plan (7). For all time points t_i there are two associated variables:

$$Ob(t_i) = \int_{t_i} O(t)dt \qquad Rc(t_i) = \int_{t_i} R(t)dt \tag{7}$$

This allows us to construct a space representing the environment for planning problems as a vectorial hyper dimensional space where each axis represents the accumulative variable associated with each objective and resource. The planning space, defined in this way, conforms to the following properties:

Property 1: The representations of the plans within the planning space are always monotonically growing functions. Given that $Ob(t)$ and $Rc(t)$ are functions defined as positive, function $p(t)$ expressed at these coordinates is constant or growing.

Property 2: In the planning space, the straight lines represent plans of constant efficiency. If the representations of the plans are straight lines, the slope of the function is constant, and coincides with the definition of the efficiency of the plan (8).

$$\frac{d}{dt} p(t) = cte \Leftrightarrow \lim_{\Delta \to 0} \frac{\Delta O(t)}{\Delta R(t)} = cte \tag{8}$$

In an n-dimensional space, the extension of the straight concept line is called a geodesic curve. In this sense, the notion of geodesic plans can be introduced, defined as those that maintain efficiency at a constant throughout their development. This way, only the plans of constant efficiency (geodesic plans) are considered, because they are the ones of minimum risk. In an environment that changes unpredictably, to consider any different plan to the geodesic plan means to accept a certain risk. The agent must search for the plan that determines a solution with a series of restrictions $F(O;R)=0$. In the plans base the plans sought are those that are initially compatible with the problem faced by the agent, with the requirements imposed on the solution according to the desires and in the current state [1]. If all the possible plans $\{p_1,...,p_n\}$ are represented within the planning space, a subset of states that the agent has already attained in the past will be obtained in order to resolve similar problems. With the mesh of points obtained (generally irregular) within the planning space and using interpolation techniques, a working hyperplan $h(x)$ can be obtained. The hyperplan encapsulates the information on the set of restrictions from restored experiences, which, by definition verify that $h(x_j)=p_j$ $j=1,...,n$ and the planning space is the dimension n). From this hyperplan, geodesic plans can be calculated and the variation calculation is then applied. Suppose, for simplicity's sake, a planning space of dimension 3 with coordinates $\{O,R_1,R_2\}$. Between the point e_0 and the objective points f_s $f=\{e_1,..., e_m\}$ and over the interpolation surface $h(x)$, the Euler Theorem [20] guarantees that the expression of the geodesic plans will be obtained by resolving the system of equations in (9), where R_i is the function accumulated R, O is the function of accumulated O and L is the distance function on the hyperplan $h(x)$, $L=\int_h dl$.

In order to obtain all the geodesic plans that, on the surface $h(x)$ and beginning at e_0, allows us to reach any of the points $e^* \in f_s f$, a condition must be imposed on the surroundings: the initial point will be $e_0=(O_0,R_0)$. Once an efficient plan is developed, the plan around it (along its trajectory) is used to create a denser distribution of geodesic plans. The tool that allows us to determine this is called the minimum Jacobi field associated with the solution set. Let $g_0:[0,1]\rightarrow S$ be a geodesic over a surface S. Let $h:[0,1]\ x[-\varepsilon,\varepsilon]\rightarrow S$ be a variation of g_0 so that for each $t \in (-\varepsilon,\varepsilon)$, the set $\{h_t(s)\}_{t\in(-\varepsilon,\varepsilon)}$: $h_t(s)$ for all $t\in(-\varepsilon,\varepsilon)$ are geodesic in S and they begin at $g_0(0)$, in other words, they conform to $h_t(0)=g_0(0)$ for all $t\in(-\varepsilon,\varepsilon)$. The differential limit of the variations is (10).

$$\begin{cases} \dfrac{\partial L}{\partial R_1} - \dfrac{d}{dO}\dfrac{\partial L}{\partial R_1} = 0 \\ \dfrac{\partial L}{\partial R_2} - \dfrac{d}{dO}\dfrac{\partial L}{\partial R_2} = 0 \end{cases} \tag{9}$$

$$\lim_{t\to 0}\{h_t(s)=g_0(s+t)\}=\lim_{t\to 0}\{h(s,t)\}=\frac{\partial g_0}{\partial t}\Big|_{(s,0)}=\frac{dg_0}{ds}\equiv J_{g_0}(s) \tag{10}$$

The term $J_{g0}(s)$ is given to the Jacobi Field of the geodesic g_0 for the set $\{g_n(x)\}_{n\in N}$, and in the same way as the definition has been constructed, it is possible to give a measurement for the distribution of the other geodesics of $\{g_n(x)\}_{n\in N}$ around g_0 throughout the trajectory. Given a set of geodesics, some of them are always g* that, within their environment, have a greater distribution than other geodesics in a neighbouring environment. This is equivalent to saying that it presents a variation in the distribution of geodesics lower than the others and therefore the Jacobi Field associated with $\{g_n(x)\}_{n\in N}$ reaches its lowest value at J_{g*}. Let's return to the CBP-BDI agent problem that, following the recuperation and variation calculation phase, contains a set of geodesic plans $\{p_1,...,p_n\}$. If the $p*$ is selected with a minimum Jacobi Field value, it can be guaranteed that in the event of interruption it will have around it a greater number of geodesic plans in order to continue. This suggests that given a problem with certain restrictions $F(O;R)=0$, the geodesic plan $p*$ with minimum associated Jacobi field associated with the set $\{g_n(x)\}_{n\in N}$ is called the most re-plan-able solution. The behaviour model G for the CBP-BDI agent is (11).

$$G(e_0, p_1,\cdots,p_n) = p^* \Leftrightarrow \exists n\in N/ J_{g_n} \equiv J_{g*} = \underset{n\in N}{Min} J_{g_n} \tag{11}$$

If the plan $p*$ is not interrupted, the agent will reach a desired state $e_j \equiv e^* \in f_s f$, $j\in\{1,...,m\}$. In the learning phase, a weighting $w_f(p)$ is stored. With the updating of weighting $w_f(p*)$, the planning cycle of the CBP motor is completed. In Figure 3, it is possible to see what happens if $p*$ is interrupted. Let's suppose that the agent has initiated a plan $p*$ but at a moment $t>t_0$, the plan is interrupted due to a change in the environment. The geodesic planning meets the conditions of the Bellman Principle of Optimality [5], in other words, each one of the plan's parts is partially geodesic between the selected points. This guarantees that if g_0 is geodesic for interrupted e_0 in

t_1, because e_0 changes to e_1, and g_1 is geodesic to e_1 that is begun in the state where g_0 has been interrupted, it follows that: $g = g_0 + g_1$ is geodesic to $e = e_0 (t_1 - t_0) + e_1 (t_2 - t_1)$ The dynamic process follows the CBP cycle recurrently: each time a plan finds itself interrupted, it generates from the state reached so far, the surroundings of the plans from the case base and adjusts them to the new problem. With this it calculates the geodesic plans and selects the one which meets the minimum conditions of the associated Jacobi field. In this way, the dynamic planning model of the agent $G(t)$ is characterised as shown in Figure 3. A minimum global Jacobi field $J(t)$ also meets Bellman's conditions of optimality [5], in other words, a minimum global Jacobi field, must select minimum Jacobi fields "in pieces" (12).

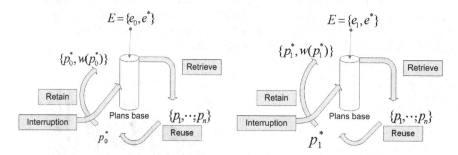

Fig. 3. Model for behaviour G(t)

If on the one hand, successive Jacobi fields generate one Jacobi field, and on the other hand, minimum Jacobi fields generate a minimum Jacobi field, the CBP-BDI agent that follows a strategy of replanning $G(t)$ as indicated to survive a dynamic environment, generates a global plan $p^*(t)$ that, faced with all possible global plans $\{p_n(t)\}_{n \in N}$, presents a minimum value in its Jacobi field $J_{g^*}(t) \equiv J_{p^*}(t)$. As such, an agent has been formally defined which in a dynamic environment seeks plans that lend it greater capacity for replanning.

$$J_{\min}(t) = \{ J_{\min}(t_1 - t_0), J_{\min}(t_2 - t_1), \cdots, J_{\min}(t_n - t_{n-1}) \}$$ (12)

5   Results and Conclusions

The system described in this paper was tested at the Tormes Shopping Mall in the city of Salamanca during 2005 and 2006. This Shopping centre has 86 different businesses including shops, restaurants, cafes, cinemas, hairdressers and a day nursery. The multiagent system prototype has been tuned and updated during this period and the initial results have been very successful from the technical and scientific point of view. The construction of the distributed prototype has been relatively easy using previously developed CBR-BDI libraries [3], [11], especially since the Mall has a Wi-Fi network and has provided the businesses with Bluetooth and RFID technology (75 readers have been installed). The formalism defined in [20] facilitates the straight mapping between the agent definition and the CBR construction. The security problem in data transmissions (data privacy) was tackled by using the FIPA https protocol and a private network to connect Shop agents with the guiding agent.

The fundamental concept when working with a CBR system is the concept of case, so it is necessary to establish a case definition. A case managed by the CBP-BDI agent, is composed of the attributes described in Table 2: the user profile - the money available to spend, the time available, the user's initial location, the user's preferences when guidance is given through the PDA interface between the options shown and the solution proposed; The guidance and the result obtained for the guidance - success, failed, user opinions, sales results. Cases can be manipulated manually or automatically by the agent during its revision stage, when the user evaluation obtained through questionnaires is given to the system. The agent plans can be generated using different strategies since the agent integrates different algorithms. The metrics mechanisms proposed in [8] facilitate the retrieval stage, but the products base and the promotions base must be defined and sorted including metrics that allow it to find similitude, such as the time expected to spend buying each product. The user profile is obtained from retail data and periodic questionnaires.

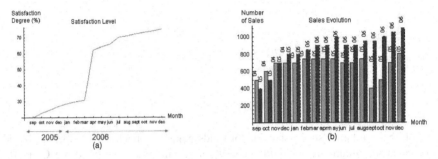

Fig. 4. Users satisfaction degree and sales evolution

The e-commerce techniques have facilitated user motivation since a user can easily find the products he/she is interested in, spend their leisure time more effectively and contact other users with whom he/she can share hobbies or opinions. So the degree of user satisfaction has been improved as observed in the surveys. The first autonomous prototype was implemented in October 2005 with a test set of 30 users and 23 business; presently there are over a 2400 different users and 62 business. The users were selected among users with specific models of terminals supporting the application (they use their own Wi-Fi, Bluetooth devices). The results obtained show that the greater part of users, nearly 67%, were people between 16 and 30 years old, while the percentage of people older than 40 is less than 3%. However there were no significant differences with respect to user gender. Figure 4(a) shows the users satisfaction level over time, which increased substantially, especially after a second prototype was launched in February 2006, that was more consistent and containing more information about promotions and special offers. At the beginning, the system obtained a low evaluation, basically due to the fact that the system was new and had some bugs; but as cases were incorporated, the products being promoted became closer to the user profile. The user satisfaction is measured from user opinions and by indirect observation on the sales results. The user opinions are obtained from a questionnaire that the user completes every month. Moreover, every time the system provides guidance, it asks the user about his/her degree of satisfaction.

Figure 4(b) shows the evolution of sales for the set of special offers, used as a reference over the years to evaluate the evolution of purchases at the commercial centre. They represent a set of 23 promotions that gradually diminish over time. Although the evolution of sales is not a significant index (it can be affected by other factors), the use of reference promotions allows us to observe the impact of the multiagent system in the mall. From this data we can see that, comparing the sales of each promotion over the time that the prototype was introduced with the sales from the previous year (within the same time period and similar social and economic conditions), the percentage of sales slightly increased. The promotion of these products through the guiding system helped to change tendencies.

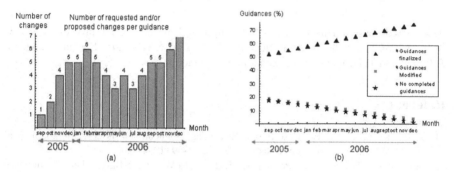

Fig. 5. Guidance system evolution

Users have noticed the utility of the dynamic replanning, since it is quite usual for them change opinions/objectives in the middle of a plan. CBP-BDI is a highly appreciated tool that optimizes the time spent in the shopping mall. Figure 5(a) shows how the number of replannings requested per visit stabilised between 3 or 4 among visitors who requested guidance. Figure 5(b) shows how the number of plans completed without a request for guidance continually increased because of the capacity of the system to learn and adapt to the interests of the users. This occurred at the same time as the number of users who did not complete the plan requested or that requested modifications to the initial plan. A guidance is composed of the problem description (user profile, money, time available, initial location of user and preferences) and the solution (guidance proposed, and result obtained after following up the guidance) given for the problem description given. As SHOMAS obtains more information about user profiles, products and habits, the system knowledge increases and the CBP-BDI agent provides more optimal plans. The users also need time to get used to the system. The proposed guiding system has been improved to be able to provide adequate guidance in a dynamic way and in execution time. In this sense it is a unique system useful for dynamic environments and open enough to be used in other environments such as health care residences, educational environments or tourist related environments.

One of the most demanding services of SHOMAS is the location of a given user by means of the RFID technology or the identification of someone with a given profile, in the same line of web services such as Match.com or similar sites. This service is used by an average of 46% of the users. The shop owners are the most reticent about using the guiding system for several reasons: (i) they do not trust the partiality of the guiding systems, since they cannot control whether it is biased or not, (ii) updating the information about products and offers of the shop agents requires specialised human resources and time, since they are not currently integrated with their software packages, (iii) they believe that the CBP-BDI agent may favour big shop stores with many offers and (iv) some of them argue that the SHOMAS may confuse some users. Nevertheless most shop managers believe that SHOMAS has more advantages than disadvantages and that the system has helped their businesses attract more customers and, in general, to sell more. They tend to argue that SHOMAS should incorporate a method that guarantees impartiality. This is our next challenge as well as an improved system evaluation in comparison to similar planning or recommender systems.

Acknowledgments. This work has been supported by the MCYT project TIC2003-07369-C02-02 and the JCyL Project JCYL-2002-05-SA104A05. Special thanks to Sokymat and Telefónica for the technology provided.

References

1. Aamodt, A., Plaza, E.: Case-Based Reasoning: foundational Issues, Methodological Variations, and System Approaches. AICOM 7, 39–59 (1994)
2. Aha, D.W., Molineaux, M., Ponsen, M.: Learning to Win: Case-Based Plan Selection in a Real-Time Strategy Game. In: Muñoz-Ávila, H., Ricci, F. (eds.) ICCBR 2005. LNCS (LNAI), vol. 3620, pp. 5–20. Springer, Heidelberg (2005)
3. Bajo, J., Corchado, J.M.: Evaluation and monitoring of the air-sea interaction using a CBR-Agents approach. In: Muñoz-Ávila, H., Ricci, F. (eds.) ICCBR 2005. LNCS (LNAI), vol. 3620, pp. 50–62. Springer, Heidelberg (2005)
4. Bellifemine, F., Poggi, A., Rimasa, G.: Developing Multi-agent Systems with JADE. In: Castelfranchi, C., Lespérance, Y. (eds.) ATAL 2000. LNCS (LNAI), vol. 1986, pp. 89–103. Springer, Heidelberg (2001)
5. Bellman, R.E.: Dynamic Programming. Princeton University Press, New Jersey (1957)
6. Bohnenberger, T., Jacobs, O., Jameson, A.: DTP meets user requirements: Enhancements and studies of an intelligent shopping guide. In: Gellersen, H.-W., Want, R., Schmidt, A. (eds.) PERVASIVE 2005. LNCS, vol. 3468, pp. 279–296. Springer, Heidelberg (2005)
7. Bratman, M.E.: Intentions, Plans and Practical Reason. Harvard University Press, Cambridge, M.A (1987)
8. Burke, R.: Knowledge-based Recommender Systems. Encyclopedia of Library & Information Systems 69(32) (2000)
9. Camacho, D., Aler, R., Borrajo, D., Molina, J.M.: Multi-agent plan based information gathering. Applied Intelligence. Springer Netherlands 25(1), 59–71 (2006)
10. Corchado, J.M., Laza, R.: Constructing Deliberative Agents with Case-based Reasoning Technology. International Journal of Intelligent Systems 18, 1227–1241 (2003)
11. Corchado, J.M., Pavón, J., Corchado, E., Castillo, L.F.: Development of CBR-BDI Agents: A Tourist Guide Application. In: Funk, P., González Calero, P.A. (eds.) ECCBR 2004. LNCS (LNAI), vol. 3155, pp. 547–559. Springer, Heidelberg (2004)
12. Cox, M.T., Muñoz-Avila, H., Bergmann, R.: Case-based planning. The Knowledge Engineering Review, vol. 00(0), pp. 1–4. Cambridge University Press, Cambridge (2005)

13. Cumby, C., Fano, A., Ghani, R., Krema, M.: Building intelligent shopping assistants using individual consumer models. In: Proc. IUI 2005 ACM, New York, pp. 323–325 (2005)
14. Eriksson, J., Finne, N.: MarketSpace: an open agent-based market infrastructure, Uppsala Master's thesis in Computing Science 106, Examensarbete DV3 (1997)
15. Fano, A.E.: Shopper's Eye: Using location-based Filtering for a shopping agent in the physical world. In: Proc. of the Second International Conference on Autonomous Agents, pp. 416–421 (1998)
16. Fonseca, S.P., Griss, M.L., Letsinger, R.: An Agent Mediated E-Commerce Environment for the Mobile Shopper, Hewlett-Packard Laboratories, Technical Report, HPL-2001-157 (2001)
17. Ga, M.: Agents in E-commerce. In: Communications of the ACM, vol. 42(3), pp. 79–80. ACM Press, New York (1999)
18. Giampapa, J.A., Sycara, K.: Conversational Case-Based Planning for Agent Team Coordination. In: Aha, D.W., Watson, I. (eds.) ICCBR 2001. LNCS (LNAI), vol. 2080, pp. 189–203. Springer, Heidelberg (2001)
19. Giampapa, J.A., Sycara, K.: Team-Oriented Agent Coordination in the RETSINA Multi-Agent System. In: AAMAS 2002 Workshop on Teamwork and Coalition Formation. Robotics Institute, Carnegie Mellon University, Pittsburgh, PA (2002)
20. Glez-Bedia, M., Corchado, J.M., Corchado, E., Fyfe, C.: Analytical Model for Constructing Deliberative Agents. Engineering Intelligent Systems 3, 173–185 (2002)
21. Hammond, K.: Case-based planning: Viewing planning as a memory task. Academic Press, Boston, MA (1989)
22. Kim, J., LaRose, R.: Interactive e-commerce: Promoting consumer efficiency or impulsivity? Journal of Computer-Mediated Communication 10 (2004)
23. Kowalczyk, R., Ulieru, M., Unland, R.: Integrating Mobile and Intelligent Agents in Advanced e-Commerce: A Survey. In: Kowalczyk, R., Müller, J.P., Tianfield, H., Unland, R. (eds.) Agent Technologies, Infrastructures, Tools, and Applications for E-Services. LNCS (LNAI), vol. 2592, pp. 295–313. Springer, Heidelberg (2003)
24. Maes, P., Guttman, R., Moukas, A.: Agents That Buy and Sell. Communications of the ACM 42(3), 81–91 (1999)
25. Muñoz-Avila, H., Aha, D.W.: On the role of explanation for hierarchical case-based planning in real-time strategy games. In: Gervás, P., Gupta, K.M. (eds.) Proceedings of the ECCBR 2004 Workshops (2004) (Technical Report 142-04)
26. Pokahr, A., Braubach, L., Lamersdorf, W.: Jadex, Implementing a BDI-Infrastructure for JADE Agents. In: EXP - In Search of Innovation (Special Issue on JADE) September 2003, vol. 3(3), pp. 76–85. Telecom Italia Lab, Turin, Italy (2003)
27. Shung, H.H.: Helping Online Customers Decide through Web Personalization. IEEE Intelligent Systems 17(6), 34–43 (2002)
28. Sokymat (2007), http://www.sokymat.com
29. Veloso, M., Muñoz-Avila, H., Bergmann, R.: Case-Based Planning: Selected Methods and Systems. AI Commun. 9(3), 128–137 (1996)
30. Yoshino, T., Muta, T., Munemori, J.: NAMBA: location-aware collaboration system for shopping and meeting. IEEE Trans. on Consumer Electronics 48(3), 470–477 (2001)

Case-Based Reasoning for Invoice Analysis and Recognition

Hatem Hamza[1,2], Yolande Belaïd[2], and Abdel Belaïd[2]

[1] ITESOFT, Parc d'Andron, Le Sequoia. 30470 Aimargues. France
[2] University Nancy 2, LORIA. 54506 Vandoeuvre-les-Nancy, France
{hamza,ybelaid,abelaid}@loria.fr

Abstract. This paper introduces the approach CBRDIA (Case-based Reasoning for Document Invoice Analysis) which uses the principles of case-based reasoning to analyze, recognize and interpret invoices. Two CBR cycles are performed sequentially in CBRDIA. The first one consists in checking whether a similar document has already been processed, which makes the interpretation of the current one easy. The second cycle works if the first one fails. It processes the document by analyzing and interpreting its structuring elements (adresses, amounts, tables, etc) one by one. The CBR cycles allow processing documents from both konwn or unknown classes. Applied on 923 invoices, CBRDIA reaches a recognition rate of 85,22% for documents of known classes and 74,90% for documents of unknown classes.

Keywords: Case-based reasoning, document case, structure case, invoice analysis, invoice interpretation, structure extraction.

1 Introduction

Form and invoice analysis systems in real production chains are often faced with a huge quantity of documents requiring a high processing speed and a continuous adaptation capacity to the structure variation. The manual and even semi-automatic solutions which consist in building manually the model of each set of new documents can no longer be used because of the heavy modeling phase they require [1].

Invoices have variations depending on many factors : the company issuing the invoice, the client, etc. Most current information to be extracted are: addresses (delivery, billing...), total amounts and table lines showing details of services, purchased products... Two types of documents occur in invoice processing:

- documents of known class i.e similar documents have been already processed;
- new documents from an unknwon class.

In two documents from the same class, information blocks (addresses, amounts, tables...) are organized in the same way and have the same relative positions in the documents. However, their absolute positions vary from a document to another, depending on the specific content of each document. Figure 1 shows two documents from the same class where the information to be extracted are gray tone

R.O. Weber and M.M. Richter (Eds.): ICCBR 2007, LNAI 4626, pp. 404–418, 2007.
© Springer-Verlag Berlin Heidelberg 2007

or boxed. We can see that the absolute position of the total amount zone changes between the documents.

For a new document from an unknown class, the problem consists in building a generic and reliable model for all the documents of this class. Figure 2 shows two invoices from different classes. We can clearly see that they have different structures. The paper is organized as the following: section 2 presents some related works. Section 3 introduces the use of CBR the system. Sections 4, 5 and 6 present CBRDIA's architecture. Finally, the seventh section shows the obtained results and their interpretation.

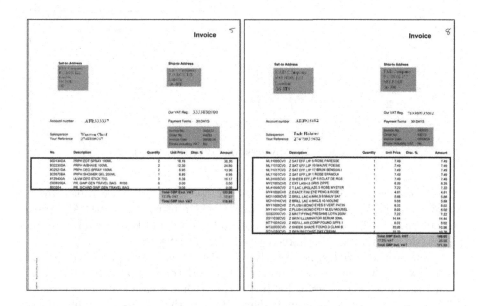

Fig. 1. Two invoices from the same class

2   Related Work

The most promising approaches are those which can process documents of either known or unknown classes [2] [3]. In [3], after a first step related to document classification, the document is interpreted via its structures (keywords) by combining two levels of knowledge: intra- and inter-classes knowledge. If the document class is recognized, the system looks for the solution using the intra-class knowledge (tags, relative positions of the related object, etc) and the inter-class knowledge (summarizing knowledge in different invoice classes). If the document is not recognized, then only inter-classes knowledge is used to interpret the extracted information. The application of this approach is however limited to isolated keywords not taking into account more frequent and important structures in forms such as tables, addresses, etc. Concerning table analysis, Belaïd presented in [4] a morphological tagging approach for invoice analysis. This approach was used

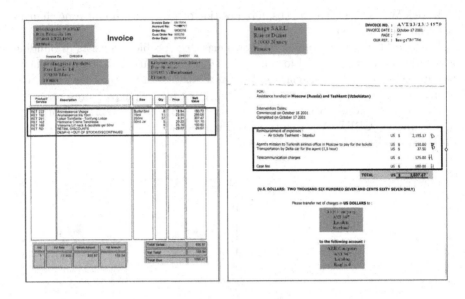

Fig. 2. Two invoices from different classes

in order to tag table columns and fields. However, the processed tables are already extracted before tagging. Contrary to these methods, CBRDIA extracts and interprets data associated with both table lines and keywords. It can also process documents from both known and unknown classes.

To our best knowledge, no directly related work has been published in CBR field. However, we can link this work to other works on textual CBR (TCBR) [5] or on CBR in image processing [6]. In our approach, our cases will be represented either by strings or graphs. Cunningham [7] shows that the use of graphs in case representation can be useful in TCBR.

Another type of related works concerns systems using multiple CBR reasoners. In CBRDIA, we will use 2 CBR reasoners (one for invoices of known class, and another for invoices of unknown class). These reasoners will be sequential. Some other approaches [8] use parallel CBR reasoners in order to enhance the system performance.

3   Case-Based Reasoning in Our Approach

CBR is a solving strategy that uses previous experiences to process new problems that have not been processed before [9].

The problems we are facing in this work are the following:

– document structure extraction: this is a difficult and time consuming problem in industry. Structure extraction is done for every document in order to be interpreted. However, when a whole set of documents (coming from the same client) has the same structuring elements (example : a table, an amount block, and an address block), then the whole set can be represented by a generic model. This is generally done by a user who takes into account a certain number of documents in order to build such a model.

- document classification: there is a continuous flow of documents that have to be processed (read and interpreted). We do not know a priori to which class of documents the processed one belongs to. It is obvious that if the system has processed a similar document before, then it is a real waste of time not to take advantage of such a knowledge. Otherwise, a new document model has to be built in order to extract the desired information.

- document analysis and interpretation: this task (interpreting words, fields, or tables) is really hard. It has to be done either by a user who supervises every document, or automatically by a reliable system. For example, interpreting the word "total" means associating it with the numerical value related to it on the document. The system, in the interpretation phase should

  • generalize easily based on the previous document processing experiences;
  • understand the current document and make profit of the extracted and interpreted information it contains;
  • be as quick as possible. If possible, we have to avoid a classical training process as other machine learning techniques;
  • self adaptable to any new class of documents. In classical machine learning techniques (example: neural networks), as soon as a new class of data appears, these techniques fail generally in recognizing it. A new learning has to be done in order to overcome these difficulties. However, in CBRDIA, when the document class is completely new, the system can find solutions (partial solutions if not total ones) by trying to exploit the previous knowledge.

For all these reasons, the choice of CBR was natural. In CBRDIA, two sorts of cases are defined: a document case and a structure case. As shown in figure 3, the flow of our approach is based on three main steps: problem elaboration, global problem solving and local problem solving.

Problem elaboration consists in indices extraction from the document. These indices are either keywords (KW) and their spatial relationships, or table rows. This problem is then solved using either global solving process or local solving one.

Global Solving (first CBR cycle on figure 3) consists in checking if a similar document case exists already. If yes, then the system solves the problem by applying the solution of the database case to this problem. Otherwise, the problem is decomposed into sub-problems, and solved via the solving of its sub-problems. The second CBR cycle corresponds to this step, and is called local solving. The use of global solving and local solving makes our system able to process any kind of invoice documents.

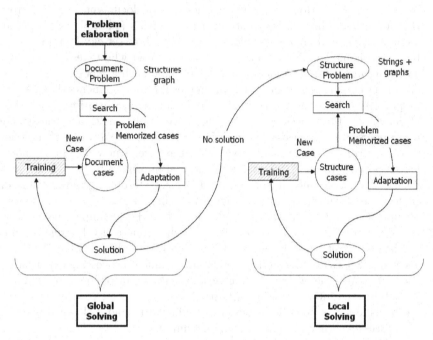

Fig. 3. CBRDIA flow

4   Problem Elaboration

The system requires the precise definition of the problem. This precision is required in every step of the flow (case retrieval, solution adaptation). The system input is a raw document given by OCR (optical character recognition). The OCR file written in XML contains the list of words and their coordinates. The document is represented by a set of words $D = W_i$, $i = 1..n$.

4.1   Data Extraction and Coding

First, each word W is given a list of attributes:

- position (coordinates in the document);
- KW: if a word in the current document matches a word in a predefined list of keywords, then it is tagged as a KW. This list is enriched gradually as new keywords are discovered;
- nature: represented by an alphabetic character. For example, 'A' for numerical, 'B' for alphabetical, etc.

In the next step, fields (F) are constituted from the set of words D by gathering neighbour words horizontally. Each successive pair of words $d(W_i, W_j)$ in F verifies $d(W_i, W_j) < \alpha$ where α is a threshold depending on the words' size. F is also characterized by a list of attributes:

- position;
- nature: the nature of a field is deduced from its words' natures. For example, if F contains an alphabetical and a numerical word, then it will be given the tag 'C' for alphanumerical.

From fields, we extract horizontal and vertical lines (HL, VL). We use the fields' neighbourhoods and the fields' alignments to constitute HL and VL. A vertical line VL is a set of fields F vertically aligned. Two vertical fields $d(F_i)$ and $d(F_j)$ are in the same vertical line if $d(F_i, F_j) < \delta$ where δ is a threshold depending on the fields' size and position. Similarly, we use a threshold for horizontal fields. A line is described by the following attributes:

- position;
- pattern: a string composed of fields' tags list. For example, if the fields' tags in the line are: 'A', 'B', 'B' and 'C', then the pattern is "ABBC". These patterns will be very helpful in the extraction of tables.

Figure 4 shows an example of a field, a HL and a VL. After these elementary information are extracted, we can extract high level structuring elements (S) which can be either pattern structures (PS) when related to tables or keyword structures (KWS) when related to local arrangements of keywords (KW). The final document problem will be defined thanks to PS and KWS.

Fig. 4. A VL in the big box, a HL in gray tone, a field in the small box

4.2   Structures Extraction

Figure 5 shows a document containing 3 KWS and a PS.

PS Extraction. PS are a list of consecutive HLs having similar patterns. This is the case of a table. Figure 5 shows a document containing a PS composed of 18 HLs having the pattern "ABAAAA". The PS detection process contains three steps:

- For each HL, we constitute a list of HL neighbours HLN using edit distance on their strings (i.e. patterns). We use a threshold (usually equal to 1 in order to accept only 1 transformation between strings) between HL patterns to find neighbours;
- The list of each HL neighbours is studied based on the fields' positions. In figure 6, the edit distance between the patterns is null, as they represent the same string "ABB". However they do not correspond to the same PS because of the difference of the spatial positions. To avoid such confusions when the edit distance is null, we take into account patterns' fields positions

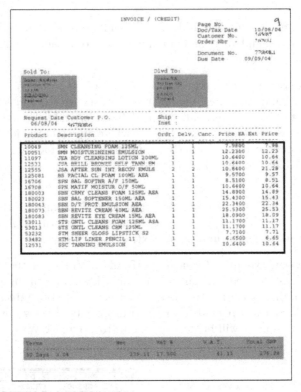

Fig. 5. An invoice containing 3 KWS and a PS

as the following. For every list HLN we compute a new matching value. This value depends on the number of exact vertical alignment of fields having the same tag. The final matching value is the ratio in (1):

$$RT = \frac{|matching\ fields|}{|fields\ in\ HLN|} \text{where } |X| \text{ is the number of elements in} X \ . \quad (1)$$

The higher RT is, the more probable HLN is a PS. In fact, if RT tends to 1, then two possibilities exist:

- $RT = 1$, HLN is a singleton (this case will be eliminated because it is meaningless for table), or HLN is a perfect table;
- $RT < 1$, meaning the case of a possible table.

– After processing the whole document, the chosen HLN is the one maximizing RT. PS is then the best HLN candidate. This method can extract tables only when there are at least two table lines in the document.

KWS Extraction. Keyword structures (KWS) are local arrangements of key-words (KW) like "road", "zip-code", "name", etc for an address. These KW

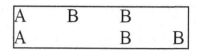

Fig. 6. Two patterns with edit distance=0

occur frequently in administrative documents and can be in several languages. KW are extracted thanks to a specific software developped by ITESOFT. Its details are outside the aim of this paper. KW can be written in different manners but have always the same meaning. For example, "total", "tot", "total amount" represent the same information but are written differently from an invoice to another. In order to avoid confusions and to be able to propose general cases, KW with the same meaning are given the same KW tag. We use graphs to represent this keyword association (keywords in vertices, and relative spatial relationships on edges). This association maintains the real positions of KW in the document as well as the semantic proximity between them. We preferred using relative positions instead of absolute positions when tagging the edges in order to have a better generalisation of a case. For example when a homogeneous set of documents is processed, it is usual that the absolute positions of a KW changes from a document to another one. However, its relative position to the other KW in the document does not change.

4.3   Document Structure Extraction

A document structure is a gathering of all its sub-element structures (PS and KWS). We use a graph for its representation. In order to have a harmonious graph representation, useful for future comparisons, we consider all the vertices visible at the same level. This means that the difference between vertices is characterized by edges which are either "spatial" (left, right, top, bottom) when they designate spatial relationships or "contain" when they designate a structure component (as between a KWS and each of its KW). This kind of graph representation gives flexibility to CBRDIA as it is just articulated around KWS and PS relative positions. It is also helpful for document comparisons (see 5.1). We preferred the graph representation to the vector representation as the latter does not take into account any position in the document. Moreover, classical vector representations do not give any information about the position in the document, nor about the relative position with another KW. In addition to all that, [10] [7] show clearly that using the graph representation gives much better results in document classification than the vector based representation. All these reasons lead us to represent KWS and documents in graphs.

4.4   Problem Enriching Using a Set of Homogeneous Documents

In the previous sections, we introduced problem elaboration starting from one single document. This can be sufficient when the extraction is done easily and when the proposed document does not contain any noise (very good OCR results, tables with multiple lines). However, this is not usually the case. In many cases, extracting a document problem without checking whether this problem is representative of the set of documents it comes from can cause many errors in the solving process.

In this paragraph, we show how to extract and to enrich a problem starting from a set of documents. A set of documents means a set of homogeneous documents i.e they are all issued by the same company, they have the same physical structure. The similarity of documents in the same set is high and processing one document can help a lot in processing the remaining documents. In order to help having available and representative problems, we use a whole set of documents in the problem elaboration process. The final problem is representative of all the problems of the processed documents. The system extracts the problem from each document in the set and adds this problem to the previous ones. As the document problems are graphs, the final problem is a graph representing all the extracted graphs. Such a graph can only be the Minimum Common Supergraph (MCS) of all the extracted graphs. Formally speaking, strating from a set of graphs G_i, $i = 1..n$ an MCS is a graph such that it has a subgraph isomorphism with every graph in G_i. This MCS is very helpful. It represents the whole class of documents and allows a better generalization in both the steps of elaboration and solving.

Bunke [11] introduces the notion of weighted MCS. It is an MCS where the vertices and edges have weights corresponding to their frequencies in the set G_i. These weights can be useful as they allow the distinction between real information and noisy information. A noisy information (a vertex which can be in our application a keyword, a KWS or a PS) is usually characterized by a very low frequency. By using a threshold, we can filter the undesired information.

The redundancy of some information in the problem enriching phase can also help finding and modelling future solutions. For example, the redundancy of the field "phone number + XX.XX.XX.XX.XX" can be helpful in the solving process. If this redundancy is detected, the solution of the KW "phone number" is known in advance, and it becomes unnecessary to look for it once the solving phase starts. similar ideas concerning problem enriching are under study.

4.5   CBRDIA Cases

CBR requires the definition of cases: a problem and its corresponding solution. Let C be a case, C= {P_C, S_C}. According to the problem elaboration step, two cases are possible:

1. Structure case which can be a KWS case or a PS case
   - KWS case: where P_KWS is the graph of keywords contained in a structure and S_KWS is the interpretation of each KW. For example, the solution of the KW "street" is the name of the street and the number corresponding to the address (example: 12 Decker street). In this case, KWS solution is the set of KW solutions. S_KWS = {S_KW} where KW is a particular case of KWS containing just one keyword;

    – PS case: where P_PS is the pattern (e.g "ABBB") representing the table
      and S_PS is the interpretation of each table column.
2. Document case: P_DC is the document graph and S_DC is the solution of all
   its structures: S_DC = {S_KWS, S_PS}. P_DC consists in the graph of all the
   structures of the document. The graph vertices are the structures or the kew-
   words contained in the structures. Two different edge labels exist. If the edges
   connect between structure vertices or between KW inside a KWS, then their
   labels are spatial labels (above, below, right, left) representing the relative
   positions of structures (arrows in full line on figure 7). Otherwise, their labels
   are "contain" type, meaning that a certain information is contained in a
   structure (arrows in dotted line on figure 7).

Figure 7 shows a simple example of a graph of a document problem.

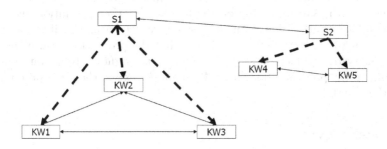

Fig. 7. Example of a document graph. KW1 to KW5 are keywords. S1 and S2 are two
KWS.

5 Global Solving

5.1 Similar Case Retrieval

For graph comparison, many measures can be used [10]. However, as we are
not only looking for accuracy, but also for a fast processing, we used Lopresti's
method called graph probing [12]. It is a fast and accurate technique to compare
graphs by measuring their degree of dissimilarity. In his paper, Lopresti applied
his method successfully on document graphs containing simple structures of lines
and words. In order to compare labelled and directed graphs, two probes PB1
and PB2 are measured:

1. PB1 = the frequency of each vertex in the graph;
2. PB2 = the frequency of each vertex' edge structure.

PB1 and PB2 are measured for the studied graph P_DC (G_1) and the Document Database (D_DB) graph (G_2). The probing distance P between the graphs
G_1 and G_2 is then (2):

$$P(G_1, G_2) = (PB1(G_1) - PB1(G_2)) + (PB2(G_1) - PB2(G_2)). \qquad (2)$$

It has to be noticed that if $P(G_1, G_2)=0$, G_1 and G_2 are not necessarily isomorphic. However, graph probing gives an approximation of the edit distance. We notice here that other types of distances are being studied.

Graph probing is then used to compare graphs and to retrive the nearest case in D_DB.

5.2   Solution Adaptation

When a similar case for P_DC (G_1) is found in D_DB (G_2), the adaptation consists first in finding for each structure in G_1 the corresponding structure in G_2. This is achieved by measuring the distance between the structures (PS or KWS) of G_1 and G_2. As the documents correspond to the same case (meaning they belong to the same set of documents), the system just copies the information about the nature (alphabetical, numerical) and the position (left on the same line, right on the same line, top on the line above) of each solution and looks for similar information in the current document. For example, if the solution corresponding to a KW "total" in G_2 case has the properties "real number + right", the system will look for a real number on the right of "total" on the same line (HL) in the processed document. If an answer exists, then it is proposed as a solution for this KW.

6   Local Solving

If no similar case exists in D_DB, the system builds a solution based on the structures already processed in others documents and stored in a special database S_DB (Structure cases database).

6.1   KWS Solving

The solving procedure acts as the following:

1. For each structure in the document, the nearest structure in the Structure Database (S_DB) is retrieved. P_KWS graph is compared to the KWS cases of S_DB. The solution of the nearest structure is adapted. Graph edit distance is used to find the nearest graphs in S_DB. Edit distance is used for graph comparison as we are really looking for graph isomorphism, or at least sub-graph isomorphism. As S_DB graphs are also small (no more than 5 vertices per graph in general), it is then better to use a more precise comparison technique than to use a faster but less accurate one like graph probing. The cost function used to compute edit distance between graphs has uniform costs for both vertices and edges edit operations as both KW and their relative positions seem to have the same importance in the graph.
2. The nearest structures' solutions are now adapted to the document structures. As the cases in the S_DB have already a correct solution, the adaptation consists in taking the solution of each KW (case of KWS) and trying to find a corresponding solution in the processed document. If a complete solution is

found for a structure, then, it can be stored in the S_DB. Otherwise, the following processing has to be done. For KW, some universal knowledge exists and it would be really a waste of time not to take advantage of it. For example, it is usual that the KW "total" is followed by a numerical. This numerical can be a real number or an integer depending on the document but its numerical nature is always valid. Following this logic, a rule basis detailing the general rules associated with keywords was built, in order to complete any partial solution of a KWS. This basis allows completing some missing KWS solutions. It has to be noticed that a rule basis is not able to solve complete cases as it does not take into account the context of the structure, and as its knowledge is very general and not related to any concrete case. If no solution can be found for a given structure, the system can ask the user to propose one.

The example on figure 8 shows a KWS which nearest KWS in S_DB solves four out of five KW. By using a rule basis, a complete solution can be found.

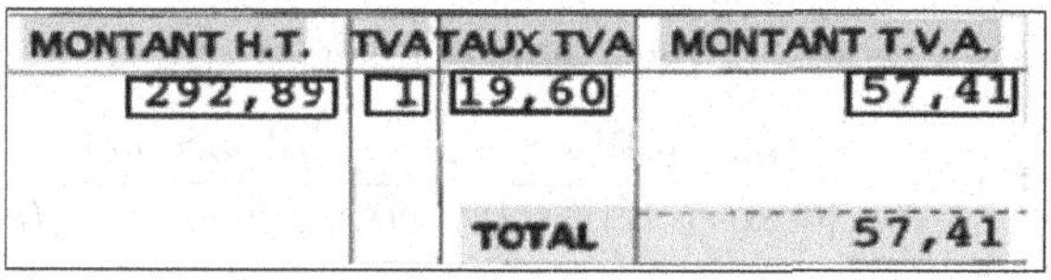

Fig. 8. A KWS. Only the KW Total is solved by the rule basis.

6.2 PS Solving

Each extracted PS (E_PS) is compared with the S_DB cases to retrieve the nearest structure. As PS are represented with strings, their patterns are compared using string edit distance. When a similar PS (C_PS) is found in S_DB, (same pattern, or with a maximum of one transformation), the table columns of E_PS are given the tags of C_PS, unless the rule between C_PS fields can not be applied on E_PS. In this case, the system tries to find the rule between E_PS fields by trying the rules in other close PS cases (close PS cases with more than one transformation) until a valid rule is found.

If no solution can be found, the user can also here propose one.

A perspective of our work is to use the table headers in order to interpret the table columns. In this way, PS cases could also be considered as KWS cases as we will use the KW found in the headers for the interpretation.

7   Experiments

7.1   The Database

The dataset is composed of 923 documents taken from different clients representing 325 different sets. The database set is divided in 2 groups:

– the first one contains 100 documents where each one has a similar case in the document database: this will help us testing the global solving;
– the second one contains 823 documents for which no associated case exists in the document database. Hence, local solving will be applied on these documents.

S_DB contained initially 300 structures. Only 20 of the tested structures have a complete similar case in S_DB. The remaining cases in S_DB are taken from several other documents which are not related to the tested documents. We have chosen to test our system in this way to show its ability to find a solution for a given problem even if it has never been studied before.

7.2   Measures

The results are described thanks to three different measures (3, 4, 5):

$$R = \frac{|right\ solutions\ in\ all\ documents|}{|desired\ solutions\ in\ all\ documents|}. \tag{3}$$

$$R\_KWS = \frac{|right\ KW\ solutions\ in\ all\ documents|}{|desired\ KW\ solutions\ in\ all\ documents|}. \tag{4}$$

$$R\_PS = \frac{|right\ PS\ fields\ in\ all\ documents|}{|desired\ PS\ fields\ in\ all\ documents|}. \tag{5}$$

A right solution corresponds to a KW's solution or to a field in a PS that has been correctly extracted and interpreted.

7.3   Results

The results are given in table 1, they are very satisfying from an industrial point of view.

Table 1. Results of CBRDIA for global solving and local solving

	R	R_KWS	R_PS
Global Solving	85.22%	79.77%	90.10%
Local Solving	74.90%	75.25%	74.80%

In global solving, the missing 14.78% correspond to 3.72% system errors and 11.06% OCR errors.

In local solving, for KWS, errors are due to:

– 12.15% system errors (bad solution, no solution found, confusion with other solutions);
– 12.59% of OCR errors.

In local solving, for PS, errors are due to:

- bad detection of table lines (11.32%) (missing lines, no detection of table);
- OCR and segmentation errors (12.67%) (e.g : 12.T instead of 12.7. Two fields are fused together which implies a wrong tag);
- bad solution (1.21%) (fields are given bad solutions).

The OCR used in our system is a professional one used by ITESOFT. OCR errors are not just due to the software performance, but they also depend on:

- the quality of documents. In our dataset, we had about 11% of documents of very poor quality (this can be caused by the original quality of the document, or by a bad scanning);
- noisy information such as missing characters.

The difference between the results of global solving and those of local solving can be explained as the following:

- In global solving, the system is processing a similar document: it has the knowledge of what it is looking for in the document. The only sources of error can be:
  - a bad tagging (words, fields);
  - a bad PS extraction;
  - a missing KWS or a missing KW;
  - OCR errors.
- However, in local solving, in addition to all the previous sources of errors, we can also notice the bad extracted solutions. This can happen when the processed structures have no very close structures in S_DB. This can deteriorate the quality of the proposed solutions.

A special case of KWS was also tested (addresses). We tested our system for KWS solving on 30 documents containing addresses. We obtained 78.33% (118/150) of good results (150 being the number of processed KW in these address blocks). We can notice that this special case exists not only in invoice documents, but also in any other administrative documents.

8   Conclusion and Future Works

A CBR approach for invoice document analysis and interpretation was proposed in this paper. CBRDIA produces good results even if the documents have never been processed by the system before. This work is still under study in several ways. We are studying the improvement of problem elaboration especially in PS extraction. We are also focusing on S_DB and D_DB indexing in order to reduce the solving time. Finally, solutions' quality is the next step in our work. Enriching S_DB and D_DB requires having high quality solutions; otherwise, a lot of noisy cases can reduce the solving process efficiency. These studies should allow CBRDIA to have better results.

References

1. Yuan, J., Xu, L., Suen, C.: Form items extraction by model matching. In: ICDAR, France (1991)
2. Sako, H., Seki, M., Furukawa, N., Ikeda, H., Imaizumi, A.: Form reading based on form-type identification and form-data recognition. In: ICDAR, Scotland (2003)
3. Cesarini, F., Francesconi, E., Gori, M., Soda, G.: Analysis and understanding of multi-class invoices. IJDAR 6(2), 102–114 (2003)
4. Belaïd, Y., Belaïd, A.: Morphological tagging approach in document analysis of invoices. In: ICPR, pp. 469–472 (2004)
5. Weber, R., Ashley, K., Bruninghaus, S.: Textual case-based reasoning. The Knowledge Engineering Review 20(3), 255–260 (2006)
6. Perner, P., Hlot, A., Richter, M.: Image processing in case-based reasoning. The Knowledge Engineering Review 20(3), 311–314 (2006)
7. Cunningham, C., Weber, R., Proctor, J.M., Fowler, C., Murphy, M.: Investigating graphs in textual case-based reasoning. In: Funk, P., González Calero, P.A. (eds.) ECCBR 2004. LNCS (LNAI), vol. 3155, pp. 573–586. Springer, Heidelberg (2004)
8. Cheetham, W., Shultz, J.: Using ensembles of binary case-based reasoners. In: Muñoz-Ávila, H., Ricci, F. (eds.) ICCBR 2005. LNCS (LNAI), vol. 3620, pp. 152–162. Springer, Heidelberg (2005)
9. Aamodt, A., Plaza, E.: Case-based reasoning: Foundational issues, methodological variations, and system approaches. In: IOS press (1994)
10. Schenker, A., Last, M., Bunke, H., Kandel, A.: Comparison of distance measures for graph-based clustering of documents. In: Hancock, E.R., Vento, M. (eds.) GbRPR 2003. LNCS, vol. 2726, pp. 202–213. Springer, Heidelberg (2003)
11. Bunke, H., Foggia, P., Guidobaldi, C., Vento, M.: Graph clustering using the weighted minimum common supergraph. In: Hancock, E.R., Vento, M. (eds.) GbRPR 2003. LNCS, vol. 2726, pp. 235–246. Springer, Heidelberg (2003)
12. Lopresti, D.P., Wilfong, G.T.: A fast technique for comparing graph representations with applications to performance evaluation. IJDAR 6(4), 219–229 (2003)

Watershed Segmentation Via Case-Based Reasoning

Maria Frucci[1], Petra Perner[2], and Gabriella Sanniti di Baja[1]

[1] Institute of Cybernetics "E.Caianiello", CNR, Pozzuoli, Italy
[2] Institute of Computer Vision and Applied Computer Science, Leipzig, Germany
m.frucci@cib.na.cnr.it, p.perner@ibai-institut.de,
g.sannitidibaja@cib.na.cnr.it

Abstract. This paper proposes a novel grey-level image segmentation scheme employing case-based reasoning. Segmentation is accomplished by using the watershed transformation, which provides a partition of the image into regions whose contours closely fit those perceived by human users. Case-based reasoning is used to select the segmentation parameters involved in the segmentation algorithm by taking into account the features characterizing the current image. We describe the different processing steps involved in a CBR-based image segmentation scheme. The segmentation parameters of the Watershed segmentation that can be controlled are explained. One possible case description based on statistical low-level features is given as well as the similarity measure. The performance of the chosen case description and the similarity measure for retrieval is assessed based on hierarchical clustering. Finally, we propose a method for the automatic evaluation of the segmentation results that will allow us to automatically select the best segmentation parameters and, thus, making the whole segmentation scheme to a closed-loop image-segmentation control scheme.

1 Introduction

Image segmentation is a necessary preliminary step for any image analysis task. This process partitions an image into a number of constituting regions. Each partition region is homogeneous with respect to a given property, while the set including any two adjacent regions is not homogeneous. Segmentation has been widely studied, as it is witnessed by the large relative literature (see, e.g., [1-5]). Different homogeneity criteria can be used, e.g., based on grey-level distribution, texture, color, and so on. In this paper we will consider grey-level distribution.

Watershed transformation (WT) is a basic tool for image segmentation exploiting both region-based and edge-detection-based methodologies (see, e.g., [6,7]). The basic idea of this segmentation scheme is to identify in the gradient image of a grey-level image a suitable set of seeds from which to perform a growing process. The growing process determines the region associated to each seed, by gathering into the region all pixels that are closer to the corresponding seed more than to any other seed, provided that a certain homogeneity in grey-level is satisfied.

Watershed segmentation is not severely affected by the drawbacks characterizing region-based and edge-detection-based segmentation methods. In fact, the seeds from which region growing is performed are detected in the gradient image of the input

R.O. Weber and M.M. Richter (Eds.): ICCBR 2007, LNAI 4626, pp. 419–432, 2007.
© Springer-Verlag Berlin Heidelberg 2007

grey-level image as the sets of pixels with locally minimal grey-level (called *regional minima*). In turn, the problem of identifying closed edges surrounding the regions of interest is solved, since the regions (and, hence, their boundaries) are determined by the growing process.

Watershed segmentation has been used in different image domains, generally producing satisfactory results, since the obtained image partition is into regions whose boundaries closely fit those perceived by human users.

One of the main problems in using the WT is the excessive fragmentation of the image into a large number of partition regions, not all perceptually meaningful. Thus, watershed segmentation generally includes a merging phase aimed at suitably reducing the number of partition regions. To this purpose, a number of measures of properties of the partition regions have to be taken into account to distinguish meaningful and non-meaningful regions, and suitable thresholds on the values of these measures have to be set. The same region properties can be adequate in different image domains, but they do not always equally contribute to obtain the best segmentation results. In some cases, the computed measures of certain properties should be weighted more than the remaining measures. To automatically identify the proper weights for the measures, it can be useful to resort to case-based reasoning (CBR).

The use of CBR for image segmentation has been already attempted successfully in the past for segmentation methods different from those based on the use of the WT. In [8], CBR has been introduced in the framework of histogram-based segmentation. In [9], CBR has been used to optimize image segmentation at the low-level stage of the process, i.e., by taking into account image acquisition conditions and image quality. In [10], CBR and dissimilarity classification methods have been considered and in [11], improving system performance by controlling the image similarity measure has been described. Other applications for image processing where CBR has been used are described in [17].

This work proposes a novel image watershed segmentation scheme employing case-based reasoning. In our approach, CBR is used to select the proper weights to be assigned to the measures of the region properties according to the current image characteristics. We assume that for images with similar image characteristics, similarly good segmentation results will be obtained by using the same weights.

This paper is organized as follows. In Section 2, we briefly discuss the general case-based approach to image segmentation. In Section 3, the watershed segmentation method proposed in [12] is sketched. In Section 4, we show how to improve the segmentation results of the algorithm [12] by using CBR. Some discussions and conclusions are given in Section 5.

2   The Case-Based Image Segmentation Approach

The segmentation problem can be seen as a classification problem, where the image at hand is compared to the images in a data-base to identify the best matching and, hence, select the segmentation criteria for the image at hand. The classifier needs a learning phase. In particular, the classifier needs to learn the mapping function between the image features and the segmentation parameters involved in the selected algorithm. Our basic idea is that there is a strong correlation between the features of an image and the obtained segmentation results. Using the same segmentation parameters for images with similar features should produce similarly good results.

The learning of the classifier should be accomplished on a large set of data, in order to build a general model for the segmentation problem. This is generally not the case, and the segmentation model should be adjusted to fit new data by means of a suitable case-base maintenance process. Though, case-base maintenance is an important topic, we will not discuss it in this communication. We remark that a general model does not always guarantee the best segmentation for each image. It guarantees an average best fit over the data-base.

Case-based reasoning can be used as basic methodology for image segmentation. The relative CBR process is shown in Fig.1.

The characteristics of an image can be, for example, some statistical features extracted from the grey-level image (mean, variance, skewness, kurtosis, variation coefficients, energy, entropy, centroid). These features are used for indexing the case-base and for retrieval of a set of cases that include images close to the current image, based on a proper image similarity measure. A case consists of the statistical features as well as the values assigned to the segmentation parameters. Among the close cases, the one maximizing image similarity with the current image is selected and the segmentation parameters adopted for this case are given to the image segmentation unit to process the current image. The output is the segmented image.

The result of the segmentation process is evaluated by the user. If the user considers the obtained result as non correct, the current image has to be added to the case-base as a new case. This means that the correct segmentation parameters have to be empirically identified.

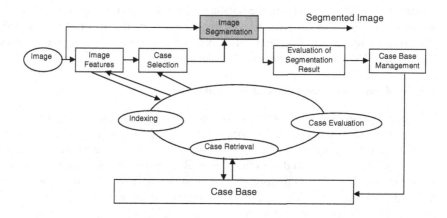

Fig. 1. Scheme of the CBR process

3   The Watershed Segmentation

The segmentation method we use in this work is based on the watershed transformation, [6]. This technique exploits both the region-based approach and edge detection.

The seeds from which to perform region growing are detected as the regional minima in the gradient image of the input grey-level image. The partition regions are determined by the growing process. This is based on the distance of any pixel from the seeds, as well as on the grey-level so generating a partition of the image into regions characterized by homogeneity in grey-level.

The mechanism according to which the watershed partition is obtained can be understood by referring to the landscape paradigm. The gradient image can be interpreted as a 3D landscape, where the grey-level of a pixel in position (x,y) is interpreted as its height. Thus, high grey-levels are mapped into mountains and low grey-levels into valleys. Pixels with locally higher grey-level identify peaks, and pixels with locally lower grey-level correspond to pits in the landscape. If the pits are pierced and the landscape is immersed in water, the landscape will start to be flooded as soon as the water level will reach the pits. The valleys that will be flooded first are those whose pits are the lowest ones, since they are reached first by the increasing level of the water. A dam is built to prevent water to spread from a catchment's basin into the close ones, wherever waters from different basins are going to meet. When the whole landscape has been covered by water, the top lines of the dams constitute the watershed lines, i.e., the boundaries of the partition regions of the input grey-level image.

Watershed segmentation can be used for a wide repertory of images and the watershed lines generally border in a satisfactory way the regions into which the image is partitioned. However, if all the regional minima detected in the gradient image are used as seeds for the growing process, the image is fragmented into a too large number of homogeneous regions, not all perceptually significant. This problem, known as over-segmentation, can be solved by selecting only a reduced, significant, set of regional minima, or by merging the obtained partition regions. In general, both seed selection and region merging are taken into account. Once the final partition is available, its regions have to be classified as belonging to either the foreground or the background [13]. This task depends on problem domain.

3.1 Seed Selection Based on Region Significance

To reduce over-segmentation, only seeds corresponding to significant regions should be detected and used during the growing process. Seed reduction can be achieved by using a filter to remove irrelevant minima, but a priori knowledge on the class of images would be necessary to design the proper filter. We use a fully automatic way to reduce the number of seeds performing well on different image domains. The method is based on the notion of significance of the regions of the watershed partition and is accomplished by means of techniques that, by using the landscape paradigm, can be called *flooding* and *digging*.

The general scheme is the following. The notion of significance is used to discriminate the significant and the non-significant regions in the initial watershed partition of the grey-level image. Flooding and digging are then used to cause disappearance of the regional minima corresponding to the non-significant regions. The watershed transform is computed again, starting from the seeds surviving flooding and digging, so that a less fragmented partition of the image is obtained. The process is iterated until no seed can be removed by flooding and digging, meaning that all surviving seeds are relevant.

The definition of significant region is crucial to obtain a meaningful partition. In [12], a new criterion was introduced to evaluate region significance in watershed partitioned images and to filter out the irrelevant seeds by flooding and digging. In particular, flooding and digging reduce the seeds in such a way to cause merging of non-significant regions during the region growing process only with selected adjacent regions.

The significance of a catchment basin was defined by taking into account the portion of the landscape where the basin is placed, i.e., was evaluated with respect to the adjacent basins. Let us consider the basin X and let Y be one of the basins adjacent to X. The pixel p at the minimal height along the ridge separating X from Y is called the *relative local overflow* of X with respect to Y and its grey-level is denoted by LO_{XY}. The local overflow pixel is the one where the dam separating X from Y should start to be built to prevent overflow from X to Y. See Fig.2.

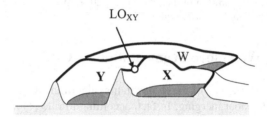

Fig. 2. Local overflow pixel for the basin X with respect to the basin Y

For a basin X, the set of pixels of X having grey-levels less than the relative local overflow LO_{XY} was considered. This set of pixels is the lake formed when the water reaches the relative local overflow pixel and is denoted by L_{XY}. Let us denote by R_X the grey-level of the pit of the basin X. With reference to Fig. 2 we can define the *depth D_{XY}* of X with respect to Y as follows:

$$D_{XY} = \max_{p \in L_{XY}} \{LO_{XY} - p\} = LO_{XY} - R_X$$

A relative *region similarity measure SM_{XY}* was also introduced, as the absolute value of the difference in altitude between the pits of X and the adjacent basin Y:

$$SM_{XY} = |R_X - R_Y|$$

The relative depth D_{XY} and the region similarity measure SM_{XY} were, then, used to evaluate the relative significance of X with respect to Y. Precisely, a basin X was termed significant with respect to Y if the following holds:

$$SM_{XY} > St \quad OR \quad D_{XY} > Dt \tag{1}$$

where *St* and *Dt* are threshold values, computed automatically by using statistics on the initial watershed partition of the grey-level image.

In Fig. 3, the watershed partition of an image is shown as an example of the performance of flooding and digging to reduce over-segmentation, With respect to the initially detected 1213 basins, only 79 basins are found in the final image.

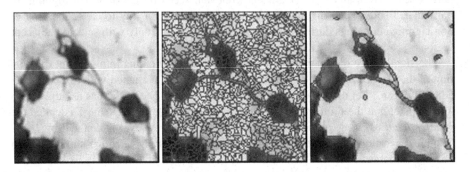

Fig. 3. Input image, left, partition of the image obtained by WT in 1213 regions, middle, segmentation by the algorithm [12] in 79 regions, right

4   Improving Watershed Segmentation by CBR

To improve the performance of the segmentation algorithm [12], we should not use a crisp test to decide about merging. In fact, according to rule (1) it is enough that one of the two measures overcomes the relative threshold, in order a region be classified as significant with respect to an adjacent region. We think that better results could be achieved if we require that both measures SM_{XY} and D_{XY} are taken into account, possibly giving different weights to their contributions. We also think that the weights should be determined by analyzing the image characteristics. Thus, we here use image characteristics and CBR to weight the influence of the two measures SM_{XY} and D_{XY}. Depending on image characteristics, we weight the influence of region similarity and of depth by means of two weights a and b, and introduce a threshold T as in the following:

$$\frac{1}{2}(a \cdot \frac{SM_{XY}}{St} + b \cdot \frac{D_{XY}}{Dt}) > T \qquad (2)$$

If at least one of the values SM_{XY}/St and D_{XY}/Dt is larger than 1, then rule (1) would classify the region X as significant with respect to the adjacent region Y. If $a=b=1$ and the threshold T is set to 0.5, rule (2) would also classify X as significant with respect to Y. If both SM_{XY}/St and D_{XY}/Dt have value larger than 1, then the threshold T in rule (2) can be set to 1 to classify X as by rule (1).

Table 1 shows possible combinations of values for a, b and T and the relative interpretations.

Table 1. Possible combinations of the values a, b and T

a	b	T	Interpretation
1.5	0,5	1	Region similarity is weighted more than depth.
1	1	0,5	Region similarity and depth are equally weighted.
0,75	1,25	0,7	Depth is weighted more than region similarity.
0,75	1,25	1,35	Region similarity is weighted less than depth, and SM_{XY} and D_{XY} are quite larger than the relative thresholds St and Dt.
1	1	0,95	Region similarity and depth are equally weighted, and SM_{XY} and D_{XY} can be smaller than the relative thresholds St and Dt.

4.1 Case Description

To use CBR we need to build our case-base. As said in Section 2, a case consists of a suitable description of an image, coupled with the best solution to its segmentation. The description of the image can be given in different ways. A possibility could be to directly store the image and compare the current image to the images stored in the cases, pixel to pixel. Some work has been done in this direction, e.g., in [14,15]. However, memory occupation and computational cost are quite large. We prefer to describe the images in terms of statistical features. These features are statistical measures of the grey levels, like mean, variance, skewness, kurtosis, variation coefficient, energy, entropy, and centroid, as suggested in [16]. These features are shown in Table 2, where the first order histogram $H(g)$ is equal to $N(g)/S$, being g the grey-level, $N(g)$ the number of pixels with grey-level g and S the total number of pixels. The image similarity is calculated on the basis of these features.

Table 2. Image Features

Feature Name	Calculation	Feature Name	Calculation
Mean	$\bar{g} = \sum_g g \cdot H(g)$	Variance	$\delta_g^2 = \sum_g (g-\bar{g})^2 H(g)$
Skewness	$g_s = \frac{1}{\delta_g^3} \sum_g (g-\bar{g})^3 H(g)$	Kurtosis	$g_k = \frac{1}{\delta_g^4} \sum_g (g-\bar{g})^4 H(g) - 3$
Variation Coefficient	$v = \frac{\delta}{\bar{g}}$	Entropy	$g_E = -\sum_g H(g)\log_2[H(g)]$
Centroid_x	$\bar{x} = \frac{\sum_x \sum_y xf(x,y)}{\bar{g}S}$	Centroid_y	$\bar{y} = \frac{\sum_x \sum_y yf(x,y)}{\bar{g}S}$

4.2 Similarity Measure

We compute the image similarity *SIM* between two images A and B in the data-base of images as the complement to 1 of the distance between A and B. The distance between A and B is computed as follows:

$$dist_{AB} = \frac{1}{k} \sum_{i=1}^{K} w_i \left| \frac{C_{iA} - C_{i\min}}{C_{i\max} - C_{i\min}} - \frac{C_{iB} - C_{i\min}}{C_{i\max} - C_{i\min}} \right|$$

where C_{iA} and C_{iB} are the values of the i-th feature of A and B, respectively, $C_{i\min}$ and $C_{i\max}$ are the minimum and maximum value respectively of the i-th feature of all images n the data-base, and w_i is the weight for the i-th feature with $w_1 + w_2 + ... + w_i + ... + w_k = 1$. In our case, we assign the same value to all weights.

4.3 Similarity Between Cases and Retrieval

Since our case base is small at the moment we assess the retrieval performance by evaluating the similarity relation between different images using clustering based on the normalized city-block metric (see Section 4.2) and the average linkage method [18]. The aim is to see how well the case description separate different cases and form groups of similar cases. The results are show in Fig. 4 for the statistical gray-level features. Our expectation was that images, for which we got the best segmentation by using the same values of the parameters, would cluster into groups of similar images. By following this idea, we have to cut the dendrogram in Fig. 4 by the cophenetic-similarity value equal to seven. In this way, the first aggregation, where images (image *Bio-1* and image *Flora-1*) having different similarity measures meet, does not form a group. The biological images *Bio-3-1, Bio-3-2, Bio-3-3, and Bio-3-4* form a cluster. The other images get more or less separate into groups with one case member only, regardless if they share the same segmentation parameters.

The results show that we can distinguish the images based on the proposed low-level image features and, thus, we are able to assign the best segmentation parameters to an input image with specific image characteristics.

From the retrieval point of view, it would be good to have only a few clusters with as many as possible case members sharing the same segmentation parameters. In fact, this would reduce the retrieval and similarity-determination time. In contrast, it is also possible to form groups having cases that do not share the same segmentation parameters, as long as it can support fast retrieval.

The hierarchy of case groups is used to single out cases that are not related to the current case. If the final node of the retrieval hierarchy is used, then searching the most similar case is accomplished within the associated group of cases, which should include the cases with the same image characteristics and the best segmentation parameters. The dendrogram shows that the similarity between all the cases is sensitive enough to achieve this task.

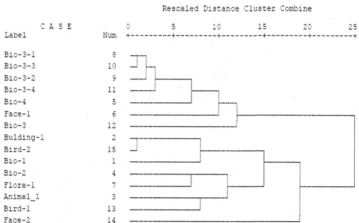

Dendrogram using Average Linkage (Within Group)

Fig. 4. Dendrogram for CBR based on statistical feature

4.4 Automatic Evaluation of the Segmentation Results

The similarity measure developed in [19] can be used for two purposes: 1) for image retrieval, based on the image matrix, and 2) for the evaluation of the segmentation results.

In this study, we use this measure for the evaluation of the segmentation results. In fact, we are interested in investigating if, by using this measure, we can achieve an objective criterion to compare not only qualitatively different segmentation outcomes. Thus, we use this similarity measure to compare the quality of the obtained segmentation result to the expected result (e.g. the segmentation manually drawn by an expert). We call this image the gold standard.

The algorithm computes the similarity between two image matrixes (see Fig. 5). According to the specified distance function, the proximity matrix is calculated, for one pixel at position r,s in image A, to the pixel at the same position in image B and to the surrounding pixels within a predefined window. Then, the minimum distance between the compared pixels is computed. The same process is done for the pixel at position r,s in image B. Afterwards, the average of the two minimal values is calculated. This process is repeated until all the pixels of both images have been processed. The final dissimilarity for the whole image is calculated from the average minimal pixel distance. The use of an appropriate window size should make this measure invariant to scaling, rotation and translation.

We used the above similarity measure to evaluate our segmentation result for the running example. The gold standard was in case A the binarized gradient image of the original image and in case B the manually labeled image. Table 3 shows the similarity-values obtained when comparing the original image to the standard watershed-based image segmentation and to the outcome of the algorithm in [12]. The highest dissimilarity was found for the pair-wise computation original-to-standard watershed.

Table 4 shows the similarity-values obtained when comparing the output of the new algorithm to the original image, in correspondence with different values for the

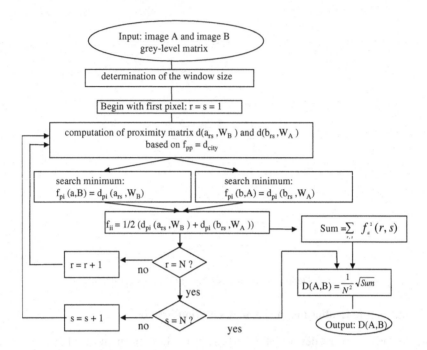

Fig. 5. Flowchart of the algorithm [19] for computing the similarity measure

parameters *a*, *b* and *T*. Based on the similarity-value we should be able to select the best segmentation parameters for the current input image. If this will work, it would also allow us to adjust the segmentation parameters by an automatic optimization procedure where the optimization function is the similarity-value.

The results in Table 4 show the best similarity value for the parameter combination *a*=0.75, *b*=1.25, and *T*=0.8. This result confirms our evaluation of the performance, done by visual observation of the results.

Furthermore the similarity values in Table 4 show that values converge to a local minimum when the best possible segmentation is achieved for the chosen parameter combination. It should be possible to guide a search strategy for the automatic selection of the best segmentation-parameter combination.

It is interesting to note that we obtain the same results for the manually labeled image and the binarized gradient image.

Table 3. Evaluation of the segmentation results for the running example, based on the similarity measure in [19], for the partitions obtained by standard watershed and by the algorithm in [12]

	Original to-original	Original-to-watershed segmentation	Original-to-segmentation by algorithm [12]
Case A	0	0.04656367	0.00808133
Case B	0	0.045201939	0.005551775

Table 4. Evaluation of the different segmentation results for the running example, based on the similarity measure in [19], for the new algorithm

Segmentation Results	Parameters *a*=1,*b*=1, *T*=0.9	Parameters *a*=1,*b*=1, *T*=0.7	Parameters *a*=1,*b*=1, *T*=0.65
Case A	0.009195196	0.008050811	0.00805929
Case B	0.006305389	0.005838306	0.00555007

Segmentation Results	Parameters *a*=0.75,*b*=1.25, *T*=0.8	Parameters *a*=1.5,*b*=0.5, *T*=0.2
Case A	0.008032165	0.008313606
Case B	0.005482262	0.006072278

5 Discussion

Our case-base includes images mainly of biological nature, like different kinds of cells. The results we have achieved are generally satisfactory. The evaluation of the results has been done by comparing the segmentation obtained by our method with the segmentation based on the similarity measure described in Section 4.4. With respect to the algorithm [12], the new method based on CBR generally performs better. The two algorithms perform mostly the same, when the case retrieved from the case-base for the image at hand suggests that the best solution is for *a*=1, *b*=1 and *T*=0,5, i.e., when region similarity and depth have the same influence and at least one out of SM_{XY}/St and D_{XY}/Dt is larger than 1. This occurs for the input image shown in the example of Fig.3. The two segmentations obtained for this image by the algorithm [12] and the new algorithm are shown in Fig. 6. In turn, the new method performs significantly better whenever image similarity suggests that the best solution for the current image is obtained with a different choice for *a*, *b* and *T*. See for example the images shown in Fig. 7. In Fig. 7 top, the image is segmented into 286 regions by the algorithm [12], while a significantly less over-segmented partition in 54 regions is obtained by using the solution *a*=1.5, *b*=0.5 and *T*=1 as suggested by taking into account the image similarity between the current image and those stored in the case-base. Analogously, for the image in Fig.7 bottom, a segmentation in 126 regions is obtained by using the solution with *a*=1, *b*=1 and *T*=0.95, while 200 regions were obtained by the algorithm [12].

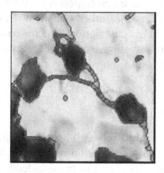 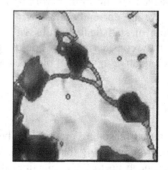

Fig. 6. Two very similar results, obtained by using the algorithm in [12], left, and the new method, right

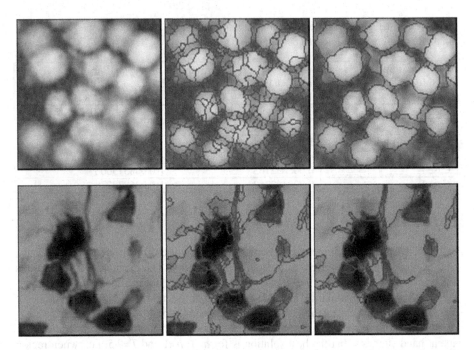

Fig. 7. Input image, left, segmentation with the algorithm [12], middle, and segmentation with the new method, right. In both top and bottom examples, a better segmentation is obtained by the new method

We have tried to use our method for a general image domain, including for example faces, animals and natural scenes. Some of these images, though appearing to the user as clearly different from the biological images in the case base, where characterized by similar statistical features. Thus, these images would be expected to be well segmented by using the same values for *a*, *b* and *T* adopted for the correspondingly similar biological images. Unfortunately, the values empirically found as those producing the best segmentation results for the non biological images did not coincide with those found via CBR. This means that to extend the validity of our method to a general image domain, further work related to image description is necessary. The alternatives we are currently considering are the use of other statistical features, or a combination of statistical features with an image description directly based on the images, or by considering also non-image information (such as the position of the camera, the relative movement of the camera, and the object category).

6 Conclusion

The case-based reasoning process can be applied to solve all aspects of images segmentation, from choosing the appropriate image segmentation method/parameters for the actual image up to the evaluation of the results, and to provide feedback to the system for performance improvement. Therefore, the model construction aspect for image segmentation can be handled very efficiently based on CBR. CBR is an incremental knowledge acquisition method as well as a reasoning method. New situations can be captured in an efficient way and the behavior of the segmentation algorithm can be efficiently studied. New situations can be made available for reasoning as soon as they have been captured by the system. This allows the construction of a model for image segmentation that is applicable to wide range of images. We have described how CBR can be applied to watershed-based image segmentation by controlling the merging process. The case image-description used for indexing and the similarity measure have been described.

More research has to be done on the definition of the proper image description. Image description based on statistical features might properly cover the information about image quality, but this is possibly not enough for watershed-based image segmentation. The introduction of texture features is a promising step in this direction and needs to be further investigated. Moreover, there might be other features, besides statistical and texture features, that could result as more appropriate.

In the future, we plan to investigate more extensively the automatic parameter selection process based on the segmentation-evaluation procedure we have proposed in Section 4.4. This is the final step we have to solve for closed-loop image segmentation control scheme.

Acknowledgements

This work has been partially supported by the Italian National Research Council, CNR, in the framework of the Short Term Mobility Program 2006.

References

1. Pal, N.R., Pal, S.K.: A review on image segmentation techniques. Pattern Recognition 26(9), 1277–1294 (1993)
2. Pham, D.L., Xu, C., Prince, J.L.: Current methods in medical image segmentation. Annual Review of Biomedical Engineering 2, 315–337 (2000)
3. Lucchese, L., Mitra, S.K.: Color Image Segmentation: A State-of-the-Art Survey, "Image Processing, Vision, and Pattern Recognition. In: Proc. of the Indian National Science Academy (INSA-A). New Delhi, India, vol. 67 A(2), pp. 207–221 (2001)
4. Cheng, H.D., Jiang, X.H., Sun, Y., Wang, J.: Color image segmentation: advances and prospects. Pattern Recognition 34, 2259–2281 (2001)
5. Freixenet, J., Muñoz, X., Raba, D., Martí, J., Cufí, X.: Yet Another Survey on Image Segmentation: Region and Boundary Information Integration. In: Heyden, A., Sparr, G., Nielsen, M., Johansen, P. (eds.) ECCV 2002. LNCS, vol. 2352, pp. 408–422. Springer, Heidelberg (2002)
6. Beucher, S., Lantuejoul, C.: Use of watersheds in contour detection. In: Proc. Int. Workshop on Image Processing, Real-Time Edge and Motion Detection/Estimation, Rennes, France (1979)
7. Beucher, S., Meyer, F.: The morphological approach of segmentation: the watershed transformation. In: Dougherty, E. (ed.) Mathematical Morphology in Image Processing, pp. 433–481. Marcel Dekker, New York (1993)

8. Perner, P.: An Architecture for a CBR Image Segmentation System. Journal on Engineering Application in Artificial Intelligence 12(6), 749–759 (1999)
9. Perner, P.: CBR Ultra Sonic Image Interpretation. In: Blanzieri, E., Portinale, L. (eds.) EWCBR 2000. LNCS (LNAI), vol. 1898, pp. 479–481. Springer, Heidelberg (2000)
10. Perner, P.: Are case-based reasoning and dissimilarity-based classification two sides of the same coin? Journal Engineering Applications of Artificial Intelligence 15(3), 205–216 (2002)
11. Perner, P., Perner, H., Müller, B.: Similarity Guided Learning of the Case Description and Improvement of the System Performance in an Image Classification System. In: Craw, S., Preece, A.D. (eds.) ECCBR 2002. LNCS (LNAI), vol. 2416, pp. 604–612. Springer, Heidelberg (2002)
12. Frucci, M.: Oversegmentation Reduction by Flooding Regions and Digging Watershed Lines. In: International Journal of Pattern Recognition and Artificial Intelligence, vol. 20(1), pp. 15–38. World Scientific, Singapore (2006)
13. Frucci, M., Arcelli, C., di Baja, G.S.: Detecting and ranking foreground regions in gray-level images. In: De Gregorio, M., Di Maio, V., Frucci, M., Musio, C. (eds.) BVAI 2005. LNCS, vol. 3704, pp. 406–415. Springer, Heidelberg (2005)
14. Zamperoni, P., Starovoitov, V.: How dissimilar are two gray-scale images. In: Proceedings of the 17th DAGM Symposium, pp. 448–455. Springer, Heidelberg (1995)
15. Wilson, D.L., Baddeley, A.J., Owens, R.A.: A new metric for grey-scale image comparision. International Journal of Computer Vision 24(1), 1–29 (1997)
16. Dreyer, H., Sauer, W.: Prozeßanalyse Berlin, Verlag Technik (1982)
17. Perner, P., Holt, A., Richter, M.: Image Processing in Case-Based Reasoning. The Knowledge Engineering Review 20(3), 311–314
18. Jain, A.K., Dubes, R.C.: Algorithms for clustering data. Prentice-Hall, Inc, Upper Saddle River, NJ, USA (1988)
19. Zamperoni, P., Starovotov, V.: How dissimilar are two gray-scale images. In: Proc. 17th DAGM Symposium, pp. 445–448. Springer, Berlin (1995)

A Case-Based Song Scheduler
for Group Customised Radio*

Claudio Baccigalupo and Enric Plaza

IIIA - Artificial Intelligence Research Institute
CSIC - Spanish Council for Scientific Research
Campus UAB, 08193 Bellaterra, Catalonia, Spain
Vox: +34-93-5809570; Fax: +34-93-5809661
{claudio,enric}@iiia.csic.es

Abstract. This paper presents a knowledge-intensive Case-Based Reasoning system to generate a sequence of songs customised for a community of listeners. To select each song in the sequence, first a subset of songs musically associated with the last song of the sequence is retrieved from a music pool; then the preferences of the audience expressed as cases are reused to customise the selection for the group of listeners; finally listeners can revise their satisfaction (or lack thereof) for the songs they have heard. We have integrated this CBR system with *Poolcasting*, a social group-based Web radio architecture in which listeners can actively contribute to the music played and influence the channels programming process. The paper introduces the Poolcasting architecture, presents the CBR technique that tailors in real-time the music of each channel for the current audience, and discusses how this approach may radically improve the group-satisfaction of the audience for a Web radio.

1 Introduction

Although digital distribution has revolutionised the way in which we buy, sell and share music, not much has changed in the way we listen to songs in shared environments. In different situations, groups of people with similar tastes gather to listen to a unique stream of music, but none of these situations is customised to the audience. In a music club, for instance, a DJ can be too busy mixing to check the reaction of the public; in a radio, broadcasters have it difficult to meet the taste of all the listeners; with a juke-box, the available records can be very limited for the audience to appreciate; in a home-party, anyone can easily monopolise the control over the music, and songs can be played in any sequence, with annoying disruptions between genres.

In this paper, we present an interactive social framework to overcome the problems of a group scenario similar to the ones above, with the goal to improve the group-satisfaction of an audience. In short, we propose a novel group-based

---

* This research is partially supported by the MID-CBR (TIN2006-15140-C03-01) project and by a MyStrands scholarship.

R.O. Weber and M.M. Richter (Eds.): ICCBR 2007, LNAI 4626, pp. 433–448, 2007.

Web radio architecture, called Poolcasting, where the music played on each channel is not pre-programmed, but influenced in real-time by the current audience. In addition, users can submit explicit preferences: via a Web interface they can request new songs to be played, evaluate the scheduled songs and send feedback about recently played ones. A main issue is how to guarantee fairness to the members of the audience with respect to the songs that are broadcast. For this purpose, we have implemented a CBR technique that schedules songs for each channel combining both musical requirements (such as variety and continuity) and listeners' preferences. In order to keep fairness in the presence of concurrent preferences, we use a strategy that favours those listeners that were less satisfied with the last songs played.

The contribution of this paper is two-fold. First we present the Poolcasting Web radio architecture, where users can interact to influence the music played. Then we present a CBR technique that, for each Web radio channel, schedules a sequence of songs customised towards the group-satisfaction of the listeners.

2   Poolcasting

Poolcasting is a novel framework providing a Web radio service, with an architecture based on group customisation and interaction. Poolcasting takes inspiration from home-parties, where participants can contribute with their own records to the *pool* of music and can control in turn which songs are played. In Poolcasting, any user can share her personal music digital library, adding her songs to *Music Pool*, and can interact via a Web interface, to evaluate the songs played and propose new songs to play (see Fig. 1). These interactions allow the sequence of songs played on each channel to be *customised* for the current listeners. Let us present an example of how a user can interact with a Poolcasting Web radio.

Example 1. Mark checks via the Web interface the list of channels of a Poolcasting radio and joins the *'80s Music Channel*, which has 3 other participants and a pool of 90 songs. The Reflex *(Duran Duran)* is currently playing, and True Blue *(Madonna)* has been scheduled to play next. Mark shares his music library: the songs he owns become part of the Music Pool of the radio. At some moment, the system has schedule which song to play after True Blue. First, it retrieves from the Music Pool a subset of songs that fit the channel context (songs from the '80s) and are musically associated with the last scheduled track; these are: Heaven Is A Place On Earth *(B. Carlisle)*, True Colors *(C. Lauper)* and Love Shack *(The B-52's)*. Next, the preferences of each listener towards these three songs are evaluated; this is done by analysing the content of each listener's library. For example, the system discovers that Mark does not have True Colors in his library, but owns other themes from C. Lauper, and has given them positive ratings; thus it deduces a preference of Mark for this song over the other two. Then, the system merges the individual preferences of all the listeners with a strategy that balances fairness; for instance, it schedules Mark's preferred song at this turn, because he has just entered the channel, but will favour someone else on the next turn.

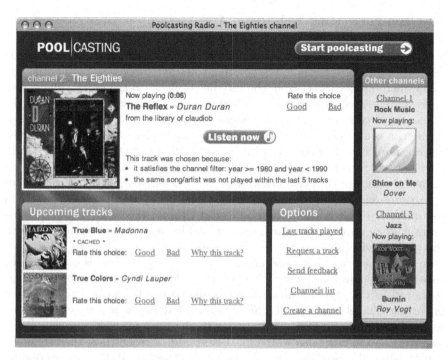

Fig. 1. The Poolcasting radio Web Interface

Using the Web interface, Mark sees that True Colors has been scheduled; he approves of this choice and sends a positive feedback, which is stored as new knowledge acquired over his preferences. Other listeners give a positive rating to this choice as well; this reinforces the knowledge that (True Blue, True Colors) is a good association of songs for the '80s Music Channel. While listening to True Colors, another listener, Lisa, recalls that her library contains Time After Time (C. Lauper) performed by Miles Davis, and figures that other participants will like to hear this track, for they will listen to an uncommon version of a known song from the Eighties. Using the Web interface, Lisa recommends this song for the channel; her proposal is accepted and after a while the song is played. Mark gets to listen to one of his favourite songs in a version he was unaware of, and all the way appreciates very much. He assigns a positive rating to this choice, increasing both the association between this and the previous song, and the reputation of Lisa as a good recommender.

Thus, Poolcasting combines both bottom-up and top-down approaches: users can contribute to the available music and influence the programming, while the actual choice of music played is taken by a technique that combines knowledge about songs' associations and listeners' preferences. In the rest of this section, we will first outline the innovative components of Poolcasting that allow listeners to influence the music played (Sect. 2.1), and next the requirements for a technique able to customise the music for the current audience (Sect. 2.2).

2.1   The Poolcasting Web Radio Architecture

The two main components of a typical Web radio are the *Music Library* (a large static collection of songs in a digital format) and the *Streaming Server* (the machine where users connect from the Internet to listen to the radio). Many Web radios have several channels; each corresponds to an Internet stream, where the Streaming Server continuously broadcasts songs from the Music Library. *Listeners* can connect to these streams with an appropriate stream-enabled media player. Two more components in a common Web radio are the *Song Scheduler* and the *Stream Generator*. The first is responsible for determining the sequence of songs for each channel, and generally is very simple, either random or time/genre-related (e.g., from 6pm to 8pm only play classic music). The second continuously retrieves the next scheduled song from the Music Library, transforms it in an uncompressed audio signal, and loads it to the Streaming Server, that will broadcast it once the previous song ends.

In the Poolcasting Web radio architecture (see Fig. 2), there is no centralised collection of audio files, but rather a virtual *Music Pool*, made of the songs contained in the personal music libraries shared by the participants. Another important difference is that the *Song Scheduler* does not just select each song to be played, but also has to connect via the Internet to the library containing that song and to download it in a local *Song Buffer*, from where the Streaming Server will read it once the previous song ends. The Song Buffer ensures that an uninterrupted music stream can be served, without gaps between songs. A central *Database* is continuously updated to keep track of the current participants, the songs they share and the channel they are listening to. Poolcasting offers a *Web Interface* where *Visitors* can check information about channels, and interact to share libraries, request songs and send feedback. The Poolcasting *Administrator*

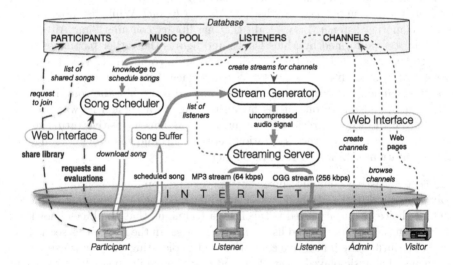

Fig. 2. Architecture of the Poolcasting Web radio

only controls the server components of the Web radio (e.g., restarting servers, administrating accesses, managing channels).

2.2 The Task of the Song Scheduler

The Song Scheduler is responsible for programming the sequence of songs for each channel, following a policy of "scheduling two songs in an advance": while song X is playing, and song Y is in the local buffer ready to be played, song Z is decided by the Song Scheduler to play after Y. Once X ends, song Y is reproduced, song Z is downloaded to the local buffer (replacing Y), and a new song is scheduled to play after Z.

The goal of the Song Scheduler is to provide a satisfactory and customised listening experience to the participants that are simultaneously listening to a channel. To achieve this goal, we argue that a combination of four properties is required: 1) no song or artist should be repeated closely on a channel (*variety*); 2) each song should be musically associated with the song it follows (*continuity*); 3) each song should match the musical preferences of the current listeners, or at least of most of them (*individual satisfaction*); 4) the more a listener is unsatisfied with the songs recently streamed, the more her preferences should influence the selection of the next songs that will be played so that, throughout the whole broadcasting, she will listen to songs she likes (*fairness*).

The advantage of the Poolcasting architecture is that user interaction allows the Song Scheduler to *model the musical preferences* of each listener and exploit them to customise the content of the channels. In fact, the *explicit evaluations* made by the users via the Web interface offer the system an overview of the listeners' preferences (e.g., Mark approves of the selection of True Colors, the system infers that he likes this song). In addition, Poolcasting is able to work *without* any user interaction, by exploiting the *implicit knowledge* contained in the user shared music libraries in the form of *listening experience* data.

3   A Case-Based Reasoning Song Scheduler

We present now the Case-Based Reasoning technique we have developed to accomplish the task of the Song Scheduler in a Poolcasting Web radio. Let $\mathcal{P}(t)$ be the set of Participants at time t, let $\mathcal{L}(P)$ be the set of songs in the library of a Participant P, and let $\mathcal{C}(t)$ be the Music Pool at time t: $\mathcal{C}(t) = \bigcup_{P \in \mathcal{P}(t)} \mathcal{L}(P)$. Let H be a channel of the Web radio; let $\phi(H)$ be the Channel Pool of H, that is, the subset of songs of $\mathcal{C}(t)$ that comply with the definition of channel H (e.g., the Channel Pool of the *'80 Music Channel* contains only songs from 1980 to 1989). Let Y be the last song scheduled on channel H. The task of the Song Scheduler is to select, among all the songs in $\phi(H)$, a song Z to schedule after Y on channel H that satisfies the four properties above. To fulfil this goal, we employ a CBR approach that comprises three steps (see Fig. 3):

1. *(Retrieve Process)* Retrieves from $\phi(H)$ a subset of songs (the *retrieved set*) either recommended by some participant via the Web interface or that have not been played recently and are musically associated with Y.

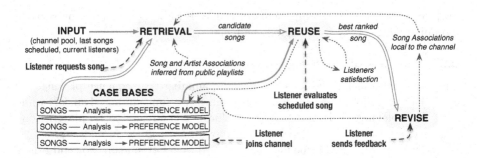

Fig. 3. The CBR schema

2. *(Reuse Process)* Ranks the retrieved set combining the preferences of the current listeners, giving more importance to those listeners less satisfied with the music recently played on H; the song that best matches the four properties of Sect. 2.2 is scheduled to play on H after Y.
3. *(Revise Process)* Listeners can evaluate the songs played on H; a positive/negative feedback increases/decreases the degree of association of this song with the previous one played, relatively to channel H.

We consider the library of each participant as a Case Base. Each case is a tuple (song, artist, preference degree), where the preference degree reflects how much a participant likes a song. In Sect. 3.1 we will explain how, when a new user joins a channel, her musical preferences are inferred from the listening experience of the songs contained in her personal music library. In Sect. 3.2 we will explain the concept of musical association and how to infer which songs or artists are associated from the analysis of a large public collection of playlists. In Sect. 3.3 we will present the Retrieve Process, that selects from the Case Bases a subset of songs to achieve the goals of variety and continuity. In Sect. 3.4 we will detail the Reuse Process, that combines individual preferences to choose a song that fairly satisfies the group as a whole. Finally (Sect. 3.5), we will present the Revise Process, where users can evaluate the songs played on each channel.

3.1   The Participants' Case Bases

Every Case Base contains the list of songs in the shared library of a Participant, and a preference degree for each song. We define, for each participant $P \in \mathcal{P}(t)$, and for each song $S \in \mathcal{L}(P)$, a *preference degree* $g(P, S)$ with values in $[-1, 1]$, where -1 means P hates S, 1 means P loves S, and 0 reflects indifference. To assess the preference degrees of P, we use her library to extract information about her listening experience, namely the rating she assigned to each song and the number of times she listened to them. We assume that the higher the rating and the higher the play count, the stronger the preference. However, the *absolute* values of rating and play count are not relevant, for a "high" play count or rating for one user (e.g., 10 times, 3 stars) could be "low" for another user. For this reason, we normalise both values according to the average listener behaviour, in the following way. Let ϱ_{min} and ϱ_{max} be the minimum and maximum possible ratings (e.g., 1 and 5 in iTunes), let $\hat{\varrho} = \frac{1}{2}(\varrho_{max} + \varrho_{min})$, let $\overline{\varrho_P}$ be the average rating assigned by P, and let $\varrho_{P,S}$ be the rating assigned by P to S; the *normalised rating* $n(P,S)$ of P for S is the function:

$$n(P,S) = \frac{2}{\varrho_{max} - \varrho_{min}} \left[\varrho_{P,S} - \hat{\varrho} - \frac{(\varrho_{P,S} - \varrho_{max})(\varrho_{P,S} - \varrho_{min})(\overline{\varrho_P} - \hat{\varrho})}{(\overline{\varrho_P} - \varrho_{max})(\overline{\varrho_P} - \varrho_{min})} \right]$$

that takes values in $[-1,1]$ and equals 1 (respectively -1) when the absolute rating for S is ϱ_{max} (respectively ϱ_{min}). For any non-rated song, we define $n(P,S) = 0$.

Let ν_{min} and ν_{max} be the minimum and maximum play counts in the library of P, let $\hat{\nu} = \frac{1}{2}(\nu_{max} + \nu_{min})$, let $\overline{\nu_P}$ be the average play count of P, and let $\nu_{P,S}$ be the play count of song S; the *normalised play count* $m(P,S)$ of S for P is:

$$m(P,S) = \frac{2}{\nu_{max} - \nu_{min}} \left[\nu_{P,S} - \hat{\nu} - \frac{(\nu_{P,S} - \nu_{max})(\nu_{P,S} - \nu_{min})(\overline{\nu_P} - \hat{\nu})}{(\overline{\nu_P} - \nu_{max})(\overline{\nu_P} - \nu_{min})} \right] .$$

We assign $m(P,S) = 0$ if P has never listened to the song S. For any $S \in \mathcal{L}(P)$ present in the library of P, we define the *preference degree of P* as: $g(P,S) = \theta n(P,S) + (1-\theta)m(P,S)$, where θ is a parameter in $[0,1]$ to give more importance to the rating or to the play count (in our current implementation, $\theta = 0.5$).

This measure can be extended to songs not included in the library of P, following this assumption: if $\mathcal{L}(P)$ does not contain a song S but contains other songs *from the same artist* of S, then the preference of P for S is estimated as her average preference for those songs (e.g., Mark has rated positively many songs by C. Lauper, we assume he will like songs by C. Lauper he doesn't own as well). Let S be a song not included in the library of P, and let $\mathcal{G}(P,S)$ be the set of songs in $\mathcal{L}(P)$ from the same artist of S: $\mathcal{G}(P,S) = \{S' \in \mathcal{L}(P) \,|\, a(S') = a(S)\}$, where the function $a(S)$ returns the artist of song S. We define the *preference degree* of P for any song S as follows:

$$g(P,S) = \begin{cases} \theta n(P,S) + (1-\theta)m(P,S) & \text{if } S \in \mathcal{L}(P), \\ \frac{1}{\#(\mathcal{G}(P,S))} \sum_{S' \in \mathcal{G}(P,S)} g(P,S') & \text{if } S \notin \mathcal{L}(P) \wedge \#(\mathcal{G}(P,S)) > 0, \\ 0 & \text{otherwise} \end{cases}$$

3.2 Musical Domain Knowledge

One of the goal of the Song Scheduler is to program on each channel a sequence of musically associated songs (*continuity*). While a human DJ knows from experience which songs are associated, we use an automatic process to extract this knowledge from a large collection of playlists available on the Web. In brief, we check which songs and artists co-occur more often in these playlists, and assume that the more the playlists where they co-occur and the closer the distance at which they occur, the higher their association. Extracting such knowledge from playlists is much better for our goal than using a content-based method (e.g., extraction of acoustic features) because playlists include cultural and social information that cannot be reduced to audio signal, and also contain songs in a specific order, which can be preserved when scheduling songs for a radio channel.

Let $s(X, Y) \in [0, 1]$ be the *song association degree* from a song Y to a song Z. Counting just the frequency with which two songs appear together in a collection of playlists is not sufficient to estimate their association degree, for some songs are quite rare, but still are strongly associated with other rare songs. One solution is to consider the association strength from song X to song Y as the conditional probability to find song Y, given a playlist that contains song X, i.e., $P(Y|X) = \frac{f(X,Y)}{f(X)}$, where $f(X)$ is the *popularity* of X (number of playlists where X appears). Notice that $P(X|Y) \neq P(Y|X)$: the relation is not symmetric. This measure is biased towards having high conditional probabilities with songs that are very popular. That is, $P(Y|X)$ may be high, as a result of the fact that Y occurs very frequently and not because X and Y are strongly associated. We correct this problem dividing $P(Y|X)$ by a quantity that depends on the popularity of Y: if Y is very popular (say, more than the average), the association degree is decreased, otherwise it is increased; the exact degree of scaling depends on the playlists and on the distribution of popularity among songs. The following formula takes into account these factors to compute the association between two songs X and Y:

$$\frac{f(X,Y)}{f(X) \cdot (f(Y)/\overline{f})^{\beta}} \tag{1}$$

where $\overline{f}$ is the average song popularity, and β is a parameter that takes a value between 0 and 1; when $\beta = 0$, the function is identical to $P(Y|X)$.

We improve this measure by taking into account how far apart two songs are in a playlist, and their relative order. We make three assumptions: 1) the farther two songs occur in a playlist, the smaller is their association; 2) if two songs are separated by more than a threshold of $\delta \geqslant 1$ songs in a playlist, their association is null; 3) any song X is more associated to the songs it follows in a playlist than to the songs it precedes. The last point can be explained as follows: our final goal is to program a channel of music by incrementally adding one song *after* the other, and since the order between songs can be meaningful (e.g., the end of a track mixes into the beginning of the next one), we endeavour to preserve it.

Let Q be a collection of playlists and $q \in Q$ be one of these playlists, $q = (S_1, S_2, \dots)$. Let X and Y be two songs; we denote as $d(q, X, Y)$ the distance that separates them in q, e.g., $d(q, S_i, S_j) = j - i$. If either X or Y does not occur in q, $d(q, X, Y) = \infty$. The songs X and Y are associated in q if $d(q, X, Y) \leqslant \delta$; formally we define their *song association degree in q* as:

$$w(q, X, Y) = \begin{cases} 0 & \text{if } |d(q, X, Y)| > \delta \\ 1/|d(q, X, Y)| & \text{if } |d(q, X, Y)| \leqslant \delta \wedge d(q, X, Y) > 0 \\ \alpha/|d(q, X, Y)| & \text{if } |d(q, X, Y)| \leqslant \delta \wedge d(q, X, Y) < 0 \end{cases}$$

where $\alpha \in (0, 1)$ is a parameter to assign higher associations to post-occurrences than to pre-occurrences. Finally, to estimate the *song association degree* between X and Y, we substitute in Eq. 1 the numerator with $\sum_{q \in Q} w(p, X, Y)$. That is, rather than accumulating 1 for each playlist q where X and Y co-occur, we accumulate $w(q, X, Y)$, which equals 1 only if Y occurs contiguously after X in q, otherwise $0 \leqslant w(q, X, Y) < 1$:

$$s(X, Y) = \frac{\sum_{q \in Q} w(q, X, Y)}{f(X)(f(Y)/\overline{f})^\beta} \ .$$

With this measure we have estimated the association for every pair of songs in a large database of playlists retrieved from the Web-based music community MyStrands (http://www.mystrands.com). We chose MyStrands because it offers a Web API called OpenStrands that helps us automate the retrieval process. The average length of the playlists was 17 songs; the average popularity was 37 for songs and 235 for artists. We set the parameters to: $\alpha = 0.75$, $\beta = 0.5$, $\delta = 3$ and ignored any song that occurred just once, to guarantee a valid statistical significance. We also discarded associations within the same artist, for their obviousness. The result was a set of 112,238 distinct songs that have a positive association with some other song; for instance, the top associated tracks found for Smoke On The Water *(Deep Purple)* were: Cold Metal *(Iggy Pop)*, Iron Man *(Black Sabbath)*, China Grove *(The Doobie Brothers)*, Crossroads *(Eric Clapton)*.

We have mined the same collection of playlists from MyStrands to gather knowledge about associated artists. Given a playlist $q = (S_1, S_2, \dots)$ and two artists A and B, we denote as $d'(q, A, B)$ the minimum distance that separates a song of A and a song of B in q, e.g., if $a(S_i) = A$ and $a(S_j) = B$, $d'(q, A, B) = j - i$. If q does not contain both a song from A and a song from B, then $d'(q, A, B) = \infty$. We define the *artist association degree in* q from A to B as: $w'(q, A, B) = \frac{1}{|d'(q, A, B)|}$ if $|d'(q, A, B)| \leqslant \delta'$, otherwise $w'(q, A, B) = 0$. Notice that the order is not important when we deal with artists. To estimate the *artist association degree* from any artist A to any artist B, we use an approach similar to the one used for the song association degree: we substitute in Eq. 1 the numerator with $\sum_{q \in Q} w'(q, A, B)$ in the following way:

$$s'(A, B) = \frac{\sum_{q \in Q} w'(q, A, B)}{f'(A)(f'(B)/\overline{f'})^\beta}$$

where $f'(A)$ is the number of playlists where any song by A appears, and $\overline{f'}$ is the average artist popularity. From the dataset of MyStrands, using $\delta' = 2$ as the maximum distance, $\alpha = 0.75$, $\beta = 0.5$, and ignoring any artist that occurred just once, we have obtained that 25,881 distinct artists have a positive association with some other artist. The value $\beta = 0.5$ was decided after several experiments, in order to obtain a nice mix of more and less popular artists in these associations. For instance, the top associated artists found for Abba were: Agnetha Faltskog, A-Teens, Chic, Gloria Gaynor, The 5th Dimension. Notice that the first two names (Agnetha Faltskog and A-Teens) are not very popular, but are very much associated with Abba: the first was their lead singer, the second is a cover band of Abba. As the sequence continues, more popular names appear, still associated with Abba, but in a weaker degree.

3.3 The Retrieve Process

This process has two subsequent steps: first each song $Z \in \phi(H)$ is rated with a *relevance value* $r(Y, Z)$ in $[0, 1]$ that expresses how much a song Z satisfies the conditions of variety and continuity; then the κ best rated songs are retrieved.

For every song Z requested via the Web interface, $r(Y, Z) = 1$, these songs are always retrieved. For every song Z either recently scheduled on H (namely, within the last ι songs) or from an artist recently scheduled on H (namely, within the last ζ songs), $r(Y, Z) = 0$, these songs are never retrieved. Notice that the values of ι and ζ are defined for each channel; for instance a "Frank Sinatra only" channel would be created with $\zeta = 0$ (artists repeated without reserve), while a "Nice Dance Mix" channel would probably have a high value for ι (songs rarely repeated).

For any other song Z (neither requested nor repeated), we define the relevance value on the basis of the musical association between Y and Z, as follows: $r(Y, Z) = s(Y, Z) + \epsilon u(Y, Z) + \epsilon^2 v(Y, Z) + \epsilon^3 s'(a(Y), a(Z))$, where $s(Y, Z)$ measures the song association from Y to Z, $u(Y, Z)$ evaluates the association from songs of the artist of Y to Z, $v(Y, Z)$ evaluates the association from songs of artists associated with the artist of Y to Z, $s'(a(Y), a(Z))$ measures the association from the artist of Y to the artist of Z, and the parameter ϵ in $[0, 1]$ controls the decreasing importance of these four conditions. Precisely, $u(Y, Z)$ is the average song association degree from every song whose artist is $a(Y)$ to Z: $u(Y, Z) = \frac{1}{\#(\mathcal{U}(Y,Z))} \sum_{W \in \mathcal{U}(Y,Z)} s(W, Z)$, where $\mathcal{U}(Y, Z) = \{W \in \mathcal{C}(t) \,|\, s(W, Z) > 0 \wedge a(Y) = a(W)\}$, and $v(Y, Z)$ is the average song association degree from every song whose artist is associated with $a(Y)$ to Z, combined with the relative artist association degree: $v(Y, Z) = \frac{1}{\#(\mathcal{V}(Y,Z))} \sum_{W \in \mathcal{V}(Y,Z)} (s(W, Z) \, s'(a(W), a(Y)))$, where $\mathcal{V}(Y, Z) = \{W \in \mathcal{C}(t) \,|\, s(W, Z) > 0 \wedge s'(a(W), a(Y)) > 0\}$.

The Retrieve process returns the first κ songs of $\phi(H)$ ranked along $r(Y, Z)$.

3.4 The Reuse Process

This process ranks the retrieved set according to the preferences of the current listeners of the channel and their "group satisfaction", and returns the best ranked song as the next song to be scheduled on the channel. The most critical challenge is how to combine different individual preferences into one group satisfaction value. To guarantee fairness among listeners, we propose a weighted average of the individual preferences, where the weight associated to each listener depends on her satisfaction about the last scheduled songs.

Let $\mathcal{O}(H, t) \subseteq \mathcal{P}(t)$ be the Participants who are listening to channel H at time t; let $\mathcal{R}(H, t) \subseteq \mathcal{C}(t)$ be the retrieved songs, and let $S \in \mathcal{R}(H, t)$ be one of these songs. The *group preference* of $\mathcal{O}(H, t)$ for S is a function $G(S, H, t)$ in $[-1, 1]$ defined by two cases:

(AVERAGE) if none of the current listeners *hates* song S (that is, all the individual preferences for S are beyond a threshold μ), then the group preference is calculated as a weighted average of the individual preferences:

$$G(S, H, t) = \frac{1}{\#(\mathcal{O}(H,t))} \sum_{P \in \mathcal{O}(H,t)} g(P, S)\,(1 - \omega(P, H, t)) \qquad (2)$$

(WITHOUT MISERY) otherwise, if $\exists P \in \mathcal{O}(H, t) : g(P, S) < \mu$, then the group preference is set to the minimum possible value: $G(S, H, t) = -1$.

The weight $\omega(P, H, t) \in [0, 1]$ in Eq. 2 is a function that biases the average in favour of the listeners more unsatisfied with the songs recently scheduled on channel H. Hereafter, we explain how the weight $\omega(P, H, t))$ is calculated. First, let us remark two important properties of this *Average Without Misery* [8] strategy: it is Pareto optimal (if at least one listener prefers S to S' and nobody prefers S' to S, then $G(S, H, t) \geqslant G(S', H, t)$) and it avoids misery: if at least one listener has a *bad* preference for S' (lower than a threshold μ), and no listener has a *bad* preference for S (lower than μ), then $G(S, H, t) \geqslant G(S', H, t)$.

The measure $\omega(P, H, t)$ estimates the individual *channel satisfaction degree* of a participant P at time t. To evaluate $\omega(P, H, t)$ we first need to know the satisfaction degree of P for each of the songs scheduled on H while P was listening. Let $\mathcal{X}(P, H, t) = (X_1, X_2, \ldots, X_z)$ be this set of songs (X_1 is the song scheduled when P entered the channel, X_z the last song scheduled), and let $X_i \in \mathcal{X}(P, H, t)$ be one of these songs, scheduled at a time $\hat{t} < t$; we define the *song satisfaction degree* of P for X_i as: $e(P, X_i, H) = g(P, X_i) - \max_{S \in \mathcal{R}(H,\hat{t})} g(P, S) + 1$. This function takes values in $[-1, 1]$ and equals 1 only when the scheduled song X_i was the most preferred song by P in the retrieved set $\mathcal{R}(H, \hat{t})$.

By combining the song satisfaction degrees of P for the songs in $\mathcal{X}(P, H, t)$ we can estimate the value of $\omega(P, H, t)$. Since satisfaction is an emotion that wears off with time, we combine the satisfaction degrees assigning more importance to the most recent songs. To achieve this goal we use a geometric series: $\sum_{i=1}^{z} \chi^{z-i}\, e(P, X_i, H)$, where $\chi \in [0, 1]$ measures the decay rate of satisfaction over time (e.g., $\chi = 0.8$). Since this series has values in $[-1, 1]$, and we require $\omega(P, H, t)$ to have values in $[0, 1]$, we rewrite the series normalised to this interval of values, and finally define the *channel satisfaction degree* for P as:

$$\omega(P, H, t) = \frac{1}{2}\left(\sum_{i=1}^{z} \frac{\chi^{z-i+1}}{1-\chi}\, e(P, X_i, H) + 1\right).$$

Depending on this value, the individual preferences of P have more or less impact on the group preference at time t: the less satisfied is a listener with the songs previously scheduled on channel H, the more the Reuse Process endeavours to satisfy her with the current selection. This strategy is much fairer than a common *Plurality Voting* strategy, which would always select the item with more individual preferences, independently from the past satisfaction of users. The strategy we propose guarantees that every listener will eventually be satisfied during the broadcasting; Plurality Voting, on the other hand, would only satisfy the majority, eventually leaving the minority totally unsatisfied with the scheduling of a channel. We show this case with an example.

Example 2. A channel H has a Channel Pool of 8 songs $\phi(H) = (S1, \ldots, S8)$ and 3 listeners $(P1, P2, P3)$, whose individual preferences $g(Pi, Sj)$ are shown in the tables:

g(Pi,Sj)	S1	S2	S3	S4
P1	**0.8**	-0.2	0	0.2
P2	**0.6**	0.2	**0.6**	-0.8
P3	-0.2	1	0.4	0.8

G(Sj,H,t1)	**0.4**	0.3	0.3	-1

g(Pi,Sj)	S5	S6	S7	S8
P1	**0.6**	0.4	-0.4	-0.6
P2	**0.6**	-0.2	0	0.4
P3	0	0.8	1	-0.8

G(Sj,H,t2)	0.08	0.15	**0.17**	-1

At a time $t1$, the Retrieve Process returns the set $\mathcal{R}(H, t1) = (S1, S2, S3, S4)$, from which we have to select a song to schedule. First, we calculate the group preference degree $G(Sj, H, t1)$ for each of these songs (we set $\mu = -0.75$ and the initial channel satisfaction weights to 0.5), and schedule $S1$ because it is the most preferred song by the group: $G(S1, H, t1) = 0.4$. Then we calculate the listeners' satisfaction degrees; since $S1$ is the preferred song of both $P1$ and $P2$, their satisfaction degree is maximum: $e(P1, S1, H) = e(P2, S1, H) = 1$; however $S1$ is not the most preferred song of $P3$, so her satisfaction degree is smaller: $e(P3, S1, H) = -0.2 - 1 + 1 = -0.2$.

At a time $t2 > t1$, the new retrieved set is $\mathcal{R}(H, t2) = (S5, S6, S7, S8)$.

This time, the channel satisfaction weights are not equal for all listeners: since $P3$ was previously unsatisfied, $P3$ is the listener with the smallest channel satisfaction: $\omega(P3, H, t2) = 0.42$, while $\omega(P1, H, t2) = \omega(P2, H, t2) = 0.9$ (we set $\chi = 0.8$). After calculating the group preference degree $G(Sj, H, t2)$ for each song in $\mathcal{R}(H, t2)$, we schedule $S7$ because it is the most preferred song by the group: $G(S7, H, t2) = 0.17$. Notice that $S7$ is the preferred song of $P3$, who fairly gets the highest satisfaction degree at this turn. On the contrary, a Plurality Voting strategy would have selected $S5$ in order to satisfy the majority of listeners ($S5$ is the preferred song at this turn of both $P1$ and $P2$), without memory of the fact that they had already been satisfied on the previous turn.

So far, the Reuse Process works without any interaction from the listeners. The retrieved set is ranked using only the *implicit knowledge* contained in the user personal libraries, and the best ranked song is scheduled. From this moment, participants can interact to explicitly state whether they like the selection made or not. As explained in Sect. 2.2, a certain time has to pass from when a song Z is scheduled to when it is actually broadcast. During this time, any listener P can send via the Web interface her explicit preference towards Z. If this occurs, the *implicit preference* $g(P, Z)$ that was stored in the Case Base of P (inferred from the music library) is replaced with this new *explicit evaluation* provided. For example, if P disapproves of the scheduling of Z, then the implicit value of $g(P, Z)$ in the Case Base of P is replaced with the explicit value -1. Next, since the Case Base has changed, the retrieved set is re-ranked to include this new value in the evaluation of the group preferences. This can lead to Z not being the most group-preferred song anymore; in this case, the scheduled song changes to the one that maximises the group preference. This process (user evaluations and re-ranking) continues until song Y starts playing on the channel. Then, Z is downloaded to the local buffer, and the CBR component restarts, to schedule the next song.

3.5 The Revise Process

While a song is playing on a channel, the Web interface shows its title, artist, cover-art, remaining time, and allows listeners to rate whether they like that song or not (see Fig. 1). The assumption is that if a user rates positively (respectively negatively) a song played on a channel, then she likes (dislikes) that song and/or the song fits (does not fit) in the sequence of music programmed for that channel. Using this feedback, Poolcasting updates both the listeners' preference models and the musical knowledge about song associations.

When a listener sends a feedback about a song, the preference model in the Case Base of P is updated with this new explicit evaluation. For example, if P had never listened to song Z and sends a positive (resp. negative) feedback about it, the system learns that P has a high (low) preference for Z, and stores in her Case Base a new preference degree $g(P, Z) = 1$ ($g(P, Z) = -1$). As a result, the Reuse Process will be influenced by this new value, and eventually will (will not) schedule other songs associated with Z.

The feedback from the listeners is also used to revise the song associations extracted from the collection of playlists, and to customise them for the current channel. Indeed, two songs can be associated in one context, and not in another; for instance (True Blue, True Colors) is a meaningful association for a *'80 Music* channel, but not for a *Cheerful Tunes* channel. For this reason, Poolcasting builds a local domain knowledge model for each channel, where song associations *relative to that channel* are stored. Initially this domain model is empty, and only the associations inferred from the external playlists are used. As long as listeners send feedback about songs played on the channel, this model is updated accordingly. For example, if song Z is played after song Y on channel H, and listeners send negative feedback about it, the system learns that (Y, Z) is not a good song association *relatively to channel H* and locally updates the value of $s(Y, Z)$. As a result, the Retrieve Process for channel H will be influenced by this new value, and eventually will refrain from re-selecting song Z as a good successor for song Y on that channel.

4   Related Work

SmartRadio [5] employs a CBR approach to provide listeners with *individual personalised* radio channels; however the goal of Poolcasting is to provide *group-customised* radio channels. AdaptiveRadio [3] is a group-based Web radio where, if a listener shows discontent for a song, no other song from that album is broadcast. Thus, interaction is limited to vetoing songs, while Poolcasting users can also promote songs. Also, musical associations exist only for songs within an album, while in this paper we have expanded the approach introduced in [2] to build an extended musical associations model that contains song and artist association degrees, inferred from the co-occurrence analysis of a large collection of playlists. Virtual Jukebox [4] is another group-based radio, where the *majority* of votes (positive or negative) determines the preference of the group for the currently playing song. Poolcasting strategy is to combine *all* the listeners' preferences, favouring users less satisfied in the recent past. This mechanism increases fairness and is also easily understandable by the public — a favourable property for a group-aggregation technique according to [7].

MusicFX [9], CoCoA-Radio [1] and Flycasting [6] are three more systems focused on generating a sequence of songs that maximises the satisfaction of a group of listeners. The first broadcasts music in a gym centre attempting to maximise the "mean happiness" of the group; the second adapts the programming of a Web radio station according to the public; the third generates a playlist for an online radio based on the listeners' request histories. Users wishing to influence the music in these systems need to *explicitly* state their preferences, either by manually rating genres/songs, submitting a playlist as a proposal or requesting specific songs to be played. Poolcasting, on the other hand, allows users to both *implicitly* influence the music played (by sharing one's personal music library) and evaluate the proposed songs, which are substituted in real time for the next best candidates in the Reuse step if the feedback is strongly negative.

A Web-based group-customised CBR system is CATS [10], that helps a group of friends find a holiday package that satisfies the group as a whole. The task of CATS is to provide a good *one-shot* solution customised for the group, while the task of Poolcasting is to provide a good *sequence* of solutions, customised for the group over time. Also, CATS contains *one* CBR process, while in Poolcasting there are *multiple* CBR processes (one for each channel). Finally, the group of users in CATS does not change during the recommendation process, while Poolcasting participants are free to enter or leave at any moment.

5   Conclusions

The contribution of this paper is two-fold: we present a novel Web radio architecture called Poolcasting and a CBR technique to customise the content of each radio channel for the current audience. Poolcasting proposes a new paradigm for Web radios, shifting from a classical monolithic approach where "One controls, many listen", to a new decentralised approach where "Many control, many listen". The system is robust in the sense that it generates satisfactory results both for passive users (inferring their implicit preferences), and for active users (resulting in more customised channels). We have developed the internal components with open source software (Apache, MySQL, icecast, liquidsoap, tunequeue)[1], and the CBR process using Perl and PHP. A Poolcasting Web radio is currently running in our Intranet with three music channels and about 20 users. Our first tests show that users are willing to listen to songs not contained in their libraries to

---

[1] Available at: apache.org, mysql.com, icecast.org, savonet.sf.net and tunequeue.sf.net.

possibly discover new music they might like; however further tests are required, possibly in a public Internet environment, to deeply evaluate properties such as average user satisfaction, individual satisfactions, or user loyalty to channels. According to the existing copyright legislation, public Web radios pay a license fee related to the number of listeners or streamed songs, but independent from where the songs are stored. As such, deploying a public Poolcasting Web radio would require the same fees currently applied to Web radios.

Our contribution to CBR has several aspects. First, the Song Scheduler works with *multiple* participants' case bases and with domain knowledge acquired from playlists containing listening experiences of a large number of users. Moreover, the collection of case bases is open and dynamic: when a user enters (resp. leaves), the system immediately integrates (removes) her case base from the system, hence it responds at each moment to the *current* radio audience. Another contribution is using the Reuse process to combine data and preferences coming from different case bases (modelling users' listening experiences). Moreover, the goal of the Reuse process is to generate a *globally good sequence* of solutions over a period of time — not just one valid "group solution" for one problem. Our approach has been to view this solution as a trade-off between desirable properties for a radio channel (variety, continuity) and community-customisation properties such as individual satisfaction and fairness. Finally, both intensive knowledge and musical preference models are used in the Retrieve and Reuse processes, while user feedback is used in the Revise process to improve the customisation by updating these models in the CBR system.

Future work includes: testing the system with different parameters, evaluating the quality of the proposed technique, dealing with the issues of copyright and privacy, introducing a reputation degree for the listeners of a channel, extending the users' preference models with other listening experience data (e.g., personal playlists, time since a song was last played). Although the work we have described is specific to Web radio, we believe that the proposed idea of satisfying a group by guaranteeing both individual preferences and fairness among users can be applied to many other contexts where a group of persons gathers to listen to the same stream of music.

References

1. Avesani, P., Massa, P., Nori, M., Susi, A.: Collaborative radio community. In: Proc. of Adaptive Hypermedia (2002)
2. Baccigalupo, C., Plaza, E.: Case-Based Sequential Ordering of Songs for Playlist Recommendation. In: Roth-Berghofer, T.R., Göker, M.H., Güvenir, H.A. (eds.) ECCBR 2006. LNCS (LNAI), vol. 4106, Springer, Heidelberg (2006)
3. Chao, D.L., Balthrop, J., Forrest, S.: Adaptive Radio: Achieving Consensus Using Negative Preferences. In: Proc. of the GROUP '05 Conference (2005)
4. Drews, C., Pestoni, F.: Virtual Jukebox. In: Proc. of the 35th Hawaii Intl. Conf. on System Sciences (2002)
5. Hayes, C., Cunningham, P., Clerkin, P., Grimaldi, M.: Programme-Driven Music Radio. In: Proc. of the ECAI '02 Conference (2002)

6. Hauver, D.B., French, J.C.: Flycasting: Using Collaborative Filtering to Generate a Playlist for Online Radio. In: Proc. of the WEDELMUSIC '01 Conf. (2001)
7. Jameson, A., Smyth, B.: What a Difference a Group Makes: Web-Based Recommendations for Interrelated Users. In: Brusilovsky, Kobsa, A., Nejdl, W. (eds.) The Adaptive Web. LNCS, vol. 4321, Springer, Heidelberg (2007)
8. Masthoff, J.: Group modeling: Selecting a sequence of television items to suit a group of viewers. User Modeling and User-Adapted Interaction 14, 37–85 (2004)
9. McCarthy, J.F., Anagnost, T.D.: MusicFX: An Arbiter of Group Preferences for Computer Supported Collaborative Workouts. In: Proc. of the 1998 Computer Supported Cooperative Work Conference (1998)
10. McCarthy, K., McGinty, L., Smyth, B., Salamó, M.: The Needs of the Many: A Case-Based Group Recommender System. In: Roth-Berghofer, T.R., Göker, M.H., Güvenir, H.A. (eds.) ECCBR 2006. LNCS (LNAI), vol. 4106, Springer, Heidelberg (2006)

Helping Software Engineers Reusing UML Class Diagrams

Paulo Gomes, Pedro Gandola, and Joel Cordeiro

AILab - CISUC, University of Coimbra, 3030 Coimbra, Portugal

Abstract. Software development is a knowledge-intensive task, with an increasing demand for higher productivity. During the design phase, the use of visual modelling languages like UML (Unified Modeling Language) are wide spread across the software industry. In this paper we present a CBR tool that helps the software engineers to reuse UML diagrams. We describe our system, REBUILDER UML, and present experimental work showing that our system decreases the number of errors made by software engineers during the design of UML diagrams.

1 Introduction

The importance of knowledge in our economy is growing. There is an increasing number of knowledge-based jobs [1,2], which need new kinds of computational tools in order to deal with an increasing amount of information. These tools must be able to share and search information and knowledge, efficiently and accurately.

Software engineering is one of such knowledge-based professions that need these kind of tools. Several attempts to help software engineers in the task of developing new systems have been done, especially in the software reuse area [3,4,5,6,7]. But software complexity and modeling languages have evolved and most of these techniques are not applicable. Nevertheless, the software engineer more than ever needs help in dealing with a crucial problem: finding relevant knowledge that can be reused.

Software development involves several different phases [8]: analysis, design, implementation, testing and integration. In each of these phases new knowledge is generated, most of it staying in the heads of the software developers. But there is also information that stays in the form of diagrams, documents, code, unit tests, and so on. This information can be transformed into knowledge and be put at the service of the organization developers. One kind of information that is most valuable for system development are UML diagrams [9]. These diagrams are widely used in software development and are an efficient and user-friendly way of modeling software. UML diagrams are mainly used in the analysis and design phase of software development, and correspond to the design of a software system.

Most of the software engineers are designers, and reason based on experience. This is a basic mechanism for designers, enabling them to reuse previous design solutions in well known problems or even in new projects. Case-Based Reasoning (CBR, see [10,11]) is a reasoning paradigm that uses experiences, in the form

R.O. Weber and M.M. Richter (Eds.): ICCBR 2007, LNAI 4626, pp. 449–462, 2007.

of cases, to perform inferences. CBR is often regarded as a methodology for developing knowledge-based systems that uses experience for reasoning about problems [12]. It is our opinion that CBR is a methodology suited for building a design system that can act like an intelligent design assistant in the design of UML diagrams.

The main idea of CBR is to reuse past experiences to solve new situations or problems. A case is a central concept in CBR, and it represents a chunk of experience in a format that can be reused by a CBR system. Usually a case comprises three main parts: problem, solution, and outcome [11]. The problem is a description of the situation that the case represents. The solution describes what was used to solve the situation described in the problem. The outcome expresses the result of the application of the solution to the problem. There can be other parts of cases, like the justification that relates problem with solution through causal relations.

At an abstract level CBR can be described by a reasoning cycle [10] that starts with the problem description, which is then transformed into a target case (or query case). The problem is provided by a system user. The first phase in the CBR cycle is to retrieve from the case library the cases that are relevant for the target case. The relevancy of a case must be defined by the system, but the most common one is similarity of features. At the end of retrieval, the best retrieved case (there are systems that retrieve more than one case, depending on the system's purpose) is returned and passed to the next phase along with the target case. In our work, cases are UML diagrams, which encode knowledge about a software system design.

This paper presents a CBR system for helping software engineers designing UML diagrams. Our system is called REBUILDER UML and deals with UML class diagrams, enabling the sharing and reuse of previously created diagrams in the development of new software systems. REBUILDER UML not only assists the software engineer as a Intelligent CASE tool, but it also functions as a knowledge management system for an organization, managing the UML diagrams developed in this organization. We have integrated our system in a UML editor and tested the system with software engineers, from which we present the experimental results.

The next section describes REBUILDER UML in greater detail, describing its architecture. Sections 3 and 4 present respectively the knowledge base and the retrieval procedure used in our system. Section 5 illustrates our work with an example of how the system can be used by software engineers. Experimental work performed with software engineers is presented in section 6, demonstrating the usefulness of REBUILDER UML. Finally section 7 makes some final remarks and presents future work for our system.

2   REBUILDER UML

REBUILDER UML is a CBR system with two main goals: assisting software engineers in developing UML diagrams, and managing the UML repository of an organization that develops software. REBUILDER UML is implemented as a plug in for Enterprise Architect (EA, www.sparxsystems.com.au), a commercial CASE tool for UML modeling, and comprises three main modules (see figure 1): the knowledge base (KB), the CBR engine, and the KB manager. The KB is the repository of knowledge that is going to be reused by the CBR engine. The system reuses UML class diagrams, which are stored as cases in the case library. The knowledge base manager enables all the knowledge stored in the system to be maintained.

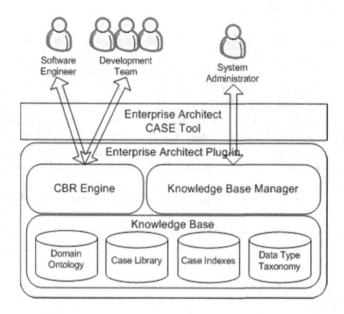

Fig. 1. The architecture of REBUILDER UML, based as a plug-in for Enterprise Architect

There are two types of users in REBUILDER UML, software engineers and the system administrator. A software engineer uses the CASE tool to model a software system in development, and s/he can use REBUILDER UML actions to reuse previous diagrams. These diagrams were developed for previous systems, by the organization in which the software engineer is integrated. The other user type is the system administrator, who has the goal of keeping the KB fine tuned and updated. Since each software engineer has a copy of the central KB, the system administrator is responsible for making new releases of the KB and installing it in the user systems. Thus, the role of the administrator is very important for REBUILDER UML to be used properly by several users, enabling the sharing of knowledge among them. Despite this, the system can also be used in a stand alone fashion, acting as an intelligent knowledge repository for a single user. In the stand alone version, the user is at the same time playing both roles, reusing knowledge and maintaining it.

The integration with EA is made by a plug-in, enabling the CBR engine to access the data model and model repository of EA. Visually the user interacts with REBUILDER UML through the main menu of EA. The user has access to the specific commands of REBUILDER UML, enabling search, browse, retrieval, reuse and maintenance operations. The next section describes in greater detail the knowledge base, showing what can be reused and how the knowledge in the KB is stored and indexed.

3   Knowledge Base

The KB comprises three different parts: the domain ontology, which represents the concepts and relations between concepts defined in the domain; the case library that stores all the UML class diagrams, called cases; the case indexes, which are associations between class diagram objects and ontology concepts.

A case in REBUILDER UML represents a specific UML class diagram (see figure 2 for an example of a class diagram). Conceptually a case comprises: a name used to identify the case within the case library; the UML class diagram that comprises all the objects in the diagram; and the file name where the case is stored. Cases are stored using XML/XMI since it is a widely used format for data exchange.

UML class diagram objects considered are: classes, interfaces and relations. A class describes an entity and it corresponds to a concept described by attributes at a structural level, and by methods at a behavioral level. A class is described by:

– a name;
– a concept in the ontology;
– a list of attributes;
– a list of methods.

The interface describes a protocol of communication for a specific class. An interface can have one or more implementations, and is described by:

– a name;
– a concept in the ontology;
– a list of methods.

A relation describes a relationship between two UML objects, and it is characterized by several attributes, which are: a name, the source object, the destination object, the relation type (association, generalization, dependency, or realization), cardinality, and aggregation. An attribute refers to a class and is characterized by a name that identifies the attribute within the class it belongs; the attribute's scope in relation to the external objects: public, private, or protected; the attribute's data type; and the attribute's default value. A method describes a request or message that can be submitted to a class, and is described by: a name that identifies the method within the class to which it belongs; the method's scope in relation to the external objects: public, private, or protected; the list of the input parameters; and the list of output parameters. A parameter can be a reference or a value that is used or generated by a class method, and is described by: a name identifying the parameter within the method to which it belongs, and the parameter's data type.

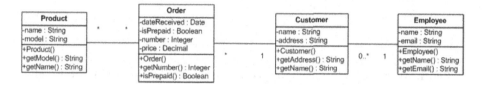

Fig. 2. An example of an UML class diagram

The domain ontology defines concepts, which are represented by words. Words that can be used to represent the same concept are called synonyms. A word associated with more than one concept is called a polysemous word. For instance, the word mouse has two meanings: it can denote a rat, or it can express a computer mouse. Besides the list of words, a concept has a list of semantic relations with other concepts in the ontology. These relations are categorized in four main types: is-a, part-of, substance-of and member-of, but the administrator can specify other types of relations. An example of part of an ontology is presented in figure 3. The domain ontology comprises three parts: the entity ontology that defines the concepts, words associated with concepts and relations; the relation ontology, where relations are defined; and the data type taxonomy, which is a simple ontology of programming data types used for semantic comparison of data types.

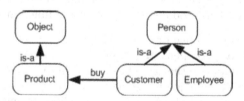

Fig. 3. An example of part of a domain ontology with concepts and relations

The ontology is used for computing the semantic distance between two concepts. Another purpose of the ontology is to index cases, and for this task, REBUILDER UML associates a concept to each diagram object (except relations). This link is then used as an index to the ontology structure, which can be used as a semantic network for case or object retrieval. Considering the diagram of figure 2 as *Case1*, figure 4 represents part of the case indexing, with objects *Product, Customer* and *Employee* indexed in the ontology. Case indexes provide

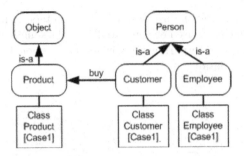

Fig. 4. An example of case indexing considering the diagram of figure 2 as Case1

a way to access the relevant case parts for retrieval without having to read all the case files from disk. Case retrieval is flexible, since the system can retrieve a complete case, using the case package, or it can retrieve only a subset of case objects, using the objects' indexes. This allows the user with the possibility to retrieve not only packages, but also classes and interfaces.

REBUILDER UML stores and manages design knowledge gathered from the software designer's activity. This knowledge is stored in a central repository, which is managed by the administrator. The basic responsibilities of the administrator are to configure the system and to decide which cases should be in the case library. Another task that s/he has to perform is to revise new diagrams submitted by the software designers.

When a diagram is submitted by a software designer as a new case candidate, the administrator has to check some items in the diagram. First the diagram must have concepts associated to the classes, interfaces and packages. This is essential for the diagram to be transformed into a case, and to be indexed and reused by the system. Diagram consistency and coherence must also be checked.

The KB Manager module is used by the administrator to keep the KB consistent and updated. This module comprises several functionalities:

KB Operations create, open or close a KB;

Case Library Manager opens the case library manager, which comprises functions to manipulate the cases in the case library, like adding new cases, removing cases, or changing the status of a case;

Ontology Manager provides to the user an editor to modify the ontology, enabling the creation and manipulation of concepts, which are used by the system to reason;

Settings adds extra configuration settings which are not present in the normal UML Editor version used by the software designers. It also enables the KB administrator to configure the reasoning mechanisms.

4   Case Retrieval

The system provides two types of retrieval: object retrieval and case retrieval. The retrieval mechanism searches the ontology structure looking for similar objects/cases and then ranks the objects/cases found, presenting them to the designer.

Retrieval comprises two phases: retrieval of a set of relevant objects/cases from the case library, and assessment of the similarity between the target problem and the retrieved objects/cases. The retrieval phase is based on the ontology structure, which is used as an indexing structure. The retrieval algorithm uses the classifications of the target object as the initial search probe in the ontology.

The query for retrieval comprises the objects selected by the user. If there is more than one object, then the systems retrieves complete diagrams (cases). If only one object is selected at the moment of the retrieval command, then the system retrieves objects from the case library. The retrieval algorithm uses the concepts of the selected objects as the initial search probe. Then the algorithm checks if there are any object indexes associated with the ontology nodes of those concepts. If there are enough indexes, the algorithm stops and returns them. Otherwise, it explores the concept nodes adjacent to the initial ones, searching for object indexes until the number of found indexes reaches the number of objects that the user wants to be retrieved.

The second step of retrieval is ranking the retrieved objects/cases by similarity with the target object(s). We have defined two similarity metrics, according to two situations: retrieval of cases (case similarity metric) or retrieval of objects (object similarity metric).

Case Similarity Metric. This metric is based on three different aspects: structural similarity between objects and relations in the query and the case; and once query objects are matched with case objects, it assesses the semantic similarity between matched objects. Basically this metric assesses structure similarity and semantic similarity of cases and its objects.

Object Similarity Metric. The object similarity metric is based on three items: concept similarity of objects being compared, inter-object similarity comprising the assessment of relation similarity between objects, and intra-object similarity that evaluates the similarity between objects' attributes and methods.

After the ranked objects/cases are presented to the user, s/he can select three different actions: copy, replace or merge. The copy action copies the selected object/case to the current diagram, where it can then be reused. The replace operation replaces the query with the selected object/case. The merge action merges the selected object/case with the query. Even if the software engineer does not use any of the retrieved objects/cases, s/he can explore the design space using the retrieved knowledge. This enables a more efficient way of designing systems and increases productivity, enabling novice engineers to get a first solution, from which they can iteratively build a better solution.

5   Example of Use

This section presents an example of how REBUILDER UML can be used by a software designer. This example shows how design knowledge can be retrieved and stored for reuse.

Suppose that a designer is starting the design of an information system for a banking company. S/he has already the system's analysis done, in the form of use cases (an UML diagram type used for describing system requirements). From these use cases, some initial entities are extracted by the designer and drawn in a new diagram. Figure 5 shows the initial class diagram, representing some of the classes identified in the system requirements and functional specifications.

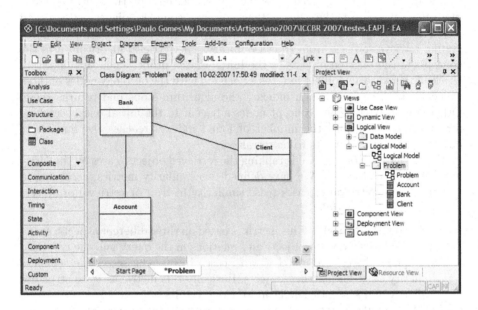

Fig. 5. The diagram used as query in the retrieval example

One of the tools available to the designer is the retrieval of similar designs from the case library. The designer can retrieve objects or diagrams. Imagine that s/he selects the package object and clicks on the retrieval command. REBUILDER UML retrieves the number of diagrams defined by the designer (in this situation three cases). Figure 6 presents the list of retrieved cases ranked by similarity. The user can then: copy, replace or merge one of the retrieved diagrams.

After the new diagram is completed (the user selected to merge the retrieved diagram with the query one), the designer can submit the diagram to the KB administrator (see figure 7). This implies that the designer considers the diagram correct and ready for being stored in the KB, for later reuse. This new diagram goes into a list of unconfirmed cases of the case library. The KB administrator has the task of examining these diagrams more carefully, deciding which diagrams are going to be transformed into cases, going to the list of confirmed cases (ready to be reused), and which are going to the list of obsolete cases not being used by the system.

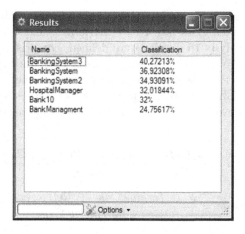

Fig. 6. The list of retrieved cases using the diagram in figure 5 as the query

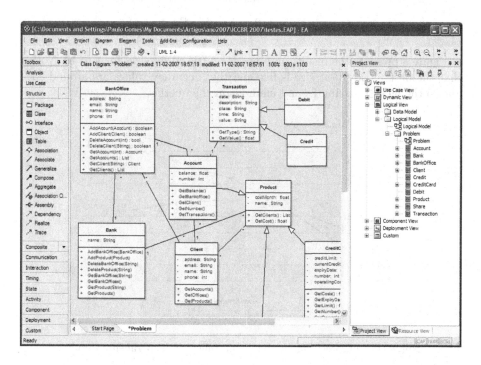

Fig. 7. The submission of a completed diagram in REBUILDER UML

6 Experiments

The experimental work developed in REBUILDER UML comprises three analysis axis: recall and precision results, retrieval time performance, and user experiments. The case base used has 29 cases, each case with an average number of 10 classes. Each class has 4 to 7 attributes, and 5 to 14 methods. In the first type of analysis 16 queries were defined, comprising only classes and relations (with an average of 4 classes and no attributes nor methods). A set of reference cases from the case base was defined for each query. The queries were then run in REBUILDER UML varying the size of the retrieval set (from 1 to 10 cases). The retrieved cases were analyzed and the following measures were computed:

$$Recall = \frac{\#(ReferenceCases \cap RetrievedCases)}{\#ReferenceCases} \tag{1}$$

$$Precision = \frac{\#(ReferenceCases \cap RetrievedCases)}{\#RetrievedCases} \tag{2}$$

$$Accuracy = \frac{\#(ReferenceCases \cap RetrievedCases)}{\#(ReferenceCases \cup RetrievedCases)} \tag{3}$$

$$F - Measure = \frac{2 * (Recall * Precision)}{(Recall + Precision)} \tag{4}$$

Figure 8 presents the results obtained for retrieval set sizes for 1 to 10. Notice that the best retrieval set size is five and that accuracy values are around 35% due to the lack of attributes and methods in the queries.

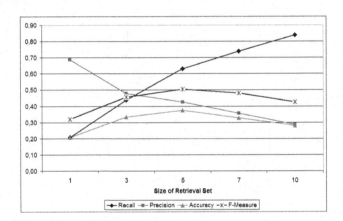

Fig. 8. Recall, precision, accuracy and f-measure experimental results

Figure 9 shows the results for the second analysis, which was the assessment of the retrieval time performance. We have executed six experiments with different case base sizes from 5 to 29. In each experiment we have run 30 queries to assess the average retrieval time of the algorithms used in REBUILDER UML. As can be seen from the figure, retrieval times are low (below 3 seconds) but further testing is needed to assess the performance with bigger case bases.

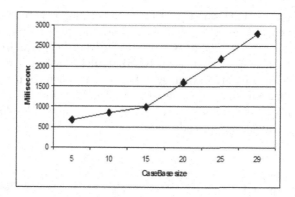

Fig. 9. Average retrieval time (milliseconds) results by query for different case base sizes

The last analysis was made with eight users with software engineering experience. Three tests were defined, comprising a natural language text describing a software system to be modelled. The first test had only one sentence and was easy to design. The second and third tests had about ten sentences and they are much more complex. The goal was for a user to design a UML class diagram corresponding to the text of each test. A reference diagram for each test was defined: the diagram for test 1 has 9 UML elements, test 2 has 36 elements and test 3 has 43 elements (when are referring to UML elements, we mean classes, relations and attributes). We have defined two test groups: one that was going to use the Enterprise Architect (EA) editor and REBUILDER UML to design the diagrams, and the second group only with EA.

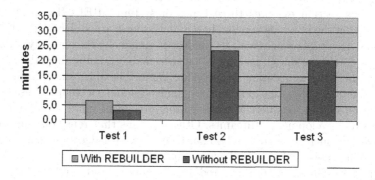

Fig. 10. Average user design time (minutes) for the three tests

We have measured the time each user needed to design each test diagram, and we also identified errors in user diagrams by comparing with the reference ones. The time results are presented in figure 10 and error results in figure 11. The time results show worse times for users with REBUILDER UML in the first two tests due to the time that users need to take in learning how to use the retrieval tools. But in the third test there is a clear improvement from the users that are using REBUILDER UML (the tests were presented in sequence, from 1 to 3). In the error results, it is clear that using REBUILDER UML and reusing cases is a major benefit for software design. Another major benefit of using our system is that all the diagrams made by users using REBUILDER UML have methods that came from the retrieved diagrams. This allows a faster development of the system being designed, due to code reuse.

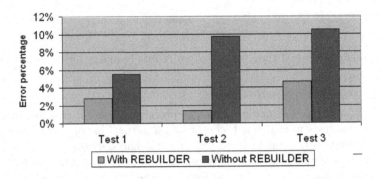

Fig. 11. Average percentage of user errors for the three tests

7   Conclusions and Future Work

REBUILDER UML descends from REBUILDER I [13,14,15], and it has two main research influences: CBR software reuse systems and software reuse systems. This section explores these types of systems. REBUILDER UML has evolved from the previous version, based on lessons learned. REBUILDER UML has some major differences with its predecessor, namely: the ontology is now specific and domain oriented, making it easier to manage, maintain and with better performance; the application architecture is more flexible, allowing the system to be used in a wide range of scenarios (single system to a company usage level); integration with a commercial UML editor, making it more suitable for usage in software development companies. Other systems that reuse diagrams do not address the multi-user issue, and do not focus on knowledge management aspect, which brings new problems and aspects into focus.

Fernández Chamizo [16] presented a CBR approach for software reuse based on the reuse and design of Object-Oriented code. Cases represent three types of entities: classes, methods and programming recipes, thus allowing the retrieval of these types of objects. Cases comprise a lexical description (problem), a solution (code) and a justification (code properties). It uses a lexical retrieval algorithm using a natural language query, and a conceptual retrieval using an entity and slot similarity measures. Deja Vu [17] is a CBR system for code generation and reuse using hierarchical CBR. Deja Vu uses a hierarchical case representation, indexing cases using functional features. The main improvement of this system is the adaptation-guided retrieval, which retrieves cases based on the case adaptation effort instead of the similarity with the target problem. CAESER [18] is another code reuse CBR tool. It works at the code level and uses data-flow analysis to acquire functional indexes. The user can retrieve cases from the case library using a prolog-like query goal, which is used by the system to retrieve similar functions. Althoff et. al. [19] have a different approach to software reuse and design. Instead of reusing code, they reuse system requirements and associated software development knowledge.

The RSL [20] is a software design system that combines several software design tools and library retrieval tools. It allows the reuse of code and design knowledge, and provides several software design tools to work the retrieved objects. RSL uses automatic indexing of components by scanning design documents and code files for specially labeled reuse component statements. Component retrieval can be done using a natural-language query, or using attribute search. Component ranking is an interactive and iterative process between RSL and the user. Borgo [21] uses WordNet [22] for retrieval of object oriented components. His system uses a graph structure to represent both the query and the components in memory. The retrieval mechanism uses a graph matching algorithm returning the identifiers of all components whose description is subsumed by the query. WordNet is also used for node matching. Most of these systems do not deal with diagrams, but directly with code, and consequently retrieval is performed at a more symbol level, instead of a graph level as ReBuilder - UML.

The system presented helps software designers build diagrams with less errors and at the same time reusing code (from the methods). It is our opinion that it also decreases the time needed to design the UML diagram, but further experimental work needs to be done. There are some limitations in REBUILDER UML that are being addressed, like ontology development. We are working on a tool for extracting ontologies semi automatically, so that it can be used to help the system administrator to develop the ontology. Another issue being addressed is the integration of tools to help the ontology management. Future work includes the development of new reasoning modules that make the system-user interaction easier. A module is being developed that intends to automatically translate natural language requirements into UML class diagrams [23,24].

References

1. Liebowitz, J.: Knowledge Management Handbook. CRC Press, New York (1999)
2. Nonaka, I., Takeuchi, H.: The Knowledge-Creating Company. Oxford University Press, New York (1995)
3. Coulange, B.: Software Reuse. Springer, London (1997)
4. Gamma, E., Helm, R., Johnson, R., Vlissides, J.: Design Patterns: Elements of Reusable Object-Oriented Software. Addison-Wesley, Reading (1995)
5. Jacobson, I., Griss, M., Jonsson, P.: Software Reuse: Architecture Process and Organization for Business Success. ACM Press, New York (1997)
6. Meyer, B.: Reusability: The case for object-oriented design. IEEE Software 4, 50–64 (1987)

7. Prieto-Diaz, R.: Status report: Software reusability. IEEE Software 3 (May 1993)
8. Boehm, B.: A Spiral Model of Software Development and Enhancement. IEEE Press, Los Alamitos (1988)
9. Rumbaugh, J., Jacobson, I., Booch, G.: The Unified Modeling Language Reference Manual. Addison-Wesley, Reading, MA (1998)
10. Aamodt, A., Plaza, E.: Case–based reasoning: Foundational issues, methodological variations, and system approaches. AI Communications 7(1), 39–59 (1994)
11. Kolodner, J.: Case-Based Reasoning. Morgan Kaufman, San Francisco (1993)
12. Althoff, K.D.: Case-based reasoning. In: Chang, S.K. (ed.) Handbook on Software Engineering and Knowledge Engineering, vol. 1, pp. 549–588. World Scientific, Singapore (2001)
13. Gomes, P., Pereira, F.C., Paiva, P., Seco, N., Carreiro, P., Ferreira, J.L., Bento, C.: Case retrieval of software designs using wordnet. In: Harmelen, F. (ed.) European Conference on Artificial Intelligence (ECAI'02), Lyon, France, IOS Press, Amsterdam (2002)
14. Gomes, P., Pereira, F.C., Paiva, P., Seco, N., Carreiro, P., Ferreira, J.L., Bento, C.: Using wordnet for case-based retrieval of UML models. AI Communications 17(1), 13–23 (2004)
15. Gomes, P.: Software design retrieval using bayesian networks and wordnet. In: Funk, P., González Calero, P.A. (eds.) ECCBR 2004. LNCS (LNAI), vol. 3155, pp. 184–197. Springer, Heidelberg (2004)
16. Fernández-Chamizo, C., González-Calero, P., Gómez-Albarrán, M., Hernández-Yánez, L.: Supporting object reuse through case-based reasoning. In: Smith, I., Faltings, B.V. (eds.) Advances in Case-Based Reasoning. LNCS, vol. 1168, pp. 150–163. Springer, Heidelberg (1996)
17. Smyth, B., Cunningham, P.: Deja vu: A hierarchical case-based reasoning system for software design. In: Neumann, B. (ed.) 10th European Conference on Artificial Intelligence (ECAI'92), Vienna, Austria, John Wiley and Sons, West Sussex, England (1992)
18. Fouqué, G., Matwin, S.: Compositional software reuse with case-based reasoning. In: 9th Conference on Artificial Intelligence for Applications (CAIA'93), IEEE Computer Society Press, Orlando, FL (1993)
19. Althoff, K.D., Birk, A., Wangenheim, C.G. v., Tautz, C.: Case–based reasoning for experimental software engineering. Technical Report 063.97/E, Fraunhofer IESE (1997)
20. Burton, B.A., Aragon, R.W., Bailey, S.A., Koehler, K.D., Mayes, L.A.: The reusable software library. IEEE Software 4, 25–32 (1987)
21. Borgo, S., Guarino, N., Masolo, C., Vetere, G.: Using a large linguistic ontology for internet-based retrieval of object-oriented components. In: 9th International Conference on Software Engineering and Knowledge Engineering, SEKE'97, Madrid, Spain, pp. 528–534. Knowledge Systems Institute, Illinois (1997)
22. Miller, G., Beckwith, R., Fellbaum, C., Gross, D., Miller, K.J.: Introduction to wordnet: an on-line lexical database. International Journal of Lexicography 3(4), 235–244 (1990)
23. Seco, N., Gomes, P., Pereira, F.C.: Using CBR for semantic analysis of software specifications. In: Funk, P., González Calero, P.A. (eds.) ECCBR 2004. LNCS (LNAI), vol. 3155, pp. 778–792. Springer, Heidelberg (2004)
24. Seco, N., Gomes, P., Pereira, F.C.: Modelling software specifications with case based reasoning. In: Sharp, B. (ed.) NLUCS, pp. 135–144. INSTICC Press (2004)

Failure Analysis for Domain Knowledge Acquisition in a Knowledge-Intensive CBR System

Amélie Cordier[1], Béatrice Fuchs[1], Jean Lieber[2], and Alain Mille[1]

[1] LIRIS CNRS, UMR 5202, Université Lyon 1, INSA Lyon, Université Lyon 2, ECL
43, bd du 11 Novembre 1918, Villeurbanne Cedex, France
{Amelie.Cordier,Beatrice.Fuchs,Alain.Mille}@liris.cnrs.fr
[2] Orpailleur team, LORIA UMR 7503 CNRS, INRIA, Nancy Universities
BP 239 54 506 Vandœuvre-lès-Nancy, France
Jean.Lieber@loria.fr

Abstract. A knowledge-intensive case-based reasoning system has profit of the domain knowledge, together with the case base. Therefore, acquiring new pieces of domain knowledge should improve the accuracy of such a system. This paper presents an approach for knowledge acquisition based on some failures of the system. The CBR system is assumed to produce solutions that are consistent with the domain knowledge but that may be inconsistent with the expert knowledge, and this inconsistency constitutes a failure. Thanks to an interactive analysis of this failure, some knowledge is acquired that contributes to fill the gap from the system knowledge to the expert knowledge. Another type of failures occurs when the solution produced by the system is only partial: some additional pieces of information are required to use it. Once again, an interaction with the expert involves the acquisition of new knowledge. This approach has been implemented in a prototype, called FRAKAS, and tested in the application domain of breast cancer treatment decision support.

1 Introduction

A case-based reasoning system (CBR [17]) relies on several containers of knowledge. The source cases are, obviously, among those containers of knowledge, but a lot of systems also use additional knowledge sources as the "domain knowledge" (also known as "domain ontology" or "domain theory"). The more correct and accurate the domain knowledge is, the better the CBR system's inferences will be.

This paper presents an approach to interactive acquisition of domain knowledge in a CBR system. More precisely, this acquisition is performed during a CBR session: the target problem is automatically solved by adaptation of the retrieved case and, after that, the solution is presented to the user who, depending on his/her expertise level, may be able to detect that the solution is not satisfactory and why that is not the case. Two kinds of failures are considered in this paper:

(1) The suggested solution is inconsistent with the expert knowledge and
(2) The suggested solution is only partially valid (the user misses some information to fully exploit it).

R.O. Weber and M.M. Richter (Eds.): ICCBR 2007, LNAI 4626, pp. 463–477, 2007.

An interactive mechanism that aims at incorporating new pieces of domain knowledge is described. The new knowledge is used to repair the failed adaptation and to prevent similar failures to occur in future reasonings. This work concerns domain knowledge acquisition during the CBR step called repairing in [17], also known as the revise step in [2]. Thus, retrieval and adaptation issues are not detailed in this paper.

The rest of the paper is organized as follows. In section 2, we present the notions, notations, and assumptions we make about CBR. Then the principles of our knowledge acquisition approach are outlined (section 3). Those principles have been implemented in a prototype called FRAKAS whose presentation in section 4 constitutes the core of the paper. An example and an algorithm show how FRAKAS assists the proposed acquisition method. Section 5 presents some related work on domain knowledge acquisition in CBR systems in comparison with the approach introduced in this paper. Finally, section 6 concludes this paper and proposes some future work.

2   Basic Notions, Notations and Assumptions on CBR

In this work, the notions of problem and solution are assumed to be well-defined. If pb is a problem (resp., sol is a solution) then pb (resp., sol) is an expression in a knowledge representation formalism representing a problem (resp., a solution) of this domain. In addition, it is assumed that there exists a binary relation that links a solution sol to a problem pb and meaning "sol is a solution of pb". In some CBR applications, this relation is only imperfectly specified. However, a finite set of pairs (srce, Sol(srce)) is still available, where srce is a problem and Sol(srce) is a solution of srce. This finite set is the *case base* and a pair (srce, Sol(srce)) is a *source case*. We also denote by DK the knowledge base containing the domain knowledge.

Reasoning from cases means solving a problem called the target problem and denoted by tgt, using the case base. This reasoning process is usually constituted of two main steps: retrieval that aims at selecting a source case deemed to be similar to the target problem and adaptation that aims at solving the target problem by using the retrieved source case. Moreover, a third step is sometimes added, namely the learning step, that can be performed automatically or in interaction with an expert. This step consists in improving the system's knowledge (cases, domain knowledge, etc.) after the adaptation of the retrieved case.

In this paper, we make four additional assumptions that we believe relevant for a CBR system. The first assumption is that the adaptation produces a result *consistent* with the domain knowledge (but not necessarily with the knowledge of the expert).

The second assumption is that there exists a computable distinction between a solution that totally solves a problem and a solution that only partially solves it. A way to distinguish between partial and non partial solutions is to split the vocabulary for representing cases in two subsets: the "abstract" vocabulary and "concrete". If a solution needs some of the abstract vocabulray in order to be represented, then this solution is said to be partial.

The third assumption is that each problem (resp., solution) coded in the CBR system represents a set of problem instances (resp., a set of solution instances).

The fourth assumption is that a problem (resp., a solution) is represented by a set of descriptors interpreted in a conjunctive way: if pb $= \{d_1, \ldots d_n\}$, then pb describes the problem whose instances satisfy each of the descriptors d_i ($i \in \{1, \ldots n\}$). This assumption is not mandatory in the approach presented in this paper but makes simpler its explanation.

The example used in this paper addresses a specific domain, namely breast cancer treatment.

3 Principles

Between the domain knowledge DK in the CBR system and the expert's knowledge, there is usually a gap. According to [15], it is impossible to fully fill this gap in most of the practical applications: this is the so-called qualification problem. Nevertheless, new knowledge can still be acquired from the expert.

The general principle of the approach described here is to perform an on-line knowledge acquisition by analyzing the adaptation failures. An on-line acquisition is performed when the system is used: the system interacts with the expert to acquire some of his/her knowledge. One can talk of acquisition by failure analysis if the interaction with the expert relies on the fact that, according to the expert, the result is, at least partially, a failure. Two kinds of failures are considered in this paper. Each of them leads to specific knowledge acquisition (though quite similar). Other kinds of failures are likely to exist but are not considered here.

First kind of failures: inconsistency of the adapted solution with the expert knowledge. The expert points out that, considering his or her domain knowledge, the assessment "Sol(tgt) solves tgt" is inconsistent. This can mean that the solution by itself is inconsistent (or unrealizable, such as the fact of transforming a cooked egg into a fresh egg) or that the solution is inconsistent with the context of the target problem (for example, if the problem tgt is "How to travel from Lyon to Belfast?" and its solution Sol(tgt) is a plan to travel from Nancy to Aberdeen).

In both situations, the expert is supposed to highlight (thanks to an appropriate interface) a part of Sol(tgt) (ideally, the "smallest" possible) that is inconsistent with his/her knowledge about the target problem. This part of the solution is a subset Inc of the set of descriptors of Sol(tgt). A first acquired knowledge (added to DK) is the fact that "Inc is false". Then, the CBR process is performed again, with the new domain knowledge.

Afterwards, the expert is required for an explanation. This explanation may be complex and our opinion is that it is very complicated (if not impossible) to completely automate this part (modeling and formalizing knowledge is the matter of knowledge engineers and requires competences that a domain expert may not have). Therefore, the expert is invited to write an explanation in plain text. The resulting document is used later by a knowledge engineer, in presence of the expert, to acquire new knowledge (that will imply, in particular, but not only, that "Inc is false").

Second kind of failures: failures caused by a partial solution. If the solution Sol(tgt) proposed after the adaptation is partial, and therefore, not fully satisfactory, the interaction with the expert may make it precise. Let SI be the set of the instances of Sol(tgt). If such an instance $s \in SI$ is judged satisfactory by the expert, it constitutes a solution to the problem tgt. If, by contrast, it is inconsistent with the expert knowledge, the expert is supposed to highlight a minimal part Inc of the descriptors of s. Then, this amounts to the same knowledge acquisition process as the one proposed for the first kind of failures: "Inc is false" is added to DK and the expert is asked for an explanation to latter support the knowledge acquisition with the expert and the knowledge engineer.

4   FRAKAS: A System for Domain Knowledge Acquisition by Interactive Analysis of Reasoning Failures in Case-Based Reasoning

FRAKAS (*FailuRe Analysis for domain Knowledge AcquiSition*) is a prototype that implements the principles introduced above with a knowledge representation in propositional logic.

4.1   Principles of the Adaptation

Formalism. The formalism used is propositional logic on a set of variables $\mathcal{V}$. Thus, DK, srce, Sol(srce), and tgt are propositional formulas on $\mathcal{V}$. $\mathcal{V}$ is partitioned in $\{\mathcal{V}_{pb}^c, \mathcal{V}_{pb}^a, \mathcal{V}_{sol}^c, \mathcal{V}_{sol}^a, \mathcal{V}_{other}\}$ where $\mathcal{V}_{pb}^x$ (resp., $\mathcal{V}_{sol}^x$) represents the variables used to represent some problems (resp., some solutions), and if $x = c$ (resp., $x = a$) then this set only contains variables said to be concrete (resp., abstract). A problem (resp., a solution) is a formula whose variables belongs to $\mathcal{V}_{pb}^c \cup \mathcal{V}_{pb}^a$ (resp., to $\mathcal{V}_{sol}^c \cup \mathcal{V}_{sol}^a$). This distinction between problem variables and solution variables allows one to express a source case as a conjunction of its problem part and its solution part: srce-case $=$ srce$\wedge$Sol(srce).

An interpretation on $\mathcal{V}$ is a function $\mathcal{I}$ that to $x \in \mathcal{V}$ associates $x^{\mathcal{I}} \in \{T, F\}$. $\mathcal{I}$ is prolongated on the set of the formulas build on $\mathcal{V}$ in the usual way (for example, $(f \wedge g)^{\mathcal{I}} = T$ iff $f^{\mathcal{I}} = T$ and $g^{\mathcal{I}} = T$). $\mathcal{I}$ is a model of f if $f^{\mathcal{I}} = T$. f implies g (resp., f is equivalent to g), noted $f \vDash g$ (resp. $f \equiv g$) if $\text{Mod}(f) \subseteq \text{Mod}(g)$ (resp., $\text{Mod}(f) = \text{Mod}(g)$). f implies (resp., is equivalent to) g modulo DK, noted $f \vDash_{DK} g$ (resp., by $f \equiv_{DK} g$) if DK $\wedge f \vDash g$ (resp., if DK $\wedge f \equiv$ DK $\wedge g$). $\text{Mod}(f)$ denotes the set of the models of f. The instances of a problem (resp., a solution) are defined here as its interpretations on $\mathcal{V}_{pb}^c \cup \mathcal{V}_{pb}^a$ (resp., on $\mathcal{V}_{sol}^c \cup \mathcal{V}_{sol}^a$).

A solution sol is partial if it is not possible to express it without any abstract variable, in other word, if there exists no f such that sol $\equiv_{DK} f$ and such that no variable of f belongs to $\mathcal{V}_{sol}^a$ [1].

Conservative adaptation. The adaptation performed by FRAKAS follows the principle of conservative adaptation that is briefly described here (see [14] for more details).

---

[1] This is checked in FRAKAS as follows. For each $\mathcal{I} \in \text{Mod}(\text{sol})$, let $\mathcal{I}^-$ be the interpretation obtained by projection of $\mathcal{I}$ on the set of variables $\mathcal{V} \backslash \mathcal{V}_{sol}^a$. Then, let sol$^-$ be a formula whose models are the $\mathcal{I}^-$'s, for $\mathcal{I} \in \text{Mod}(\text{sol})$. Then the test sol $\equiv_{DK}$ sol$^-$ is done; sol can be written without any abstract solution variable (i.e., sol is not partial) iff this test holds.

This approach to adaptation consists in doing minimal changes on the source case in order to be coherent with both the target problem and the domain knowledge. This adaptation is formalized based on the notion of revision operator [11]: a revision operator $\circ$ associates to two knowledge bases ψ and μ that entails μ and the knowledge base $\psi \circ \mu$ which, intuitively, is obtained by a minimal change on ψ to be consistent with μ. In the framework of propositional logic, the conservative adaptation of a case `srce-case` to solve a problem `tgt`, given the domain knowledge DK and a revision operator $\circ$ is:

$$\mathtt{CA_\circ}(\mathtt{DK}, \mathtt{srce\text{-}case}, \mathtt{tgt}) = (\mathtt{DK} \wedge \mathtt{srce\text{-}case}) \circ (\mathtt{DK} \wedge \mathtt{tgt})$$

A solution `Sol(tgt)` can be deductively inferred. From a practical viewpoint, Dalal's revision operator, noted $\circ_\mathrm{D}$ [11], is used. $\circ_\mathrm{D}$ is defined as follows. Let `dist` be the Hamming distance between interpretations on $\mathcal{V}$ ($\mathtt{dist}(\mathcal{I}, \mathcal{J})$ is the number of $x \in \mathcal{V}$ such as $x^{\mathcal{I}} \neq x^{\mathcal{J}}$) and let $G^\lambda(\psi)$ be the formula (for $\lambda \geq 0$ and ψ a formula) such that:

$$\mathtt{Mod}(G^\lambda(\psi)) = \{\mathcal{J} \mid \mathcal{J} \colon \text{interpretation on } \mathcal{V} \text{ such as exists}$$
$$\mathcal{I} \in \mathtt{Mod}(\psi) \text{ with } \mathtt{dist}(\mathcal{I}, \mathcal{J}) \leq \lambda\}$$

(This defines $G^\lambda(\psi)$ up to the logical equivalence, which is enough since we adhere to the principle of irrelevance of syntax, saying that whenever $f \equiv g$, an artificial reasoning system using knowledge f makes the same inferences –up to logical equivalence– as the same system using g instead of f.) For ψ and μ two formulas such that at least the latter is satisfiable, $\psi \circ_\mathrm{D} \mu$ is defined as being $G^\Delta(\psi) \wedge \mu$ where Δ is the smallest value such as $G^\Delta(\psi) \wedge \mu$ is satisfiable. Intuitively, $\psi \circ_\mathrm{D} \mu$ is obtained by generalizing ψ minimally (according to the scale $(\{G^\lambda\}_\lambda, \vDash)$) to be consistent with μ.

Example. Léon is about to invite Thècle and wants to prepare her an appropriate meal. His target problem can be specified by the characteristics of Thècle about food. Let us assume that Thècle is vegetarian (denoted by the propositional variable v) and that she has other characteristics (denoted by o) not detailed in this example: $\mathtt{tgt} = v \wedge o$. From his experience as a host, Léon remembers that he had invited Simone some time ago and he thinks that Simone is very similar to Thècle according to food preferences, except that she is not a vegetarian: $\mathtt{srce} = \neg v \wedge o$. He had proposed to Simone a meal with salad (s), beef (b) and a dessert (d), and she was satisfied by the two formers but has not eaten the dessert. Thus Léon has retained the case ($\mathtt{srce}, \mathtt{Sol(srce)}$) with $\mathtt{Sol(srce)} = s \wedge b \wedge \neg d$. Besides that, Léon has some general knowledge about food: he knows that beef is meat, that meat and tofu are protein-based food, that tofu is not meat, and that vegetarians do not eat meat. Thus, his domain knowledge is

$$\mathtt{DK} = b \rightarrow m \quad \wedge \quad m \rightarrow p \quad \wedge \quad t \rightarrow p \quad \wedge \quad \neg t \vee \neg m \quad \wedge \quad v \rightarrow \neg m$$

On this example, conservative adaptation produces the following result:

$$\mathtt{CA_{\circ_D}}(\mathtt{DK}, \mathtt{srce\text{-}case}, \mathtt{tgt}) \equiv_{\mathrm{DK}} \underbrace{v \wedge o}_{\mathtt{tgt}} \wedge \underbrace{s \wedge \neg m \wedge p \wedge \neg d}_{\mathtt{Sol(tgt)}}$$

if Léon follows `Sol(tgt)`, he will propose to Thècle a dinner with a salad, a main course with proteins but no meat (for example, a tofu-based dish) and no dessert.

4.2 Study of an Example Through FRAKAS

The example described in details in this section comes from the research project KA-SIMIR whose framework is knowledge management and decision support in oncology [8][2]. A problem is given by the description of a patient suffering from breast cancer. A solution is a therapy. In this example, the successive states of the domain knowledge are denoted by DK_0, DK_1, etc.

Example specification. Jules is a man suffering from breast cancer with other characteristics not detailed here (in particular, the fact that the decision is made after the surgery that has removed the tumor, and the fact that the hormone receptors are positive). It can be noticed that this example comes from a real example, that has been simplified and for which the first name of the patient has been changed. It is modeled by the problem $\texttt{tgt} = \texttt{man} \wedge \texttt{other-charac}$.

If M_1 and M_2 are two sets of interpretations, $\text{dist}(M_1, M_2)$ denotes the minimum of the values $\text{dist}(\mathcal{I}_1, \mathcal{I}_2)$, for $\mathcal{I}_1 \in M_1$ and $\mathcal{I}_2 \in M_2$. As argued in [14], the following criterion for retrieval (following the principle of adaptation-guided retrieval [19], for the conservative adaptation based on $\circ_D$) can be given: the source case $\texttt{srce-case}^1$ has to be preferred to the source case $\texttt{srce-case}^2$ when $\Delta^1 < \Delta^2$, with $\Delta^i = \text{dist}(\text{Mod}(\texttt{srce-case}^i), \text{Mod}(\texttt{tgt}))$ ($i \in \{1, 2\}$).

It is assumed that exists a source case $\texttt{srce-case} = (\texttt{srce}, \text{Sol}(\texttt{srce}))$ such that $\texttt{srce} = \texttt{woman} \wedge \texttt{other-charac}$. This source case corresponds to a woman having the same characteristics as Jules, except for her gender. This source case has been retrieved because it is very similar to $\texttt{tgt}$ according to a (conservative) adaptation-guided retrieval criterion defined in [14].

The solution of this problem is $\text{Sol}(\texttt{srce}) = \texttt{FEC-50} \wedge \texttt{Rad-50Gy} \wedge \texttt{ovariectomy}$: this treatment corresponds to a cure of FEC 50 (a chemotherapy drug), a breast radiotherapy with a dose of 50 Gy, and an ovariectomy (ovary ablation), that has an anti-oestrogen effect and, so, constitutes a hormone therapy. There are other anti-oestrogen treatments, such as the treatment with tamoxifen and the one with anti-aromatases. The knowledge presented above, together with the fact that men are not women can be formalized by

$$DK_0 = (\neg\texttt{woman} \vee \neg\texttt{man}) \wedge (\texttt{FEC-50} \rightarrow \texttt{chemotherapy}) \wedge$$
$$(\texttt{Rad-50Gy} \rightarrow \texttt{radiotherapy}) \wedge (\texttt{ovariectomy} \rightarrow \texttt{anti-oestro}) \wedge$$
$$(\texttt{tamoxifen} \rightarrow \texttt{anti-oestro}) \wedge (\texttt{anti-aromatases} \rightarrow \texttt{anti-oestro}) \wedge$$
$$(\texttt{anti-oestro} \rightarrow \texttt{hormone-therapy})$$

Moreover, it is assumed that:

$$\mathcal{V}^c_{\texttt{sol}} = \{\texttt{FEC-50}, \texttt{Rad-50Gy}, \texttt{ovariectomy}, \texttt{tamoxifen}, \texttt{anti-aromatases}\}$$
$$\mathcal{V}^a_{\texttt{sol}} = \{\texttt{chemotherapy}, \texttt{radiotherapy}, \texttt{anti-oestro}, \texttt{hormone-therapy}\}$$

---

[2] The medical knowledge presented here has been simplified and should not be considered correct from a medical viewpoint.

The conservative adaptation gives:

$$\text{CA}_{\circ_D}(\text{DK}_0, \texttt{srce-case}, \texttt{tgt}) = (\text{DK}_0 \wedge \texttt{srce} \wedge \text{Sol}(\texttt{srce})) \circ_D (\text{DK}_0 \wedge \texttt{tgt})$$
$$\equiv_{\text{DK}_0} \texttt{man} \wedge \texttt{other-charac} \wedge \texttt{FEC-50} \wedge \texttt{Rad-50Gy} \wedge \texttt{ovariectomy}$$

Knowledge acquisition following a detection, by the expert, of inconsistency of the solution with his/her knowledge. The result of the conservative adaptation is presented to the expert (figure 1). This latter is in charge of determining if the solution is consistent with his/her knowledge. In this example, this is not the case (type 1 failures) and he/she checks a set of literals such that their conjunction is inconsistent with his/her knowledge. He checks $\texttt{man}$ and $\texttt{ovariectomy}$ since he/she knows that it is not possible to do an ovariectomy on men (cf. figure 1). Therefore, $\text{Inc}_1 = \texttt{man} \wedge \texttt{ovariectomy}$ is false and $\neg\text{Inc}_1$ can be added to the domain knowledge:

$$\text{DK}_1 = \text{DK}_0 \wedge \neg\text{Inc}_1 \equiv \text{DK}_0 \wedge (\neg\texttt{man} \vee \neg\texttt{ovariectomy})$$

Moreover, the expert is asked to provide an explanation, and he/she proposes the following one:

Text 1: *To make an ablation of ovaries on a person, it is necessary that this person has ovaries, which is not the case for men.*

Then, the system performs a new adaptation:

$$\text{CA}_{\circ_D}(\text{DK}_1, \texttt{srce-case}, \texttt{tgt}) \equiv_{\text{DK}_1} \texttt{man} \wedge \texttt{other-charac} \wedge \texttt{FEC-50} \wedge \texttt{Rad-50Gy}$$
$$\wedge \neg\texttt{ovariectomy} \wedge \texttt{anti-oestro}$$

(the conservative adaptation does not keep the ovariectomy, since it is in contradiction with $\text{DK}_1 \wedge \texttt{man}$ but keeps the idea of an anti-oestrogen treatment).

Knowledge acquisition for making a partial solution precise. Then, the result of the second adaptation is presented to the expert. This latter, first indicates that the solution is consistent with his/her knowledge. Thus, there is no first type failure, but there is a second type failure: the type of anti-oestrogen treatment should be precised. Indeed, $\texttt{anti-oestro} \in \mathcal{V}_{\text{sol}}^a$ and there exists no formula f that does not contain any variable of $\mathcal{V}_{\text{sol}}^a$ that is equivalent to $\text{CA}_{\circ_D}(\text{DK}_1, \texttt{srce-case}, \texttt{tgt})$ modulo DK. In this situation, the set of interpretations of $\text{CA}_{\circ_D}(\text{DK}_1, \texttt{srce-case}, \texttt{tgt})$ is presented to the expert who points out the ones that are inconsistent with his/her knowledge (cf. figure 2) and, for each of them, a set of literals whose conjunction Inc is inconsistent with his/her knowledge. In this example, 2 of the 4 interpretations (the first and the fourth on the figure) are inconsistent. From the first one, the expert makes a selection that corresponds to

$$\text{Inc}_{2.1} = \neg\texttt{ovariectomy} \wedge \neg\texttt{tamoxifen} \wedge \neg\texttt{anti-aromatases} \wedge \texttt{anti-oestro}$$

And he/she explains it by text 2 and FRAKAS adds $\neg\text{Inc}_{2.1}$ to the domain knowledge:

Text 2: *The only therapies that are possible and permitted in my hospital for an anti-oestrogen treatment are the ovariectomy, the tamoxifen, and the anti-aromatases.*

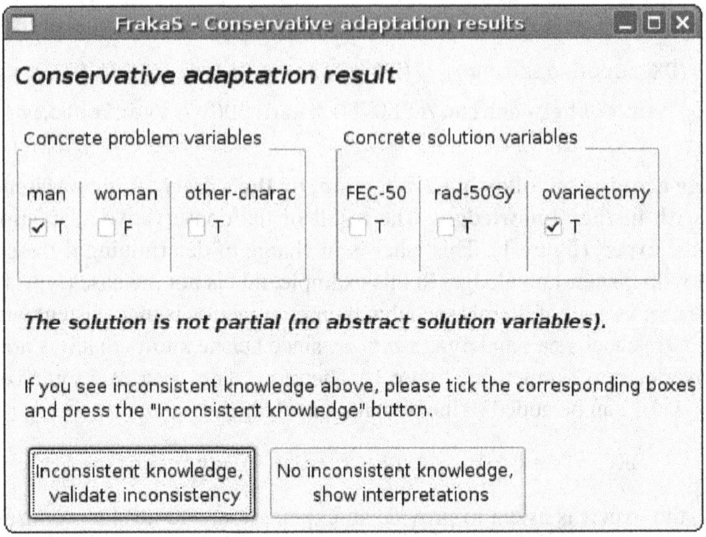

(a) Display of $CA_{o_D}(DK_0, \texttt{srce-case}, \texttt{tgt})$

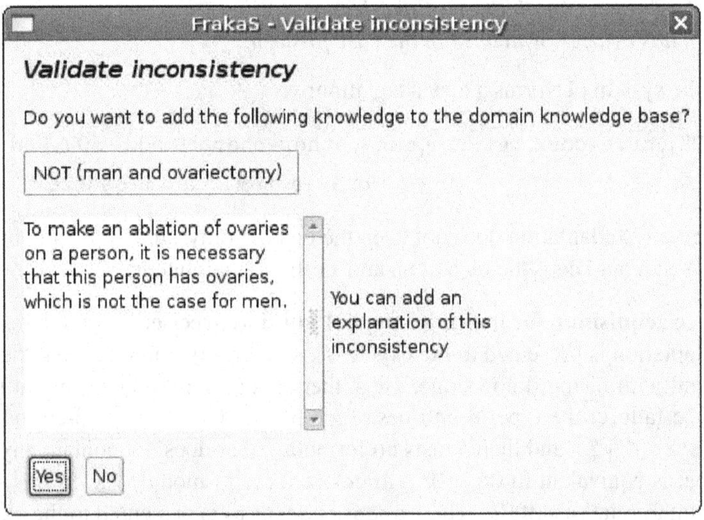

(b) The expert validates the acquired knowledge and provides an explanation

Fig. 1. First solution presented to the expert ($CA_{o_D}(DK_0, \texttt{srce-case}, \texttt{tgt})$) and his/her feedback, in the form of checked boxes (a). Plain text explanation provided by the expert (b).

$$DK_2 = DK_1 \wedge \neg Inc_{2.1}$$

$$\equiv DK_1 \wedge \texttt{anti-oestro} \rightarrow \begin{pmatrix} \texttt{ovariectomy} \vee \texttt{tamoxifen} \\ \vee \texttt{anti-aromatases} \end{pmatrix}$$

For the other interpretation that is inconsistent with the expert knowledge, Inc is $Inc_{2.2} = \texttt{tamoxifen} \wedge \texttt{anti-aromatases}$ that is explained by text 3.

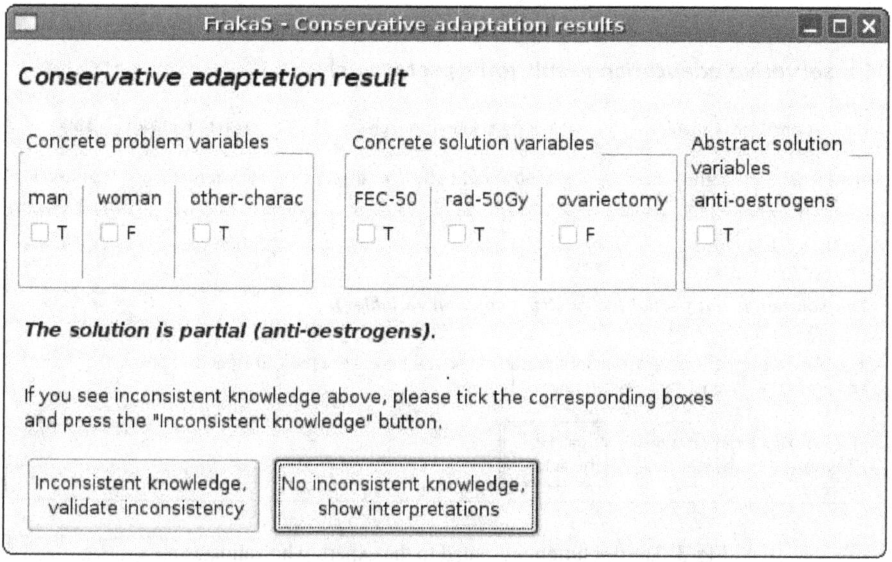

(a) Display of $CA_{o_D}(DK_1, \texttt{srce-case}, \texttt{tgt})$ that is judged by the expert to be consistent

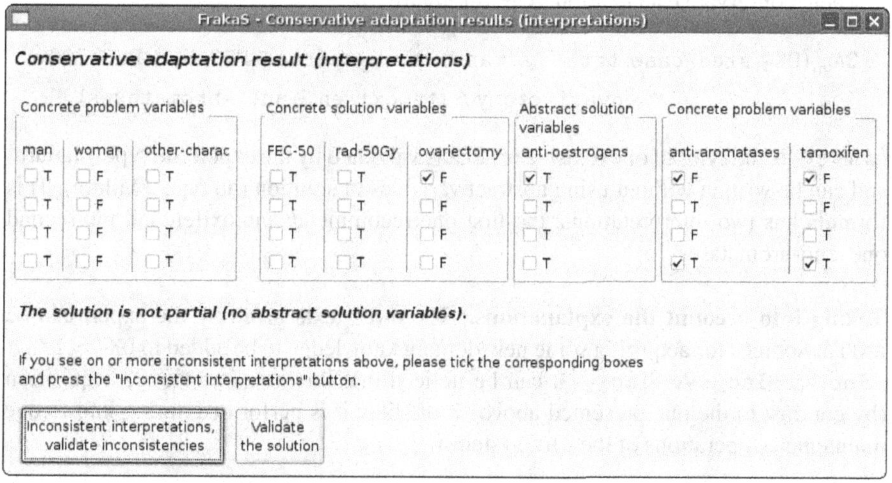

(b) Display of the interpretations of $CA_{o_D}(DK_1, \texttt{srce-case}, \texttt{tgt})$ and the feedback of the expert on the interpretations he/she rejects

Fig. 2. Second solution presented to the expert and his/her feedback (only the checking box part)

Text 3: *A given hormone therapy should not use at the same time tamoxifen and anti-aromatases.*

$$DK_3 = DK_2 \wedge \neg Inc_{2.2} \equiv DK_2 \wedge (\neg\texttt{tamoxifen} \vee \neg\texttt{anti-aromatases})$$

Then, $\neg Inc_{2.2}$ is added to DK_2.

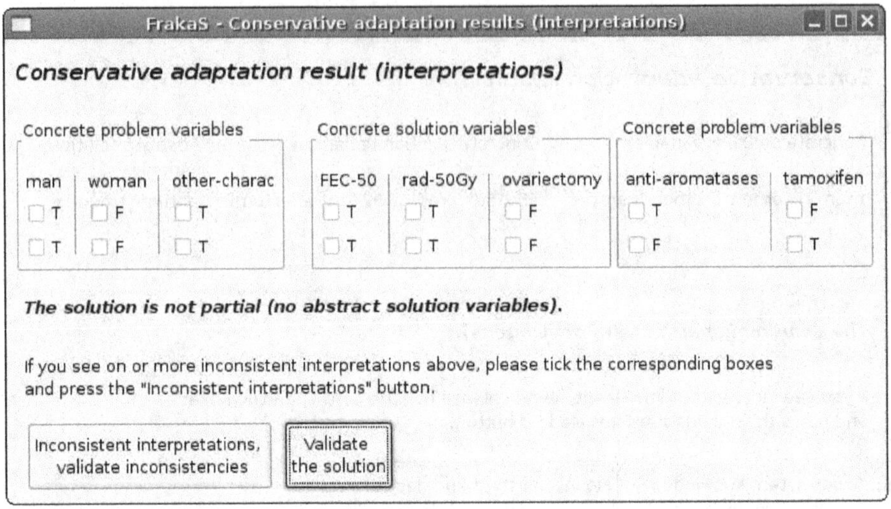

Fig. 3. Third solution presented to the expert, who validates it

Then, conservative adaptation gives (cf. figure 3):

$$CA_{o_D}(DK_3, \text{srce-case}, \text{tgt}) \equiv_{DK_3} \text{man} \land \text{other-charac} \land \text{FEC-50} \land \text{Rad-50Gy}$$
$$\land \neg \text{ovariectomy} \land (\text{tamoxifen} \oplus \text{anti-aromatases})$$

(where $\oplus$ is the symbol of exclusive or) that is validated by the expert (no type 1 failure) and can be written without using abstract variables of solution (no type 2 failure). This formula has two interpretations: the first one recommends tamoxifen and the second one, anti-aromatases.

Taking into account the explanations. The three texts given by the expert can be used as sources for acquiring some new domain knowledge to be added to $DK_3 = DK_0 \land \neg Inc_1 \land \neg Inc_{2.1} \land \neg Inc_{2.2}$. It can be noticed that this new knowledge acquisition (by contrast to the one presented above) is off-line; it is performed during knowledge maintenance operations of the CBR system.

Taking into account the first text. In this text, a knowledge engineer can establish the following knowledge, thanks to discussions with the expert:

- A man does not have ovaries ($f_1 = \text{man} \rightarrow \neg\text{has-ovaries}$);
- If a person has to be treated by ovariectomy, then this person must have ovaries ($f_2 = \text{ovariectomy} \rightarrow \text{has-ovaries}$);
- A woman who has already had an ovariectomy does not have her ovaries any more ($f_3 = \text{antecedent-ovariectomy} \rightarrow \neg\text{has-ovaries}$).

f_1 and f_2 formalize the text 1. f_3 comes from an answer of the expert to the following question asked by the knowledge engineer: "Are there women that do not have ovaries?"

Then, the state of the domain knowledge is:

$$DK_4 = DK_3 \wedge f_1 \wedge f_2 \wedge f_3$$

It can be noticed that during this phase, the vocabulary of the CBR system is enriched. It can also be noticed that $DK_0 \wedge f_1 \wedge f_2 \models DK_0 \wedge \text{Inc} = DK_1$: f_1 and f_2 explain Inc_1 that has to be a consequence of their conjunction. But, the additional knowledge f_3 enables to solve correctly the problem $\text{tgt}' = \text{woman} \wedge \text{antecedent-ovariectomy} \wedge \text{other-charac}$ by adaptation of the same source case:

$\text{CA}_{\text{Op}}(DK_4, \text{srce-case}, \text{tgt}') \equiv_{DK_4} \text{woman} \wedge \text{antecedent-ovariectomy} \wedge \text{other-charac}$
$\wedge \text{FEC-50} \wedge \text{Rad-50Gy} \wedge \neg\text{ovariectomy} \wedge (\text{tamoxifen} \oplus \text{anti-aromatases})$

Taking into account the second text. From the second text, the following fact can be acquired: when an anti-oestrogen treatment is required it is necessarily either an ovariectomy or a treatment with tamoxifen or anti-aromatases:

$$f_4 = \text{anti-oestro} \rightarrow (\text{ovariectomy} \vee \text{tamoxifen} \vee \text{anti-aromatases})$$

Nevertheless, this does not add new knowledge to what has already been acquired: $f_4 \equiv \neg\text{Inc}_{2.1}$. Does it imply that the second text is useless? No, since it highlights the fact that the knowledge f_4 (or $\neg\text{Inc}_{2.1}$) is *contextual*: it holds in the framework of the expert's hospital but a discussion with the expert points out that there exist other types of anti-oestrogen treatments. Therefore, it is important to avoid using this knowledge $\neg\text{Inc}_{2.1}$ in another medical context.

Taking into account the third text. A formalization of the third text gives $f_5 = \neg\text{tamoxifen} \vee \neg\text{anti-aromatases}$ but this does not enrich the domain knowledge: $f_5 \equiv \neg\text{Inc}_{2.2}$.

4.3   Main Algorithm of FRAKAS

Input: a problem tgt, a case base, and a domain knowledge DK

begin (algorithm)
   The case retrieval with target problem tgt gives the source case $(\text{srce}, \text{Sol}(\text{srce}))$.
   $\text{Sol}(\text{tgt}) \leftarrow \text{Adaptation}(DK, (\text{srce}, \text{Sol}(\text{srce})), \text{tgt})$
   / Taking into account type 1 failures */*
   while the user finds that $\text{tgt} \wedge \text{Sol}(\text{tgt})$ is inconsistent with his/her knowledge
      The user points out the failure Inc and gives a textual explanation.
      $DK \leftarrow DK \wedge \neg\text{Inc}$
      The textual explanation is stored for off-line knowledge acquisition.
      $\text{Sol}(\text{tgt}) \leftarrow \text{Adaptation}(DK, (\text{srce}, \text{Sol}(\text{srce})), \text{tgt})$
   end (while)
   / Taking into account type 2 failures */*
   if $\text{Sol}(\text{tgt})$ is not partial **then** exit
   while the user finds inconsistency is some interpretations of $\text{tgt} \wedge \text{Sol}(\text{tgt})$

for each inconsistent interpretation $\mathcal{I}$
    The user points out the failure Inc and gives a textual explanation.
    DK $\leftarrow$ DK $\wedge$ ¬Inc
    The textual explanation is stored for off-line knowledge acquisition.
end (for)
    Sol(tgt) $\leftarrow$ Adaptation(DK, (srce, Sol(srce)), tgt)
  end (while)
end (algorithm)

5 Discussion and Related Work

By storing solved problems, CBR allows one to obtain solution hypothesis to new problems even in weak or incomplete theory domains. Meanwhile, these solutions may be non appropriate because of a lack of sufficient knowledge, leading to reasoning failures. Thus, many research work address the learning component in CBR systems which has been studied along several perspectives. One of these perspectives characterizes the different kinds of knowledge containers targeted by the learning process [16]: cases, similarity knowledge, adaptation knowledge and domain knowledge. Another perspective characterizes the knowledge source used by the learning process [21].

Some approaches use the content of the knowledge containers, in particular those who rely on machine-learning techniques in order to explicit hidden knowledge [10; 6; 7]. Other approaches, by contrast, aim at acquiring new knowledge that is not already in the system through interactions with the environment [4; 13]. FRAKAS can be classified in this second category. Learning takes place during the use of the system and aims at acquiring domain knowledge. The evaluation of the adapted solution may highlight the fact that it does not meet the requirements of the target problem. In this situation, a reasoning failure occurs that can be treated by a learning from failures process. The expert is involved in the process of identifying inconsistent parts of the solution whose negation constitutes new knowledge.

Among related approaches, the CHEF system [9], a case-based planner in the cooking domain, can be cited. CHEF uses a causal model to test an adapted plan. In case of failure, CHEF generates an explanation to guide the repair of the solution. Then, the learning process sets appropriate indexes in order to avoid a later retrieval of the faulty plan in similar circumstances. Besides case-based planning, CHEF inspired many subsequent lines of research based on explanations in order to search for failure causes, propose the associated repairs of the case solution, and modify the knowledge involved in the failure. Among work conducted on explanations, the METAAQUA system [5] provides a taxonomy of failure causes associated to explanations in order to determine appropriate learning strategies. CREEK's reasoning and learning models [1] are built upon explanations in a knowledge-intensive context and [20] stresses the importance of explanations in the machine-learning process (and also for human learning and understanding).

In FRAKAS, textual explanations are used offline by knowledge engineers and domain experts to maintain domain knowledge. But FRAKAS also interacts with an expert during the reasoning process in a simple manner to point out faulty knowledge and gives the opportunity to add a textual explanation. A parallel may be established between FRAKAS and the relevance feedback principle [18] of information retrieval where items are emphasized or weakened depending on user feedback. In relevance feedback, users are marking documents as relevant to their needs and this gives information to the information retrieval system on how to modify the query for better further retrievals. In FRAKAS, the user marks inconsistent knowledge which is integrated to domain knowledge and further adaptation is retried thanks to this modification. This kind of interaction is quite simple and intuitive for the user while it gives minimal but useful information to the system to enhance the process.

6   Conclusion and Future Work

This paper presents an approach for acquiring domain knowledge based on reasoning failures of a CBR system. This work is restricted to a framework where a system produces solutions that are consistent with its domain knowledge, as it is the case, for instance, when based on conservative adaptation. Two kinds of failures are considered. The first one is characterized by a conflict between the solution inferred by the CBR system and knowledge of the domain expert (though it is consistent with domain solutions). An analysis of this failure highlights the faulty descriptors which led to the conflict and then, add new domain knowledge. The second kind of failures is characterized by the fact that the solution is only partial: some information needed to make it usable is missing. If an analysis of solution instances shows that some of them are conflicting, the result of this analysis is used to acquire new knowledge. Furthermore, textual explanations provided by the expert constitute also a starting point for acquiring new knowledge or even to clarify the context of some knowledge pieces. This approach has been implemented in FRAKAS, a prototype based on propositional logic. This formalism has been chosen because it is a simple one for expressing inconsistencies, but the ideas presented here should be transposable to other formal frameworks (e.g. descriptions logics and fuzzy logics).

The work described in this paper is only in an early stage. Several further research directions may be considered. First, FRAKAS has to be improved to be usable in real-world situations: the core example of the paper is a use case of FRAKAS that we have designed (by simplifying a real medical situation). In a practical way, for the KASIMIR project, the system should be confronted to cancer specialists under the assistance of computer scientists. This entails to work on the interface ergonomics of FRAKAS and to the optimization of several parts of the code of FRAKAS. It would be interesting to study the opportunity of selecting relevant interpretations and relevant variables in order to reduce the complexity and to make the work of the expert easier.

Moreover, since the KASIMIR system is based on a description logic formalism (see [3]), it will be necessary either to implement translation procedures between propositional logic and description logic (these procedures are necessarily approximate) or to implement a new version of FRAKAS based on description logic.

We also need to go further into the failures of the second kind. Indeed, in our example, an interaction with the expert was sufficient to handle it but it may not be always the case. Suppose for example that there exists a great number of anti-oestrogen treatments, ao_1, ao_2, ... ao_n, it will be tedious to enumerate them all and thus to obtain the knowledge `anti-oestro` $\rightarrow$ $ao_1 \vee ao_2 \vee \ldots \vee ao_n$. It seems more reasonable that the adaptation process provides such kind of result: "anti-oestrogen treatment, such as one based on tamoxifen or anti-aromatases".

Finally, an underlying assumption of this work is that domain knowledge is at any time consistent with expert's knowledge. This does not necessarily hold: DK may be "approximately true" (true in most situations but not all). In this case, when adding a new knowledge f to DK, a conflict of DK $\wedge$ f may occur. Consequently, such a conflict must be detected (which is not difficult). One could go further and propose to merge these two knowledge bases, by using a merging operator (see for example [12]). In particular, if one considers that DK can be revised, but f must be kept, one can use a revision operator instead of the ordinary conjunction: instead of $DK_{i+1} = DK_i \wedge f$, we would have $DK_{i+1} = DK_i \circ f$. This may occur if the use of FRAKAS leads first to the approximative knowledge $\neg Inc$ and then to the formula f which models the textual explanation given by the expert. This latter point needs to be studied thoroughly.

References

1. Aamodt, A.: A Knowledge-Intensive, Integrated Approach to Problem Solving and Sustained Learning. Doctoral dissertation, University of Trondheim, Norway (1991)
2. Aamodt, A., Plaza, E.: Case-based Reasoning: Foundational Issues, Methodological Variations, and System Approaches. AI Communications 7(1), 39–59 (1994)
3. Baader, F., Calvanese, D., McGuinness, D., Nardi, D., Patel-Schneider, P.: The Description Logic Handbook. Cambridge University Press, cambridge, UK (2003)
4. Cordier, A., Fuchs, B., Mille, A.: Engineering and Learning of Adaptation Knowledge in Case-Based Reasoning. In: Staab, S., Svátek, V. (eds.) EKAW 2006. LNCS (LNAI), vol. 4248, pp. 303–317. Springer, Heidelberg (2006)
5. Cox, M.T., Ram, A.: Introspective multistrategy learning: On the construction of learning strategies. Artificial Intelligence 112, 1–55 (1999)
6. Craw, S., Wiratunga, N., Rowe, R.C.: Learning adaptation knowledge to improve case-based reasoning. Artificial Intelligence 170(16–17), 1175–1192 (2006)
7. d'Aquin, M., Badra, F., Lafrogne, S., Lieber, J., Napoli, A., Szathmary, L.: Case Base Mining for Adaptation Knowledge Acquisition. In: Proceedings of the 20th International Joint Conference on Artificial Intelligence (IJCAI'07), pp. 750–755. Morgan Kaufmann, Inc, San Francisco (2007)
8. d'Aquin, M., Lieber, J., Napoli, A.: Adaptation Knowledge Acquisition: a Case Study for Case-Based Decision Support in Oncology. Computational Intelligence (an International Journal) 22(3/4), 161–176 (2006)
9. Hammond, K.J.: Explaining and Repairing Plans That Fail. AI Magazine 45(1–2), 173–228 (1990)
10. Hanney, K., Keane, M.T.: Learning Adaptation Rules From a Case-Base. In: Smith, I., Faltings, B. (eds.) Advances in Case-Based Reasoning. LNCS, vol. 1168, pp. 179–192. Springer, Berlin (1996)
11. Katsuno, H., Mendelzon, A.: Propositional knowledge base revision and minimal change. Artificial Intelligence 52(3), 263–294 (1991)
12. Konieczny, S., Lang, J., Marquis, P.: DA^2 merging operators. Artificial Intelligence 157(1-2), 49–79 (2004)

13. Leake, D.B., Kinley, A., Wilson, D.C.: Learning to Integrate Multiple Knowledge Sources for Case-Based Reasoning. In: Proceedings of the 15th International Joint Conference on Artificial Intelligence (IJCAI'97), pp. 246–251 (1997)
14. Lieber, J.: Application of the Revision Theory to Adaptation in Case-Based Reasoning: the Conservative Adaptation. In: Proceedings of the 7th International Conference on Case-Based Reasoning. LNCS, vol. 4626, pp. 224–238. Springer, Heidelberg (2007)
15. McCarthy, J.: Epistemological Problems of Artificial Intelligence. In: Proceedings of the 5th International Joint Conference on Artificial Intelligence (IJCAI'77, Cambridge (Massachussetts), pp. 1038–1044 (1977)
16. Richter, M.M.: The Knowledge Contained in Similarity Measures. In: Aamodt, A., Veloso, M.M. (eds.) Case-Based Reasoning Research and Development. LNCS, vol. 1010, Springer, Heidelberg (1995)
17. Riesbeck, C.K., Schank, R.C.: Inside Case-Based Reasoning. Lawrence Erlbaum Associates, Inc., Hillsdale, New Jersey (1989)
18. Rocchio, J.J.: Document Retrieval Systems – Optimization and Evaluation. PhD thesis, Harvard University (March 1966)
19. Smyth, B., Keane, M.T.: Experiments On Adaptation-Guided Retrieval In Case-Based Design. In: Aamodt, A., Veloso, M. (eds.) Case-Based Reasoning Research and Development. LNCS, vol. 1010, pp. 313–324. Springer, Heidelberg (1995)
20. Sørmo, F., Cassens, J., Aamodt, A.: Explanation in Case-Based Reasoning –Perspectives and Goals. Artificial Intelligence Review 24(2), 109–143 (2005)
21. Wilke, W., Vollrath, I., Althoff, K.-D., Bergmann, R.: A Framework for Learning Adaptation Knowedge Based on Knowledge Light Approaches. In: Proceedings of the Fifth German Workshop on Case-Based Reasoning, pp. 235–242 (1997)

Classify and Diagnose Individual Stress Using Calibration and Fuzzy Case-Based Reasoning

Shahina Begum, Mobyen Uddin Ahmed, Peter Funk, Ning Xiong,
and Bo von Schéele

Department of Computer Science and Electronics
Mälardalen University,
SE-72123 Västerås, Sweden
{firstname.lastname}@mdh.se

Abstract. Increased exposure to stress may cause health problems. An experienced clinician is able to diagnose a person's stress level based on sensor readings. Large individual variations and absence of general rules make it difficult to diagnose stress and the risk of stress-related health problems. A decision support system providing clinicians with a second opinion would be valuable. We propose a novel solution combining case-based reasoning and fuzzy logic along with a calibration phase to diagnose individual stress. During calibration a number of individual parameters are established. The system also considers the feedback from the patient on how well the test was performed. The system uses fuzzy logic to incorporating the imprecise characteristics of the domain. The cases are also used for the individual treatment process and transfer experience between clinicians. The validation of the approach is based on close collaboration with experts and measurements from 24 persons used as reference.

1 Introduction

Today everyday life for many people contain many situations that may trigger stress or result in an individual living on an increased stress level under long time. It is known that high level of stress may cause serious health problems. Different treatments and exercises can reduce this stress. Since one of the effects of stress is that the awareness of the body decreases, it is easy to miss signals such as high tension in muscles, unnatural breathing, blood-sugar fluctuations and cardiovascular functionality. It may take many weeks or months to become aware of the increased stress level, and once it is noticed, the effects and unaligned processes, e.g. of the metabolic processes, may need long and active behavioural treatment to revert to a normal state [25]. For patients with high blood pressure and heart problems high stress levels may be directly life-endangered. A system determining a person's stress profile and potential health problems would be valuable both in a clinical environment as second opinion or in a home environment as part of a stress management program.

A well known fact is that finger temperature has a correlation with stress for most people, but large individual fluctuations make it difficult to use a traditional diagnosis system. In this paper we propose a system that uses case-based reasoning (CBR) and fuzzy logic along with a calibration phase. CBR [1, 9] is a method based on learning

R.O. Weber and M.M. Richter (Eds.): ICCBR 2007, LNAI 4626, pp. 478–491, 2007.
© Springer-Verlag Berlin Heidelberg 2007

from similar cases and since this is spread practiced in clinical work, it is a method readily accepted by many clinicians. The calibration phase helps to determine a number of parameters that are important inputs both for a clinician to make the final diagnosis and treatment plan and also for the following system to classify the severity of the current stress level and makes a prognosis of its development so counter measures and treatment can be chosen.

2 Background

2.1 Stress Medicine

Psycho-physiology addresses the relation between psychology and physiology. Stress medicine is a branch of Psycho-physiology where the treatment of stress-related dysfunctions is studied. In psychology stress is defined as a condition caused by different factors in which human beings are inclining to change the existing normal stable state. When we react to certain events or facts it may produce stress. Stress may in worst case cause severe mental and physical problems that are often related to psychosomatic disorders, coronary heart disease etc. [24].

2.2 Establishing a Person's Stress Profile

We will give a brief description of the standard procedure followed by the clinicians to establish a person's stress profile without going into clinical details, and only give a general understanding of the test procedure. Measurement of the finger temperature is taken using a temperature sensor connected to a computer during stress conditions as well as in non-stressed (relaxed) conditions as shown in fig.1.

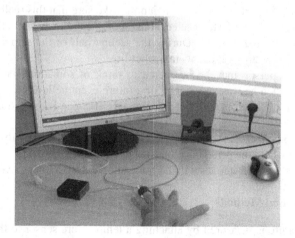

Fig. 1. Taking finger temperature measurement using a temperature sensor

Adjustments before starting the test conditions are achieved under the base-line measurement conditions, by securing a stable room temperature and allowing time for a person to adjust from the outdoor temperature (if the person has been outside

recently). Thus it allows a person to stabilize the hand temperature and then tempera-
tures are measured following a standard procedure (table 1).

Table 1. Measurement procedure used to create an individual stress profile

Test step	Observation time	Con/Parameter	Finger temp	Notes
1.	3 min	Base Line		
2.	2 min	Deep Breath		
3.	2+2 min	Verbal Stress		
4.	2 min	Relax		
5.	2 min	Math stress		
6.	2 min	Relax		

Step1 may be seen as indicating the representative level for the individual when
he/she is neither under strong stress nor in a relax state. Sometimes clinicians let the
person to read a neutral text during this step. A clinician not only identifies an individual's basic finger temperature, but also notes fluctuations and other effects, e.g.
disturbances in the environment or observes person's behaviour.

During step2 the person breaths deeply which under guidance normally causes a
relax state. Also how quickly the changes occur during this step is relevant and
recorded together with observed fluctuations.

Step 3 is initiated with letting a person tell about some stressful events they experienced in life. It is important for the clinician to make sure that this really is a stressful
event, since some persons instead select some more neutral event or tell about a challenge they were excited to solve. During the second half of the step a person thinks
about some negative stressful events in his/her life.

In step 4, the person may be instructed to think of something positive, either a
moment in life when he was very happy or a future event he looks forward to experiencing (this step may be difficult for a depressed person and adjusted accordingly by
the clinicians).

Step 5 is the math stress step; it tests the person's reaction to directly induced stress
by the clinician where the person is requested to count backwards.

Finally, the relaxation step tests if and how quickly the person recovers from stress.

2.3 Materials and Methods

Finger temperature is measured by attaching a temperature sensor to the little finger.
The signal from the sensor contains the pattern of the finger temperature during different stress and relaxed conditions. An example of the finger temperature measurements is shown in fig. 2 demonstrating the variations on finger temperature.

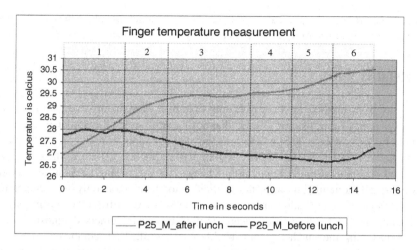

Fig. 2. Variations on finger temperature before and after lunch

Clinical studies show that when talking about any stressful events/experience finger temperature decreases and in extreme cases it decreases up to 5 to 10 degrees of Celsius. Recalling a minor misunderstanding could even decrease the temperature by 1 degree [13]. However, this effect of changes varies for different persons. Ideally the temperature is monitored repeatedly during a longer period, e.g. a week, to determine the temperature consistency or pattern for the person. This pattern could be different for different persons, e.g. some may have lowest representative temperature at 22C while for another person 28C may be the lowest. Changes in temperature before and after meal can be pronounced in some individuals, but for persons with some food allergy no changes or a decrease may occur. In general, temperature associated with stress may vary from 15.5 degree Celsius to 37.2 degree Celsius in a normal room temperature (20C to 23C).

The procedure described above for establishing a person's stress profile is used as a standard procedure in the clinical work in patients with stress related dysfunctions and an experienced clinician evaluates these measurements during the different test conditions to make an initial diagnosis. This diagnosis is complex and based on long experience and tacit knowledge [19]. The approach proposed here is based on feature extraction from temperature signals and case-based reasoning to detect appearance of stress and fuzzy set theory to tackle imprecision of input given by patient or clinician as well as imprecision of the domain.

2.3.1 Fuzzy Logic and Case-Based Reasoning

Fuzzy case-based reasoning is useful for some applications in representing cases where the information is imprecise [17, 18]. It is possible to define inexact medical entities as fuzzy sets. For a fuzzy set, the idea of fuzziness is initiated by the assignment of an indicator function (membership function) that may range from values 0-1. Also in retrieving cases fuzzy set theory can be useful for matching similarities between the existing cases and the current case. Fuzzy CBR matches the cases in terms of degrees of similarities between attribute values of previous cases and a new case instead the traditional Boolean matching. Several matching algorithms have been proposed [5, 26 and 7] to retrieve cases in fuzzy CBR systems.

3   Related Work

CBR has been applied in the psycho-physiological domain in several studies. For example, a procedure using CBR for diagnosing stress-related disorder was put forwarded by Nilsson et al. [15] where stress-related disorders were diagnosed by classifying the heart rate patterns. A CBR system was outlined in [2] where the cases were fuzzified depends on finger temperature changes for diagnosing stress in the psycho-physiological domain, but it is not sufficient to depend on only the temperature changes for classifying individual sensitivity to stress. Apart from the psycho physiological domain, CBR techniques were applied in several others diagnosis/classification tasks in the medical domain. Montani et al. [23] combines case-based reasoning, rule-based reasoning, and model-based reasoning to support therapy for diabetic patients. AUGUSTE [14] project was developed for diagnosis and treatment planning in Alzheimer's disease. MNAOMIA [3] was developed for the domain of psychiatry. CARE-PARTNER [4] was used in stem cell transplantation. BOLERO [12] is a successfully applied medical CBR diagnosis system in diagnosing pneumonias using fuzzy set theory for representing uncertain and imprecise values. A CBR technique with fuzzy theory is used for the assessment of coronary heart disease risk [22]. All these projects and others [8, 21, and 16] show significant evidence of successful application of CBR techniques in the medical domain.

4   Classification

Before defining the severity of stress for a person we consider the variation of the finger temperature with stress and define three categories such as: a. finger temperature decreases with increasing stress which is the most common situation, b. finger temperature increases with increasing stress and c. little or no changes i.e., remains in the stable situation when a person is experienced with stress which is exceptional but might happened for some persons. In such cases the clinical expertise is important, and also similar cases in a case library may give important clues on explaining the result. As the treatment advised for the different groups would be different this categorization provides valuable information for selecting the treatment procedure for each individual.

4.1   Classify Individual Sensitivity to Stress

According to the clinical experts step 3 and step 4 (table 1) are the most significant steps to classify a person's sensitivity to stress. Step 3, verbal stress is defined as reactions during lab stress conditions and step 4 which is a relaxation step soon after finishing the stress condition in step 3, is to see how quickly a person recover or cope with stress. We find that different persons behave differently in step 3, (talking about and thinking about a negative event) some have a very sharp drop in finger temperature, others a slow drop, a few have no drop in temperature (i.e. after lunch). Also some persons quickly recover in phase 4 (thinking positive event) others have slow increase in temperature, a few just continue dropping. According to the clinicians the later may be an indication of being more sensitive to stress, but in some cases there are normal explanations for these cases (i.e. a person having an exam after the test or being very hungry) and they are probably not needing treatment, but if this pattern is repeatedly consistent, then there may be a problem that need some treatment. Also a stressed person may not reach a stable or relaxed state if the body is misadjusted. This can be caused by different illnesses or by long periods of increased stress. One indication of such an increased stress level may be that the difference between a stressed state (step 3) and a relaxed state (step 4) is small. The time it takes for a person to switch from one state to another state is relevant information for a clinician, e.g. a person who still has a finger temperature level that corresponds to stressed state after spending time on relaxation exercises may need a different treatment than a person quickly reaching a finger temperature corresponding to a relaxed state. This kind of reasoning is what clinicians often doing, weighting different information. Therefore, the shape or 'behaviour' in step 3 and 4 are significant to classify a person's sensitivity to stress.

We propose to introduce "degree of change" as a measurement for finger temperature change. A low value, e.g. zero or close to zero is no change or stable in finger temperature. A high value indicating a steep slope upwards indicates a fast increase in finger temperature, while a negative angle, e.g. -20° indicates a steep decline. Together with clinicians we have agreed on a standardisation of the slope to make changes visible and patients and situations easier to compare. The proposal is that the X axis in minutes and the Y axis in degrees Celsius, hence a change during 1 minute of 1 degree gives a "degree of change" of 45° see fig.3.

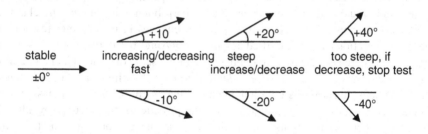

Fig. 3. Example of visualisations of temperature change, X axis minutes, Y axis 0.5 degree Celsius and clinicians response

Decrease of temperature may be an indication of stress and how steep the change is also of importance for the clinicians. Using negative angles make this more obvious and give the clinician a terminology to reason about change. This is shown in figure 4 as text under the arrows.

If a clinician classifies temperature change we have to be aware that this also is context dependent, e.g. -17° decline may be classified "decreasing fast" for one patient and "steep decrease" for another. This is important e.g. when explaining a case to a clinician or explaining the differences and similarities between two cases.

In a test step both the average drop and the steepest drop during a time frame are relevant. The first step in the decision support system is to translate the curves into relevant sections of interest and calculate their angles as illustrated for step 3 in fig.4.

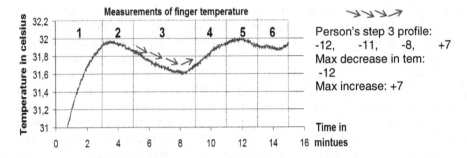

Fig. 4. The visualisations of temperature change and clinician's response

This notation makes it also easier to compare different person's differences and similarities during the test cycle, despite that their finger temperature differs widely.

4.2 Fuzzy Classification

Furthermore, improved classification is possible by using fuzzification of these angles. Instead of using the sharp distinction we can use the fuzzy membership function (mf) because this change of finger temperature in step 3 and step 4 is highly individual and difficult to make any sharp boundaries among the classified regions. For example in step 3, 10 degrees of changes in temperature towards the negative direction can be classified as *'fast decreasing'* but in real life a person who has the 13 degrees of changes in temperature in the same direction can be classified as the same level of severity (*fast decreasing*) by the clinician. An experienced clinician does this with his own judgment. So the sharp distinction to classify individual sensitivity to stress might not always provide us the accurate result. The fuzzy membership functions are applied to generate a more smooth distinction among the sensitivity levels to classify stress. By doing this a person can be diagnosed as having multiple severity levels of stress simultaneously whereas with different degrees.

In figure 5 an example is shown where the levels of severity of stress are defined (linguistic classifications) as too steep, steep, fast increasing/decreasing and stable depend on the 'degrees of changes' of the finger temperature in both positive and negative directions (i.e. -45 degree to +45 degree) with a set of fuzzy membership functions.

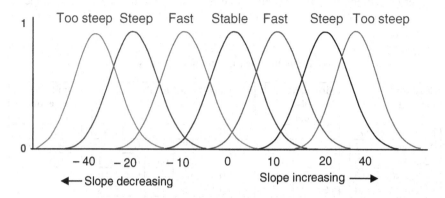

Fig. 5. Membership functions for different levels of sensitivity of stress for the similar individuals

5 Fuzzy Case-Based Reasoning

Initial case library was build using some reference cases from the experts then the new cases are adapted and retained manually by the expert. The output from the calibration phase is used to create an individual case. This case will contain the derivative values of various important steps. We consider the temperature from step 3 to step 5 because these are the most significant steps to determine the sensitivity to stress according to the expert. Each step is divided in one minute time interval (4 minutes step 3 is divided into four time windows) and the derivative is calculated for each window. These values along with other attributes (gender, different between ceiling and floor temperature, etc) are stored into the case library with different weight values.

5.1 Similarity Matching

The retrieval step is especially essential in medical applications since missed similar cases may lead to less informed decision. The reliability and accuracy of the diagnosis systems depend on the storage of cases/experiences and on the retrieval of all relevant cases and their ranking. Similarity measurement is taken to assess the degrees of matching and create the ranked list containing the most similar cases retrieved by equation 1.

$$Similarity \quad (C,S) = \sum_{f=1}^{n} w_f * sim \ (C_f, S_f) \tag{1}$$

Where; C is the current case, S is a stored case in the case library, w is the normalized weight, n is the number of the attributes in each case, f is the index for an individual attribute and *sim* is the local similarity function for attribute f in case C and S.

For the numeric attribute values, the distances between two attributes values are calculated through the Euclidean distance shown in equation 2.

$$sim \ (C_f, S_f) = \left| C_f - S_f \right| \tag{2}$$

After calculating the distance, this value is compared with the similarity values as depicted in table 2 where the similarity values for different matrices are defined by the expert.

Table 2. Different matrices for the similarity values

Similarity for step			Similarity for ceiling/floor			Hours since last meal							Similarity for gender		
Distance	sim			sim		T/S	0	1	2	3	>4			m	f
0-2 degree	1		>0,3	1		0	1	0.8	0.6	0.4	0		m	1	0.5
>2 and <4	0.8		0,3 -0,5	0.8		1	0.8	1	0.8	0.6	0.4		f	0.5	1
>4 and <6	0.6		0,5-0,7	0.4		2	0.6	0.8	1	0.8	0.6				
>6 and <8	0.4		<0,7	0		3	0.4	0.6	0.8	1	0.8				
>8 and <10	0.2					>4	0	0.4	0.6	0,8	1				
>10	0														

So, finally the global similarity is calculated as a weighted sum of local similarities. An example is shown in table 3 where a current case is compared with two other stored cases (C_92 and C_115) in the case library.

Table 3. Similarity matching between cases

Attributes	Local weight	Normalized weight	Current case	Stored case C_92	Similarity Function	Weighted similarity	Stored case C_115	Similarity function	Weighted similarity
Gender	5	0.05	M	M	1.00	0.05	F	0.50	0.03
Hours since last meal	10	0.11	1	3	0.60	0.07	1	1.00	0.11
Room Temp	7	0.08	20	21	1.00	0.08	21.00	1.00	0.08
Step_3_part_1	7	0.08	-17.09	-1.39	0.00	0.00	-14.39	0.60	0.05
Step_3_part_2	7	0.08	-6.38	-10.91	0.60	0.05	-8.11	1.00	0.08
Step_3_part_3	7	0.08	-7.62	-7.55	1.00	0.08	-7.55	1.00	0.08
Step_3_part_4	7	0.08	1.52	3.15	1.00	0.08	3.15	1.00	0.08
Step_4_part_1	7	0.08	16.58	1.08	0.00	0.00	5.08	0.00	0.00
Step_4_part_2	7	0.08	8.34	6.34	1.00	0.08	7.13	1.00	0.08
Step_5_part_1	6	0.07	-8.66	-2.17	0.40	0.03	-6.17	0.40	0.03
Step_5_part_2	6	0.07	-9.44	-1.77	0.40	0.03	-1.77	0.80	0.05
Diff cealing /floor	9	0.10	0.75	0.59	1.00	0.10	0.59	1.00	0.10
				Global Similarity for C_92		0.67	Global Similarity for C_115		0.80

Here, the *Local weight (LW)* is defined by the experts, *Normalized weight (NW)* is calculated by the equation 3 where i=1 to n number of attributes, *Similarity function* calculates the similarity between attributes of the current case and the stored cases using the equation 2 and comparing the similarity values from the table 3, *Weighted similarity* for each attribute is defined by the normalized weight multiply the output of the similarity function, *Global similarity* between the cases are calculated as weighted sum of local similarities using the equation 1.

$$NW_i = \frac{LW_i}{\sum_{i=1}^{n} LW_i} \tag{3}$$

In table 3 the global similarity between the current case and case C_92 is 67% and current case and case C_115 is 80%.

5.2 Fuzzy Matching

The representation of a similarity value using a matrix as shown in table 2 often shows a sharp distinction which often provides an unrealistic solution. Moreover, multiple if-then rules are needed to implement the matrices. Fuzzy similarity matching is used to reduce this sharp distinction which also helps to avoid multiple rules. A triangular membership function replaces the crisp input attribute with the membership grade of 1. The width of the membership functions (*mf*) are provided by the expert's of the domain.

For example, in table 3 the attribute '*Step3_part2*' of the current case and the old case have the values -6.3 and -10.9 respectively. The weight of the *mf* is fuzzified with 50% in each side as shown in fig.6. For the current case the lower and upper bounds are -9.45 and -3.15 represented with an *mf* of grade 0. The input value is -6.3 with the *mf* grade of 1. The old case has the lower and upper bounds -16.35 and -5.45 with an *mf* grade of 0 and the input is -10.9 with an *mf* grade of 1.

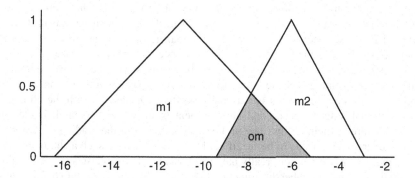

Fig. 6. Similarity matching using membership functions

The similarity between the old cases and the new case is calculated using the overlapping areas between the two fuzzy values in their membership functions [6]. The similarity equation is defined as-

$$S_{m_1 m_2} = \min(om/m_1, om/m_2) \tag{4}$$

Here m_1 is the area of one attribute value with one membership function and m_2 is associated with the second membership function and the overlapping area is denoted as om. In fig.6, m_1=5.45, m_2=3.15 and om=0.92 where height is defined from the intersection point of the two fuzzy membership functions. So from the equation 4, the local similarity is *min (0.17, 0.29)* =0.17 and *max* is 0.29. If the *mfs* are considered as 100% fuzzified then minimum local similarity will be 0.34 and maximum will be 0.58 which is close to the value of table 3. In this way the user has option both for tuning the *mfs* and choosing the min/max in the similarity function depends on the requirements. When the overlapping areas become bigger then the similarity between the two attributes will also increase and for a completely matched attributes similarity will be 1.

The system returns a ranked list with the most similar cases. Cases are sorted according to the percentage where 100% means the perfect match and represented the solution with the classification shown in the previous section. From the table 3, case C_115 has higher rank than C_92 that is the current case is more similar to the case C_115. A threshold value can be defined and modified by the user to get a list of similar cases and this list of cases are treated as candidate cases. From these candidate cases a case can be proposed by the user as an acceptable case and that can be reused to solve the new problem. If necessary, the solution for this acceptable case is revised by the expert that is often important in the medical domain. Finally, the current problem with confirmed solution is retained as a new case and added to the case library. In terms of adaptation any changes can be done by the expert before adding it into the case library and this could be done manually.

5.3 Reliability of the Test

Once the decision support system suggests a number of similar cases it is important for the clinician to know how reliable the similarity estimate is. One valuable indication of reliability in diagnosing stress is how well the person succeeded in doing the different test assignments or how sure a clinician is on a given value or judgment. Such input will make the foundation of a confidence factor [7] for a case.

A person can grade the severity of a stressful event (step 3) he/she was thinking by using a Visual Analogue Scale (-5 to +5) where +5 is very severe traumatic memory while 0 is not stressful and -5 is extremely positive. Discussing with the clinical experts and analysing the grade and measurement from the 24 persons it is clear that they are aware of their success rate in the specific step. But the grading does not have a high accuracy and needs to be fuzzified due to many factors such as humans tend to give a precise answer without really having a basis for this "preciseness". The value is fuzzified using two membership functions (Fig. 7). The left linear mf (from -2 to +5) represents the fuzzy values for the negative range (rate of failure in test) and the right linear mf (from -5 to +2) represents the positive range (success in test) in the universe of discourse (-5 to +5) for the fuzzy variable scale. This will give a value for the success rate in some degrees of mf instead of just a precise value and also reduce the number of rules to one.

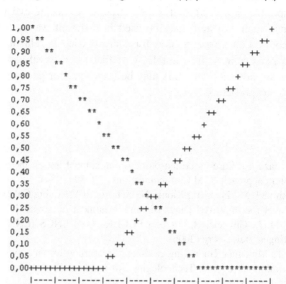

Fuzzy Value: State for Negative and Positive Rate of Test Step
Linguistic Value: negativeRate (*), positiveRate (+)

Fig. 7. Membership function of the positive and negative success rate of test

For example in table 3, the current case (CC) and case C_92 and C_115 have the success rate for the test step 3,4, and 5 are CC(7,3,6), C_92(5,6,5) and C_115(8,4,3) respectively. On an average the differences in success rate between CC and C_92 is 2 and CC and C_115 is 1.6. Suppose the global similarity between CC and other two cases are same then according to their rating of success the case C_92 will get more preference. Besides the same global similarities, this rating helps the clinician able to take a closer look at the suggested cases when the global similarities among them are different.

6 Summary and Conclusions

We have presented a decision support system based on a case-based method using a calibration procedure and fuzzy membership functions. Integration of CBR with fuzzy set theory enables the system to handle impreciseness in input features and domain knowledge in a way understood and accepted by the clinicians. The calibration phase also assists to individualize the system. The system extracts key features from the finger temperature signal and classifies individual sensitivity to stress. This provides important information to the clinician to make a decision about individual treatment plan. One of the strengths of the method is that it bears similarities with how the clinicians work manually and when clinicians are confronted with the concepts and functionality of the decision support system it is readily accepted by them. This support is valuable since clinicians are willing to participate actively in the project and validate the results. Our hope is that the classification system can be developed to a tool used by people that need to monitor their stress level during every day situations for health reasons. Such a system may be used in different ways: to monitor stress levels that are reported back to clinicians for analysis used in relaxation exercises or actively notify a person, in some suitable way, that stress levels are increased and counter measures are advisable and this may be important for patients with increased risk of stroke or heart problems.

References

1. Aamodt, A., Plaza, E.: Case-based reasoning: Foundational issues, methodological variations, and system approaches. AI Communications , 39–59 (1994)
2. Begum, S., Ahmed, M., Funk, P., Xiong, N., Scheele, B.V.: Using Calibration and Fuzzification of Cases for Improved Diagnosis and Treatment of Stress. In: Roth-Berghofer, T.R., Göker, M.H., Güvenir, H.A. (eds.) ECCBR 2006. LNCS (LNAI), vol. 4106, pp. 113–122. Springer, Heidelberg (2006)
3. Bichindaritz, I.: Mnaomia: Improving case-based reasoning for an application in psychiatry. In: Applications of Current Technologies. Artificial Intelligence in Medicine, pp. 14–20. AAAI, California (1996)
4. Bichindaritz, I., Kansu, E., Sullivan, K.M.: Case-based reasoning in care-partner: Gathering evidence for evidence-based medical practice. In: Smyth, B., Cunningham, P. (eds.) EWCBR 1998. LNCS (LNAI), vol. 1488, pp. 334–345. Springer, Heidelberg (1998)
5. Bonissone, P., Cheetham, W.: Fuzzy Case-Based Reasoning for Residential Property Valuation. In: Handbook on Fuzzy Computing (G 15.1), Oxford University Press, Oxford (1998)
6. Dvir, G., Langholz, G., Schneider, M.: Matching attributes in a fuzzy case based reasoning. Fuzzy Information Processing Society , 33–36 (1999)
7. Funk, P., Olsson, E., Bengtsson, M., Xiong, N.: Case-Based Experience Reuse and Agents for Efficient Health Monitoring, Preventive, and Corrective Actions. In: proceedings of the 19th International Congress on Condition Monitoring and Diagnostic Engineering Management, Sweden (2006)
8. Gierl, L.: ICONS: Cognitive basic functions in a case-based consultation system for intensive care. In: Andreassen, S., et al. (eds.) Proceedings of Artificial Intelligence in Medicine, pp. 230–236 (1993)
9. Watson, I.: Applying Case-Based Reasoning: Techniques for Enterprise Systems. Morgan Kaufmann Publishers Inc, 340 Pine St, 6th floor, San Fransisco, CA 94104, USA (1997)
10. Jaczynski, M., Trousse, B.: Fuzzy Logic for the retrieval step of a case-based reasoner. In: Haton, J.-P., Manago, M., Keane, M.A. (eds.) Advances in Case-Based Reasoning. LNCS, vol. 984, pp. 313–322. Springer, Heidelberg (1995)
11. Linkens, D.A., Abbod, M.F., Mahfouf, M.: Department of Automatic Control and Systems Engineering. University of Sheffield, Sheffield S1 3JD, United Kingdom (1988)
12. Lopez, B., Plaza, E.: Case-based learning of strategic knowledge Machine Learning. In: Kodratoff (ed.) Machine Learning - EWSL-91. LNCS (LNAI), vol. 482, pp. 398–411. Springer, Heidelberg (1991)

13. Lowenstein, T.: Stress and Body Temperature (Last referred on May 2006) (1995), http://www.cliving.org/stress.htm.

14. Marling, C., Whitehouse, P.: Case-based reasoning in the care of Alzheimer's disease patients. Case-Based Research and Development, 702–715 (2001)

15. Nilsson, M., Funk, P., Olsson, E., Von Schéele, B.H.C., Xiong, N.: Clinical decision-support for diagnosing stress-related disorders by applying psychophysiological medical knowledge to an instance-based learning system. Artificial Intelligence in Medicine , 159–176 (2006)

16. Perner, P., Gunther, T., Perner, H., Fiss, G., Ernst, R.: Health Monitoring by an Image Interpretation System- A System for Airborne Fungi Identification. In: Perner, P., Brause, R., Holzhütter, H.-G. (eds.) ISMDA 2003. LNCS, vol. 2868, pp. 64–77. Springer, Heidelberg (2003)

17. Plaza, E., Lopez de R., M.: A case-based apprentice that learns from fuzzy examples. Methodologies for Intelligent Systems 5, 420–427 (1990)

18. Plaza, E., Arcos, J-L.: A reactive architecture for integrated memory-based learning and reasoning. In: Richter, Wess, Altho, Maurer (eds.) Proceedings First European Workshop on Case-Based Reasoning, vol. 2, pp. 329–334 (1993)

19. Polanyi, M.: Tacit knowing. In: Marx, M.H., Goodson, F.E. (eds.) Theories in Contemporary Psychology, 2nd edn. pp. 330–344. Macmillan, New York (1966)

20. Rissland, E., Skalak, D.: Combining case-based and rule-based reasoning: A heuristic approach. In: Proceedings IJCAI-89, Detroit, MI, pp. 524–530 (1989)

21. Schmidt, R., Gierl, L.: Prognostic Model for Early Warning of Threatening Influenza Waves. In: Proceedings of the 1st German Workshop on Experience Management, pp. 39–46 (2002)

22. Schuster, A.: Aggregating Features and matching Cases on Vague Linguistic Expressions. In: Proceedings of International Joint Conferences on Artificial Intelligence, pp. 252–257 (1997)

23. Montani, S., Magni, P., Roudsari, A.V., Carson, E.R., Bellazzi, R.: Integrating Different Methodologies for Insulin Therapy Support in Type 1 Diabetic Patients. In: Quaglini, S., Barahona, P., Andreassen, S. (eds.) AIME 2001. LNCS (LNAI), vol. 2101, pp. 121–130. Springer, Heidelberg (2001)

24. Stress. In: Encyclopædia Britannica. Retrieved September 24, 2006, from Encyclopædia Britannica Online (2006), http://www.britannica.com/eb/article-9069962

25. Von Schéele, B.H.C., von Schéele, I.A.M.: The Measurement of Respiratory and Metabolic Parameters of Patients and Controls Before and After Incremental Exercise on Bicycle: Supporting the Effort Syndrome Hypothesis. Applied Psychophysiology and Biofeedback 24, 167–177 (1999)

26. Wang, W.J.: New similarity measures on fuzzy sets and on elements. Fuzzy Sets and Systems, 305–309 (1997)

Prototypical Cases for Knowledge Maintenance in Biomedical CBR

Isabelle Bichindaritz

University of Washington, 1900 Commerce Street, Box 358426,
Tacoma, WA 98402, USA
ibichind@u.washington.edu

Abstract. Representing biomedical knowledge is an essential task in biomedical informatics intelligent systems. Case-based reasoning (CBR) holds the promise to represent contextual knowledge in a way that was not possible before with traditional knowledge-based methods. One main issue in biomedical CBR is dealing with the rate of generation of new knowledge in biomedical fields, which often makes the content of a case base partially obsolete. This article proposes to make use of the concept of prototypical case to ensure that a CBR system would keep up-to-date with current research advances in the biomedical field. Prototypical cases have served various purposes in biomedical CBR systems, among which to organize and structure the memory, to guide the retrieval as well as the reuse of cases, and to serve as bootstrapping a CBR system memory when real cases are not available in sufficient quantity and/or quality. This paper presents knowledge maintenance as another role that these prototypical cases can play in biomedical CBR systems.

1 Introduction

Case-based reasoning is a valued knowledge management and reasoning methodology in biomedical domains because it founds its recommendations on contextual knowledge. This type of knowledge is much more detailed and to the point for solving clinical problems, and allows to account for some of the complexity inherent to working in clinical domains [11]. Cases play an essential role in medical training and medical expertise acquisition, and a comprehensive set of CBR systems in medicine now has been built and evaluated successfully [11]. Their usefulness in clinical settings has been showed for decision-support, explanation, and quality control [11]. If the value of contextual, instance-based knowledge, is not in question, main issues for CBR methodology are how to keep up with the rate of generation of new biomedical knowledge, and how to maintain the *currency* of the knowledge represented as cases in a case base [22]. The system presented here proposes to automate the process of maintaining the currency of the knowledge represented in cases through maintenance prototypical cases, which can be mined from current biomedical literature. In the system presented in this article, prototypical cases serve as a structuring mechanism for the case base. They also guide the different steps of the reasoning process, for example the retrieval and the reuse. During reuse, current medical recommendations,

R.O. Weber and M.M. Richter (Eds.): ICCBR 2007, LNAI 4626, pp. 492–506, 2007.

represented in prototypical cases mined from biomedical literature, guide the reuse of past cases and automatically revise obsolete recommendations from past cases.

The prototypical case structure adopted here is the one chosen for the Mémoire project, which is presented in the next section. The third section explains the role of case-based knowledge to represent contextual knowledge in biomedicine. The fourth section summarizes how prototypical cases can capture latest advances in biomedical literature, through a text mining mechanism. The fifth section presents how prototypical cases can serve as preserving the currency of a case base. A detailed example is presented in the sixth section. It is followed by a discussion and a conclusion.

2 Mémoire Project

The goal of the Mémoire project [7] at the University of Washington is to provide a framework for the creation and interchange of cases, concepts, and CBR systems in biology and medicine. This project extends on previous case-based decision-support systems developed by the same team, namely MNAOMIA in psychiatry [5] and Care Partner in stem cell transplantation [7].

The cornerstone of the knowledge acquisition process has been the conception of prototypical cases, called clinical pathways in this system. This prototypical case structure has been proposed in Mémoire as a generic prototypical case representation structure [7]. The clinical pathways, 112 of them having been implemented in a previous test version of the system, correspond to clinical diagnostic categories for the most part, some of them corresponding also to essential signs and symptoms requiring specific assessment or treatment actions. The clinical pathways are knowledge structures represented from a domain ontology, namely: all diseases, functions (also known as signs and symptoms), labs, procedures, medications, sites, and planning actions. Most of the terms naming these objects are standardized using the Unified Medical Language System (UMLS) [16]. Terms not corresponding to objects in the UMLS have been added to the domain specific ontology, such as all the planning actions used in the *treatment* part of a prototypical case.

An example of a prototypical case is provided in a next section in Fig. 4. It shows that a prototypical case, mostly a diagnostic category or disease, such as here chronic graft versus host disease affecting the liver, which is a complication of stem-cell transplantation, comprises three parts:

1. A list of *findings*, corresponding to signs and symptoms.
2. A *diagnosis assessment plan*, which is a plan to follow for confirming (or informing) the suspected diagnosis.
3. A *treatment plan*, which is a plan to follow for treating this disease when confirmed, or a solution when the pathway does not correspond to a disease.

The diagnosis assessment part and the treatment part can also be seen as simplified algorithms, since they use IF-THEN-ELSE structures, and LOOP structures, as well as SEQUENCE structures of actions in time. When instantiated with actual patients' data, this knowledge structure allows for sophisticated adaptation.

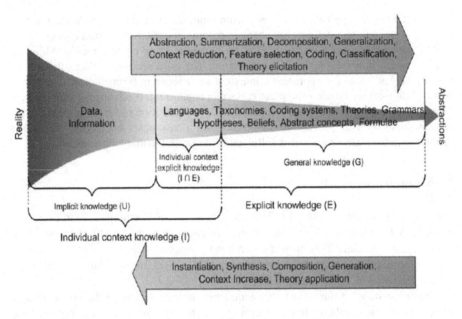

Fig. 1. The knowledge spectrum in biomedical informatics [17]

3   Cases as Contextual Knowledge

One of the main motivations for the development of case-based reasoning systems in biomedicine is that cases, as traces of the clinical experience of the experts, play a unique and irreplaceable role for representing knowledge in these domains. Recent studies, presented here, have worked at better formalizing this specific role. These studies explain that the gold standard for evaluating the quality of biomedical knowledge relies on the concept of evidence [17]. Pantazi et al. propose an extension of the definition of *biomedical evidence* to include knowledge in individual cases, suggesting that the mere collection of individual case facts should be regarded as evidence gathering [17] (see Fig. 1). To support their proposal, they argue that the traditional, highly abstracted, hypothesis centric type of evidence that removes factual evidence present in individual cases, implies a strong *ontological commitment* to methodological and theoretical approaches, which is the source of the never-ending need for *current* and *best* evidence, while, at the same time, offering little provision for the reuse of knowledge disposed of as obsolete. By contrast, the incremental factual evidence about individuals creates, once appropriately collected, a growing body of context-dependent evidence that can be reinterpreted and reused as many times as possible.

Currently, the concept of evidence most often refers to an abstract proposition derived from multiple, typically thousands of cases, in the context of what is known as a *randomized controlled trial*. Hypothesis forming is the cornerstone of this kind of biomedical research. Hypotheses that pass an appropriately selected statistical test become evidence. However, the process of hypothesis forming also implies a commitment to certain purposes (e.g., research, teaching, etc.), and inherently postulates ontological and conceptual reductions, orderings and relationships. All these are direct results of the particular conceptualizations of a researcher who is influenced by experience, native language, background, etc. This reduction process will always be prone to errors as long as uncertainties are present in our reality. In addition, even though a hypothesis may be successfully verified statistically and may become evidence subsequently, its applicability will always be hindered by our inability to fully construe its complete meaning. This meaning is defined by the complete context where the hypothesis was formed and which includes the data sources as well as the context of the researcher who formed the hypothesis [17].

The discussion about commitment to research designs, methodological choices, and research hypotheses led Pantazi et al. to propose to extend the definition and the understanding of the concept of evidence in biomedicine and align it with an intuitively appealing direction of research: *case-based reasoning* (CBR) [18]. From this perspective, the concept of evidence, traditionally construed on the basis of knowledge applicable to populations, is evolved to a more complete, albeit more complex construct which emerges naturally from the attempt to understand, explain and manage unique, individual cases. This new perspective of the concept of evidence is surprisingly congruent with the current acceptation of the notion of evidence in forensic science for instance. Here, by evidence, one also means, besides general patterns that apply generally to populations, the recognition of any spatio-temporal form (i.e., pattern, regularity) in the context of a case (e.g., a hair, a fibre, a piece of clothing, a sign of struggle, a finger print, the reoccurrence of a certain event) which may be relevant to the solution to that case. This new view where a body of evidence is incremental in nature and accumulates dynamically in form of facts about individual cases is a striking contrast with traditional definitions of biomedical evidence. Case evidence, once appropriately collected, represents a history that can be reinterpreted and reused as many times as necessary. But most importantly, the kind of knowledge where the "what is", i.e., case data, is regarded as evidence can be easily proven to be less sensitive to the issues of *recency* (i.e., current evidence) and *validity* (i.e., best evidence) [17].

4 Prototypical Case Mining

If the value of CBR in biomedical domains is becoming more and more established, the complexity of these domains has led researchers to develop novel methodologies. For example ProCaseMiner system addresses the issue of maintaining the currency of the knowledge in a case base. This system (see Fig. 2) mines for prototypical cases from biomedical literature [8]. A selection of documents for a given medical domain is the input to this system. Pertinent documents may be literature articles, but also textual clinical practice guidelines, and medical case studies. It is important that such documents should all be related to a given domain.

ProConceptMiner core component is the RelationshipMiner, which mines for triples *<concept-1, relationship-1,2, concept-2>* from a text. It also attaches a condition to a triple when it finds it to represent the information that IF a condition occurs, then an action or test is undertaken. This can be represented as *<concept-1, relationship-1,2, concept-2>* IF *<concept-3, relationship-3,4, concept-4>*. An example can be *<Patient, startTreatment, PrednisoneAndCyclosporineTherapy>* IF *<absent, property_of, ImmunosuppressantAgentNOS>*. This structure is called a triple pair.

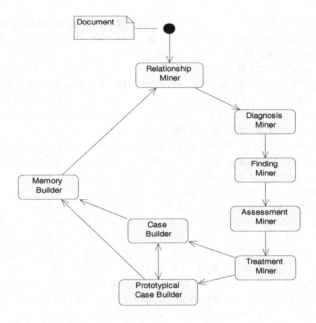

Fig. 2. ProConceptMiner architecture

ProConceptMiner interprets the results from RelationshipMiner, a component mining for the triples structures previously introduced, by successively mining for diagnoses in DiagnosisMiner, findings in FindingMiner, assessments in Assessment-Miner, and treatments in TreatmentMiner. Following, it builds cases from these results in CaseBuilder or PrototypicalCaseBuilder. In some cases, learnt relationships will be associated with conditions, signaling a prototypical case, and in others the absence of these conditions will signal a practice case. Generally, from medical articles and clinical practice guidelines, the learnt artifact will be a prototypical case. From clinical case studies, the learnt artifact will be a practice case. After learning cases from a single document, a next step is to consolidate results across documents. It is called MemoryBuilder [8].

5 Prototypical Cases for Knowledge Maintenance

Mémoire integrates clinical cases and the prototypical cases mined from literature to achieve a case-based reasoning goal. This system relies on a generic prototypical case representation to perform its case-based reasoning and to maintain its knowledge.

5.1 Case Representation

The elements of the representation language are those of semantic networks:

- A *domain ontology*, which is the set of *class symbols* (also called concepts in the UMLS [16]) C, where C_i and C_j denote elements of C. Specific subdomains are for example findings (signs and symptoms, noted F_i), tests and procedures (A_i), and planning actions (P_i).

- *A set of individual symbols* (also called instances) I, where i and j denote elements of I. Among these, some refer to instances of classes, others to numbers, dates, and other values. Instances of a class C_i are noted aC_i.

- *A set of operator symbols* O, permits to form logical expressions composed of classes, instances and other values, and relationships. Prototypical cases and clinical cases are expressed this way, and such a composition permits to represent complex entities in a structured format. The set of operators comprises the following:

$\wedge$ (AND)
$\vee$ (OR)
ATLEAST n
ATMOST n
EXACTLY n
IF

Prototypical cases are expressed as *<problem situation, solution>*, where *problem situation* is expressed in the object-oriented knowledge representation language above as a composition of instances with operators and where *solution* also has the same representation, but adds other operators to express conditional expressions (*IF*):

$$\begin{array}{ll} \text{problem situation} = & \Theta\ aF_i \{ <att_i,\ val_i> \} \\ \text{solution} = & \Theta\ aA_i \{ <att_i,\ val_i> \} \\ & \Theta\ aP_i \{ <att_i,\ val_i> \} \end{array}$$

with for prototypical cases: $\Theta \in O$, the default value being $\vee$ for prototypical cases, and for clinical cases: $\Theta \in \{\wedge\}$, the default value being $\wedge$ for clinical cases.

The default representation for clinical cases is the same as for prototypical cases, except that the only connector available here is the connector $\wedge$ both for problem situation and for solution because a case is not abstracted.

5.2 Memory Organization

The memory of the system is organized in several layers, where the prototypical cases index the clinical cases (see Fig. 3). Several kinds of prototypical cases may be available:

- The *expert prototypical cases*, which were provided by the experts when the system was built. They represent the knowledge of the experts in the form of cases that summarize the clinical experience of the experts. These cases also provide a structure to the memory, and organize the clinical/experiential cases so as to facilitate the search through the memory.

- The *maintenance prototypical cases*, which provide the updates coming from the literature. These may be reviewed by humans as well – regular staff or experts. The role of these cases is to maintain the knowledge represented in the case base.

- The *learnt prototypical cases*, which are learnt through conceptual clustering from the cases that enrich the memory over time [6]. These prototypical cases have for main role to facilitate the search through the memory, like the expert prototypical cases, as well as a role of suggesting research questions [5].

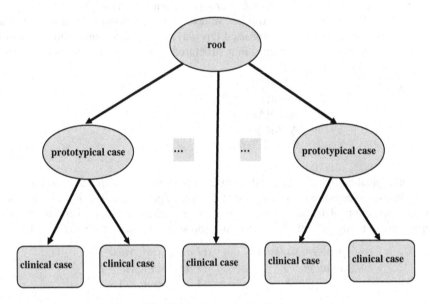

Fig. 3. Memory organization

5.3 Reasoning Process

The reasoning process starts with the presentation to the system of a new problem to solve. This system is capable of handling the wide variety of problems that physicians can face when they take care of patients, and the first task of the system is to determine the nature of the problem to solve. Classically, the reasoning of the system proceeds through the following steps [1]:

[1] Interpretation: Given the description of a patient problem, the system constructs, by interpretation, the initial situation expressed in the knowledge representation language of the system (see [5] for more details about this interpretation phase). Abstraction is the main reasoning type used here, and in particular temporal abstraction to create trends from time-stamped data. Numerical values are abstracted into qualitative values. Let c_c be the target patient case to solve, represented as a conjunction of findings:

$$c_c \quad = \quad \Theta \ aF_i \{ \ <att_i, val_i> \ \}$$

[2] Prototype-guided retrieval: The case-base is searched for prototypical cases and cases matching this new problem to solve through case-based retrieval. The result is a set containing both cases and prototypical cases. Let CS be this conflict set: $CS = \{ c_i, p_j \}$ where the c_i are cases and the p_j are prototypical cases. Cases are only retrieved directly if they are not indexed under a prototypical case – which is rare.

[3] **Conflict resolution (R_r):** The following hierarchy of reuse is followed:

I.	reuse expert prototypical cases
II.	reuse maintenance prototypical cases
III.	reuse learnt prototypical cases
IV.	reuse cases

Nevertheless, the first criterion to choose the entity to reuse is the number of problem description elements matched. The entities are ranked by decreasing number of matched problem description elements with the target case to solve. The similarity measure used for ranking is the following:

$$sim(x_i, x_j) = \frac{\sum_{r=1}^{n} sim(aF_r(x_i), aF_r(x_j))}{n} \qquad (1)$$

where aF_r are description elements, representing instances of findings, x_i and x_j are two cases, and $sim(aF_r(x_i), aF_r(x_j)) = 1$ if these findings instances have compatible attribute / value combinations, and 0 otherwise.

Most of the time, the most similar entity is a prototypical case. The retrieval is then guided by the prototypical case(s) ranked highest, and the clinical cases indexed under this prototypical case are retrieved and ranked by decreasing similarity with the target case to solve. If no clinical case is available, the prototypical case will be reused.

[4] **Prototype-guided reuse:** The reuse of a prototypical case entails evaluating the preconditions of any IF-THEN statement, keeping only those that are satisfied, and selecting the solution steps in an ordered manner directed by the *order* attribute attached to each assessment or treatment class (see Fig. 4). The reuse of a clinical case is guided by the expert or maintenance prototypical case so that the prototypical case can substitute, add, or delete recommendations from the case.

[5] **Retain:** When the solution is complete, and after feedback from the application, it is memorized with the target case solved.

The system provides recommendations represented as instances of assessments and/or planning actions.

6 Examples

This section illustrates the system reasoning on two examples: one example of a prototypical case as sole basis for the system recommendations, and one example of prototypical case guided retrieval and reuse.

GastrointestinalDiagnoses : LiverChronic GVHD (-----------------)

Findings

Connector	Finding Name	Snomed code	(Properties, Values)	Importance	Level
	(JaundiceNOS	M-57610		H	
OR	Nausea	F-52760		M	
OR	Anorexia	F-50015		M	
OR	Malaise	F-01220		M	
OR	Fever	F-03003		M	
OR	PainNOS	F-A2600	site=RightUpperQuadrantAbdomen	M	
OR	Stool	T-59666	color=light	M	
OR	Urine	T-70060	color=dark	M	
OR	Hepatomegaly	D5-81220		M	
OR	Ascites	D5-70400		M	
OR	PeripheralEdema)	M-36330		M	
AND	HepatoToxicDrug			H	A

Diagnosis Assessment

Connector	Procedure Name	Snomed code	(Properties, Values)	Importance	Order
	HepaticFunctionPanel	P3-09100	finding=AlkalinePhosphataseMeasurement (ALKP)(P3-71350) result=elevated OR finding=ASTMeasurement(AST)(P3-72000) result=elevated OR finding=ALTMeasurement(ALT)(P3-71220) result=elevated OR finding=LDHMeasurement(LDH)(P3-73380)result=elevated	C	1
AND	HepatitisPanel	P3-09110	finding=HepatitisPanelMeasurement(P3-64000) result=negative	H	1
AND	UltrasonographyAbdom enNOS (USNABD)	P5-BB200	finding=Normal	H	1
AND	CBC	P3-30100	Finding = Eosinophils result = elevated	H	1
IF HepatitisCA ntigenMeasu rement(P3-64054) .resul t = Positive	HCVRNAMeasurement	P3-64050	finding=negative AND synonym= HCVMeasurement	H	2
IF HepatitisBA ntigen Measuremen t(P3-64021) result=Positi ve	HBVDNAMeasurement		finding=negative	H	2
AND	OralExamination	P8-00200	finding=abnormal	H	3
AND	BiopsyOfLipNOS	P1-51300	finding=Positive diagnosis=SkinChronicGVHD	H	3
AND	BiopsyOfSkin	P1-40303	finding=Positive diagnosis=SkinChronicGVHD	H	3
AND	SchirmerTearTest	P2-A0016V	finding=Decreased	H	3
IF all above are negative	BiopsyOfLiver	P1-5B300	finding=positive diagnosis=LiverChronicGVHD	N	4
	RequestGIConsult				

Treatment Plan

Condition/Connector	Planning Action Name	(Properties, Values)	Order
IF ImmunosuppressantAgentNOS(C-79000) =Absent	StartPDNCSPTherapy		1
IF ImmunosuppressantAgentNOS=Present	StartSalvageRxProtocol		1
	LimitHepatotoxicDrugs		1
IF PDN=present and patient.condition=stable	ConsiderUDCARxProtocol		1

Fig. 4. *LiverChronicGVHD* prototypical case representation with its list of findings (corresponding to diagnoses), its list of diagnosis assessment steps, and its list of treatment actions

6.1 Example 1

A patient consults his doctor about new symptoms occurring after his transplant. The patient's symptoms are: *Nausea, Malaise,* and *PainNOS* localized in the upper right portion of the abdomen. The physician records the main complaint of the patient, which is the unusual abdominal pain and reviews the drugs the patient is taking, as well as his chart with the latest labs and physical exams. The patient is not taking any immunosuppressant drug, nor any hepato-toxic drug.

Prototype guided retrieval. The three symptoms of the patient each trigger several prototypical cases:

- *Nausea* triggers 18 prototypical cases: *LiverChronicGVHD, HepatitisAcuteNOS, LiverDrugToxicity, GastricChronicGVHD, GastricHemorrhage, ColonChronicGVHD, DrugInducedNauseaAndVomiting, DuodenalChronicGVHD, EsophagealChronicGVHD, EsophagealInfection, IntestinalDrugToxicity, AdrenalInsufficiency, UrethralInfection, BladderInfection, RecurrentNonHodgkin'sLymphoma, NonInfectiousPericarditisNOS, AcuteCholecystitis,* and *Hypomagnesemia.*
- *Malaise* triggers 4 prototypical cases: *LiverChronicGVHD, HepatitisAcuteNOS, LiverDrugToxicity,* and *InfectiousMononucleosis.*
- *PainNOS* in *RightUpperQuadrant* triggers 4 prototypical cases: *LiverChronicGVHD, LiverDrugToxicity, HepatitisAcuteNOS,* and *AcuteCholecystitis.*

The similarity measure ranks highest *LiverChronicGVHD* and *HepatitisAcuteNOS*, because *LiverDrugToxicity* is ruled out by the fact that the patient is not taking any hepato-toxic drug. Therefore the cases chosen to base the reuse are: *LiverChronicGVHD* (see Fig. 4 for this prototypical case) and *HepatitisAcuteNOS*.

In this particular example, the system does not retrieve the cases indexed under these prototypical cases because all the features describing the case to solve are accounted for in the prototypical cases. Most of the time though the actual clinical cases would be retrieved, since they would often match some of the features not present in a prototypical case.

Prototype guided reuse. The reuse in this case combines the diagnosis assessment and eventually the treatment plan of two prototypical cases: *LiverChronicGVHD* and *HepatitisAcuteNOS*.

The diagnosis assessment proceeds in four stages, as indicated by the range of *order* in the *LiverChronicGVHD* prototypical case (from 1 to 4, rightmost column in Fig, 4):

- First, request a *HepaticFunctionPanel*, a *HepatitisPanel*, an *UltrasonographyAbdomenNOS*, and a *CBC*. The first steps of diagnosis assessment for both *LiverChronicGVHD* and *HepatitisAcuteNOS* being the same, the system does not propose any additional procedures to be performed yet.
- Second, after the results have come in, and if they have the values indicated in the case, proceed with *HCVRNAMeasurement* if *HepatitisCAntigenMeasurement* was positive, and with *HBVDNAMeasurement* if *HepatitisBAntigenMeasurement* was positive. The patient tested negative for hepatitis, therefore these procedures are not requested.
- Third, request an *OralExamination*, a *BiopsyOfLipNOS*, a *BiopsyOfSkinNOS*, and a *SchirmerTearTest*. The patient undertook all of these, and tested positive for *SkinChronicGVHD* in his lip biopsy.

- Fourth, because the patient tested positive for *SkinChronicGVHD*, he will not have to undergo *BiopsyOfLiver*, and his diagnosis of *Liver-ChronicGVHD* is established.

Case ID#395

Findings

Finding Name	Snomed code	(Properties, Values)	Importance	Level
Nausea	F-52760		M	
Malaise	F-01220		M	
PainNOS	F-A2600	site=RightUpperQuadrantAbdomen	M	
ThermalSensitivity		Site=MouthNOS	M	

Diagnosis Assessment

Procedure Name	Snomed code	(Properties, Values)	Date
HepaticFunctionPanel	P3-09100		12/1/2002
HepatitisPanel	P3-09110		12/1/2002
CBC	P3-30100		12/1/2002
OralConsult	P8-00200		12/1/2002
OralExamination	P8-00200		12/1/2002
BiopsyOfLipNOS	P1-51300		12/1/2002

Fig. 5. A clinical case

The treatment plan starts in this prototypical case only after the diagnosis is established because of the order of 1 indicated in the rightmost column of the treatment plan (see Fig. 4). If the order had been 0, some treatment would have started just by triggering this case. Since the patient is not taking any immunosuppressant drug, he will be placed on prednisone and cyclosporine therapy (*StartPDNCSPTherapy*). The other actions are eliminated because their preconditions are not met (*StartSalvageRx-Protocol*), and not yet met (*ConsiderUDCARxProtocol*). If later the patient condition is stable, the third statement will be considered: *ConsiderUDCARxProtocol*.

6.2 Example 2

The clinical case is the same as in the previous example, although there is one more symptom: *ThermalSensitivity*. The patient experiences exacerbated sensitivity to hot or cold food, which he notices as being different from the ordinary (see Fig. 5).

Prototype guided retrieval. The four symptoms of the patient each trigger prototypical cases:

- *Nausea* triggers 18 prototypical cases: *LiverChronicGVHD, HepatitisAcuteNOS, LiverDrugToxicity, GastricChronicGVHD, GastricHemorrhage, ColonChronicGVHD, DrugInducedNauseaAndVomiting, DuodenalChronicGVHD, EsophagealChronicGVHD, EsophagealInfection, IntestinalDrugToxicity, AdrenalInsufficiency, UrethralInfection, BladderInfection, RecurrentNonHodgkin'sLymphoma, NonInfectiousPericarditisNOS, AcuteCholecystitis*, and *Hypomagnesemia*.
- *Malaise* triggers 4 prototypical cases: *LiverChronicGVHD, HepatitisAcuteNOS, LiverDrugToxicity*, and *InfectiousMononucleosis*.

- *PainNOS* in *RightUpperQuadrant* triggers 4 prototypical cases: *Liver-ChronicGVHD, LiverDrugToxicity, HepatitisAcuteNOS,* and *AcuteCholecystitis*.
- *ThermalSensitivity* triggers 1 prototypical case: *OralChronicGVHD*.

Again, the similarity measure ranks highest *LiverChronicGVHD* and *HepatitisAcuteNOS*, because *LiverDrugToxicity* is ruled out by the fact that the patient is not taking any hepato-toxic drug. *OralChronicGVHD* ranks lower, nevertheless the system keeps it because one symptom is not accounted for by the other prototypical cases: *ThermalSensitivity*.

The cases indexed under these prototypical cases are then retrieved, and case *ID#395* is ranked first because the findings match perfectly those of the new clinical case. Therefore this case, indexed under *LiverChronicGVHD* since this is the diagnosis ultimately associated with this case, is chosen as the candidate for reuse (see Fig. 6).

Prototype guided reuse. The reuse takes the assessment and treatment plans from case *ID#395*. It also takes the diagnosis under which this case is indexed: *LiverChronicGVHD* – since this case was ultimately indexed under this diagnosis. *LiverChronicGVHD* prototypical case is more recent than case *ID#395*.

The system determines that the assessment plan for this case should be updated to include *UltrasonographyAbdomenNOS* as recommended for assessing this disease, therefore the recommended assessment plan is the following:

HepaticFunctionPanel   (*from   LiverChronicGVHD   prototypical   case   &
                            from case ID#395*)
HepatitisPanel   (*from LiverChronicGVHD prototypical case & from case ID#395*)
CBC   (*from LiverChronicGVHD prototypical case & from case ID#395*)
UltrasonographyAbdomenNOS(USNABD)
                     (*from LiverChronicGVHD prototypical case*)
OralConsult   (*from case ID#395*)
OralExamination   (*from case ID#395*)
BiopsyOfLipNOS   (*from case ID#395*)

Therefore the recommendations of the system have been generated mostly from the clinical case, but have also taken into account the prototypical case recommendation since this literature-based case is more recent than the clinical case.

7 Discussion

This section discusses the roles of prototypical cases in CBR. Generalized cases are named in varied ways, such as prototypical cases, abstract cases, prototypes, stereotypes, templates, classes, categories, concepts, schemas, and scripts – to name the main ones [13]. Although all these terms refer to slightly different concepts, they represent structures that have been abstracted or generalized from real cases either by a CBR system, or by an expert. When these prototypical cases are provided by a domain expert, this is a knowledge acquisition task [3]. More frequently, they are learnt from actual cases. In CBR, prototypical cases are often learnt to structure the memory.

Many authors mine for *prototypes*, and simply refer to *induction* for learning these, such as in CHROMA [2]. Bellazzi et al. organize their memory around prototypes [4]. either acquired from an expert, or induced from a large case base. Schmidt and Gierl point that prototypes are an essential knowledge structure to fill the gap between general knowledge and cases in medical domains [21]. The main purpose of this prototype learning step is to guide the retrieval process and to decrease the amount of storage by erasing redundant cases. A generalization step becomes necessary to learn the knowledge contained in stored cases for the antibiotic therapy domain [21].

Others specifically refer to *generalization,* so that their prototypes correspond to generalized cases [12, 15, 20]. For example Portinale and Torasso in ADAPTER organize their memory through E-MOPs learnt by generalization from cases for diagnostic problem-solving [20]. E-MOPs carry the common characteristics of the cases they index, in a discrimination network of features used as indices to retrieve cases. Maximini et al. have studied the different structures induced from cases in CBR systems [13]. They define three types of cases. A point case is what we refer to as a real case. The values of all its attributes are known. A generalized case is an arbitrary subspace of the attribute space. There are two forms: the attribute independent generalized case, in which some attributes have been generalized (interval of values) or are unknown, and the attribute dependent generalized case, which cannot be defined from independent subsets of their attributes [13].

Yet other authors refer to *abstraction* for learning abstract cases. Branting proposes case abstractions for its memory of route maps [9]. The abstract cases, which also contain abstract solutions, provide an accurate index to less abstract cases and solutions. Perner also learns prototypes by abstracting cases [19].

Finally, many authors learn *concepts* through *conceptual clustering.* MNAOMIA [5, 6] learns concepts and trends from cases through *conceptual clustering.* Time representation plays a major role in this system, as in biomedical CBR in general [14]. Perner learns a hierarchy of classes by *hierarchical conceptual clustering,* where the concepts represent clusters of prototypes [19].

Dìaz-Agudo and Gonzàlez-Calero use *formal concept analysis* (FCA) – a mathematical method from data analysis - as another induction method for extracting knowledge from case bases, in the form of *concepts* [10].

The system presented here also uses prototypical cases to organize its memory, direct its retrieval and its adaptation. Its originality lies in reusing both clinical cases and prototypical cases, judiciously combining their recommendations to build more up-to-date recommendations. The prospect of using prototypical cases for case base maintenance is also novel. In addition, the mining process for mining prototypical cases from the literature is innovative in CBR, and is explained in [8]. Next steps for this research are to conduct a formal evaluation and qualitative validation study. The development of this system, based on mining knowledge from documents, allows for rapid deployment in a clinical environment, which will facilitate this validation study.

8 Conclusion

This system proposes to keep a case base up-to-date by automatically learning prototypical cases from biomedical literature. These prototypical cases are an important memory structure upon which the system relies for guiding its retrieval and reuse steps. These prototypical cases, called maintenance prototypical cases, provide a method for enabling a case base to naturally evolve and follow the otherwise overwhelming flow of biomedical advances. Coupled with the concept of mining prototypical cases from biomedical literature, this methodology moves a step forward in the direction of automatically building and maintaining case bases in biomedical domains. Future areas of research are to study how prototypical cases learnt from clinical cases, from the experts, and from the literature can complement one another, and how the reasoner can take advantage of the knowledge provided by each in a harmonious way.

References

1. Aamodt, A., Plaza, E.: Case-Based Reasoning: Foundational Issues, Methodologies Variations, and Systems Approaches. In: AI Communications, vol. 7(1), pp. 39–59. IOS Press, Amsterdam (1994)
2. Armengo, E., Plaza, E.: Integrating induction in a case-based reasoner. In: Keane, M., Haton, J.P., Manago, M. (eds.) Proceedings of EWCBR 94, pp. 243–251. Acknosoft Press, Paris (1994)
3. Bareiss, R.: Exemplar-Based Knowledge Acquisition. Academic Press, Inc. San Diego, CA (1989)
4. Bellazzi, R., Montani, S., Portinale, L.: Retrieval in a Prototype-Based Case Library: A Case Study in Diabetes Therapy Revision. In: Smyth, B., Cunningham, P. (eds.) EWCBR 1998. LNCS (LNAI), vol. 1488, pp. 64–75. Springer, Heidelberg (1998)
5. Bichindaritz, I.: A case based reasoner adaptive to several cognitive tasks. In: Aamodt, A., Veloso, M.M. (eds.) Case-Based Reasoning Research and Development. LNCS, vol. 1010, pp. 391–400. Springer, Heidelberg (1995)
6. Bichindaritz, I.: Case-Based Reasoning and Conceptual Clustering: For a Co-operative Approach. In: Watson, I., Fahrir, M. (eds.) Progress in Case-Based Reasoning. LNCS, vol. 1020, pp. 91–106. Springer, Heidelberg (1995)
7. Bichindaritz, I.: Mémoire: Case-based Reasoning Meets the Semantic Web in Biology and Medicine. In: Funk, P., González Calero, P. (eds.) ECCBR 2004. LNCS (LNAI), vol. 3155, pp. 47–61. Springer, Heidelberg (2004)
8. Bichindaritz, I.: Prototypical Case Mining from Biomedical Literature. Applied Intelligence (in press) (2007)
9. Branting, K.L.: Stratified Case-Based Reasoning in Non-Refinable Abstraction Hierachies. In: Leake, D., Plaza, E. (eds.) Case-Based Reasoning Research and Development. LNCS, vol. 1266, pp. 519–530. Springer, Heidelberg (1997)
10. Dìaz-Agudo, B., Gonzàlez-Calero, P.: Classification Based Retrieval Using Formal Concept Analysis. In: Aha, D., Watson, I. (eds.) ICCBR 2001. LNCS (LNAI), vol. 2080, pp. 173–188. Springer, Heidelberg (2001)
11. Holt, A., Bichindaritz, I., Schmidt, R.: Medical Applications in Case-based Reasoning. The Knowledge Engineering Review 20(03), 289–292 (2005)

12. Malek, M., Rialle, V.: A Case-Based Reasoning System Applied to Neuropathy Diagnosis. In: Kene, M., Haton, J.P., Manago, M. (eds.) Proceedings of EWCBR 94, pp. 329–336. Acknosoft Press, Paris (1994)

13. Maximini, K., Maximini, R., Bergmann, R.: An Investigation of Generalized Cases. In: Ashley, K.D., Bridge, D.G. (eds.) ICCBR 2003. LNCS, vol. 2689, pp. 261–275. Springer, Heidelberg (2003)

14. Montani, S., Portinale, L.: Accounting for the Temporal Dimension in Case-Based Retrieval: a Framework for Medical Applications. Computational Intelligence 22(3-4), 208–223 (2006)

15. Mougouie, B., Bergmann, R.: Similarity Assessment for Generalized Cases by Optimization Methods. In: Craw, S., Preece, A.D. (eds.) ECCBR 2002. LNCS (LNAI), vol. 2416, pp. 249–263. Springer, Heidelberg (2002)

16. National Library of Medicine: The Unified Medical Language System (Last access: 2005-04-01) (1995), http://umls.nlm.nih.gov

17. Pantazi, S.V., Arocha, J.F.: Case-based Medical Informatics. BMC Journal of Medical Informatics and Decision Making 4(1), 19–39 (2004)

18. Pantazi, S.V., Bichindaritz, I., Moehr, J.R.: The Case for Context-Dependent Dynamic Hierarchical Representations of Knowledge in Medical Informatics. In: Proceedings of ITCH'07 (in press) (2007)

19. Perner, P.: Different Learning Strategies in a Case-Based Reasoning System for Image Interpretation. In: Smyth, B., Cunningham, P. (eds.) EWCBR 1998. LNCS (LNAI), vol. 1488, pp. 251–261. Springer, Heidelberg (1998)

20. Portinale, L., Torasso, P.: An Integrated Diagnostic System Combining Case-Based and Abductive Reasoning. In: Aamodt, A., Veloso, M.M. (eds.) Case-Based Reasoning Research and Development. LNCS, vol. 1010, pp. 277–288. Springer, Heidelberg (1995)

21. Schmidt, R., Gierl, L.: Experiences with Prototype Designs and Retrieval Methods in Medical Case-Based Reasoning Systems. In: Smyth, B., Cunningham, P. (eds.) EWCBR 1998. LNCS (LNAI), vol. 1488, pp. 370–381. Springer, Heidelberg (1998)

22. Wilson, D., Leake, D.B.: Mainting Case Based Reasoners: Dimensions and Directions. Computational Intelligence Journal 17(2), 196–213 (2001)

Case-Based Support for Library Reference Services

Yen Bui

College of Information Science and Technology, Drexel University
Philadelphia, Pennsylvania, U.S.A.
yb37@drexel.edu

Abstract. This paper reports on the results of the first phase of the development of a knowledge management system that provides assistance to reference librarians. This system would employ the parallel use of expert knowledge and case-based retrieval of similar existing question/answer (QA) pairs. CBR is used to store, organize, and represent these QAs in such a way that they could be offered as suggested solutions. The first phase involves testing the possibility of categorizing reference questions in the knowledge base into case-groups and combining attribute matching with text similarity in the similarity measure. Here, CBR is used in a new field which is not domain-specific, and where the level of variability among the potentially high volume of textual cases can be both major and minor. Questions are used in the similarity measure, and the solutions are the paired answers of the retrieved questions.

Keywords: Library reference services, knowledge representation.

1 Introduction

Reference librarians are the connection between the library's knowledge repository and the public. Hummelshoj [3, p. 13] argues that the "development of community information services with maximum human support is crucial for users' access to and use of information". However, the tremendous growth in information resources presents challenges to the reference librarians who need to find ways to provide searching assistance to the public. We propose that a Case-based Reasoning (CBR) type of retrieval could be useful in helping the librarians find similar types of questions and the previously worked-out answers could be reused and adapted. This paper reports on the first phase of a project involving the development of a knowledge management system that provides assistance to reference librarians. This project would employ the use of expert knowledge and case-based retrieval of existing question/answer (QA) pairs, in a parallel manner, to enhance the process of knowledge transfer. CBR is used to store, organize and represent existing QAs in a repository in such a way that they could be offered as suggested solutions to the users of the system. This means the premise of a CBR framework could be used to manage knowledge and advance the transfer of knowledge from one population (the experts) to another (the non-experts, which could be people who are in the field but are not necessarily familiar with the particular area of knowledge being studied). The

R.O. Weber and M.M. Richter (Eds.): ICCBR 2007, LNAI 4626, pp. 507–516, 2007.
© Springer-Verlag Berlin Heidelberg 2007

intended users of this system are new reference librarians and those who work in small libraries where a one-person reference desk is the norm. The system also has the potential to be applied for internal corporate knowledge management such as in a corporate library. This first phase involves testing the possibility of categorizing reference questions in a knowledge base into case-groups, and the similarity measure is based on category matching combined with a measure of free text matching. The scope is limited to general medical information at this time.

2 Related Works

There is a large volume of literature on both theoretical research and practical usage of Case-based Reasoning. At its most fundamental, the framework of CBR is premised on the natural form of human reasoning and learning from prior experience [7]. The knowledge base consists of individual cases built from episodes encountered previously [10]. When the user enters a new case, the system uses similarity assessment techniques to search for one or more cases in its repository that best match this new case. The system then gives each of the associated outcomes a score based on the similarity measure. CBR also has the capability of adapting new cases which do not have a good match into its knowledge base thereby enhancing the repository.

Artificial intelligence methodologies, which include CBR, have offered beneficial results when the environment is well structured with adequately defined processes or case characteristics; however this leaves out areas where the experiences are very rich but available only in natural language text [4]. In addition, attempts at utilizing AI methods have not been as successful at the higher strategic level [8], or in environments where there is a high level of case variability which can cause the number of cases to potentially grow to an unmanageable level. Consequently, the application of CBR has been relatively fewer for tasks in social science domains or is usually limited to smaller case bases [5].

Efforts to address problems associated with natural language knowledge bases in Textual CBR have made significant progress in the last ten years. Weber et al. [9] identify four main areas associated with Textual CBR:

- Assessing similarity between textually represented cases
- Mapping texts to structured case representations
- Adapting textual cases
- Automatic generation of representation.

One of the earlier works in Textual CBR is *SPIRE* [2][6] which combines CBR and Information Retrieval (IR) where CBR is used as an interface to a deeper IR engine. On the flip side of this approach, Burke et al. [1] introduce the system *FAQ Finder* where IR is used first to filter the information before feeding it to a CBR system. *FAQ Finder* is a question-answering system which retrieves existing documents in the frequently-asked question files. *FAQ Finder* works in two stages – the first stage utilizes an existing IR technique called *SMART* to narrow down the potential matches for a question posed in natural language. Once a match has been chosen by the user,

CBR is used in the next stage to find matched questions in this chosen area. The authors use statistical similarity, semantic similarity, and coverage to arrive at the final score. Lenz et al. [4] argue that CBR usually focuses on a particular domain and therefore should employ knowledge from that domain. The authors apply this principle on a hotline and help desk application. Case representation is done using Case Retrieval Net (CRN) where a set of Information Entities (IEs) are used to automatically characterize a case. The IEs are compiled with domain specific keywords, expressions, codes, numbers, etc. They found that the performance of the system degrades if components of less-intensive domain knowledge are not included in the similarity measure, and if structural information is not represented explicitly.

Our approach differs from these previous works in that the knowledge is transformed into case-groups which are well structured, but free text is also allowed in a limited sense for the purpose of improving flexibility and enhanced retrievability. CBR and IR therefore are not used sequentially as in SPIRE or FAQ Finder, but incorporated into one step - the similarity measure is based not only on the matching attributes (i.e. categories), but also on some level of text similarity. Document analysis of the knowledge base is used to determine the most appropriate categories. We believe that the additional work in categorizing existing cases will significantly improve precision and recall, and the trade-off is worthwhile. This methodology is especially suitable where the knowledge base is already categorized to some extent, such as in the case of the Internet Public Library[1] (IPL). Reference questions submitted to the IPL are pre-categorized before they are distributed to librarians who will research the answers.

The area of library reference QA service is an unstructured environment. A new reference question usually does not match well with previous ones, both because the questions use natural language and also because questions tend to differ slightly from each other, even though they may be about the same situation. However, library reference questions have the characteristic that while the questions may vary a great deal depending on how the questions are phrased, the underlying basis of these questions can fit into a well defined structure. It is likely that the solutions to these questions may be very similar, either regarding the reference resources cited or the strategies used in the search process. In this kind of an environment, it would be very beneficial to explore how the acquired knowledge can be structured, represented and organized for retrieval in a CBR system. The reliance on past experience provides a ready body of knowledge for reference services. However, the high variation among the cases makes it problematic regarding retrieval. If the restriction is too high, we miss many applicable cases; on the other hand, a lower restriction leads to too many cases getting retrieved and hence effectively makes the retrieval set not very useful. A CBR prototype was built to test the possibility of classifying the domain knowledge into types of reference questions along with the appropriate typical solutions. A new case entered into the system by the user would be compared against cases in the library to find those which are of the same type. The purpose is to impose some structure on a repository which has many cases of minor variations.

---

[1] The Internet Public Library, http://www.ipl.org

3 Methodology

Transcripts of pairs of question/answer (QA) from the e-reference service Question Point[2] are made available to the public courtesy of the New York Public Library. A PHP program was written to retrieve approximately 100 pairs of reference questions and answers related to general medical information from this website. The keywords used to filter the returned items were "health, medical, medicine, medication, drugs, prescriptions, doctors, hospital". Each returned pair includes the question and the answer (or compiled answer if it came from a chat session). This knowledge base then was examined to determine applicable and representative groups or types, and each case in the CBR library was determined to belong to one or more of these groups. An organizational structure called "case-type" is introduced where "case-type" refers to how reference questions of similar type are grouped together based on similar characteristics. CBR's similarity assessment techniques were then used to find the appropriate case-types in the repository and retrieve the associated solutions.

Of the 100 pairs retrieved, 36 were eliminated because either they did not fall within the scope of the research or the answers were not usable, leaving 64 pairs for analysis. Figure 1 shows an example of a retrieved question/answer pair from QuestionPoint.

3.1 Data Analysis and Categorization

The purpose of the data analysis was to determine if it would be possible to classify reference questions into cases for storage in a knowledge base. The requirement was that the data needed to be categorized in some way so that they could be representative and retrievable. Among the issues considered were: 1) how general or specific should the categories be, 2) how could the questions/categories be represented in the database so that they would work best with the similarity assessment mechanism of a CBR system, 3) how could the categories and sub-categories be designed so that it would facilitate both retrieval and user input. 4) One other important consideration had to do with the lack of strong structure and variability of reference questions - most questions could fit into some categories, however they were usually not exactly the same but were different in some minor ways. How then could this type of minor variations be accommodated among the questions?

Transcripts of the reference questions/answers were analyzed to investigate the content and determine the appropriate categorization scheme. The documents retrieved were first scanned to identify all potential key terms. Then we continued to refine these key terms until we arrived at the most suitable and representative categorization coding. The questions were examined and categorized into types of questions according to this scheme. The more specific details in the questions were used to build the subcategories. The intention was to give some structure to the high level of variability associated with reference questions.

---

[2] http://www.questionpoint.org/crs/servlet/org.oclc.home.BuildPage

Last Update:	2006-04-13 23:12:00.0
Question:	Patron needs to know what drugs use equine estrogens. She knows about Premarin. Are there others? Needs drug names and companies that manufacture them.
Answer:	We were only able to find two other drugs in the Physician's Desk Reference (PDR) in this category. They are named "Prempro" and "Premphase". They are described as conjugated estrogens/medroxyprogesterone acetate tablets. They are listed in the following strengths: Prempro 0.3mg/1.5 mg Prempro 0.45 mg/1.5 mg Prempro 0.625 mg/2.5 mg Prempro 0.625 mg/5 mg Premphase - This may be a derivative of Premarin. We were not able to determine the difference between the two. The company that manufactures both of these is named Wyeth Pharmaceuticals, Philadelphia, PA.. In addition to the PDR, the Seattle Public Library has the following resources which cover this topic. These books are located on the 5th floor of the Central Library. 1. "Complete guide to prescription & non-prescription drugs." by HP Books, c1983- Call #: 615.1 C73865 2. "The Essential guide to prescription drugs." by Harper & Row, c1977- Call #: 615.1 L852E 3. "Prescription drugs" by the editors of Consumer guide. Call#: 615.1 P925
Keywords:	estrogen, horses, drugs, nonprescription
This material is from the QuestionPoint Global Knowledge Base	

Fig. 1. Sample of a pair of QA retrieved from QuestionPoint

Seven (7) main categories were identified: *Treatment, Statistics, Historical Information, Disease, Drugs/Medication, Definition,* and *General.* Five of these categories were constructed as structured type where user could only select from a list of allowable values (namely the subcategories). We believe that this restriction on input will produce more accurate retrieval. The lists also included the values "na" (not assigned) and "other". The value "other" was used to allow the user to enter a case when it fits within a type but does not have a specific match within a category. In this case, the returned solution was intended to be more general and presumably contains information that is generic to that category. The category *Definition* took textual entries since it appears likely that definition of medical terms should be found in similar reference resources, and similar terms such as "breast cancer" or "prostate cancer" could benefit from similar solutions. The user would also have the option of selecting choice(s) in more than one category, such as *treatment* = "AIDS" and *disease* = "AIDS".

The category *General* deserves special mention. Even when the categories are broken down into more specific subcategories, there are still variations in the questions which belong to the same category. The category *General* allows for free text entry, and partial word matching criteria is used to assess similarity, i.e. based on the percentage of words matched within the entire text. However, this attribute should have lower weight than others due to its more flexible entries. In other words, the system used both a taxonomy-based category and a level of free text matching. The issue of weight assignment will be discussed further below.

Table 1 shows the final classification scheme for the questions. The coding is based on only 64 pairs of question/answer, so the list is understandably not comprehensive.

Table 1. Categorization Scheme – Categories (in bold) and their allowable values are listed underneath

Treatment	Disease	Drugs/Medication
Diabetes	AIDS	Approved drugs
Hepatitis-c	Smallpox	Historical
AIDS	Hepatitis-c	Properties
Hyperhydrosis	Malaria	AIDS
Prostate cancer	Breast cancer	Malaria
Other	GRICE	Temazepam
	Diabetes	Norplant
	Sarcoidosis	Aspirin
	Other	Other
Historical Information	**Statistics**	**Definition** (free text)
Hospital	Drugs/medication	
Person	Death-rate	
Disease	Disease	**General** (free text)
Drugs/medication	Medical-records	
Experiment	Other	
Medical-procedures		
Other		

For the answer part of the question/answer pair, the text was screened for resources and any indication of strategies used. Resources were easy to find and easy to code because they were usually readily identifiable and could simply be listed the way they appeared in the text. Ideally, the information should be normalized as much as possible. For example, when two answers cited the same resource but only one provided a website, the URL should be included in both answers. However, this step was not done since the prototype was intended only to test how classification of the knowledge base can produce effective retrieval results in an unstructured environment. Unfortunately, there was not much information on strategy from the retrieved QA pairs. Occasionally, the responder to the e-reference question includes the keywords she/he uses in a search, and these rare cases were most commonly associated with Google searches.

Table 2. Sample Coding of 2 pairs of question/answer

Question	Answer*
Drugs (Other) General (which drugs use equine estrogens	Physician's Desk Reference (PDR) Complete Guide to prescription & non-prescription drugs (book)
Statistics (death-rate) Treatment (Hepatitis C) Disease (Hepatitis C) General (Hepatitis C, infectious disease)	New York Public Library, Manhattan Branch (http://www.nypl.org/branch/central_units/mm/midman.html) Center for Disease Control (FAQs) Gale Encyclopedia of Medicine Medline Plus and HOAH Google ("hepatitis c") => CDC, National Center for Infectious Diseases, The Hepatitis Info Network, National Institute of Diabetes & Digestive & Kidney Diseases

The answers have been abbreviated for a cleaner presentation

3.2 Weighting Scheme

The design purpose was to match the new case with one or more of the pre-determined types of questions. This means that most of the times, the target case would have a match of only one of the structured categories and possibly some partial match in the General category. The weights for all the categories were therefore assigned an equal weight, with the exception of General (free text) which had a lower weight equal to 1/2 the weight of the other categories. We also needed to ensure that when the value "na" (not assigned) was entered for a category, this would not bump up the score inappropriately. For example, if the new case was of the *Treatment* type, it would correctly have a match in the *Treatment* category, but it would also match cases in the library which have "na" in some of the other categories and would give an artificially high score, as well as failing to properly distinguish the cases. To overcome this problem, rules were used to set variable weights depending on the values of the attributes. The rules in essence assigned the weight to 0 when the value is "na". This weighting scheme was used for all the attributes with the exception of the categories *General* and *Definition* which are of type text.

A new reference question would be matched against "cases" in the knowledge base (i.e. existing questions) and scores would be assigned using the above weighting scheme. The threshold was set at 30% so that trivial matches would be eliminated from the retrieval set, but cases with lower matching scores would still be available for evaluation.

4 Discussion and Results

Each of the 64 cases was in turn used for testing along with 5 new test cases. The overall results show a consistency of retrieved cases. It is expected that when a case is run as a test case, this case itself should be the top return because it represents an exact match. This was true in all cases. Since the cases were represented by well-structured categories, the matched cases in the knowledge base were retrieved and assigned the appropriate scores. The usual report of the percentage of cases retrieved correctly therefore is not the main issue. Instead, we feel it is more interesting to show what kind of matching was assigned what score. Table 3 lays out how the scores correspond to how the categories of the test case match with existing cases. For example, when the test case matches with an existing case in three of the structured categories and also in the *General* category, the existing case is retrieved and given a score of 93. The results indicate that when there are mismatched categories, the scores are lowered. Further, it appears that the *General* category contributes more to the final score than intended, and some adjustment would be necessary.

Table 3. Scores and Matchability

Matching Categories	Score	No. Occurences
3 structured categories & "General" category	93	1
2 structured categories & "General"	90	6
3 structured categories	86	1
1 structured category & "General"	83	30
2 structured categories	80	2
1 structured category	67	26
• "General" (perfect match) • 1 category & "General" & 1 mismatched category	50	39
"General" (not perfect match)	33 - 48	26

As an illustration, when a new case is entered with *Historical Information*=other, *Drugs/Medication*=historical, and *General*=" ", and others = na (not assigned) the following results were retrieved:

Score	Case	Treat-ment	Statistics	Historical Info	Disease	Drugs/Med	Definition	General
90	C2	na	na	Other	na	historical	na	
50	c20	na	na	Drugs	na	historical	na	
40	c76	na	na	Other	na	na	na	sweden
40	c88	na	na	Other	na	na	na	Educ of women

The results are encouraging. They show that data from an unstructured environment could be represented in a knowledge repository in such a way that they could be reused. It is possible to classify reference questions into categories so that they could be represented and retrieved appropriately when a similar new question is encountered. Regarding accuracy, the prototype produces the correct results. The retrieval set includes cases with similar features as intended by the design. The scores assigned to the retrieved cases are also mostly appropriate; however, the weighting scheme could be adjusted to test other scoring considerations.

While the prototype does show that similar questions are retrieved appropriately, there are limitations to the data and the coding. The data come from transcripts of compiled questions and answers. Since the solutions (i.e. the answers) are obtained from a database of an e-reference service where questions are worked on by many different librarians who may or may not be familiar with medical reference information, the answers are inconsistent. Similar questions have answers that are different in content and style as well as refer to different resources. Another limitation has been mentioned previously – there is very little information regarding strategies, or why and how resources are selected. In addition, the dataset includes only 64 pairs of question/answer and therefore the classification scheme is not comprehensive.

5 Conclusions and Future Work

The results show that it is possible to employ the CBR technology in a domain where the knowledge base has cases that have various levels of variability. The technique of grouping cases into case-types to impose a structure on the high number of potential minor variations works as intended, and the addition of free text matching adds some flexibility to the similarity assessment. Cases retrieved fit into the right type. The use of a mixture of a taxonomy and free text helps enhance the retrieval results.

Work is still ongoing to analyze more QA pairs from an e-reference database to produce a richer and fitter categorization scheme. We are planning on testing the prototype on the QA database of the Internet Public Library. Additional work also includes further strengthening the categorization of cases, doing a survey to establish how different or similar reference librarians categorize reference questions, adjusting the weighting scheme, considering the possibility of using a Natural Language Processing tool for the categorizing process, and adaptation of new and modified cases.

References

1. Burke, R.D., Hammond, K.J., Kulyukin, V.A., Lytinen, S.L., Tomuro, N., Schoenberg, S.: Question Answering from Frequently Asked Question Files: Experiences with the FAQ Finder System. Technical Report. UMI Order Number: TR-97-05., University of Chicago (1997)
2. Daniels, J.J., Rissland, E.L.: What You Saw Is What You Want: Using Cases to Seed Information Retrieval. In: Leake, D.B., Plaza, E. (eds.) Case-Based Reasoning Research and Development. LNCS, vol. 1266, pp. 325–336. Springer, Heidelberg (1997)
3. Hummelshoj, M.: Web-Based Reference Services and Community Information -The Role of Public Libraries. In: 11th NI&D Conference, Spring for information, Reykjavik (2003)

4. Lenz, M., Hubner, A., Kunze, M.: Question Answering with Textual CBR. In: Andreasen, T., Christiansen, H., Larsen, H.L. (eds.) FQAS 1998. LNCS (LNAI), vol. 1495, pp. 236–248. Springer, Heidelberg (1998)
5. Redmond, M., Line, C.B.: Empirical Analysis of Case-Based Reasoning and Other Prediction Methods in a Social Science Domain: Repeat Criminal Victimization. In: Ashley, K.D., Bridge, D.G. (eds.) ICCBR 2003. LNCS, vol. 2689, pp. 452–464. Springer, Heidelberg (2003)
6. Rissland, E.L., Daniels, J.J.: The Synergistic Application of CBR to IR. Artificial Intelligence Review: Special Issue on the use of AI in Information Retrieval 10(5-6), 441–475 (1996)
7. Schank, R.C., Abelson, R.P.: Scripts, Plans, Goals, and Understanding. Erlbaum, Mahwah (1977)
8. Srikantaiah, T.K., Koenig, M. (eds.): Knowledge Management for the Information Professional. American Society for Information Science (2000)
9. Weber, R., Ashley, K., Bruninghaus, S.: Textual Case-Based Reasoning. The Knowledge Engineering Review 20(3), 255–260 (2006)
10. Weber, R., Kaplan, R.: Knowledge-based Knowledge Management. In: Jain, R., Abraham, A., Faucher, C., Jan van der Zwaag, B. (eds.) Innovations in Knowledge Engineering. International Series on Advanced Intelligence, vol. 4, pp. 151–172. Advanced Knowledge International, Adelaide (2003)

Knowledge Extraction and Summarization for an Application of Textual Case-Based Interpretation

Eni Mustafaraj[1], Martin Hoof[2], and Bernd Freisleben[1]

[1] Dept. of Mathematics and Computer Science, University of Marburg
{eni,freisleb}@informatik.uni-marburg.de
[2] Dept. of Electrical Engineering, Fachhochschule Kaiserslautern
m.hoof@et.fh-kl.de

Abstract. This paper presents KES (Knowledge Extraction and Summarization), a new knowledge-enhanced approach that builds a case memory out of episodic textual narratives. These narratives are considered as generated probabilistically by the structure of the task they describe. The task elements are then used to construct the structure of the case memory. The KES approach is illustrated with examples and an empirical evaluation of a real-world scenario of textual case-based interpretation for a technical domain.

1   An Application of Textual Case-Based Interpretation

Janet Kolodner has described *interpretive* Case-Based Reasoning (CBR) as "a process of evaluating situations or solutions in the context of previous experience" [11, p. 86]. She argues that this evaluation can be performed by means of comparing and contrasting a new situation to old experiences. A defining aspect of interpretive CBR is the fact that a reasoner cannot be content with the recall of only one previous situation, as it is often sufficient in some CBR applications. Rather, for the reasoner it is important to have at disposal a few cases for both comparison and contrasting, so that the argumentation has a more solid foundation. A classical example of a CBR system that uses the compare-and-contrast strategy for case-based interpretation is Kevin Ashley's system HYPO [1].

HYPO, aside from its elaborated reasoning strategies, displays another characteristic which is not very common to more recent CBR systems: The features used to represent the cases are not part of the original case representation. Indeed, the original cases are documents written in natural language describing a legal dispute; while the internal cases are a set of some very abstract domain concepts (known as issues and factors). These domain concepts have been created by highly knowledgeable professionals in the domain of trade secret law. Thus, discovering these concepts in the original documents is not easy, particularly when some of them need to be inferred from text, as the example in Figure 1 shows, where, while factor (f2) can be directly found in text, factor (f4) needs to be inferred. In fact, extensive research from Brünninghaus & Ashley

R.O. Weber and M.M. Richter (Eds.): ICCBR 2007, LNAI 4626, pp. 517–531, 2007.
© Springer-Verlag Berlin Heidelberg 2007

Original Text: Whiz had signed a nondisclosure agreement with Amexxco in which he undertook to maintain confidentiality with respect to all of Amexxco's trade secrets.

Factors:
(f2) Agreed-Not-To-Disclose   (in text)
(f4) Nondisclosure-Agreement-Specific   (inferred)

Fig. 1. Applying factors to a legal case. Source [1, p. 762].

[3,4] has demonstrated that trying to assign these factors to textual documents automatically is a very hard task.

Creating an application of interpretive CBR requires both highly specialized domain-knowledge (in order to create indexes for the cases) as well as considerable manual effort in assigning these indexes to cases (because automatic methods are not yet able to perform satisfactorily). This high burden of knowledge engineering could be the reason why there are almost no other CBR interpretive approaches in the literature, particularly in the situations when the original cases are in textual form.

Meanwhile, knowledge-lean approaches that have been investigated in the Textual CBR (TCBR) literature, despite being able to extract features for indexing cases with no need of knowledge engineering, cannot produce features that are so self-telling as the features of HYPO, because the automatically extracted features, even when in the form of logical propositions (as e.g., in [23]), do not make explicit their underlying semantic meaning

In our research work, we attempt a middle way between knowledge-rich and knowledge-lean approaches to the indexing problem. On the one hand (similar to knowledge-lean approaches), we do not ask domain experts to provide domain-specific indexes for the cases, but rather, try to acquire them directly from text. On the other hand (similar to knowledge-rich approaches), the acquiring process is performed as a semi-supervised learning, that is, a classifier learns to identify phrases in the text as instances of some abstract concepts related to task knowledge (these concepts are referred to as knowledge roles). Task knowledge is a knowledge source external to the corpus of documents, but it is readily available (that is, we do not need domain expert to identify knowledge roles).

To concretize our approach, we initially present examples from a technical domain where the interpretive TCBR approach has been applied.

1.1   Interpreting Monitoring Processes

The scenario considered in this paper comes from the technical domain, concretely, the domain of predictive maintenance services for electrical machines. To prevent the breakdown of electrical machines during operation, several components of the machines are periodically monitored by means of different tests and measurements.

The graphics shown in Figure 2 are the result of performing one (out of many) of the measurements constituting the monitoring/diagnostic process for assessing the condition of the insulation system of an electrical machine. The textual evaluations (shown on the side of the graphics) are part of diagnostic reports compiled by service providers of diagnostic services. We are in possession of a corpus of such reports and are using it for evaluating new research ideas for interpretive TCBR. The final goal is to extract valuable pieces of knowledge from these textual evaluations and organize them in a way that enables the less experienced users to correctly interpret results of such monitoring procedures.

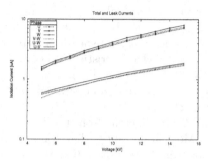

The measured current values lie in the normal area. The recorded curves (current values as a function of the measuring voltage) are mainly uniform. Compared to previous measurements, the characteristic values have not significantly changed. Weak points in the insulation can be derived neither from the curves nor from the calculated characteristic values.

(a) Normal condition

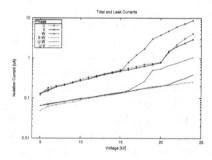

The measured total and leak current values lie in the expected area for the present insulation system. The recorded curves (current values as a function of the measuring voltage) of the individual phases are up to 1.5 times the nominal voltage practically identical and show a uniform, linear course. In the higher voltage area, at all phases a stronger increase of the total current and of the leak current at phase W is detected, which indicates a conducting dirtiness of winding, at phase W particularly in the area of phase separation. Actions: Renewed cleaning of the winding, phase lead, and connections within 1–2 years.

(b) Problematic condition

Fig. 2. Two monitoring measurements for the insulation system of two different machines and their respective textual evaluations written by human experts. The text is translated from German, the original language of the reports.

Monitoring is a very common task in many technical domains, medicine, or financial markets, because it serves to the purposes of condition-based maintenance, prevention of diseases, or prediction of future trends. The common thread of monitoring tasks, independently of the domains, is that one or many entities are kept under observation either periodically or permanently. The behavior of some predefined parameters that characterize some aspect of the observed entities is then analyzed and the findings are interpreted based on previous knowledge and the current context. However, because the observed entities are part of complex environments with a strong stochastic nature, interpretation knowledge is based on both experience and background knowledge. The experience knowledge for the monitoring task is compatible with the compare-and-contrast strategy, because the interpretation of a new situation must refer to previous situations of the same or other similar entities under observation.

1.2   Characteristics of Text

Diagnostic reports are written by professionals and have an official nature, so that the used language is grammatically correct and articulate. The grammaticality aspect of the text is important to our approach, because it allows the use of natural language processing (NLP) tools such a part-of-speech taggers or syntactic parsers. Although grammaticality is not a characteristic of all corpora used in TCBR systems (such as informal notes [21] or e-mails [22]), many other corpora of documents display such a feature, for instance, legal cases, reports of aviation incidents, product manuals, news articles, etc.

The textual evaluations shown in Figure 2 are different from the types of text commonly used in TCBR approaches. Most importantly, they contain no explicit problem description and problem solution. Rather, each text is a snapshot. It narrates the condition of an entity in a particular time and place, giving explanations that evaluate this condition. Therefore, we refer to such textual evaluations as *episodic textual narratives*.

The episodic narratives have several interesting characteristics that can be exploited during the design of a TCBR approach. First, they always consider the same entities, again and again, that is, they contain repetitive information. Second, the narration of the episodes follows the temporal and causal order of the described events. Thus, each episode can be represented in a concise form by the list of participating events. Finally, when narratives are concerned with a specific task, such as in the case of *monitoring*, the vocabulary used in a narrative can be abstracted in terms of the semantic categories that describe the task. We will return to these characteristics and discuss them in more detail in Section 3.

The remainder of the paper is organized in the following way. In Section 2, available approaches for constructing knowledge containers in TCBR are discussed. Our central idea of regarding episodic narratives as generated by task structure is elaborated in Section 3. It follows in Section 4 a discussion of the *knowledge extraction and summarization* approach. An empirical evaluation for a real-world corpus of episodic narratives can be found in Section 5. The paper is concluded with a discussion of related research and some ideas of future work.

2   Knowledge Containers in TCBR

From the four knowledge containers identified by Michael Richter, research in TCBR has been in general concerned with only two of them: indexing vocabulary and similarity knowledge. In constructing these containers, two generic trends can be noticed throughout TCBR research, to which we refer to as knowledge-lean and knowledge-rich approaches. Knowledge-lean approaches, such as PSI [23] and Sophia [15] tap into knowledge that can be found inside the corpus of documents only. The only external sources that they use are a list of common stop-words and a stemmer. All knowledge-lean approaches consider text documents as bag-of-words, every word as a feature, and represent documents as vectors in the feature space, with either binary or other types of weights. Then, different kinds of feature selection or extraction methods are adopted to reduce the dimensionality of the representation and find discriminative features that capture the underlying semantics of the documents. The most striking aspect of knowledge-lean approaches is that they are domain and language independent and employ only statistical and machine learning tools for knowledge extraction. However, none of the proposed knowledge-lean approaches has been used in concrete TCBR scenarios, and their evaluation has shown that the methods are good for text clustering, text classification, and document retrieval in general.

Knowledge-rich approaches instead are tightly bound to a specific domain and reasoning task and use all available knowledge sources, like domain experts, thesauri, glossaries, domain ontologies, etc., in order to acquire indexing vocabulary and similarity knowledge. The knowledge layers approach of Lenz [12], which has been used in many real-world or research systems is an example of a knowledge-rich approach. The research of Brünninghaus & Ashley [3,4] and Gupta et al.[9] are other examples.

In our view, the majority of the existing TCBR approaches considers only two of the three characteristics that an indexing vocabulary should have, characteristics that have been described by Kolodner ([11], p. 195):

1. Indexing has to anticipate the vocabulary a retriever might use.
2. Indexing has to be by concepts that are normally used to describe the items being indexed, whether they are surface features or something abstract.
3. Indexing has to anticipate the circumstances in which a retriever is likely to want to retrieve something (i.e., the task context in which it will be retrieved).

Indeed, by using as the source of knowledge the documents itself, and by assuming that they have been written by a large group of users over an extended period of time, it can be ensured that almost the whole surface vocabulary of a given domain is captured. However, by failing to consider the specific task contexts in which users need to use the TCBR system, the problem of information overload on the user side is not handled. One of the goals of our research is to propose a balanced approach, which does not aim at decreasing knowledge engineering efforts at the cost of increasing information overload for users. Therefore, we explicitly consider task knowledge as a knowledge source for building knowledge containers for the TCBR approach.

3   Task Structure as Generator of Episodic Narratives

Several explicit or implicit assumptions lay at the roots of TCBR research. Concretely, every text document is considered as one case, which also has a structure of the kind <problem description, problem solution>, for example, as a pair of question and answer, document title and document body, or legal dispute and court decision. Furthermore, it is assumed that every case belongs to a unique situation or topic, so that each case has the potential for reuse on its own (independently of other cases). Finally, it can also be noticed that the circumstances in which a document has been created are either not known or not considered.

The mentioned assumptions can be regarded as constraints, able to promote the aplicability of the CBR approach. However, it cannot be expected that they always hold. Therefore, we are trying to build a TCBR approach that departs from such assumpttions, seeing this as a constraint relaxation process:

- One document needs not necessarily be equaled to one case.
- Documents might display no explicit division in a problem description and a problem solution.
- Reuse of case knowledge needs not be confined to a singular case.

While departing from such traditional assumptions, we bring into attention the following assumptions:

- A text document can be considered as the probabilistic output of some underlying, interconnected event types (or topics), instead of being regarded as a mere container of some information entities.
- A *case* can be considered as the chain of the interconnected participants in related events. Thus, a document will contain as many cases as there are groups of related events that do not intersect.
- Redundancy of information that results from describing the same events again and again can be exploited to distinguish among prototypical and exemplar cases.

To clarify these hypotheses, we give examples from the TCBR scenario built upon the episodic textual narratives shown in Figure 2. Such narratives are written every time the monitoring task is performed, and the communicative structure of the narratives follows the structure of the task. In concrete terms, this means the following. Consider that the monitoring task for maintenance purposes could be structured in the following way:

1. Some parameters of a specific object or process (which is under monitoring) are observed.
2. The nature of the findings is explained (e.g., what is the reason for a positive or negative finding).
3. If the findings are evaluated as negative for the observed object, then actions to improve the situation are recommended.

These three steps of the task structure can be represented in terms of three event types: Observe, Explain, and Act. Since we assume that the task structure is mirrored in the communication structure of the narratives, we expect to find verbalizations of such events in the narratives. Thus, the task structure can be regarded as the underlying source that generated the narratives describing different instances of task execution.

Although the description of the task structure might appear arbitrary, in building it, we made use of the task templates of the CommonKADS methodology, a knowledge engineering methodology for building knowledge systems [20]. Its repository of task templates contains generic task descriptions for the two major groups of knowledge tasks: analytic and synthetic tasks (such as classification, diagnosis, planning, design, etc.). Our task model is a combination of the terminology used to describe the tasks of Monitoring and Diagnosis. In CommonKADS the elements of the task templates are referred to as *knowledge roles*. Knowledge roles are just a denotation for task elements, and different terms can be adopted according to the terminology most known to domain users. For the described approach we have used the following knowledge roles: observed_object, finding, explanation, evaluation, location, action, time, etc. It can be noticed that the knowledge roles are not related to a specific domain, but rather, reflect the nature of the task only.

An important relation exists between events and knowledge roles in the textual narratives. Events encapsulate relations between knowledge roles. So, an Observe event connects an observed_object with a finding, an Explain event connects a finding with an explanation and evaluation, and an Act event connects an action with a location or time.

By using events and their constituting knowledge roles, it is possible to represent narratives and cases in an abstract conceptual form, which permits a comparison at a more generic level than that of specific domain terms.

For example, the narrative of Figure 2a that contains four observation events (one for every sentence) can be represented as a series of such events: [Observe, Observe, Observe, Observe], or the narrative of Figure 2b can be regarded as consisting of three cases, as shown in Figure 3.

It can be noticed in Figure 3 that in creating a case, the components of several events are combined. For instance, in Case 3, the combination consists in the events of Observe, Explain, and Act.

The reason for representing the narratives once as sequences of events and once as sets of cases is the derived practical value. In this way, narratives can be compared among them both at a generic and at a specific level. Alternatively, we can think of the narratives as compound cases, which permit comparison at different levels of granularity.

The question now is how to automatically transform narratives from their original form to an event and role based representation organized in cases. To this purpose, we have built an approach for *knowledge extraction and summarization*.

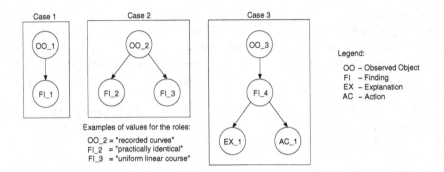

Fig. 3. Examples of cases constructed as chains of knowledge roles

4   Knowledge Extraction and Summarization

An advantageous characteristic of a corpus of episodic narratives generated by a task structure is redundancy. Because the same task is performed continuously over entities of the same nature (e.g., in the examples of Figure 2, the same monitoring process is carried out for different electrical machines), repetitiveness will be present both in vocabulary and communication structure. Although redundancy is usually regarded as harmful in CBR (particularly during the retrieval step), it is beneficial to the goals of extracting and summarizing knowledge from the corpus.

4.1   Knowledge Extraction

Knowledge extraction is concerned with extracting from the narratives those textual phrases that correspond to knowledge roles. In our work, we have considered knowledge extraction as the post-processing phase of an annotation process. That is, initially all narratives are annotated with knowledge roles, and then the annotated phrases are extracted from text forming pairs of attribute-value (where the attribute is a knowledge role and its value a textual phrase).

In previous publications, we have presented a framework named LARC (Learning to Assign knowledge Roles to textual Cases), which is an active learning framework that combines machine learning and NLP methods to perform the annotation process. Due to space restrictions, the description of LARC in this paper will be short, thus, we direct the interested reader to [13] for a detailed account. LARC was inspired by computational linguistic research, particularly, the task of semantic role labeling [5].

Compared to the knowledge-lean and knowledge-rich approaches discussed in Section 2, LARC falls somewhere in-between the two. That is, LARC differently from knowledge-lean approaches uses several external knowledge sources (therefore, we refer to it as knowledge-enhanced), however, differently from knowledge-rich approaches, these sources are not domain-specific (e.g., for the shown scenario, no sources that have to do with electrical machines have been used). Concretely, the following sources are exploited:

- A part-of-speech tagger (e.g TreeTagger, Brill Tagger, etc.)
- A statistical syntactical parser (e.g. Stanford Parser, Sleepy Parser, etc.)
- A list of verbs clustered in groups with the same meaning (e.g. VerbNet, FrameNet, etc.)
- Task templates and knowledge roles from CommonKADS

The only moment in which a domain expert needs to be involved in the knowledge extraction process (although this is not strictly necessary) is during the bootstrapping of the active learning process.

In broad lines, LARC works in the following way. During the preprocessing, the whole corpus is tagged, verbs are extracted, and the most frequent ones are paired with their semantic category, which is nothing else but the event type (e.g. Observe, Explain, etc.). Each event type is also associated with some possible knowledge roles. Every sentence in the corpus is syntactically parsed, and based on the derived parse tree, a set of features is constructed, which will be used during the learning. Naturally, during the parsing, a sentence will be divided in several phrases. The goal of learning is to build a classifier that will label such phrases either with a knowledge role or with a None label. During the learning, LARC chooses some sentences for manual annotation. The sentences are selected by following an active learning strategy, so that to maximize the accuracy of the classifier and to minimize the number of sentences to annotate. The Salsa annotating tool [8], a graphical environment that assigns roles per mouse-click, was used for annotation.

In the experiments reported in [13], we have shown that with only four iterations of 10 sentences per time, it was possible to achieve an F-measure of 0.85 ($recall = 0.8, precision = 0.9$) in the labeling of knowledge roles for a corpus of narratives as those in Figure 2. Repeated 10-fold cross-validation over the whole training corpus (without active learning strategy) had shown that the F-measure cannot pass the mark of 0.92, thus, the F-measure for only 40 sentences with active learning is to be considered as very good. With the Salsa tool, the manual annotation of 40 sentences needs only 1 hour of work. Clearly, if desired, more sentences can be annotated to achieve the mark 0.92.

4.2 Knowledge Summarization

After the knowledge extraction step, the extracted pieces of knowledge need to be brought together at a micro and a macro level. This means that, initially, cases within a narrative need to be created, and thereafter collapsed together in the creation of a case memory. The creation of cases within narratives is simple. To do that, we make use of the quintessential sequence of the task structure: Observe, Explain, Act. This means that each case will be about one observed_object only, the findings related to it, and their respective explanations and actions. This is exactly what was shown in Figure 3, where the sentences of the Figure 2b were organized in three different cases. Thus, for every narrative, the sentences (or clauses) are processed one after the other, trying to fill the basic template of the case. The minimal case should have at least values for the two primary fields OO and FI. Case creation proceeds automatically, by following a set of simple heuristic rules.

While case creation needs only a bit of programming, case memory creation is a more complex process, because it needs to consider similarities and relations within the domain. However, remaining true to our resolution to not use any kind of domain-specific knowledge, case memory creation is also an approach that exploits only corpus knowledge and generic task knowledge. Before explaining how this works, we return to the issue of task-based indexing.

Task-Based Indexing. As mentioned in Section 2, Kolodner regarded as an important aspect the fact that "indexing should anticipate the task context in which it will be retrieved". Therefore, we take in consideration the circumstances in which the users of the TCBR system will need assistance. Concretely, consider the scenario introduced from the beginning: the interpretation of monitoring results. Suppose that the user faces the graphic of Figure 2b and has to formulate an evaluation for it. If the user has some experience, she will directly formulate an observation about a parameter of the graph and what it is atypical for it (e.g., "the current values are rising"). The reason for formulating such and observation is that the user would like to have possible explanations for the atypical finding. Once similar findings are found in the case memory, the related explanations and actions would also be retrieved. However, a user that is not very experienced may not be able to see that there is something atypical in the graphic, that is, the user will face a common problem in diagnostic situations, known as "missing the symptoms". Therefore, such a user might also need help in finding out which type of atypical findings are related to each parameter.

What is important in the described scenario is that the information need of the users follows the causal relationships between the knowledge roles. So, a user needs to go from an observed_object to a finding, from a finding to an explanation, or from a finding to another co-occurring finding. This means that an indexing based on types of observed_object and the nature of finding (positive or negative, typical or atypical) is more important than an indiscriminative indexing that does not consider the semantic category of the terms (i.e., the knowledge roles) and does not follow the reasoning trace of the users (i.e., if a user enters as a query an observed_object, she is actually interested on types of finding related to it). By not having a fixed division in problem description and problem solution, every attribute of the case representation can be used to retrieve a successive attribute, permitting a more efficient reuse of case knowledge. However, some attributes might be more useful than others during the quering time.

Probabilistic Task Content Modeling. Suppose that it was decided (based on the task and the goals) that indexing should be focused on two attributes: observed_object and finding. On the other hand, recall that during the knowledge extraction process, hundreds of phrases corresponding to these attributes have been extracted. Because of the redundancy phenomenon that we have frequently mentioned, many of these phrases will have either the same or similar meaning. To see that, consider the two first sentences in Figure 2a and Figure 2b:

[$_{OO}$ The measured current values] lie [$_{FI}$ in the normal area]
[$_{OO}$ The measured total and leak current values] lie [$_{FI}$ in the expected area]

Despite some differences in the verbalization of the OO and FI roles, it is clear that the meaning of the two sentences is the same. There will be hundreds of such sentences in the corpus, and we are interested that the phrases that are semantically related are grouped together. In order for such grouping to be useful for TCBR purposes, we model the process of text generation with a Markov Model, as shown in Figure 4. Such a modeling is inspired by research in computational lingusitics, for example [2]. Concretely, each of the knowledge roles is considered as a state that depends upon the preceding state. Then, every state is responsible of generating textual phrases based on its vocabulary (in the figure, the big circles represent the vocabulary of each state, whereas the small circles represent unique phrases from the training corpus).

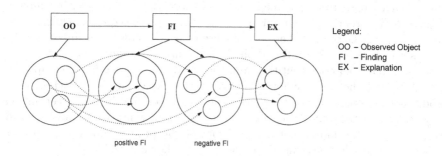

Fig. 4. Knowledge roles as states of the probabilistic model

Following Rabiner[16], the model shown in Figure 4 is a Hidden Markov Model (HMM), where, however, the states are known due to the annotation process with LARC. The parameters of HMM state transition distribution and emission distributions can be estimated directly from the annotated corpus using the formulas described in [2]. We refer to the HMM model as the *probabilistic task content model* (PTCM), because it models the content of the narratives in terms of the task structure.

The advantage of PTCM lies in its dual nature: it is a graph as well as a joint probability distribution. Within KES, the graph is seen as a case memory that connects nodes that have a type of relation based on the event type they participate. The symbol emission distributions are used to find the state that corresponds to an entered query as well as the most similar node. The outgoing edges are then followed to retrieve the phrases that correspond to the desired answer.

Although the graph component of PTCM reminds one of the *Case Retrieval Net* [12] (which was a source of inspiration for the model), they differ in many aspects: the nature of nodes, the nature of connecting arcs, the approach of building the network, as well as the retrieval process. PTCM is also different from another TCBR approach that uses graphs for representing documents [6], because the latter approach does not create a case memory.

Once built, the PTCM can be used for different purposes related to discovering knowledge in the case base. An interesting use is as a classifier for the semantic orientation of finding phrases, namely, classifying these phrases as positive and negative, according to their meaning. The classification is performed without any use of domain lexical knowledge. The classifier takes into consideration only conditional distributions of state emissions in the model. Due to space restrictions, we refer the interested reader to [14] for details in this issue.

5   Empirical Evaluation

Using KES, we created a case memory from a corpus of 490 episodic narratives. Episodes have in average 60 words and 4.6 event types. The representation of narratives as sequences of events permits to find the *prototypical narrative*, which corresponds to a machine in a normal condition (such as the example in Figure 2a The representation for such a narrative is the sequence [Observe, Observe, Observe, Observe], where every Observe event type has a different value for its role observed_object. Based on the structure of the *prototypical narrative*, these four observed_object entities were selected as start-nodes for the graph representation of the case memory. The subgraphs expanding from each of these nodes are directed, in order to model the causal relationships between knowledge roles. For the four observed_object nodes, a representative term is selected, too, based on the most frequent headword of the phrases annotated with the label OO. The selected terms (in German[1]) are shown in Table 1.

KES will be evaluated with respect to its major goals:

- how much it reduces the information load on the user side
- how useful it is to case-based interpretation

To measure the reduction of information load, we calculate the *compression ratio* achieved by the case memory, which indicates how many term occurrences in the corpus are collapsed to one node in the case memory. A high compression ratio means that the user has not to inspect all occurrences separately. For instance, having grouped all phrases connected with the four OO types under the respective node achieves the largest compression in the case memory, with an average ratio of 790 : 1 (the number of occurrences of a term versus the number of nodes under which these terms are collected).

In order to serve to the goal of performing case-based interpretation, it is important that the CBR system retrieves several and *different* cases that would

---

[1] These terms ae shown in German, because English translations are not single words.

Table 1. Compression ratio for the root nodes of the case-memory

Node Type	Compression Ratio
OO_1 = 'Stromwert'	1003 : 1
OO_2 = 'Kurve'	969 : 1
OO_3 = 'Kennwert'	702 : 1
OO_4 = 'Kurvenverlauf'	485 : 1

support the creation of a new argument or evaluation. We argued previously in the paper that the described task of monitoring is one of those tasks that can benefit from case-based interpretation. This means that a user will need to look at several existing cases in order to choose those pieces of knowledge that apply best to a given context. An example could be, for instance, to enter as query a phrase describing a finding and have the system output different possible explanation phrases.

Table 2. Recall and Precision values for the retrieval results

Method	Recall	Precision
LSI	0.57	0.62
KES	0.81	0.85

In the PTCM model, the finding nodes have been grouped into two clusters of positive and negative orientation (refer to Figure 4). Negative findings are those nodes that are succeeded by explanation and action nodes. Then, a good criterion for measuring the success of case-based interpretation would be to check whether it can retrieve appropriate and diverse explanations when entering as query a negative finding. In order to do that, we proceeded in this way. Thirty narratives that contained cases with negative findings were selected, and the five most frequent explanations from the remaining cases were identified for each negative finding. The case memory is created every time with a leave-one-out schema (i.e., withholding the narrative used for querying).

In order to have a competitive comparison scale, we implemented a baseline retrieval system based on the LSI (latent semantic indexing) approach [7]. This is appropriate, because of the conceptual similarity between latent concepts and hidden states. Furthermore, Wiratunga et al. [23] have demonstrated with their experiments that LSI performs generally better than a TCBR approach such as PSI.

The average values for recall and precision of the two compared approaches in the task of retrieving explanations for phrases of negative findings are given in Table 2. The better results of KES are statistically significant according to the Wilcoxon signed-ranked test. By exploring the retrieved narratives from LSI, we found that they are similar to one-another. This is different to what KES does (and what we are testing), that is, retrieving diverse explanations, and this explains the unsatisfactory results of LSI. Meanwhile, the performance of

KES is not optimal, due to inaccuracies introduced by the different levels of text processing (parsing, annotation, etc.).

6   Discussion

The presented KES approach serves the purpose of automatically creating a case memory, whenever text documents in the form of episodic textual narratives are available. If narratives are created within the framework of a task performance (e.g. engineers performing monitoring or physicians performing diagnosis), the task structure can be considered responsible of generating the episodic narratives. Because task structure is far less variable than the natural language used to describe task instantiations, the few elements of task structure (i.e. event types and knowledge roles) can be used as attributes for authoring cases. The values for these attributes are extracted and grouped automatically by KES, according to their semantic meaning.

We regard the success of KES as a proof of the value of NLP tools and techniques in developing TCBR systems. Although NLP is regarded by many TCBR researchers as an evil that must be avoided, our experience has been very positive, and we believe that current research trends in computational linguistics can largely contribute to the development of TCBR systems aiming at the "beyond retrieval" target.

Another aspect that contributes to the success of KES is the event-oriented perspective that we have adopted. Actually, some simple elements of such a perspective have previously appeared in [3] (roles and propositional phrases) and [9] (ontology of relationships between events). However, they were not applied to the entirety of text. While we are aware of the fact that many text documents will not have an underlying task structure that generates them, still, an underlying script or plan for generating a document may generally exist. Thus, an important venue for future research is the extension of KES to tackle other types of documents, possibly by automatically capturing the underlying source that has generated the documents.

As a final note, our work is partly inspired by early research in the field of story understanding and case memory construction, concretely, the fundamental work of Roger Schank [18,19], Janet Kolodner [10], and many others. However, we have only retained the spirit of such work, since our approach does not utilize any ad-hoc sources, such as the *Conceptual Dependency* of Schank [17] that was the basis of all processing tools and representation structures used, for instance, in building the Cyrus system of Kolodner [10].

References

1. Ashley, K.: Reasoning with cases and Hypotheticals in HYPO. Int. J. Man-Machine Studies 34, 753–796 (1991)
2. Barzilay, R., Lee, L.: Catching the Drift: Probabilistic Content Models, with Applications to Generation and Summarization. In: Proc. of NAACL-HLT, pp. 113–120 (2004)

3. Brüninghaus, S., Ashley, K.: The Role of Information Extraction for Textual CBR. In: Aha, D.W., Watson, I. (eds.) ICCBR 2001. LNCS (LNAI), vol. 2080, pp. 74–89. Springer, Heidelberg (2001)
4. Brüninghaus, S., Ashley, K.: Reasoning with textual cases. In: Muñoz-Ávila, H., Ricci, F. (eds.) ICCBR 2005. LNCS (LNAI), vol. 3620, pp. 137–151. Springer, Heidelberg (2005)
5. Carreras, X., Màrquez, L.: Introduction to the CoNLL-2005 Shared Task: Semantic Role Labeling. In: Proc. of 9th Co-NLL, pp. 152–165 (2005)
6. Cunningham, C., Weber, R., Proctor, J., Fowler, C., Murphy, M.: Investigating Graphs in Textual Case-Based Reasoning. In: Funk, P., González Calero, P.A. (eds.) ECCBR 2004. LNCS (LNAI), vol. 3155, pp. 573–586. Springer, Heidelberg (2004)
7. Deerwester, S., et al.: Indexing by Latent Semantic Analysis. Journal of the American Soc. Of Information Science 41(6), 391–407 (1990)
8. Erk, K., Kowalski, A., Padó, S.: The Salsa Annotation Tool-Demo Description. In: Proc. of the 6th Lorraine-Saarland Workshop, pp. 111–113 (2003)
9. Gupta, K., Aha, D.: Towards Acquiring Case Indexing Taxonomies from Text. In: Proc. of the 17th FLAIRS Conference, pp. 59–73. AAAI Press, California (2004)
10. Kolodner, J.: Retrieval and Organizational Strategies in Conceptual Memory: A Computer Model. Lawrence Erlbaum Associates, Mahwah (1984)
11. Kolodner, J.: Case-Based Reasoning. Morgan Kaufmann, San Francisco (1993)
12. Lenz, M.: Case Retrieval Nets as a Model for Building Flexible Information Systems. PhD Thesis, Humboldt Universität zu Berlin (1999)
13. Mustafaraj, E., Hoof, M., Freisleben, B.: Mining Diagnostic Text Reports by Learning to Annotate Knowledge Roles. In: Kao, A., Poteet, S. (eds.) Natural Language Processing and Text Mining, pp. 45–69. Springer, Heidelberg (2006)
14. Mustafaraj, E., Hoof, M., Freisleben, B.: Probabilistic Task Content Modeling for Episodic Textual Narratives. In: Proc. of 20th FLAIRS, AAAI Press, California (2007)
15. Patterson, D., Rooney, N., Dobrynin, V., Galushka, M.: Sophia: A novel approach for Textual Case-Based Reasoning. In: Proc. of 19th IJCAI, pp. 15–21 (2005)
16. Rabiner, L.: A Tutorial on Hidden Markov Models and Selected Applications in Speech Recognition. Proc. of IEEE 77(2), 257–286 (1989)
17. Schank, R.: Conceptual Information Processing. North Holland (1975)
18. Schank, R., Abelson, R.: Scripts, Plans, Goals and Undertanding. Lawrence Erlbaum Associates, Mahwah (1977)
19. Schank, R.: Dynamic Memory: A Theory of Reminding and Learning in Computers and People. Cambridge University Press, Cambridge (1982)
20. Schreiber, G., Akkermans, H., Anjewierden, A., de Hoog, R., Shadbolt, N., Van de Velde, W., Wielinga, B.: Knowledge Engineering and Management: The CommonKADS Methodology. The MIT Press, Cambridge (2000)
21. Varma, A.: Managing Diagnostic Knowledge in Text Cases. In: Aha, D.W., Watson, I. (eds.) ICCBR 2001. LNCS (LNAI), vol. 2080, pp. 622–633. Springer, Heidelberg (2001)
22. Wiratunga, N., Koychev, I., Massie, S.: Feature Selection and Generalisation for Retrieval of Textual Cases. In: Funk, P., González Calero, P.A. (eds.) ECCBR 2004. LNCS (LNAI), vol. 3155, pp. 806–820. Springer, Heidelberg (2004)
23. Wiratunga, N., Lothian, R., Chakraborti, S., Koychev, I.: Textual Feature Construction from Keywords. In: Muñoz-Ávila, H., Ricci, F. (eds.) ICCBR 2005. LNCS (LNAI), vol. 3620, pp. 118–128. Springer, Heidelberg (2005)

Author Index

Lecture Notes in Artificial Intelligence (LNAI)

Vol. 4410: A. Branco (Ed.), Anaphora: Analysis, Algorithms and Applications. X, 191 pages. 2007.

Vol. 4399: T. Kovacs, X. Llorà, K. Takadama, P.L. Lanzi, W. Stolzmann, S.W. Wilson (Eds.), Learning Classifier Systems. XII, 345 pages. 2007.

Vol. 4390: S.O. Kuznetsov, S. Schmidt (Eds.), Formal Concept Analysis. X, 329 pages. 2007.

Vol. 4389: D. Weyns, H.V.D. Parunak, F. Michel (Eds.), Environments for Multi-Agent Systems III. X, 273 pages. 2007.

Vol. 4384: T. Washio, K. Satoh, H. Takeda, A. Inokuchi (Eds.), New Frontiers in Artificial Intelligence. IX, 401 pages. 2007.

Vol. 4371: K. Inoue, K. Satoh, F. Toni (Eds.), Computational Logic in Multi-Agent Systems. X, 315 pages. 2007.

Vol. 4369: M. Umeda, A. Wolf, O. Bartenstein, U. Geske, D. Seipel, O. Takata (Eds.), Declarative Programming for Knowledge Management. X, 229 pages. 2006.

Vol. 4342: H. de Swart, E. Orłowska, G. Schmidt, M. Roubens (Eds.), Theory and Applications of Relational Structures as Knowledge Instruments II. X, 373 pages. 2006.

Vol. 4335: S.A. Brueckner, S. Hassas, M. Jelasity, D. Yamins (Eds.), Engineering Self-Organising Systems. XII, 212 pages. 2007.

Vol. 4334: B. Beckert, R. Hähnle, P.H. Schmitt (Eds.), Verification of Object-Oriented Software. XXIX, 658 pages. 2007.

Vol. 4333: U. Reimer, D. Karagiannis (Eds.), Practical Aspects of Knowledge Management. XII, 338 pages. 2006.

Vol. 4327: M. Baldoni, U. Endriss (Eds.), Declarative Agent Languages and Technologies IV. VIII, 257 pages. 2006.

Vol. 4314: C. Freksa, M. Kohlhase, K. Schill (Eds.), KI 2006: Advances in Artificial Intelligence. XII, 458 pages. 2007.

Vol. 4304: A. Sattar, B.-h. Kang (Eds.), AI 2006: Advances in Artificial Intelligence. XXVII, 1303 pages. 2006.

Vol. 4303: A. Hoffmann, B.-h. Kang, D. Richards, S. Tsumoto (Eds.), Advances in Knowledge Acquisition and Management. XI, 259 pages. 2006.

Vol. 4293: A. Gelbukh, C.A. Reyes-Garcia (Eds.), MICAI 2006: Advances in Artificial Intelligence. XXVIII, 1232 pages. 2006.

Vol. 4289: M. Ackermann, B. Berendt, M. Grobelnik, A. Hotho, D. Mladenič, G. Semeraro, M. Spiliopoulou, G. Stumme, V. Svátek, M. van Someren (Eds.), Semantics, Web and Mining. X, 197 pages. 2006.

Vol. 4285: Y. Matsumoto, R.W. Sproat, K.-F. Wong, M. Zhang (Eds.), Computer Processing of Oriental Languages. XVII, 544 pages. 2006.

Vol. 4274: Q. Huo, B. Ma, E.-S. Chng, H. Li (Eds.), Chinese Spoken Language Processing. XXIV, 805 pages. 2006.

Vol. 4265: L. Todorovski, N. Lavrač, K.P. Jantke (Eds.), Discovery Science. XIV, 384 pages. 2006.

Vol. 4264: J.L. Balcázar, P.M. Long, F. Stephan (Eds.), Algorithmic Learning Theory. XIII, 393 pages. 2006.

Vol. 4259: S. Greco, Y. Hata, S. Hirano, M. Inuiguchi, S. Miyamoto, H.S. Nguyen, R. Słowiński (Eds.), Rough Sets and Current Trends in Computing. XXII, 951 pages. 2006.

Vol. 4253: B. Gabrys, R.J. Howlett, L.C. Jain (Eds.), Knowledge-Based Intelligent Information and Engineering Systems, Part III. XXXII, 1301 pages. 2006.

Vol. 4252: B. Gabrys, R.J. Howlett, L.C. Jain (Eds.), Knowledge-Based Intelligent Information and Engineering Systems, Part II. XXXIII, 1335 pages. 2006.

Vol. 4251: B. Gabrys, R.J. Howlett, L.C. Jain (Eds.), Knowledge-Based Intelligent Information and Engineering Systems, Part I. LXVI, 1297 pages. 2006.

Vol. 4248: S. Staab, V. Svátek (Eds.), Managing Knowledge in a World of Networks. XIV, 400 pages. 2006.

Vol. 4246: M. Hermann, A. Voronkov (Eds.), Logic for Programming, Artificial Intelligence, and Reasoning. XIII, 588 pages. 2006.

Vol. 4223: L. Wang, L. Jiao, G. Shi, X. Li, J. Liu (Eds.), Fuzzy Systems and Knowledge Discovery. XXVIII, 1335 pages. 2006.

Vol. 4213: J. Fürnkranz, T. Scheffer, M. Spiliopoulou (Eds.), Knowledge Discovery in Databases: PKDD 2006. XXII, 660 pages. 2006.

Vol. 4212: J. Fürnkranz, T. Scheffer, M. Spiliopoulou (Eds.), Machine Learning: ECML 2006. XXIII, 851 pages. 2006.

Vol. 4211: P. Vogt, Y. Sugita, E. Tuci, C.L. Nehaniv (Eds.), Symbol Grounding and Beyond. VIII, 237 pages. 2006.

Vol. 4203: F. Esposito, Z.W. Raś, D. Malerba, G. Semeraro (Eds.), Foundations of Intelligent Systems. XVIII, 767 pages. 2006.

Vol. 4201: Y. Sakakibara, S. Kobayashi, K. Sato, T. Nishino, E. Tomita (Eds.), Grammatical Inference: Algorithms and Applications. XII, 359 pages. 2006.

Vol. 4200: I.F.C. Smith (Ed.), Intelligent Computing in Engineering and Architecture. XIII, 692 pages. 2006.

Vol. 4198: O. Nasraoui, O. Zaïane, M. Spiliopoulou, B. Mobasher, B. Masand, P.S. Yu (Eds.), Advances in Web Mining and Web Usage Analysis. IX, 177 pages. 2006.

Vol. 4196: K. Fischer, I.J. Timm, E. André, N. Zhong (Eds.), Multiagent System Technologies. X, 185 pages. 2006.

Vol. 4188: P. Sojka, I. Kopeček, K. Pala (Eds.), Text, Speech and Dialogue. XV, 721 pages. 2006.

Vol. 4183: J. Euzenat, J. Domingue (Eds.), Artificial Intelligence: Methodology, Systems, and Applications. XIII, 291 pages. 2006.

Vol. 4180: M. Kohlhase, OMDoc – An Open Markup Format for Mathematical Documents [version 1.2]. XIX, 428 pages. 2006.

Vol. 4177: R. Marín, E. Onaindía, A. Bugarín, J. Santos (Eds.), Current Topics in Artificial Intelligence. XV, 482 pages. 2006.